The Economics of Over-the-Counter Markets

The Economics of Over-the-Counter Markets

A TOOLKIT FOR THE ANALYSIS OF DECENTRALIZED EXCHANGE

JULIEN HUGONNIER

BENJAMIN LESTER

PIERRE-OLIVIER WEILL

PRINCETON UNIVERSITY PRESS
PRINCETON AND OXFORD

Published by Princeton University Press
41 William Street, Princeton, New Jersey 08540
99 Banbury Road, Oxford OX2 6JX

press.princeton.edu

Library of Congress Cataloging-in-Publication Data

Names: Hugonnier, Julien, author. | Lester, Benjamin, author. | Weill, Pierre-Olivier, author.
Title: The economics of over-the-counter markets : a toolkit for the analysis of decentralized exchange / Julien Hugonnier, Benjamin Lester, and Pierre-Olivier Weill.
Description: Princeton : Princeton University Press, [2025] | Includes bibliographical references and index.
Identifiers: LCCN 2024040976 (print) | LCCN 2024040977 (ebook) | ISBN 9780691236285 (hardback) | ISBN 9780691236292 (ebook)
Subjects: LCSH: Over-the-counter markets. | BISAC: BUSINESS & ECONOMICS / Economics / Macroeconomics | BUSINESS & ECONOMICS / Finance / General
Classification: LCC HG4521 .H87 2025 (print) | LCC HG4521 (ebook) | DDC 332.6–dc23/eng/20241120
LC record available at https://lccn.loc.gov/2024040976
LC ebook record available at https://lccn.loc.gov/2024040977

British Library Cataloging-in-Publication Data is available

Editorial: Joe Jackson, Emma Wagh
Production Editorial: Elizabeth Byrd
Jacket: Ben Higgins
Production: Danielle Amatucci
Publicity: William Pagdatoon
Copyeditor: Stephen Beitel

Jacket image: Alexey Avdeev / iStock

This book has been composed in Arno Pro

The views expressed in this book are solely those of the authors and do not necessarily reflect the views of the Federal Reserve Bank of Philadelphia or the Federal Reserve System. Any errors or omissions are the responsibility of the authors.

Printed in the United States of America

10 9 8 7 6 5 4 3 2 1

MIX
Paper
FSC FSC® C183721

To Laurence and Louise.
J.H.

To Amy, Isabel, and Sam.
B.R.L.

To Tatiana, my love, soulmate, and teacher,
whose light was extinguished too early.
P.-O.W.

CONTENTS

LIST OF FIGURES

LIST OF TABLES

ACKNOWLEDGMENTS

We owe a great debt to our professors and supervisors, exceptional scholars who have patiently passed on to us part of their knowledge and taught us how to approach research questions. We are particularly grateful to Philippe Artzner, Andrew Atkeson, Bruno Biais, Ken Burdett, Darrell Duffie, Jan Eeckhout, Stéphane Gregoir, Monique Jeanblanc, Patrice Poncet, Andrew Postlewaite, Tom Sargent, Steve Shreve, Dimitri Vayanos, and Randy Wright.

This book builds on two decades of research on OTC markets and related topics with many coauthors, including Gara Afonso, Manuel Amador, Roc Armenter, Adrien d'Avernas, Tony Berrada, Saki Bigio, Braz Camargo, Assa Cohen, Pierre Collin Dufresne, Jérôme Dugast, Chris Edmond, Andrea Eisfeldt, Johan Hombert, Mahyar Kargar, Teddy Kim, Dmitry Kramkov, Yiting Li, David Lindsay, Shuo Liu, Ricardo Lagos, Semyon Malamud, Erwan Morellec, Sébastien Plante, Rodolfo Prieto, Guillaume Rocheteau, Pascal Saint Amour, Ali Shourideh, Semih Üslü, Stijn Van Nieuwerburgh, Venky Venkateswaran, Ludo Visschers, Ronald Wolthoff, Tsz-Nga Wong, Ariel Zetlin-Jones, and Diego Zúñiga. We thank these coauthors for the insights that came out of our joint research, many of which appear (in one form or another) in this text.

Several people contributed directly to this book. We thank Mariano Palleja for his research assistance in compiling the stylized facts in chapter 2, and Chang He for sharing her corporate bond dealer network figure. We are also extremely grateful to Lian Chen, Eduardo Davila, Ali Haider Ismail, Darius Nik Nejad, Alex Maciocco, Vincent Maurin, and especially Semih Üslü for providing detailed comments and suggestions on various chapters.

Last but not least, we would like to thank students from the Ecole Polytechnique Fédérale de Lausanne, the University of Pennsylvania, the University of California, Los Angeles, the University of Lausanne, the Paris School of Economics, and Universidad de Los Andes for working with us through the years, attending the classes that grew into this book, and contributing to search and microstructure theory, including Daniel Andrei, Adrien d'Avernas, Paula Beltran, Adrien Bilal, Huifeng Chang, Anton Cheremukhin, Julien Cujean, Joel David, Nicolas Gauderon, Tomas Geelen,

Andreas Gulyas, Santiago Franco, Alessio Galuzzi, Corey Garriott, Ekaterina Gurkova, Michael Hasler, Chang He, Wenjing He, Kykle Herkenoff, Ali Haider Ismal, Mahyar Kargar, Kei Kawakami, Masanori Kashiwagi, Patrick Kiefer, Ioannis Kospentaris, Noah Kwicklis, Lucie Lebeau, Jiasun Li, David Lindsay, Jiaer Liu, Shuo Liu, Alexis Marchal, Sean McCrary, Theodore Naff, Mariano Palleja, Ana Luisa Pessoa de Araujo, Remy Praz, Paulina Restrepo, Joao Ritto, Juan Sagredo, Shihan Shen, Marcus Studart, Liyan Shi, Venky Venkateswaran, Yilin Wang, Menghan Xu, Linlin Ye, Mengbo Zhang, and Junyuan Zou.

Julien, Ben, and Pierre-Olivier
Lausanne, Philadelphia, and Los Angeles
June 10, 2024

LIST OF ABBREVIATIONS

BIS	Bank for International Settlements
CD	customer-to-dealer
DC	dealer-to-customer
DD	dealer-to-dealer
FINRA	Financial Industry Regulatory Authority
GFC	Global Financial Crisis
HJB	Hamilton-Jacobi-Bellman
IID	independently and identically distributed
MSRB	Municipal Securities Rulemaking Board
ODE	ordinary differential equation
OTC	over-the-counter
RFQ	request for quote
SEF	Swap Execution Facility
SPNE	Subgame Perfect Nash Equilibrium
TRACE	Trade Reporting and Compliance Engine

LIST OF NOTATIONS

$\mathbf{R}$	Set of real numbers
$\mathbf{R}_+$	Set of nonnegative real numbers
$\mathbf{R}_{++}$	Set of strictly positive real numbers
$\mathbf{N}$	Set of integer numbers
$\mathrm{cl}(A)$	Closure of the set $A \in \mathbf{R}$
$\mathrm{conv}(A)$	Convex hull of the set $A \in \mathbf{R}$
$\mathcal{D} = (\underline{\delta}, \overline{\delta})$	Open interval of utility flows
$\mathrm{cl}(\mathcal{D}) = [\underline{\delta}, \overline{\delta}]$	Closure of $\mathcal{D}$
$\mathcal{B} = \mathcal{B}(E)$	Space of bounded functions from E into $\mathbf{R}$
$\mathcal{C} = \mathcal{C}(E)$	Space of continuous functions from E into $\mathbf{R}$
$F(\cdot)$	Distribution on $\mathcal{D}$
$F(\cdot\|\delta)$	Conditional distribution on $\mathcal{D}$
$\mathrm{supp}(F)$	Support of a distribution
$\mathbf{F} = (F(\cdot\|\delta))_{\delta \in \mathcal{D}}$	Collection of conditional distributions
$x^+ = \max\{x, 0\}$	Positive part of a real number
$x^- = \max\{-x, 0\}$	Negative part of a real number
$\|x\| = x^- + x^+$	Absolute value of a real number
$x \wedge y = \min\{x, y\}$	Minimum of two real numbers
$x \vee y = \max\{x, y\}$	Maximum of two real numbers
$x \propto y$	Proportionality: $\exists c > 0$ such that $x = cy$
$\mathbf{1}_{\{A\}}$	Indicator equal to 1 on A and zero otherwise
$f(\delta_+) = \lim_{x \downarrow \delta} f(x)$	Right limit of the function f at the point δ
$f(\delta_-) = \lim_{x \uparrow \delta} f(x)$	Left limit of the function f at the point δ
$\Delta f(\delta) = f(\delta_+) - f(\delta_-)$	Jump of the function f at the point δ

$\|f\| = \sup_\delta \|f(\delta)\|$	The supremum norm of a function f
$f_q(t, q)$	Derivative of a function $f(t, q)$ with respect to q
$\dot{f}(t, q)$	Time derivative of a function $f(t, q)$
$\mathbf{P}[A]$	Probability of A
$\mathbf{P}[A\|B]$	Probability of A conditional on B
$\mathbf{E}[x]$	Expectation of the random variable x
$\mathbf{E}[x\|A]$	Expectation of x conditional on A
$\mathbf{E}_t[x] = \mathbf{E}[x\|\mathcal{F}_t]$	Expectation of x conditional on the σ-field $\mathcal{F}_t$
$\mathbf{E}_\delta[H] = \mathbf{E}[H\|\delta_0 = \delta]$	Expectation of a functional $H = H(\delta_t : t \geq 0)$ conditional on $\delta_0 = \delta$
$\mathbf{E}^F[g(x)]$	Expectation of $g(x)$ given that $x \rightsquigarrow F$
$\mathbb{F} = \{\mathcal{F}_t\}_{t\geq 0}$	Filtration

1

Introduction

Securities are traded in one of two types of market structures: centralized exchanges or decentralized over-the-counter (OTC) markets. Standard models in financial economics, however, are largely designed to study centralized exchanges, and ignore many of the key frictions that affect asset prices, liquidity, and fragility in OTC markets. This oversight is significant because OTC markets are both *large* and *important*: they are at least as large as those markets that are organized as centralized exchanges, and play a crucial role in the functioning of our modern financial system. Moreover, OTC markets are fundamentally *different* than exchanges along a number of key dimensions, including the information available to market participants, the institutions and technologies they use to trade with one another, and the methods they use to determine the terms of trade.

Over the past two decades, in recognition of the dissonance between standard models and the realities of OTC markets, economists have developed new models that are capable of analyzing empirical regularities in the data and providing theoretical predictions for policy proposals and technological innovations in OTC markets. At the time of writing, this large and growing area of research is missing a graduate-level textbook—a synthesis of existing methods and results that can familiarize scholars with the literature and convey the basic technical skills they need to jump-start their own research on the topic. Our objective with this book is to provide such a synthesis. We take the reader on a deep dive into the economics of OTC markets, developing a unified framework that encompasses many of the key theoretical developments in this growing literature and, where possible, relating these developments to recent policy debates and empirical findings that are emerging from the availability of bigger and better data sets.

1.1 OTC Markets Are Large and Important

Many assets trade in OTC markets. Commonly cited examples include fixed income securities, such as corporate and government debt, and derivatives such as asset-backed securities, interest rate swaps, and foreign-exchange forward contracts. Most short-term funding markets also operate as OTC markets, including the markets for fed funds and repurchase agreements or *repos*. In addition, a number of markets for non-financial assets also operate OTC, such as the markets for used capital (e.g., commercial aircraft) and real estate. In fact, even a sizeable fraction of equity trading volume is executed through some form of OTC market.

The total supply of publicly listed securities traded in OTC markets in 2021 was about USD66 trillion, which was approximately 50% more than the supply of securities traded on centralized exchanges. In addition to being large, a number of OTC markets play key roles within the architecture of our current financial system. For example, the fed funds and repo markets are crucial cogs in the process of monetary policy transmission in the United States. Similarly, the secondary market for U.S. Treasuries, which also operates OTC, is central for the provision of liquidity and the allocation of capital across financial institutions. Finally, the U.S. corporate and municipal bond markets are a critical source of funding for large firms, cities, and states.

Given these crucial roles, it is not surprising that OTC markets have been at the center of recent financial crises. For example, the markets for various types of derivatives, such as mortgage-backed securities and credit default swaps, were ground zero for the Global Financial Crisis (GFC) that unfolded in 2007–2008. More recently, the financial system teetered on the edge of a crisis as severe dislocations in the markets for Treasuries and corporate bonds appeared at the onset of the COVID-19 pandemic in March 2020.

1.2 OTC Markets Are Different from Centralized Exchanges

There are many differences between OTC markets and centralized exchanges, and many dimensions of heterogeneity *within* each category. Therefore, it is helpful to highlight a few key differences between the two, often competing, types of market arrangements.

As Dodd [2012] highlights, many exchanges trace their origins to a physical location, such as the New York Stock Exchange or the Chicago Board of Trade, where transactions were executed according to a particular set of rules and traditions. Though these exchanges have largely migrated to virtual platforms, trades are still organized centrally, through a limit-order book that allows for both communication and trade execution to occur on a multilateral basis. As a result, most exchanges feature pretrade price transparency: prices at which one can sell (the *bid* price) or buy (the *ask* or *offer* price) are continuously updated and communicated to all participants. These posted prices are *firm*, rather than negotiable. Finally, most exchanges feature posttrade price transparency: the prices and quantities of completed transactions are also continuously communicated to market participants.

OTC markets, in contrast, are decentralized. They are typically not located in a particular location, but rather represent what Dodd [2012] describes as a network of trading relationships, often (but not always) organized through a set of intermediaries or *broker-dealers*. Without a centralized limit-order book, most OTC markets do not feature pretrade price transparency. In particular, in the absence of publicly available bid and ask prices, investors have to *search* for quotes to buy or sell a particular quantity of an asset. Traditionally, search occurred on a bilateral basis, in the sense that investors contacted intermediaries one at a time. Though some OTC markets have introduced electronic platforms that allow investors to search on a multilateral basis—running auctions with a small number of dealers—trading in OTC markets remains fragmented. As a result, the terms of trade continue to vary across transactions and often depend on the identities of the counterparties. OTC markets traditionally did not feature posttrade price transparency either, though recent regulations—such as the Trade Reporting and Compliance Engine (TRACE) in the United States and the Markets in Financial Instruments Directive (MiFID) regulations in Europe—have been enacted to collect and share the terms of trade in completed transactions, albeit with some delay.

1.3 A Paradigm to Study OTC Markets

The unique structure, size, and central role of OTC markets in the financial system have prompted policymakers to confront a number of important issues. For example, in the early 2000s, concerns over a lack of transparency and competition in OTC markets prompted new regulations in the markets for corporate and municipal bonds, whereby certain market participants (mainly dealers) were required to report the price and quantity of their transactions soon after they occurred [Bessembinder and Maxwell, 2008]. With the collapse of several OTC markets during the GFC of 2007–2008, policymakers were faced with a new set of questions: How should they respond when trade collapses in an important OTC market? Should the government engage in ex post interventions, such as large-scale asset purchases? What regulations should be put in place ex ante to prevent such market failures in the future? Should OTC markets be forced to migrate to a centralized exchange?

More recently, economists have debated whether post-GFC regulations put in place to promote financial stability—such as stricter capital and liquidity requirements—have had the unintended consequence of reducing liquidity in certain OTC markets. For example, as Duffie [2012a] argues, intermediaries in OTC markets (i.e., dealers) have to use their balance sheets to provide liquidity to investors: they buy assets, hold them for a period of time as inventory, and resell them later, hopefully at a higher price. Therefore, policies that make it more expensive to hold assets reduce the dealers' incentives to provide liquidity, thereby increasing transaction costs and reducing market depth. These concerns materialized dramatically at the onset of the COVID-19 crisis, when various fixed income markets were subject to unprecedented selling pressures that dealers were unable or unwilling to absorb [Kargar, Lester, Lindsay, Liu, Weill, and Zúñiga, 2021]. In the wake of this crisis, regulators have been tasked with understanding the trade-off between promoting financial stability and maintaining liquidity in OTC markets.

Traditional models of financial markets are not appropriate to address these policy issues and, more generally, to analyze the functioning of OTC markets. Indeed, the vast majority of the asset pricing literature is based on the perfectly competitive Walrasian paradigm, in which investors submit their demand and supply curves to a fictitious auctioneer who sets a market-clearing price for multilateral trade. While this model of equilibrium prices and allocations is quite similar to centralized exchanges in practice, it bears little resemblance to OTC markets.

In particular, the Walrasian paradigm recognizes neither the decentralized nature of trade in OTC markets nor the crucial role that intermediaries play in facilitating trade and providing liquidity. Indeed, the fictitious auctioneer in the background of the Walrasian model leaves little room for understanding a variety of arrangements and institutions that have evolved to overcome the spatial and informational frictions inherent to over-the-counter trading. The Walrasian paradigm also ignores a key dimension of market quality in OTC markets, namely the *time* it takes investors to find a counterparty and trade. Last, but not least, models that ignore the decentralized (and, often, bilateral) nature of interactions among market participants are ill-suited to understand the sources of private information in OTC markets and the implications for prices and allocations.

To address these shortcomings, scholars interested in OTC markets have stepped away from the Walrasian paradigm and built new theoretical market settings to capture the key features of OTC markets. While various approaches have emerged, our objective in this book is to provide a unified treatment of one important strand of this literature that is now sufficiently mature to warrant its own textbook: the search-theoretic approach.

We start, in chapter 2, by discussing a number of empirical regularities that are common across many OTC markets, using data from the corporate bond market as a leading example. This introductory chapter is intended to establish a set of stylized facts and motivate the theoretical frameworks that we develop throughout the book.

Then, in chapter 3, we introduce the dynamic problem of an investor with time-varying preferences who searches for an acceptable price to trade, taking as given that price offers are drawn at random arrival dates from an exogenous distribution. This analysis is a crucial building block of the equilibrium models that follow. It also provides an opportunity to introduce and develop a number of technical tools and results, such as dynamic programming and Hamilton-Jacobi-Bellman (HJB) equations, that are used throughout the text. More generally, we aim for the book to be as self-contained as possible, minimizing the number of results and techniques that the reader needs to find elsewhere.

Understanding the basic decision problem of an individual investor sets the stage for chapters 4 and 5, where we present what we view as the two workhorse search-theoretic models of OTC markets. The first, which we refer to as the model of *semicentralized* OTC markets, considers an environment where investors with heterogeneous preferences and asset holdings periodically get the opportunity to trade with a dealer, who has access to a frictionless interdealer market. This model is meant to capture dealer-intermediated OTC markets, such as the U.S. corporate bond market, where most (if not all) trades are executed through intermediaries, who are able to reallocate assets through a relatively efficient interdealer market. The second model, which we call the *pure decentralized* market, considers an environment without dealers, where investors periodically meet and trade directly with other investors. This model is best applied to OTC markets such as the U.S. Fed Funds market, where financial institutions trade directly with other financial institutions, without any dedicated intermediaries or dealers. The analysis of these two workhorse models, and the various extensions and generalizations described below, derive in large part from Hugonnier, Lester, and Weill [2022], which itself extends the seminal contributions of Duffie, Gârleanu, and Pedersen [2005, 2007].

The remainder of the book builds off of these two workhorse models to create richer frameworks, which can be used to address a variety of important issues and questions. The first extension addresses the fact that both workhorse models described above abstract from the intensive margin of trade—that is, trade size—by assuming that assets are indivisible. In chapter 6, we relax this assumption and characterize the equilibrium in a semicentralized market setting with divisible asset holdings, as in Gârleanu [2009] and Lagos and Rocheteau [2009]. This extension allows us to study, among other things, the relationship between transaction costs and trade size.

Another important simplifying assumption in the model of semicentralized markets is that dealers trade among themselves in a frictionless, competitive market. While this is a good approximation of some dealer-intermediated OTC markets, it abstracts from the process of reallocation within the dealer sector, which is known to be frictional in some important OTC markets. For example, in their study of the U.S. municipal bond market, Li and Schürhoff [2019] document that trades between customers often involve long chains of trades within the dealer sector. Moreover, they show that the length of these *intermediation chains*, and the characteristics of the dealers who participate in them, have systematic relationships with the size of the transaction costs that investors pay. To study the importance of frictions *within* the dealer sector, chapter 7 develops a model in which investors trade with dealers, who themselves trade in a frictional interdealer model, as in Hugonnier, Lester, and Weill [2020].

Next, in chapter 8, we take a deep dive into the price-setting mechanisms that are used to determine the terms of trade between investors and dealers. We first explore the microfoundations of the bargaining game that is employed in the workhorse models described above, and then explore two alternative price-setting mechanisms. First, we consider a game based on the model of Burdett and Judd [1983], which is meant to capture the multilateral "request for quote" (RFQ) system that prevails on many of the increasingly popular electronic OTC trading platforms. Second, we analyze a framework where investors *direct* their search according to the prices posted by dealers, as in Moen [1997] and Burdett, Shi, and Wright [2001]. The latter extension is important for understanding, e.g., the trade-off that has been documented between trading cost and the speed of execution.

Given the central role of OTC markets in recent financial crises, it is also important to study how OTC markets perform in times of stress, which requires going beyond the analysis of steady-state equilibria. We tackle this problem in chapter 9, where we study the nonstationary dynamics of our semicentralized benchmark in response to a shock that generates a sudden surge in selling pressure. We characterize the optimal inventory accumulation of dealers as they attempt to "lean against the wind," and derive the subsequent implications for asset prices, trading volume, and overall market resilience.

Up until this point in the book, we maintained the assumption that trade occurs under perfect information. In particular, this means that both parties to a transaction observe their counterparty's *private value* for the asset, and that they are symmetrically informed about the quality—the *common value* component—of the asset. However, OTC markets are often considered to be "opaque": trade is decentralized with a lack of public signals or benchmarks that aggregate information. It is thus important to study the effects of asymmetric information over both private and common values. We tackle these two cases in chapters 10 and 11, respectively. We study how information and search frictions can combine to reduce trading volume and even cause markets to freeze; how the deleterious effects of private information can be exacerbated by search frictions; and how policymakers can intervene to help correct the distortions that arise from asymmetric information.

Finally, in chapter 12, we develop a theoretical model to make progress on several fundamental questions regarding the microstructure of financial markets. In particular, economists have long struggled to understand *why* some asset markets are organized through centralized exchanges while others trade OTC, and whether one type of structure generates higher welfare than the other [see, e.g., Rust and Hall, 2003]. Though there are many dimensions to this question, and many possible theoretical frameworks to study it, we contribute to the discussion by developing a model in which investors *choose* whether to trade through a centralized exchange or through an OTC market. We identify conditions under which the OTC market is too large or too small, and analyze how the optimal market structure depends on the primitives of the economy.

1.4 Some Final Notes

Before jumping in, we think it is worthwhile to discuss the way we have chosen to write the book and its relationship to other books in the literature. To start, we should emphasize that there are several different approaches to studying OTC markets, each with its own advantages and disadvantages. For example, a growing literature using network theory has evolved alongside—and, in some rare instances, made contact with—the literature using search theory to study OTC markets [see, e.g., Malamud and Rostek, 2017; Atkeson, Eisfeldt, and Weill, 2015]. While one would obviously like to cover all approaches to studying OTC markets, we have chosen to be narrow yet deep, as opposed to broad and, by necessity, more shallow. For the same reasons, we do not cover the small, but important literature that studies OTC markets in a broader macroeconomic context, by analyzing the *interaction* between prices and allocations in OTC markets and the decisions and/or outcomes in other areas of the economy.

These choices allow us to develop and extend a single theoretical framework throughout the book. We believe this approach has several advantages. First, from a pedagogical point of view, we are able to provide a unified discussion of existing work with a consistent set of assumptions and notation. Second, by incorporating a number of earlier studies into the context of a unified framework, we uncover several deep theoretical connections between seemingly different modeling approaches and assumptions within the literature. Finally, by showing how to modify our workhorse models with various extensions, our analysis equips the reader with a versatile framework that can be further extended and manipulated to conduct empirical, quantitative, and theoretical research.

Next, it is worth pointing out that we have striven to make this book self-contained by including nearly all the technical results *and the corresponding proofs* that one needs to understand our theoretical analysis. This makes the book well suited for graduate students and other researchers who are interested in the details of solving this class of models, along with other related search models that are used in labor economics, monetary economics, and industrial organization. However, the book is also written for those with more applied interests who desire an "off-the-shelf" model of OTC markets; wherever possible, we present or propose exercises on simplified special cases of our general framework, and also indicate the theoretical deep dives that can be skipped by the reader with more applied interests.

Finally, let us end this introduction with a discussion of related textbooks. Major references in the field of market microstructure include O'Hara [1995], Amihud, Mendelson, and Pedersen [2005], Hasbrouck [2007], and Foucault, Pagano, and Roell [2013]. We add to these important contributions by focusing on the recent literature addressing market liquidity from the point of view of search theory. The only earlier book on the search-theoretic approach to OTC markets is the Princeton Lectures of Duffie [2012b]. The present book has a different objective: we aim to provide a more systematic overview of the literature, including new methodological developments, applications, and empirical evidence. As such, it is a self-contained reference for a semester class on the topic. In addition, our work is related to several other important books on search theory, including Pissarides [2000], Shimer [2010], and Petroky-Nadeau and Wasmer [2017]—who use search theory to study labor economics—and Nosal and Rocheteau [2011], who present the search-theoretic approach to monetary economics. Our treatment should be viewed as complementary to these books, with a new focus on financial market applications and a significant number of new technical results to support our exploration.

2

OTC Market Facts

This introductory chapter sets the stage for our subsequent theoretical analyses by providing a number of empirical observations about OTC markets. To start, section 2.1 describes some general facts, including the overall size of global OTC markets and several important dimensions of heterogeneity across these markets that are relevant for our theoretical models.

In the remainder of the chapter, we document a series of stylized facts about a specific market—namely, the market for U.S. corporate bonds. First, in section 2.2, we describe the Trade Reporting and Compliance Engine (TRACE) data set and the standard procedure for cleaning the data and making it suitable for empirical economic analysis. Then, in section 2.3, we describe the patterns of trade in this market: the characteristics of trades, the process of intermediation, and estimates of the time it takes to complete a trade. Section 2.4 then offers a discussion of how to measure trading costs, and reports a number of their empirical properties.

The corporate bond market is a natural market to study for several reasons. For one, as noted above, it is a large OTC market and plays a key role in the allocation of capital in the U.S. corporate sector. In addition, since the TRACE data is publicly available, this market has been studied extensively. Lastly, the market structure of the U.S. corporate bond market is similar to that of several other large OTC markets. Importantly, the regularities we glean from this market motivate a number of modeling considerations throughout the book, and provide a quantitative benchmark for those interested in taking this class of models to the data.

2.1 The Basics

2.1.1 How Large Are OTC Markets?

Figure 2.1 breaks down the supply of publicly listed U.S. securities that were traded on exchanges (dark) and in OTC markets (light) in the year 2021. It reveals that a wide

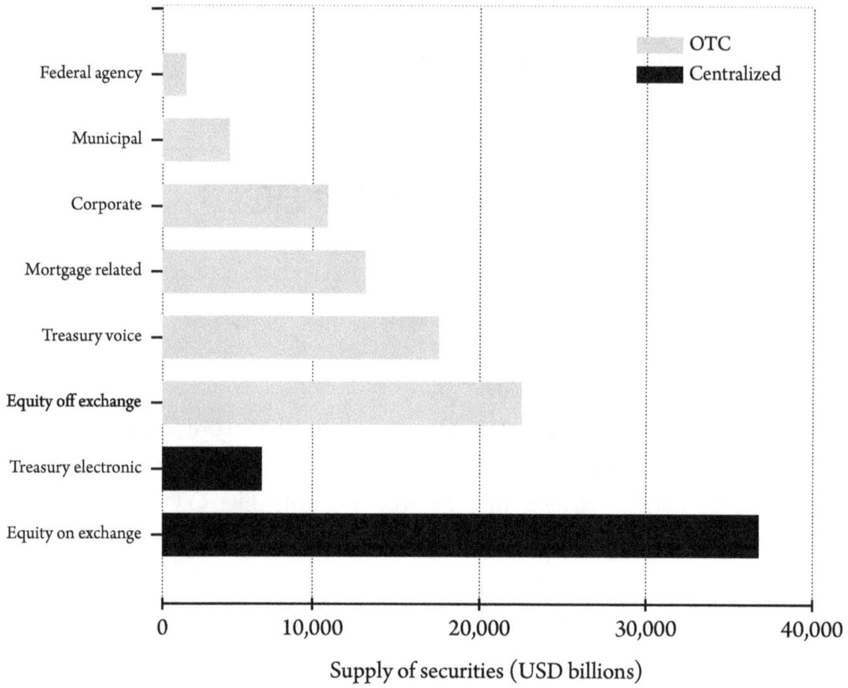

FIGURE 2.1. Supply of U.S. securities

This figure reports the supply of different types of publicly listed U.S. securities across centralized exchanges and OTC markets in billions of US dollars. See Online appendix A of Weill [2020] for a description of the data and method.

variety of securities trade OTC, most notably those in the fixed-income segment. Some securities, namely equities and Treasuries, actually trade in both OTC markets and exchanges. The figure illustrates that OTC markets are extremely large: the total supply of publicly listed securities traded in OTC markets was about USD66 trillion, which was approximately 50% more than the supply of assets traded on exchanges in 2021.

In addition to the securities listed in figure 2.1, several prominent classes of derivative products also trade OTC. According to the Bank for International Settlements (BIS), which regularly publishes global OTC derivative statistics, the two largest classes of OTC derivatives are interest rate and foreign exchange derivatives, with a combined traded notional value of close to USD700 trillion in the first semester of 2023. Many important credit markets also operate over the counter, including the Federal Funds market [Ashcraft and Duffie, 2007], the market for short-term loans between banks and money market funds [Beltran, 2021], and a significant portion of the market for repurchase agreements [Eisenschmidt, Ma, and Zhang, 2024]. Finally, many nonfinancial assets trade OTC, such as used capital [Gavazza, 2011a], real estate [Han and Strange, 2015], and even ideas [Silveira and Wright, 2010].

2.1.2 Heterogeneity Across OTC Markets

No two OTC markets are exactly alike. One key dimension of heterogeneity is that some markets have designated intermediaries who handle most of the trading volume, while others do not. For example, most of the volume in the U.S. corporate bond market is executed through dealers, whereas banks in the Fed Funds market tend to trade directly with one another without the help of a designated intermediary.

OTC markets also differ according to the protocols used to solicit quotes and/or determine the terms of trade. In many OTC markets, investors request quotes to buy or sell on a bilateral basis, contacting dealers or other investors sequentially and bargaining over the terms of trade. However, several markets have introduced platforms that allow investors to solicit requests for quotes (or RFQs) from multiple dealers at once. Using these new platforms, investors essentially conduct auctions that determine the price at which they trade.

The network of trading relationships also differs substantially across OTC markets. In some OTC markets, investors trade with a wide range of different counterparties, depending on their immediate trading needs, and the resulting network of relationships is relatively dispersed. In other markets, however, investors trade almost exclusively with a small number of counterparties with whom they have long-term relationships, so that the resulting network exhibits a so-called core-periphery structure.

Still another important dimension of heterogeneity across OTC markets is the method by which trades are settled or cleared. More specifically, some OTC markets specify that trades are settled bilaterally, so that counterparty risk is borne exclusively by the parties involved in a given trade. Alternatively, some markets have introduced a third party called a "central counterparty" (CCP) to assist in clearing the transfer of funds and assets and to collectively insure market participants against counterparty risk.

While each of these dimensions of heterogeneity across OTC markets has potentially interesting economic implications, we are not able to analyze all of them in this book, in part because the literature has not yet settled on a suitably unified framework. As a result, in the theoretical analyses that follow, we will focus on some specific features of OTC markets, such as whether they are intermediated by dealers and how investors solicit quotes, and leave other dimensions of heterogeneity, like the method by which trades clear, for future work.

2.1.3 OTC Market Data

Since OTC markets historically provided little pretrade and posttrade price transparency, transaction data was much less readily available than data from markets that operated through an exchange. However, in the last two decades, regulatory efforts to improve transparency have fostered the availability of data for several important OTC markets in the United States. For example, dealers trading corporate bonds, as well as various asset-backed securities, are now required to report transactions to the Trade Reporting and Compliance Engine (TRACE), which are aggregated and disseminated to the public after a short delay. Similar data is collected in the municipal bond market by the Municipal Securities Rulemaking Board (MSRB). These new datasets offer investors a benchmark for the valuations of the securities they seek to trade and, more importantly for our purposes, enable researchers to empirically study trading activity, transaction costs, and intermediation in OTC markets.

In the remainder of this chapter, we document a number of empirical regularities for one particular dealer-intermediated OTC market: the market for U.S. corporate bonds. We choose this market for several reasons. First, as noted above, it is a large and important market. Second, the data on corporate bonds has been made widely available and offers a relatively long time series of prices and quantities traded. Third, there are well-documented algorithms available for cleaning and analyzing this data. Finally, since this market has been widely studied, there are a number of stylized facts that have been established in the academic literature.

To be clear, we do not intend to provide an exhaustive list of stylized facts. Rather, our goal is to establish some general properties of the corporate bond market—many of which are shared by other OTC markets—and to motivate the models that follow. In particular, we describe how customers trade with dealers and the process by which securities are reallocated within the dealer sector. We document that trading costs are often substantial; that they vary significantly depending on the characteristics of the bond, and on both the size and the direction of the trade; and that there is a considerable amount of dispersion in trading prices after controlling for observables. At this stage, we resist the temptation to formulate economic interpretations of these facts, choosing instead to explore these empirical regularities within the context of the theoretical frameworks we develop in subsequent chapters.

2.2 U.S. Corporate Bond Market Data

2.2.1 Data

In July 2002, the Financial Industry Regulatory Authority (FINRA) introduced the TRACE, which requires dealers to report all transactions within fifteen minutes of execution. These transaction reports include the time of the trade, a unique identifier for the bond that was traded, the trade size, the transaction price, the side of the trade on which the dealer participated, and some information about the counterparty. Since most trades in the corporate bond market involve at least one dealer, these reports constitute a near-comprehensive record of all secondary-market transactions in U.S. corporate bonds.

Upon receiving these TRACE reports, FINRA disseminates the information to the investment and academic communities with varying levels of details. For example, while FINRA does not collect information about customers, different versions of the dataset provide varying levels of information about the identity of the dealer(s) involved in a transaction. The various versions of the TRACE data also differ with respect to top-coding: some versions only report trading volume up to a cap of USD5 million for investment-grade bonds and USD1 million for high-yield bonds. The academic version of the dataset that we study here is one of the most detailed available: it is not top-coded and provides anonymized identifiers that allow one to follow a dealer's transactions over time.

2.2.2 Cleaning the Data

Dick-Nielsen [2014, 2019] describes a cleaning process for the TRACE data that has become standard in the academic literature. The data must be cleaned for several reasons. First, dealers sometimes correct their initial reports, perhaps because some details were entered incorrectly in the system or because the transaction was canceled. As a result, some transactions are associated with several reports: the original, and the subsequent corrections or cancellation. Second, each interdealer transaction appears twice in the dataset because both dealers are required to report their trades. As a result, one must remove these duplicate reports so that each transaction appears only once, with the most up-to-date information about the terms of trade. Third, one often removes bonds with exotic features, such as convertibility or foreign currency denomination, so as to keep the sample homogeneous. Fourth, since trading activity differs markedly for newly issued bonds and bonds close to maturity, one typically removes trades that occur within two months of a bond's issuance and less than one year to its maturity. Focusing on trades for bonds outside of the beginning and end of their lifespan allows us to focus on trading activity when it has reached a relatively stationary level, as envisioned in the steady-state equilibrium of the models studied in this book.

Since the TRACE dataset is continuously growing, the implementation of the basic algorithm proposed in Dick-Nielsen [2014] has become increasingly time-consuming. To overcome this computational challenge, Palleja [2022] developed an alternative, recursive algorithm that is sufficiently efficient to be run on a laptop computer. In this chapter, we apply this novel algorithm to the academic version of the TRACE data for the two-year window of 2016 and 2017, which contains more than 14 million transactions.

2.3 Trading Activity

2.3.1 Basic Facts

The first four rows of table 2.1 provide some of the characteristics of bonds traded during these two years. On average, bonds in the sample are about four years removed from issuance and have approximately eight years to maturity. The average coupon rates and yield spreads are around 4 to 5 percent, though yield spreads vary substantially based, in part, on differences in credit risk.

Next, the middle section of table 2.1 provides insight into the frequency and size of trades. The first observation is that individual bonds do not trade very often: the average bond trades a little more than 700 times per year. Assuming that there are about 250 trading days, this means that the average bond trades less than three times per day. There is, however, a lot of dispersion: bonds at the 5th percentile trade only eight times per year, while bonds at the 95th percentile trade approximately 3,000 times. Consistent with these observations, the average yearly turnover is close to 50%, but ranges from about 2% at the 5th percentile to more than 140% at the 95th percentile. By contrast the World Bank reports that the average turnover for U.S. equities over the same period was about 105% [World Federation of Exchanges database, n.d.]. The table also reveals that trade sizes are large—with an average of nearly USD500,000—and that there is considerable dispersion in the size of trades. Presumably, a significant portion of this dispersion reflects heterogeneity among market participants, with retail investors trading small quantities of bonds and institutional investors trading larger blocks.

Finally, the bottom section of table 2.1 reports statistics for three separate segments of the market: the customer-to-dealer (CD) segment that records sales of bonds by customers to dealers; the dealer-to-customer (DC) segment that records sales by dealers to customers; and the dealer-to-dealer (DD) segment that records interdealer trades. The DC and CD turnover are approximately equal, implying that most of what dealers buy from customers is sold to other customers, and not absorbed into the inventory of the dealer sector as a whole. At the same time, DD turnover is substantial as well. This reflects the fact that, when a customer sells an asset to a dealer, this asset is often retraded between dealers before being reallocated to another customer. Finally, note that trade size differs across market segments. Indeed, DD trades tend to be much smaller

Table 2.1. Trading activity statistics from TRACE, 2016–2017

Variables	Obs.	Mean	P5	P25	P50	P75	P95
Bond age (year)	14,246,209	3.84	0.42	1.51	2.99	5.01	10.11
Time to maturity (year)	14,246,209	8.11	1.57	3.67	5.74	8.67	26.60
Coupon rate (pp)	14,246,127	4.72	2.05	3.25	4.50	6.00	8.00
Yield spread (pp)	14,133,403	3.89	0.40	0.87	1.62	3.49	10.14
All - Trades per bond-year	19,810	719.14	8.00	70.00	254.00	781.00	2,986.00
All - Yearly turnover (pp)	19,810	48.75	1.98	14.74	33.82	63.84	142.91
All - Trade par value ($K)	14,246,209	475.00	3.00	10.00	25.00	150.00	2,500.00
CD - Trades per bond-year	19,810	174.25	2.00	19.00	69.00	195.00	700.55
CD - Yearly turnover (pp)	19,810	19.89	0.56	5.34	13.23	26.52	60.79
CD - Trade par value ($K)	3,451,841	815.75	2.00	10.00	35.00	350.00	5,000.00
DC - Trades per bond-year	19,810	244.82	2.00	23.00	89.00	265.00	993.55
DC - Yearly turnover (pp)	19,810	19.22	0.36	5.22	12.78	25.61	58.91
DC - Trade par value ($K)	4,849,866	562.35	3.00	10.00	28.00	200.00	3,000.00
DD - Trades per bond-year	19,810	300.08	2.00	21.00	87.00	305.00	1,293.55
DD - Yearly turnover (pp)	19,810	9.63	0.12	1.79	5.33	12.17	32.25
DD - Trade par value ($K)	5,944,502	205.86	2.00	10.00	23.00	90.00	1,000.00

In this table the notations *pp* and *$K* refer to percentage points and to USD 1,000, respectively. The variables have different numbers of observations because they are calculated using different samples.

Table 2.2. Distribution of volume across dealers

Market segment	30%	60%	90%	100%
Total dealer-customer volume	4	8	29	1,161
CD volume	4	8	26	1,086
DC volume	4	8	32	1,040
Interdealer volume	8	21	72	1,228

than trades between customers and dealers. Moreover, there is an asymmetry in trade size between customers and dealers: CD trades are, on average, larger than DC trades. Since CD and DC turnover are approximately equal, this mechanically means that there are more CD trades than DC trades, which suggests that customers tend to split their trades more often when they buy than when they sell.

2.3.2 *Intermediation*

Given the substantial volume of trade between dealers, several researchers have explored the process of reallocation that occurs within the intermediation sector. In particular, Li and Schürhoff [2019] have shown that, in the market for municipal bonds, dealers trade together along so-called *intermediation chains.* A chain begins when a customer sells to a dealer (a CD trade), which is followed by a series of DD trades until a dealer resells to a customer (a DC trade). We can use the trading volume data in table 2.1 to derive a rough estimate of the length of these intermediation chains in the corporate bond market. To do so, let $\bar{n}$ denote the number of dealers in a typical intermediation chain, so that the number of DD trades in a chain is $\bar{n} - 1$. Assuming, for simplicity, that CD and DD trades have the same size, the ratio of DD to CD volume is $\bar{n} - 1$. In the data, this ratio is approximately equal to 0.5, implying that the average length of intermediation chains in the corporate bond market is $\bar{n} = 1.5$. Finally, table 2.1 reveals that DD trades are typically smaller than CD and DC trades, which suggests that intermediation chains often involve splitting up the initial block into smaller quantities that are easier to trade.

Existing empirical studies have documented substantial heterogeneity in the frequency with which dealers participate in intermediation chains and in their typical position within a chain. Table 2.2 reports that trading volume is very unevenly distributed across dealers: Among all trades between customers and dealers, 90% of the volume is accounted for by about 30 dealers (out of the 1,161 active dealers). Concentration is also substantial in the DD segment of the market, though less pronounced—approximately 90% of the volume is concentrated among 72 dealers. Concentration in the interdealer segment is related to an observation made by Hollifield, Neklyudov, and

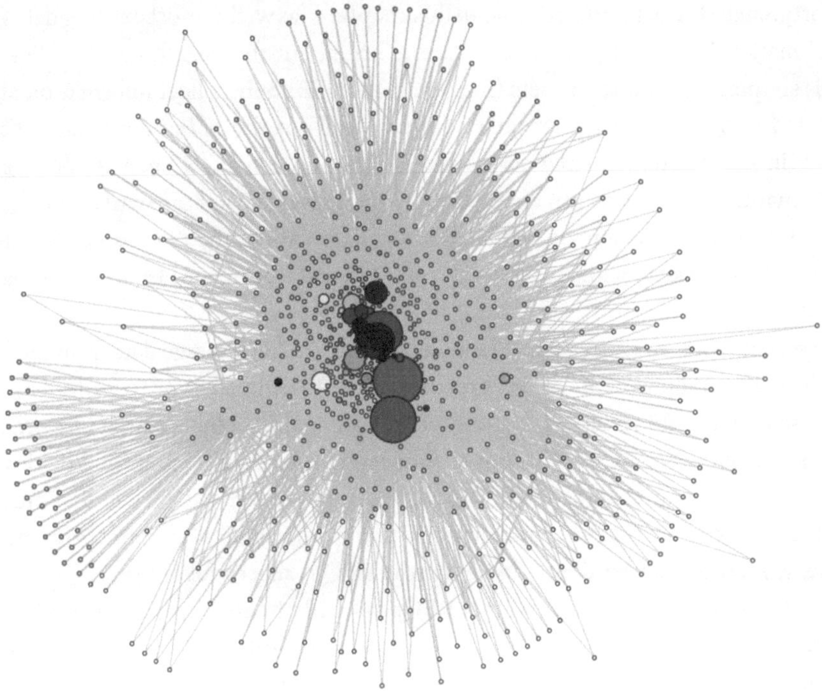

FIGURE 2.2. The network of interdealer trades

This figure illustrates the core-periphery structure of the interdealer network. Nodes in the graph represent dealers, edges represent trades, and the size and shade of the nodes reflect the number and size of executed trades.

Spatt [2017] and Li and Schürhoff [2019], among others, that interdealer markets have a *core-periphery* network structure. That is, there is a core of large dealers who trade actively with each other and a periphery of small dealers who mostly trade with the core. Figure 2.2 confirms this observation by plotting the network of interdealer trades in our two-year sample. In the picture, each node represents a dealer, and the size of the node is proportional to the number of trades executed. The picture reveals that dealers in the core trade frequently and that they are often in the middle of an intermediation chain, whereas dealers in the periphery trade less often and typically find themselves at one end of a chain.

2.3.3 *Trading Delays*

A premise of the search models that we study in this book is that investors in OTC markets have to find a counterpart to trade and, hence, executing a trade can take time.

Unfortunately, the data studied so far in this chapter—as well as most existing data from OTC markets—cannot provide direct evidence about this search process. The reason is simple: since most datasets (including TRACE) only collect information about executed transactions, they are only informative about the *end* of a *successful* search. This is in sharp contrast with data from other frictional markets, such as labor or real estate markets, where one can observe how long sellers stay on the market. For example, labor market data contains detailed information about the duration of search for unemployed workers, while residential real estate datasets record time on the market for listed homes.

In recent work, Kargar, Lester, Plante, and Weill [2023] leverage data from the leading electronic trading platform for corporate bonds to estimate time to trade. The data they use contains information about when investors initiate their search by sending a request for quotes (RFQ) and about the subsequent responses submitted by dealers. The data is unique in that it contains all of the details for each RFQ, including the time at which it occurred, the bond and quantity that the investor wanted to trade, and the replies from dealers, regardless of whether the RFQ is successful or not.

Kargar et al. [2023] document that RFQs fail fairly frequently: investors reject the offers they receive (or, less frequently, don't receive any offers) about 30% of the time. When this occurs, investors often come back to the market and send additional RFQs for the same quantity of the same bond. Kargar et al. [2023] interpret these repeat attempts as evidence of sequential search in the market for corporate bonds. After correcting for biases, they estimate that, after an unsuccessful RFQ, it takes about two to three days for investors to complete a trade. They show that time to trade varies considerably depending on the trade and investor characteristics, as well as the state of the market. For example, they document that it takes longer to trade larger quantities, that attempts to sell are completed faster than attempts to buy, and that certain customers who appear to be more connected to the dealer sector trade substantially faster than other customers who have fewer connections.

2.4 Trading Costs

2.4.1 Measurement

Measuring trading costs in OTC markets is a challenging task. In contrast to exchanges, where prevailing bid and ask prices are available at all times, round-trip trading costs in OTC markets have to be constructed from trades between customers and dealers that are recorded at different points in time. Moreover, as noted above, it is often hours (or even days or weeks) between consecutive CD and DC trades for a particular bond.

There are a number of different methodologies that have been proposed to overcome the challenge of measuring trading costs. In what follows, we use the methodology of Choi, Huh, and Seunghun Shin [2024] because it has a close theoretical counterpart in the models we study throughout the book. Specifically, we calculate the markup (markdown) that dealers charge customers who buy (sell) relative to a reference interdealer price. To compute this reference interdealer price at the bond-day level, we calculate the volume-weighted average interdealer price of a particular bond on a given day. Then, for all trades in the same bond on the same day, we let the trading cost be the percentage markup (if the dealer sells to a customer) or markdown (if the dealer buys from a customer) relative to this reference price.

Since we only consider CD and DC trades that can be matched with a DD trade on the same bond-day, the sample is selected. Table 2.3 provides summary statistics. Comparing with the last rows of table 2.1, one sees that about 14% of the full sample of CD and DC trades could not be matched to a reference interdealer price. However, the resulting sample does not seem to be dramatically selected; for example, the distribution of turnover in the restricted sample is quite similar to that in the overall sample.

The table reveals information about the typical magnitude and variation in trading costs. For example, it shows that the median one-way trading cost is 18 bps. The trading cost at the 5th percentile is actually negative—a phenomenon that Choi et al. [2024] interpreted as customer liquidity provision—while the trading cost at the 95th percentile exceeds 200 bps.

2.4.2 The Determinants of Trading Costs

Following the methodology of Edwards, Harris, and Piwowar [2007], we study the empirical determinants of trading costs using regression analysis, including fixed effects for day, dealer, and the industry of the bond's issuer. The results are reported in table 2.4.

The first two lines of the table reveal that transaction costs increase with the age and time to maturity of the bond being traded. The next lines show that transaction costs are higher for riskier bonds, as measured by the yield spread or by credit rating. Note that the relationship between transaction cost and credit rating is economically quite significant: the difference in trading cost between a bond in the highest and the lowest credit rating bins is more than 40 bps on average. The next lines confirm that transaction costs decrease with trade size. This relationship is economically significant, but also nonlinear: relative to the omitted microtrade category, all trades above USD100,000 have a similar discount of approximately 15 bps.

Table 2.3. Properties of trades in the selected trading cost sample

	Observations	Mean	P5	P25	P50	P75	P95
Bond age (year)	7,098,957	3.79	3.43	1.50	2.96	4.93	9.73
Time to maturity (year)	7,098,957	7.83	1.55	3.63	5.68	8.49	26.00
Coupon rate (pp)	7,098,940	4.64	2.00	3.20	4.45	5.95	7.88
Yield spread (pp)	7,045,916	3.71	0.38	0.83	1.55	3.38	9.69
Trades per bond-year	19,293	429.97	6.00	50.00	175.00	485.00	1,712.00
Yearly turnover (pp)	19,293	39.74	1.48	11.33	26.74	52.62	119.74
Trade par value ($K)	7,098,957	541.07	2.00	10.00	25.00	125.00	3,000.00
Transaction cost (bp)	7,098,957	47.42	−21.72	1.99	17.78	65.84	215.28

Table 2.4. Transaction cost regression

Independent Variable	Coefficient	Standard Error
Bond age	0.5247***	(0.0985)
Time to maturity	2.189***	(0.0698)
Yield spread	0.4447***	(0.0642)
Credit rating		
IG (A-BBB)	5.285***	(0.8990)
HY (BB-B)	25.02***	(1.1320)
HY (CCC-D)	42.78***	(1.7710)
Trade size		
Odd lot (>100K-1M)	−13.94***	(0.3290)
Round lot (>1M-5M)	−17.30***	(0.4252)
5M and above	−13.38***	(0.4046)
Dealer-Customer (DC)	9.588***	(0.5208)
Agency	−3.035***	(0.4425)
Agency × DC	−12.98***	(0.6454)
Day FE	Yes	
Dealer FE	Yes	
Issuer industry FE	Yes	
Observations	6,896,251	
Adjusted R^2	0.36189	

Bond age and time to maturity are expressed in years while yield spreads are expressed in percentage points, and transaction costs in basis points. Credit ratings are split into four bins, of which IG (AAA–AA) is used as a baseline. Similarly, trade sizes, expressed in US dollars, are split into four bins, with micro (0–100k) CD trades used as a baseline. Bond-day clustered standard errors are presented in parenthesis with superscripts *,**, and *** denoting statistical significance at 10%, 5%, and 1%, respectively. Detailed credit ratings are obtained from the Mergent Fixed Income Security Database (FISD).

We noted earlier that there is an asymmetry between the trade size of DC and CD trades—namely, that DC trades are smaller than CD trades. Moving down the table reveals that there is a similar asymmetry between transaction costs. In particular, we find that DC trades are more expensive, by about 10 bps, than CD trades.

Finally, the last lines of table 2.4 introduce an important distinction between two types of transactions that dealers facilitate. The first type is called a *risky principal* (or just *principal*) trade, when a dealer buys bonds from a customer on her own account, holds them in inventory for some period of time, and then sells to a different customer. The second type of transaction is called an *agency* trade. Under this trading arrangement, the dealer is essentially a matchmaker: she does not use her own inventory capacity to facilitate the trade, but rather matches a customer who wants to sell with a customer who wants to buy (much like a real estate agent).

Empirical studies typically identify agency trades by finding pairs of trades, one CD trade and one DC trade, that are reported in rapid succession for the same quantity of the same bond. Intuitively, when a dealer facilitates an agency trade, she buys from one customer, sells immediately to another, and reports the two trades to TRACE at the same time. After distinguishing between these two types of trades in our data, table 2.4 reveals that agency trades are less costly than principal trades, and that the effect is twice as large for DC trades than for it is CD trades.

2.4.3 Dealer-to-Dealer vs. Customer-to-Dealer Frictions

How large are the frictions in the DD segment relative to the CD/DC segments? One way to answer this question is to compare the realized dispersion of prices in the DD market to that of prices in the CD/DC markets.

Figure 2.3 plots a histogram of the level of dispersion in the DC/CD and DD market segments. To generate this figure, we compute the realized dispersion of log prices in the DD market and in the CD/DC market at the bond-day level. For each bond, we restrict our attention to days in which there are at least 10 trades in each market segment, which obviously biases the sample toward relatively active bonds. Despite this bias, the figure clearly suggests that dispersion is significantly lower in the DD segment, which has a mean of about 40 bps, while the CD/DC segment has a mean of about 74 bps. Clearly, the *level* of dispersion reflects both the arrival of news about fundamental values and frictions. However, the *difference* in dispersion is likely to reflect differences in frictions.

One could argue that some of this difference reflects sample selection, since the two segments are active for different bonds at different times. To address this concern, we regress our measure of realized price dispersion on a market segment indicator (DD or CD/DC), trade-size category dummies, as well as bond and day fixed effects. Interestingly, the results of this regression, which are reported in table 2.5, suggest an even larger difference between the price dispersion in the two segments—about 44 bps—which is close to the size of the median round-trip trading cost paid by customers.

2.5 Notes and References

While there have been some early studies of OTC markets, such as Garbade and Silber [1976], much of the empirical research on the topic traces back to the early 2000s, when trade-level data first became available for some OTC markets. Seminal

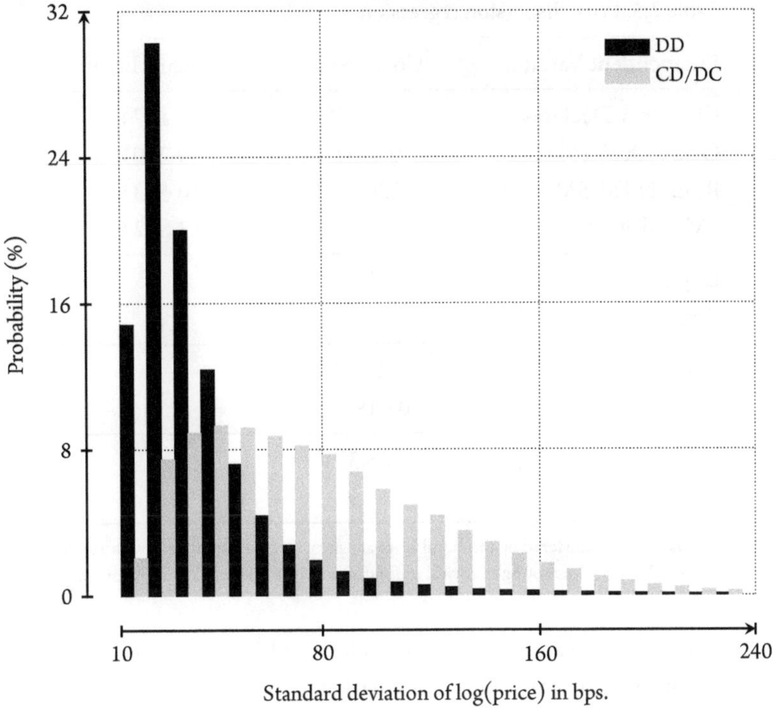

FIGURE 2.3. Price dispersion in the corporate bond market

This figure illustrates the extent of price dispersion in the DD and CD/DC segments of the U.S. corporate bond market over the period 2016–2017.

contributions include Edwards, Harris, and Piwowar [2007] for the U.S. corporate bond market; Green, Hollifield, and Schürhoff [2006] for the U.S. municipal bond market; and Ashcraft and Duffie [2007] for the federal funds market. The literature has grown significantly since then, particularly in certain fixed-income markets [see the survey by Bessembinder, Spatt, and Venkataraman, 2020].

While it is impossible to do justice to every paper in this extensive literature, it is worthwhile to mention some of the markets and economic phenomena that have been studied empirically, and that we will discuss later in the book. Bao, Pan, and Jiang [2011], Friewald and Nagler [2019], and He, Khorrami, and Song [2022] document certain dimensions of commonality in illiquidity across corporate bonds. Bessembinder, Maxwell, and Venkataraman [2006], Goldstein, Hotchkiss, and Sirri [2007], Bessembinder and Maxwell [2008], and Asquith, Covert, and Pathak [2013] study the impact of regulations promoting price transparency on OTC market liquidity.

Table 2.5. Price dispersion regression

Independent Variable	Coefficient	Standard Error
Customer-Dealer	43.69***	(1.147)
Odd (100K-1M)	0.6941***	(0.250)
Round (1M-5M)	2.808***	(0.533)
5M and above	−17.02***	(2.562)
Day FE	Yes	
Bond FE	Yes	
Observations	182,969	
Adjusted R^2	0.61971	
% Vol	25.3	
% Trades	15.9	

Standard errors clustered at the bond level are presented in parenthesis with superscripts *,**, and *** denoting statistical significance at 10%, 5%, and 1% respectively.

Hendershott and Madhavan [2015] and O'Hara and Zhou [2021] study the rise of electronic platforms in the corporate bond market. Afonso, Kovner, and Schoar [2014] and Hendershott, Li, Livdan, and Schürhoff [2020] offer evidence on the importance of trading relationships in the fed funds and U.S. corporate bond markets, respectively. Bessembinder, Jacobsen, Maxwell, and Venkataraman [2018], Adrian, Boyarchenko, and Shachar [2017], Trebbi and Xiao [2017], Choi, Huh, and Seunghun Shin [2024] and Bao, O'Hara, and Zhou [2018] study the adverse impact of balance sheet constraints and other regulations on bond market liquidity, while Dick-Nielsen, Feldhütter, and Lando [2012], Friewald, Jankowitsch, and Subrahmanyam [2012], Di Maggio, Kermani, and Song [2017], Dick-Nielsen and Rossi [2019], O'Hara and Zhou [2021], and Kargar, Lester, Lindsay, Liu, Weill, and Zúñiga [2021] study the performance of OTC markets under stress. Foley-Fisher, Gissler, and Verani [2019] study security lending in the corporate bond market, while Li, O'Hara, Rapp, and Zhou [2023] analyze the effects of the recent trend toward exchanging portfolios instead of individual bonds. Credit derivative markets have been studied empirically in Arora, Gandhi, and Longstaff [2012], Siriwardane [2019], and Riggs, Onur, Reiffen, and Zhu [2018] using proprietary data. Finally, Kondor and Pinter [2022] and Pinter, Wang, and Zou [2021] exploit a unique feature of data from the UK bond market—the ability to track the identity of customers over time—to study the importance of customers' identities on trading outcomes.

3

Sequential Search for Assets

In this chapter, we study a dynamic decision problem in the style of McCall [1970] but in the context of an over-the-counter (OTC) asset market instead of a labor market. The analysis of this benchmark problem allows us to introduce many of the objects and techniques that will be used throughout the text, and also serves as a crucial building block for the equilibrium models that we consider in later chapters. The techniques discussed in this chapter are also useful more generally to formulate and solve the dynamic optimization problems that naturally arise in search-and-matching models of OTC markets.

Section 3.1 introduces the model: an individual investor searches for the best price to sequentially buy and sell an asset, taking as given the arrival rate of trading opportunities and the distribution of price offers. Section 3.2 formally defines the associated stochastic control problem and provides a proof of the dynamic programming principle. Section 3.3 derives the solution to this optimization problem by analyzing the associated Bellman equation. Section 3.4 introduces the related concept of the Hamilton-Jacobi-Bellman (HJB) equation.

3.1 The Model

The models we consider throughout the book are cast in continuous time over an infinite horizon, and are subject to uncertainty represented by a probability space $(\Omega, \mathcal{F}, \mathbf{P})$ equipped with a filtration $\mathbb{F} = \{\mathcal{F}_t\}_{t\geq 0}$ that captures the gradual resolution of uncertainty. While the precise specification of these elements may vary across models, we maintain the assumption that $\mathbb{F}$ satisfies the usual conditions of right-continuity and completion.

3.1.1 The Investor

We consider an infinitely lived investor who is risk-neutral and discounts the future at rate $r > 0$. The investor can hold zero or one unit of an asset and enjoys a utility flow $q_t\delta_t\,dt$ from holding $q_t \in \{0, 1\}$ units at date $t \geq 0$, so that the lifetime utility derived from a sequence of asset holdings is

$$\mathbf{E}\left[\int_0^\infty e^{-rt} q_t \delta_t dt\right].$$

The utility flow δ_t characterizes the investor and is thus often referred to as his *type* when we later consider models with heterogeneous investors.

We assume that δ_t takes values in some bounded interval, $\mathcal{D} \equiv (\underline{\delta}, \overline{\delta})$, and evolves according to a continuous Markov jump process that can be described as follows: Starting from $\delta \in \mathcal{D}$, the process remains constant until the first jump of a Poisson process with intensity $\gamma > 0$. At that point in time, the utility flow is reset to some value $\delta' \in \mathcal{D}$ that is drawn from a cumulative distribution function $F(\cdot|\delta)$, and the same cycle begins anew. Figure 3.1 illustrates a sample path of the utility flow process, and appendix A.6 provides a brief introduction to Markov jump processes.

In our framework, the set $\mathcal{D}$ of *potential* utility flows is always assumed to be an open interval. However, the set of *accessible* utility flows, defined as the smallest closed set A such that

$$F(A|\delta_0) \equiv \int_{\underline{\delta}}^{\overline{\delta}} \mathbf{1}_{\{A\}} dF(x|\delta_0) = 1, \qquad \forall \delta_0 \in \mathcal{D},$$

merely has to be contained in $\mathcal{D}$. Thus, the set of accessible utility flows can be an open or closed interval, a collection of isolated points, or a countable union of intervals and isolated points. This assumption, which we maintain throughout the text, serves several purposes. First, as we formally establish in appendix A.2, it guarantees that the distribution functions that we consider do not have mass points on the boundary of $\mathcal{D}$, which considerably simplifies the manipulation of integrals. Second, it allows us to consider transient states from which the utility flow may start but to which it never returns. We exploit this opportunity in chapter 9 to study the transition dynamics of an OTC market following an aggregate shock. Third, this level of generality allows for a unified treatment of all the distributions considered in the literature.

Example 3.1: As a first example, consider the case in which the set of accessible states consists of two points, as in Duffie, Gârleanu, and Pedersen [2005, 2007]. Formally, let $\delta_L < \delta_H$ be a pair of points in $\mathcal{D}$ and consider the cumulative distribution function

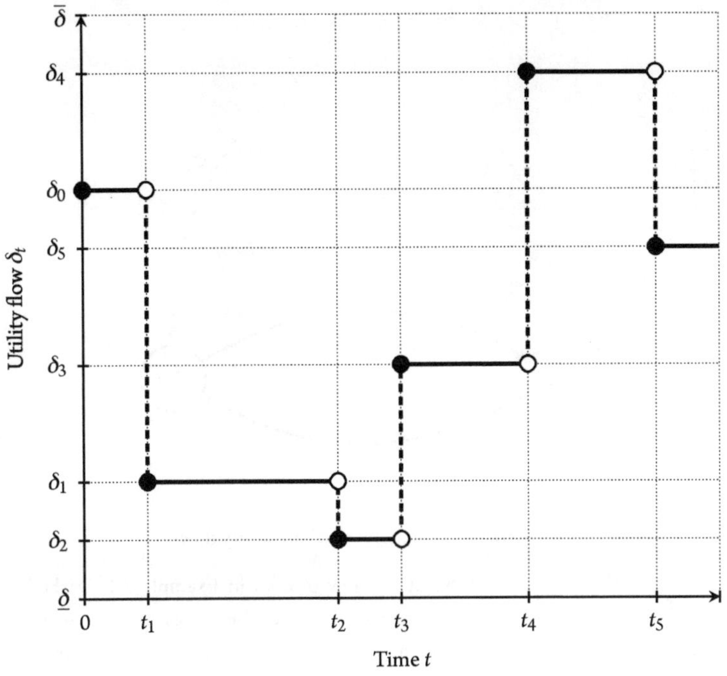

FIGURE 3.1. A sample path of the utility flow process

Along the illustrated path, the utility flow jumps from δ_i to $\delta_{i+1} \sim F(\cdot|\delta_i)$ at time t_{i+1}. The time intervals between jumps, $t_{i+1} - t_i$, are the realizations of a sequence of independent exponential random variables with arrival rate γ.

given by

$$F(\delta) = f_L \mathbf{1}_{\{\delta_L \leq \delta\}} + f_H \mathbf{1}_{\{\delta_H \leq \delta\}} = \begin{cases} 0, & \delta < \delta_L, \\ f_L, & \delta_L \leq \delta < \delta_H, \\ 1, & \delta \geq \delta_H, \end{cases} \tag{3.1}$$

for $f_L, f_H > 0$ such that $f_L + f_H = 1$. The behavior of the corresponding utility flow process is illustrated in figure 3.2. Starting from a transient state δ that lies outside the set of accessible utility flow $\{\delta_L, \delta_H\}$, the process remains idle for an exponentially distributed time with mean $1/\gamma$ and then jumps either to δ_L with probability

$$\Delta F(\delta_L) \equiv F(\delta_L) - \lim_{x \uparrow \delta_L} F(x) = F(\delta_L) - F(\delta_L-) = f_L$$

or to δ_H with probability $\Delta F(\delta_H) = 1 - f_L = f_H$. Following this first reset, the utility

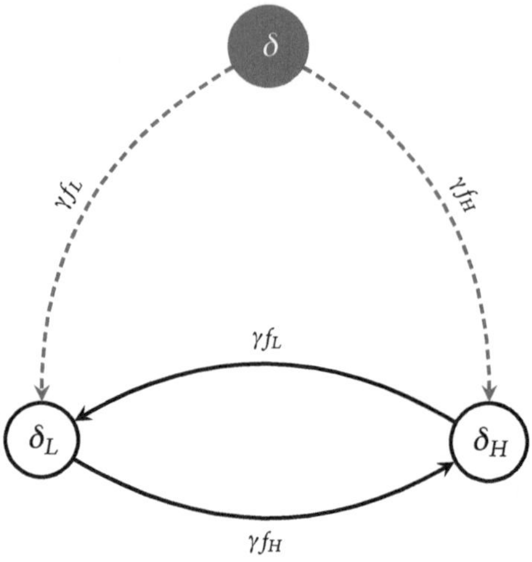

FIGURE 3.2. Transitions of the utility flow

This figure illustrates the dynamics of the utility flow process in Example 3.1. Dashed arrows indicate transitions from a transient state δ to either of the accessible states $\{\delta_L, \delta_H\}$ while solid arrows indicate transitions between accessible states. The annotation of each arrow gives the intensity with which the transition occurs.

flow process then cycles between the accessible states with transitions from the high state δ_H to the low state δ_L occurring at rate γf_L and opposite transitions occurring at rate γf_H.

***Example* 3.2:** As a second example, let $\mathcal{D} = (0, 1)$ and $F(x|\delta) = x$. In this case, the set of potential and accessible utility flows are the same. There are no mass points and each new utility flow, x, is drawn independently from the current utility flow, δ, according to a uniform distribution on $(0, 1)$.

3.1.2 *Trading Opportunities*

Over time, the investor randomly meets counterparties that present him with opportunities to buy or sell. To model this feature, we assume that the jumps of a Poisson process N_{1t} with intensity $\lambda_1 > 0$ the investor receives an offer to sell at a price drawn from a cumulative distribution $G_1(\cdot|\delta)$ on some bounded interval $\mathcal{P} = (\underline{\pi}, \overline{\pi})$. Symmetrically, we assume that the jump times of another, independent, Poisson process N_{0t} with intensity $\lambda_0 > 0$ the investor receives offers to buy at a price drawn from a cumulative distribution $G_0(\cdot|\delta)$ that is also defined on the interval $\mathcal{P}$.

In this chapter, we take the price distributions $\mathbf{G}_0 = \{G_0(\cdot|\delta) : \delta \in \mathcal{D}\}$ and $\mathbf{G}_1 = \{G_1(\cdot|\delta) : \delta \in \mathcal{D}\}$ as exogenously given, without explaining where these distributions come from or why they might depend on the investor's utility flow. However, in subsequent chapters, we show that our assumptions turn out to be natural equilibrium outcomes when investors bargain over terms of trade with potential counterparties.

3.2 The Sequential Search Problem

In this section, we briefly study the optimal stochastic control formulation of the sequential search problem. Note that this is pedagogically more advanced material; the reader may prefer to skip it at first pass, and proceed directly to the analysis of the Bellman equation in section 3.3. However, there are several reasons to present the stochastic control problem first. For one, as a matter of logic, it is the primitive optimization program that the investor seeks to solve. Second, it allows us to formally establish the dynamic programming principle that serves as a basis for the derivation of the Bellman equation. Finally, it delivers *a priori* properties of the value function that narrow down the functional space in which the solution to the Bellman equation lies, and thereby unlocks the power of contraction mapping arguments.

3.2.1 *Formulation*

In the sequential search problem, the investor selects a trading strategy that prescribes whether or not to trade when given the opportunity. Formally, a trading strategy is represented by a stochastic process

$$\alpha : \Omega \times \mathbf{R}_+ \to \{0, 1\}$$

that is adapted to the filtration $\mathbb{F}$ generated by the observation of utility flows, meeting times, and price offers. If the strategy is such that $\alpha_s(\omega) = 1$, then it prescribes that the investor should trade, if an opportunity to do so materializes at time $s \geq 0$ in state $\omega \in \Omega$. If, instead, $\alpha_s(\omega) = 0$ then the investor will not trade. The requirement that the strategy be adapted to $\mathbb{F}$ guarantees that the investor cannot condition her behavior on future events, but allows her strategy to depend in arbitrary ways on present and past information. Importantly, this means that the trading decision at time s depends on the price offered at that time. In what follows, we denote by $\mathcal{A}$ the set of all trading strategies available to the investor.

If the investor holds $q_t \in \{0, 1\}$ units of the asset at time $t \geq 0$ and uses a strategy α, then his holdings evolve according to

$$dq_s^\alpha = \alpha_s(1 - q_{s-}^\alpha)dN_{0s} - \alpha_s q_{s-}^\alpha dN_{1s}, \qquad q_t^\alpha = q_t,\ s \geq t.$$

To understand this evolution equation, assume first that the investor currently owns the asset ($q_{s-}^\alpha = 1$) and receives an opportunity to trade. If $dN_{0s} = 1$, then the investor receives an opportunity to buy and no trade occurs, since the investor can only hold one unit of the asset. Alternatively, if $dN_{1s} = 1$ then the investor receives an opportunity to sell at some price, and the investor can either accept by setting $\alpha_s = 1$ or reject by setting $\alpha_s = 0$. If the investor rejects the offer, he remains an owner until the next trading opportunity arrives.

The execution of a strategy α generates a stream of cash flows, corresponding to the revenues from asset sales and payments from asset purchases. Given the evolution of the holdings process, these cash flows can be written as

$$-P_s dq_s^\alpha = \alpha_s P_s q_{s-}^\alpha dN_{1s} - \alpha_s P_s(1 - q_{s-}^\alpha)dN_{0s},$$

where the offered price P_s is drawn from the distribution $G_{q_{s-}^\alpha}(x|\delta_s)$. The first term in this equation is the revenue that the investor obtains upon selling a unit of the asset, and the second term is the payment she makes upon buying. Hence, the lifetime utility associated with a strategy $\alpha \in \mathcal{A}$, starting with asset holding q_t and utility flow δ_t at time $t \geq 0$, can be written as

$$V^\alpha(q_t, \delta_t) = \mathbf{E}_t\left[\int_t^\infty e^{-r(s-t)}\left(q_s^\alpha \delta_s ds - P_s dq_s^\alpha\right)\right],$$

where $\mathbf{E}_t = \mathbf{E}[\cdot|\mathcal{F}_t]$ denotes an $\mathcal{F}_t$-conditional expectation. Putting it all together shows that the *sequential search problem* is given by

$$V(q_t, \delta_t) = \sup_{\alpha \in \mathcal{A}} V^\alpha(q_t, \delta_t). \tag{3.2}$$

Note that the value function is well defined for all $\delta \in \mathcal{D}$, i.e., for all potential utility flows and not just for those that are accessible. In the context of Example 3.1, this means that the value function is defined for all utility flows in $\mathcal{D}$ and not just for the high and low utility flows.

Given our assumptions and (3.2), we can establish the following a priori property of the value function.

***Proposition* 3.3:** The value function $V : \{0, 1\} \times \mathcal{D} \to \mathbf{R}$ is bounded.

Proof. Since $\mathcal{D}$ and $\mathcal{P}$ are bounded we have that

$$|q_s^\alpha \delta_s| ds + |P_s dq_s^\alpha| \leq \hat{\delta} ds + \hat{p}\,(dN_{0s} + dN_{1s})$$

for some constants $\hat{p}, \hat{\delta} \geq 0$. Therefore,

$$|V^\alpha\left(q_t, \delta_t\right)| \leq \mathbf{E}_t\left[\int_t^\infty e^{-r(s-t)}\left(\hat{\delta} ds + \hat{p}\,(dN_{0s} + dN_{1s})\right)\right]$$
$$= \frac{1}{r}\left(\hat{\delta} + \hat{p}(\lambda_0 + \lambda_1)\right),$$

where the equality follows from standard properties of Poisson processes that we review in appendix A.5. The result then follows by taking the supremum over $\alpha \in \mathcal{A}$ on both sides. □

The reason why boundedness is an important property to establish a priori is that it allows us to apply elementary contraction mapping arguments that are only valid in spaces of bounded functions; see Stokey and Lucas [1989] and appendix A for a review.

3.2.2 The Dynamic Programming Principle

The classical approach to stochastic control problems such as (3.2) relies on Richard Bellman's [1957] principle of optimality to derive a recursive equation for the value function. In informal terms, this principle states that a control strategy is optimal if and only if, for any time $\tau \geq 0$, it is optimal to use this control strategy until τ and then behave optimally forever after. The following proposition establishes the validity of this principle for the sequential search problem and shows that it holds not only at fixed times but also at stopping times, i.e., at random times τ whose occurence is gradually revealed over time, in the sense that $\{\tau \leq t\} \in \mathcal{F}_t$ for all $t \geq 0$. This generality is necessary because, as we will see in section 3.3, the natural times at which to apply the dynamic programming principle are the stopping times at which the investor changes utility flow or meets a trading partner.

Proposition 3.4: The value function $V : \{0, 1\} \times \mathcal{D} \to \mathbf{R}$ satisfies the principle of dynamic programming:

$$V(q_t, \delta_t) = \sup_{\alpha \in \mathcal{A}} \mathbf{E}_t\left[\int_t^\tau e^{-r(s-t)}\left(q_s^\alpha \delta_s ds - P_s dq_s^\alpha\right) + e^{-r(\tau - t)} V(q_\tau, \delta_\tau)\right] \qquad (3.3)$$

for any stopping time $\tau \geq t$ of the filtration $\mathbb{F}$.

Proof. Recall that

$$V^{\alpha}(q_t,\delta_t)=\mathbf{E}_t\left[\int_t^{\infty} e^{-r(s-t)}\left(q_s^{\alpha}\delta_s ds-P_s dq_s^{\alpha}\right)\right]$$

denotes the continuation utility generated by using the strategy $\alpha\in\mathcal{A}$ starting from the state (q_t,δ_t) at time $t\geq 0$, and that

$$V(q_t,\delta_t)=\sup_{a\in\mathcal{A}} V^{\alpha}(q_t,\delta_t) \tag{3.4}$$

denotes the value function. If $\tau\geq t$ is an arbitrary stopping time of $\mathbb{F}$, then (3.4) and the law of iterated expectations imply that

$$\begin{aligned}V^{\alpha}(q_t,\delta_t)&=\mathbf{E}_t\left[\int_t^{\tau} e^{-r(s-t)}\left(q_s^{\alpha}\delta_s ds-P_s dq_s^{\alpha}\right)+e^{-r(\tau-t)}V^{\alpha}(q_\tau,\delta_\tau)\right]\\&\leq\mathbf{E}_t\left[\int_t^{\tau} e^{-r(s-t)}\left(q_s^{\alpha}\delta_s ds-P_s dq_s^{\alpha}\right)+e^{-r(\tau-t)}V(q_\tau,\delta_\tau)\right],\end{aligned}$$

and taking the supremum over $\alpha\in\mathcal{A}$ on both sides gives

$$V(q_t,\delta_t)\leq\sup_{\alpha\in\mathcal{A}}\mathbf{E}_t\left[\int_t^{\tau} e^{-r(s-t)}\left(q_s^{\alpha}\delta_s ds-P_s dq_s^{\alpha}\right)+e^{-r(\tau-t)}V(q_\tau,\delta_\tau)\right].$$

To establish the reverse inequality, fix $t\geq 0$ and let $\tau\geq t$ be a stopping time. By definition of the supremum, we know that for every constant $\varepsilon>0$ and state of nature $\omega\in\Omega$, there exists a strategy $\alpha^{(\varepsilon,\omega)}$ such that

$$\left(V^{\alpha^{(\varepsilon,\omega)}}(q_\tau,\delta_\tau)\right)(\omega)\geq(V(q_\tau,\delta_\tau))(\omega)-e^{r(\tau(\omega)-t)}\varepsilon. \tag{3.5}$$

Now consider the process defined by

$$\hat{\alpha}_s(\omega)=\mathbf{1}_{\{s<\tau(\omega)\}}\alpha_s(\omega)+\mathbf{1}_{\{s\geq\tau(\omega)\}}\alpha_s^{(\varepsilon,\omega)}(\omega)$$

for an arbitrary $\alpha\in\mathcal{A}$. A technical argument that is beyond our scope shows that $\hat{\alpha}$ is adapted and thus can be used as a control; see, for example, Bertsekas and Shreve [1978]. In particular, we have that

$$\left(V^{\hat{\alpha}}(q_\tau,\delta_\tau)\right)(\omega)=\left(V^{\alpha^{(\varepsilon,\omega)}}(q_\tau,\delta_\tau)\right)(\omega)\geq(V(q_\tau,\delta_\tau))(\omega)-e^{r(\tau(\omega)-t)}\varepsilon$$

for every $\omega \in \Omega$. Combining this observation with (3.4), (3.5), and the law of iterated expectations then shows that

$$V(q_t, \delta_t) \geq V^{\hat{\alpha}}(q_t, \delta_t)$$
$$= \mathbf{E}_t \left[\int_t^\tau e^{-r(s-t)} \left(q_s^\alpha \delta_s ds - P_s dq_s^\alpha\right) + e^{-r(\tau-t)} V^{\hat{\alpha}}(q_\tau, \delta_\tau) \right]$$
$$\geq \mathbf{E}_t \left[\int_t^\tau e^{-r(s-t)} \left(q_s^\alpha \delta_s ds - P_s dq_s^\alpha\right) + e^{-r(\tau-t)} V(q_\tau, \delta_\tau) \right] - \varepsilon.$$

The conclusion now follows by taking the supremum over $\alpha \in \mathcal{A}$ on both sides and letting $\varepsilon \to 0$. □

Remark 3.5: Throughout the text, we implicitly assume that all the functions we work with are appropriately measurable in their arguments. This technical condition is mostly harmless, but there are cases where some care is needed. In particular, the value function of a dynamic stochastic optimization problem is not necessarily measurable [Stokey and Lucas, 1989, chap. 9], but this property is needed to define the expectation of the continuation utility in the proof of the dynamic programming principle. In the class of models that we consider, this measurability property can be verified a priori but the required arguments, based on measurable selection theorems, are very technical and thus beyond our scope. We refer the interested reader to Bertsekas and Shreve [1978] and El Karoui [1981, 3.47] for a detailed treatment.

3.3 The Bellman Equation

3.3.1 Derivation

To obtain the Bellman equation associated with the sequential search problem, we apply the dynamic programming principle (3.3) at a well-chosen stopping time. Specifically, assume that the investor starts with utility flow $\delta \in \mathcal{D}$ and consider the stopping time defined by

$$\tau \equiv \min\left\{\tau_\gamma, \tau_0, \tau_1\right\},$$

where τ_γ denotes the arrival time of the next change in utility flow, τ_0 denotes the arrival time of the next opportunity to buy, and τ_1 denotes the arrival time of the next opportunity to sell. In words, the stopping time τ is the arrival time of the *first* of these three events.

Consider first the case in which the investor holds the asset. Since the utility flow and asset holdings remain constant on the interval $[0, \tau)$ it follows from the dynamic programming principle (3.3) that

$$V(1,\delta) = \sup_{\alpha\in\mathcal{A}} \mathbf{E}\left[\int_0^\tau e^{-rs}\delta ds + e^{-r\tau}\left(V(q_\tau^\alpha, \delta_\tau) + \mathbf{1}_{\{\tau=\tau_1\}}\alpha_\tau P_\tau\right)\right], \tag{3.6}$$

where $\alpha_\tau \in \{0, 1\}$ encodes the trading decision of the investor upon being offered to sell the asset at price P_τ. Combining the definition of τ with the law of iterated expectations shows that the expectation on the right-hand side can be written as

$$\begin{aligned}
&\mathbf{E}\left[\int_0^\tau e^{-rs}\delta ds\right] + \mathbf{E}\left[\mathbf{1}_{\{\tau=\tau_0\}}e^{-r\tau}V(1,\delta)\right] \\
&\qquad + \mathbf{E}\left[\mathbf{1}_{\{\tau=\tau_\gamma\}}e^{-r\tau}\int_{\underline{\delta}}^{\overline{\delta}} V(1,x)dF(x|\delta)\right] \\
&\qquad + \mathbf{E}\left[\mathbf{1}_{\{\tau=\tau_1\}}e^{-r\tau}\int_{\underline{\pi}}^{\overline{\pi}} \left(V(1-\alpha_\tau,\delta) + \alpha_\tau p\right) dG_1(p|\delta)\right].
\end{aligned}$$

Substituting this expression back into (3.6) and maximizing pointwise over $\alpha_\tau \in \{0, 1\}$ shows that the value function of the investor-owner satisfies

$$\begin{aligned}
V(1,\delta) = &\mathbf{E}\left[\int_0^\tau e^{-rs}\delta ds\right] + \mathbf{E}\left[\mathbf{1}_{\{\tau=\tau_0\}}e^{-r\tau}V(1,\delta)\right] \\
&+ \mathbf{E}\left[\mathbf{1}_{\{\tau=\tau_\gamma\}}e^{-r\tau}\int_{\underline{\delta}}^{\overline{\delta}} V(1,x)dF(x|\delta)\right] \\
&+ \mathbf{E}\left[\mathbf{1}_{\{\tau=\tau_1\}}e^{-r\tau}\int_{\underline{\pi}}^{\overline{\pi}} \max\left\{V(1,\delta), V(0,\delta) + p\right\} dG_1(p|\delta)\right].
\end{aligned} \tag{3.7a}$$

We refer to this equation as the *Bellman equation*.

On the right-hand side of (3.7a), the first term is the present value of the utility flow that the owner enjoys until time τ, while the three remaining terms capture the present value of the continuation utility that the investor derives at time τ, depending on the nature of the event. If $\tau = \tau_0$, then the event is an opportunity to buy and the continuation utility is simply given by $V(1, \delta)$ because the investor already owns an asset and cannot purchase any more. If $\tau = \tau_\gamma$, then the event is a reset of the investor's utility flow, in which case the continuation utility is given by $V(1, x)$, where x is drawn from the distribution $F(\cdot|\delta)$. Finally, if $\tau = \tau_1$, then the event is an opportunity to sell and the continuation utility,

$$\max_{\alpha\in\{0,1\}} \left(V(1-\alpha,\delta)+\alpha p\right) = \max\left\{V(1,\delta), V(0,\delta)+p\right\},$$

reflects the fact that the investor sells if the offered price p is large enough and otherwise remains an owner until the next trading opportunity.

Proceeding in a similar way shows that the Bellman equation for the value function of the investor when he does not hold the asset is

$$\begin{aligned} V(0,\delta) &= \mathbf{E}\left[\mathbf{1}_{\{\tau=\tau_1\}}e^{-r\tau}V(0,\delta)\right] \\ &\quad + \mathbf{E}\left[\mathbf{1}_{\{\tau=\tau_\gamma\}}e^{-r\tau}\int_{\underline{\delta}}^{\overline{\delta}} V(0,x)dF(x|\delta)\right] \\ &\quad + \mathbf{E}\left[\mathbf{1}_{\{\tau=\tau_0\}}e^{-r\tau}\int_{\underline{\pi}}^{\overline{\pi}} \max\left\{V(0,\delta), V(1,\delta)-p\right\} dG_0(p|\delta)\right]. \end{aligned} \tag{3.7b}$$

The interpretation of the three terms on the right-hand side of this equation is similar to that of the terms on the right-hand side of (3.7a), with the obvious difference that the investor does not enjoy any utility flow when he does not hold the asset. In particular, the quantity inside the integral in the last term gives the continuation utility that the investor derives if the event that occurs at date τ is an opportunity to buy the asset at price $p \in \mathcal{P}$:

$$\max_{\alpha\in\{0,1\}} \left(V(\alpha,\delta)-\alpha p\right) = \max\left\{V(0,\delta), V(1,\delta)-p\right\}.$$

A key insight from the Bellman equations is that the trading decisions of the investor are fully determined by the *reservation value*

$$R(\delta) \equiv V(1,\delta) - V(0,\delta).$$

In words, the reservation value is the difference between the value of owning the asset and not owning it, given optimal trading behavior. Indeed, (3.7a) shows that, upon meeting a buyer, the investor sells if and only if the offered price is greater than $R(\delta)$. Similarly, (3.7b) shows that, upon meeting a seller, the investor buys if and only if the asked price is less than $R(\delta)$. Subtracting (3.7b) from (3.7a) reveals that the reservation function solves the autonomous equation given by

$$
\begin{aligned}
R(\delta) = \mathbf{E}\left[\int_0^{\tau} e^{-rs}\delta ds\right] &+ \mathbf{E}\left[\mathbf{1}_{\{\tau=\tau_\gamma\}} e^{-r\tau} \int_{\underline{\delta}}^{\overline{\delta}} R(x) dF(x|\delta)\right] \\
&+ \mathbf{E}\left[\mathbf{1}_{\{\tau=\tau_0\}} e^{-r\tau} \int_{\underline{\pi}}^{\overline{\pi}} \min\left\{p, R(\delta)\right\} dG_0(p|\delta)\right] \\
&+ \mathbf{E}\left[\mathbf{1}_{\{\tau=\tau_1\}} e^{-r\tau} \int_{\underline{\pi}}^{\overline{\pi}} \max\left\{p, R(\delta)\right\} dG_1(p|\delta)\right], \quad (3.8)
\end{aligned}
$$

where the last two lines follow by noting that

$$
\begin{aligned}
V(1,\delta) - \max\left\{V(1,\delta) - p, V(0,\delta)\right\} &= \min\left\{p, V(1,\delta) - V(0,\delta)\right\} \\
&= \min\left\{p, R(\delta)\right\},
\end{aligned}
$$

and

$$
\max\left\{p + V(0,\delta), V(1,\delta)\right\} - V(0,\delta) = \max\left\{p, R(\delta)\right\}.
$$

An important takeaway from (3.8) is that future buying and selling opportunities have opposite effects on the reservation value. For example, the value of selling opportunities is captured by the term inside the integral on the third line,

$$
\max\left\{p, R(\delta)\right\} = R(\delta) + \max\left\{p - R(\delta), 0\right\} \geq R(\delta).
$$

The fact that this term is larger than $R(\delta)$ implies that the option value of searching for a higher selling price increases the investor's current reservation value, i.e., the minimum price at which the investor is willing to sell the asset. In contrast, the term inside the integral on the second line,

$$
\min\left\{p, R(\delta)\right\} = R(\delta) - \max\left\{R(\delta) - p, 0\right\} \leq R(\delta),
$$

implies that buying opportunities have the opposite effect on the reservation value. This is because the option value of searching for a lower price to buy makes the investor less willing to buy in the first place, and thus decreases his willingness to pay for the asset or, equivalently, his reservation value.

3.3.2 Existence, Uniqueness, and Properties of the Solution

From Proposition 3.3, we know that the functions $V(0,\delta)$ and $V(1,\delta)$ are bounded and satisfy (3.7). Let $\mathcal{B}$ denote the space of bounded functions on $\mathcal{D}$. If we show that the system of equations characterizing these functions admits a unique solution in

$\mathcal{B} \times \mathcal{B}$, then this unique solution will automatically coincide with the value functions of the investor. As a first step toward this objective, we analyze the autonomous equation (3.8) satisfied by the reservation value function.

The definition of τ as the minimum of three exponential random variables, along with the results of appendix A.3, implies that

$$\begin{aligned}\mathbf{E}\int_0^\tau e^{-rs}ds &= \mathbf{E}\left[\mathbf{1}_{\{\tau=\tau_0\}}\frac{e^{-r\tau}}{\lambda_0}\right] = \mathbf{E}\left[\mathbf{1}_{\{\tau=\tau_\gamma\}}\frac{e^{-r\tau}}{\gamma}\right] \\ &= \mathbf{E}\left[\mathbf{1}_{\{\tau=\tau_1\}}\frac{e^{-r\tau}}{\lambda_1}\right] = \frac{1}{r+\gamma+\lambda_0+\lambda_1} \equiv \psi.\end{aligned} \tag{3.9}$$

Substituting these expressions into (3.8) then shows that the equation for the reservation value is equivalent to the fixed point problem

$$\begin{aligned}R(\delta) = T[R](\delta) \equiv \psi\Bigg\{\delta + \gamma\int_{\underline{\delta}}^{\overline{\delta}} R(x)dF(x|\delta) \\ + \lambda_0\int_{\underline{\pi}}^{\overline{\pi}} \min\left\{p, R(\delta)\right\} dG_0(p|\delta) \\ + \lambda_1\int_{\underline{\pi}}^{\overline{\pi}} \max\left\{p, R(\delta)\right\} dG_1(p|\delta)\Bigg\}.\end{aligned} \tag{3.10}$$

Since $V(0,\delta)$ and $V(1,\delta)$ are bounded, we know a priori that the reservation value function is also bounded, which allows us to rely on standard fixed point results to analyze the existence, uniqueness, and structural properties of solutions to the reservation value equation.

Proposition 3.6: There exists a unique solution to (3.10) in $\mathcal{B}$.

Proof. As is easily seen, T is nondecreasing and maps $\mathcal{B}$ into itself. Furthermore, because

$$m\left\{g(\delta)+a, p\right\} \le a + m\left\{g(\delta), p\right\}, \quad \forall (m, a) \in \{\min, \max\} \times \mathbf{R}_+,$$

we have that

$$T[g+a](\delta) - Tg(\delta) \le \psi(\gamma+\lambda_0+\lambda_1)a, \qquad \forall a \ge 0.$$

Since $\psi(\gamma+\lambda_0+\lambda_1) < 1$, this establishes that Blackwell's sufficient conditions for a contraction in Proposition A.2 are satisfied, and the result now follows from the Banach fixed point (see Theorem A.3 in appendix A). □

Next, we establish monotonicity and continuity of the reservation value function. To this end, we require precise assumptions about the distributions of utility flows and price offers. Intuitively, for the reservation value function to be increasing (continuous) in δ it is necessary that its integrals against $dF(x|\delta)$ and $dG_q(x|\delta)$ be increasing (continuous) in the conditioning variable. The following definition describes the specific assumptions that we require.

***Definition* 3.7:** Let $\mathbf{H} = \{H(\cdot|\delta) : \delta \in \mathcal{D}\}$ denote a collection of distributions on $\mathcal{D}$ and consider the integral operator

$$(h \in \mathcal{B}) \mapsto Mh(\delta) \equiv \int_{\underline{\delta}}^{\overline{\delta}} h(x) dH(x|\delta).$$

Then the collection $\mathbf{H}$ is persistent (has the Feller property) if M maps the set of bounded and nondecreasing (continuous) functions into itself.

The notion of persistence that we use is sometimes also referred to as monotonicity. To understand this definition, consider the collection of distributions $\mathbf{F} = \{F(\cdot|\delta) : \delta \in \mathcal{D}\}$ that governs the transitions of utility flows. If the collection $\mathbf{F}$ is persistent, then

$$F(y|\delta') \leq F(y|\delta), \qquad \forall \left(y, \delta, \delta'\right) \in \mathcal{D}^3 \text{ such that } \delta \leq \delta',$$

so that the probability of drawing a utility flow lower than any given threshold decreases as the current utility flow increases. This condition means that the family $\mathbf{F}$ is increasing in the first-order stochastic dominance sense, and classical results that we review in appendix A.2 show that this seemingly weaker condition is in fact equivalent to persistence.

Equipped with these concepts of monotonicity and continuity, we can now establish additional, key properties of the reservation value function.

***Corollary* 3.8:** Assume that the collections $\mathbf{F}$, $\mathbf{G}_0$, and $\mathbf{G}_1$ are persistent (respectively, have the Feller property). Then the reservation value function $R : \mathcal{D} \to \mathbf{R}$ is strictly increasing (respectively, continuous).

Proof. If g belongs to the set $\mathcal{B}^{\uparrow} \subset \mathcal{B}$ of nondecreasing bounded functions, then it follows from the assumption of persistence that the function $Tg(\delta)$ is strictly increasing. Hence, the operator T maps $\mathcal{B}^{\uparrow}$ into itself. Since the latter set is closed in $\mathcal{B}$ and T is a contraction, it follows from Corollary A.4 that the unique fixed point is nondecreasing. Hence, on the right-hand side of the fixed point equation (3.10), the first function is strictly increasing in δ, and the other functions are nondecreasing. Since, by definition, $R(\delta)$ is equal to the sum of these functions, it is strictly increasing.

Similarly, if g belongs to the set $\mathcal{B}_c \subset \mathcal{B}$ of bounded continuous functions, then the Feller property guarantees that the function $Tg(\delta)$ is continuous and therefore that the operator T maps $\mathcal{B}_c$ into itself. Since the latter set is closed in $\mathcal{B}$ and T is a contraction, the result again follows from Corollary A.4. □

The analysis so far has focused on the characterization of the reservation value function, $R(\delta)$. However, to fully solve the sequential search problem, we need to take a step back and solve for the value function itself, $V(q, \delta)$.

Proposition 3.9: There exists a unique solution to (3.7) in $\mathcal{B} \times \mathcal{B}$. If the collections $\mathbf{F}$, $\mathbf{G}_0$, and $\mathbf{G}_1$ are persistent (respectively, have the Feller property) then the value functions $V(q, \cdot) : \mathcal{D} \to \mathbf{R}$ are nondecreasing (respectively, continuous).

Proof. Given $R(\delta)$, the Bellman equation (3.7) splits into a pair of autonomous fixed point problems given by

$$V(q,\delta) = S_q[V](q,\delta) \equiv \psi \left\{ q\delta + (\lambda_0 + \lambda_1)V(q,\delta) + \gamma \int_{\underline{\delta}}^{\overline{\delta}} V(q,x)\, dF(x|\delta) \right.$$

$$\left. + \lambda_q \int_{\underline{\pi}}^{\overline{\pi}} \left((1-2q)\left(R(\delta) - p\right)\right)^+ dG_q(p|\delta) \right\}.$$

By inspection, it is clear that S_q maps the space $\mathcal{B}$ into itself and satisfies

$$\|S_q g - S_q h\| \leq (\gamma + \lambda_0 + \lambda_1)\psi \|g - h\|,$$

where $\|\cdot\|$ denotes the sup norm. Since $(\gamma + \lambda_0 + \lambda_1)\psi < 1$, it follows that S_q is a contraction on $\mathcal{B}$ and thus admits a unique fixed point in that space. The rest of the proof is similar to that of Corollary 3.8. □

3.3.3 *Comparative Statics of Reservation Values*

The next two results establish comparative statics of reservation values with respect to the meeting intensities and the collection of distributions from which new utility flows and offered prices are drawn.

Proposition 3.10: Reservation values are increasing in λ_1 and decreasing in λ_0.

Proof. Denote by T_{λ_0,λ_1} and R_{λ_0,λ_1} the operator in (3.10) and its unique bounded fixed point indexed by the intensities λ_0 and λ_1. Using the definition of T_{λ_0,λ_1} and the elementary inequalities

$$\min\{p, h(\delta)\} \leq h(\delta) \leq \max\{p, h(\delta)\},$$

we deduce that, for any $\varepsilon > 0$,

$$T_{\lambda_0+\varepsilon,\lambda_1}h \leq \frac{T_{\lambda_0,\lambda_1}h + \varepsilon\psi \cdot h}{1+\varepsilon\psi} \leq T_{\lambda_0,\lambda_1+\varepsilon}h.$$

From the proof of Proposition 3.6, we know that $T : \mathcal{B} \to \mathcal{B}$ is a nondecreasing contraction. Therefore, the operator S_ε defined by the middle expression in the inequality above is also a nondecreasing contraction on $\mathcal{B}$ and it thus follows from Corollary A.6 that its unique bounded fixed point b satisfies

$$R_{\lambda_0+\varepsilon,\lambda_1}(\delta) \leq b(\delta) \leq R_{\lambda_0,\lambda_1+\varepsilon}(\delta).$$

To complete the proof, it remains to show that b coincides with R_{λ_0,λ_1}. Indeed, the definition of S_ε and the fixed point property imply that

$$b = S_\varepsilon(b) = \frac{T_{\lambda_0,\lambda_1}b + \varepsilon\psi \cdot b}{1+\varepsilon\psi} = T_{\lambda_0,\lambda_1}b$$

is a fixed point of T_{λ_0,λ_1}, and the desired result now follows from the fact that a contraction admits a unique fixed point. □

Proposition 3.11: Reservation values are increasing in **F**, $\mathbf{G}_0$, and $\mathbf{G}_1$ with respect to first-order stochastic dominance between collections of persistent distributions.

Proof. We give a detailed proof of monotonicity in **F**. The other two results are established in a similar way. Let $T_{\mathbf{F}}$ denote the operator in (3.10) indexed by **F** and let $R_{\mathbf{F}}$ denote its unique bounded fixed point. If $\overline{\mathbf{F}}$ is another persistent collection of distributions such that

$$\overline{F}(x|\delta) \leq F(x|\delta), \qquad \forall (x,\delta) \in \mathcal{D}^2,$$

then Proposition A.13 implies that we have

$$\int_{\underline{\delta}}^{\overline{\delta}} h(x)dF(x|\delta) \leq \int_{\underline{\delta}}^{\overline{\delta}} h(x)d\overline{F}(x|\delta),$$

and thus $T_{\mathbf{F}}h \le T_{\overline{\mathbf{F}}}h$ for all $h \in \mathcal{B}^{\uparrow}$. Since the collection $\overline{\mathbf{F}}$ is persistent, Corollary 3.8 implies that the function $R_{\overline{\mathbf{F}}}(\delta)$ is strictly increasing. Therefore, we may use the inequality above with the test function $h = R_{\overline{\mathbf{F}}}$ to obtain

$$(T_{\mathbf{F}}R_{\overline{\mathbf{F}}}) \le (T_{\overline{\mathbf{F}}}R_{\overline{\mathbf{F}}}) = R_{\overline{\mathbf{F}}}.$$

The desired comparative static now follows from Corollary A.6 by noting that the operator $T_{\mathbf{F}}$ is nondecreasing. □

The comparative statics of reservation values with respect to the collections **F**, $\mathbf{G}_0$, and $\mathbf{G}_1$ are fairly intuitive. For example, a first-order stochastic dominant shift in **F** increases the investor's average utility flow from holding the asset, and thus increases his reservation value. Turning to the distribution of price offers, a first-order stochastic dominant shift in $\mathbf{G}_1$ increases the price that the investor expects to obtain in exchange for his asset in the future—that is, it increases the option value of searching to sell. In accordance with the discussion of option values in (3.8) above, this increases the investor's reservation value and thus makes him less inclined to sell today. A first-order stochastic dominant shift in $\mathbf{G}_0$ increases the price that the investor expects to pay for the asset in the future, which *decreases* the option value of searching to buy. Since this option value contributes negatively to the reservation value, an upward shift in the distribution of ask prices also leads to an increase in the investor's reservation value and thus makes the investor more likely to buy today.

The option value interpretation of (3.8) also provides a natural explanation for the comparative statics with respect to the meeting intensities. For example, an increase in λ_1 means that the investor receives more frequent opportunities to exercise his option to sell the asset when he owns it. This mechanically raises the value of this selling option and thus the reservation value. Symmetrically, an increase in λ_0 implies that the investor has more frequent opportunities to exercise his option to buy when he is a nonowner. This raises the option value of buying and thus lowers the reservation value since this option carries a negative sign in (3.8).

Note that if buying and selling opportunities share the same arrival rate, then the net effect of a change in the meeting intensity parameter $\lambda = \lambda_0 = \lambda_1$ is ambiguous and depends on the details of the investor's utility flows and price offers, as we discuss in the next example.

3.3.4 An Explicit Example

To illustrate the above results, consider a version of the sequential search problem where the distribution $F(\cdot|\delta) \equiv F(\cdot)$ does not depend on the investor's current utility flow, and assume that

$$\lambda_0 G_0(p|\delta) = \lambda_1 G_1(p|\delta) = \lambda \mathbf{1}_{\{P \leq p\}}$$

for some $\lambda > 0$ and P, so that all trading opportunities arrive at the same speed and entail the same offered price P.

RESERVATION VALUE

Under this specification, the Bellman equation reduces to

$$\begin{aligned} R(\delta)/\psi &= \delta + \gamma \mathbf{E}^F [R(\delta)] + \lambda (\min\{R(\delta), P\} + \max\{R(\delta), P\}) \\ &= \delta + \gamma \mathbf{E}^F [R(\delta)] + \lambda (P + R(\delta)), \end{aligned} \tag{3.11}$$

where

$$\mathbf{E}^F [R(\delta)] = \int_{\underline{\delta}}^{\overline{\delta}} R(x) dF(x)$$

denotes the average reservation value across the investor population. Taking this constant as given and solving (3.11) yields

$$R(\delta) = \frac{\delta + \lambda P + \gamma \mathbf{E}^F [R(\delta)]}{r + \gamma + \lambda}. \tag{3.12}$$

Integrating against $dF(\delta)$ on both sides of this equation then shows that the average reservation value is explicitly given by

$$\mathbf{E}^F [R(\delta)] = \frac{\mathbf{E}^F [\delta] + \lambda P}{r + \lambda}.$$

Substituting this identity back into (3.12), we finally obtain that

$$R(\delta) = \frac{\lambda}{r + \lambda} P + \frac{r}{r + \lambda} D(\delta),$$

where

$$rD(\delta) \equiv \frac{r + \lambda}{r + \lambda + \gamma} \delta + \frac{\gamma}{r + \lambda + \gamma} \mathbf{E}^F [\delta].$$

Exercise 3.13 shows that this function satisfies

$$\mathbf{E}_\delta \int_0^\tau e^{-rt} (\delta_t - rD(\delta)) \, dt = 0 \tag{3.13}$$

where the random time τ is independent of the investor's utility flow and exponentially distributed with rate λ. In other words, $rD(\delta)$ represents the *flow* certainty equivalent of the utility that an investor with utility flow δ derives by holding the asset until the next trading opportunity. Correspondingly, $D(\delta)$ is the present discounted value of this flow certainty equivalent.

This expression reveals that the reservation value converges to P as $\lambda \to \infty$. This is intuitive: if search frictions vanish, then the investor is in constant contact with a continuum of potential trading partners who all value the asset at P. As a result, the investor's reservation value is equal to P, regardless of his current utility flow. At the other extreme, as $\lambda \to 0$ search frictions intensify and the expression above reveals that the reservation value function satisfies

$$\lim_{\lambda \to 0} R(\delta) = \lim_{\lambda \to 0} D(\delta) = \mathbf{E}_\delta \left[\int_0^\infty e^{-rt} \delta_t dt \right],$$

where the last equality follows by letting $\tau = \infty$ in (3.13). This conclusion is also quite intuitive: the limit above is simply the present value of the utility flows of an investor who holds the asset and never trades. Therefore, this equality states that the reservation value of the asset to an investor who cannot trade is simply the buy-and-hold value of the asset.

THE OPTIMAL STRATEGY

To analyze the optimal trading strategy induced by the reservation value function, we distinguish between three cases depending on the price at which the investor can buy or sell. If the price is such that

$$P \leq R(\underline{\delta}; P) \Leftrightarrow P \leq D(\underline{\delta}),$$

then the reservation value of all investors is higher than the price and the optimal strategy consists of buying at the first opportunity and never selling. Symmetrically, if the price $P \geq R(\overline{\delta}; P)$—or, equivalently, $P \geq D(\overline{\delta})$—then the reservation value of all investors is lower than the price and the optimal strategy consists of selling at the first opportunity and never buying. Finally, if the price lies in the interval $(P(\underline{\delta}), P(\overline{\delta}))$ then there exists a unique solution in $\mathcal{D}$ to the indifference condition

$$R(\delta^*) = P \Leftrightarrow \delta^* = \mathbf{E}^F[\delta] + \left(\frac{r+\gamma+\lambda}{r+\lambda} \right) \left(rP - \mathbf{E}^F[\delta] \right),$$

which prescribes the following optimal strategy: upon meeting a seller, an investor should buy only if her utility flow is higher than δ^*; and, upon meeting a buyer, an investor should sell only if her utility flow is lower than δ^*.

Combining Lemma A.17 and Proposition A.37 shows that the solution to the Bellman equation (3.11) can be represented as

$$R(\delta) = \mathbf{E}_\delta \left[\int_0^\infty e^{-(r+\lambda)t} \left(\delta_t + \lambda P\right) dt \right] = \mathbf{E}_\delta \left[\int_0^\tau e^{-rt} \delta_t dt + e^{-r\tau} P \right], \qquad (3.14)$$

where the random time τ is independent of the investor's utility flow and exponentially distributed with rate λ. In words, this equation shows that in this example the reservation value is the expected utility associated with holding the asset until time τ and then selling at price P.

This simple representation highlights the dual effect of a change in the arrival rate of trading opportunities. To see this, assume that the price and utility flows are nonnegative. An increase in λ means that τ tends to be smaller, which implies that the investor enjoys his utility flow over a shorter period in (3.14) and, thus, reduces his reservation value since $\delta_t \geq 0$. However, a smaller τ also implies that the investor receives the price earlier, which tends to increase his reservation value since $P \geq 0$. Which of the two effects dominates ultimately depends on the utility flow of the investor. When the utility flow is high relative to the price, then the first effect dominates and the reservation value is a decreasing function of the meeting intensity. The opposite is true when the utility flow is low.

3.4 The Hamilton-Jacobi-Bellman Equation

An alternative—but ultimately equivalent—equation for the value function can be derived by applying the dynamic programming principle over a fixed time interval of vanishing length, rather than over the random time interval until the next trading opportunity or type change. The resulting equation is commonly referred to as the Hamilton-Jacobi-Bellman equation (HJB).

3.4.1 A Heuristic Derivation

We start with a heuristic derivation of the HJB equation. Specifically, let us apply the dynamic programming principle over a time interval of length h, for some small h. Then, up to negligible terms, the Bellman equation for an investor who holds $q = 1$ units of the asset is given by

$$\begin{aligned} V(1,\delta) = \frac{1}{1+rh} \Bigg(& \delta h + \gamma h \int_{\underline{\delta}}^{\overline{\delta}} V(1,x)\, dF(x|\delta) \\ & + \lambda_1 h \int_{\underline{\pi}}^{\overline{\pi}} \max\left\{V(0,\delta) + p, V(1,\delta)\right\}\, dG_1(p|\delta) \\ & + (1 - \gamma h - \lambda_1 h) V(1,\delta) \Bigg). \end{aligned}$$

The multiplicative term $1/(1+rh) \simeq e^{-rh}$ is the discount factor over the time interval of length h. The first term in the parenthesis, δh, is the utility flow enjoyed by the asset owner during that time interval. The second term arises because, with probability $1-e^{-\gamma h} \simeq \gamma h$, the investor draws a new utility flow. The third term arises because of trading opportunities, and the last term arises because, with probability $e^{-(\gamma+\lambda_1)h} \simeq 1-(\gamma+\lambda_1)h$, the investor neither changes utility flow nor receives a trading opportunity.

Collecting the two terms multiplied by γh and the two terms multiplied by $\lambda_1 h$, we obtain

$$V(1,\delta) = \frac{1}{1+rh}\Bigg(\delta h + V(1,\delta) + \gamma h \int_{\underline{\delta}}^{\overline{\delta}} (V(1,x) - V(1,\delta))\, dF(x|\delta)$$

$$+ \lambda_1 h \int_{\underline{\pi}}^{\overline{\pi}} \max\left\{p + V(0,\delta) - V(1,\delta), 0\right\} dG_1(p|\delta)\Bigg).$$

Multiplying both sides by $1+rh$, canceling $V(1,\delta)$ from the resulting equation, and dividing by h yields

$$rV(1,\delta) = \delta + \gamma \int_{\underline{\delta}}^{\overline{\delta}} (V(1,x) - V(1,\delta))\, dF(x|\delta)$$
$$+ \lambda_1 \int_{\underline{\pi}}^{\overline{\pi}} \max\left\{p + V(0,\delta) - V(1,\delta), 0\right\} dG_1(p|\delta) \tag{3.15}$$

This equation is the HJB equation for the value function of an owner. A similar argument shows that the corresponding equation for the value function of a nonowner is given by

$$rV(0,\delta) = \gamma \int_{\underline{\delta}}^{\overline{\delta}} (V(0,x) - V(0,\delta))\, dF(x|\delta)$$
$$+ \lambda_0 \int_{\underline{\pi}}^{\overline{\pi}} \max\left\{V(1,\delta) - V(0,\delta) - p, 0\right\} dG_0(p|\delta)$$

These equations are typically interpreted in the following way. The left-hand side of (3.15) represents the flow of annuity value $rV(1,\delta)$ received by an owner. The right-hand side of (3.15) breaks down this flow value into three components. First, an owner enjoys utility flows at rate δ. Second, with intensity γ, the owner draws a new utility flow, with a net change in value given by $V(1,x) - V(1,\delta)$ if the new utility flow is x. Third, with intensity λ_1, the owner receives an opportunity to sell, with net utility given by $\max\{p + V(0,\delta) - V(1,\delta), 0\}$ if the offered price is p.

Subtracting the HJB equation for $V(0,\delta)$ from that for $V(1,\delta)$, we obtain the HJB equation for the reservation value:

$$
\begin{aligned}
rR(\delta) = \delta + \gamma \int_{\underline{\delta}}^{\overline{\delta}} \big(R(x) - R(\delta)\big)\, dF(x|\delta) \\
+ \lambda_1 \int_{\underline{\pi}}^{\overline{\pi}} \max\big\{p - R(\delta), 0\big\}\, dG_1(p|\delta) \\
- \lambda_0 \int_{\underline{\pi}}^{\overline{\pi}} \max\big\{R(\delta) - p, 0\big\}\, dG_0(p|\delta).
\end{aligned}
$$

This equation admits a similar interpretation to the one derived earlier in the chapter. In particular, note that the option value of selling (on the second line) and of buying (on the third line) have opposite signs in the equation and thus have opposite effects on the reservation value.

3.4.2 The Formal Derivation

In this section we derive the HJB equations formally, i.e, without making any heuristic approximations. Proposition 3.4 implies that, if $t < h$, then

$$
e^{-rt} V(q_t, \delta_t) = \sup_{\alpha \in \mathcal{A}} \mathbf{E}_t \left[\int_t^h e^{-rs} \left(q_s^\alpha \delta_s ds - P_s dq_s^\alpha \right) + e^{-rh} V(q_h^\alpha, \delta_h) \right].
$$

Subtracting the left side from the right, dividing by the length $h - t$ of the time interval, and letting $h \to t$, we deduce that the value function satisfies

$$
rV(q_t, \delta_t) = \sup_{\alpha \in \mathcal{A}} \frac{1}{dt} \mathbf{E}_t \left[dV(q_t^\alpha, \delta_t) + q_t \delta_t dt - P_t dq_t^\alpha \right]. \tag{3.16}
$$

This alternative formulation of the HJB equation reveals that the continuation utility flow of the investor—given by the maximand on the right—is lower than the discount rate r applied to the value function unless the investor uses an optimal strategy, in which case the two are equalized.

Mathematically, this formulation can be interpreted as a local version of the *martingale principle of optimality*, a close relative of the dynamic programming principle [for a survey, see Davis, 1979]. In particular, the martingale principle of optimality characterizes V as the unique function such that

$$
e^{-rt} V(q_t^\alpha, \delta_t) + \int_0^t e^{-rs} \left(q_s^\alpha \delta_s ds - P_s dq_s^\alpha \right)
$$

is a supermartingale along any strategy $\alpha \in \mathcal{A}$ and a martingale under the optimal strategy, so that any strategy but the optimal one leads to an expected decrease in the present value of future net utility flows.

To further elucidate the properties of the HJB equation, note that, over a small time interval starting at date t, the investor switches utility flow from δ_t to x with probability $\gamma\, dF(x|\delta_t)dt$ and meets a compatible counterparty who offers him to trade at some price p with probability $\lambda_{q_t^\alpha} dG_{q_t^\alpha}(p|\delta_t)dt$. Therefore, it follows from the definition of the reservation value that the expectation on the right of (3.16) is given by

$$\frac{1}{dt}\mathbf{E}_t\left[dV(q_t^\alpha,\delta_t) - P_t dq_t^\alpha\right] = \gamma \int_{\underline{\delta}}^{\overline{\delta}} \left(V(q_t,x) - V(q_t,\delta_t)\right) dF(x|\delta_t)$$
$$+ \lambda_{q_t} \int_{\underline{\pi}}^{\overline{\pi}} \alpha_t\left(1-2q_t\right)\left(R(\delta_t) - p\right) dG_{q_t}(p|\delta_t).$$

Substituting this expression into (3.16) and maximizing over $\alpha_t \in \{0, 1\}$ shows that the HJB equation can be written compactly as

$$rV(q,\delta) = q\delta + \gamma \int_{\underline{\delta}}^{\overline{\delta}} (V(q,x) - V(q,\delta))dF(x|\delta)$$
$$+ \lambda_q \int_{\underline{\pi}}^{\overline{\pi}} \left(\left(1-2q\right)\left(R(\delta)-p\right)\right)^+ dG_q(p|\delta), \tag{3.17}$$

where (q, δ) denotes a generic state in $\{0, 1\} \times \mathcal{D}$ and $x^+ \equiv \max\{x, 0\}$ denotes the positive part of a real number x. Finally, subtracting the above equation with $q = 0$ from its counterpart with $q = 1$, we conclude that the reservation value function satisfies

$$rR(\delta) = \delta + \gamma \int_{\underline{\delta}}^{\overline{\delta}} (R(x) - R(\delta))dF(x|\delta)$$
$$- \lambda_0 \int_{\underline{\pi}}^{\overline{\pi}} \left(R(\delta)-p\right)^+ dG_0(p|\delta) + \lambda_1 \int_{\underline{\pi}}^{\overline{\pi}} \left(p - R(\delta)\right)^+ dG_1(p|\delta). \tag{3.18}$$

The HJB equations (3.17) and (3.18) can be interpreted as time derivatives of the Bellman equations (3.7) and (3.8). Therefore, they provide a decomposition of the rate of change of the value functions into different net utility flows. In particular, the left side of (3.18) represents the annuitized reservation value $rR(\delta)$, whereas the four terms on the right side capture the expected utility flows associated with holding the asset, changing utility flow, exercising the option to sell, and exercising the option to buy. Like the Bellman equation, the HJB equation highlights the opposite impact of buying and selling opportunities on the reservation value.

3.4.3 The Time-Dependent Case

Up to this point, we have assumed that the arrival rates $(\gamma, \lambda_0, \lambda_1)$ and the collections of distributions $(\mathbf{F}, \mathbf{G}_0, \mathbf{G}_1)$ are time independent, so that the value function and the induced reservation values are also time independent. This assumption is natural in a steady-state environment, but it precludes us from studying out-of-steady-state dynamics and convergence to the steady state—situations in which the parameters of the sequential search problem, and hence the optimal strategy, depend on time. We now briefly discuss how to extend the results above to the time dependent case.

Suppose that $F_t(\cdot|\delta)$ and $G_{t,q}(\cdot|\delta)$ are time dependent but maintain the assumption of constant arrival rates. By inspection it is clear that all the results of sections 3.2 through 3.3.1 continue to hold in this more general setting, provided that we index the distributions and value functions by time. In particular, (3.8) now writes as

$$R_t(\delta) = \mathbf{E}\left[\int_t^{\tau} e^{-r(s-t)}\delta\, ds\right] + \mathbf{E}\left[\mathbf{1}_{\{\tau=\tau_\gamma\}} e^{-r(\tau-t)} \int_{\underline{\delta}}^{\overline{\delta}} R_\tau(x)\, dF_\tau(x|\delta)\right]$$
$$+ \mathbf{E}\left[\mathbf{1}_{\{\tau=\tau_0\}} e^{-r(\tau-t)} \int_{\underline{\pi}}^{\overline{\pi}} \min\left\{p, R_\tau(\delta)\right\} dG_{\tau,0}(p|\delta)\right]$$
$$+ \mathbf{E}\left[\mathbf{1}_{\{\tau=\tau_1\}} e^{-r(\tau-t)} \int_{\underline{\pi}}^{\overline{\pi}} \max\left\{p, R_\tau(\delta)\right\} dG_{\tau,1}(p|\delta)\right]. \tag{3.19}$$

Integrating over the conditional distribution of the random time τ, given in appendix A.3, we obtain that

$$R_t(\delta) = \int_t^{\infty} e^{-(s-t)\frac{1}{\psi}} \Big\{ \delta + \gamma \int_{\underline{\delta}}^{\overline{\delta}} R_s(x)\, dF_s(x|\delta) \tag{3.20}$$
$$+ \lambda_0 \int_{\underline{\pi}}^{\overline{\pi}} \min\left\{p, R_s(\delta)\right\} dG_{s,0}(p|\delta)$$
$$+ \lambda_1 \int_{\underline{\pi}}^{\overline{\pi}} \max\left\{p, R_s(\delta)\right\} dG_{s,1}(p|\delta) \Big\}\, ds,$$

with the constant ψ defined as in (3.9). Starting from this equation, the same arguments as in the stationary case can be used to establish the existence and uniqueness of the solution, and to show that the structural properties and comparative statics results of sections 3.3.2 and 3.3.3 all extend to the time-dependent case, provided that we work in the space of bounded functions on $\mathbf{R}_+ \times \mathcal{D}$ rather than in the space $\mathcal{B}$.

Since the right-hand side of (3.19) is absolutely continuous in time, it is clear that the reservation value function inherits this property and, thus, admits a time derivative $\dot{R}_t(\delta)$ almost everywhere. Differentiating (3.20) with respect to time and using that derivative shows that

$$
\begin{aligned}
R_t(\delta)/\psi = \delta + \dot{R}_t(\delta) + \gamma \int_{\underline{\delta}}^{\overline{\delta}} R_t(x) dF_t(x|\delta) \\
+ \lambda_0 \int_{\underline{\pi}}^{\overline{\pi}} \min\left\{p, R_t(\delta)\right\} dG_{t,0}(p|\delta) \\
+ \lambda_1 \int_{\underline{\pi}}^{\overline{\pi}} \max\left\{p, R_t(\delta)\right\} dG_{t,1}(p|\delta)
\end{aligned}
$$

at almost every point of $\mathbf{R}_+ \times \mathcal{D}$. Comparing this equation with its stationary counterpart (3.10) reveals that the only adjustment required to account for time dependence is the addition of a time derivative in the definition of the Bellman operator. A similar adjustment is also needed in the HJB equation. Indeed, since the value function is time dependent, we have that

$$
\begin{aligned}
\frac{1}{dt}\mathbf{E}_t\left[dV_t(q_t^\alpha, \delta_t) - P_t dq_t^\alpha\right] = \dot{V}_t(q_t, \delta_t) + \gamma \int_{\underline{\delta}}^{\overline{\delta}} \left(V_t(q_t, x) - V_t(q_t, \delta_t)\right) dF_t(x|\delta_t) \\
+ \lambda_{q_t} \int_{\underline{\pi}}^{\overline{\pi}} \alpha_t \left(1 - 2q_t\right) \left(R_t(\delta_t) - p\right) dG_{t,q_t}(p|\delta_t).
\end{aligned}
$$

Proceeding as in the stationary environment of section 3.4.2 then shows that the time-dependent version of the HJB equation is given by

$$
\begin{aligned}
rV_t(q, \delta) = \dot{V}_t(q, \delta) + q\delta + \gamma \int_{\underline{\delta}}^{\overline{\delta}} \left(V_t(q, x) - V_t(q, \delta)\right) dF_t(x|\delta) \\
+ \lambda_q \int_{\underline{\delta}}^{\overline{\delta}} \left(\left(1 - 2q\right) \left(R_t(\delta) - p\right)\right)^+ dG_{t,q}(p|\delta)
\end{aligned}
$$

for the value function and

$$rR_t(\delta) = \dot{R}_t(\delta) + \delta + \gamma \int_{\underline{\delta}}^{\overline{\delta}} (R_t(x) - R_t(\delta))\, dF(x|\delta)$$

$$- \lambda_0 \int_{\underline{\pi}}^{\overline{\pi}} \left(R_t(\delta) - p\right)^+ dG_{t,0}(p|\delta) + \lambda_1 \int_{\underline{\pi}}^{\overline{\pi}} \left(p - R_t(\delta)\right)^+ dG_{t,1}(p|\delta)$$

for the reservation value function. Comparing these two equations with their stationary counterparts reveals that here again the only required adjustments are to properly index the value functions and distributions by time and to add a derivative of the value function on the right-hand side.

3.5 Exercises

Exercise 3.12: Derive the Bellman equation and the HJB equation for the reservation value function with the addition of any of the following features:

1. A fixed cost ϕ upon each transaction.
2. A probability $\xi \in [0, 1]$ that each desirable trade fails.
3. A transaction cost equal to a fraction $\chi \in [0, 1]$ of the gain from trade.
4. A random draw of the next meeting intensity upon each meeting.

Verify that, under appropriate conditions, the existence, uniqueness, and qualitative properties we established in the text extend to these cases.

Exercise 3.13: The goal of this exercise is to show that

$$rD(\delta) = \frac{A(\delta)}{B} \equiv \frac{\mathbf{E}_\delta\left[\int_0^\tau e^{-rt}\delta_t dt\right]}{\mathbf{E}_\delta\left[\int_0^\tau e^{-rt} dt\right]} = \frac{\gamma \mathbf{E}^F[\delta] + (r+\lambda)\,\delta}{r+\gamma+\lambda}$$

where τ is independent of δ_t and exponentially distributed with rate λ.

1. Write the HJB equation that $A(\delta)$ satisfies. Solve for $\mathbf{E}^F\left[A(\delta')\right]$ and $A(\delta)$.
2. Write the HJB equation that B satisfies and calculate B.
3. Calculate $A(\delta)/B$ and conclude.

Exercise 3.14: Consider the same setting as in the example of section 3.3.4. Provide an explicit solution for the value function $V(q, \delta)$ and verify that this function is increasing in δ, λ, γ, and $\mathbf{E}^F\left[\delta\right]$.

Exercise 3.15: Consider the same setting as in the example of section 3.3.4. Find conditions on the exogenous parameters under which $R(\underline{\delta}) \geq \lim_{\lambda \to 0} R(\overline{\delta})$ so that the reservation value dominates the buy-and-hold value associated with any utility flow. Explain why such a situation can be seen as an OTC market version of the speculative premium first modelled by Harrison and Kreps [1978].

Exercise 3.16: Consider the same setting as in the example of section 3.3.4 but with (3.1) and assume that the investor starts from either δ_L or δ_H so that his utility flow takes values in $\{\delta_L, \delta_H\}$. Provide a necessary and sufficient condition on P under which the optimal strategy is to sell when meeting a buyer in state δ_L, to buy when meeting a seller in state δ_H, and otherwise to do nothing.

3.6 Notes and References

The sequential search problem that we consider in this chapter is very similar to the classic McCall [1970] model in labor economics, and its textbook presentation in Ljungqvist and Sargent [2012]. The key difference is that, in the McCall [1970] model, the worker who searches for a job is always on the supply side of the market. In an OTC market, by contrast, the investor alternates between the demand and the supply side of the market, depending on his trading needs. As shown in this chapter, this implies that OTC market valuations depend on two option values (to buy and to sell assets) rather than just one option value (to sell labor) in the labor market.

This chapter introduces three equivalent ways to analyze the investor's sequential search problem: using the stochastic control formulation in section 3.2, using a Bellman equation in section 3.3, and using the HJB equation in section 3.4. In practice, depending on the problem at hand, each of these approaches may turn out to be the most insightful and tractable.

As a matter of logic, the stochastic control formulation should always be viewed as the primitive definition of the optimization problem. In contrast, the Bellman and HJB equations should be viewed as auxiliary tools for solving this problem. In this chapter we have explicitly proved the *necessity* of the Bellman equation. In many cases researchers skip this step to directly analyze and solve the Bellman or HJB equations. This is mathematically acceptable as long as the analysis is concluded by an explicit verification argument. That is, one must show that the value function and strategy obtained from the Bellman or HJB equation solve the investor's primitive stochastic control problem. This verification argument almost always goes through the same standard steps. See Brémaud [1981, Theorem VII.T1] and Addendum IX of Weill [2007] for an OTC market application.

Garbade and Silber [1976] were among the first to apply the sequential search model to financial markets, documenting and exploring the causes of price dispersion in the Treasury market from both a theoretical and empirical perspective. In the early literature studying market microstructure, several authors built on the conceptual framework proposed by Demsetz [1968] to study optimal trading strategies when opportunities to buy and sell assets arrived at random according to a Poisson process; see, for example, Garman [1976] and Amihud and Mendelson [1980]. Burdett and O'Hara [1987] develop a model of block trade.

Our formulation of the sequential search problem is explicitly designed to study the literature following the seminal contribution of Duffie, Gârleanu, and Pedersen [2005]. This line of research has largely assumed that investors have linear preferences with time-varying utility flows from consuming the dividends that arise from holding an asset. While this type of assumption is standard in many areas of the search-theoretic literature, it is less common in asset pricing. However, several authors have offered microfoundations and/or natural interpretations of this assumption in an asset market context. For example, Duffie, Gârleanu, and Pedersen [2002] and Hugonnier [2012] show that heterogeneous utility flows can derive from heterogeneous beliefs about the distribution of the asset's payoffs. An alternative microfoundation, formalized in Duffie, Gârleanu, and Pedersen [2007], Vayanos and Weill [2008], and Praz [2015], establishes that heterogeneous utility flows across investors can arise from heterogeneous hedging needs. To see why, suppose investors are risk averse and hold an outside portfolio of asset B (say, Treasuries) that is correlated with the asset of interest A (say, corporate bonds). Then large holdings of asset B depress the marginal value of holding asset A, generating a small value of δ in our framework [see the empirical study of Newman and Rierson, 2003]. Finally, if investors have to finance consumption by selling assets in OTC markets [as in, e.g., Geromichalos and Herrenbrueck, 2016], then heterogeneous consumption opportunities translate into heterogeneous indirect utilities for assets.

Though most of our analysis maintains the convenient assumption of linear preferences, in most cases we allow for a fairly general distribution over the set of accessible points of the utility flow process, which allows us to unify the different specifications that have been studied in the literature. These include the special case of two points in the models of Duffie, Gârleanu, and Pedersen [2005] and Weill [2008], among others; the case of a finite collection of accessible points in which utility flows follow a Markov chain, as in Lagos and Rocheteau [2009] and Lagos, Rocheteau, and Weill [2011]; and the case of a continuum of accessible points considered by Hugonnier, Lester, and Weill [2022].

In this chapter, as in the rest of the book, the parameter λ is interpreted as the rate at which an investor makes contact with a counterparty. However, one could also interpret this parameter as the rate at which an investor monitors the market. This is fruitful because one can then apply the techniques developed in this book to centralized markets as well. Under this interpretation, limit orders represent the trading interest of "absent traders, while they attend to business elsewhere" [Harris, 2003, section 4.4.5]; examples of papers in this area include Rosu [2009], Biais and Weill [2009], Biais, Hombert, and Weill [2014], and Dugast [2018].

4

Semicentralized Markets

In this chapter we study equilibrium prices, trading volume, and allocations under a market structure that we refer to as a *semicentralized* OTC market. In a nutshell, we assume that the market is populated by two classes of agents: investors and dealers. Dealers can trade among themselves in a frictionless market but investors can only trade through dealers. As in chapter 3, investors have to sequentially search for a dealer with whom to trade. After contacting a dealer, we assume that the ensuing bid and ask prices are determined by Nash bargaining within each meeting between an investor and a dealer. Figure 4.1 illustrates the basic market structure.

The semicentralized framework is attractive for at least two reasons. First, it captures some of the key features of real-world OTC markets in a simple way. For example, in many OTC markets, such as the U.S. corporate bond market discussed in chapter 2, investors trade almost exclusively through dealers, so that almost all of the trading volume is made up of investor-to-dealer trades and dealer-to-dealer trades. Moreover, the interdealer market is typically more competitive than the investor-dealer market. This was also demonstrated in chapter 2, where we documented that interdealer trades of corporate bonds exhibit significantly less price dispersion than investor-dealer trades. The second attractive feature of the semicentralized market structure is that it turns out to be extremely tractable. As a result, this model offers a simple and transparent account of the effects of search and bargaining frictions on prices and allocations. Furthermore, and as we establish in later chapters, this workhorse model can be extended and enriched in a variety of ways without sacrificing its tractability.

The chapter is organized as follows. Section 4.1 introduces the model. Section 4.2 then derives the frictionless, competitive equilibrium, which is the benchmark against which we evaluate the impact of search and bargaining frictions. Section 4.3 studies asset demand, taking the interdealer price as given. Section 4.4 then determines the interdealer price in equilibrium and compares it to its frictionless counterpart. Section 4.5 derives the empirical implications of the model for various observable

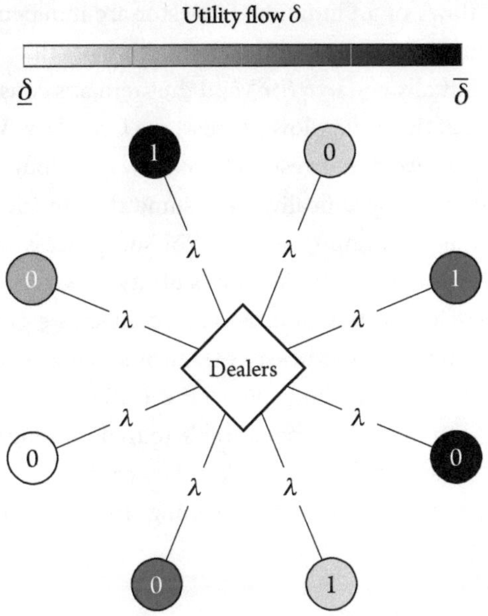

FIGURE 4.1. Semicentralized OTC market

This figure illustrates the structure of a semicentralized over-the-counter market in which heterogeneous investors holding zero or one unit of the asset meet dealers randomly over time and bargain bilaterally on the terms of trade.

outcomes, including liquidity yield spread and trading costs. Section 4.6 studies a variant of the model in which investors and dealers form lasting relationships that allow for the instantaneous execution of multiple trades over time.

4.1 The Model

We consider a continuous-time, infinite-horizon model with a measure one of investors and a measure one of dealers. Investors are risk neutral, discount the future at rate $r > 0$, and derive utility over two goods: an asset in positive supply $s \in (0, 1)$ and a numéraire good. Agents can produce (consume) the numéraire good at a constant marginal cost (utility) that is normalized to one.

Each investor can hold either zero or one unit of the asset and enjoys a utility flow $\delta_t dt$ from holding one unit of the asset at time $t \geq 0$. The utility flow of each investor is independent from that of any other investor and follows a Markov jump process with arrival rate γ and reset distribution $F(\delta)$ on some open interval $\mathcal{D} = (\underline{\delta}, \overline{\delta})$. Hence, relative to the model of chapter 3, we make the simplifying assumption that the successive utility flows of an individual investor are independent and identically distributed (iid). Finally, we assume that the distribution of utility flows across the population of investors is initially equal to $F(\delta)$ and thus remains constant since $F(\delta)$ is the stationary distribution of the utility flow process: see Corollary A.41 in appendix A.

We start from the premise that investors have no way of contacting each other and must trade through dealers. Specifically, we assume that an investor contacts a randomly selected dealer at the jump times of a Poisson process with intensity λ. The contact times are independent of the investor's utility flow process and independent across the population of investors. Conditional on contact, we assume that an investor and a dealer determine the terms of a possible trade by solving a simple Nash bargaining game in which the dealer has bargaining power $\theta \in (0, 1)$.

Dealers cannot hold any inventory but are able to trade among themselves instantly, at all times, in a frictionless Walrasian market. Hence, the market structure is *semi-centralized* in the sense that search and bargaining frictions only affect transactions between investors and dealers.

4.2 The Frictionless Benchmark

As a first step toward the solution to the semicentralized market, it is helpful to derive prices and allocations in the frictionless benchmark where investors have continuous access to a Walrasian market. Since the distribution of utility flows across investors is constant, one can show that the equilibrium price P in this frictionless market must be constant (a corollary of Exercise 4.6 below). As a result, the optimization problem of an individual investor is given by

$$V(q, \delta) = \sup_{\vartheta \in \mathcal{Q}_q} \mathbf{E}_\delta \left[\int_0^\infty e^{-rt} \left(\vartheta_t \delta_t dt - P d\vartheta_t \right) \right],$$

where $\mathcal{Q}_q$ denotes the set of $\{0, 1\}$-valued processes of bounded variations with initial value equal to $\vartheta_0 = q$. Integrating by parts (which is licit here as ϑ_t has bounded variations and $e^{-rt}P$ is bounded and continuous) shows that this problem can be equivalently stated as

$$V(q, \delta) = Pq + \sup_{\vartheta \in \mathcal{Q}_0} \mathbf{E}_\delta \left[\int_0^\infty e^{-rt} q_t \left(\delta_t - rP \right) dt \right].$$

This intuitive formulation shows that the optimal strategy is determined as if, in every small time interval $(t, t + h]$, the investor was choosing whether to purchase a unit of the asset at the beginning of the interval before reselling it at the end. Indeed, if the investor chooses to purchase the asset, then she enjoys utility flow $\delta_t h$ but incurs the holding cost

$$\left(P - \frac{P}{1+rh}\right) \simeq rPh,$$

and comparing these flows shows that, taking the price as given, the investor's optimal asset holdings satisfy

$$q_t^\star \begin{cases} = 0 & \text{if } \delta_t < \delta^\star, \\ \in \{0,1\} & \text{if } \delta_t = \delta^\star, \\ = 1 & \text{if } \delta_t > \delta^\star, \end{cases}$$

where the constant $\delta^\star \equiv rP$ is referred to as the *marginal type*, i.e. the utility flow of an investor who is indifferent between trading or not trading.

Aggregating this optimality condition across investors and using the fact that the cross-sectional distribution of utility flows is equal to $F(\delta)$ at all times shows that market clearing imposes two conditions. First, the marginal type must lie in the convex hull of the support of $F(\delta)$, for otherwise all investors would be on the same side of the market at all times. Second, the marginal type must be a solution to

$$s \in [1 - F(\delta^\star), 1 - F(\delta^\star -)], \tag{4.1}$$

where $F(\delta^\star -) \equiv \lim_{\delta \uparrow \delta^\star} F(\delta)$ is the left-limit of the cumulative distribution function at $\delta^\star$. The left-hand side is the supply while the interval on the right-hand side is the evaluation of the aggregate demand correspondence given P and the induced marginal utility flow $\delta^\star = rP$. In particular, the lower bound of the interval is obtained when only investors with utility flows $\delta > \delta^\star$ purchase the asset, while the upper bound is obtained when all investors with utility flows $\delta \geq \delta^\star$, including those at $\delta^\star$ who are indifferent, purchase the asset.

The inclusion (4.1) shows that the marginal type is a quantile of the distribution of utility flows at level $1 - s$. Such a quantile is uniquely defined except in the nongeneric case where the distribution is equal to $1 - s$ over an open set. Given a solution $\delta^\star$, the corresponding price

$$P = \frac{\delta^\star}{r} = \int_0^\infty e^{-rt} \delta^\star dt \tag{4.2}$$

capitalizes the value of the utility flows derived by a hypothetical investor who remains at the marginal type forever.

Next, we solve for the equilibrium asset allocation. Let $\delta^\star$ be a solution to (4.1) and denote by

$$\pi^\star = \mathbf{1}_{\{\Delta F(\delta^\star)=0\}} + \mathbf{1}_{\{\Delta F(\delta^\star)\neq 0\}} \frac{F(\delta^\star) - (1-s)}{\Delta F(\delta^\star)}$$

the fraction of investors with utility flow equal to $\delta^\star$ who must hold the asset to clear the market. With this notation, we have that the distribution of utility flows among owners is

$$\begin{aligned}\Psi_1(\delta) &= \mathbf{1}_{\{\delta\geq\delta^\star\}} \left(F(\delta) - F(\delta^\star) + \pi^\star \Delta F(\delta^\star)\right) \\ &= \mathbf{1}_{\{\delta\geq\delta^\star\}} \left(F(\delta) - (1-s)\right) = \max\left\{0, F(\delta) - (1-s)\right\}. \end{aligned} \tag{4.3}$$

Importantly, this expression does not depend on the choice of a marginal type, so that the distribution is unique even when the marginal type is not. Correspondingly, we can solve for the distribution of utility flows among investors who do not hold the asset, $\Psi_0(\delta)$. Indeed, since the measures of holders and nonholders must add up to the population distribution we have

$$\Psi_0(\delta) + \Psi_1(\delta) = F(\delta),$$

and it immediately follows that

$$\Psi_0(\delta) = F(\delta) - \Psi_1(\delta) = \min\left\{F(\delta), 1-s\right\}. \tag{4.4}$$

To summarize, a steady-state equilibrium of the frictionless benchmark consists in a marginal utility flow $\delta^\star$ satisfying (4.1), a price P satisfying (4.2), and distributions $\Psi_0(\delta)$ and $\Psi_0(\delta)$ satisfying (4.3) and (4.4), respectively.

To close this section, let us briefly discuss trading volume in the frictionless benchmark. Since market participants can buy and sell simultaneously, trading volume is indeterminate in the Walrasian market. Nonetheless, we can pin down the minimum volume that must be traded to support the equilibrium. Indeed, at all times the flow of sell orders must be at least

$$\gamma s F(\delta^\star -),$$

which is the flow of owners who find it strictly optimal to sell because their utility flow has just been reset to some $\delta < \delta^\star$. By the same token, the flow of buy orders must be at least equal to the flow

$$\gamma\,(1-s)\left(1 - F(\delta^\star)\right)$$

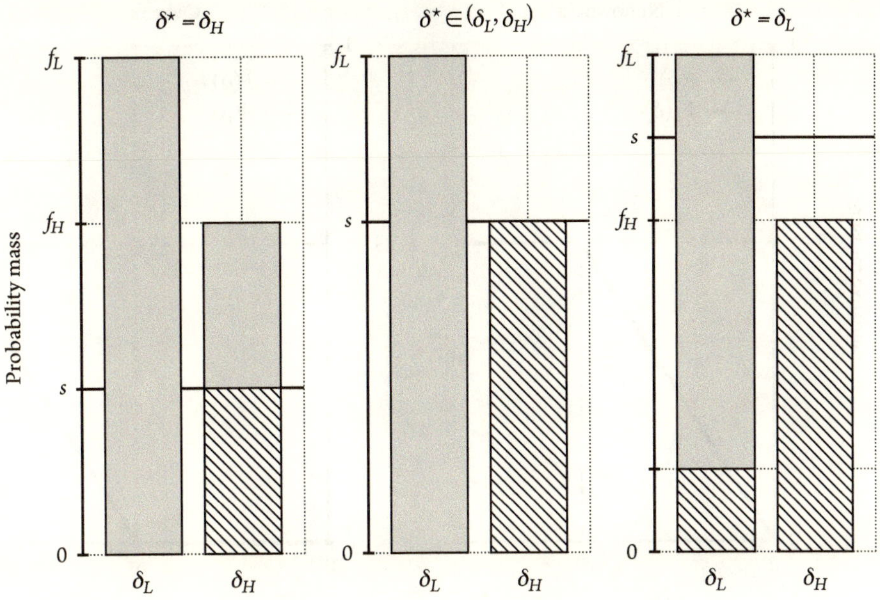

FIGURE 4.2. Frictionless allocation with two types

This figure illustrates the frictionless equilibrium distribution of utility flows among owners (hatched) and nonowners (solid) in each of the paremeter configurations of Example 4.1. To produce the figure we fix $f_H = 0.4$ and vary $s \in \{0.2, 0.4, 0.5\}$.

of nonowners who find it strictly optimal to buy because their utility flow has just been reset to some $\delta > \delta^\star$. It follows that the minimum volume in the frictionless market is given by

$$\nu^\star \equiv \gamma \max\left\{sF(\delta^\star -), (1-s)F(\delta^\star)\right\}.$$

Exercise 4.7 below offers a detailed, step-by-step derivation of this lower bound on the equilibrium trading volume.

Example 4.1: To illustrate the frictionless equilibrium consider the two-point distribution from Example 3.1, where

$$F(\delta) = f_L \mathbf{1}_{\{\delta_L \leq \delta\}} + f_H \mathbf{1}_{\{\delta_H \leq \delta\}}$$

for some $\delta_L < \delta_H$ and $f_L, f_H > 0$ such that $f_L + f_H = 1$. In this specification, three cases may occur depending on the parameter configuration. If the mass of investors with high utility flow exceeds the asset supply, as in the left panel of figure 4.2, then the marginal

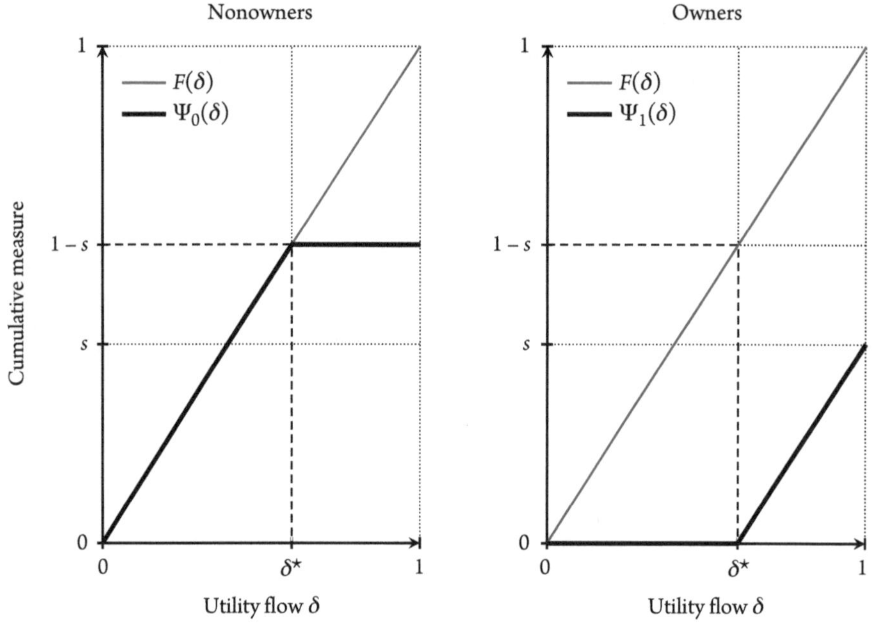

FIGURE 4.3. Frictionless equilibrium with uniform types

This figure illustrates the frictionless equilibrium distribution of utility flows among owners (right panel) and nonowners (left panel) in a continuous model with supply $s = 0.4$ and a reset distribution $F(\delta) = \delta$ on $\mathcal{D} = (0, 1)$ so that $\delta^\star = 0.6$.

type is uniquely defined by $\delta^\star = \delta_H$. In this case, the minimal flow of trades is $\gamma s f_L$ and the equilibrium prescribes that the asset should be held by a randomly selected fraction s/f_H of investors with utility flow δ_H. Alternatively, if the asset supply exceeds the mass of investors with utility flow δ_H, as in the right panel of the figure, then the marginal type is uniquely defined by $\delta^\star = \delta_L$. In this case, the minimal flow of trades is $\gamma(1-s)f_H$, and the asset should be held by all investors with utility flow δ_H and a randomly selected fraction $(s - f_H)/f_L$ of investors with utility flow δ_L.

Finally, in the nongeneric case in which the asset supply coincides with the mass of investors with utility type δ_H, we have that any $\delta^\star \in [\delta_L, \delta_H]$ defines a marginal type. In that case, the equilibrium allocation naturally requires that the entire supply be in the hands of investors at δ_H, and the minimal flow of trades is $\gamma s(1-s)$ regardless of the marginal utlity flow.

Example 4.2: Consider the class of models where the distribution of utility flow resets is continuous and strictly increasing. In any such model, the marginal type is uniquely determined by the inverse relation

$$F(\delta^\star) = 1 - s \Leftrightarrow \delta^\star = F^{-1}(1-s).$$

As a result, the flow of trades must exceed $\gamma s(1-s)$, and the equilibrium allocation prescribes that the asset should only be held by investors with utility flow larger than the marginal type. See figure 4.3 for an illustration with $s = 0.4$ and a uniform distribution on the unit interval.

4.3 Asset Demand

We now return to the semicentralized model with search frictions. As a first step toward the characterization of equilibrium, we study the optimization problem of an investor who takes as given the interdealer price. We first derive the solution to the bargaining problem between the investor and a dealer, taking as given the relevant outside options. Then, we use the solution to the bargaining problem as a building block to derive the Hamilton-Jacobi-Bellman (HJB) equation associated with the investor's optimization problem. We provide a closed-form solution to the resulting equation, which in turn delivers an explicit characterization of the optimal strategy as a function of the interdealer price and the investor's utility flow.

4.3.1 Bargaining between an Investor and a Dealer

Consider a meeting between a dealer and an owner with utility flow $\delta \in \mathcal{D}$. Since investors cannot hold more than one unit, the only possible trade is that the investor sells her asset to the dealer at some bid price $B(\delta)$, which will be determined as the outcome of a Nash bargaining game. If the sale occurs, then the investor becomes a nonowner and receives the continuation utility

$$B(\delta) + V(0, \delta),$$

where $V(q, \delta)$ denotes the value function of an investor in state (q, δ). Otherwise, the investor remains an owner and receives the continuation utility $V(1, \delta)$. Hence, the investor's net utility from trading with the dealer is

$$B(\delta) + V(0, \delta) - V(1, \delta) = B(\delta) - R(\delta),$$

where, as in chapter 3, $R(\delta)$ denotes the reservation value of the investor as a function of her utility flow.

On the other side of the transaction, the dealer's net utility from the trade is $P - B(\delta)$. As a result, the total surplus from the trade is given by the difference between the interdealer price P and the reservation value of the investor, i.e.,

$$(P - B(\delta)) + (B(\delta) - R(\delta)) = P - R(\delta).$$

If the surplus is negative, then there are no gains from trade and the investor simply walks away. If there are gains from trade, then the investor and the dealer split the surplus according to the solution of the generalized Nash bargaining program:

$$\max_{B \in [R(\delta), P]} \ (P - B)^{\theta} \, (B - R(\delta))^{1-\theta} \, .$$

Since the dealer's bargaining power, θ, lies in $(0, 1)$, the objective function of this program is concave in B on the feasible interval $[R(\delta), P]$. Therefore, the first-order condition

$$0 = \frac{d}{dB} \left((P - B)^{\theta} \, (B - R(\delta))^{1-\theta} \right)$$

is necessary and sufficient for an interior maximum, and solving this equation shows that the bid price is given by a convex combination of the interdealer price and the investor's reservation value:

$$B(\delta) = \theta R(\delta) + (1 - \theta) \, P. \tag{4.5}$$

Intuitively, if $\theta \approx 1$ then the dealer has most of the bargaining power and the bid price is close to the reservation value of the investor, which is the price that would be set by a fully discriminating monopsonist. Alternatively, if $\theta \approx 0$ then the dealer has almost no bargaining power and the bid price approaches the competitive interdealer price.

Consider next a meeting between a dealer and a generic nonowner with utility flow $\delta \in \mathcal{D}$. In such a meeting, the only possible trade is that the investor buys from the dealer. As in the analysis above, this trade occurs if and only if the surplus $R(\delta) - P$ is nonnegative, in which case the ask price is

$$A(\delta) \equiv \operatorname*{argmax}_{A \in [P, R(\delta)]} \ (A - P)^{\theta} \, (R(\delta) - A)^{1-\theta} = \theta R(\delta) + (1 - \theta) \, P. \tag{4.6}$$

Note that the bid and the ask are given by the same formula, so that the price at which a given investor can trade with dealers depends on his utility flow but not on the direction of the trade. As we will see below, this feature leads to a significant simplification of the HJB equation, which is ultimately responsible for the tractability of the semicentralized market model.

We close this section by observing that the results of the Nash bargaining protocol are consistent with the setting of chapter 3, where we assumed that an investor with a higher utility flow tends to trade at higher prices. Indeed, we will show below that the reservation value function is increasing, which implies that the cumulative price distributions faced by the investor in the semicentralized market,

$$G_q(x|\delta) = \mathbf{1}_{\{x \geq A(\delta)\}} = \mathbf{1}_{\{x \geq B(\delta)\}} = \mathbf{1}_{\{x \geq \theta R(\delta) + (1-\theta)P\}}, \tag{4.7}$$

are increasing with respect to δ in the first-order stochastic dominance sense. Note, however, that here the price distributions are partially endogenous, as they depend on the (yet undetermined) reservation value function.

4.3.2 Reservation Values

Substituting $\lambda_q = \lambda$ and (4.7) into (3.17) shows that the HJB equation for the investor's value function is given by

$$rV(q,\delta) = q\delta + \gamma \int_{\underline{\delta}}^{\overline{\delta}} \big(V(q,x) - V(q,\delta)\big)\, dF(x)$$
$$+ \lambda q \max\{B(\delta) - R(\delta), 0\} + \lambda(1-q)\max\{R(\delta) - A(\delta), 0\}.$$

Subtracting this equation with $q = 0$ from its counterpart with $q = 1$, and substituting the bid and ask prices given in (4.5) and (4.6), then shows that the reservation value function satisfies

$$rR(\delta) = \delta + \gamma \int_{\underline{\delta}}^{\overline{\delta}} (R(x) - R(\delta))\, dF(x) \tag{4.8}$$
$$+ \lambda(1-\theta)\max\{P - R(\delta), 0\} - \lambda(1-\theta)\max\{R(\delta) - P, 0\}.$$

Since this functional equation is a special case of (3.10), we can derive the existence, uniqueness, and basic features of its solution from the results of Proposition 3.6 and Corollary 3.8.

Proposition 4.3: The reservation value equation (4.8) admits a unique solution in $\mathcal{B}$ that is both continuous and strictly increasing in utility flows.

Comparing (4.8) to its sequential search counterpart (3.18) reveals that trading through dealers with bargaining power θ is payoff-equivalent to trading in the interdealer market, but with a reduced intensity

$$\lambda_\theta \equiv \lambda\,(1-\theta).$$

To understand why, recall that Nash bargaining is payoff-equivalent to a static game in which the dealer makes a take-it-or-leave it offer with probability θ and the investor makes a take-it-or-leave-it offer with probability $1-\theta$. For the investor, receiving the offer is payoff-equivalent to not trading, while making the offer is payoff-equivalent to trading in the interdealer market. As a result, what ultimately matters for reservation values is not the physical contact rate, λ, but the adjusted contact rate, λ_θ, that reflects the combined likelihood of meeting a dealer and being able to make an offer. Hence, even if investors are able to contact dealers quickly, search frictions can have a large impact on valuations if dealers have sufficient bargaining power.

Before moving on to the construction of the equilibrium, we perform some manipulations of equation (4.8) that deliver several alternative representations, as well as an explicit solution for the reservation value function. While these derivations may appear a bit tedious, they turn out to be quite useful down the road, as they shed light on the trading incentives of investors and simplify the characterization of the equilibrium. As a first step, since

$$\max\{P-R(\delta),0\}-\max\{R(\delta)-P,0\}=P-R(\delta),$$

note that we can rewrite (4.8) as

$$rR(\delta)=\delta+\lambda_\theta\,(P-R(\delta))+\gamma\int_{\underline{\delta}}^{\overline{\delta}}(R(x)-R(\delta))\,dF(x). \tag{4.9}$$

Combining Proposition A.37 with basic properties of exponential random variables reported in Lemma A.17 reveals that the unique bounded solution to this functional equation can be represented as

$$\begin{aligned} R(\delta) &= \mathbf{E}_\delta\left[\int_0^{\tau_\theta} e^{-rt}\delta_t dt + e^{-r\tau_\theta}P\right] \\ &= \mathbf{E}_\delta\left[\int_0^{\infty} e^{-(r+\lambda_\theta)t}\,(\delta_t+\lambda_\theta P)\,dt\right], \end{aligned} \tag{4.10}$$

where the expectations are conditional on the initial utility flow $\delta_0=\delta$ and τ_θ is an exponentially distributed variable with intensity equal to the bargaining-adjusted contact rate λ_θ.

Equation (4.10) shows that the reservation value can be computed as the present value of the utility flows derived by holding the asset until making contact with the interdealer market and then selling it at the interdealer price. A key insight of this representation is again that the relevant contact rate reflects *both* the search and the bargaining frictions in the market.

To derive a second useful representation of the reservation value function, recall the elementary identity

$$e^{-r\tau_\theta}P = P + \left(e^{-r\tau_\theta} - 1\right)P = P - \int_0^{\tau_\theta} e^{-rt}\, rP\, dt.$$

Substituting this identity into (4.10) reveals that

$$R(\delta) = P + \mathbf{E}_\delta\left[\int_0^{\tau_\theta} e^{-rt}\,(\delta_t - rP)\, dt\right]. \tag{4.11}$$

This representation highlights that the only reason reservation values differ from the interdealer price is the presence of search and bargaining frictions: the second term is nonzero precisely because the adjusted contact time is strictly positive, so that investors cannot trade instantaneously at the interdealer price P. In particular, as the meeting rate $\lambda \to \infty$, the contact time $\tau_\theta \to 0$ and hence the reservation value $R(\delta) \to P$. Intuitively, if the investor is constantly in contact with dealers, then her reservation value is the interdealer price at all times regardless of her utility flow. Alternatively, as $\lambda \to 0$ or $\theta \to 1$, the adjusted contact time $\tau_\theta \to \infty$ and so

$$\lim_{\lambda_\theta \to 0} R(\delta) = \mathbf{E}_\delta\left[\int_0^{\infty} e^{-rt}\delta_t dt\right].$$

At this limit, investors are effectively in autarky: Either they never meet a dealer ($\lambda = 0$) or, when they do, the dealer extracts all the surplus ($\theta = 1$). Therefore, they are indifferent between trading and not trading and their reservation values are simply equal to the autarky values.

Another insight from (4.11) that we will use later to solve for the equilibrium price in the interdealer market is that

$$R(\delta) = P \Leftrightarrow P = D(\delta), \tag{4.12}$$

where

$$rD(\delta) = \frac{\mathbf{E}_\delta\left[\int_0^{\tau_\theta} e^{-rt}\delta_t dt\right]}{\mathbf{E}_\delta\left[\int_0^{\tau_\theta} e^{-rt} dt\right]}$$

is the unique solution to

$$\mathbf{E}_\delta \int_0^{\tau_\theta} e^{-rt}\,(\delta_t - x)\, dt = 0.$$

In words, the quantity $rD(\delta)$ represents the *flow* certainty equivalent of the utility that an investor with utility flow δ derives by holding the asset until the next bargaining-adjusted contact time. Since the latter is independent from the investor's utility flow, we have that

$$r\mathbf{E}_\delta\left[\int_0^{\tau_\theta} e^{-rt}dt\right]=1-\mathbf{E}\left[e^{-r\tau_\theta}\right]=\frac{r}{r+\lambda_\theta},$$

where the second equality follows from Lemma A.17. Substituting back into (4.10) reveals that the reservation value function can be expressed as a convex combination of the interdealer price and the present value $D(\delta)$ of receiving the certainty equivalent flow in perpetuity, i.e.,

$$R(\delta)=\frac{\lambda_\theta}{r+\lambda_\theta}P+\frac{r}{r+\lambda_\theta}D(\delta). \tag{4.13}$$

To derive an explicit solution for $D(\delta)$ we now proceed as follows (see Proposition A.37 for a similar argument in a more general context). Integrating against the reset distribution $dF(\delta)$ on both sides of (4.9) shows that

$$(r+\lambda_\theta)\,\mathbf{E}^F\left[R(\delta)\right]=\mathbf{E}^F\left[\delta\right]+\lambda_\theta P,$$

where

$$\mathbf{E}^F\left[g(\delta)\right]\equiv\int_{\underline{\delta}}^{\overline{\delta}} g(x)dF(x) \tag{4.14}$$

denotes the mean of $g(\delta)$ under the assumption that δ is distributed according to $F(x)$. This identity implies that the average reservation value across the population of investors is explicitly given by

$$\mathbf{E}^F\left[R(\delta)\right]=\frac{\mathbf{E}^F\left[\delta\right]+\lambda_\theta P}{r+\lambda_\theta}$$

regardless of the arrival rate γ of preference shocks. Substituting back into (4.9) and comparing with (4.13), we finally obtain that

$$R(\delta)=\frac{\lambda_\theta}{r+\lambda_\theta}P+\frac{1}{r+\lambda_\theta}\left(\frac{r+\lambda_\theta}{r+\gamma+\lambda_\theta}\delta+\frac{\gamma}{r+\gamma+\lambda_\theta}\mathbf{E}^F\left[x\right]\right). \tag{4.15}$$

This implies in particular that

$$rD(\delta)\equiv\frac{r+\lambda_\theta}{r+\gamma+\lambda_\theta}\delta+\frac{\gamma}{r+\gamma+\lambda_\theta}\mathbf{E}^F\left[x\right].$$

Together with (4.13), this explicit solution confirms the continuity and strict monotonicity predicted by Proposition 4.3 but also permits a more detailed analysis. In particular, it shows that reservation values are linear with a slope

$$R'(\delta) = \frac{1}{r+\gamma+\lambda_\theta}. \tag{4.16}$$

Note that this derivative is independent from the reset distribution $F(\delta)$ and monotone decreasing in r, γ, and λ_θ, so that an investor's utility flow matters less for her reservation value as she becomes more impatient, as she changes types more often, and as she contacts dealers more frequently. The linearity of the reservation value function and its independence from the reset distribution reflect the fact that all investors are equally likely to contact a dealer. As such, these properties are specific to the semi-centralized market setting. In particular, we will see in chapters 5 and 8 that, when investors can choose their contact rate with dealers or meet each other in a frictional market, the marginal reservation value $R'(\delta)$ varies to reflect the different trading opportunities of each investor in the market.

4.4 Equilibrium

In this section we use the optimal trading behavior of investors to construct the equilibrium allocation of assets across the population of investors and the equilibrium price in the interdealer market. As a first step, we derive a convenient formulation of the market clearing condition.

4.4.1 Market Clearing

The optimal trading behavior of investors follows directly from our analysis of the reservation value function: conditional on meeting a dealer, an asset owner with utility flow δ weakly prefers to sell if and only if his reservation value is such that $R(\delta) \leq P$, while a nonowner with utility flow δ weakly prefers to buy if and only if his reservation value is such that $R(\delta) \geq P$.

An immediate consequence of this trading strategy at the aggregate level is that *in equilibrium* it must hold that $R(\delta') \leq P \leq R(\delta'')$ for some δ', δ'' in the support of $F(\delta)$, as otherwise all investors would be on the same side of the market at all times. Since the reservation value function is continuous and strictly increasing, by Proposition 4.3, this observation implies that in any equilibrium there exists a unique utility flow $\delta^\star \in \mathcal{D}$ such that $R(\delta^\star) = P$ and $R(\delta) \leq P$ if and only if $\delta \leq \delta^\star$. The traditional approach to pin down this *marginal* type would be to derive the allocation induced by a given value of $\delta^\star$ and then to vary this threshold until the allocation is stationary and consistent with market clearing. However, and as noted by Lagos and Rocheteau [2009], the specific features of the semicentralized market setting allow us to circumvent this approach by directly computing the gross demand and supply induced by a given marginal type.

Since all investors meet dealers at the same rate, it follows from the law of large numbers that the joint distribution of utility flows and asset holdings among the group of investors who meet dealers at a given instant is the same as in the whole population. In particular, the marginal distribution of utility flows in that group is $F(\delta)$, with a proportion s of owners. Hence, over a small time interval of length h, the gross asset supply in the interdealer market is λsh. On the other hand, given $\delta^\star$ we have that the postcontact asset holdings of an investor with utility flow $\delta \in \mathcal{D}$ must satisfy

$$q \begin{cases} = 0, & \text{if } \delta < \delta^\star, \\ \in \{0, 1\} & \text{if } \delta = \delta^\star, \\ = 1, & \text{if } \delta > \delta^\star. \end{cases}$$

This implies that, over a small time interval of length h, the gross demand for assets in the interdealer market lies in

$$\lambda h \left[1 - F(\delta^\star), 1 - F(\delta^\star -)\right].$$

Equating gross supply and demand, we conclude that the marginal type is a solution to the inclusion

$$\delta^\star \in \mathcal{S} \text{ such that } s \in \left[1 - F(\delta^\star), 1 - F(\delta^\star -)\right], \tag{4.17}$$

where $\mathcal{S}$ denotes the convex hull of the support of $F(\delta)$. This simple expression of the market clearing condition pins down the marginal type as a quantile of the reset distribution $F(\delta)$ at level $1 - s$ and, therefore, establishes the *existence* and *generic uniqueness* of the equilibrium.

Condition (4.17) also shows that the marginal type does not depend on the contact rate with dealers λ in our semicentralized market setting. In fact, this requirement is exactly the same as in the frictionless benchmark of section 4.2 because, at each instant, the group of investors who are matched with dealers effectively participate in a frictionless market. This, however, does *not* imply that search frictions do not matter for prices and allocations in a semi-centralized market. It only means that, over a short time interval, search frictions do not affect the postcontact asset holdings of those investors who contact a dealer. But search frictions do affect both the allocation and the valuation of those investors who do not get matched with a dealer. In particular, search frictions imply that there are *misallocated* investors with utility flow $\delta < \delta^\star$ ($\delta > \delta^\star$) who hold (don't hold) the asset because they have switched utility flow but have not yet been able to contact a dealer with whom to trade.

4.4.2 Asset Allocation

To precisely understand the impact of search frictions on the asset allocation, consider the cumulative measure $\Phi_q(\delta)$ of investors who hold q units of the asset and have utility flow in the interval $(\underline{\delta}, \delta]$. In a steady-state equilibrium these measures must satisfy three conditions. First, they must add up to the distribution of utility flows across the whole population:

$$\Phi_0(\delta) + \Phi_1(\delta) = F(\delta), \qquad \delta \in \mathcal{D}. \tag{4.18}$$

Second, they must enforce market clearing in the sense that the total measure of owners must equal the asset supply:

$$\Phi_1(\overline{\delta}) \equiv \lim_{\delta \uparrow \overline{\delta}} \Phi_1(\delta) = s. \tag{4.19}$$

Third, these measures must be consistent with stationarity, which requires that the inflow to and outflow from any group of investors be equalized at all times. Specifically, let us define $\lambda_q(\delta)$ to be the trading intensity of an investor who holds $q \in \{0, 1\}$ units of the asset and has utility flow δ. With this notation, the stationarity condition can be formally written as

$$\int_B (\gamma s dF(\delta) + \lambda_0(\delta)\, d\Phi_0(\delta)) = \int_B (\gamma d\Phi_1(\delta) + \lambda_1(\delta)\, d\Phi_1(\delta)) \tag{4.20}$$

for all Borel sets $B \subseteq \mathcal{D}$. This stationary condition holds in all the models we consider in this book, albeit with different market structures and, thus, different trading intensity functions. The left-hand side is the inflow into the group of owners with utility flow in B, whereas the right-hand side is the outflow from that group. The inflow is itself the sum of two terms. The first term, $\gamma s dF(\delta)$, is the inflow induced by preference shocks. Indeed, at each instant a measure $\gamma s = \gamma \Phi_1(\overline{\delta})$ of owners receive a preference shock that resets their utility flow to some $\delta \in B$ with probability $dF(\delta)$. The second term, $\lambda_0(\delta) d\Phi_0(\delta)$, is the inflow due to asset purchase. The two terms that compose the outflow on the right-hand side have a similar interpretation.

In the semicentralized market setting of this chapter, the trading intensity function $\lambda_q(\delta)$ takes a very simple form:

$$\lambda_q(\delta) \begin{cases} = \lambda q & \text{if } \delta < \delta^\star, \\ \in [0, \lambda] & \text{if } \delta = \delta^\star, \\ = \lambda(1-q) & \text{if } \delta > \delta^\star. \end{cases} \tag{4.21}$$

This expression allows us to pin down the equilibrium allocation by stating condition (4.20) for two well-chosen groups of investors. First, consider investors with utility flow in $B = (\underline{\delta}, \delta]$ for some $\delta < \delta^\star$. Equation (4.21) shows that the trading intensities of investors with utility flow in that set are given by $\lambda_1(x) = 0$ and $\lambda_0(x) = \lambda$. Therefore, it follows from (4.20) that

$$\Phi_1(\delta) = \frac{\gamma}{\gamma+\lambda} sF(\delta), \qquad \delta < \delta^\star. \tag{4.22}$$

Next, consider the group of investors with utility flow in $B = (\delta, \overline{\delta})$ for some fixed $\delta \geq \delta^\star$. Equation (4.21) shows that the trading intensities of such investors are simply given by $\lambda_1(x) = 0$ and $\lambda_0(x) = \lambda$. Therefore, (4.20) implies that

$$\Phi_1(\overline{\delta}) - \Phi_1(\delta) = \frac{\gamma s + \lambda}{\gamma + \lambda} (1 - F(\delta)), \qquad \delta \geq \delta^\star,$$

and substituting (4.19) we obtain that

$$\Phi_1(\delta) = \frac{\gamma}{\gamma+\lambda} sF(\delta) + \frac{\lambda}{\gamma+\lambda} (F(\delta) - (1-s)), \qquad \delta \geq \delta^\star. \tag{4.23}$$

Finally, combining (4.22) and (4.23) while keeping in mind that $\delta^\star$ is a quantile of the distribution of utility flows at the level $1 - s$, we obtain an expression that is valid across all utility flows:

$$\Phi_1(\delta) = \frac{\gamma}{\gamma+\lambda} sF(\delta) + \frac{\lambda}{\gamma+\lambda} \Psi_1(\delta), \tag{4.24}$$

where $\Psi_1(\delta)$ is the frictionless allocation in (4.3). Importantly, this expression depends neither on the choice of a marginal type $\delta^\star$ satisfying (4.17) nor on the specification of the trading intensities of marginal investors (see Exercises 4.8 and 4.9). This shows that the allocation is always unique—even in the nongeneric cases where the marginal type is not.

Equation (4.24) shows that the equilibrium allocation arises from the convex combination of two distributions: the distribution that obtains from randomly allocating assets across the population, $sF(\delta)$, and the efficient distribution that results from allocating assets to those investors who value them most, $\Psi_1(\delta)$. The weights in this combination depend on λ and γ only through their ratio $\phi \equiv \gamma/\lambda$. This constant measures the arrival rate of trading opportunities relative to that of preference shocks and controls the efficiency of the allocation. Indeed, it follows directly from (4.3) and (4.24) that

$$\frac{\partial \Phi_1(\delta)}{\partial \phi} = \frac{sF(\delta) - \Psi_1(\delta)}{(1+\phi)^2} \geq 0$$

and

$$\lim_{\phi \to 0} \Phi_1(\delta) = \Psi_1(\delta) \leq sF(\delta) = \lim_{\phi \to \infty} \Phi_1(\delta).$$

Therefore, the distribution of utility flows among asset owners starts from the efficient allocation of the frictionless benchmark at $\phi = 0$ and then decreases monotonically in the sense of first-order stochastic dominance to reach the purely random allocation when $\phi \to \infty$. Intuitively, as ϕ decreases, investors either have more opportunities to trade (if λ increases) or find themselves needing to trade less often (if instead γ decreases). In both cases, the market is better able to channel assets toward investors with high utility flows, which reduces the impact of search frictions.

Note that the efficient allocation can be obtained even in the presence of search frictions ($\lambda < \infty$) provided that the arrival rate of preference shocks γ approaches zero. This is because, with permanent utility flows, nonowners with $\delta \geq \delta^\star$ (owners with $\delta < \delta^\star$) will acquire (sell) the asset upon their first meeting with a dealer and then hold on to it (remain asset free), so that the trading volume is zero in the steady state.

Example 4.4: To illustrate the results above, figure 4.4 plots the cumulative measures $\Phi_q(\delta)$ in a semicentralized market where the reset distribution is uniform on the unit interval, the supply is $s = 0.4$, and $\phi = 1$ so that preference shocks and trading opportunities arrive at the same speed.

Comparing the distributions to their frictionless counterparts shows that the impossibility to trade immediately after a preference shock makes the equilibrium less efficient by pushing the distribution among owners up and to the left, so that there are investors with $\delta < \delta^\star$ who would not hold the asset in the frictionless benchmark but do so in the semicentralized market. In this numerical example, the steady-state measure of these *misallocated* investors is $\Phi_1(\delta^\star) = 0.12$, which implies that $0.12/s = 30\%$ of existing assets are in the wrong hands at any point in time.

Symmetrically, the left panel shows that search frictions push the distribution among nonowners down and to the right, so that nonowners tend to have higher utility flows in the environment with search frictions. In particular, at any point in time, there is a mass $\Phi_0(\overline{\delta}) - \Phi_0(\delta^\star) = 0.12$ of investors with utility flow $\delta > \delta^\star$ who would be owners in the frictionless market but are not in the semicentralized market because

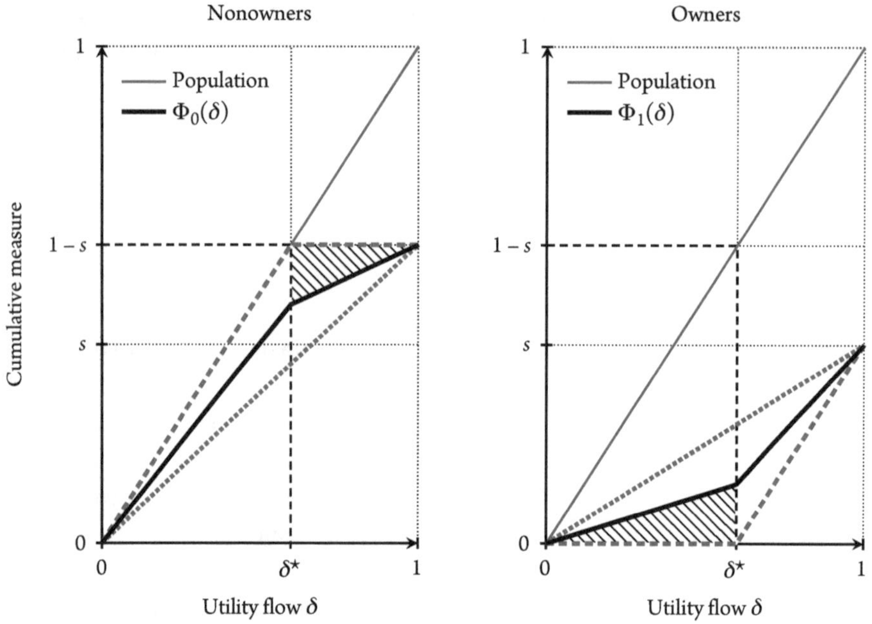

FIGURE 4.4. The equilibrium allocation in the semicentralized market

This figure illustrates the equilibrium distribution of utility flows among owners (right panel) and nonowners (left panel) in a model with $\lambda/\gamma = 1$, asset supply $s = 0.4$, and uniform distribution $F(\delta) = \delta$ on $\mathcal{D} = (0, 1)$. In each panel, the solid line represents the population distribution, the thick dashed line represents the frictionless benchmark, the dash-dotted line represents the purely random case where $\phi \to 0$, and the hatched region represents the misallocated investors.

they have not been able to locate a dealer since the occurence of their last preference shock.

4.4.3 The Interdealer Price

To complete the construction of the equilibrium, we now determine the price of the asset in the interdealer market. From the characterization of the marginal type, we know that $P \equiv R(\delta^\star)$, i.e., that the price is given by the reservation value of the asset to an investor with current utility flow equal to the marginal type. Therefore, it immediately follows from (4.12) and (4.15) that

$$P = R(\delta^\star) = D(\delta^\star) = \frac{\delta^\star}{r} - \frac{\gamma}{r\,(r+\gamma+\lambda_\theta)}\left(\delta^\star - \mathbf{E}^F\left[\delta\right]\right), \tag{4.25}$$

where $\mathbf{E}^F[\cdot]$ is defined in (4.14). This expression shows that the interdealer price is the sum of the price $\delta^\star/r$ in the frictionless benchmark and a correction term that reflects the frictions at play in the semicentralized market environment. Specifically, a direct calculation shows that

$$\lim_{\lambda_\theta \to \infty} P = \frac{\delta^\star}{r}$$

and

$$\lim_{\lambda_\theta \to 0} P = \frac{\delta^\star}{r} - \frac{\gamma\left(\delta^\star - \mathbf{E}^F[\delta]\right)}{r(r+\gamma)} = \mathbf{E}_{\delta^\star}\left[\int_0^\infty e^{-rt}\delta_t dt\right].$$

Moreover, one can easily show that

$$\frac{\partial P}{\partial \lambda_\theta} \propto -\frac{\partial P}{\partial \gamma} \propto \left(\delta^\star - \mathbf{E}^F[\delta]\right),$$

so that the direction of the price deviation and its comparative statics are entirely determined by the difference between the marginal type and the average utility flow in the population of investors, $\delta^\star - \mathbf{E}^F[\delta]$. Figure 4.5 illustrates for an example with a uniform distribution of utility flows.

To understand these results, recall from chapter 3 that the reservation value function contains two components related to future trading opportunities. First, part of the value of acquiring an asset derives from the option to sell it at a later date. Frictions, however, reduce this value and make investors less willing to pay for the asset—that is, frictions introduce an *illiquidity discount*. When frictions ease, the investor is able to exercise the option to sell more quickly, the illiquidity discount declines, and his reservation value rises. Second, by acquiring an asset now, the investor derives value from the fact that he *doesn't* have to search for an asset later if he receives a positive shock to his utility flow. Unlike the option value of reselling, the presence of frictions actually increases this component of the investor's reservation value—that is, frictions introduce what we call a *scarcity premium*. As frictions vanish, this scarcity premium declines, since it becomes less valuable to not have to search for the asset in the future.

Whether the illiquidity discount or scarcity premium dominates depends on the asset supply. When the average utility flow $\mathbf{E}^F[\delta]$ is smaller than the marginal utility flow $\delta^\star$, which occurs if and only if the supply is large, then the illiquidity discount effect described above dominates, since the investor is more likely to receive a preference shock that makes him want to exercise the option to sell the asset. Hence the asset price is below the price in the frictionless benchmark and increases as frictions vanish—either because the meeting rate increases or because the frequency of preference shocks

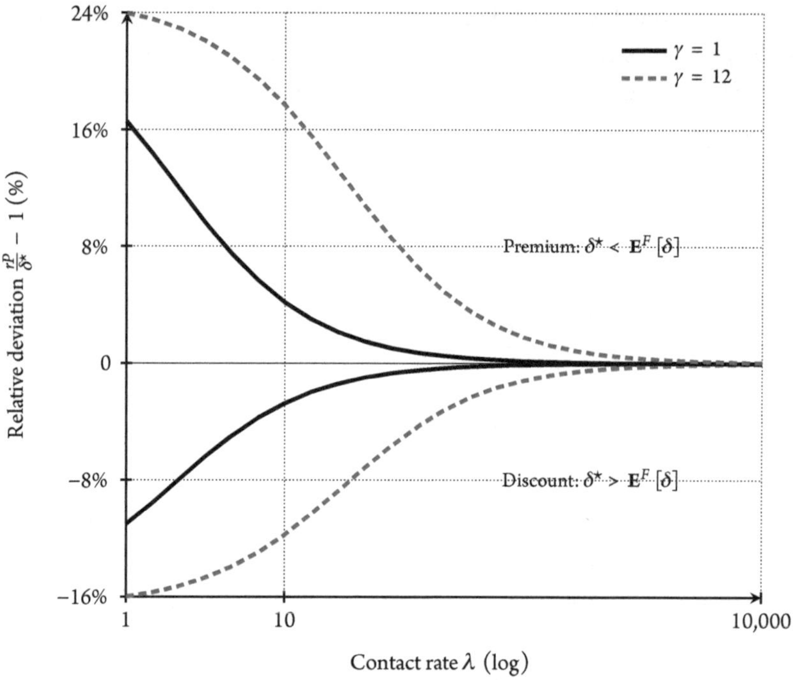

FIGURE 4.5. The interdealer price

This figure illustrates the behavior of the interdealer price in a model with a uniform distribution $F(\delta) = \delta$ on $\mathcal{D} = (0, 1)$. The bottom panel shows the relative deviation from the frictionless price as a function of λ in a market where $\delta^\star = 1 - s = 0.6 > \mathbf{E}^F[\delta]$ and either $\gamma = 1$ (solid) or $\gamma = 12$ (dashed). The top panel plots the same quantities but in a market where the marginal type $\delta^\star = 0.4$ is lower than the average.

declines. Alternatively, when $\mathbf{E}^F[\delta] > \delta^\star$ then the scarcity premium effect dominates, since the investor is more likely to receive a preference shock that makes him want to own the asset. In this case, the presence of frictions makes the investor more willing to pay for the asset now, raising his reservation value and hence pushing the equilibrium price above $P = \delta^\star / r$. As frictions vanish, however, the reduction in the scarcity premium outweighs the reduction in the illiquidity discount and the equilibrium price falls.

In either case, the price approaches the Walrasian price as the bargaining-adjusted meeting rate $\lambda_\theta \to \infty$. An intriguing implication of (4.25), however, is that the price can exceed or fall short of the buy-and-hold price

$$\lim_{\lambda_\theta \to 0} D(\delta) = \mathbf{E}_\delta \left[\int_0^\infty e^{-rt} \delta_t dt \right] = \frac{\delta}{r} + \frac{\gamma}{r(r+\gamma)} \left(\mathbf{E}^F[\delta] - \delta \right) \tag{4.26}$$

for *any* investor in the market. For example, as $s \to 0$ we have that the marginal type converges to the upper bound of the support of the distribution $F(\delta)$, and it thus follows from (4.25) and (4.26) that

$$\min_{\delta\in\mathcal{S}}\left(P - \lim_{\lambda_\theta\to 0} D(\delta)\right) \to \max_{\delta\in\mathcal{S}} \frac{\gamma\lambda_\theta(\delta - \mathbf{E}^F[\delta])}{r(r+\gamma)(r+\gamma+\lambda_\theta)} \geq 0.$$

The opposite conclusion obtains when $s \to 1$, in which case the interdealer price lies below the buy-and-hold value of any investor. To understand these results, recall from chapter 3 that the reservation value is not determined by the value of buying and holding forever. Instead, it is determined by the value of buying and then *following an optimal strategy* that requires the investor to sell whenever possible if $\delta < \delta^\star$ and to buy whenever possible if $\delta > \delta^\star$.

4.4.4 *Sequential Representation of Reservation Values*

To close this section, we discuss an insightful representation of *equilibrium* reservation values. In equilibrium, the interdealer price P must coincide with the reservation value $R(\delta^\star)$ of an investor at the marginal type. Substituting this condition into (4.9) shows that, *in equilibrium*, the reservation value function solves

$$\begin{aligned} rR(\delta) &= \delta + \lambda_\theta\left(R(\delta^\star) - R(\delta)\right) + \gamma \int_{\underline{\delta}}^{\overline{\delta}} (R(x) - R(\delta))\, dF(x) \\ &= \delta + (\gamma + \lambda_\theta) \int_{\underline{\delta}}^{\overline{\delta}} (R(x) - R(\delta))\, d\hat{F}(x), \end{aligned}$$

with the auxiliary distribution defined by

$$\hat{F}(\delta) = \frac{\gamma}{\gamma+\lambda_\theta} F(\delta) + \frac{\lambda_\theta}{\gamma+\lambda_\theta} \mathbf{1}_{\{\delta\geq\delta^\star\}}.$$

Combining this equation with Proposition A.37 of appendix A.6 then delivers the following explicit representation.

Proposition 4.5: In equilibrium,

$$R(\delta) = \mathbf{E}_\delta\left[\int_0^\infty e^{-rt}\hat{\delta}_t dt\right], \tag{4.27}$$

where the market valuation process $(\hat{\delta}_t)_{t\geq 0}$ is a Markov jump process with constant jump intensity $\gamma + \lambda_\theta$ and reset distribution $\hat{F}(\delta)$.

The proposition refers to $\hat{\delta}_t$ as the *market valuation* process because it takes into account not only the physical changes of utility flows of an investor, but also his trading opportunities. To describe this process note that, during a small interval of length h, the market valuation can change for two reasons. First, a preference shock arrives with probability γh, in which case a new utility flow is drawn from $F(x)$. Second, a trading opportunity arrives with probability $\lambda_\theta h$, in which case the market valuation jumps to the marginal type so that the reservation value jumps to the interdealer price.

Representations such as (4.27) are standard in classical asset pricing, where private asset values are obtained as the present value of cash flows under an auxiliary probability constructed from marginal rates of substitution. The emergence of such a representation in a decentralized financial market can be viewed as a generalization of the concept of the marginal investor that accounts for search and bargaining frictions. Indeed, in the frictionless benchmark, we have $\lambda_\theta/\gamma \to \infty$ and it follows that the market valuation is constant and equal to the marginal type. By contrast, in the semi-centralized trading environment, the market valuation is stochastic and differs from the marginal type because, following a negative preference shock, every owner is forced to enjoy a depressed utility flow until a dealer can be contacted.

4.4.5 Summary

The above derivations deliver a complete description of the equilibrium in the semi-centralized market setting. Specifically, the equilibrium is generically unique and composed of

- The interdealer price P in (4.25).
- The reservation value function $R(\delta)$ in (4.15).
- The asset allocation captured by the measures $\Phi_q(\delta)$ in (4.24),

where the marginal type $\delta^\star$ is the generically unique solution to the market clearing condition (4.17).

4.5 Equilibrium Implications

We now use the explicit characterization of the equilibrium to study the effects of search and bargaining frictions on several common measures of liquidity: trading volume, the bid-ask spread, and the yield spread.

To simplify the exposition, we *assume in this section that the distribution of utility flows is continuous*—so that the measure of investors who are indifferent between buying or selling is zero at all times—and guide the reader through the general case in the end-of-chapter exercises. This assumption has two important consequences that we use repeatedly throughout this section: it implies that the cumulative measures $\Phi_q(\delta)$ are continuous and it guarantees that $F(\delta^\star) = 1 - s$ at any marginal type.

4.5.1 *Trading Volume*

In equilibrium, the instantaneous order flows originating from investors who meet a dealer and either sell or buy are equal and given by

$$\lambda\Phi_1(\delta^\star) = \lambda\left(1 - s - \Phi_0(\delta^\star)\right) = \frac{\lambda}{\gamma + \lambda}\gamma s(1 - s), \tag{4.28}$$

where the equalities follow from (4.18), (4.24), and the assumed continuity of $F(\delta)$. In contrast, when the distribution of utility flows is continuous, example 4.2 shows that the flow of trades required to clear markets in the frictionless benchmark is $\gamma s(1 - s)$. Therefore, (4.28) shows that search frictions reduce trading volume by a factor $\lambda/(\gamma + \lambda)$. Note that this factor approaches 1 as $\phi = \gamma/\lambda \to 0$ because search frictions create a bottleneck that slows down asset reallocation relative to the frictionless benchmark unless utility flows are permanent in which case there is no trade.

4.5.2 *Trading Costs*

One of the most common measures of market liquidity is the bid-ask spread, which is commonly defined as the cost of a *round-trip* transaction, i.e., an asset purchase followed by an asset sale. The semicentralized framework offers a coherent theory of the bid-ask spread based on search and bargaining frictions. Indeed, with search frictions, dealers generate a surplus by offering investors the opportunity to rebalance their portfolios; and with bargaining power, they extract part of this surplus in the form of the bid-ask spread. In this section, we derive the equilibrium bid-ask spread and study how it depends on the severity of the frictions and the preferences of the investors.

Recall that, upon meeting a dealer, owners with utility flow δ weakly prefers to sell if and only if $\delta \le \delta^\star$, in which case the price they receive is

$$B(\delta) = \theta R(\delta) + (1 - \theta)P = \theta R(\delta) + (1 - \theta)R(\delta^\star),$$

where we have used (4.25). Moreover, since $F(\delta)$ is continuous, we have that the distribution of utility flows among owners who prefer to sell is

$$\frac{\Phi_1(\min\{\delta, \delta^\star\})}{\Phi_1(\delta^\star)} = \frac{F(\min\{\delta, \delta^\star\})}{F(\delta^\star)} \equiv F\left(\delta \middle| \delta \le \delta^\star\right). \tag{4.29}$$

Hence, the average transaction cost incurred by an investor who sells—or the average *bid-to-interdealer spread*—can be written as

$$P-\overline{B}=\int_{\underline{\delta}}^{\delta^{\star}}(P-B(\delta))\frac{d\Phi_1(\delta)}{\Phi_1(\delta^{\star})}=\mathbf{E}^F\left[P-B(\delta)\mid\delta\leq\delta^{\star}\right] \tag{4.30}$$

$$=\theta\mathbf{E}^F\left[R(\delta^{\star})-R(\delta)\middle|\delta\leq\delta^{\star}\right]=\frac{\theta\mathbf{E}^F\left[\delta^{\star}-\delta|\delta\leq\delta^{\star}\right]}{r+\gamma+\lambda_\theta},$$

where $\mathbf{E}^F\left[\cdot\mid\delta\leq\delta^{\star}\right]$ denotes an integral against the distribution in (4.29) and the last equality follows from (4.16), which shows that the reservation value function is linear in utility flow with slope $1/\left(r+\gamma+\lambda_\theta\right)$.

Notice that the average bid-to-interdealer spread is equal to zero when dealers have no bargaining power, since in that case investors can sell at the interdealer price. When $\theta>0$, the average bid-to-interdealer spread is strictly positive and decreasing in the adjusted contact rate, λ_θ, so that the cost of selling the asset increases as trading frictions become more severe. Also note that the spread gets larger when asset owners experience larger declines in utility flow upon becoming sellers—i.e., more extreme distress costs—as captured by the conditional expectation $\mathbf{E}^F\left[\delta^{\star}-\delta|\delta\leq\delta^{\star}\right]$. Finally, note that the average selling cost is decreasing in the arrival rate of preference shocks. Intuitively, as γ increases, utility flows become less persistent and differences in reservation values across investors shrink. As a result, the gains from trade created by reallocating the asset are diminished and the spread declines.

Symmetrically, using (4.6) and (4.24) together with the assumed continuity of $F(\delta)$ shows that the average *ask-to-interdealer spread* is

$$\overline{A}-P=\mathbf{E}^F\left[A(\delta)-P\middle|\delta>\delta^{\star}\right] \tag{4.31}$$

$$=\theta\mathbf{E}^F\left[R(\delta)-R(\delta^{\star})\middle|\delta>\delta^{\star}\right]=\frac{\theta\mathbf{E}^F\left[\delta-\delta^{\star}|\delta>\delta^{\star}\right]}{r+\gamma+\lambda_\theta}.$$

Comparing (4.30) and (4.31) reveals an important empirical implication of this class of model: the bid-to-interdealer spread and the ask-to-interdealer spread are not necessarily symmetric. The reason why the spreads charged to buyers and sellers may be different is that these costs depend on the average gains from trade above and below the marginal type $\delta^{\star}$, which in turn reflect the (possibly asymmetric) shape of the distribution of utility flows.

The asymmetry of transaction costs on the bid and the ask sides of the market is empirically relevant. Indeed, we saw in chapter 2 that customers pay larger transaction costs when they buy than when they sell. Through the lens of the model considered here, this indicates that the difference $|\delta - \delta^\star|$ tends to be larger above $\delta^\star$ than below. See chapter 2 for a more detailed discussion.

Finally, combining (4.30) and (4.31) shows that, in a semicentralized market setting, the average *bid-ask spread* is explicitly given by

$$\overline{A} - \overline{B} = \frac{\theta}{r+\gamma+\lambda_\theta}\left(\mathbf{E}^F\left[\delta \middle| \delta > \delta^\star\right] - \mathbf{E}^F\left[\delta \middle| \delta \leq \delta^\star\right]\right).$$

Intuitively, this expression shows that the average bid-ask spread is equal to the surplus between the average buyer and seller, and thus proportional to the difference between the utility flows of the average buyer and the average seller. Following the same logic as above, the average bid-ask spread is increasing in the bargaining power of dealers, increasing in the severity of the trading frictions, and decreasing in the arrival rate of preference shocks.

4.5.3 Liquidity Yield Spreads

The yield spread of a fixed-income instrument is composed of one component related to risk and one component related to liquidity. The model studied here delivers a simple, intuitive formula for the liquidity component. In particular, we define the liquidity yield spread, ℓ, as the solution to

$$\frac{\delta^\star}{r+\ell} = P = R(\delta^\star).$$

In words, the liquidity yield spread is the adjustment to the discount rate that makes the value of utility flows to a perpetually marginal investor equal to the interdealer price. Substituting this definition into (4.25) and simplifying yields

$$\frac{\ell}{r+\ell} = \frac{\gamma}{r+\gamma+\lambda_\theta}\left(1 - \mathbf{E}^F\left[\delta/\delta^\star\right]\right). \tag{4.32}$$

Note that the liquidity yield spread can be either positive or negative, which follows from our finding that trading frictions have ambiguous effects on the interdealer price. In particular, the yield spread is positive when $\delta^\star > \mathbf{E}^F[\delta]$, which corresponds to the case in which the asset trades at a discount relative to the frictionless benchmark.

Assuming for the sake of discussion that the spread is positive, as received wisdom suggests, we see that several factors contribute to a larger spread. The first is larger values of γ, which correspond to more frequent preference shocks. The second is more severe search frictions or greater bargaining power for dealers, as captured by the adjusted contact rate λ_θ. Finally, the theory predicts that larger yield spreads are associated with more extreme distress costs, as measured by the difference between the marginal type and the average utility flow $\delta^{\star} - \mathbf{E}^{F}[\delta]$.

Interestingly, (4.32) shows that the liquidity yield spread can be positive even if investors have all the bargaining power and, thus, do not appear to incur a transaction cost when they trade with dealers. The reason is that the price still capitalizes the present value of the distress costs that investors will incur while waiting for an opportunity to trade with dealers. This observation stands in contrast with traditional formulas for asset pricing with transaction costs, such as Amihud and Mendelson [1986], in which yield spreads capitalize the present value of transaction costs incurred by successive buyers.

4.6 Trading Relationships

The random matching mechanism that underlies the semicentralized market setting assumes that, after executing a trade, an investor and a dealer part ways and never meet again. This simplifies the analysis but ignores the fact that, in practice, investors tend to form relationships with dealers that allow them to bypass search frictions and obtain better terms of trade. In this section, we briefly outline a variant of the semicentralized model that incorporates the possibility of such long-term relationships.

4.6.1 The Model

We consider the same economic environment as in previous sections of this chapter but with a different modeling of relationships. Specifically, we assume that instead of parting ways after negotiating a trade, a dealer and an investor remain connected for some period of time. As a result, the population of investors is now composed of two types: *matched* and *unmatched* investors.

An unmatched investor becomes matched at rate $\lambda \geq 0$. Upon matching, an investor and a dealer bargain over a lump-sum fee, which allows the investor to trade instantly at the interdealer price until the end of the relationship, which occurs at rate $\beta \geq 0$. After the relationship ends, the investors cannot trade until she meets a new dealer. In particular, no transaction can be executed at the breakup time. We assume that a dealer can be simultaneously matched with several investors, but that an investor can be matched with at most one dealer at a time. As before, we denote by $\theta \in [0, 1]$ the bargaining power of dealers relative to investors and, to simplify the presentation, we assume throughout this section that the distribution of utility flow is *continuous*.

The model we present in this section assumes that every meeting between a dealer and an unmatched investor initiates a long-term relationship, which implies that all transactions occur at the interdealer price. This admittedly stark assumption can be relaxed by assuming that only a fraction of such meetings lead to a relationship, while the remaining fraction generate at most one trade, as in the previous sections. In this case, the model would produce two types of trades: relationship trades that occur at the interdealer price and spot trades (with dispersed prices) that result from one-off meetings between investors and dealers. See Exercise 4.11 for the analysis of such a model.

4.6.2 Asset Demand

Let $V(q,\delta)$ denote the value function of an *unmatched* investor with current utility flow δ who holds q units of the asset, and $M(q,\delta)$ denote the value function of an otherwise identical *matched* investor. Using integration by parts as in section 4.2 shows that

$$\begin{aligned}M(q,\delta) &= \sup_{\vartheta\in\mathcal{Q}_q} \mathbf{E}_\delta\left[\int_0^\sigma e^{-rt}\left(\vartheta_t\delta_t dt - Pd\vartheta_t\right) + e^{-r\sigma}V(\vartheta_\sigma,\delta_\sigma)\right]\\ &= qP + \sup_{\vartheta\in\mathcal{Q}_0} \mathbf{E}_\delta\left[\int_0^\sigma e^{-rt}\vartheta_t\left(\delta_t - rP\right)dt + e^{-r\sigma}\left(V(\vartheta_\sigma,\delta_\sigma) - \vartheta_\sigma P\right)\right],\end{aligned}$$

where P is the interdealer price; σ is an exponential random time, with rate β, at which the relationship ends; and $\mathcal{Q}_q$ denotes the set of $\{0,1\}$ —valued processes of bounded variation that start from q. Integrating against the distribution of σ inside the expectation and maximizing the result pointwise over ϑ_t yields

$$\begin{aligned}M(\delta) &\equiv M(0,\delta) = M(q,\delta) - qP\\ &= \mathbf{E}_\delta\left[\int_0^\infty e^{-(r+\beta)t}\left((\delta_t - rP + \beta(R(\delta_t) - P))^+ + \beta V(0,\delta_t)\right)dt\right],\end{aligned}$$

where

$$R(\delta) \equiv V(1,\delta) - V(0,\delta)$$

denotes the reservation value of an unmatched investor. The key implication of this expression is that a matched investor holds the asset if and only if his utility flow is such that

$$\delta \geq rP + \beta(P - R(\delta)). \tag{4.33}$$

To understand this condition, it suffices to compare the instantaneous costs and benefits of holding an asset for a matched investor with utility flow δ. Over a small time interval of length h, the benefit is approximately δh, whereas the cost is approximately equal to

$$\beta h\left(P-e^{-rh}R(\delta)\right)+(1-\beta h)\left(P-e^{-rh}P\right)\approx(rP+\beta(P-R(\delta)))\,h.$$

This expression shows that the cost depends on whether the relationship ends or continues. If the relationship ends, which occurs with probability βh, then the investor pays the interdealer price P at the beginning of the time interval, and receives the unmatched reservation value at the end. If the relationship continues, which occurs with probability $1-\beta h$, then the investor pays and receives the interdealer price at the beginning and at the end of the time.

Importantly, (4.33) shows that the demand of matched investors is fully determined by the unmatched reservation value $R(\delta)$. To compute this function, note that the surplus generated by a meeting between a dealer and an unmatched investor is

$$M(q,\delta)-V(q,\delta)=M(\delta)+qP-V(q,\delta).$$

Therefore, the HJB equation for the value function of an unmatched investor is

$$rV(q,\delta)=q\delta+\lambda_\theta\left(M(\delta)+qP-V(q,\delta)\right)+\gamma\mathbf{E}^F\left[V(q,x)-V(q,\delta)\right],$$

where $\lambda_\theta=\lambda(1-\theta)$ denotes the bargaining-adjusted meeting intensity. Using this equation to compute the difference $R(\delta)=V(1,\delta)-V(0,\delta)$ shows that the unmatched reservation value satisfies

$$rR(\delta)=\delta+\lambda_\theta\left(P-R(\delta)\right)+\gamma\mathbf{E}^F\left[R(x)-R(\delta)\right].$$

Comparing this equation to (4.8) reveals that the reservation value function in the model with long-term relationships is the same as in the model with instantaneous relationships. This is due to the fact that $M(\delta,1)-M(\delta,0)=P$: when an investor contacts a dealer, the pair has instantaneous access to the interdealer market, so the value of owning the asset vs. not owning it is just equal to the price of the asset, P. This was true before when investors and dealers could only engage in spot trade, and continues to be true now that they can form relationships. In particular, proceeding as in section 4.3.2 shows that

$$R(\delta)=\frac{\lambda_\theta P}{r+\lambda_\theta}+\frac{1}{r+\gamma+\lambda_\theta}\left(\delta+\frac{\gamma\mathbf{E}^F[x]}{r+\lambda_\theta}\right), \tag{4.34}$$

and it follows that the demand of matched investors who take the interdealer price as given can be expressed as

$$\hat{q}(\delta; P) \equiv \mathbf{1}_{\left\{\delta > \hat{\delta}(P)\right\}}$$

with the threshold

$$\hat{\delta}(P) \equiv rP + \frac{\gamma\beta\left(rP - \mathbf{E}^F[x]\right)}{(r+\lambda_\theta)(r+\gamma+\beta+\lambda_\theta)}. \tag{4.35}$$

This expression naturally converges to the asset demand of the semicentralized market as the average duration of trading relationships $1/\beta$ decreases to zero, and to the frictionless asset demand as the average bargaining-adjusted duration of unmatched periods $1/\lambda_\theta$ decreases to zero.

Whether shorter relationships (smaller $1/\beta$) reduce asset demand (larger $\hat{\delta}(P)$) depends on the sign of $rP - \mathbf{E}^F[x]$. If this quantity is positive, then a reduction in the duration of relationships reduces demand, and otherwise it increases it. The intuition is similar to the case of spot trade. An investor's demand is driven by two considerations. First, while she remains in a relationship, the investor compares the rental cost of the asset, rP, with her current utility flow, δ. Second, as she anticipates that the relationship may terminate, the investor compares the rental cost with her expected utility flow over the period between termination and the next opportunity to form a relationship. This expected utility flow depends on both δ and $\mathbf{E}^F[x]$. If $\mathbf{E}^F[x]$ is smaller than rP, then the investor expects a relatively low utility flow upon termination, which increases the threshold type $\hat{\delta}(P)$ and reduces demand, the more so when the relationship has a shorter duration.

4.6.3 *Asset Allocation*

Since relationships are created at rate λ and destroyed at rate β, the distributions of utility flows $(\Phi_m(\delta), \Phi_u(\delta))$ within the population of matched and unmatched investors must satisfy the inflow-outflow equation

$$(\gamma+\lambda)\Phi_u(\delta) = \gamma\Phi_u(\bar{\delta})F(\delta) + \beta\Phi_m(\delta) \tag{4.36}$$

subject to the consistency condition

$$\Phi_u(\delta) + \Phi_m(\delta) = F(\delta).$$

The term on the left of (4.36) captures exits from the group of unmatched investors with utility flow lower than δ that result from preference shocks and matching with dealers. The two terms on the right-hand side of (4.36) capture entrants into the group of unmatched investors that result from preference shocks and relationship breakups, respectively.

Solving this system shows that the distributions of utility flows in the population of matched and unmatched investors are simply scaled versions of the distribution in the overall population:

$$\Phi_m(\delta) = F(\delta) - \Phi_u(\delta) = \frac{\lambda F(\delta)}{\beta + \lambda}.$$

Next, since matched investors participate in a frictionless market, we have that the distribution of utility flows among matched asset owners is given by the efficient allocation

$$\Phi_{m1}(\delta) = \Phi_m(\bar{\delta})\left(F(\delta) - 1 + s_m\right)^+, \tag{4.37}$$

where the constant $s_m \equiv \Phi_{m1}(\bar{\delta})/\Phi_m(\bar{\delta})$ denotes the asset supply per capita in the population of matched investors. On the other hand, the inflow-outflow equation for the distribution among unmatched owners is given by

$$(\gamma + \lambda)\Phi_{u1}(\delta) = \gamma\Phi_{u1}(\bar{\delta})F(\delta) + \beta\Phi_{m1}(\delta) \tag{4.38}$$

subject to the market clearing condition

$$\Phi_{u1}(\bar{\delta}) + \Phi_{m1}(\bar{\delta}) = s. \tag{4.39}$$

Substituting (4.39) into (4.38) evaluated at $\bar{\delta}$ reveals that $s_m = s$, so that the supply per capita in the populations of matched and unmatched investors is the same as in the overall population.

Plugging this constant back into (4.37), substituting the result into (4.38), and solving then gives

$$\Phi_{u1}(\delta) = \frac{s\beta}{\beta + \lambda}\left(\frac{\gamma}{\gamma + \lambda}F(\delta) + \frac{\lambda}{s(\gamma + \lambda)}\left(F(\delta) - 1 + s\right)^+\right).$$

To understand this expression, note that at any given time the population of unmatched owners can be split into two groups. A fraction $\lambda/(\gamma + \lambda)$ of unmatched owners have the same utility flow as when their match broke up, and the distribution of utility flows in that group is the frictionless one. On the other hand, the distribution of utility flows among the remaining unmatched owners coincides with the population distribution because investors in that group have experienced one or more preference shocks since the breakup of their last trading relationship. A similar intuition naturally also applies to the asset allocation (4.24) of the model with instantaneous relationships.

Finally, combining this expression with (4.37) shows that the distribution of utility flows among *all* owners is

$$\Phi_1(\delta) \equiv \Phi_{u1}(\delta) + \Phi_{m1}(\delta)$$
$$= \frac{\gamma\beta}{(\beta+\lambda)(\gamma+\lambda)} sF(\delta) + \left(1 - \frac{\gamma\beta}{(\beta+\lambda)(\gamma+\lambda)}\right)(F(\delta) - 1 + s)^+,$$

This expression shows that, as in previous sections, the allocation is a convex combination of the purely random allocation that would prevail absent trading and the efficient allocation that would prevail absent search frictions. The weights in this combination reflect the frictions at play in the market and can be easily compared to those of the semicentralized model with instantaneous relationships. In particular, since

$$\frac{\gamma\beta}{(\beta+\lambda)(\gamma+\lambda)} < \frac{\gamma}{\gamma+\lambda},$$

the above combination puts less weight on the purely random allocation, and it follows that lasting relationships improve the efficiency of the allocation. The intuition is simple: With long-term relationships only unmatched investors are subject to misallocation, and the asset allocation within that group is the same as in the semicentralized market with instantaneous relations. Therefore, the market with long-term relationships is less prone to misallocation.

4.6.4 *The Interdealer Price*

For a given interdealer price P, the aggregate flow of demand received by the dealer sector at any given point in time is

$$\lambda\left(\Phi_{u0}(\bar{\delta}) - \Phi_{u0}(\hat{\delta}(P))\right) + \gamma\Phi_{m0}(\bar{\delta})\left(1 - F(\hat{\delta}(P))\right),$$

where the first term is the demand from unmatched nonowners with utility flow above $\hat{\delta}(P)$ who have just met a dealer and the second term captures the demand from matched nonowners whose utility flow has just been reset to some value above $\hat{\delta}(P)$. Similarly, the aggregate flow of asset supply received by the dealer sector is

$$\lambda\Phi_{u1}(\hat{\delta}(P)) + \gamma\Phi_{m1}(\bar{\delta})F(\hat{\delta}(P)).$$

Equating the two and using

$$\Phi_{n0}(\delta) + \Phi_{n1}(\delta) = \Phi_n(\delta), \qquad (n,\delta) \in \{u,m\} \times \mathcal{D}$$

reveals that the market clearing condition boils down to

$$\hat{\delta}(P) = \delta^\star \equiv F^{-1}(1-s).$$

Using (4.35) to invert this relation shows that the equilibrium interdealer price is explicitly given by

$$P = \frac{\beta}{r+\beta+\lambda_\theta} P_\infty + \frac{r+\lambda_\theta}{r+\beta+\lambda_\theta} P^\star,$$

where

$$P_\infty \equiv \frac{\gamma}{r+\gamma+\lambda_\theta} \mathbf{E}^F[\delta/r] + \frac{r+\lambda_\theta}{r+\gamma+\lambda_\theta} P^\star$$

denotes the interdealer price in the market with only instantaneous relationships (see (4.25)) and $P^\star \equiv \delta^\star/r$ denotes the frictionless price. An immediate implication is that the deviation between the interdealer price with long-term relationships and the frictionless price,

$$\begin{aligned} P - P^\star &= \frac{\beta}{r+\beta+\lambda_\theta} \left(P_\infty - P^\star\right) \\ &= \frac{\beta\gamma}{r(r+\beta+\lambda_\theta)(r+\gamma+\lambda_\theta)} \left(\mathbf{E}^F[\delta] - \delta^\star\right), \end{aligned}$$

has the same sign but a smaller magnitude than the deviation that prevails in the market without long-term relationships. In particular, in both models, there is a net liquidity discount if and only if $\delta^\star$ exceeds the average utility flow, and the magnitude of this discount decreases with the average duration of relationships.

4.7 Exercises

Exercise 4.6: Consider the frictionless model of section 4.2 with a continuous $F(\delta)$ and assume that the initial distribution of utility flows in the population is given by some continuous $F_0(\delta)$.

1. Calculate the distribution $F_t(\delta)$ of utility flows at every $t \geq 0$.
2. Derive the investor's objective function when the price is a bounded and continuously differentiable function $p : \mathbf{R}_+ \to \mathbf{R}$ instead of a constant.
3. Derive the equilibrium equation for the marginal type $\delta_t^\star$ at every $t \geq 0$.

4. Show that the equilibrium price $p_t^\star$ satisfies an ordinary differential equation (ODE) and derive an explicit expression for the unique bounded solution to this equation.

Exercise 4.7: Consider the frictionless benchmark of section 4.2 and assume that investors can only trade immediately after receiving a preference shock. Recall that, in equilibrium, owners with utility flow $\delta < \delta^\star$ strictly prefer to sell, nonowners with utility flow $\delta > \delta^\star$ strictly prefer to buy, and investors with utility flow $\delta = \delta^\star$ are indifferent between buying and selling.

Denote by $\alpha_q \in [0, 1]$ the fraction of investors holding q units of the asset who trade after drawing utility flow $\delta^\star$.

1. Calculate the sell and buy order flows as functions of α_1 and α_0.
2. Use the market clearing condition (the equality of buy and sell order flows) to derive an condition that links α_1 and α_0.
3. Show that this equilibrium condition admits infinitely many solutions in $[0, 1]^2$. Explain why.
4. Derive the solution that minimizes trading volume.

Exercise 4.8: Consider a semicentralized model with a general distribution in which the marginal type $\delta^\star$ is unique and such that $\Delta F(\delta^\star) \neq 0$. Denote by $\alpha_q \in [0, 1]$ the fraction of investors holding q units who trade after drawing utility flow $\delta^\star$.

1. Calculate the sell and buy order flows as functions of α_1 and α_0.
2. Use the market clearing condition (the equality of buy and sell order flows) to derive the equilibrium condition that links α_1 and α_0.
3. Show that this condition admits infinitely many solutions in $[0, 1]^2$. Under what condition can we have $\alpha_0 = 0$ or $\alpha_1 = 0$?
4. Derive the solution that minimizes trading volume as well as the induced trading volume.
5. Derive the solution that maximizes trading volume under the assumption that each meeting results in at most one trade.

Exercise 4.9: Consider a semicentralized model with a general distribution in which the marginal type $\delta^\star$ is unique and such that $\Delta F(\delta^\star) \neq 0$. Let (α_0, α_1) be as in Exercise 4.8 and assume that we choose these execution probabilities to minimize trading volume.

1. Show that the distribution of utility flows within the groups of owners who would trade upon meeting a dealer is given by

$$\frac{1}{m}\left(\mathbf{1}_{\{\delta<\delta^\star\}}dF(\delta)+\mathbf{1}_{\{\delta=\delta^\star\}}\beta\Delta F(\delta^\star)\right)$$

for some constants m and β to be determined.
2. Use the previous result to derive the average bid-to-interdealer spread.
3. Proceed as in the two previous questions to derive the distribution of utility flows in the group of nonowners who would trade upon meeting a dealer, the average ask-to-interdealer spread, and the average bid-ask spread

Exercise 4.10: We have shown in the text that an increase in λ_θ increases the interdealer price if and only if $\delta^\star > \mathbf{E}^F[\delta]$. The goal of this exercise is to develop more intuition for this result based on the marginal investor's option value of search. The starting point of the analysis is the equation

$$rR(\delta)=\delta+\gamma\left(\mathbf{E}^F\left[R(\delta')\right]-R(\delta)\right)+\lambda_\theta\left(P-R(\delta)\right)$$

satisfied by the reservation value function.

1. Show that, for the marginal investor,

$$\frac{\partial R}{\partial\lambda_\theta}(\delta^\star)\propto\mathbf{E}^F\left[\frac{\partial R}{\partial\lambda_\theta}(\delta)\right].$$

Argue that this means that the marginal investor does not care about the option value of continuing search. Explain why.
2. Show that

$$\mathbf{E}^F\left[\frac{\partial R}{\partial\lambda_\theta}(\delta)\right]=\mathbf{E}^F\left[(P-R(\delta))^+\right]-\mathbf{E}^F\left[(R(\delta)-P)^+\right].$$

Interpret this formula in terms of search options to sell and buy upon the next preference shock.
3. Use the logic of search options to provide an explanation of the effect of a reduction in frictions on the interdealer price.

Exercise 4.11: Consider the same model of long-term relationships as in section 4.6 but assume that only a fraction $\pi\in[0,1]$ of meetings between unmatched investors and dealers lead to a long-term relationship.

1. Show that a matched investor holds the asset if and only if his utility flow is such that (4.33) holds.

2. Show that equation (4.34) continues to hold and use it to determine the asset demands of matched and unmatched investors.
3. Determine the distribution of utility flows $\Phi_{nq}(\delta)$ in the populations of matched ($n = m$) and unmatched ($n = u$) investors with holding $q \in \{0, 1\}$.
4. Compute the equilibrium interdealer price and study its dependence on the probability π that a meeting initiates a lasting relation.
5. Compute the trading volume generated by one-off meetings and the trading volume generated by relationships.

4.8 Notes and References

There is a long history of using search models of decentralized trade to study equilibrium asset pricing and intermediation. A nonexhaustive list includes Rubinstein and Wolinsky [1987], Yavaş [1992], Gehrig [1993], Spulber [1996], Li [1998], LeRoy and Krainer [2002], Rust and Hall [2003], Shevchenko [2004], and Masters [2007], among many others. The specific model studied in this chapter was originally introduced by Duffie, Gârleanu, and Pedersen [2005]. While they assume that investors could have just two possible utility flows, $\delta \in \{\delta_L, \delta_H\}$, in this chapter we generalize their analysis to the case of an arbitrary distribution of utility flows.

The semicentralized market model takes one element of the market structure as exogenous—namely, that interdealer trades are frictionless while customer-to-dealer trades are subject to search frictions. A related market structure emerges endogenously in Farboodi, Jarosch, and Shimer [2022]. In their model, after making a costly choice of search intensity, identical investors contact each other at random in a market subject to search frictions. In equilibrium, they find that ex ante homogeneous investors actually choose different search intensities and, if search costs are linear, the set of equilibrium search intensities is unbounded. Hence, in this case, an infinitesimally small fraction of investors have infinite search intensity, so that the equilibrium behavior of these investors endogenously resembles that of the dealers in this chapter.

Also note that, with a frictionless interdealer market, the assumption that dealers cannot hold inventory is without loss of generality for the analysis of the steady-state equilibrium. Indeed, as long as dealers are not the final holders of the asset—in the sense that their utility flows are sufficiently small relative to those of investors—they find it optimal to hold no inventory. However, as we show later, it is important to allow for dealer inventories in the steady-state analysis of environments where the interdealer market is frictional (chapters 5 and 7) and in the analysis of out-of-steady-state dynamics following an aggregate liquidity shock (chapter 9).

The semicentralized market model uses a particular matching function, which determines the mapping between the masses of various types of market participants and the total (flow) number of meetings between them. In the formulation studied in this chapter, this function is simply $\lambda\mu_i$, where μ_i is the mass of investors, so that each investor meets a dealer at rate $\lambda\mu_i/\mu_i = \lambda$. In applications of search models to other markets, it is commonly assumed that the matching function has constant returns to scale. While this assumption is supported by empirical evidence in labour markets [Petrongolo and Pissarides, 2001], it seems less appropriate in the context of financial markets due to the presence of scale effects such as the positive relationship between issue size (or asset supply) and various measures of liquidity. For this reason, some of the literature has considered matching functions that exhibit increasing returns [such as Pagano, 1989; Vayanos and Wang, 2007; Weill, 2008; Vayanos and Weill, 2008; Shen, Wei, and Yan, 2020] and [Sambalaibat, 2022]. A related matching technology with scale effects arises in the so-called "stock-flow" models of Coles and Smith [1992], An and Zheng [2018], and An [2019], in which the inflow of new participants on one side of the market matches with unmatched participants on the other side of the market. In this environment, trading delays arise not from search frictions per se, but rather because each buyer is only willing to purchase a finite collection of assets, drawn at random according to some point process. As a result, the demand for any particular asset takes time to materialize and, in equilibrium, a stock of buyers and sellers is waiting in the market for suitable counterparties to arrive.

Another difference between search-theoretic models of labor and of financial markets is that the former treat matches as being long-term relationships while the latter almost always assume that matches are dissolved immediately after the parties decide whether or not to trade. In some OTC markets, this is clearly counterfactual, as certain investors appear to repeatedly trade with the same counterparty. This observation draws attention to the need for better models of relationships in OTC markets; the simple model of section 4.6 is inspired by Maciocco [2023], who develops a closely related framework with divisible asset holdings to study relationship vs. spot trading of municipal bonds.

This chapter focuses on the case of a *single* asset trading in an OTC market, which is highly tractable and constitutes an important step in understanding the impact of OTC market frictions on liquidity and asset prices. Korenok, Kospentaris, and Lightle [2024] have recently proposed an experimental evaluation of the model-implied relationship between trading speed and prices. Consistent with the model, they find that an increase in the trading speed causes a rise (fall) in the price when the supply is small (large). However, to further test the theory in a nonexperimental setting, one would need to establish closer contact with *cross-sectional* empirical evidence. For example, Amihud, Mendelson, and Pedersen [2005, chap. 3] document the cross-sectional relationship between risk-adjusted returns and measures of liquidity such as turnover, volume, or bid-ask spreads, while Amihud and Mendelson [1991] provide evidence that liquidity is related to violations of no-arbitrage relationships. To fully address these patterns, one would ideally want to incorporate multiple assets into the model, to explain why an investor's ability to choose between payoff-equivalent assets does not undo an arbitrage relationship or equalize risk-adjusted return differentials. Search-theoretic models that address these questions include Vayanos and Wang [2007], Weill [2008], Vayanos and Weill [2008], Sambalaibat [2022], Milbradt [2017], Üslü and Velioğlu [2019], and Li and Yu [2021].

In this chapter—as in the remainder of this book—we study OTC markets *in isolation* from the rest of the economy. However, an important strand of the literature analyzes OTC markets *within a broader macroeconomic context,* which is important for at least two reasons. First, it shows that OTC market frictions matter for broader economic questions. Second, it makes normative analyses more meaningful, since it can account for the welfare of all economic agents and not only that of OTC market participants. We highlight several branches of this literature. The new monetarist literature [see Nosal and Rocheteau, 2011, for an overview] considers a general equilibrium framework in which agents exchange assets for money in an OTC market, before exchanging money for goods and services in a separate market; see, for example, Geromichalos and Herrenbrueck [2016], Lagos and Zhang [2019a,b, 2020], Geromichalos, Herrenbrueck, and Salyer [2016], Mattesini and Nosal [2016], and Lebeau [2019]. A large literature focuses on the cost of capital of firms that issue debt in OTC markets; see, for example, He and Milbradt [2014], Hugonnier, Malamud, and Morellec [2015], Chen, Cui, He, and Milbradt [2018], d'Avernas [2017], Arseneau, Rappoport, and Vardoulakis [2017], Bethune, Sultanum, and Trachter [2019], Cui and Radde [2020], Roh [2019], Kozlowski [2018], and Chang [2022]. Bianchi and Bigio [2022], Bigio and Sannikov [2019], and Malamud and Schrimpf [2017] incorporate OTC markets into larger macroeconomic models to analyze the impact of monetary policy on aggregate outcomes. Finally, an emerging literature utilizes some of the models developed in this book to study international implications; see, for example, Geromichalos and Jung [2018], Malamud and Schrimpf [2018], Bianchi, Bigio, and Engel [2018], Passadore and Xu [2018], and Chaumont [2018].

5

Pure Decentralized Markets

The semicentralized OTC market model of chapter 4 is a good benchmark for dealer-intermediated markets where frictions in the interdealer market are small relative to frictions between investors and dealers. However, several important OTC markets are not dealer intermediated, such as the fed funds market. Moreover, even in markets where trade does occur through a dealer sector, it is often the case that the interdealer market itself is subject to significant frictions. To accomodate the analysis of such unintermediated markets, and as a first step toward modeling frictional interdealer markets, we develop in this chapter a model where market participants meet and trade bilaterally subject to search and bargaining frictions.

5.1 The Model

As in previous chapters, we consider a continuous-time, infinite-horizon model of an economy populated by a unit mass of risk-neutral investors who discount the future at rate $r > 0$ and derive utility from holding an asset with fixed supply $s \in (0, 1)$. Each investor can hold either zero or one unit of the asset and enjoys a utility flow $\delta_t dt$ from holding the asset at time $t \geq 0$. The utility flow of each investor is independent from that of any other investor and follows a Markov jump process with arrival rate γ and reset distribution $F(\delta)$ on some open interval $\mathcal{D} = (\underline{\delta}, \overline{\delta})$. As in chapter 4 we assume that preference shocks are iid across investors, and that the cross-sectional distribution of utility flows in the population is equal to $F(\delta)$ at all times.

Unlike in chapter 4, we assume that investors trade bilaterally as illustrated in figure 5.1. Specifically, we assume that investors participate in a fully decentralized market where each investor is matched with another at the jump times of a Poisson process with intensity λ. Conditional on contact, two investors with opposite asset holdings determine the terms of a possible trade by solving a Nash bargaining game in which the investor who owns the asset (and may want to sell it) has bargaining power $\theta_1 \in (0, 1)$

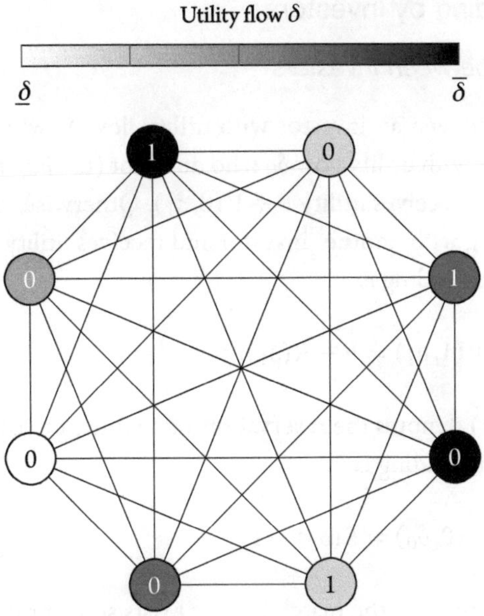

FIGURE 5.1. Decentralized OTC market

This figure illustrates the structure of a decentralized over-the-counter market in which heterogeneous investors holding zero or one unit of the asset meet each other randomly over time to bargain over the terms of a possible trade.

and the investor who does not own an asset (and may want to buy one) has bargaining power $\theta_0 = 1 - \theta_1$.

We denote by $V(q, \delta)$ the value function of an investor in state (q, δ) and by $\Phi_q(\delta)$ the measure of investors who hold $q \in \{0, 1\}$ units of the asset and have utility flow $\delta' \leq \delta$. These cumulative measures are to be determined endogenously in equilibrium subject to

$$\Phi_0(\delta) + \Phi_1(\delta) = F(\delta), \qquad \forall \delta \in \mathcal{D}, \tag{5.1}$$

and the market clearing condition

$$\Phi_1(\overline{\delta}) \equiv \lim_{\delta \uparrow \overline{\delta}} \Phi_1(\delta) = s, \tag{5.2}$$

which ensure, respectively, that the cross-sectional distribution of utility flows is consistent with the population distribution $F(\delta)$ and that the mass of owners equals the asset supply.

5.2 Optimal Trading by Investors

5.2.1 *Bargaining between Investors*

Consider a match between an investor with utility flow δ_1 who owns the asset (the *seller*) and an investor with utility flow δ_0 who does not (the *buyer*). If a trade occurs at price P, then the seller receives utility $P + V(0, \delta_1)$. Otherwise, she remains an owner until her next meeting with another investor and receives utility $V(1, \delta_1)$. Hence, the seller's net utility from trading is

$$(P + V(0, \delta_1)) - V(1, \delta_1) = P - R(\delta_1),$$

where, as before, $R(\delta)$ denotes the reservation value function. By the same token, the buyer's net utility from trading is

$$(V(1, \delta_0) - P) - V(0, \delta_0) = R(\delta_0) - P.$$

There are gains from trade in the match if there exists some price P at which both the seller and the buyer are willing to trade, i.e., such that $P - R(\delta_1) \geq 0$ and $R(\delta_0) - P \geq 0$. One can easily verify that this is so if and only if the reservation value of the buyer exceeds that of the seller, $R(\delta_0) \geq R(\delta_1)$, in which case the transaction price is taken to maximize the Nash product

$$P(\delta_0, \delta_1) = \underset{P \in [R(\delta_1), R(\delta_0)]}{\operatorname{argmax}} \; (P - R(\delta_1))^{\theta_1} \, (R(\delta_0) - P)^{\theta_0}.$$

Since the bargaining powers θ_q lie in $(0, 1)$, the objective function is concave in P on the feasible interval. Therefore, the first-order condition

$$0 = \frac{d}{dP} (P - R(\delta_1))^{\theta_1} \, (R(\delta_0) - P)^{\theta_0}$$

is necessary and sufficient for an interior maximum. Solving this equation shows that the bid price is given by a convex combination of reservation values:

$$P(\delta_0, \delta_1) = \theta_0 R(\delta_1) + \theta_1 R(\delta_0). \tag{5.3}$$

Intuitively, if $\theta_1 \approx 1$, then the seller has most of the bargaining power and the price is close to the reservation value of the buyer, which is the best price possible within the match from her point of view. On the contrary, if $\theta_1 \approx 0$, then the seller has almost no bargaining power and, as a result, the price approaches his reservation value.

5.2.2 Reservation Values: Basic Properties

Fix a pair of cumulative measures $(\Phi_0(\delta), \Phi_1(\delta))$ satisfying the consistency and market clearing conditions (5.1) and (5.2). Proceeding as in section 3.3.1 shows that the reservation value function of an investor who takes these cumulative measures as given satisfies the Bellman equation:

$$R(\delta) = \mathbf{E}\Bigg[\int_0^\tau \delta e^{-rt} dt + e^{-r\tau}\Bigg(\mathbf{1}_{\{\tau=\tau_\gamma\}}\int_{\underline{\delta}}^{\overline{\delta}} R(x)\,dF(x) \qquad (5.4)$$

$$+\mathbf{1}_{\{\tau=\tau_0\}}\int_{\underline{\delta}}^{\overline{\delta}} \max\{R(\delta), P(x,\delta)\}\frac{d\Phi_0(x)}{1-s}$$

$$+\mathbf{1}_{\{\tau=\tau_1\}}\int_{\underline{\delta}}^{\overline{\delta}} \min\{R(\delta), P(\delta,x)\}\frac{d\Phi_1(x)}{s}\Bigg)\Bigg],$$

where τ_γ is an exponential random variable with rate γ that represents the time until the arrival of a preference shock, τ_q is an exponential random variable with rate

$$\lambda\Phi_q(\overline{\delta}) = \begin{cases} \lambda s & \text{if } q=1, \\ \lambda(1-s) & \text{if } q=0, \end{cases}$$

that counts the time until the next meeting with a randomly selected investor holding q units of the asset, and $\tau = \min\{\tau_0, \tau_1, \tau_\gamma\}$.

Substituting the price defined in (5.3) into (5.4) reveals that the Bellman equation can equivalently be written as

$$R(\delta) = \mathbf{E}\Bigg[\int_0^\tau \delta e^{-rt} dt + e^{-r\tau}\Bigg(\mathbf{1}_{\{\tau\neq\tau_\gamma\}}R(\delta) \qquad (5.5)$$

$$+\mathbf{1}_{\{\tau=\tau_\gamma\}}\int_{\underline{\delta}}^{\overline{\delta}} R(x)dF(x)$$

$$+\mathbf{1}_{\{\tau=\tau_0\}}\int_{\underline{\delta}}^{\overline{\delta}} \theta_1\,(R(x)-R(\delta))^+\,\frac{d\Phi_0(x)}{1-s}$$

$$-\mathbf{1}_{\{\tau=\tau_1\}}\int_{\underline{\delta}}^{\overline{\delta}} \theta_0\,(R(x)-R(\delta))^-\,\frac{d\Phi_1(x)}{s}\Bigg)\Bigg].$$

This equation shows that, in contrast with the semicentralized market of chapter 4, reservation values in the pure decentralized market model depend directly on the joint cross-sectional distribution of asset holdings and utility flows, as summarized by the measures $\Phi_0(\delta)$, and $\Phi_1(\delta)$. To understand this difference, note that investors in the semicentralized market, trade with homogeneous counterparties (dealers) who all have access to the same outside options through the frictionless interdealer market. As a result, both the rate and the price at which an investor trades do not depend directly on $\Phi_0(\delta)$, and $\Phi_1(\delta)$ in the semicentralized market, though the equilibrium interdealer price, of course, depends on distributional consideration. This is no longer true in the decentralized market because, conditional on an investor's current utility flow, heterogeneity in the reservation values of potential counterparties affects both the likelihood and the terms of trades.

A direct implication of this observation is that the joint distribution of asset holdings and utility flows across the population of investors—which is an infinite-dimensional object—is a state variable for reservation values. In most cases, this would make the analysis considerably more complicated. However, the analysis here remains fully tractable because, as we establish in the following proposition, the optimal trading strategy is purely ordinal.

Proposition 5.1: Equation (5.5) admits a unique solution and this function is bounded, strictly increasing, and Lipschitz continuous on $\mathcal{D}$. In particular, the optimal strategy of an investor is to buy from any owner whose utility flow is smaller than her own, and to sell to any nonowner whose utility flow is larger than her own.

Proof. To start, note that the desired result *does not follow* from Proposition 3.6 and Corollary 3.8, because the trading terms in (5.5) depend on the reservation value function not only at δ but at all utility flow levels. Therefore, we do not even know a priori that the reservation value function $R(\delta)$ is bounded and we have to establish that property from first principles.

Integrating on both sides of (5.5) against the distribution of the random time τ and simplifying the result shows that $R : \mathcal{D} \to \mathbf{R}$ is a solution to (5.4) if and only if it is a fixed point of the operator defined by

$$T[g](\delta) \equiv \frac{1}{r}\left(\delta + U[g](\delta)\right) = \frac{1}{r}\left[\delta + \gamma \int_{\underline{\delta}}^{\overline{\delta}} \left(g(x) - g(\delta)\right) dF(x)\right.$$

$$\left. + \lambda\theta_1 \int_{\underline{\delta}}^{\overline{\delta}} \left(g(x) - g(\delta)\right)^+ d\Phi_0(x) - \lambda\theta_0 \int_{\underline{\delta}}^{\overline{\delta}} \left(g(x) - g(\delta)\right)^- d\Phi_1(x)\right].$$

To establish that any fixed point is strictly increasing, assume toward a contradiction that $R : \mathcal{D} \to \mathbf{R}$ is a fixed point of T such that $R(\delta) \leq R(\delta')$ for some $\delta > \delta'$. Since the maps $y \mapsto \pm\left(R(x)-y\right)^{\pm}$ are both weakly decreasing, we have that

$$R(\delta) \leq R(\delta') \Rightarrow U[R](\delta) \geq U[R](\delta'), \tag{5.6}$$

and therefore

$$R(\delta) = \frac{1}{r}\left(\delta + U[g](\delta)\right) > \frac{1}{r}\left(\delta' + U[R](\delta')\right) = R(\delta'),$$

where the equalities follow from the fixed point property. This provides the required contradiction and thus shows that any fixed point of T is strictly increasing. Combining this property with (5.6) we then deduce that any fixed point of T satisfies

$$0 \leq R(\delta) - R(\delta') = \frac{1}{r}\left(\delta - \delta' + U[R](\delta) - U[R](\delta')\right) \leq \frac{1}{r}\left(\delta - \delta'\right)$$

for all $\delta' \leq \delta$. Interchanging the roles of δ and δ' establishes that any such function is Lipschitz continuous with modulus no larger than $1/r$. Since $\mathcal{D}$ is bounded, this implies that any fixed point of T is bounded and it now only remains to show that such a fixed point is unique.

Assume that $R : \mathcal{D} \to \mathbf{R}$ is a fixed point of T. Since such a function is bounded and strictly increasing we have that

$$U[R](\delta) = V[R](\delta) - R(\delta)V[1](\delta), \qquad \forall \delta \in \mathcal{D},$$

with the operator

$$V[g](\delta) \equiv \int_{\underline{\delta}}^{\overline{\delta}} g(x)\Big(\gamma\, dF(x) + \lambda\theta_1 \mathbf{1}_{\{x \geq \delta\}} d\Phi_0(x) + \lambda\theta_0 \mathbf{1}_{\{x \leq \delta\}} d\Phi_1(x)\Big),$$

and it follows that R is a bounded fixed point of

$$S[g](\delta) \equiv \frac{1}{r + V[1](\delta)}\left(\delta + V[g](\delta)\right).$$

As is easily seen, S maps the space $\mathcal{B}$ of bounded functions into itself. On the other hand, a direct calculation shows that, if $(g, h) \in \mathcal{B}^2$, then

$$\left\|S[g] - S[h]\right\| = \left\|\frac{V[g] - V[h]}{r + V[1]}\right\| \leq \left\|\frac{V[1]}{r + V[1]}\right\| \left\|g - h\right\|.$$

Since $r > 0$ and $\gamma \leq V[1] \leq \gamma + \lambda$, it follows that S is a contraction on $\mathcal{B}$, and the existence and uniqueness of a fixed point now follows from the Banach fixed point theorem A.3. □

5.2.3 Reservation Values: Explicit Expressions

Building on the necessary conditions of Proposition 5.1, we now derive explicit expressions for the reservation value function of an investor who takes the cumulative measures $\Phi_0(\delta)$ and $\Phi_1(\delta)$ as given. These different expressions are convenient for analyzing the effects of changes in the environment on reservation values and the subsequent implications for equilibrium prices. In addition, comparing these expressions to those of chapter 4 delivers key insights about the effects of bilateral search frictions.

THE SEQUENTIAL REPRESENTATION

Since the reservation value function is strictly increasing, proceeding as in section 3.4.2 shows that the Hamilton-Jacobi-Bellman (HJB) equation can be written as

$$rR(\delta) = \delta + \gamma \int_{\underline{\delta}}^{\overline{\delta}} (R(x) - R(\delta))\, dF(x) + \lambda\theta_1 \int_{\delta}^{\overline{\delta}} (R(x) - R(\delta))\, d\Phi_0(x)$$
$$+ \lambda\theta_0 \int_{\underline{\delta}}^{\delta} (R(x) - R(\delta))\, d\Phi_1(x). \tag{5.7}$$

This expression highlights once again that, in the presence of search frictions, the reservation value of an investor is affected by her utility flow, the arrival of preference shocks, and two distinct option values: the option of reselling the asset at a later date, which increases her reservation value; and the foregone option value of buying at a later date, which depresses it.

To derive a sequential (or expected value) representation of reservation values, consider the family of conditional distributions defined by

$$\hat{F}(x|\delta) = \frac{\Pi(x, \delta)}{\Pi(\overline{\delta}, \delta)}, \qquad (x, \delta) \in \mathcal{D}^2, \tag{5.8}$$

with the function

$$\Pi(x, \delta) \equiv \gamma F(x) + \lambda\theta_1 \left(\Phi_0(x) - \Phi_0(\delta)\right)^+ + \lambda\theta_0\Phi_1\left(\min\{x, \delta\}\right). \tag{5.9}$$

Using these objects, we can now rewrite the HJB equation for the reservation value function as

$$rR(\delta) = \delta + \Pi(\overline{\delta}, \delta) \int_{\underline{\delta}}^{\overline{\delta}} (R(x) - R(\delta))\, d\hat{F}(x|\delta). \tag{5.10}$$

Combining this equation with Proposition A.37 of appendix A.6 delivers the following explicit representation of the unique solution.

Proposition 5.2: The reservation value function is given by

$$R(\delta) = \mathbf{E}_\delta \left[\int_0^\infty e^{-rt} \hat{\delta}_t dt \right], \tag{5.11}$$

where $(\hat{\delta}_t)_{t\geq 0}$ is a Markov jump process with jump rate $\hat{\lambda}(\delta) \equiv \Pi(\bar{\delta}, \delta)$ and reset distribution $\hat{F}(x|\delta)$.

Proof. The result follows by applying Proposition A.37 to (5.10). □

As in the semicentralized market model of chapter 4, we refer to $\hat{\delta}_t$ as the *market valuation* process. This process takes into account not only the preference shocks that affect an investor over time, but also the arrival of trading opportunities. Specifically, over a small time interval of length h, the market valuation in the decentralized market can change for three reasons. First, a preference shock arrives with probability γh, in which case a new utility flow is drawn from the distribution $F(x)$. Second, a sale is executed with a probability $\lambda\theta_1(1 - s - \Phi_0(\delta))h$ that combines the physical arrival rate of a buyer with utility flow higher than δ and the share θ_1 of the surplus that the seller retains. Third, a purchase occurs with a probability $\lambda\theta_0\Phi_1(\delta)h$ that combines the physical arrival rate $\lambda\Phi_1(\delta)h$ of a seller with utility flow lower than δ and the share θ_0 of the surplus that the buyer retains.

Comparing the market valuation process to its semicentralized counterpart in Proposition 4.5 shows that bilateral trading induces serial correlation into the market valuation process. This occurs because, conditional on an investor's utility flow, the heterogeneity in the utility flows of her potential counterparties in the decentralized market directly influences the likelihood and the terms of possible trades.

THE DIFFERENTIAL REPRESENTATION

Since the reservation value function is strictly increasing and Lipschitz continuous by Proposition 5.1, we know that

$$R(x) - R(\delta) = \int_\delta^x \sigma(x) dx \tag{5.12}$$

for some bounded, but not necessarily continuous, function $\sigma(x) > 0$ that we interpret as a measure of the local trading surplus in a neighborhood of utility flow x. Differentiating both sides of (5.7) and solving the resulting equation reveals that the local surplus is explicitly given by

$$\sigma(\delta) = \frac{1}{r + \gamma + \lambda\theta_1(1 - s - \Phi_0(\delta)) + \lambda\theta_0\Phi_1(\delta)}. \tag{5.13}$$

Since the denominator in this expression is the sum of the discount rate r and the jump rate of the market valuation process $\Pi(\overline{\delta},\delta)$, the local surplus can be viewed as the present value of a unit flow of utility to be received until the random time $\hat{\tau}$ of the first jump in the market valuation process:

$$\sigma(\delta) = \mathbf{E}_\delta\left[\int_0^{\hat{\tau}} e^{-rt}dt\right].$$

Such a representation of the local surplus also holds in the semi-centralized market of chapter 4. However, in that case, Proposition 4.5 shows that the jump rate of the market valuation process is $\gamma + \lambda_\theta$, so that the local surplus $1/(r+\gamma+\lambda_\theta)$ is constant. Here again, the difference between the two settings can be traced to the fact that investors in the semicentralized market trade with a homogeneous counterparty—and thus only face timing uncertainty—whereas investors in the pure decentralized OTC market face uncertainty regarding both the timing of trading opportunities and the characteristics of future trading partners.

Substituting (5.12) into (5.7) and changing the order of integration delivers an explicit expression for the reservation value function in terms of exogenous variables and the joint distribution of asset holdings and utility flows that investors take as given. We summarize this expression in the following proposition.

Proposition 5.3: The reservation value function is

$$R(\delta) = \frac{\delta}{r} - \int_{\underline{\delta}}^{\delta} \sigma(x)\Pi(x,\delta)\frac{dx}{r} + \int_{\delta}^{\overline{\delta}} \sigma(x)\left(\Pi\left(\overline{\delta},\delta\right) - \Pi(x,\delta)\right)\frac{dx}{r},$$

with $\Pi(x,\delta)$ and $\sigma(\delta)$ as in (5.9) and (5.13), respectively.

5.3 Equilibrium

In this section, we characterize the steady-state distribution of asset holdings and utility flows in the population of investors, and derive the unique steady-state equilibrium of the pure decentralized market model.

5.3.1 Equilibrium Distributions

In a steady-state equilibrium, the cumulative measures $\Phi_1(\delta)$ and $\Phi_0(\delta)$ must be consistent with the optimal trading behavior of investors and with the usual stationarity conditions, which require that the inflow to and outflow from any group of investors coincide at all times. Mathematically, the stationarity conditions require that

$$\int_B (\gamma s dF(\delta) + \lambda_0(\delta)\, d\Phi_0(\delta)) = \int_B (\gamma\, d\Phi_1(\delta) + \lambda_1(\delta)\, d\Phi_1(\delta))$$

for any Borel set $B \in \mathcal{D}$, where $\lambda_q(\delta)$ is the trading intensity of an investor with utility flow δ who owns q units of the assets. The gross inflow on the left-hand side of this equation consists of two terms. The first is the inflow of owners who receive a preference shock that resets their utility flow to some new value $x \in B$. The second term represents the inflow from trading. Similarly, the gross outflow on the right-hand side is the sum of the flow of investors in B who exit because of a preference shock and the outflow from trading.

Since there are strict gains from trade if and only if a nonowner with type δ_0 meets an owner with type $\delta_1 < \delta_0$, the trading intensities can be written as

$$\lambda_0(\delta) = \lambda\Phi_1(\delta-),$$

$$\lambda_1(\delta) = \lambda\,(1 - s - \Phi_0(\delta)),$$

where we assume that investors only trade when there are strict gains from doing so. This assumption clearly has no effect on reservation values. It does not impact the allocation either, since a trade between investors with $\delta_0 = \delta_1$ changes the identity of the owner but not its utility flow.

Proceeding as in section 4.4.2 we determine the equilibrium asset allocation by substituting the trading intensities above into the stationarity condition for a well-chosen group of investors. Specifically, considering the group of investors with utility flow in the set $B = (\underline{\delta}, \delta]$ yields

$$\gamma s F(\delta) + \lambda \int_{\underline{\delta}}^{\delta} \Phi_1(x-) d\Phi_0(x) \tag{5.14}$$

$$= \gamma\Phi_1(\delta) + \lambda \int_{\underline{\delta}}^{\delta} (1 - s - \Phi_0(x))\, d\Phi_1(x).$$

Changing the order of integration in the last term on the right-hand side of (5.14) yields

$$\lambda \int_{\underline{\delta}}^{\delta} \big(1 - s - \Phi_0(x)\big) d\Phi_1(x) = \lambda \int_{\underline{\delta}}^{\delta} \int_{\underline{\delta}}^{\overline{\delta}} \mathbf{1}_{\{x<y\}} d\Phi_0(y) d\Phi_1(x)$$

$$= \lambda \int_{\underline{\delta}}^{\overline{\delta}} \int_{\underline{\delta}}^{\delta} \mathbf{1}_{\{x<y\}} d\Phi_1(x) d\Phi_0(y)$$

$$= \lambda \int_{\underline{\delta}}^{\delta} \Phi_1(y-) d\Phi_0(y) + \lambda\Phi_1(\delta)\,(1 - s - \Phi_0(\delta)),$$

where we used that $\Phi_0(\overline{\delta}) = 1 - s$ and, for the last equality, decomposed the integral over the intervals $(\underline{\delta}, \delta]$ and $(\delta, \overline{\delta}]$.

Note that the first term on the last line of the equation above cancels with the last term on the first line of (5.14). The intuition is that trades between an owner with utility flow $x < \delta$ and a nonowner with utility flow $x < y \leq \delta$ create no net inflow into the set of owners with utility flow less than δ. Indeed, the x investor sells and leaves the set, while the y investor buys and enters. On net, there is only outflow due to owners with utility flow $x \leq \delta$ who sell to nonowners with utility flow $y > \delta$. The resulting inflow-outflow equation thus simplifies to

$$\gamma s F(\delta) = \gamma \Phi_1(\delta) + \lambda \Phi_1(\delta)\,(1 - s - \Phi_0(\delta))\,.$$

Substituting the consistency condition (5.1) into this expression and rearranging shows that, in a steady-state equilibrium, we must have

$$-\lambda \Phi_1(\delta)\,(1 - s - F(\delta) + \Phi_1(\delta)) + \gamma\,(sF(\delta) - \Phi_1(\delta)) = 0. \tag{5.15}$$

This equation for the cumulative measure is surprisingly easy to solve, for three reasons. First, it is autonomous in the sense that the equation for $\Phi_1(\delta)$ is independent from $\Phi_1(x)$ for all $x \neq \delta$. Second, it is quadratic. Third, it does not impose any conditions on the underlying distribution of utility flows. By contrast, differentiating (5.15) reveals that the equations for *measures* (instead of the *cumulative measures*) exhibit dependences across utility flows, which makes the solution more difficult to derive and analyze in all but the simplest cases (see Exercise 5.13).

The next proposition shows that (5.15) uniquely pins down the equilibrium distribution and provides comparative statics.

Proposition 5.4: In a steady-state equilibrium

$$\Phi_1(\delta) = F(\delta) - \Phi_0(\delta) = \ell(F(\delta)) \tag{5.16}$$

with the function

$$\ell(x) \equiv -\tfrac{1}{2}\,(1 - s + \phi - x) + \sqrt{\phi s x + \tfrac{1}{4}\,(1 - s + \phi - x)^2} \tag{5.17}$$

and the constant $\phi \equiv \gamma/\lambda$. In particular, the measure $\Phi_1(\delta)$ is increasing in the asset supply s as well as increasing and concave in ϕ.

Proof. The definition of ϕ and (5.15) imply that, for any utility flow $\delta \in \mathcal{D}$, the measure $x = \Phi_1(\delta)$ is a solution to

$$x^2 + x(1 - s + \phi - F(\delta)) - \phi s F(\delta) = 0.$$

The first part then follows by deriving the unique positive solution to this quadratic equation and the second by differentiating this solution. □

As in the semicentralized market setting, the steady-state distributions of utility flows among owners and nonowners only depend on the arrival rates of meetings and type switches through the ratio $\phi = \gamma/\lambda$, which measures the severity of search frictions in the market. Indeed, Proposition 5.4 shows that as ϕ increases—either because bilateral meetings become less frequent or because investors change utility flows more often—the equilibrium allocation becomes less efficient, in that owners tend to have lower utility flows. Furthermore, writing (5.15) as

$$\Phi_1(\delta) = \frac{\phi s F(\delta)}{1 - s - \Phi_0(\delta) + \phi}$$

reveals that the distribution converges to $sF(\delta)$ as $\phi \to \infty$, so that ownership and utility flows become independent. In this limit, it must be that either $\gamma \to \infty$ or $\lambda \to 0$, so that either utility flows become infinitely volatile or trading becomes impossible. In either case, the market is unable to reallocate assets across investors and, as a result, misallocation builds up unchecked until the point where the asset is uniformly distributed across investors.

At the other extreme, (5.16) implies that $\Phi_1(\delta)$ converges to its frictionless counterpart in (4.3) as $\phi \to 0$, i.e.,

$$\lim_{\phi \to 0} \Phi_1(\delta) = \Psi_1(\delta) = (F(\delta) - (1 - s))^+ . \tag{5.18}$$

This asymptotic efficiency result is intuitive: either $\lambda \to \infty$, so that search frictions vanish; or $\gamma \to 0$, so that the utility flows of all investors become constant. In the latter case, the OTC market will always achieve the efficient allocation given enough time as long as the meeting rate $\lambda > 0$.

To illustrate the effect of search frictions on the equilibrium distributions, figure 5.2 plots the cumulative measures $\Phi_q(\delta)$ as functions of $\delta \in \mathcal{D} = (0, 1)$ for different values of ϕ in the setting of Example 4.4, where the asset supply $s = 0.4$ and the distribution of utility flows is uniform. The figure confirms that the decentralized market becomes more efficient as ϕ decreases, in the sense that the distribution of utility flows among owners gradually shifts down and to the right, and reaches the frictionless allocation in the limit where investors either trade instantly or have permanent utility flows. From a

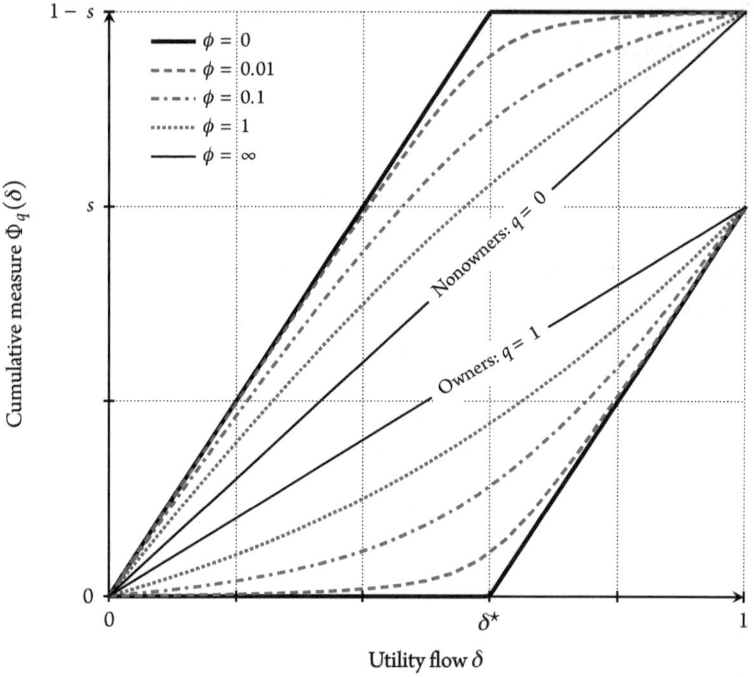

FIGURE 5.2. The equilibrium allocation in the decentralized market

This figure illustrates the equilibrium distribution of utility flows among owners and nonowners for different values of $\phi = \gamma/\lambda$ in the pure decentralized market model with asset supply $s = 0.4$ and a uniform distribution of utility flows on $\mathcal{D} = (0, 1)$.

quantitative point of view, the figure shows that the deviations from the efficient allocation can be sizable. For example, even if $\phi = 1$, so that investors meet and change type at the same frequency (dotted lines), the mere asynchronicity of these events implies that almost half of the asset supply is held by investors who would not be owners absent frictions.

5.3.2 Convergence to the Efficient Allocation

To further analyze the effect of search frictions on the equilibrium allocation, we can study the exact rate at which the equilibrium allocation converges to the efficient allocation. Consider first utility flows $\delta < \delta^\star$, where

$$\delta^\star = \inf\{\delta \in \mathcal{D} : F(\delta) \geq 1 - s\}$$

is the *marginal type* defined in section 4.2, i.e., the threshold above which all investors are owners in the frictionless equilibrium. Writing (5.15) as

$$\frac{\Phi_1(\delta)}{\phi} = \frac{sF(\delta)}{1-s-\Phi_0(\delta)+\phi}$$

and taking the limit as $\phi \to 0$ on both sides reveals that

$$\Phi_1(\delta) = \Psi_1(\delta) + \frac{sF(\delta)\phi}{1-s-F(\delta)} + o(\phi), \tag{5.19}$$

where the equality follows from the fact that the cumulative measure of nonowners $\Phi_0(\delta) \to \Psi_0(\delta) = F(\delta)$ for all $\delta < \delta^\star$ as $\phi \to 0$.

Remark 5.5 (Small o and Big O): In the equation above, the asymptotic notation

$$f(x) \in o(g(x)) \quad \text{as } x \to \infty$$

means that g grows much faster than f in the sense that $f(x)/g(x)$ goes to zero as x goes to infinity. Formally,

$$\forall c > 0 : \exists x_0 \text{ such that } |f(x)| \leq c|g(x)| \text{ for all } x \geq x_0. \tag{5.20}$$

By contrast, the asymptotic notation

$$f(x) \in O(g(x)) \quad \text{as } x \to \infty$$

only requires that $f(x)/g(x)$ remains bounded as x approaches infinity and, thus, relaxes the definition (5.20) by replacing the condition that $\forall c : \exists x_0$ by the less stringent requirement that $\exists(c, x_0)$.

Consider next the case of utility flows *strictly* above the marginal type. Writing the functional equation (5.15) as

$$\frac{1}{\phi}(1-s-F(\delta)+\Phi_1(\delta)) = \frac{sF(\delta)-\Phi_1(\delta)}{\Phi_1(\delta)},$$

and taking the limit as $\phi \to 0$ yields

$$\Phi_1(\delta) = \Psi_1(\delta) - \frac{(1-s)(1-F(\delta))\phi}{1-s-F(\delta)} + o(\phi), \tag{5.21}$$

where the equality follows from the fact that the cumulative measure of owners $\Phi_1(\delta) \to \Psi_1(\delta) = F(\delta) - (1-s)$ for all $\delta > \delta^\star$ as $\phi \to 0$.

Finally, consider convergence *at* the marginal type. If the distribution is discontinuous at $\delta^\star$ then $F(\delta^\star) > 1 - s$, and it follows that (5.21) continues to hold. If instead the distribution is continuous at $\delta^\star$, then

$$\frac{(\Phi_1(\delta^\star))^2}{\phi} = \frac{1}{\phi}\Phi_1(\delta^\star)\left(1 - s - \Phi_0(\delta^\star)\right) = s(1-s) - \Phi_1(\delta^\star),$$

where the second equality follows from (5.15) evaluated at $\delta^\star$. Taking the limit on both sides shows that

$$\Phi_1(\delta^\star) = \sqrt{s(1-s)\phi} + o\left(\sqrt{\phi}\right). \tag{5.22}$$

This expansion reveals that when the underlying distribution is continuous at the marginal type—so that there are heterogeneous investors whose utility flows lie in a neighbourhood of $\delta^\star$—then convergence to the efficient allocation is much slower at the marginal type than away from it. In particular, comparing the above limits, we see that the allocation converges at rate ϕ for values of δ away from the marginal type, but only converges at rate $\sqrt{\phi}$ around the marginal type. We will see in the next section that this slower convergence arises because of an equilibrium feedback loop between the investors' trading intensities and the distribution of utility flows among owners and nonowners.

5.3.3 *Summary of the Equilibrium*

A full characterization of the unique steady-state equilibrium readily follows from the above results. In particular, this equilibrium is composed of the reservation value function $R(\delta)$ characterized in Proposition 5.3 and of the joint distributions of utility flows and asset holdings $\Phi_q(\delta)$ characterized in Proposition 5.4. Note that uniqueness follows because we established the monotonicity of reservation values from first principles, taking arbitrary distributions as given, rather than guessing and verifying that such an equilibrium exists, as is often done in the literature.

5.4 Equilibrium Implications

In the remainder of this chapter, we exploit the explicit characterization of the steady-state equilibrium to explore the model's implications. As a first step, we study how the trading intensity of an investor depends on his utility flow and asset holdings. In particular, investors with low utility flows are mostly nonowners in the steady state, who rarely buy, but those few owners with low values of δ tend to sell quickly. Symmetrically, investors with high utility flows are mostly owners who rarely find a counterparty to trade, whereas nonowners with high values of δ will typically find a trading partner and purchase the asset quickly. Hence, in equilibrium, we observe that investors with more extreme utility flows trade quickly, but less frequently, and most often in the same direction.

In contrast, investors with utility flows close to the marginal type of the frictionless benchmark find willing counterparties regardless of their asset holdings: asset owners find nonowners with larger utility flows who want to buy, and nonowners find owners with lower utility flows who are willing to sell. Hence, investors with utility flows around the marginal type trade more frequently and in both directions.

What makes these trading patterns interesting is that they resemble the behavior of different categories of market participant in practice. Namely, investors with more extreme utility flow resemble customers who buy and hold, or sell and remain assetless for long periods of time. Likewise, investors with utility flows close to the marginal types resemble intermediaries or dealers, who buy and resell quickly, with other dealers and with customers.

These trading patterns have important aggregate implications. In particular, we show that investors with utility flows near the marginal type of the frictionless benchmark are more likely to be involved in any given trade and, therefore, account for a disproportionate amount of trading volume. As a result, even though the search process that generates meetings is random, the aggregate patterns of trade that emerge in equilibrium are not. Specifically, we establish that a *core-periphery* trading network emerges endogenously despite the fact that investors are ex ante homogeneous.

5.4.1 Trading Intensities

Consider a nonowner with utility flow process δ_t. In equilibrium, the arrival rate of a *strictly* profitable trading opportunity for this investor—i.e., his *buying intensity*—is the random process defined by the product of the arrival rate of a meeting and the probability that the counterparty is an owner with a strictly lower utility flow:

$$\lambda_0(\delta_t) \equiv \lambda \Phi_1(\delta_t -). \tag{5.23a}$$

Similarly, the arrival rate of strictly profitable trading opportunities, or *selling intensity,* for an owner with utility flow process δ_t is given by the product of the arrival rate of a meeting and the probability that the randomly selected counterparty is a nonowner with a higher utility flow:

$$\lambda_1(\delta_t) \equiv \lambda \left(\Phi_0(\bar{\delta}) - \Phi_0(\delta_t)\right) = \lambda\,(1 - s - \Phi_0(\delta_t))\,. \tag{5.23b}$$

Since $\Phi_1(\delta)$ is nondecreasing, nonowners with higher utility flows have a higher buying intensity, and thus tend to remain asset-less for shorter periods of time. By the same logic, since $1-s-\Phi_0(\delta)$ is nonincreasing, owners with higher utility flows trade less often, and thus tend to hold the asset over longer periods. The following lemma provides additional, intuitive comparative statics results for the equilibrium trading intensities.

Lemma 5.6: The trading intensity is increasing in s for buyers, decreasing in s for sellers, and increasing in λ for both buyers and sellers.

Proof. A direct calculation using (5.1) and (5.23) shows that

$$\lambda\frac{\partial^2\lambda_q(\delta)}{\partial\lambda^2}=\phi^2\left(q\frac{\partial^2\Phi_1(\delta)}{\partial\phi^2}+(1-q)\frac{\partial^2\Phi_1(\delta-)}{\partial\phi^2}\right),$$

and we know from Proposition 5.4 that $\Phi_1(\delta)$ is concave in ϕ. Therefore, the trading intensities are concave in λ with

$$\begin{aligned}\frac{\partial\lambda_q(\delta)}{\partial\lambda}&\geq\lim_{\lambda\to\infty}\frac{\partial\lambda_q(\delta)}{\partial\lambda}=q\,(1-s-F(\delta))\\&+\lim_{\phi\to 0}\left\{q\left(\Phi_1(\delta)-\phi\frac{\partial\Phi_1(\delta)}{\partial\phi}\right)+(1-q)\left(\Phi_1(\delta-)-\phi\frac{\partial\Phi_1(\delta-)}{\partial\phi}\right)\right\}\\&\geq q\,(1-s-F(\delta))+q\Psi_1(\delta)+(1-q)\Psi_1(\delta-)\\&=q\,(1-s-\Psi_0(\delta))+(1-q)\Psi_1(\delta-)\geq 0,\end{aligned}$$

where the first equality follows from the definition of ϕ, the second inequality follows from (5.18) and the fact that $\Phi_1(\delta)$ is concave as a function of ϕ, and the last equality follows from the market clearing condition.

The positive relation between the supply and the buying intensity follows from Proposition 5.4. Turning to the selling intensity, note that

$$\frac{\partial^2\lambda_1(\delta)}{\partial s^2}=\lambda\frac{\partial^2\ell(F(\delta))}{\partial s^2}=\frac{2\gamma F(\delta)(1-F(\delta))}{\left((1-s+\phi-F(\delta))^2+4s\phi F(\delta)\right)^{3/2}}\geq 0.$$

Hence, the selling intensity is convex in s and combining this property with (5.16) reveals that

$$\frac{\partial\lambda_1(\delta)}{\partial s}\leq\left.\frac{\partial\lambda_1(\delta)}{\partial s}\right|_{s=1}=\frac{\gamma(F(\delta)-1)}{\phi+F(\delta)}\leq 0,$$

which completes the proof. □

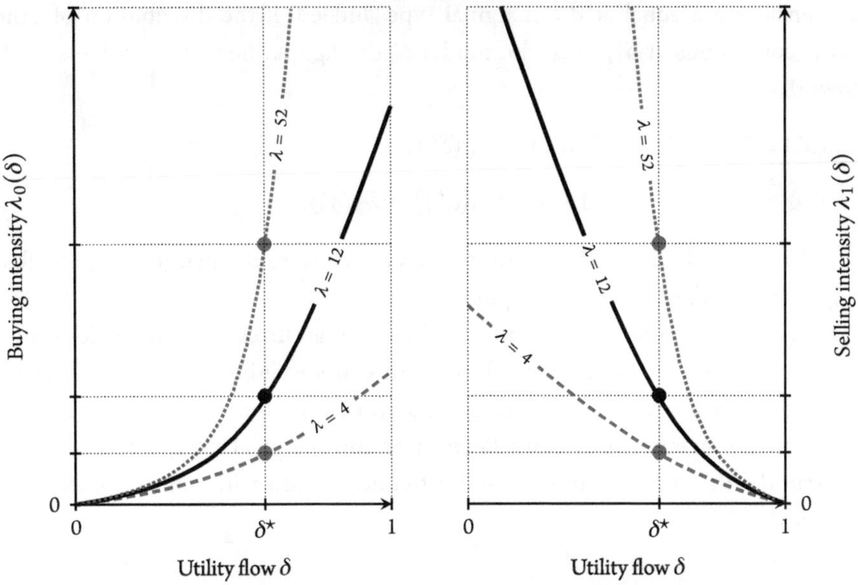

FIGURE 5.3. Equilibrium trading intensities

This figure plots the buying (left panel) and selling (right panel) intensities as functions of utility flow for different values of the meeting intensity λ in the pure decentralized market model with asset supply $s = 0.4$, arrival rate of preference shocks $\gamma = 1$, and a uniform distribution of utility flows on the set $\mathcal{D} = (0, 1)$. On each curve, the • indicates the trading intensity at the marginal type.

To illustrate the results above, figure 5.3 plots the trading intensities for different meeting rates ranging from $\lambda = 4$ (quarterly meetings) to $\lambda = 52$ (weekly meetings) in the environment of figure 5.2. The figure confirms the monotonicity of the trading intensities and highlights the role of the marginal type. In particular, it shows that, as λ decreases, the trading intensities fall more—and more sharply—for owners above the marginal type and for nonowners below it. To understand this result, recall from section 5.3.2 that the equilibrium asset allocation approaches the efficient allocation as search frictions vanish. Since

$$\Psi_1(\delta^\star - \varepsilon) = 1 - s - \Psi_0(\delta^\star + \varepsilon) = 0, \qquad \varepsilon > 0,$$

this convergence implies that owners with utility flow $\delta \gg \delta^\star$ and nonowners with utility flow $\delta \ll \delta^\star$ have essentially no willing counterparties to trade with, and it follows that their trading intensities are very low.

By contrast, the figure shows that owners with $\delta \ll \delta^\star$ and nonowners with $\delta \gg \delta^\star$ trade fast because they have many willing counterparties. It also reveals that the intensities are equal at the marginal type. Indeed, if the distribution of utility flows is continuous at $\delta^\star$, as in the model of the figure, then $F(\delta^\star) = 1 - s$, and it follows that

$$\lambda_0(\delta^\star) = \lambda\Phi_1(\delta^\star) = \lambda\left(F(\delta^\star) - \Phi_0(\delta^\star)\right)$$
$$= \lambda\left(1 - s - \Phi_0(\delta^\star)\right) = \lambda_1(\delta^\star).$$

Hence, buyers and sellers whose utility flows are close to the marginal type will, on average, trade at similar speeds in equilibrium.

Taken together, these trading patterns show that an investor's type endogenously determines his role in the market: those with extreme utility flows emerge as natural *customers* who trade infrequently and mostly in the same direction; while those with more moderate utility flows near the marginal type emerge as natural *intermediaries* who buy and sell more frequently and with approximately equal intensities.

5.4.2 Misallocation

The trading patterns discussed above have important implications for *misallocation*, defined as the extent to which the equilibrium asset allocation differs from its frictionless counterpart. To elicit these implications, consider the cumulative misallocation measure defined by

$$M(\delta) \equiv \int_{\underline{\delta}}^{\delta} \mathbf{1}_{\{x<\delta^\star\}} d\Phi_1(x) + \int_{\underline{\delta}}^{\delta} \mathbf{1}_{\{x>\delta^\star\}} d\Phi_0(x)$$
$$= \lim_{x\uparrow\delta^\star} \Phi_1\left(\min\{x, \delta\}\right) + \max\left\{0, \Phi_0(\delta) - \Phi_0(\delta^\star)\right\}.$$

This cumulative measure is the sum of two types of misallocation: the mass of investors with utility flow in $(\underline{\delta}, \delta] \cap (\underline{\delta}, \delta^\star)$ who would strictly prefer to not hold an asset in a frictionless environment, but do so in the presence of search frictions; and the mass of investors with utility flow in $(\delta^\star, \delta]$ who would own the asset in a frictionless market environment, but do not in the presence of search frictions.

Since $\Phi_1(\delta)$ is increasing in ϕ for all $\delta \in \mathcal{D}$ (Proposition 5.4), it follows that the total mass of misallocated assets

$$\mathbf{m} \equiv M(\overline{\delta}) = 1 - s - F(\delta^\star) + \Phi_1(\delta^\star) + \Phi_1(\delta^\star -)$$

is naturally increasing in the severity of the search friction. See the left panel of figure 5.4 for an illustration in the same environment as in figure 5.3.

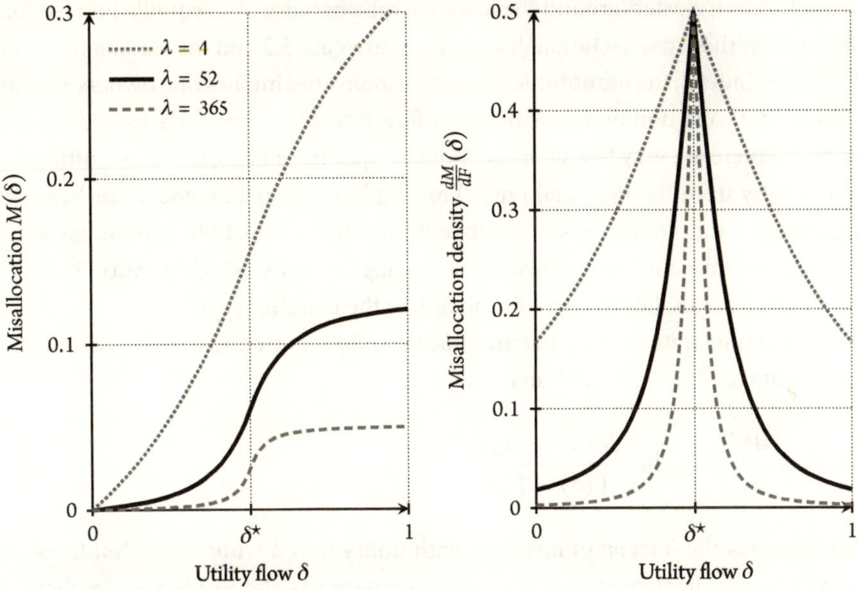

FIGURE 5.4. Equilibrium misallocation

This figure plots the misallocation (left panel) and the misallocation density (right panel) as functions of utility flow for different values of the meeting rate λ in the pure decentralized market model with asset supply $s = 0.5$, arrival rate of preference shocks $\gamma = 1$, and a uniform distribution of utility flows on the interval $\mathcal{D} = (0, 1)$.

The following result formally establishes that misallocation concentrates around the marginal type as search frictions vanish.

Proposition 5.7: In equilibrium

$$\lim_{\phi \to 0} \frac{M(\delta^\star + a) - M(\delta^\star - b)}{\mathbf{m}} = 1 \tag{5.24}$$

for any constants $a, b > 0$ such that $(\delta^\star - b, \delta^\star + a) \subset \mathcal{D}$.

Proof. Equations (5.19), (5.21), and (5.22) jointly imply that

$$M(\delta^\star + a) - M(\delta^\star - b) = C_0\phi + \mathbf{1}_{\{\Delta F(\delta^\star)=0\}} 2\sqrt{s(1-s)\phi} + o\left(\sqrt{\phi}\right),$$

$$\mathbf{m} = C_1\phi + \mathbf{1}_{\{\Delta F(\delta^\star)=0\}} 2\sqrt{s(1-s)\phi} + o\left(\sqrt{\phi}\right),$$

for some constants C_i that depend on $(a, b, s, \delta^\star, F)$ but not on ϕ. Combining these approximations yields (5.24). □

Misallocation clusters around the marginal type because of an equilibrium feedback loop between the cross-sectional distributions in figure 5.2 and the trading intensities in figure 5.3. Indeed, the monotonicity of these intensities implies that owners with utility flow $\delta \ll \delta^\star$ and nonowners with utility flow $\delta \gg \delta^\star$ are both able to trade quickly. As a result, there are very few such investors in equilibrium and, therefore, little misallocation away from the marginal type. This implies that asset owners just below the marginal type and nonowners just above it have few compatible counterparties. As a result, these investors experience a low trading intensity, which, in turn, induces a higher degree of misallocation in the vicinity of the marginal type.

To further illustrate the fact that misallocation clusters around the marginal type, we can compute the Radon-Nikodym density

$$m(\delta) \equiv \frac{dM}{dF}(\delta) = \lim_{x \uparrow \delta} \frac{M(\delta) - M(x)}{F(\delta) - F(x)}, \tag{5.25}$$

which captures the *fraction* of investors with utility flow δ whose asset holdings with search frictions differ from their frictionless counterparts. Proposition 5.4 implies that, when the underlying distribution of utility flows is continuous, this density is simply given by

$$m(\delta) = \mathbf{1}_{\{\delta < \delta^\star\}} \ell'(F(\delta)) + \mathbf{1}_{\{\delta \geq \delta^\star\}} \left(1 - \ell'(F(\delta))\right),$$

with the function $\ell(x)$ defined in (5.17). Since this function is convex, it is clear that the misallocation density is single peaked with a maximum either at the marginal type or just below it, which confirms that investors near the marginal type are those for whom misallocation is the most prevalent. In fact, the definition of $\ell(x)$ implies that

$$\Delta m(\delta^\star) = 1 - 2\ell'(1-s) = \frac{(1-2s)\sqrt{\phi}}{\sqrt{\phi + 4s(1-s)}},$$

so that the misallocation density is continuous at the marginal type if and only if $s = 0.5$ (as in figure 5.4) or $\phi = 0$, and reaches its maximum at the marginal type if and only if the asset supply $s \leq 0.5$.

To conclude this section, note that the above properties of misallocation arise in a decentralized market environment because the equilibrium trading intensities differ across utility flows. Indeed, when all investors trade with equal speed, as in the semi-centralized market of chapter 4, the misallocation measure is proportional to the underlying distribution of utility flows and, as a result, its density is constant across utility flows.

5.4.3 Trading Volume

The concentration of misallocation translates into a concentration of trading volume among the group of investors with utility flows near the marginal type. To see this, consider the function

$$V(B) \equiv \lambda \int_{B\times B} \mathbf{1}_{\{\delta_1<\delta_0\}} d\Phi_0(\delta_0) d\Phi_1(\delta_1), \tag{5.26}$$

which represents the flow rate of strictly profitable trades between investors with utility flows in the Borel set $B \subseteq \mathcal{D}$. When the distribution of utility flows is continuous, we can use integration by parts to write the aggregate trading volume as

$$\mathbf{v} \equiv V(\mathcal{D}) = \lambda \Phi_1(\delta^\star)(1-s-\Phi_0(\delta^\star)) + \lambda \int_{\underline{\delta}}^{\delta^\star} \left(\Phi_0(\delta^\star) - \Phi_0(\delta)\right) dM(\delta)$$
$$+ \lambda \int_{\delta^\star}^{\overline{\delta}} \left(\Phi_1(\delta) - \Phi_1(\delta^\star)\right) dM(\delta),$$

with the cumulative misallocation measure $M(\delta)$ defined in (5.25). The first term on the right-hand side captures trades between owners in $[0, \delta^\star]$ and nonowners in $[\delta^\star, 1]$. Absent frictions these would be the only trades executed. With frictions, however, there are additional inframarginal trades, captured by the second and third terms. In particular, the second term accounts for trades between owners with utility flows $\delta < \delta^\star$ and nonowners in $[\delta, \delta^\star]$, while the third term accounts for trades between nonowners with utility flows $\delta > \delta^\star$ and owners in $[\delta^\star, \delta]$. This formula highlights the role of misallocation in generating excess volume and suggests that near-marginal investors, who are subject to greater misallocation, are likely to have a larger contribution to volume. This is confirmed in the next proposition.

Proposition 5.8: If the distribution of utility flows is continuous then

$$\mathbf{v} = \gamma s(1-s)\left[(1+\phi)\log\left(1+\frac{1}{\phi}\right) - 1\right] \tag{5.27}$$

is strictly increasing in λ with

$$\lim_{\lambda\to\infty} \mathbf{v} = \infty \quad \text{and} \quad \lim_{\lambda\to\infty} \frac{V(B)}{\mathbf{v}} = 1$$

for any interval $B = (a, b] \subseteq \mathcal{D}$ that strictly contains $\delta^\star$.

Proof. By Proposition 5.4 we know that $\Phi_1(\delta) = F(\delta) - \Phi_0(\delta) = \ell(F(\delta))$, where the function $\ell(x)$ is defined by (5.17) and satisfies

$$\ell(0) = \ell(1) - s = 0$$

as well as

$$\lambda\,(1 - s - x + \ell(x)) = \frac{\gamma(1-s)(s-\ell(x))}{\phi s + \ell(x)}.$$

Since the distribution $F(\delta)$ is continuous, we can combine these identities with (5.26) and the change of variable $y = \ell(F(\delta))$ to obtain

$$\mathbf{v} = \int_{\underline{\delta}}^{\overline{\delta}} \lambda\,(1 - s - F(\delta) + \ell\,(F(\delta)))\, d\ell\,(F(\delta)) = \int_0^1 \frac{\gamma(1-s)(s-y)}{\phi s + y} dy.$$

Equation (5.27) and the required comparative statics follow, respectively, by integration and differentiation. Furthermore, since

$$\lim_{\phi\to 0}\,(1+\phi)\log\left(1 + \frac{1}{\phi}\right) = \infty,$$

we have that $\lim_{\lambda\to\infty} \mathbf{v} = \infty$ and it now suffices to prove that the volume of trades executed by investors with utility flows in the set $B^c = \mathcal{D}\backslash B$ remains bounded as the meeting rate diverges. The structure of B ensures that

$$\begin{aligned} V(B^c) &= \lambda \int_b^{\overline{\delta}} (1 - s - \Phi_0(\delta))\, d\Phi_1(\delta) \\ &\quad + \lambda \int_{\underline{\delta}}^{a} (1 - s - \Phi_0(b) + \Phi_0(a) - \Phi_0(\delta))\, d\Phi_1(\delta) \end{aligned}$$

for some constants $a < \delta^\star < b$, which in turn implies that

$$V(B^c) \le \lambda s(1 - s - \Phi_0(b)) + \lambda(1-s)\Phi_1(a).$$

The desired result now follows by letting $\lambda \to \infty$ on both sides and using the asymptotic expansions in (5.19) and (5.21). □

In addition to providing a closed-form expression in the continuous case, Proposition 5.8 establishes two key results. First, trading volume is unbounded as $\lambda \to \infty$. By contrast, the trading volume per unit of time is finite in the equilibrium of the frictionless benchmark. Therefore, the fully decentralized market can generate arbitrarily large excess volume relative to the frictionless benchmark, as long as search frictions are sufficiently benign.

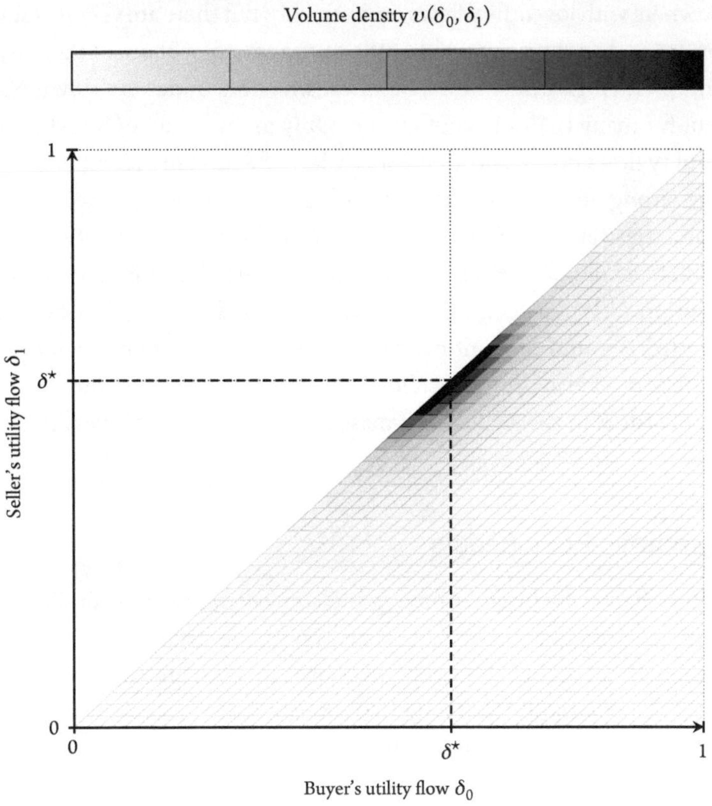

FIGURE 5.5. Contribution to trading volume

This figure plots the volume density as a function of the buyers' and sellers' utility flows in the pure decentralized market model with $\phi = \gamma/\lambda = 0.05$, asset supply $s = 0.4$, and a uniform distribution of utility flows on the unit interval.

Second, trading volume is for the most part generated by investors near the marginal type who assume the role of intermediaries. As a result, the trading network has an endogenous core-periphery structure. To illustrate this phenomenon, figure 5.5 plots the contribution of each owner/nonowner pair to the equilibrium trading volume in our base case model,

$$\nu(\delta_0, \delta_1) = \mathbf{1}_{\{\delta_1 < \delta_0\}} \frac{d\Phi_0}{dF}(\delta_0) \frac{d\Phi_1}{dF}(\delta_1) = \mathbf{1}_{\{\delta_1 < \delta_0\}} \ell'(F(\delta_1))(1 - \ell'(F(\delta_0))).$$

From the figure, one can see that investors with extreme utility flows account for a small fraction of trades and, therefore, lie at the periphery of the trading network. For example, owners with low utility flows trade quickly, but there are very few such owners in equilibrium and so they contribute little to the trading volume. Likewise, there are many owners with high utility flows, but these investors trade very slowly and thus do not account for many trades in equilibrium. Only in the group of investors with near-marginal utility flows do we find a sufficiently large fraction of individuals who are *both* holding the wrong portfolio and able to meet suitable counterparties at a reasonably high rate, and these are the investors who make up the core of the network.

The result that volume diverges when frictions vanish depends on two assumptions: the distribution of type is continuous, and investors do not trade when indifferent. Namely, if $F(\delta)$ is a sum of point masses then the trading volume no longer diverges as search frictions vanish. But if we allow investors to trade when they are indifferent (i.e., when investors in the same point mass meet), then one recovers the divergence result.

5.5 Asymptotic Price Effects

We close this chapter by briefly studying the convergence of the equilibrium trading prices as the meeting rate $\lambda \to \infty$. This analysis is important for two reasons. First, this fast trading limit is the empirically relevant case in many markets, where trading speeds are finite but steadily becoming faster. Second, this analysis highlights the effect of investor heterogeneity on equilibrium prices. In particular, we show that heterogeneity magnifies the price impact of frictions, and that this impact is more pronounced on price levels than on price dispersion.

Since the proofs of the results in this section are lengthy and technical—but also rather elementary—we omit them and instead refer the interested reader to the appendixes of Hugonnier, Lester, and Weill [2022] for details.

5.5.1 *The Frictionless Limit*

As a first step, we establish that the reservation values of all investors converge to the frictionless equilibrium price as search frictions vanish.

Lemma 5.9: $\lim_{\lambda\to\infty} R(\delta) = p^\star = \delta^\star/r$ for all $\delta \in \mathcal{D}$.

To understand this result, consider the market-valuation process defined in Proposition 5.2. From the analysis of section 5.3.2 we know that, as frictions vanish, it becomes very easy for an investor with utility flow $\delta < \delta^\star$ ($\delta > \delta^\star$) to sell (buy) but a lot more difficult to buy (sell). Specifically, (5.19) and (5.21) imply that the trading intensities are such that

$$\lim_{\lambda\to\infty} \lambda_q(\delta) = \infty \Leftrightarrow (1-2q)\left(\delta-\delta^\star\right) > 0,$$

and combining this property with (5.8) and (5.9) reveals that the jump rate and reset distribution of the market valuation process satisfy

$$\lim_{\lambda\to\infty} \left(1/\hat{\lambda}(\delta)\right) = \lim_{\lambda\to\infty} \left(\hat{F}(x|\delta) - \mathbf{1}_{\{x\le\delta^\star\}}\right) = 0, \quad \forall (x,\delta) \in \mathcal{D}^2.$$

This implies that the market valuation process converges to $\delta^\star$ as frictions vanish, and it now follows from (5.11) that all reservation values converge to the frictionless equilibrium price.

5.5.2 Price Level near the Frictionless Limit

To analyze the behavior of prices near the frictionless limit, we study the rate at which the market-valuation process converges to the marginal type. This analysis yields the following result.

Proposition 5.10: Assume that $F(\delta)$ is continuously differentiable in a neighborhood of $\delta^\star$ on which $F'(\delta)$ is bounded away from zero. Then,

$$R(\delta) = p^\star + \frac{\pi/r}{F'(\delta^\star)}\left(\frac{1}{2}-\theta_0\right)\left(\frac{\gamma s(1-s)}{\theta_0\theta_1}\right)^{\frac{1}{2}}\frac{1}{\sqrt{\lambda}} + o\left(\frac{1}{\sqrt{\lambda}}\right) \tag{5.28}$$

for all utility flows $\delta \in \mathcal{D}$.

The first term in the expansion follows directly from Lemma 5.9. The main result of the proposition is the second term, which determines the deviation of reservation values from the frictionless price. To calculate this term, we center the market valuation process around the marginal type and scale the result by $\sqrt{\lambda}$. This delivers an auxiliary process $\hat{x}_t \equiv \sqrt{\lambda}(\hat{\delta}_t - \delta^\star)$ whose limiting distribution can be derived explicitly, and the second term of the expansion is then obtained by calculating the limit of

$$\sqrt{\lambda}\left(R(\delta)-p^\star\right) = \mathbf{E}_{\sqrt{\lambda}(\delta-\delta^\star)}\left[\int_0^\infty e^{-rt}\hat{x}_t dt\right].$$

As can be seen from (5.28), the price deviation depends on three features of the decentralized market model. The first is the equilibrium mass of misallocated assets, as measured by the term

$$\frac{1}{2}\mathbf{m} = \Phi_1(\delta^\star) \approx \left(\frac{\gamma s(1-s)}{\lambda}\right)^{\frac{1}{2}}.$$

The second is the relative bargaining power of investors, which determines the sign of the price deviation: if $\theta_0 > 1/2$ then the asset is traded at a discount, and if $\theta_0 < 1/2$ it is traded at a premium. When buyers and sellers have equal bargaining powers, the correction term vanishes, so that all reservation values are well approximated by the frictionless equilibrium price.

The third feature of the market that matters for the price deviation is the slope of the distribution at the marginal type, $F'(\delta^\star)$. This quantity measures the heterogeneity among investors near the marginal type. To see this, consider a distribution G that is *more heterogeneous* than F in the sense that $G(\delta) \geq F(\delta)$ if and only if $\delta < \delta_0$ for some δ_0. As discussed by Chateauneuf, Cohen, and Meilijson [2004], this definition of heterogeneity is very intuitive as it simply requires that G be obtained from F by shifting probability mass to the left in the interval $[0, \delta_0]$ and to the right in the interval $[\delta_0, 1]$. If, in addition, the two distributions induce the same marginal type and satisfy the conditions of Proposition 5.10, then $G'(\delta^\star) \leq F'(\delta^\star)$, so that the price deviation implied by the more heterogeneous distribution is larger in absolute value.

To further emphasize the role of investor heterogeneity, we can also derive the convergence rate of reservation values when the underlying distribution is discontinuous at the marginal type.

Proposition 5.11: Assume that $\Delta F(\delta^\star) > 0$. Then

$$R(\delta) = p^\star + \frac{\xi(\delta)}{\lambda} + o\left(\frac{1}{\lambda}\right)$$

for some function $\xi : \mathcal{D} \to \mathbf{R}$ that is independent of the meeting intensity.

To confirm that the difference in convergence rates is economically significant, we compare the relative price deviation implied by the uniform distribution of our baseline example to that implied by a two-point distribution, chosen to keep the marginal and average investors the same as in the baseline case. The left panel of figure 5.6 shows that, when investors meet twice a day on average ($\lambda = 500$), the deviation is 6% for the continuous distribution and only 0.5% for the corresponding discrete distribution. When meetings occur 20 times per day on average ($\lambda = 10{,}000$), the deviation is about 1.5% for the continuous distribution but essentially zero for the discrete distribution. Why is there such a quantitatively large difference in the price impact of search frictions? Our analysis shows that this difference is driven by a fundamental economic difference between the two classes of distributions: the elasticity of asset demand at the marginal type is infinite with a discrete distribution and finite with a continuous one.

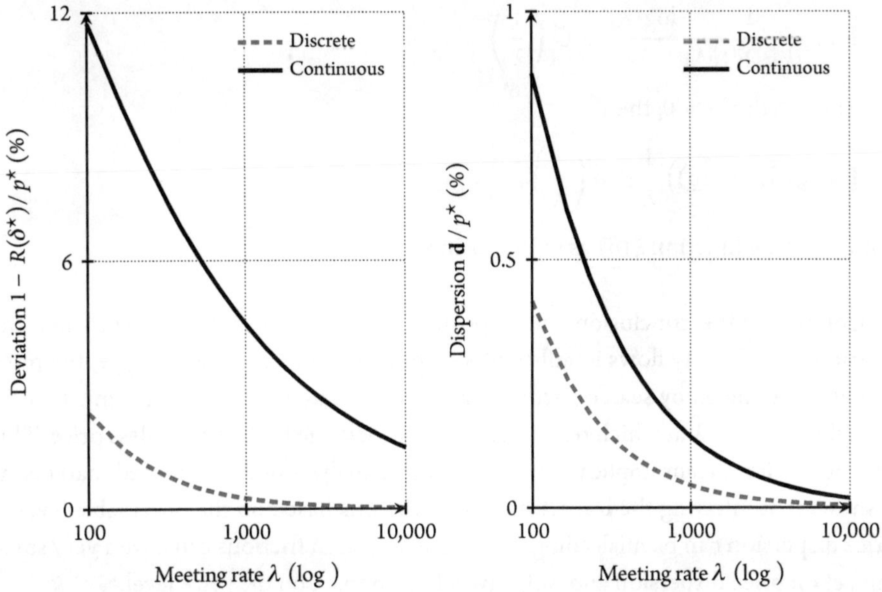

FIGURE 5.6. Equilibrium deviation and dispersion of prices

This figure plots the relative deviation from the frictionless equilibrium price (left panel) and the relative price dispersion (right panel) as functions of the meeting rate for the baseline model of figure 5.3 with bargaining power $\theta_0 = 0.75$ and a model with a two-point distribution constructed to have the same mean and the same marginal type as the uniform distribution of the baseline model.

5.5.3 Price Dispersion near the Frictionless Limit

A key implication of Proposition 5.11 is that, to a first-order approximation, there is no price dispersion when the distribution of utility flows is smooth around the marginal type. This can be seen by noting that the correction term in (5.28) does not depend on the investor's utility flows. Hence, in order to obtain results about the impact of frictions on the price dispersion

$$\mathbf{d} \equiv R(\overline{\delta}) - R(\underline{\delta}) = \int_{\underline{\delta}}^{\overline{\delta}} \sigma(x) dx,$$

it is necessary to work out higher-order terms.

Proposition 5.12: If $F(\delta)$ is twice continuously differentiable in a neighborhood of $\delta^\star$ on which $F'(\delta)$ is bounded away from zero, then

$$\mathbf{d} = \frac{1}{2\theta_0\theta_1 F'(\delta^\star)} \frac{\log(\lambda)}{\lambda} + O\left(\frac{1}{\lambda}\right).$$

If instead $\Delta F(\delta^\star) > 0$, then

$$\mathbf{d} = \left(\xi(\bar{\delta}) - \xi(\underline{\delta})\right) \frac{1}{\lambda} + o\left(\frac{1}{\lambda}\right),$$

with the same function $\xi(\delta)$ as in Proposition 5.12.

Comparing the conclusions of Propositions 5.10 and 5.12 shows that, when the distribution of utility flows is sufficiently smooth around the marginal type, the price dispersion induced by search frictions vanishes at a rate $\log(\lambda)/\lambda$ that is much faster than the rate $1/\sqrt{\lambda}$ at which reservation values converge to the frictionless price. This finding has important implications for empirical analysis of decentralized markets, as it shows that inferring the impact of search frictions based on the observable level of price dispersion can be misleading. In particular, search frictions can have a very small impact on price dispersion and, yet, have a large impact on the price level.

This finding is illustrated in figure 5.6. Comparing the two panels, one sees clearly that the price dispersion induced by search frictions vanishes much faster than the price deviation. For instance, when investors meet twice a day on average, the discount implied by our baseline model is 6% but the corresponding price dispersion is about 20 times smaller. One can also see from the figure that, in accordance with Proposition 5.12, price dispersion is larger with a continuous distribution than with a discrete distribution.

5.6 Exercises

Exercise 5.13: Consider the same model as in the text.

1. Show that in a steady-state equilibrium $\Phi_1(\delta) = \ell(F(\delta))$ for some smooth function $\ell : [0, 1] \to [0, s]$.
2. Derive an algebraic equation for the function $\ell(x)$.
3. Assume that $F(\delta)$ is absolutely continuous. Derive an integro-differential equation for the density $\phi_1(\delta) = \Phi_1'(\delta)$.

Exercise 5.14: In a seminal paper, Harrison and Kreps [1978] define *speculation* as a situation where the right to resell an asset makes investors willing to pay more for it than they would agree to pay if obliged to hold it forever. This exercise briefly explores conditions under which such a behavior occurs in the decentralized market.

1. Argue that speculation occurs if and only if

$$\min_{(\delta,x)\in\mathcal{D}^2} \{\theta_1 R(\delta) + \theta_0 R(\delta \wedge x) - B(\delta)\} \geq 0,$$

where $B(\delta)$ denotes the buy-and-hold value of the asset. What is the counterpart of this condition in the frictionless benchmark?

2. Provide an explicit expression for $B(\delta)$.
3. Show that speculation arises in the equilibrium of the frictionless benchmark if and only if

$$\delta^\star \geq \frac{r}{r+\gamma}\bar{\delta} + \frac{\gamma}{r+\gamma}\mathbf{E}^F[\delta] \tag{5.29}$$

and argue that this condition is equivalent to an upper bound on the asset supply s.

4. Show that if (5.29) holds, then speculation occurs in the equilibrium of the decentralized market for all sufficiently low values of $\phi = \gamma/\lambda$.

Exercise 5.15: Denote by $\eta > 0$ the random amount of time until the next trade of a given investor and define $g_q(\delta) \equiv \mathbf{E}_{q,\delta}[\eta]$.

1. Use the law of iterated expectations to show that

$$g_q(\delta) = \mathbf{E}_{q,\delta}\left[\mathbf{1}_{\{\eta\leq\tau_\gamma\}}\eta + \mathbf{1}_{\{\eta>\tau_\gamma\}}\left(\tau_\gamma + \mathbf{E}^F[g_q(x)]\right)\right], \tag{5.30}$$

where τ_γ denotes the exponentially distributed time until the investor's next preference shock.

2. Argue that

$$\mathbf{P}_{q,\delta}\left[u \geq \eta \in dt | \tau_\gamma = u\right] = \mathbf{1}_{\{t\leq u\}}\lambda_q(\delta)e^{-\lambda_q(\delta)t}dt.$$

Use this expression together with (5.30) and the exponential distribution of the random time τ_γ to show that

$$g_q(\delta) = \frac{1}{\gamma+\lambda_q(\delta)}\mathbf{E}^F\left[1 + \frac{\gamma}{\gamma+\lambda_q(x)}\right]^{-1}.$$

3. Use the above result to show that the expected trading delay is increasing in utility flow for sellers, decreasing in utility flow for buyers, and increasing in $\phi = \gamma/\lambda$ for all investors.

Exercise 5.16: Assume that the conditions of Proposition 5.12 hold true and define the welfare cost of search friction as

$$\mathbf{w} \equiv \int_{\underline{\delta}}^{\overline{\delta}} x \left(d\Psi_1(x) - d\Phi_1(x) \right),$$

where $\Psi_1(\delta)$ denotes the distribution of utility flows among asset owners in the frictionless benchmark. Show that

$$\mathbf{w} = \frac{\gamma s(1-s)}{F'(\delta^\star)} \frac{\log \lambda}{\lambda} + O\left(\frac{1}{\lambda}\right)$$

and combine this expansion with the result of Proposition 5.12 to conclude that, when the meeting rate is sufficiently large, the unobserved welfare cost of frictions may be approximated by the observed amount of price dispersion.

5.7 Notes and References

This chapter largely follows ?Hugonnier, Lester, and Weill [2022], which generalized the formulation of pure decentralized trade in Duffie, Gârleanu, and Pedersen [2007] to the case of an arbitrary distribution of utility flows. Another important contribution in this literature was made by Afonso and Lagos [2015a], who study a model with pure decentralized trade with two key differences: first, they allow investors to hold multiple (integer) units of the asset, rather than $\{0, 1\}$; and second, they study a finite horizon model, intended to capture end-of-day trading dynamics in the federal funds market. Among many other results, Afonso and Lagos [2015a] first made the observation that, in a pure decentralized market with heterogeneity, investors with intermediate marginal utility flows endogenously emerge as intermediaries.

A number of studies have extended the pure decentralized market model by including other dimensions of heterogeneity to understand the characteristics that make a market participant likely to emerge as an intermediary. For examples, Neklyudov [2019], Üslü [2019], and Farboodi, Jarosch, and Shimer [2022] consider environments in which investors differ with respect to their trading speed. In equilibrium, they find that investors who meet others more quickly will endogenously have reservation values near the median, and thus provide intermediation services to others. In Farboodi, Jarosch, Menzio, and Wiriadinata [2018], the same is true of investors with high bargaining power. In Bethune, Sultanum, and Trachter [2019], investors are heterogeneous with respect to their ability to observe the utility flows of their counterparties—interpreted as their expertise—and show that investors with more expertise endogenously emerge as intermediaries. Other papers in this literature include Atkeson, Eisfeldt, and Weill [2015], Sagi [2021], Colliard and Demange [2021], Chang and Zhang [2018], Shen, Wei, and Yan [2020], Tse and Xu [2021], Yang and Zeng [2019], Üslü and Velioğlu [2019], Liu [2024], and Gabrovski and Kospentaris [2021].

From a methodological point of view, some of the techniques we used to characterize the equilibrium in this chapter build on earlier work from models of on-the-job search. In particular, Burdett and Mortensen [1998] and Postel-Vinay and Robin [2002] developed models in which workers move along a job ladder from low- to high-productivity firms, much like assets in our OTC market model are reallocated from low- to high-valuation investors. The dynamics differ, however, because firms in on-the-job search models can grow without bound, subject to a flow constraint: they hire or lose only one worker at a time. In models of decentralized asset markets, by contrast, investors are typically assumed to hold at most a finite number of assets, but they face no flow constraints: they are free to trade any number of assets in a single transaction.

6

Divisible Asset Holdings

In this chapter, we extend the semicentralized OTC market model to allow for divisible asset holdings. In particular, we relax the previous assumption that investors can take just two asset positions, and instead assume that they can choose any quantity q. This is an important extension because it allows us to explore the relationships between frictions, transaction costs, and *trade size*.

In section 6.1, we outline the model and the assumptions we impose on preferences, before describing the equilibrium in a frictionless benchmark in section 6.2. Section 6.3 goes on to characterize the equilibrium with frictions, including the investors' optimal trading strategies, the equilibrium interdealer price, and the asset allocation. In the process of deriving these results, we establish economic and technical connections between this model and those considered in previous chapters.

Next, in section 6.4, we study special cases that can be solved in closed form. These special cases are important in that they provide tractable workhorse models that have been studied and extended in the existing literature. They also reveal a key, novel prediction of the model—namely, that search frictions lead investors to reduce the size of their trades. More specifically, we show that search frictions cause investors to demand fewer assets when their marginal utility is high, and to supply fewer assets when it is low. However, despite these clear implications for trade size quantities, we show that the ultimate effect of search frictions on asset prices is ambiguous, since the supply and demand curves shift in the same directions.

Section 6.5 shows that the model can be easily extended to accommodate multiple dimensions of ex ante heterogeneity among investors: e.g., investors who differ ex ante in their trading speed, their bargaining power, or the frequency with which they receive preference shocks. Finally, in section 6.6, we explore implications for the relationship between transaction costs and trade sizes. We first show that, with ex ante homogeneous investors, proportional transaction costs are increasing with trade size, contrary to the empirical evidence reported in chapter 2. However, ex ante heterogeneity in speed can reconcile the model with this evidence. Second, we show that, under the standard assumption that preference draws arc iid, the model has the counterfactual prediction that purchases and sales have the same average size.

6.1 The Model

The model is the same as in chapter 4, except that an investor can hold any quantity of asset $q \in Q \equiv [q_0, \infty)$. Later in the chapter, we consider several natural cases corresponding to different values of q_0, including the unrestricted case where $q_0 = -\infty$ and no short-selling case where $q_0 = 0$.

An investor with asset holdings q and utility type $\delta \in \mathcal{D} \subseteq \mathbf{R}_+$ derives flow utility $u(q, \delta)$, which is assumed to be strictly concave in $q \in Q$ and twice continuously differentiable on $Q \times [\underline{\delta}, \overline{\delta}]$. We also assume that

$$u_{q\delta}(q, \delta) > 0, \qquad (q, \delta) \in Q \times [\underline{\delta}, \overline{\delta}],$$

so that an increase in $\delta \in \mathcal{D}$ creates a positive shift in asset demand. To ensure that demand is well defined at any price, we assume that

$$\lim_{q \to \infty} u_q(q, \overline{\delta}) \leq 0 < u_q(s, \underline{\delta}).$$

Finally, we require that the lower bound on asset holdings $q_0 < s$, so that the constraint set Q is compatible with market clearing.

6.2 The Frictionless Benchmark

As in chapter 4, we start with a derivation of the equilibrium when the market is frictionless, i.e., when investors have continuous access to a competitive market. As in the previous analysis, we focus on the steady state, in which the interdealer market price, P, is constant.

Integrating by parts, as in section 4.2, reveals that the value function of an investor with utility flow δ and asset holdings q satisfies

$$V(q, \delta) = qP + \sup_{\vartheta \in \mathcal{Q}(Q)} \mathbf{E}_\delta \left[\int_0^\infty e^{-rt} \left(u(\vartheta_t, \delta_t) - r\vartheta_t P \right) dt \right],$$

where $\mathcal{Q}(Q)$ denotes the set of adapted holdings processes with values in Q. Maximizing pointwise with respect to ϑ_t below the integral shows that the optimal asset holding of the investor with utility flow δ satisfies the necessary and sufficient first-order condition given by

$$u_q(q,\delta) \leq rP, \quad \text{with "=" if } q > q_0. \tag{6.1}$$

The analysis of this condition, which is left to the reader in Exercise 6.7, delivers the following elementary properties of asset demand.

Lemma 6.1: Equation (6.1) admits a unique solution $q^\star(\delta,P)$ for all $\delta \in \mathcal{D}$ and $P > 0$. Furthermore, the map $(\delta,P) \mapsto q^\star(\delta,P)$ is continuous, increasing with respect to $\delta \in \mathcal{D}$, strictly decreasing with respect to P over the set $q^\star(\delta,P) > q_0$, and satisfies both $q^\star(\delta,0) > s$ and $q^\star(\delta,\infty) = q_0$ for all $\delta \in \mathcal{D}$.

The equilibrium interdealer price is determined by imposing the market clearing condition

$$\int_{\underline{\delta}}^{\overline{\delta}} q^\star(\delta,P)dF(\delta) = s,$$

which requires that the aggregate asset demand coincides with the exogenous supply. Combining Lemma 6.1 and the dominated convergence theorem shows that the demand on the left-hand side is continuous, strictly decreasing in the interdealer price as long as $q^\star(\delta,P) > q_0$ for some strictly positive measure of investors, and satisfies

$$\lim_{P\to\infty} \int_{\underline{\delta}}^{\overline{\delta}} q^\star(\delta,P)dF(\delta) = q_0 < s < \lim_{P\to 0} \int_{\underline{\delta}}^{\overline{\delta}} q^\star(\delta,P)dF(\delta).$$

Therefore, the existence of a unique market clearing price follows from the intermediate value theorem.

6.3 Equilibrium in the Semicentralized Market

Next, we turn to the derivation of equilibrium in the semicentralized market where investors meet dealers at rate $\lambda \geq 0$.

6.3.1 *Asset Demand*

The Hamilton-Jacobi-Bellman (HJB) equation for the value function $V(q,\delta)$ of an investor with asset holdings $q \in Q$ and utility flow $\delta \in \mathcal{D}$ is given by

$$\begin{aligned}(r+\gamma)V(q,\delta) &= u(q,\delta) + \gamma \mathbf{E}^F\left[V(q,x)\right] \\ &\quad + \lambda\left(V(q',\delta) - T' - V(q,\delta)\right),\end{aligned} \tag{6.2}$$

where q' is the investor's posttrade asset holdings and T' is the transfer that she makes to the dealer for this transaction. As in earlier chapters, we assume that these objects solve a generalized Nash bargaining problem:

$$(q', T') \in \underset{(\hat{q},\hat{T})\in Q\times\mathbf{R}}{\operatorname{argmax}} \left\{ \left(V(\hat{q},\delta) - V(q,\delta) - \hat{T}\right)^{1-\theta} \left(\hat{T} - P\left(\hat{q}-q\right)\right)^{\theta} \right\}.$$

The first term in the Nash product is the net utility of the investor, while the second is the net profit of the dealer, i.e., the transfer made by the investor net of the cost of executing the transaction on the interdealer market.

Changing variables from $\hat{T}$ to the net profit $\hat{\Pi} \equiv \hat{T} - P\left(\hat{q} - q\right)$ reveals that the bargaining problem can be equivalently stated as

$$(q', \Pi') \in \underset{(\hat{q},\hat{\Pi})\in Q\times\mathbf{R}}{\operatorname{argmax}} \left\{ \left(V(\hat{q},\delta) - V(q,\delta) - P(\hat{q}-q) - \hat{\Pi}\right)^{1-\theta} \hat{\Pi}^{\theta} \right\}.$$

Since $\hat{q}$ only appears in the first term of the Nash product, it is clear that the optimal posttrade asset holdings maximizes the total surplus:

$$q' \in \underset{\hat{q}\in Q}{\operatorname{argmax}} \left\{ V(\hat{q},\delta) - V(q,\delta) - P(\hat{q}-q) \right\}.$$

Moreover, maximizing over $\hat{\Pi}$ reveals that the dealer appropriates a fraction θ of the maximum surplus:

$$\Pi' = \theta \max_{\hat{q}\in Q} \left\{ V(\hat{q},\delta) - V(q,\delta) - P(\hat{q}-q) \right\}.$$

In words, the solution to the Nash bargaining problem specifies that the quantity traded, $q' - q$, maximizes the joint surplus between the investor and the dealer, while the transfer T is such that the dealer receives a fraction θ of the surplus. These results are standard and jointly follow from the Pareto optimality of Nash bargaining solutions, and from the quasi-linearity of preferences.

Substituting these objects into the HJB equation (6.2) and making use of our previous notation $\lambda_\theta = \lambda(1-\theta)$ for the bargaining adjusted meeting rate, we obtain that the value function solves

$$\begin{aligned} rV(q,\delta) = u(q,\delta) + \gamma \mathbf{E}^F \left[V(q,x) - V(q,\delta)\right] \\ + \lambda_\theta \max_{\hat{q}\in Q} \left\{ V(\hat{q},\delta) - P(\hat{q}-q) - V(q,\delta) \right\}. \end{aligned} \tag{6.3}$$

In the indivisible holdings models of previous chapters, the optimal strategy was fully determined by the reservation value $V(1,\delta) - V(0,\delta)$, so that we did not need to actually compute the value functions. This convenient property remains true here. However, since asset holdings are infinitely divisible, the characterization is now based on the marginal value

$$V_q(q,\delta) \equiv \frac{\partial V}{\partial q}(q,\delta)$$

rather than on the reservation value.

To make this point, let $(q,h) \in Q \times \mathbf{R}$ be such that $q+h \in Q$ and consider the difference quotient

$$\Delta V(h,q,\delta) \equiv \frac{V(q+h,\delta)-V(q,\delta)}{h}.$$

Subtracting the HJB equation evaluated at the points $(q+h,\delta)$ and (q,δ) shows that this function solves

$$r\Delta V(h,q,\delta) = \Delta u(h,q,\delta) \\ + \lambda_\theta(P-\Delta V(h,q,\delta)) + \gamma \mathbf{E}^F\left[\Delta V(h,q,x) - \Delta V(h,q,\delta)\right],$$

where $\Delta u(h,q,\delta)$ denotes the corresponding difference quotient of the utility flow function. By inspection, this equation has exactly the same structure as equation (4.9) for the reservation value function in the indivisible holdings model, except that the source term δ is replaced by $\Delta u(h,q,\delta)$. Therefore, it admits the same explicit solution, namely

$$\begin{aligned}\Delta V(h,q,\delta) &= \mathbf{E}_\delta\left[\int_0^{\tau_\theta} e^{-rt}\Delta u(h,q,\delta_t)dt + e^{-r\tau_\theta}P\right] \\ &= \frac{1}{r+\gamma+\lambda_\theta}\left(\Delta u(h,q,\delta) + \frac{\gamma}{r+\lambda_\theta}\mathbf{E}^F\left[\Delta u(h,q,x)\right]\right) + \frac{\lambda_\theta}{r+\lambda_\theta}P,\end{aligned}$$

where τ_θ is an exponential time with parameter λ_θ. Letting $h \to 0$ on both sides and using the smoothness of the utility flow to justify the interchange of limits and expectations, we conclude that

$$\begin{aligned}V_q(q,\delta) &= \lim_{h\to 0}\Delta V(h,q,\delta) \\ &= \mathbf{E}_\delta\left[\int_0^{\tau_\theta} e^{-rt}u_q(q,\delta_t)dt\right] + \frac{\lambda_\theta}{r+\lambda_\theta}P \qquad (6.4) \\ &= \frac{1}{r+\gamma+\lambda_\theta}\left(u_q(q,\delta) + \frac{\gamma}{r+\lambda_\theta}\mathbf{E}^F\left[u_q(q,x)\right]\right) + \frac{\lambda_\theta}{r+\lambda_\theta}P.\end{aligned}$$

Our assumptions on the utility flow immediately ensure that this marginal value is continuous in (q, δ), strictly increasing in δ, and strictly decreasing in q. This, in turn, implies that the value function is strictly concave in q and it follows that the unique solution to the maximization problem on the second line of the HJB equation (6.3),

$$\max_{\hat{q}\in Q} \left\{V(\hat{q},\delta) - P(\hat{q}-q) - V(q,\delta)\right\} = \max_{\hat{q}\in Q} \int_q^{\hat{q}} \left(V_q(\vartheta,\delta) - P\right) d\vartheta,$$

is fully characterized by the first-order condition

$$V_q(q',\delta) \leq P, \text{ with "=" if } q' > q_0. \tag{6.5}$$

In view of (6.4) and our assumptions regarding the utility flow, it is clear that the marginal value satisfies

$$\lim_{q\to\infty} V_q(q,\delta) \leq P.$$

As we now state formally, it follows that the target holdings enjoy the same qualitative properties as their frictionless counterparts.

Lemma 6.2: Equation (6.5) admits a unique solution $q^\star(\delta, P)$ for all $\delta \in \mathcal{D}$ and $P > 0$. Furthermore, the map $(\delta, P) \mapsto q^\star(\delta, P)$ is continuous, increasing with respect to $\delta \in \mathcal{D}$, strictly decreasing with respect to P over the set $q^\star(\delta, P) > q_0$, and satisfies both $q^\star(\delta, 0) > s$ and $q^\star(\delta, \infty) = q_0$ for all $\delta \in \mathcal{D}$.

Proof. The proof follows the same steps as in Exercise 6.7. □

6.3.2 *Market Clearing and the Interdealer Price*

To obtain the equilibrium interdealer price, we need to clear markets among the group of investors who are in contact with dealers at a given point in time. As in the model with restricted asset holdings, we do so by equating the gross (rather than net) supply and demand during a small interval. This allows us to determine the market clearing price without explicitly deriving the distribution of asset holdings in the population of investors.

Over a small time interval of length h, the gross supply is equal to the mass of assets held by those investors who are in contact with a dealer. Since contact times are independent and identical across investors, this mass is simply equal to the product $(\lambda h) \cdot s$ of the measure of investors who contact the market, λh, and the average holding per capita in the population, s.

On the other side of the market, the gross demand from investors with utility flow δ is equal to $(\lambda h dF(\delta)) \cdot q^\star(\delta, P)$: the product of the measure of investors with utility type δ who contact a dealer, $\lambda h dF(\delta)$, and the quantity that each of them demands, $q^\star(\delta, P)$. Integrating across utility types yields the aggregate gross demand, and equating the result with the gross supply reveals that the market clearing condition can be stated as

$$s = \int_{\underline{\delta}}^{\overline{\delta}} q^\star(\delta, P) dF(\delta). \tag{6.6}$$

As in the frictionless case, the regularity properties of the investors' optimal asset holdings allow us to establish the existence of an equilibrium.

Lemma 6.3: There is a unique $P > 0$ solving the market-clearing condition (6.6).

6.3.3 Asset Allocation

We now characterize the joint equilibrium distribution of utility types and asset holdings. Let $\Phi(q, \delta)$ denote the measure of investors with asset holdings less than q and utility type less than δ. Clearly, the support of the equilibrium distribution of asset holdings is contained in $\bar{Q} \times \mathcal{D}$ with $\bar{Q} \equiv \left[q^\star(\underline{\delta}), q^\star(\overline{\delta})\right]$.

As a first step toward the characterization of this joint distribution, we derive the marginal distribution of holdings across investors by computing the measure of investors with holdings less than a given $q \in \bar{Q}$,

$$\int_{Q \times \mathcal{D}} \mathbf{1}_{\{q' \leq q\}} d\Phi(q', \delta').$$

The stationarity condition that equalizes the *gross* inflow into and outflow from the group of investors who hold less than q units is

$$\lambda \int_{\mathcal{D}} \mathbf{1}_{\{q^\star(\delta') \leq q\}} \, dF(\delta') = \lambda \int_{Q \times \mathcal{D}} \mathbf{1}_{\{q' \leq q\}} \, d\Phi(q', \delta'), \tag{6.7}$$

where we have suppressed the explicit dependence of $q^\star(\delta)$ on P to simplify notation. The left-hand side is the gross inflow generated by all investors with *optimal holdings* less than q who contact dealers, whereas the right-hand side is the gross outflow that is generated by all investors with *current holdings* less than q who contact dealers.

Since the target holdings are nondecreasing, we clearly have that

$$q^\star(\delta') \leq q \Leftrightarrow \delta' \leq \delta^\star(q) \equiv \sup\{\delta \in \mathcal{D} : q^\star(\delta) \leq q\}, \tag{6.8}$$

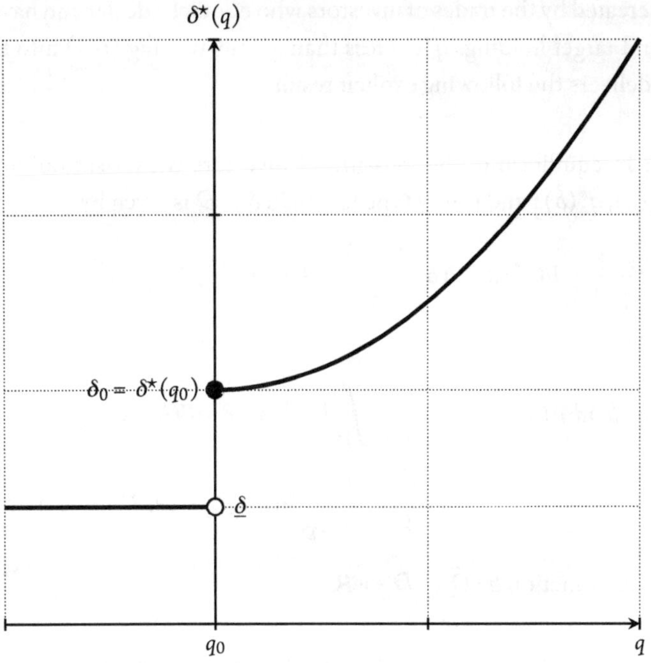

FIGURE 6.1. The function $\delta^\star(q)$

In this figure, the jump from $\underline{\delta}$ to $\delta^\star(q_0)$ that occurs at the point q_0 corresponds to the interval of utility types for which the constraint that $q \geq q_0$ is binding.

with the convention that $\delta^\star(q) = \underline{\delta}$ if this set is empty; see figure 6.1 for an illustration. Introducing the function $\delta^\star(q)$ greatly facilitates the derivation of the entire distribution. In particular, it follows from (6.7) that

$$\int_{Q\times\mathcal{D}} \mathbf{1}_{\{q' \leq q\}} d\Phi(q', \delta') = F\left(\delta^\star(q)\right).$$

Using this result, we can write the inflow-outflow equation for the cumulative measure $\Phi(q, \delta)$ simply as

$$(\gamma + \lambda)\Phi(q, \delta) = \gamma F(\delta^\star(q))F(\delta) + \lambda \int_{\mathcal{D}} \mathbf{1}_{\{\delta' \leq \delta \text{ and } q^\star(\delta') \leq q\}} dF(\delta'). \tag{6.9}$$

The left-hand side of this expression is the gross outflow from investors with utility type less than δ and asset holdings less than q who either change utility type or contact dealers. On the right-hand side, the first term is the gross inflow from investors with holdings less than q who draw a new utility type less than δ, while the second term is the gross inflow created by the trades of investors who contact a dealer and have utility type less than δ and target holdings $q^\star(\delta)$ less than q. Substituting (6.8) into this equation and solving delivers the following explicit result.

Lemma 6.4: In equilibrium, the measure of investors with asset holdings less than $q \in \bar{Q} = [q^\star(\underline{\delta}), q^\star(\bar{\delta})]$ and utility type less than $\delta \in \mathcal{D}$ is given by

$$\Phi(q,\delta) = \frac{\gamma}{\gamma+\lambda} F(\delta^\star(q)) F(\delta) + \frac{\lambda}{\gamma+\lambda} F\left(\min\left\{\delta, \delta^\star(q)\right\}\right).$$

Moreover,

$$\int_{\bar{Q}\times\mathcal{D}} h(q',\delta') d\Phi(q',\delta') = \frac{\lambda}{\gamma+\lambda}\int_{\mathcal{D}} h(q^\star(\delta),\delta) dF(\delta) + \frac{\gamma}{\gamma+\lambda}\int_{\mathcal{D}\times\mathcal{D}} h(q^\star(\delta),\delta') dF(\delta) dF(\delta') \tag{6.10}$$

for any bounded function $h : \bar{Q} \times \mathcal{D} \to \mathbf{R}$.

Proof. The formula for $\Phi(q,\delta)$ follows directly from (6.9) while (6.10) follows from Exercise 6.9. □

While the most beautiful part of the lemma is the explicit formula for the steady-state equilibrium distribution, its most useful part is formula (6.10) for calculating expectations relative to this distribution. This formula follows from an intuitive change of variable: instead of indexing an investor by her asset holdings, q, we index her by the utility type δ' she had at the time of her last trade, when she chose to hold $q^\star(\delta') = q$. With this change of variable in mind, the formula admits the following interpretation. At the last trading opportunity, the investor's utility type was δ with probability $dF(\delta)$. The first term on the right-hand side of (6.10) accounts for the possibility that, with probability $\lambda/(\gamma+\lambda)$, the utility type has not changed since, while the second accounts for the possibility that, with probability $\gamma/(\gamma+\lambda)$, the investor's utility type has changed and is now equal to δ' with probability $dF(\delta')$.

6.4 Closed-Form Examples

In this section we discuss specifications leading to closed-form solutions. These offer transparent insights about the economic forces at play in the model, and have proven important in various applications of this model.

6.4.1 Quadratic Utility Flow

As a first example, we consider the quadratic specification

$$u(q,\delta) = \mu q + \alpha\sigma q\left(\delta - \frac{1}{2}\sigma q\right) \tag{6.11}$$

defined over $(q,\delta) \in \mathbb{R} \times \mathcal{D}$. As several others have argued (see the references cited in the notes at the end of the chapter), this specification can be viewed as an approximation of a model with constant absolute risk aversion. Namely, in the utility flow function, the constants μ and σ^2 are interpreted as the average and variance of the asset dividend; the parameter α corresponds to the absolute risk aversion of the investor; and the time-varying utility type δ is related to the covariance between the asset dividend and the rest of the investor's portfolio. If this covariance is negative (positive), then holding assets helps hedge these other risks, so that the utility type δ is positive (negative).

Elementary calculations using (6.4) show that, under this specification, the marginal value function satisfies

$$(r+\lambda_\theta)V_q(q,\delta) = \mu + \lambda_\theta P + \alpha\sigma\left(rD(\delta) - \sigma q\right), \tag{6.12}$$

where the function

$$D(\delta) \equiv \frac{(r+\lambda_\theta)\,\delta + \gamma\mathbf{E}^F[x]}{r\,(r+\gamma+\lambda_\theta)} \tag{6.13}$$

is defined as in chapter 4. Substituting (6.12) into the first-order condition (6.5) shows that the optimal asset holdings are given by

$$q^\star(\delta,P) = \max\left\{q_0;\ \frac{\mu + r\,(\alpha\sigma D(\delta) - P)}{\alpha\sigma^2}\right\}. \tag{6.14}$$

Consider first the unconstrained case where $q_0 \equiv -\infty$. Integrating both sides of the expression above against $dF(\delta)$, using the fact that $\mathbf{E}^F[D(x)] = \mathbf{E}^F[x/r]$, and setting the resulting expression equal to the asset supply shows that the equilibrium price is explicitly given by

$$rP = \mu + \alpha\sigma\left(\mathbf{E}^F[x] - \sigma s\right).$$

This formula has the standard interpretation that the price is equal to the risk-adjusted present value of future cash flows and exhibits intuitive comparative statics. In particular, the interdealer price is increasing in the average cash flow μ, decreasing in the asset supply s, and decreasing in both the risk aversion α and the amount of risk σ if and only if $\mathbf{E}^F[x] < \sigma s$.

The most striking property of the above equilibrium price is that it *does not* depend on the parameter λ_θ, which measures the level of frictions. This implies that when investors have quadratic utility flow and are not subject to a short-selling constraint, the equilibrium price is equal to its frictionless counterpart. This does not mean, of course, that search frictions do not matter for equilibrium. In particular, given that the price does not depend on λ_θ in equilibrium, it follows from (6.14) that the target holdings satisfy

$$\frac{\partial q^\star(\delta)}{\partial \lambda_\theta} \propto \frac{\partial D(\delta)}{\partial \lambda_\theta} \propto \left(\delta - \mathbf{E}^F\left[x\right]\right).$$

Hence, when λ_θ increases and search frictions decline, investors with higher-than-average utility type demand more assets, while investors with lower-than-average δ supply more assets. This creates two opposing effects on the net asset demand, which cancel out exactly. As a result, in equilibrium, investors trade larger sizes but the price stays the same.

However, this result is not robust to the introduction of a short-selling constraint, because only one of the two effects operates when the constraint is binding. Indeed, as λ_θ increases, investors with higher-than-average utility types, who hold $q > q_0$, demand even more. Yet investors with lower-than-average utility types, who hold $q = q_0$ because of a binding constraint, *cannot* supply more. The net effect is an increase in demand and, thus, an increase in the equilibrium price. This can be shown formally by noting that the optimal asset holding becomes strictly convex as a function of $D(\delta)$ when the short-selling constraint binds, and that an increase in the meeting rate λ_θ creates a mean-preserving increase in $D(\delta)$.

6.4.2 Isoelastic Utility Flow

Assume next that $Q = (0, \infty) \supseteq \mathcal{D}$ and consider the isoelastic utility flow function given by

$$u(q, \delta) = \left(\frac{q^{1-\alpha} - 1}{1-\alpha}\right)\delta$$

for some constant elasticity parameter $\alpha > 0$, with the usual convention that $u(q, \delta) = \log(q)\delta$ if $\alpha = 1$. In this specification, the same calculations as above show that the marginal value function is

$$V_q(q, \delta) = \frac{\lambda_\theta P}{r + \lambda_\theta} + \frac{r}{r + \lambda_\theta} q^{-\alpha} D(\delta),$$

with the same function $D(\delta)$ as in (6.13). Since $q_0 = 0$ the target asset holdings is always interior and equal to

$$q^\star(\delta, P) = \left(\frac{D(\delta)}{P}\right)^{\frac{1}{\alpha}}. \tag{6.15}$$

Finally, clearing the market as in (6.6) shows that the equilibrium interdealer price is given by

$$P = s^{-\alpha}\mathbf{E}^F\left[D(x)^{\frac{1}{\alpha}}\right]^{\alpha}.$$

As in the quadratic case, we find that as frictions weaken, investors with higher-than-average δ increase their demand, while investors with lower-than-average δ increase their supply. Which of these two effects dominates depends on the relative risk aversion coefficient α. If $\alpha < 1$, then the optimal asset holding in (6.15) is a convex function of the certainty equivalent utility flow $D(\delta)$. As a result, the effect of an increase in λ_θ is stronger for investors with higher-than-average δ and the demand effect dominates. The opposite is true if $\alpha > 1$. When $\alpha = 1$, the two effects exactly cancel out, so that search frictions have no impact on price, similar to the quadratic utility flow case.

6.4.3 *The Indivisible Holdings Limit*

At first glance, the model with divisible holdings may appear fundamentally different from the model with indivisible holdings. It turns out, however, that the two are intimately related. One can see the connection in the examples above, where the certainty equivalent utility flow $D(\delta)$—which is at the center of the indivisible holdings model—plays a pivotal role in the divisible holdings model. Before proceeding, we now explore this connection in greater depth. In particular, we establish that the indivisible holdings model can be viewed as the limit of the divisible holdings model for a class of flow utility functions.

Perhaps the easiest way to formally make this point would be to consider the Leontief utility flow function given by

$$u(q, \delta) = \min\{q, 1\}\delta.$$

Since an investor with such preferences would optimally choose to hold zero or one unit of the asset, the analysis of equilibrium is exactly the same as in earlier chapters of this book. Note, however, that the Leontief utility flow does not satisfy the regularity assumptions maintained in this chapter: it is neither differentiable at $q = 1$ nor strictly concave. Arguably, the optimality of a $\{0, 1\}$ asset position relies on these departures from regularity. To address this criticism, one can go a step further and consider a sequence of smooth utility flows of the form

$$u_n(q,\delta) = m_n(q)\delta, \qquad n \geq 1,$$

where $m_n(q)$ satisfies the regularity assumptions of this chapter for each n and converges uniformly on compact sets to the Leontief utility flow as $n \to \infty$. In this case, $\{0, 1\}$ holdings are nearly optimal for large n. See Exercise 6.10 for a detailed argument. Taken together, these continuity results show that the equilibrium with indivisible holdings can be viewed as an approximation of the equilibrium with divisible holdings, with an appropriately chosen utility flow function.

6.5 Ex-Ante Heterogeneity

In this section, we briefly outline an extension of the divisible holdings model in which investors are ex ante heterogeneous in that they differ with respect to their contact intensity λ, their bargaining power $1-\theta$, their preference shock intensity γ, and the distribution of their preference shocks via a parameter ξ. As we argue in section 6.6.1 below, this extension helps reconcile the model with the stylized facts about the relation between trade size and transaction costs. More generally, introducing this heterogeneity offers a richer model that can match many features of transaction data.

To incorporate this form of ex ante heterogeneity into the semicentralized model with divisible asset holdings, we denote by

$$\chi \equiv (\lambda, \theta, \gamma, \xi)$$

the *ex ante type* of an investor and assume that the parameter χ is distributed across the population according to some distribution $G(\chi)$ on a bounded set $\mathcal{X} \subseteq \mathbf{R}_+ \times (0,1) \times \mathbf{R}_+ \times \mathbf{R}$. Proceeding as in the previous model shows that the target holdings of an investor of type (δ, χ) are uniquely determined by the first-order condition

$$V_q(q', \delta, \chi) \leq P, \quad \text{with “=” if } q' > q_0,$$

where

$$V_q(q, \delta, \chi) = \frac{\lambda_\theta}{r+\lambda_\theta} P + \frac{u_q(q,\delta)}{r+\gamma+\lambda_\theta}$$
$$+ \frac{\gamma}{(r+\lambda_\theta)(r+\gamma+\lambda_\theta)} \int_{\underline{\delta}}^{\overline{\delta}} u_q(q,x)\,dF(x|\xi)$$

represents the investor's marginal value function.

In this generalized environment, the measure of assets held by investors of ex ante type χ is

$$s(\chi, P) \equiv \int_{\mathcal{D}} q^{\star}(\delta, \chi, P)dF(\delta|\xi),$$

and the interdealer price is obtained by equalizing the asset supply s and the measure of assets held by investors of all types:

$$s = \int_{\mathcal{X}} s(\chi, P)dG(\chi) = \int_{\mathcal{X}\times\mathcal{D}} q^{\star}(\delta, \chi, P)dF(\delta|\xi)dG(\chi).$$

The difference between this condition and (6.6) is that $s(\chi, P)$ is endogenous and different from s in general because ex ante different investors may have different target holdings even if they have the same utility type. The same arguments as those used before establish the existence and uniqueness of the equilibrium interdealer price in this generalized model.

6.6 Empirical Implications

6.6.1 *Trade Size and Proportional Transaction Costs*

As we discussed in chapter 2, a well-known fact about OTC markets is that large trades appear to be associated with lower transaction costs per unit. Since the model with divisible asset holdings generates testable predictions about the relation between trade size and proportional transaction costs, we now discuss this empirical relationship—along with other, related properties—through the lens of the model.

To do so, consider the model of section 6.5, in which investors are ex ante heterogeneous in terms of fixed characteristics, $\chi = (\lambda, \theta, \gamma, \xi)$. Suppose an investor of type (δ, χ) has holdings $q < q^{\star}(\delta)$; the analysis of the reverse case is symmetric. If this investor meets a dealer before experiencing a preference shock, she buys $q^{\star}(\delta) - q$ units of the asset and pays a fee equal to a fraction θ of the trade surplus. Therefore, the proportional transaction cost paid by this investor is equal to a fraction θ of the surplus per unit traded:

$$\theta\left(\frac{V(q^{\star}(\delta), \delta) - V(q, \delta)}{q^{\star}(\delta) - q} - P\right). \tag{6.16}$$

Figure 6.2 provides some graphical intuition. The hump-shaped curve in the figure is the net value $V(q, \delta) - Pq$ of holding q units of the asset. This function is strictly concave in q and reaches a global maximum at the optimal holding, $q^{\star}(\delta)$. For any q, the

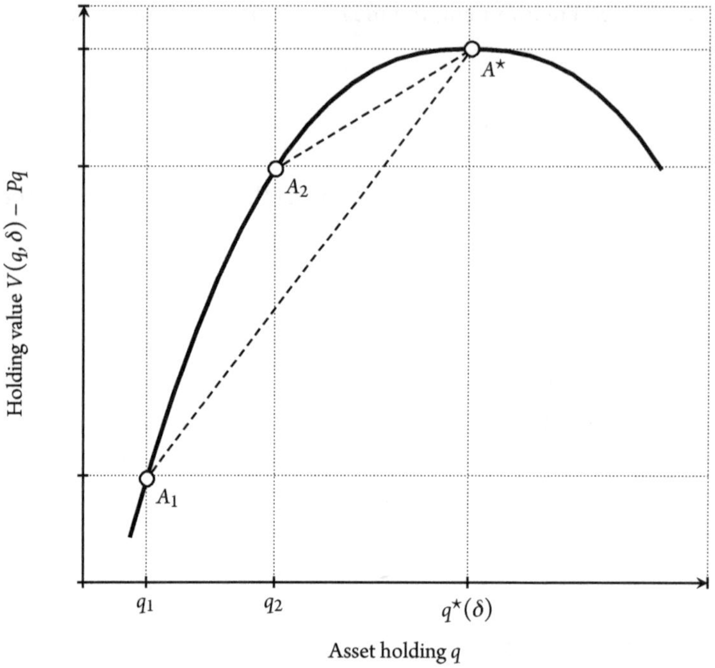

FIGURE 6.2. Transaction cost and trade size

This figure illustrates the relationship between transaction costs and trade size, holding the optimal demand constant.

proportional transaction cost (6.16) is equal to the product of the bargaining power, θ, and the slope of the line segment between the starting point

$$(q, V(q, \delta) - Pq)$$

and the target point

$$(q^\star(\delta), V(q^\star(\delta), \delta) - Pq^\star(\delta)).$$

Clearly, if the initial holding q is closer to $q^\star(\delta)$, then the quantity purchased and the slope are both smaller. For example, an investor with current asset holding q_1, represented by the point A_1, will trade to the point $A^\star$ and pay a proportional transaction cost equal to θ times the slope of the segment $A_1A^\star$. Similarly, an investor with current asset holding $q_2 > q_1$, represented by the point A_2, will purchase only

$$q^\star(\delta) - q_2 < q^\star(\delta) - q_1$$

units of the asset and will pay a smaller proportional transaction cost, equal to θ times the slope of the segment $A_2A^\star$.

The figure clearly shows that, keeping the target holdings $q^\star(\delta)$ fixed, the proportional transaction cost paid by the investor is increasing as a function of trade size, $q^\star(\delta) - q$. The economic intuition is simple and relies on two observations. First, the *marginal* value $V_q(q, \delta)$ is decreasing in q, so that the first unit traded has a marginal value that is increasing in the total quantity traded. Second, the proportional transaction cost is equal to a fixed fraction θ of the *average* surplus from trading. Taken together, this means that, if an investor's current holding, q, is further away from her optimal holding, $q^\star(\delta)$, then she pays a larger proportional transaction cost.

The above discussion shows that the divisible holdings model generates an increasing relationship between proportional transaction costs and trade size *conditional* on an investor's utility type, δ, and characteristics, χ. However, this theoretical prediction does not apply directly to our empirical observations, since the regression analyses in chapter 2 do not control for investors' fixed characteristics, which constitute unobserved heterogeneity. To understand the effects of such unobserved heterogeneity, figure 6.3 plots the model-predicted relationship between trade size and transaction costs across different types of investors; as we explain below, these different upward-sloping lines could be generated by different values of λ, holding all else equal.

However, just because *each* line is upward sloping does not imply that the data observed by an econometrician will exhibit a positive correlation between trade size and proportional transaction cost, since different types of investors tend to trade different quantities. For example, under certain parameter values, investors who meet dealers more frequently trade larger quantities, on average. In this case, the unconditional relationship between trade size and transaction costs will appear downward sloping, as illustrated by the dashed line in figure 6.3. Indeed, the empirical findings of Pinter, Wang, and Zou [2021] find just this pattern. Using data from the U.K. bond markets, they document a negative unconditional relation between trade size and proportional transaction costs, which becomes positive after they control for customers' fixed characteristics. Unfortunately, such investor-specific controls are currently not feasible in U.S. data because customers are not identified.

To make this point more formally, consider the special case of a quadratic utility flow, as in (6.11), and assume that the lower bound $q_0 = -\infty$ so that asset holdings are unconstrained. In this case, the marginal value function given by (6.12) is linear in q. As a result, the value function is quadratic and admits an exact second-order Taylor expansion:

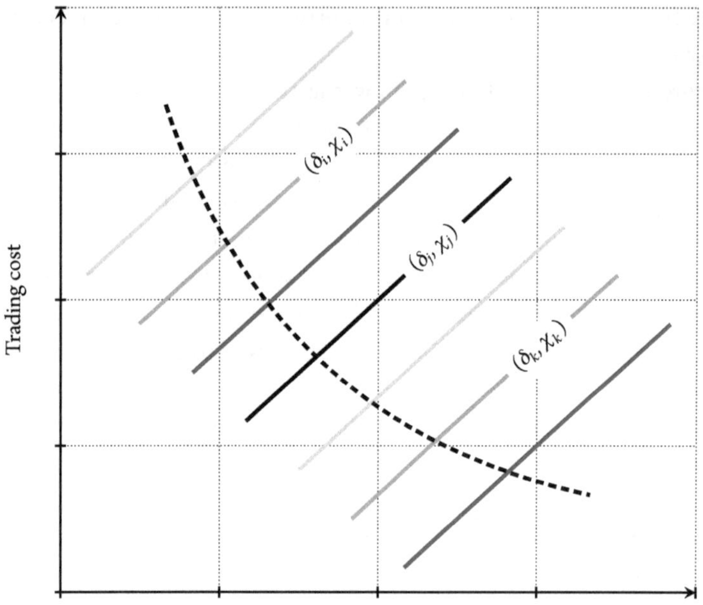

FIGURE 6.3. The relationship between trade size and cost

In this figure each upward-slopping line represents the empirical relationship between trade size and trading cost, controlling for the current utility type of the investor, δ, as well as the investor's fixed characteristics, $\chi = (\lambda, \theta, \gamma, \xi)$. The downward-slopping dotted curve represents the relationship obtained without controlling for the current utility type of the investor.

$$V(q^\star(\delta), \delta) - V(q, \delta)$$
$$= V_q(q^\star(\delta), \delta)\left(q^\star(\delta) - q\right) - \frac{1}{2} V_{qq}(q^\star(\delta), \delta)\left(q^\star(\delta) - q\right)^2.$$

Absent constraints, the optimality of $q^\star(\delta)$ implies that the first derivative at the target level of holdings is given by

$$V_q(q^\star(\delta), \delta) = P.$$

Using (6.4) and (6.12), one can also show that

$$V_{qq}(q, \delta) = -\frac{\alpha\sigma^2}{r + \lambda_\theta}.$$

The next lemma then follows from (6.16) and the Taylor expansion.

Lemma 6.5: With quadratic utility flows, the proportional transaction cost paid by an investor with utility type δ and characteristics $\chi = (\lambda, \theta, \gamma, \xi)$ is

$$\frac{\alpha\sigma^2\theta}{2(r+\lambda_\theta)}|q^\star(\delta) - q|. \tag{6.17}$$

In particular, the proportional transaction cost is a linear and increasing function of trade size conditional on χ.

According to this lemma, the divisible holdings model predicts that the unconditional relationship between trade size and transaction cost is increasing when investors have homogeneous characteristics. However, when investors have heterogeneous characteristics, (6.17) suggests that heterogeneity in the meeting rate λ and/or the bargaining power θ could make the unconditional relationship a decreasing one. Indeed, (6.17) and our previous results show that a larger bargaining-adjusted contact rate λ_θ increases trade size and reduces proportional transaction costs when size is held constant. Figure 6.3 illustrates this point: Each increasing line segment represents a trade size/transaction cost (6.17) schedule for a different value of λ_θ. In particular, larger values of λ_θ shift the schedule to the southeast of the figure. Exercise 6.11 confirms this observation by providing conditions under which the net effect is negative in a model with heterogeneous meeting rates. This theoretical result is in line with a conjecture of Edwards, Harris, and Piwowar [2007] that the negative relationship between trade size and trading cost is likely due to heterogeneity in negotiation power.

6.6.2 *Buy-Sell Symmetry*

In chapter 2 we also documented that, in the U.S. corporate bonds market, the size of customers' purchases tends to be smaller than that of their sales. Since the dollar value of purchases is approximately equal to that of sales, it follows that the *number* of customer purchases exceeds the number of sales. In this section we show that the model with divisible holdings cannot account for this asymmetry under the assumption that utility draws are independent and identically distributed: it implies that the number of customer purchases is equal to the number of customer sales.

To make this point, let φ_p and φ_s denote the flow rates of purchases and sales defined by

$$\varphi_p \equiv \lambda \int_{Q\times\mathcal{D}} \mathbf{1}_{\{q<q^\star(\delta)\}} d\Phi\left(q,\delta\right),$$

$$\varphi_s \equiv \lambda \int_{Q\times\mathcal{D}} \mathbf{1}_{\{q>q^\star(\delta)\}} d\Phi\left(q',\delta'\right).$$

In words, the flow rate of purchases φ_p (of sales φ_s) counts the number of meetings between dealers and investors with current asset holdings that are strictly smaller (larger) than their target level. Note that the sum of φ_s and φ_p provides information about the mass M of misallocated investors:

$$\varphi_p + \varphi_s = \lambda \int_{Q\times\mathcal{D}} \mathbf{1}_{\{q\neq q^\star(\delta)\}} d\Phi\left(q,\delta\right) = \lambda M.$$

Indeed, the expectation formula given by (6.10) allows us to derive explicit expressions for the rates $\left(\varphi_p,\varphi_s\right)$, and thus also for the mass M, which we summarize in the following lemma.

Lemma 6.6: In equilibrium,

$$\varphi_s = \varphi_p = \frac{\gamma\lambda}{2(\gamma+\lambda)}\left(1 - F(\delta^\star(q_0))^2 - \sum_{\delta>\delta^\star(q_0)} (\Delta F(\delta))^2\right) \tag{6.18}$$

and the mass of misallocated investors is $M = 2\varphi_s/\lambda$.

Before embarking on the proof, let us first provide some intuition for (6.18). The formula is particularly easy to understand in the special case where the distribution of utility type $F(\delta)$ has no atoms and the short-selling constraint is slack. In this case, $\delta^\star(q_0) = \underline{\delta}$ and, therefore,

$$\varphi_s = \varphi_p = \frac{\gamma\lambda}{2\left(\gamma+\lambda\right)}.$$

Intuitively, when the distribution of utility flows is continuous, the fraction of investors seeking to trade is equal to $\gamma/(\gamma+\lambda)$. This is because γ is the intensity with which an investor changes utility type and wants to trade, while λ is the intensity with which an investor manages to trade. The $1/2$ factor arises because half of the investors purchase, and the other half sell.

When the distribution is continuous but the constraint binds for some utility types, the flow of trade is reduced by a factor $1 - F(\delta^\star(q_0))^2$. For example an investor who already holds q_0 units of the asset and has utility type $\delta < \delta^\star(q_0)$ may switch to an even lower utility type $\delta' < \delta$, but will not be able to sell because of the binding short-selling constraint. Symmetrically, this investor may switch to a higher utility type δ' and not find it optimal to increase his position because δ' remains below the critical utility type $\delta^\star(q_0)$.

Finally, to understand the sum within the parentheses in equation (6.18), consider the case where the distribution $F(\delta)$ has atoms. In this case, there is an additional reduction in trade flows because, when an investor has utility type δ and experiences a preference shock, she may draw $\delta' = \delta$ with a strictly positive probability, $\Delta F(\delta) > 0$, and thus not want to trade. This further reduces the trade flow relative to the case of a continuous distribution. We now provide the formal proof.

Proof. Applying formula (6.10) with the bounded function defined by

$$h(q,\delta) = \mathbf{1}_{\{q<q^\star(\delta)\}}$$

shows that the flow rate of purchases is given by

$$\begin{aligned}\varphi_p &= \frac{\lambda}{\gamma+\lambda}\int_{\mathcal{D}}\left(\lambda \mathbf{1}_{\{q^\star(\delta')<q^\star(\delta')\}} + \gamma\int_{\mathcal{D}} \mathbf{1}_{\{q^\star(\delta)<q^\star(\delta')\}} dF(\delta)\right) dF(\delta') \\ &= \frac{\gamma\lambda}{\gamma+\lambda}\int_{\mathcal{D}^2} \mathbf{1}_{\{q^\star(\delta)<q^\star(\delta')\}} dF(\delta) dF(\delta'), \qquad (6.19)\end{aligned}$$

where the second equality follows from the fact that the first integral is equal to zero. The same calculations applied to the function

$$h(q,\delta) = \mathbf{1}_{\{q>q^\star(\delta)\}}$$

show that the flow rate of sales is

$$\varphi_s = \frac{\gamma\lambda}{\gamma+\lambda}\int_{\mathcal{D}^2} \mathbf{1}_{\{q^\star(\delta')<q^\star(\delta)\}} dF(\delta) dF(\delta').$$

Relabeling δ as δ' and vice versa, it becomes clear that $\varphi_p = \varphi_s$. To derive the formula in the statement, note that

$$\left\{(\delta,\delta') : q^\star(\delta) < q^\star(\delta')\right\} = \left\{(\delta,\delta') : \delta' > \max\left(\delta, \delta^\star(q_0)\right)\right\}.$$

Therefore, it follows from (6.19) that

$$\frac{\gamma+\lambda}{\lambda}\varphi_p = F(\delta^\star(q_0))(1-F(\delta^\star(q_0))) + \int_{\delta^\star(q_0)}^{\bar{\delta}} dF(\delta)(1-F(\delta)),$$

and the standard integration-by-parts formula for Lebesgue-Stieltjes integrals (see for example Carter and Van Brunt [2000, Theorem 6.2.2]) shows that the last integral can be computed as

$$\int_{\delta^\star(q_0)}^{\bar{\delta}} dF(\delta)(1-F(\delta)) = \frac{1}{2}(1-F(\delta^\star(q_0)))^2 - \frac{1}{2}\sum_{\delta>\delta^\star(q_0)} (\Delta F(\delta))^2.$$

Collecting terms gives the formula of the lemma. □

To summarize, the model of semicentralized trade with divisible holdings and iid utility draws does not generate the buy-sell asymmetry observed in the data. However, as we describe in the notes at the end of the chapter, recent work by Cohen, Kargar, Lester, and Weill [2023] reveals that the model *can* generate this asymmetry with the addition of a relatively natural modification that requires that dealers hold assets as inventory before selling them to investors.

6.7 Exercises

Exercise 6.7: In this exercise we study the frictionless equilibrium with divisible asset holdings of section 6.2.

1. Establish the properties stated in Lemma 6.1.
2. Derive the market clearing price explicitly when investors have quadratic utility flow, as in section 6.4.1, and when they have isoelastic utility flow, as in section 6.4.2.
3. Derive the equilibrium distribution $\Phi(q, \delta)$ and characterize its support.

Exercise 6.8: In this exercise we explore a direct approach to the study of the HJB equation (6.3). Because standard contraction mapping theorems apply to spaces of bounded functions, we initially restrict the domain of asset holdings. Specifically, we fix an interval $\bar{Q} \subseteq [q_{\min}, q_{\max}]$ where

$$q_{\min} \leq \arg\min_{q \in Q} \left\{u(q, \underline{\delta}) - rP\right\} \leq \arg\max_{q \in Q} \left\{u(q, \overline{\delta}) - rP\right\} \leq q_{\max}$$

and consider the restricted HJB equation

$$rV(q, \delta) = u(q, \delta) + \gamma \mathbf{E}^F \left[V(q, \delta') - V(q, \delta)\right] \qquad (6.20)$$
$$+ \lambda_\theta \left(Pq - V(q, \delta)\right) + \lambda_\theta \max_{\vartheta \in [q_{\min}, q_{\max}]} \{V(\vartheta, \delta) - P\vartheta\},$$

defined over $(q, \delta) \in \bar{Q} \subseteq \times \mathcal{D}$. This HJB equation differs from the unrestricted one, (6.3), in two ways. First, its domain is the compact interval $\bar{Q}$ instead of the unbounded set $Q = [q_0, \infty)$. Second, investors are constrained to choose asset holdings in the bounded interval $[q_{\min}, q_{\max}]$.

1. Show that (6.20) defines a contraction mapping on the space of bounded functions defined over $\bar{Q} \times \mathcal{D}$.
2. Show that (6.20) has a unique solution in this space of bounded functions defined over $\bar{Q} \times \mathcal{D}$. Show that this solution is continuous in (q, δ) and, for each $\delta \in \mathcal{D}$, increasing and concave in $q \in \bar{Q}$.

3. Show that the solution can be extended to the domain $Q = [q_0, \infty)$.
4. Let

$$M(\delta) \equiv \lambda_\theta \max_{\theta \in [q_{\min}, q_{\max}]} \{V(\vartheta, \delta) - P\vartheta\}.$$

Show that the solution satisfies

$$V(q,\delta) = \frac{\lambda_\theta}{r+\lambda_\theta} Pq + \frac{1}{r+\gamma+\lambda_\theta}\left(u(q,\delta) + M(\delta) + \frac{\gamma}{r+\lambda_\theta}\mathbf{E}^F\left[u(q,\delta') + M(\delta')\right]\right). \tag{6.21}$$

5. Show that the constraint $\vartheta \in [q_{\min}, q_{\max}]$ does not bind: given the possibility to choose an asset holding $\vartheta \in Q$, the investor finds it optimal to choose $\vartheta \in [q_{\min}, q_{\max}]$. Conclude that the solution just constructed satisfies the unrestricted HJB equation (6.3).
6. Show that $V(q, \delta)$ is differentiable with respect to q and use (6.21) to derive an explicit expression for the marginal value function.

Exercise 6.9: The goal of this exercise is to prove formula (6.10) for calculating the moments of the stationary distribution Φ. To this end we rely on the change-of-variable formula given by Bogachev [2007, Theorem 3.6.1], which, in terms of our notation, can be stated as

$$\int_{\mathcal{D}\times\mathcal{D}} h \circ T(\delta',\delta)\, d\Psi(\delta',\delta) = \int_{[q^\star(\underline{\delta}), q^\star(\overline{\delta})]\times[\underline{\delta},\overline{\delta}]} h(q,\delta) d\left[\Psi \circ T^{-1}\right](q,\delta).$$

for any bounded function $h(q,\delta)$ on $[q^\star(\underline{\delta}), q^\star(\overline{\delta})] \times \mathcal{D}$, any bounded mapping $T : \mathcal{D}^2 \to [q^\star(\underline{\delta}), q^\star(\overline{\delta})] \times \mathcal{D}$, and any measure Ψ on the product $\mathcal{D} \times \mathcal{D}$.

1. Define

$$T(\delta',\delta) \equiv \left(q^\star(\delta'), \delta\right)$$

and

$$\Psi(\delta',\delta) \equiv \frac{\gamma}{\gamma+\lambda} F(\delta)F(\delta') + \frac{\lambda}{\gamma+\lambda} F(\min\{\delta',\delta\}).$$

Show that the equilibrium distribution satisfies $\Phi = \Psi \circ T^{-1}$.

2. Show that

$$\Psi(\delta',\delta) = \frac{\gamma}{\gamma+\lambda}\int_{\underline{\delta}}^{\delta'} dF(y)\int_{\underline{\delta}}^{\delta} dF(x) + \frac{\lambda}{\gamma+\lambda}\int_{\underline{\delta}}^{\delta}\int_{\underline{\delta}}^{\delta'} d\varepsilon_{\{x\}}(y)dF(x),$$

where $d\varepsilon_{\{x\}}(y)$ denotes the Dirac measure at x.

3. Combine the results of questions 1 and 2 to establish formula (6.10).

Exercise 6.10: Let $q_0 = 0$ and consider the utility flow function given by

$$u(q,\delta) \equiv \left\{ 1 - \frac{\log\left(1 + e^{1/\varepsilon(1-q^{1-\varepsilon}/(1-\varepsilon))}\right)}{\log\left(1+e^{1/\varepsilon}\right)} \right\} \delta$$

for some constant $\varepsilon \in (0,1)$.

1. Show that this function is strictly increasing and strictly concave in q, twice continuously differentiable with $u_{q\delta} > 0$, and satisfies Inada conditions.
2. Show that this utility flow function can be extended by continuity at the point $\varepsilon = 0$ to $u(\delta, q) = \delta \min\{q, 1\}$.
3. Use the theorem of the maximum to study the behavior of the target holdings function $q^\star(\delta, P|\varepsilon)$ as $\varepsilon \to 0$.
4. Assume that δ is distributed according to a continuous distribution $F(\delta)$. Study the equilibrium price and allocation as $\varepsilon \to 0$. How do these objects relate to the equilibrium studied in chapter 4?
5. Answer the same question as above but when the distribution is discrete with just two atoms, δ_L and δ_H.

Exercise 6.11: For this exercise assume that investors can have only two utility types, $\delta_L < \delta_H$, and have a quadratic utility flow function.

1. Study the frictionless price.
2. Suppose that all investors have the same λ. Show that the interdealer price is equal to the frictionless price.
3. Suppose that investors differ in their λ according to some distribution $G(\lambda)$ on a compact set $\Lambda \subseteq [0,\infty)$. Show that the interdealer price is equal to the frictionless price.
4. Argue that, in equilibrium, investors with meeting rate λ always trade the same size, $q^\star(\delta_H) - q^\star(\delta_L)$. Derive an explicit formula for this trade size and show that it is increasing in λ.
5. Derive a formula for the proportional transaction cost paid by an investor with meeting rate λ. Is that transaction cost always decreasing in λ? Why? Derive a condition on the parameters of the model for the transaction cost to be decreasing in λ.

6.8 Notes and References

The divisible asset holdings model of this chapter is designed to nest several contributions. Our derivation of equilibrium in section 6.3 is most closely related to Lagos and Rocheteau [2009]. The special case of quadratic utility flow in section 6.4.1 is due to Gârleanu [2009] and we note that several authors, including Duffie, Gârleanu, and Pedersen [2007], Vayanos and Weill [2008], and Praz [2015] have derived microfoundations for this functional form using exponential utility. The alternative formulation with isoelastic utility flow in section 6.4.2 is a special case of Lagos and Rocheteau [2009]. In addition, the derivation of the asset allocation and the equilibrium in the model with ex ante heterogeneous investors is based on Pinter and Üslü [2021], while the divisible asset holdings approximation of section 6.4.3 was proposed by Biais, Hombert, and Weill [2014].

In terms of testable implications that emerge from this class of models, the discussion of the relationship between trade size and proportional transaction costs, in section 6.6.1, extends results and discussions found in Lagos and Rocheteau [2009]. The symmetry (or lack thereof) of buys vs. sells, in section 6.6.2, is due to Cohen, Kargar, Lester, and Weill [2023]. They show that a natural way to generate asymmetry is to assume that dealers can buy any quantity from customers but they can only sell assets that they already hold in inventory—what they call a "inventory-in-advance" constraint.

It is worth noting that our discussion of the relationship between search frictions and asset prices is in line with results derived elsewhere on the impact of transaction costs on demand and prices. At a high level, these studies find that transaction costs make investors want to trade less—they buy and sell smaller quantities—which shifts supply and demand in the same direction, so that the net effect on demand is indeterminate. This indeterminacy was noted in, e.g., Rostek and Weretka [2015], who study an environment in which transaction costs are induced by price impact (see p. 2959, footnote 20).

We conclude with two remarks. First, as we hope this chapter illustrates, the semicentralized market model is quite flexible and can be extended in a variety of ways to better tackle OTC market data. Recent examples of extensions that have been taken to the data, using either calibration or structural estimation, include Feldhütter [2012], Pinter and Üslü [2021], Cohen et al. [2023], Wu [2021], and Palleja [2022]. Second, while we focused here on extending the *semicentralized* market model to allow for divisible asset holdings, several important papers have done the same with *pure decentralized* markets. These include Afonso and Lagos [2015a], Üslü [2019], Brancaccio and Kang [2022], Üslü and Velioğlu [2019], Wong and Zhang [2022], Coen and Coen [2022], and Lagos and Navarro [2023], among others.

7

Frictional Intermediation

In this chapter we develop a model of a two-tiered OTC market with customers and dealers. As in the semicentralized OTC market model of chapter 4, customers in this model periodically experience preference shocks and search for a dealer with whom to bargain and trade one unit of the asset. The key innovation relative to this benchmark is that, in order to reproduce some salient characteristics of trade data, we assume that *the interdealer market is itself an OTC market.* More specifically, instead of assuming that dealers trade in a frictionless market, we model the dealer sector as a purely decentralized OTC market similar to that of chapter 5.

This rich, yet fully tractable, framework allows us to confront a number of recently documented empirical regularities about the OTC intermediation process. In particular, we show that the model generates endogenous intermediation chains and that, consistent with the data, dealers differ with respect to their position within these chains, the frequency and direction of their trades, and their contribution to trading volume. To quantify important unobservable characteristics of the market—including the bargaining power of agents and the rate at which they contact counterparties—we then calibrate the model to data from the market for municipal bonds, which is among the most active OTC markets in the United States.

7.1 The Model

As in previous chapters, we consider a continuous-time, infinite-horizon model of an economy populated by risk-neutral agents who discount the future at some rate $r > 0$ and derive utility from holding a durable asset with supply equal to $s > 0$. The market for this asset is populated by two groups of agents who can each hold zero or one unit of the asset: a continuum of *dealers* with mass $m > 0$, and a continuum of investors or *customers* with mass normalized to 1. We assume that

$$m < s < 1$$

so that i) the dealer sector has a smaller mass than the customer sector and ii) the customer sector is large enough to absorb the total supply of assets, but the dealer sector is not. The latter restriction simplifies the analysis but has no bearing on the key results of this chapter.

Each agent enjoys a utility flow δ_t from holding the asset at time $t \geq 0$. The utility flow process of a given agent depends on whether she is a customer or a dealer but is independent from that of any other agent. Specifically, we assume that the utility flow of a customer follows a Markov jump process with arrival rate $\gamma > 0$ and a *discrete* reset distribution with two atoms,

$$F_c(\delta) = \mathbf{1}_{\{\delta_L \leq \delta\}} f_L + \mathbf{1}_{\{\delta_H \leq \delta\}} f_H,$$

for some $\delta_L < \delta_H$ and $f_j \in (0, 1)$ with $f_L + f_H = 1$. On the other hand, dealers have heterogeneous but *permanent* utility flows that are distributed according to a *continuous* distribution $F(\delta)$ on some open interval $\mathcal{D} \equiv (\underline{\delta}, \overline{\delta})$.

There are two matching technologies that provide opportunities for trade between agents: each dealer contacts another randomly selected dealer at rate $\lambda > 0$ and a randomly selected customer at rate $\rho > 0$, which implies that a given customer is contacted by a randomly selected dealer at rate ρm. These matching technologies capture, in a simple way, the observation that the interdealer market appears to have less friction than the customer-to-dealer market (see section 2.4 in chapter 2). Finally, we assume that customers cannot contact each other directly and thus can trade only through the dealers. This assumption is imposed primarily for simplicity, but it is also consistent with the observation that, in practice, there are few direct trades between customers in most OTC markets. See, for example, table 2.1 in chapter 2 for data on the corporate bond market.

When two agents are matched and there are gains from trade, they bargain over the price of the asset. As in previous chapters, we take the outcome to be the generalized Nash bargaining solution. In a dealer-to-dealer match, the bargaining power of a dealer with asset holding $q \in \{0, 1\}$ is set to $\theta_q \in (0, 1)$, with $\theta_0 + \theta_1 = 1$, while in a customer-to-dealer match the bargaining power of the dealer is set to $\theta \in (0, 1)$.

Figure 7.1 illustrates the flow of customers (double arrows) and the potential flows of assets (single arrows). As is clear from the figure, trades between customers must necessarily be intermediated by dealers. However, whether or not some dealers find it optimal to intermediate these transactions is ultimately an equilibrium outcome.

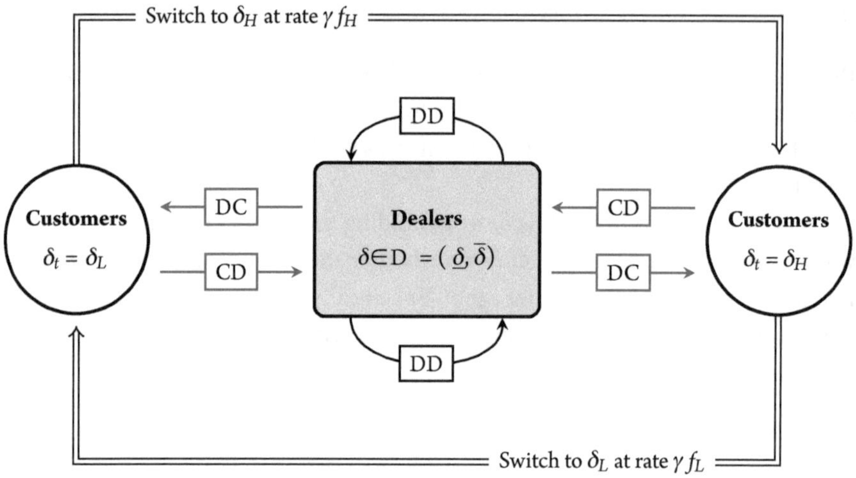

FIGURE 7.1. Flows of agents and assets

This figure illustrates the flows of customers (double arrows) and the *potential* flows of assets (single arrows) resulting from trades among dealers (DD) and between customers and dealers (CD|DC).

7.2 Optimal Trading Behavior

7.2.1 Notations

Denote by $V(q, \delta)$ the value function of a dealer with utility flow $\delta \in \mathcal{D}$ who holds q units of the asset, and by $W(q, \delta_j)$ the value function of a customer with utility flow $\delta_j \in \{\delta_L, \delta_H\}$ who holds q units of the asset. As in previous chapters, the *reservation value* of an agent is defined as the difference between the value of owning and not owning an asset, i.e.,

$$R(\delta) \equiv V(1, \delta) - V(0, \delta)$$

for dealers, and

$$C_j \equiv W(1, \delta_j) - W(0, \delta_j), \quad \text{with} \quad j \in \{L, H\},$$

for customers. Given our assumed bargaining protocol and the existence of gains from trade, the price at which a dealer with utility flow δ trades with a customer with utility flow δ_j is

$$\theta C_j + (1 - \theta) R(\delta). \tag{7.1}$$

Likewise, a dealer with utility flow x who owns the asset will sell to a dealer with utility flow δ who does not own the asset at price

$$\theta_0 R(x) + \theta_1 R(\delta), \tag{7.2}$$

provided that the nonowner values the asset more than the owner in the sense that his reservation value is higher than that of the owner.

Denote by $\Phi_q(x) \in [0, m]$ the measure of dealers who have utility flow $\delta \leq x$ and hold q units of the asset, and by $\mu_{jq} \in [0, 1]$ the measure of customers with utility flow $\delta_j \in \{\delta_L, \delta_H\}$ who hold q units of the asset. These measures will be endogenously determined in equilibrium, subject to

$$f_j = \mu_{j0} + \mu_{j1}, \qquad j \in \{L, H\}, \tag{7.3a}$$

$$mF(\delta) = \Phi_0(\delta) + \Phi_1(\delta), \qquad \delta \in \mathcal{D}, \tag{7.3b}$$

$$s = \mu_{L1} + \mu_{H1} + \Phi_1(\bar{\delta}). \tag{7.3c}$$

Equations (7.3a) and (7.3b) simply require that the joint steady-state distributions of utility flows and asset holdings be consistent with the exogenous cross-sectional distributions of utility flows in the populations of customers and dealers. Equation (7.3c) is a market-clearing condition that ensures that the measure of agents (customers and/or dealers) who own the asset is equal to the total supply of assets.

7.2.2 Reservation Values

In this section we take as given a set of distributions such that (7.3) holds and determine the resulting value functions for all agents in the market.

Using (7.1) and (7.2) shows that the Hamilton-Jacobi-Bellman (HJB) equation that governs the optimal behavior of dealers is given by

$$\begin{aligned} rV(q,\delta) = q\delta &+ \sum_{j \in \{L,H\}} \rho\mu_{j,1-q}\theta\left((2q-1)\left(C_j - R(\delta)\right)\right)^+ \\ &+ \lambda \int_{\underline{\delta}}^{\bar{\delta}} \theta_q\left((2q-1)\left(R(x) - R(\delta)\right)\right)^+ \frac{d\Phi_{1-q}(x)}{m}. \end{aligned} \tag{7.4}$$

This equation is easily interpreted. For example, a dealer with $q = 1$ and utility flow δ enjoys that utility flow until one of two events occurs. First, with intensity $\rho\mu_{j0}$, the dealer contacts a customer nonowner with utility flow δ_j. If there are gains from trade, then the dealer sells and receives a fraction θ of the trade surplus $C_j - R(\delta)$. Second, with intensity λ, the dealer contacts another dealer, who is a nonowner of type

x with probability $d\Phi_0(x)/m$. If there are gains from trade, then the owner sells to the nonowner and receives a fraction θ_1 of the trade surplus $R(x) - R(\delta)$.

Subtracting (7.4) with asset holding $q = 0$ from its counterpart with $q = 1$ shows that the reservation value function of dealers satisfies

$$rR(\delta) = \delta + \rho\theta \sum_{j \in \{L,H\}} \left(\mu_{j,0}\left(C_j - R(\delta)\right)^+ - \mu_{j,1}\left(R(\delta) - C_j\right)^+\right) \tag{7.5}$$
$$+ \lambda\theta_1 \int_{\underline{\delta}}^{\overline{\delta}} (R(x) - R(\delta))^+ \frac{d\Phi_0(x)}{m}$$
$$- \lambda\theta_0 \int_{\underline{\delta}}^{\overline{\delta}} (R(\delta) - R(x))^+ \frac{d\Phi_1(x)}{m}.$$

Notice that, as with reservation value equations in previous chapters, there are both positive and negative terms on the right-hand side of (7.5) because the dealer's reservation value takes into account two opposing option values from continuing to search. On the one hand, a dealer who acquires the asset gains the option of searching for another dealer or a customer who will pay even more, and this option increases the dealer's reservation value. On the other hand, a dealer who acquires the asset forgoes the option of searching for a dealer or a customer who might sell at an even lower price, and this decreases her reservation value.

Similar steps show that the reservation value C_j of a customer with current utility flow $\delta_j \in \{\delta_L, \delta_H\}$ satisfies

$$rC_j = \delta_j + \sum_{k \in \{L,H\}} \gamma f_k \left(C_k - C_j\right) \tag{7.6}$$
$$+ \rho m(1-\theta) \int_{\underline{\delta}}^{\overline{\delta}} \left(\left(R(x) - C_j\right)^+ \frac{d\Phi_0(x)}{m} - \left(C_j - R(x)\right)^+ \frac{d\Phi_1(x)}{m}\right).$$

There are two key differences between the reservation values of dealers and customers that are evident in (7.5) and (7.6). First, customers switch types, as indicated by the second term on the right of (7.6), while dealers do not. Second, customers do not trade directly with other customers and, therefore, only have the option to search for dealers if they want to adjust their holdings.

The next result establishes fundamental properties of reservation values that hold regardless of the distributions of types and asset holdings.

Proposition 7.1: There exists a unique triple $(C_L, C_H, R(\delta))$ that solves the system of reservation value equations given by (7.5) and (7.6). Furthermore, $C_L < C_H$ and the function $R : \mathcal{D} \to \mathbf{R}$ is continuous, bounded, and strictly increasing.

Proof. The method we use to establish this proposition is similar to that we used in chapters 4 and 5 with one important difference: since there are two classes of agents, we are now dealing with a *system* of functional equations rather than with a single functional equation. To circumvent this difficulty we fix an open interval $\overline{\mathcal{D}}$ containing $\{\delta_L, \delta_H\} \cup \mathcal{D}$ and reformulate the system as a single fixed-point equation over the set of functions from $\{c, d\} \times \overline{\mathcal{D}}$ to $\mathbf{R}$. The proofs then essentially work as in the one-dimensional case. See Hugonnier, Lester, and Weill [2020, appendix A] for details. □

7.2.3 Trading Patterns and Equilibrium Configurations

The monotonicity of reservation values established in Proposition 7.1 implies that, irrespective of the underlying distributions, the optimal trading strategies share two key features. The first is that customers follow a *reservation dealer* strategy: they sell only to dealers with sufficiently high utility flows, and buy only from dealers with sufficiently low utility flows. The second is that, in a meeting between a dealer-owner of type δ and a dealer-nonowner of type δ', there are strictly positive gains from trade *if and only if* $\delta' > \delta$. As a result, once assets enter the dealer sector, they are optimally traded along *intermediation chains* from dealers with low utility flows to dealers with higher utility flows until they are finally sold to a customer.

These individual trading patterns in turn have aggregate implications for the type of equilibria that may exist. Specifically, as we illustrate in figure 7.2, they imply that there are six possible configurations depending on the position of the interval of dealer reservation values, $[R(\underline{\delta}), R(\overline{\delta})]$, relative to the interval between customer reservation values, $[C_L, C_H]$. If these sets do not intersect, as in the configurations labeled NT_0 and NT_1 in the figure, then all dealers are willing to trade with all customers but only in one direction: they only sell in NT_0 and only buy in NT_1. As a result, in a steady-state equilibrium with one of these configurations, dealers are either all owners (NT_1) or all nonowners (NT_0). In both cases, they all remain inactive, or dormant, so we refer to such equilibria simply as *no-trade* equilibria.

If the two sets intersect, as in configurations AI_1–AI_4, then dealers with reservation values in $[C_L, C_H]$ (solid) are willing to buy the asset from low-type customers and to sell to high-type customers, whereas dealers with reservation values outside that interval (dashed segment) are willing to execute trades with *all* customer types but only in one direction. Therefore, in a steady-state equilibrium with such a configuration of reservation values, the latter group does not trade while the former provides *active intermediation*: dealers in the active group buy assets from customer owners who recently switched to the low type, then trade the asset among themselves at increasing prices along an intermediation chain, and eventually resell to customer nonowners who recently switched to the high type.

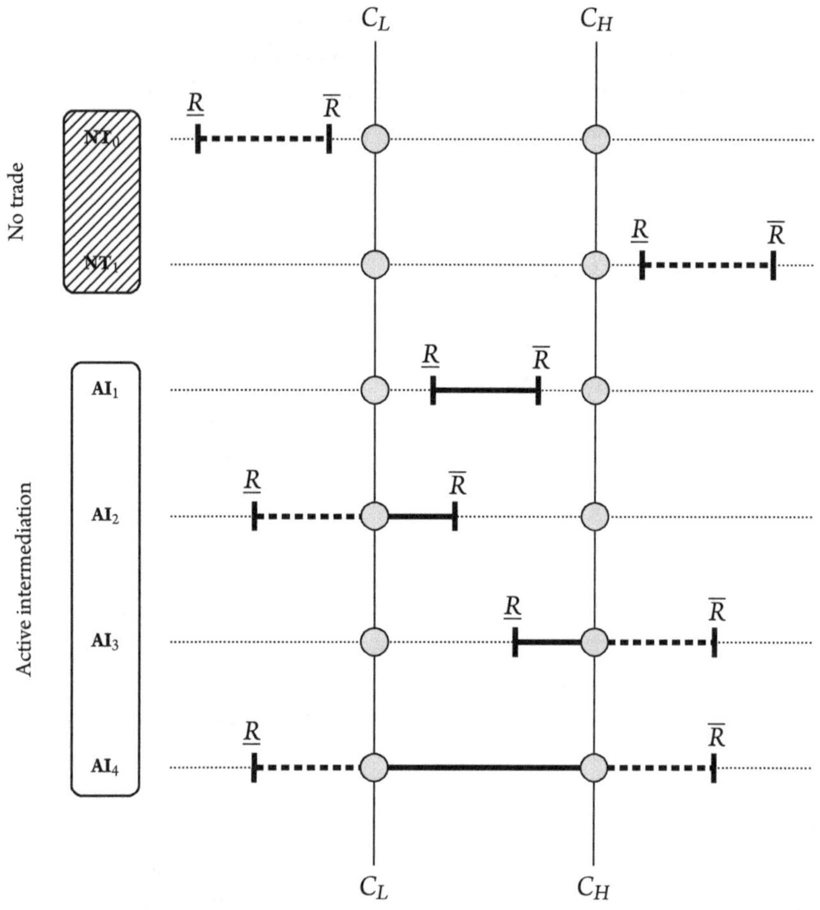

FIGURE 7.2. Equilibrium configurations of reservation values

This figure illustrates the possible equilibrium configurations of the reservation values $[\underline{R}, \overline{R}] \equiv [R(\underline{\delta}), R(\overline{\delta})]$ of dealers and $\{C_L, C_H\}$ of customers. In each configuration the solid segment indicates the set of active dealers while the dashed segments indicate the set of inactive, or dormant, dealers.

7.3 Equilibrium

7.3.1 Parameterized Equilibrium Distributions

The discussion above, along with the monotonicity of reservation values, implies that in any steady-state equilibrium there are constants

$$(\delta_0, \delta_1) \in \mathcal{D}_a \equiv \left\{(x, y) \in \mathcal{D}^2 : x \leq y\right\}$$

such that dealers with utility flows in $(\underline{\delta}, \delta_0)$ are nonowners who do not trade; dealers with utility flow in $[\delta_0, \delta_1]$ provide active intermediation by buying from low-type customers and selling to high-type customers; and dealers with utility flows in $(\delta_1, \overline{\delta})$ are owners who do not trade. This, in turn, suggests that a natural way to construct a steady-state equilibrium is to first solve for the distributions of types and asset holdings induced by an arbitrary pair $(\delta_0, \delta_1) \in \mathcal{D}_a$, and then to endogenously determine (δ_0, δ_1) by requiring that only dealers with utility flows in $[\delta_0, \delta_1]$ find it weakly optimal to provide active intermediation.

To implement this approach, fix an arbitrary pair $(\delta_0, \delta_1) \in \mathcal{D}_a$ and consider the stationary distributions of utility flows and asset holdings induced by the trading and holding patterns described above. Given (7.3a) and (7.3b), it is enough to solve for two of the four customer measures, say (μ_{L1}, μ_{H0}), and one of the distributions among dealers, say $\Phi_1(\delta)$. Correspondingly, it is sufficient to state only three inflow-outflow equations. Namely, the two measures of customers and the distribution among dealer-owners must satisfy

$$\gamma \left(f_L \mu_{H1} - f_H \mu_{L1}\right) = \rho m \left(\Phi_0(\delta_1) - \Phi_0(\delta_0)\right) \mu_{L1}, \tag{7.7a}$$

$$\gamma \left(f_H \mu_{L0} - f_L \mu_{H0}\right) = \rho m \left(\Phi_1(\delta_1) - \Phi_1(\delta_0)\right) \mu_{H0}, \tag{7.7b}$$

and

$$\begin{aligned} \lambda \Phi_1(\delta) \left(\Phi_0(\delta_1) - \Phi_0(\delta)\right) = {} & \rho m \left(\Phi_0(\delta) - \Phi_0(\delta_0)\right) \mu_{L1} \\ & - \rho m \left(\Phi_1(\delta) - \Phi_1(\delta_0)\right) \mu_{H0} \end{aligned} \tag{7.7c}$$

for all $\delta \in [\delta_0, \delta_1]$ subject to (7.3), and

$$\Phi_1(\delta) = 0, \qquad \delta \leq \delta_0, \tag{7.7d}$$

$$\Phi_1(\delta) - \Phi_1(\delta_1) = m(F(\delta) - F(\delta_1)), \qquad \delta \geq \delta_1. \tag{7.7e}$$

In both (7.7a) and (7.7b), the left-hand side is the net inflow from preference shocks while the right-hand side captures the net outflow from trading with dealers whose utility flows lie in the interval $[\delta_0, \delta_1]$. Similarly, in (7.7c) the left-hand side represents the outflow from interdealer trades, given that dealers with utility flows in $[\delta_0, \delta_1]$ trade among themselves in a frictional OTC market, and the right-hand side is the net inflow from dealers with utility flows in $(\delta_0, \delta]$ who enter the set by buying from low-type customer-owners or exit by selling to high-type customer-nonowners. Finally, (7.7d) and (7.7e) are boundary conditions that account for the fact that, under the assumed configuration, all dealers with utility flow below δ_0 (above δ_1) are nonowners (owners).

The following proposition provides closed-form expressions for the unique solution to this system of equations. To state the result, let

$$G(z) \equiv -\frac{1}{2}\left(m_0 - mz + \varrho(\mu_{L1} + \mu_{H0})\right) + \frac{1}{2}\sqrt{\left(m_0 - mz + \varrho(\mu_{L1} + \mu_{H0})\right)^2 + 4\varrho\mu_{L1}mz}, \tag{7.8}$$

where the ratio $\varrho \equiv \rho m/\lambda$ measures the speed of dealer-to-customer trading relative to that of interdealer trading and m_q denotes the mass of active dealers holding $q \in \{0, 1\}$ units of the asset.

***Proposition* 7.2:** The unique solutions to (7.3) and (7.7) are continuous functions of the pair $(\delta_0, \delta_1) \in \mathcal{D}_a$ that are explicitly given by

$$\mu_{L1} = f_L - \mu_{L0} = \frac{\gamma f_L f_H m_1}{\rho m_0 m_1 + \gamma(m_0 f_L + m_1 f_H)},$$

$$\mu_{H0} = f_H - \mu_{H1} = \frac{\gamma f_L f_H m_0}{\rho m_0 m_1 + \gamma(m_0 f_L + m_1 f_H)},$$

and

$$\Phi_1(\delta) = mF(\delta) - \Phi_0(\delta) = \begin{cases} 0 & \text{if } \delta \le \delta_0, \\ G\left(F(\delta) - F(\delta_0)\right) & \text{if } \delta_0 < \delta \le \delta_1, \\ m_1 + m\left(F(\delta) - F(\delta_1)\right) & \text{if } \delta > \delta_1, \end{cases}$$

where

$$m_1 = \Phi_1(\delta_1) - \Phi_1(\delta_0),$$

$$m_0 = \Phi_0(\delta_1) - \Phi_0(\delta_0) = m\left(F(\delta_1) - F(\delta_0)\right) - m_1,$$

and the constant m_1 is the unique solution to

$$s = m_1 + m(1 - F(\delta_1)) + f_H + \frac{\gamma f_L f_H(m_1 - m_0)}{\rho m_0 m_1 + \gamma(m_0 f_L + m_1 f_H)}$$

in the interval $[0, m]$.

7.3.2 Equilibrium Existence and Basic Properties

We now exploit the results above to construct an equilibrium. Proposition 7.2 establishes that any pair $(\delta_0, \delta_1) \in \mathcal{D}_a$ induces joint distributions of utility flows and asset holdings. Taking these distributions as given allows all agents in the model to compute their reservation values, and these reservation values in turn determine with whom each agent finds it optimal to trade. In particular, they pin down the interval of dealers who find it optimal to be active,

$$\left[\hat{\delta}_0, \hat{\delta}_1\right] = \left\{\delta \in \mathcal{D} : \min\left\{C_L, R(\bar{\delta})\right\} \leq R(\delta) \leq \max\left\{C_H, R(\underline{\delta})\right\}\right\},$$

and an equilibrium is reached if this set coincides with the interval of active dealers that we started with. Formally, a pair $(\delta_0, \delta_1) \in \mathcal{D}_a$ gives rise to a steady-state equilibrium if and only if it solves the two-dimensional fixed-point problem

$$\delta_0 = \hat{\delta}_0 = \min\left\{\delta \in \mathcal{D} : R(\delta) \geq \min\left\{C_L, R(\bar{\delta})\right\}\right\},$$

$$\delta_1 = \hat{\delta}_1 = \max\left\{\delta \in \mathcal{D} : R(\delta) \leq \max\left\{C_H, R(\underline{\delta})\right\}\right\},$$

where reservation values are implicit functions of the distributions as described in Proposition 7.1 and distributions are implicit functions of (δ_0, δ_1) as described in Proposition 7.2. To prove that such a fixed point exists, we show in Hugonnier, Lester, and Weill [2020] that the mapping $(\delta_0, \delta_1) \mapsto (\hat{\delta}_0, \hat{\delta}_1)$ from the compact set $\mathcal{D}_a$ into itself is continuous and then apply Brouwer's fixed-point theorem to obtain the following conclusion.

***Theorem* 7.3:** There exists a steady-state equilibrium.

The existence of an equilibrium does not imply trade. In the model, whether dealers find it optimal to engage in active intermediation is ultimately an equilibrium outcome, and one may be concerned that the above application of Brouwer's fixed-point theorem only picks up no-trade equilibria, which are common in search-theoretic environments (see, e.g., Diamond [1971]). The next proposition sheds light on the incentives to intermediate by providing necessary and sufficient conditions under which at least some dealers trade with customers. To state the result let

$$B_j \equiv \mathbf{E}\left[\int_0^t e^{-rt}\delta_t dt \,\middle|\, \delta_0 = \delta_j\right] = \frac{r\delta_j + \gamma \mathbf{E}^{F_c}[\delta]}{r(r+\gamma)}$$

denote the buy-and-hold value of an asset to a customer with current utility flow equal to $\delta_j \in \{\delta_L, \delta_H\}$.

Proposition 7.4: A no-trade equilibrium with configuration NT_0 as depicted in the top panel of figure 7.2 exists if and only if

$$\frac{\overline{\delta}+\rho\theta(1-s)\mathbf{E}^{F_c}[B_j]}{r+\rho\theta(1-s)} \leq B_L, \tag{7.9}$$

whereas a no-trade equilibrium with configuration NT_1 exists if and only if

$$\frac{\underline{\delta}+\rho\theta(s-m)\mathbf{E}^{F_c}[B_j]}{r+\rho\theta(s-m)} \geq B_H. \tag{7.10}$$

In particular, all steady-state equilibria induce active intermediation by at least some dealers if and only if (7.9) and (7.10) both fail.

Conditions (7.9) and (7.10) are obtained by considering the configurations that lead to no-trade equilibria, and checking whether some dealers have incentive to intermediate rather than stay inactive. For example, in configuration NT_0, dealers do not hold any asset and do not purchase from customers. Since reservation values are strictly increasing, such an equilibrium can only exist if dealers with the highest utility flow have no incentive to buy from low-type customers. A direct calculation shows that, in configuration NT_0, the reservation value of dealers with utility flow $\overline{\delta}$ is

$$R(\overline{\delta}|\mathrm{NT}_0) \equiv \frac{\overline{\delta}+\rho\theta(1-s)\mathbf{E}^{F_c}[B_j]}{r+\rho\theta(1-s)},$$

where the terms featuring the contact rate ρ account for the fact that *if* a dealer with utility flow $\overline{\delta}$ held an asset he would sell it at the first occasion to anyone in the mass $1-s$ of customer-nonowners. Comparing this reservation value to the buy-and-hold value of low-type customers yields (7.9).

Similarly, in the equilibrium associated with configuration NT_1, the reservation value of low-type dealers is

$$R(\underline{\delta}|\mathrm{NT}_1) \equiv \frac{\underline{\delta}+\rho\theta(s-m)\mathbf{E}^{F_c}[B_j]}{r+\rho\theta(s-m)},$$

where the terms featuring ρ account for the fact that if a dealer with utility flow $\underline{\delta}$ was without an asset he would buy one from anyone in the mass $s-m$ of customer-owners. Condition (7.10) then follows by comparing this reservation value to the buy-and-hold value of high-type customers.

Note that (7.9) and (7.10) also provide intuitive comparative statics. In particular, they show that the dealers' incentives to intermediate increase—in the sense that both inequalities become tighter—as the contact rate ρ between customers and dealers increases, as the bargaining power θ of dealers increases, as the spread $B_H - B_L$ between the buy and hold values of the two types of customers increases, and as the mass m of dealers decreases.

A natural question is whether the steady-state equilibrium is unique. While we are not able to answer this question in full generality, we provide easily verifiable sufficient conditions as well as explicit expressions for the resulting equilibrium in the next theorem.

***Theorem* 7.5:** Assume that

$$r\left(rB_H - \overline{\delta}\right) \geq (\lambda\theta_0 - \rho m(1-\theta))^- \left(\overline{\delta} - \mathbf{E}^F[\delta]\right) \tag{7.11a}$$

and

$$r\left(\underline{\delta} - rB_L\right) \geq (\lambda\theta_1 - \rho m(1-\theta))^- \left(\mathbf{E}^F[\delta] - \underline{\delta}\right). \tag{7.11b}$$

Then the steady-state equilibrium is unique and has $[\delta_0, \delta_1] = \mathrm{cl}(\mathcal{D})$ so that all dealers are active. In this case

$$R(\delta) = R(\underline{\delta}) + \int_{\underline{\delta}}^{\delta} \sigma(x)dx,$$

with the local interdealer surplus function

$$\frac{1}{\sigma(\delta)} \equiv r + \rho\theta\left(\mu_{L1} + \mu_{H0}\right) + \frac{\lambda\theta_0}{m}\Phi_1(\delta) + \frac{\lambda\theta_1}{m}\left(\Phi_0(\overline{\delta}) - \Phi_0(\delta)\right), \tag{7.12}$$

and the reservation values of dealers with the lowest utility flow, low-type customers, and high-type customers solve the linear system given by

$$rR(\underline{\delta}) = \underline{\delta} + \rho\theta\left(C_H - R(\underline{\delta})\right)\mu_{H0}$$
$$- \rho\theta\left(R(\underline{\delta}) - C_L\right)\mu_{L1} + \frac{\lambda\theta_1}{m}\int_{\underline{\delta}}^{\overline{\delta}} (m_0 - \Phi_0(x))\sigma(x)dx$$

and

$$rC_L = \delta_L + \gamma\left(C_H - C_L\right)f_H$$
$$+ \rho(1-\theta)\left(m_0\left(R(\underline{\delta}) - C_L\right) + \int_{\underline{\delta}}^{\overline{\delta}} (m_0 - \Phi_0(x))\sigma(x)dx\right)$$

$$rC_H = \delta_H + \gamma\,(C_L - C_H) f_L \\ + \rho(1-\theta)\left(m_1 \left(R(\underline{\delta}) - C_H\right) + \int_{\underline{\delta}}^{\overline{\delta}} (m_1 - \Phi_1(x))\sigma(x)dx \right),$$

where the measures of customers and active dealers are defined as in Proposition 7.2, albeit with the thresholds $\delta_0 = \underline{\delta}$ and $\delta_1 = \overline{\delta}$.

Conditions (7.11a) and (7.11b) ensure that, regardless of the distributions, the reservation values of agents satisfy

$$C_L \leq R(\underline{\delta}) < R(\overline{\delta}) \leq C_H$$

so that all equilibria are in configuration AI_1 of figure 7.2. In this case, there are no dormant dealers and the equilibrium trading patterns are independent of reservation values. Therefore, the equilibrium distributions correspond to the interval of active dealers $[\delta_0, \delta_1] = \mathrm{cl}(\mathcal{D})$ and can be derived independently of the reservation values of agents, which clearly ensures the uniqueness of the steady-state equilibrium.

7.4 The Intermediation Process

Building on our equilibrium characterization, we now derive a number of key statistics of interest in the empirical literature. The benefits of doing so are threefold. First, it allows us to explore the qualitative relationships between various endogenous outcomes, and to better understand how they are affected by features of the environment, including the preferences of agents and the technologies that determine the matching and bargaining processes. Second, the simple expressions we derive facilitate the calibration of the model, which we use in section 7.5 to study the municipal bond market. Lastly, these derivations provide a toolkit for the quantitative analysis of other markets, where transaction-level data may just (or soon) become available.

Throughout this section, we restrict our attention to model parameters that are consistent with an equilibrium in which all dealers are active (e.g., parameters satisfying the conditions of Theorem 7.5). This is without much loss for the analysis that follows since, by definition, the characteristics and behavior of dormant dealers are not observable. Therefore, any steady-state equilibrium with active intermediation and dormant dealers is observationally equivalent to another in which all dealers are active. In particular, if we trim out dormant dealers, adjust the contact rates by the share of active dealers, and remove from the total supply the assets held by dormant dealers, then the full participation equilibrium of the modified environment delivers the same transactions and prices as the original environment. In this sense, our analysis is unaffected by this restriction. However, it is worth noting that this restriction may entail some loss for other interesting questions. For example, analyzing changes in the size of the dealer sector requires studying regions of the parameter space where $|\delta_0 - \delta_1| < |\mathcal{D}|$ so that the willingness of dealers to intermediate is sensitive to market conditions.

7.4.1 Trading Intensities and Inventory Durations

In a steady-state equilibrium where all dealers are active, a customer-owner sells his asset to dealers at rate ρm_0 while a customer-nonowner buys from dealers at rate ρm_1. Therefore, basic properties of exponential random variables imply that, conditional on not first changing utility flow, the expected time required for a low-type customer to sell is

$$\frac{1}{\rho m_0 + \gamma f_H},$$

and the expected time required for a high-type customer to buy is

$$\frac{1}{\rho m_1 + \gamma f_L}.$$

Naturally, both of these average durations are decreasing in the contact rate ρ and the masses of active dealers (m_0, m_1). Note that they are also decreasing in the rates at which customers transition between utility flows, $(\gamma f_L, \gamma f_H)$. This is because of selection: as preference shocks arrive more frequently, the set of customers who trade before changing utility flows becomes more selected toward those who trade quickly.

The rate at which a dealer buys or sells an asset depends on his utility flow. In particular, a dealer-nonowner with utility flow δ buys at a rate

$$\Lambda_0(\delta) \equiv \rho \mu_{L1} + \frac{\lambda}{m} \Phi_1(\delta),$$

which is the sum of the rate at which he buys from low-type customer-owners, $\rho \mu_{L1}$, and the rate at which he buys from dealer-owners with lower utility flows than his own, $(\lambda/m)\Phi_1(\delta)$. Similarly, a dealer-owner with utility flow δ sells at a rate

$$\Lambda_1(\delta) \equiv \rho \mu_{H0} + \frac{\lambda}{m} (m_0 - \Phi_0(\delta)), \tag{7.13}$$

which combines the rate at which he sells to high-type customers and the rate at which he sells to dealers with higher utility flows than his own. Since $\Phi_q(\delta)$ is nondecreasing in δ, dealers with utility flows close to either $\underline{\delta}$ or $\overline{\delta}$ meet fewer willing counterparties and thus trade at a slower pace than dealers with more moderate utility flows.

A key indicator of market liquidity is the average amount of time it takes a dealer-owner to sell an asset or, equivalently, the average inventory duration in the dealer sector.

Lemma 7.6: The average inventory duration is

$$\int_{\underline{\delta}}^{\overline{\delta}} \frac{1}{\Lambda_1(\delta)} \left(\frac{d\Phi_1(\delta)}{m_1} \right) = \frac{1}{\rho\mu_{H0}} \left(1 - \frac{\chi}{2(1+\chi)} \right), \tag{7.14}$$

where the constant

$$\chi \equiv \frac{\lambda m_0}{m} \frac{1}{\rho\mu_{H0}} = \frac{\lambda m_1}{m} \frac{1}{\rho\mu_{L1}} \tag{7.15}$$

measures the intensity with which dealers contact other dealers relative to that with which they meet customers.

Proof. Equations (7.7a)–(7.7c) imply that

$$\frac{1}{\Lambda_1(x)} = \frac{1}{\rho\mu_{H0}} \left(\frac{\rho m \mu_{L1} + \lambda \Phi_1(x)}{\rho m \mu_{L1} + \lambda m_1} \right).$$

Substituting this identity below the integral in (7.14) and implementing the change of variable $z = \Phi_1(x)/m_1$ then gives

$$\int_{\underline{\delta}}^{\overline{\delta}} \frac{1}{\Lambda_1(x)} \left(\frac{d\Phi_1(x)}{m_1} \right) = \frac{1}{\rho\mu_{H0}} \int_0^1 \left(\frac{1+\chi z}{1+\chi} \right) dz,$$

and the result now follows by computing this integral. □

The formula (7.14) for the average inventory duration explicitly accounts for two effects. First, dealer-owners are heterogeneous and each utility flow δ is subject to a different inventory duration, $1/\Lambda_1(\delta)$. Second, the distribution $\Phi_1(\delta)$ of utility flows across dealer-owners is endogenous: dealers with high utility flows and, thus, long inventory durations are overrepresented among owners, relative to the underlying distribution.

Interestingly, equation (7.14) reveals that the average inventory duration does *not* go to zero as $\lambda \to \infty$ (and so $\chi \to \infty$), which clearly illustrates that the endogenous distribution can be a crucial determinant of average inventory duration. Indeed, the distribution of utility flows among dealer-owners, as measured by $\Phi_1(\delta)$ on the left-hand side of (7.14), becomes nearly efficient as search frictions in the interdealer market vanish. As a result, even though there are increasingly more meetings between dealer-owners and nonowners, more and more of these meetings have no gains from trade.

Interestingly, this implies that as $\lambda \to \infty$ the equilibrium of our model does not converge to that of Duffie, Gârleanu, and Pedersen [2005] (see example 4.1 in chapter 4), where the interdealer market is frictionless and inventory duration is zero. This is because, in Duffie et al. [2005], a dealer who buys an asset can immediately locate a dealer who is in contact with a customer-buyer. In the limit of our model, a dealer who purchases an asset can also immediately locate some other dealer-nonowner, but the probability that this dealer is also in contact with a customer-buyer is zero.

***Remark* 7.7:** In the comparative statics above, we are varying λ while holding (m_0, m_1) and (μ_{H0}, μ_{L1}) constant. By doing so we are implicitly assuming that the equilibrium values of these objects do not depend on λ, which is indeed the case as long as all dealers remain active in the region where we vary λ. It is easy to see that this assumption holds if we choose parameters that satisfy the conditions of Theorem 7.5 *for some* λ^*, which then also ensures that $[\delta_0, \delta_1] = \text{cl}(\mathcal{D})$ *for all* $\lambda \geq \lambda^*$.

7.4.2 Trading Volume

We next derive the volume of trade generated in a steady-state equilibrium, broken down into trades between customers and dealers and trades executed within the dealer sector. Given our equilibrium characterization, the total volume traded between customers and dealers is simply

$$\text{Vol}_{CD|DC} \equiv \rho\,(m_0\mu_{L1} + m_1\mu_{H0}) \tag{7.16}$$

$$= 2\rho m_0 \mu_{L1} = \frac{2\rho m_0 m_1 \gamma f_L f_H}{\rho m_0 m_1 + \gamma\,(m_0 f_L + m_1 f_H)},$$

where the second equality follows from the fact that the inflow of assets into the dealer sector, $\rho m_0 \mu_{L1}$, must equal the outflow, $\rho m_1 \mu_{H0}$, and the third equality follows from Proposition 7.2. Note that $\text{Vol}_{CD|DC}$ depends on the arrival rate of preference shocks, the dealer-customer (DC) contact rate, the asset supply, and the size of the dealer sector, but does not depend on the dealer-dealer (DD) contact rate λ because low-type customer-owners and high-type customer-nonowners trade with all dealers in the equilibrium we are studying.

Since a dealer with utility flow δ buys at rate $(\lambda/m)\Phi_1(\delta)$ from other dealers, we have that the volume of interdealer trades is

$$\text{Vol}_{DD} = \frac{\lambda}{m}\int_{\underline{\delta}}^{\overline{\delta}} \Phi_1(\delta)\,d\Phi_0(\delta). \tag{7.17}$$

The continuity of the distribution of dealers' utility flows and the same change of variable as in the proof of Lemma 7.6 allow us to characterize interdealer trading volume in closed form.

Lemma 7.8: The interdealer trading volume is

$$\text{Vol}_{DD} = \rho m_0 \mu_{L1} \left\{ \left(1 + \frac{1}{\chi}\right) \log(1+\chi) - 1 \right\},$$

where $\chi > 0$ is defined as in (7.15).

Proof. Proceeding as in the proof of Lemma 7.6 shows that the trading volume among dealers can be expressed as

$$\text{Vol}_{DD} = \rho m_0 \mu_{L1} \int_0^1 \chi \left(\frac{1-z}{1+z\chi} \right) dz$$

and the result follows by computing this integral. □

The explicit formulas for $\text{Vol}_{CD|DC}$ and Vol_{DD} deliver intuitive comparative statics. For example, Lemma 7.8 reveals that an increase in the dealer-dealer contact rate λ, which results in an increase in χ, will increase the volume of interdealer trade. In addition, these expressions imply that if customer-dealer (CD) and dealer-dealer volumes are observable—as in most dealer-intermediated OTC markets—then one can uniquely identify the parameter χ, which, as we show next, is a sufficient statistic for a number of key objects of interest in the empirical literature.

7.4.3 Intermediation Chains

Figure 7.3 illustrates an intermediation chain, which starts when an asset is sold by a low-type customer to a dealer. We say that this dealer is the first dealer in the chain and denote his utility flow by $\delta^{(1)}$. If this first dealer meets a high-type customer-nonowner, then he sells her the asset and the chain stops. Otherwise, the first dealer sells to another dealer with a higher utility flow, $\delta^{(2)}$, and the chain continues. We denote by $\mathbf{n}$ the random length of the intermediation chain defined as the number of dealers participating in the chain, and by $\delta^{(k)}$ the utility flow of the kth dealer in the chain, for $k \in \{1, \ldots, \mathbf{n}\}$.

The following key result allows us to derive a number of key statistical properties of intermediation chains.

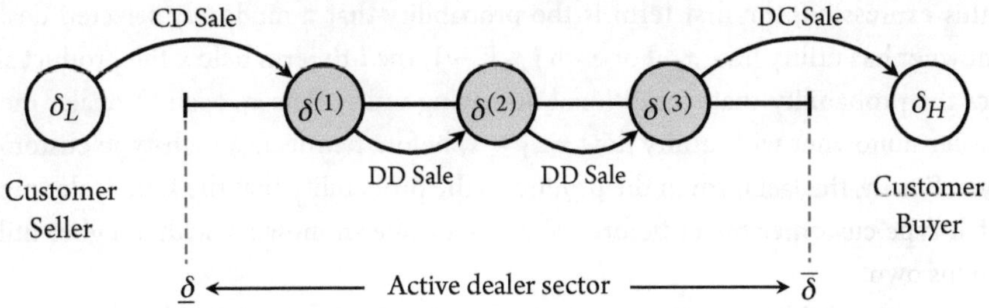

FIGURE 7.3. An intermediation chain

This figure illustrates an intermediation chain of length $\mathbf{n} = 3$ that starts when the asset is sold by a low-type customer to a dealer with utility flow $\delta^{(1)}$ and ends after $\mathbf{n} - 1 = 2$ successive interdealer trades when it is sold to a high-type customer by a dealer with utility flow $\delta^{(3)} = \delta^{(\mathbf{n})}$.

Proposition 7.9: The joint equilibrium distribution of the length of a chain and the utility flows of the participating dealers is

$$\mathbf{P}\left[\{\mathbf{n}=k\}\bigcap_{i=1}^{k}\left\{\delta^{(i)}\in dx_i\right\}\right]=\frac{1}{\chi}\prod_{i=1}^{k}\left(-d\log\Lambda_1(x_i)\right) \tag{7.18}$$

for all $k \geq 1$ and $x_1 \leq x_2 \leq x_3 \cdots \leq x_k$, where $\chi > 0$ and the function $\Lambda_1(x)$ are defined as in equations (7.13) and (7.15).

Proof. The proof proceeds by induction. For intermediation chains of length equal to 1, we have that

$$\mathbf{P}\left[\{\mathbf{n}=1\}\cap\left\{\delta^{(1)}\in dx_1\right\}\right]=\frac{\rho\mu_{H0}}{\Lambda_1(x_0)}\frac{d\Phi_0(x_1)}{m_0}=-\frac{1}{\chi}d\left(\log\Lambda_1(x_1)\right).$$

Each step in the induction process then relies on the Markovian structure of intermediation chains: conditional on the utility flows of the first i dealers in the chain, the probability distribution over the utility flows of the remaining $\mathbf{n} - i$ dealers only depends on $\delta^{(i)}$. See Hugonnier, Lester, and Weill [2020, appendix B] for details and Exercise 7.15 below for a different approach. □

To gain some intuition for the joint distribution characterized in (7.18), it is useful to rewrite the right-hand side of (7.18) as

$$\left(\frac{d\Phi_0(x_1)}{m_0}\right)\prod_{i=1}^{k-1}\left[\left(1-\frac{\rho\mu_{H0}}{\Lambda_1(x_i)}\right)\frac{d\Phi_0(x_{i+1})}{m_0-\Phi_0(x_i)}\right]\left(\frac{\rho\mu_{H0}}{\Lambda_1(x_k)}\right).$$

In this expression, the first term is the probability-that a randomly selected dealer-nonowner has utility flow x_1. For each $i \le k-1$, the i-th term below the product sign gives the probability that, conditional on having utility flow x_i, the i-th dealer meets a dealer-nonowner with utility flow $x_{i+1} \ge x_i$ before he meets a high-type customer-buyer. Finally, the last term in the product is the probability that the k-th dealer meets a high-type customer-buyer before he meets a dealer-nonowner with a higher utility than his own.

Proposition 7.9 has direct implications for a number of statistics related to intermediation chains, many of which have counterparts in the data. For example, in Corollary 7.10 below, we derive the distribution of chain length by integrating the joint distribution (7.18) over $x_1 \le x_2 \le \ldots \le x_k$. In Lemma 7.12, we derive the distribution over the utility flows of the first and last dealer in a chain, conditional on chain length, which allows us to study the relationship between markup and chain length.

Corollary 7.10: The length of intermediation chains follows a zero-truncated Poisson distribution:

$$\mathbf{P}[\mathbf{n}=k] = \frac{\log(1+\chi)^k}{\chi k!}, \qquad k \ge 1. \tag{7.19}$$

In particular, the average chain length is $\mathbf{E}[\mathbf{n}] \equiv \left(1+\frac{1}{\chi}\right)\log(1+\chi)$.

The lemma reveals that the distribution of intermediation chain length depends only on the composite parameter χ. Hence, if dealer-owners meet dealer-nonowners faster than high-type customer-nonowners, then χ increases and the distribution undergoes a first-order stochastic-dominant shift.

Lemma 7.8 and Corollary 7.10 reveal that the volume among dealers, the volume between customers, and the average chain length are related by

$$\text{Vol}_{DD} = \frac{1}{2}\left(\mathbf{E}[\mathbf{n}]-1\right)\text{Vol}_{CD|DC}.$$

To understand this intuitive relationship, consider an example in which there are two dealers, on average, per chain. In this case, every CD transaction generates on average one DD and one DC transaction, so that the DD volume equals half the total volume between customers and dealers.

Next, we turn to the distribution of volume within the dealer sector. To study this distribution, we define the volume generated by a representative dealer with utility flow δ as

$$\mathcal{V}(\delta) \equiv \sum_{q=0,1} \Lambda_q(\delta) \frac{d\Phi_q(\delta)}{m\, dF(\delta)} \tag{7.20}$$

$$= \Lambda_1(\delta) G'(mF(\delta)) + \Lambda_0(\delta)(1 - G'(mF(\delta))),$$

where the second equality follows from Proposition 7.2. The analysis of this object leads to the following results.

Proposition 7.11: The function $\mathcal{V}(\delta)$ is single peaked on $\mathcal{D}$ with a global maximum at the utility flow $\hat{\delta}$ of the dealer with the most balanced trading intensities:

$$\hat{\delta} \equiv \arg\min_{x \in \mathcal{D}} |\Lambda_0(x) - \Lambda_1(x)|.$$

In particular, the function $\mathcal{V}(\delta)$ is monotone increasing if and only if $1 + \chi \leq m_0/m_1$ and monotone decreasing if and only if $1 + \chi \leq m_1/m_0$.

Proof. A direct calculation using (7.8) shows that

$$\frac{\partial \mathcal{V}(\delta)}{\partial(mF(\delta))} = \frac{\lambda\,(\Lambda_1(\delta) - \Lambda_0(\delta))\,\Lambda_0(\delta)\Lambda_1(\delta)}{m(\Lambda_0(\delta) + \Lambda_1(\delta))^3},$$

and the result follows by observing that the difference $\Lambda_1(\delta) - \Lambda_0(\delta)$ is monotone decreasing. □

The proposition reveals that dealers with more balanced buying and selling intensities account for more volume. This implies that the dealers who generate the most volume are not necessarily those who buy or sell assets the fastest. For example, dealers with utility flow $\underline{\delta}$ are quickest to sell, as they have the largest selling intensity but rarely trade because, in equilibrium, they are mostly nonowners. Similarly, dealers with utility flow $\overline{\delta}$ are quickest to buy but they seldom do so because, in equilibrium, most of them are owners. This creates a strong composition effect in (7.20) that ultimately reduces the share of trading volume generated by dealers.

In empirical studies of OTC markets, trading volume correlates with many other aspects of trading behavior. For example, the findings of Li and Schürhoff [2019] suggest that dealers toward the end of intermediation chains account for a larger proportion of trading volume. To make our model consistent with this observation, one should pick parameters such that $\mathcal{V}(\delta)$ is monotonically increasing. According to Proposition 7.11, this occurs if and only if $1 + \chi \leq m_0/m_1$, which requires that most dealers be nonowners and that the interdealer contact rate λ be not too large. Intuitively, in this case, all dealers sell faster than they buy, so that dealers with utility flow $\overline{\delta}$—who are slowest to sell and fastest to buy—have the most balanced trading intensities and thus generate the most trading volume.

7.4.4 Markups

To conclude this section, we study the implications of our model for a common measure of market liquidity: the spread between the price at which a dealer buys an asset from a customer and the price at which a potentially different dealer eventually resells it to a another customer.

Consider an intermediation chain that starts when the asset is purchased from a low-type customer by a dealer with utility flow $\delta^{(1)} = \delta$ and ends when the same asset is sold to a high type customer by a dealer with a higher utility flow $\delta^{(\mathbf{n})} = \delta' \geq \delta$. Following Li and Schürhoff [2019], among others, we define the *markup* along such an intermediation chain as

$$M\left(\delta, \delta'\right) \equiv \frac{\theta(C_H - C_L) + (1-\theta)(R(\delta') - R(\delta))}{\theta C_L + (1-\theta)R(\delta)}.$$

In an environment with homogeneous dealers, the markup reflects the market power of dealers and the gains from trade between customers with low and high utility flows. In our environment, there is an additional force contributing to the markup because the reservation value of the dealer who buys an asset is at least weakly smaller than the reservation value of the dealer who sells it. In any trade, the price is increasing in the valuations of both the buyer and the seller. Hence, the markup increases as the spread between the valuation of the initial buyer and the final seller widens.

The model also has precise predictions about the distribution of the utility flows of the dealers who trade with customers, and how these distributions are affected by the length of intermediation chains. Specifically, exploiting Proposition 7.9 allows us to derive the following result.

Proposition 7.12: Conditional on the length of the chain, the distribution of the utility flows of the last and first dealers are explicitly given by

$$\mathbf{P}\left[\delta^{(\mathbf{n})} \leq \delta \middle| \mathbf{n} = k\right] = \left(\frac{\Lambda(\underline{\delta}, \delta)}{\Lambda(\underline{\delta}, \overline{\delta})}\right)^k,$$

$$\mathbf{P}\left[\delta^{(1)} \leq \delta \middle| \mathbf{n} = k\right] = 1 - \left(\frac{\Lambda(\delta, \overline{\delta})}{\Lambda(\underline{\delta}, \overline{\delta})}\right)^k,$$

respectively, where the function

$$\Lambda(\delta, \delta') \equiv \log \Lambda_1(\delta) - \log \Lambda_1(\delta') \tag{7.21}$$

is monotone decreasing in δ and monotone increasing in δ'.

The proposition reveals that an increase in chain length creates a negative first-order stochastic-dominant shift in the utility flow of the first dealer and a positive shift in the utility flow of the last dealer in the chain. An immediate consequence is that the expected reservation value of the first dealer in the chain is decreasing in k, while the expected reservation value of the last dealer in the chain is increasing in k. Hence, our model predicts that assets traded through longer intermediation chains should, on average, be associated with lower bid prices and higher ask prices. This suggests that the markup should be larger along longer intermediation chains. Unfortunately, this natural ordering is difficult to establish analytically because the utility flows of the dealers along the chain are statistically related. In particular, if the utility flow of the first dealer is larger, then that of the last dealer is also larger, and both move the bid and the ask in the same direction.

7.5 Quantitative Analysis

In this final section, we use the above framework to conduct a quantitative analysis of an OTC market that shares many of the fundamental features of our model—namely, the market for *municipal bonds*. This analysis highlights how our explicit results can be used to calibrate the parameters of the model to key moments from transaction-level data. Using the calibrated model, we quantify the relative importance of search frictions, market power, and preference heterogeneity in explaining market outcomes. Our quantitative analysis also offers the opportunity to study the welfare cost of search frictions and the share of rents appropriated by the dealer sector.

7.5.1 *Evidence from the Municipal Bond Market*

The municipal bonds market is an ideal laboratory for quantitatively exploring our model of frictional intermediation. It is a large OTC market with many dealers and many bonds, where the vast majority of trades are executed via telephone. As a result, the market is highly fragmented and search frictions are commonly thought to be significant. Since broker-dealers have been required to report their trades to the Municipal Securities Rulemaking Board (MSRB), a number of empirical studies, such as Green, Hollifield, and Schürhoff [2006, 2007] and Li and Schürhoff [2019], have used this data to provide a detailed account of the intermediation process in the municipal bond market.

Table 7.1. Empirical distributions of intermediation chain length, markups, and markup shares reproduced from Li and Schürhoff [2019, tables VI and XII]

Length **n**	Frequency (%)	Markup (bps.)	Markup shares of dealers (%) #1	#2	#3	#4	#5	#6	#7
1	77.23	185	100	·	·	·	·	·	·
2	13.25	194	43	57	·	·	·	·	·
3	7.60	226	29	23	48	·	·	·	·
4	1.52	292	22	21	19	39	·	·	·
5	0.33	326	19	9	25	12	34	·	·
6	0.06	357	17	8	13	24	8	32	·
7	0.01	371	17	6	12	14	12	8	31

These studies depict a process of reallocation via intermediation chains in which a dealer purchases a block of bonds, holds them in inventory for some time while searching for a buyer, and eventually resells them, either to a customer or to another dealer. Importantly, these studies highlight that there is considerable heterogeneity across dealers in terms of their typical position within an intermediation chain, the prices at which they trade, the frequency with which they buy and sell, and their contribution to trading volume. Our model, with a decentralized interdealer market and rich heterogeneity across dealers, is a natural starting point for studying these relationships, many of which have no counterparts in standard search-based models.

Although the model has implications for a wide range of stylized facts, we focus our analysis on the empirical distribution of intermediation chain lengths, markups, and markup shares, as these moments illustrate most clearly the economic mechanisms. To highlight the granular nature of the data and the moments we target, table 7.1 summarizes the empirical evidence provided by Li and Schürhoff [2019]. The table shows that chains can involve up to $\mathbf{n} = 7$ dealers, though the vast majority (99.6%) involve $\mathbf{n} = 4$ or fewer. The markups are large and increase steeply with chain length: based on the empirical frequencies shown in the table, we find that the average markup is 191.5 bps, and that the beta of markups with respect to chain length is 23 bps. Finally, the table shows that dealers at the beginning and end of intermediation chains capture most of the intermediation markup, although their combined shares decrease with the length of the chain.

7.5.2 *Calibration of the Model*

The calibration proceeds in two steps. First, we assign values to the parameters that determine the allocation of assets across customers and dealers and, hence, the frequency of trade and volume—what we call *demographics*. Given our closed-form equilibrium characterization, this step is accomplished by hand: we simply use the equilibrium conditions to back out the parameter values that correspond to the data targets we choose. Second, we assign values to the parameters that determine reservation values, markups, and the splits of markups along intermediation chains. This step is carried out numerically but nonetheless builds on the characterization of the equilibrium distributions to speed up computations.

DEMOGRAPHICS PARAMETERS

The vector of parameters that pin down the equilibrium demographics is given by $\{s, m, \rho, \lambda, \gamma, f_H\}$. As a first step toward the calibration of this vector, we identify a target for the per capita supply s. In the model, agents hold and trade blocks of identical size. To map the data to our model, we first normalize the supply of municipal bonds, A, by the average size of a block, Q. Following Green et al. [2007] we set $Q = \$206,989$, which is the average interdealer trade size of seasoned municipal securities for the 2000–2004 period. Focusing on the same period, we then use the Flow of Funds data to calculate the average par value of bonds held directly or indirectly by households, which yields an estimate for A of just over USD2.3 trillion.

Second, to express the number of blocks per capita, we need to estimate the number of participating customers, N. We do so by assuming that half of the household population is a potential direct or indirect participant in the municipal bond market. This implies a value of $N = 54{,}187{,}500$ and, combining these figures, we obtain an estimate of the supply per capita:

$$s = \frac{A}{N \times Q} = 0.2058.$$

Next, we set targets for the rates $\rho\mu_{H0}$ and $\lambda(m_0/m)$ at which dealers contact customer-buyers or dealer-buyers, respectively. To do so we rely on two key moments reported by Li and Schürhoff [2019]: The average inventory duration of dealers, 3.3 days, and the average length of intermediation chains, 1.34. It is intuitive that these targets identify the contact intensities. Indeed, the average inventory duration depends on the *total* arrival rate of potential buyers—i.e., the sum of the contact rates—while the average length of intermediation chains depends on the relative likelihood of meeting a customer before a dealer, i.e., on the ratio χ of the contact rates. Using the formulas for the average inventory duration and average chain length in Lemma 7.6 and Corollary 7.10, we obtain $\rho\mu_{H0} = 58.89$ and $\lambda(m_0/m) = 50.75$.

Our fourth target is the rate ρm_0 at which low-type customers sell to dealers. Since the MSRB only collects data from dealers, we do not have a direct target from the municipal bond market. Existing empirical studies of the corporate bond market, which is widely considered to be more liquid than the municipal bond market, also lack data to identify this parameter and have used a wide range of values, from as little as one day to as many as ten: see, for example, Kargar, Lester, Plante, and Weill [2023] for evidence on search times in the corporate bond market. We choose a median target of five days, which implies that $\rho m_0 = 50$.

Our fifth target is a measure of asset turnover, calculated as the ratio of the value of dealer-to-customer sales to the total supply. Again, using figures from Green et al. [2007] for the period 2000–2004 yields

$$\frac{\text{DC Sales (\$)}}{\text{Supply (\$)}} = \frac{\rho m_1 \mu_{H0}}{s} = 0.411.$$

To complete the identification we set the asset supply equal to the fraction of high-type customers: $f_H = s$. This choice has several desirable features. First, as in several examples [e.g., Duffie et al., 2007; Vayanos and Weill, 2008], it implies that high-type customers are the marginal buyers in the frictionless benchmark, so that illiquidity creates a price discount rather than a premium. Second, and as already noted, this choice implies that high-volume dealers are located toward the end of intermediation chains, which is consistent with the findings of Li and Schürhoff [2019].

These six targets define a system of six nonlinear equations that admits a unique feasible solution [see Hugonnier et al., 2020, appendix E]. The parameters that solve this system are reported in the top panel of table 7.2. They imply, in particular, that a customer switches from the high utility flow to the low utility flow every two years on average; that customers are in contact with dealers every 3.25 days; that dealers are in contact with each other every 3.2 days, and that, as a result of the frictional intermediation process, a fraction $m_1/s = 0.71\%$ of the asset supply is held in inventory by dealers at any point in time. The latter figure was not explicitly targeted but is consistent with the fact that broker-dealers total inventories (which may include holdings for purposes other than marketmaking) amounted to about 1% of the asset supply over the 2000–2004 period according to the Flow of Funds data.

The implied value of the composite parameter $\chi = 0.8737$ pins down not only the average chain length but the entire distribution of chain lengths, which we report in figure 7.4 and in the third column of table 7.3. As one can see from the figure, the empirical and model-implied distributions have a similar shape—with most intermediation chains involving a single dealer—though the empirical distribution is slightly more dispersed and more skewed than its model-implied counterpart.

Table 7.2. Calibrated parameters

Demographic parameters		
s	Supply per capita	0.2058
f_H	Measure of high-type customers	0.2058
γ	Type-switching intensity	0.5267
m	Relative size of the dealer sector	0.0041
ρm	Customer-dealer contact rate	76.87
λ	Dealer-dealer contact rate	78.04
Preferences and bargaining parameters		
r	Discount rate	0.05
θ_0	Dealer-to-dealer bargaining power	0.5
θ	Dealer-to-customer bargaining power	0.971
δ_L	Utility flow of low-type customers	$0.457\delta_H$
δ_H	Utility flow of high-type customers	0.05
$\overline{\delta}$	Upper bound of dealers' utility flow	$0.11\delta_H$
$\underline{\delta}$	Lower bound of dealers' utility flow	$0.8\delta_H$

PREFERENCE AND BARGAINING PARAMETERS

Given the values of the demographic parameters, we now turn to the calibration of the parameters

$$\left\{r, \theta, \theta_0, \delta_L, \delta_H, \underline{\delta}, \overline{\delta}, F(\delta)\right\}$$

that determine reservation values and, thus, markups. To facilitate this process we first impose a few *a priori* restrictions. We fix the interest rate $r = 5\%$ and let $\theta_0 = \theta_1 = 0.5$, so that dealers have symmetric bargaining power in interdealer meetings. Furthermore, we normalize the utility flow of high-type customers to $\delta_H = r$, so that the Walrasian asset price is equal to one, and assume that the utility flow of low-type customers is equal to the dealers' average utility flow. Lastly, we assume that the distribution of dealers' flow utility flow is uniform, so that the latter restriction simply amounts to $\delta_L = (\underline{\delta} + \overline{\delta})/2$.

After imposing these restrictions, there are three remaining parameters to calibrate: the mean δ_L of the distribution of dealers' utility flow, the dispersion $\overline{\delta} - \underline{\delta}$ of dealers' utility flows, and the bargaining power θ of dealers when trading with customers. To calibrate these parameters, we target the liquidity yield spread, the average markup, and the sensitivity of the markup to chain length. Specifically, we target a liquidity yield

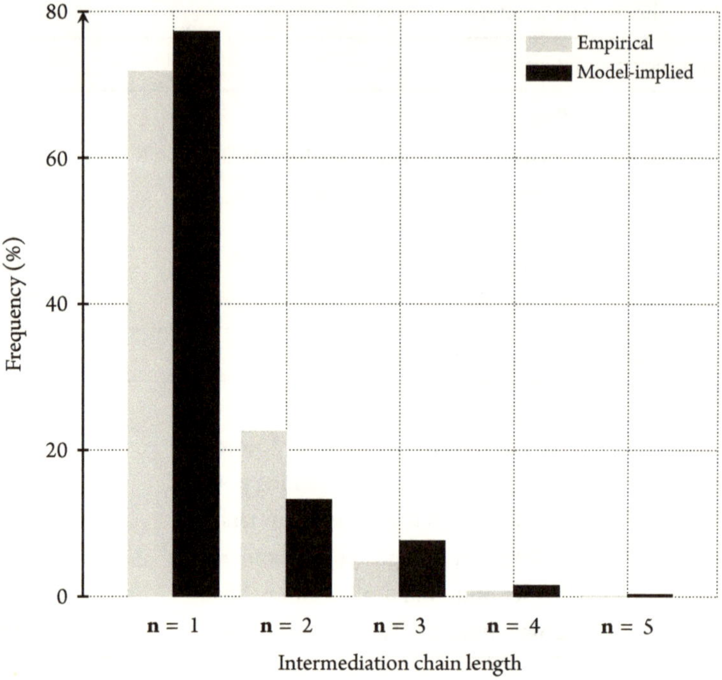

FIGURE 7.4. Distribution of intermediation chain lengths

Empirical distribution reproduced from Li and Schürhoff [2019, tables VI] and model-implied distribution given the demographic parameters in the top panel of table 7.2.

spread of 140 bps, the average of the pre- and postcrisis measure documented in Ang, Bhansali, and Xing [2014]. Next, we target an average markup of 191.5 bps, as implied by table 7.3. Finally, we target a key moment of the joint distribution of markup and chain length: the beta of a regression of markup on chain length estimated to be about 23 bps from the data shown in table 7.3.

To perform the calibration we need model-implied equivalents of the yield spread, the average markup, and the slope of markups relative to the length of intermediation chains. In keeping with the empirical literature we compute the liquidity spread as $\delta_H/\overline{P} - r$, where

$$\overline{P} \equiv \frac{\int_{\underline{\delta}}^{\overline{\delta}} d\Phi_1(x) \int_x^{\overline{\delta}} d\Phi_0(y) \left(\theta_0 R(x) + \theta_1 R(y)\right)}{\int_{\underline{\delta}}^{\overline{\delta}} d\Phi_1(x) \int_x^{\overline{\delta}} d\Phi_0(y)}$$

Table 7.3. Empirical and model-implied moments

	Frequency		Markup		Markup shares of dealers (%)							
	Data	Model	Data	Model	Data				Model			
n	(%)	(%)	(bps.)	(bps.)	#1	#2	#3	#4	#1	#2	#3	#4
1	77.23	71.87	185	192.52	100	·	·	·	100	·	·	·
2	13.25	22.56	194	192.57	43	57	·	·	63.8	36	·	·
3	7.60	4.72	226	192.59	29	23	48	·	63.6	0.5	35.8	·
4	1.52	0.74	292	192.60	22	21	19	39	63.4	0.4	0.4	35.6

This table reproduces the empirical distribution of chain lengths, the average total markup, and the average share of each dealer within chains of length 1 to 4 from Li and Schürhoff [2019, tables VI and XII] and compares these moments with their (rounded) model-implied counterparts evaluated at the parameters of table 7.2.

is the average price of interdealer trades in the model. The statistics relative to markups require the calculation of expectations of the form

$$\Pi_{ik} \equiv \mathbf{E}\left[\frac{P^{(i)}}{P^{(0)}}\middle|\mathbf{n}=k\right],$$

where

$$P^{(0)} = \theta C_L + (1-\theta)R\left(\delta^{(1)}\right)$$

is the price at which the first dealer in the intermediation chain buys the asset from a low-type customer, and

$$P^{(i)} = \begin{cases} \theta C_H + (1-\theta)R\left(\delta^{(i)}\right) & \text{if } i = \mathbf{n}, \\ \theta_0 R\left(\delta^{(i)}\right) + \theta_1 R\left(\delta^{(i+1)}\right) & \text{otherwise,} \end{cases}$$

is the price at which the i-th dealer resells it. Indeed, with this notation we have that the average markup in chains of length k is

$$M_k \equiv \sum_{i=1}^{k} (\Pi_{ik} - \Pi_{i-1k}) = \Pi_{kk} - \Pi_{1k}.$$

Since the prices $P^{(i)}$ are convex combinations of reservation values, it is clear that the computation of any Π_{ik} reduces to that of two integrals that are each integrated against the joint distribution of a pair $(\delta^{(1)}, \delta^{(j)})$ conditional on the chain length. The following corollary to Proposition 7.9 provides an explicit expression for this distribution and thus allows for an efficient computation of the required moments.

Corollary 7.13: Conditional on $\mathbf{n}=k\geq 2$, the joint distribution of the utility flows of the first and the i-th dealer in a chain is given by

$$\mathbf{P}\left[\left\{\delta^{(1)}\in dx_1\right\}\cap\left\{\delta^{(i)}\in dx_i\right\}\middle|\mathbf{n}=k\right]$$
$$=\frac{\Lambda(x_1,x_i)^{i-2}\Lambda(x_i,\overline{\delta})^{k-i}}{\Lambda(\underline{\delta},\overline{\delta})^k/k!}\frac{d\left(\log\Lambda_1(x_1)\right)d\left(\log\Lambda_1(x_i)\right)}{(i-2)!(k-i)!}$$

for all $2\leq i\leq k$.

Proof. Proposition 7.18 and Exercise 7.17 below show that

$$\mathbf{P}\left[\{\mathbf{n}=k\}\cap\left\{\delta^{(1)}\in dx_1\right\}\cap\left\{\delta^{(i)}\in dx_i\right\}\right]$$
$$=\Lambda(x_1,x_i)^{i-2}\Lambda(x_i,\overline{\delta})^{k-i}\frac{d\left(\log\Lambda_1(x_1)\right)d\left(\log\Lambda_1(x_i)\right)}{\chi(k-i)!(i-2)!}.$$

The desired conclusion follows by dividing both sides by the unconditional probability in (7.19) and noting that $1+\chi=\Lambda(\underline{\delta},\overline{\delta})$. □

The liquidity yield spread and the average markup allow us to identify the utility flow of low-type customers δ_L and the bargaining power θ. This is not immediately obvious, as one might expect that an increase in distress cost (a lower δ_L) or a decrease in the bargaining power of customers (a higher θ) would induce an increase in both the yield spread and the markup. What delivers identification is the observation that the bargaining power has a greater impact on the markup than on the yield spread. This is obvious in a simple example: if all dealers have the same utility flow, and if the bargaining power is zero, then the markup is also zero. Yet, the yield spread is positive because customers who buy an asset have to be compensated for not being able to immediately resell when they switch to a low utility flow. While we are not able to formally to establish this result, we can check local identification numerically, as in the left panel of figure 7.5, which confirms that the locus of pairs (θ,δ_L) that match the target markup level is steeper than the locus of pairs that match the yield spread.

Finally, to identify the dispersion in dealers' utility flows, we attempt to match the beta of markup with respect to chain length. As a consequence of Proposition 7.12, we expect the model to produce a positive beta that increases with the dispersion of dealers' utility flows. As an illustration, let us start with no-dealer heterogeneity ($\underline{\delta}=\overline{\delta}$) and set $(\theta,\delta_L)=(0.9728,0.01571)$ so that the model exactly matches the target liquidity yield spread and the target markup. Starting from this parameter configuration we then progressively increase the dispersion of dealers' utility flows, keeping the mean

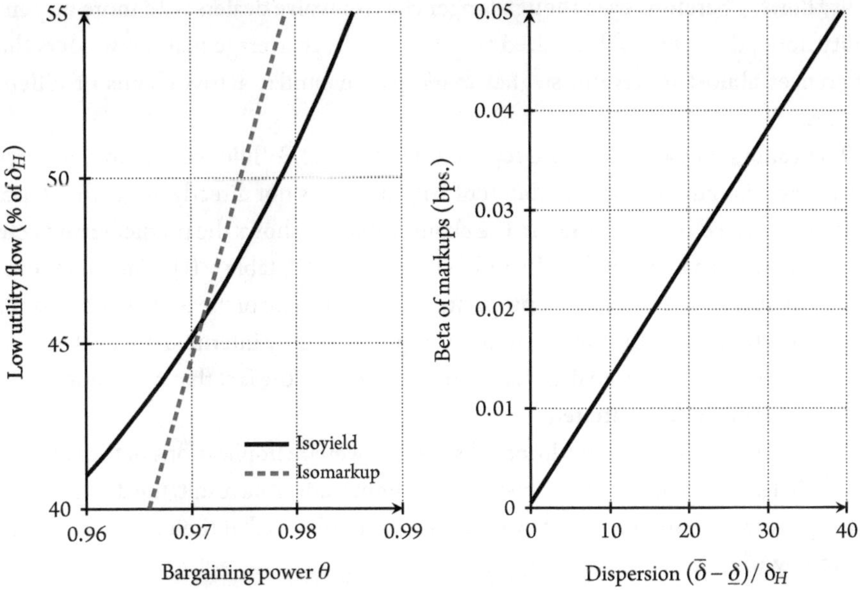

FIGURE 7.5. Identification of the model

The left panel plots the isoyield and isomarkup schedules, i.e., the locus of pairs (θ, δ_L) that match the target average markup and the observed yield spread, respectively. The right panel plots the slope of markups with respect to chain length as a function of the dispersion in the utility flows of dealers.

$\delta_L = (\underline{\delta} + \overline{\delta})/2$ the same, and vary only θ to match the average markup. The results, shown in the right panel of figure 7.5, confirm that the beta of markup to chain length is positive and increasing in dispersion. However, the magnitude is very small. Thus, dispersion in the utility flows of dealers fails to generate a quantitatively and economically significant statistical relationship between the size of the markup and the length of the intermediation chain.

The intuition behind this quantitative finding is clear. Given the calibrated values of the demographic parameters, generating a large average markup requires endowing the dealers with almost all of the bargaining power. Recall that the spread between the first and last price in a chain of length $\mathbf{n}$ is

$$\theta\,(C_H - C_L) + (1-\theta)\left(R(\delta^{(\mathbf{n})}) - R(\delta^{(\mathbf{1})})\right).$$

As θ increases, this difference depends increasingly more on the reservation values of customers and less on that of dealers. In particular, as $\theta \to 1$ the equilibrium converges to the so-called Diamond [1971] paradox in which prices are independent of dealers' utility flows. Therefore, even though longer chains involve dealers with more dispersed utility flows, the value of θ required to generate a large average markup renders these differences almost irrelevant, so that markups are similar across chains of different lengths.

The calibrated parameters are reported in table 7.2. While our calibration targets the average markup in chains of different length, it does not directly target the share of markups received by each dealer in the chain. Table 7.3 shows the predicted and actual split of markups as reported by Li and Schürhoff [2019, table VII]. The table reveals that the first and the last dealer appropriate the largest share of the total markup, similar to what is observed in the data. The share appropriated by intermediate dealers in the model is, however, much smaller than in the data, due to the fact that reservation values of dealers are very concentrated.

To conclude this section we briefly discuss the welfare implications of the calibrated model. If dealers are absent, then customers cannot trade. As a result, the distribution of holdings across customers is purely random, and it follows that their aggregated utility is given by

$$\mathcal{U}_0 = \frac{s}{r}\mathbf{E}^{F_c}[\delta] = \frac{s}{r}\left(\delta_L + \pi_H(\delta_H - \delta_L)\right).$$

On the other hand, when dealers are present they collectively own m_1 assets that are spread across types according to the equilibrium distribution $\Phi_1(\delta)$. Therefore, the aggregated utility derived by customers and dealers is given by

$$\begin{aligned}\mathcal{U} &= \sum_{j,q} \mu_{jq} W(q,\delta_j) + \sum_q \int_{\underline{\delta}}^{\overline{\delta}} V(q,\delta)d\Phi_q(\delta)\\ &= \sum_j \left(\mu_{j1}C_j + f_j W(0,\delta_j)\right) + \int_{\underline{\delta}}^{\overline{\delta}} R(\delta)d\Phi_1(\delta) + \int_{\underline{\delta}}^{\overline{\delta}} V(0,x)mdF(x),\end{aligned}$$

where $W(q,\delta_j)$ and $V(q,\delta)$ denote the equilibrium value functions of customers and dealers (see Exercise 7.16 below). Finally, as search frictions vanish, the aggregated utility converges to the first best welfare $\mathcal{U}_* = \frac{s}{r}\delta_H$.

Substituting the calibrated parameters into these expressions reveals that, despite the frictions that plague the intermediation process, the OTC market is quite efficient as it realizes

$$\frac{\mathcal{U} - \mathcal{U}_0}{\mathcal{U}_* - \mathcal{U}_0} = 98.14\%$$

of the gains from trade. Despite their very bargaining power, customers appropriate about 71% of the welfare gain $\mathcal{U}-\mathcal{U}_0$ generated by the presence of active dealers, and the remainder is captured by the dealers who intermediate these trades. As we discussed in section 5.5.3, however, the fact that the market is nearly efficient does not necessarily imply that price discounts are small. In fact, given that the Walrasian price is $\delta_H/r=1$, we have that the illiquidity discount ranges from 21.2% for low-type customers to 23% for high-type customers.

7.6 Exercises

Exercise 7.14: Show that

$$\int_{\underline{\delta}}^{\overline{\delta}} \mathcal{V}(\delta)mdF(\delta)=\mathrm{Vol}_{CD|DC}+2\mathrm{Vol}_{DD}$$

and explain why this quantity exceeds the sum of (7.16) and (7.17).

Exercise 7.15: Consider the full-participation steady-state equilibrium of section 7.4 and denote by

$$g_\alpha(\delta)\equiv\mathbf{E}\left[e^{-\alpha\mathbf{n}}\middle|\delta^{(1)}=\delta\right] \tag{7.22}$$

the Laplace transform at $\alpha>0$ of the chain length conditional on the utility flow of the first dealer.

1. Show that

$$e^{\alpha}g_\alpha(\delta)=\mathbf{E}\left[\mathbf{1}_{\{\tau_c\le\tau_d\}}\right]+\mathbf{E}\left[\mathbf{1}_{\{\tau_c>\tau_d\}}g_\alpha(\delta_0)\middle|\delta_0\ge\delta\right],$$

   where δ_0 is the utility flow of a randomly selected dealer-nonowner, τ_c is an exponential variable with intensity $\rho\mu_{H0}$, τ_d is an exponential variable with intensity $\Lambda_1(\delta)-\rho\mu_{H0}$, and all three variables are independent.

2. Reduce (7.22) to the integral equation

$$g_\alpha(\delta)\Lambda_1(\delta)=e^{-\alpha}\left[\rho\mu_{H0}+\frac{\lambda}{m}\int_{\delta}^{\overline{\delta}}g_\alpha(x)d\Phi_0(x)\right]$$

   and use this equation to verify that

$$g_\alpha(\delta)=\sum_{k=1}^{\infty}\frac{e^{-\Lambda(\delta,\overline{\delta})-\alpha k}\Lambda(\delta,\overline{\delta})^{k-1}}{(k-1)!}$$

with the function $\Lambda(\delta, \delta')$ defined as in (7.21). Use this result to show that, conditional on the utility flow of the first dealer being δ, the variable $\mathbf{n}-1$ is Poisson distributed with parameter $\Lambda(\delta, \overline{\delta})$.

3. Combine the above result and the fact that $\delta^{(1)}$ is distributed according to $d\Phi_0(\delta)/m_0$ to derive the joint distribution of $(\mathbf{n}, \delta^{(1)})$ and to provide another proof of Corollary 7.10.

Exercise 7.16: Consider the full-participation steady-state equilibrium of section 7.4. Show that the value functions of nonowners that are required for the welfare calculations are given by

$$W(0,\delta_L) = \frac{\rho(1-\theta)\gamma f_H}{\rho(1-\theta)(r+\gamma f_H)} \cdot W(0,\delta_H),$$

$$W(0,\delta_H) = \frac{\rho(1-\theta)(r+\gamma f_H)}{r(r+\gamma)}\left[m_1(C_H - R(\underline{\delta})) + \int_{\underline{\delta}}^{\overline{\delta}} \sigma(x)\Phi_1(x)dx\right],$$

and

$$V(0,\delta) = \frac{1}{r}\left[\rho\mu_{L1}\theta\,(R(\delta)-C_L) + \frac{\lambda\theta_0}{m}\int_{\underline{\delta}}^{\delta}\sigma(x)\Phi_1(x)dx\right],$$

with the marginal reservation value $\sigma(x)$ defined as in (7.12).

Exercise 7.17: Use an induction argument to show that

$$\int_{[\underline{\delta},\overline{\delta}]^k} \mathbf{1}_{\{a\le x_1\le x_2\le \ldots \le x_k \le b\}} \prod_{i=1}^{k}\left(-d\log\Lambda_1(x_i)\right) = \frac{1}{k!}\Lambda(a,b)^k$$

for all $\underline{\delta} \le a \le b \le \overline{\delta}$ and $k \in \mathbb{N}$. Combine this result with Proposition 7.9 to establish Corollary 7.10 and Proposition 7.12.

7.7 Notes and References

The model studied in this chapter was first developed in Hugonnier, Lester, and Weill [2020]. The equilibrium construction and the existence proof are slightly different, however. Specifically, in Hugonnier et al. [2020] we formulated the fixed-point problem in terms of the masses of inactive dealers

$$k_0 \equiv \Phi_0(\delta_0),$$

$$k_1 \equiv \Phi_1(\bar{\delta}) - \Phi_1(\delta_1),$$

whereas the formulation in this chapter concentrates on the utility flows that determine the set of active dealers, (δ_0, δ_1). Despite this small difference, since the parameterized equilibrium distributions are continuous, the existence of the former fixed point implies that of the latter and, therefore, Theorem 7.3 follows from the existence result in the original paper.

The quantitative analysis of the model with frictional intermediation also follows from Hugonnier et al. [2020]. They show that, through the lens of the model, generating the observed level of markups requires endowing dealers with most of the bargaining power relative to customers, which in turn makes it hard to match the steep, positive relationship between intermediation chain length and markups. In addition to highlighting this tension, the framework also suggests a natural extension to resolve it. Specifically, Hugonnier et al. [2020] offer an alternative formulation of the model in which dealers differ not in their flow valuations, but rather in their ability to locate customers with high willingness to pay for the asset. This extension preserves the key qualitative properties of the benchmark model but resolves the tension discussed above. It also illustrates that the solution techniques developed in this chapter extend to other forms of heterogeneity, and that exploring the quantitative implications of the model can help to distinguish between different forms of heterogeneity.

The quantitative analysis in this chapter is just one example of the growing literature that takes OTC market models to the data. One strand has followed Duffie, Gârleanu, and Pedersen [2007] and complemented their theoretical analyses with calibration exercises. Early examples include Vayanos and Weill [2008], who study the spread between the yields of "on-the-run" and "off-the-run" bonds, and Gavazza [2011b], who studies prices in the secondary market for leasing commercial aircraft. More recently, He and Milbradt [2014], Chen, Cui, He, and Milbradt [2018], and d'Avernas [2017] have used OTC market models to decompose credit spreads into default and liquidity components. Afonso and Lagos [2015b], Armenter and Lester [2017], Afonso, Armenter, and Lester [2019], Bianchi and Bigio [2022], and Lagos and Navarro [2023] also calibrate various OTC market models to quantitatively evaluate the effects of monetary policy on interest rates in the federal funds market. Other examples include Kozlowski [2018], who offers a quantitative analysis of maturity choice when debt is traded in OTC markets; Passadore and Xu [2018] and Chaumont [2018], who study sovereign spreads; and Buchak, Matvos, Piskorski, and Seu [2022], who study the emergence of dealer-intermediated trade in the housing market. Pagnotta and Philippon [2018], in contrast, offer normative results by conducting welfare analysis in an environment where exchanges compete by offering different execution speeds.

A second important literature has focused on structural estimation of search and/or network models of OTC markets. Many of these studies face a dual challenge: the models must be rich enough to confront the data, and the data must be sufficiently detailed to identify the parameters unique to this class of models. Among the first papers in this area is Feldhütter [2012], who uses a structural model to identify periods of strong selling pressure in the corporate bond market. Other papers studying debt markets include Brancaccio, Li, and Schurhoff [2017], who study the incentives to learn about order flow in the municipal bond market; Hendershott, Li, Livdan, and Schürhoff [2020], who study the formation of dealer-client relationships in the corporate bond market and the consequences for welfare; Brancaccio and Kang [2022], who study the relationship between search frictions in the municipal bond markets and the incentives to issue complex securities; Wu [2021], who uses a structural model to demonstrate that trading delays have increased in the corporate bond market as a result of regulation; Pinter and Üslü [2021], who compare the size of frictions in the U.K. corporate and government bond markets; Palleja [2022], who proposes a measure of transaction costs in a model that accounts for investors' choice between agency and principal trades; and Coen and Coen [2023], who study the impact of dealer heterogeneity on liquidity in the U.K. corporate bond market. Structural estimations of models designed to study other OTC markets include Gavazza [2016], who studies the welfare impact of intermediaries in the secondary market for commercial aircraft; and Allen, Clark, and Houde [2019], who study the welfare impact of search frictions in the mortgage market. Other quantitative studies, including those that estimate network and static dealer markets, have been conducted by Gofman [2014], Gofman [2017], Liu [2020a], Beltran [2021], Craig and Ma [2022], Eisfeldt, Herskovic, Rajan, and Siriwardane [2023], and Allen and Wittwer [2023].

8

Price-Setting Mechanisms

In chapter 4 we assumed that the terms of trade in bilateral meetings between investors and dealers were determined by Nash bargaining. In this chapter, we first deepen our understanding of the relation between the Nash bargaining solution and the underlying economic environment, and then explore several alternative mechanisms for price determination.

Specifically, in section 8.1 we study the strategic foundations of the Nash bargaining solution and show that it obtains as the equilibrium of an explicit bargaining game in which investors and dealers make alternating offers. We highlight several features of the economic environment that endogenously determine the share of the surplus appropriated by investors and dealers.

Then, in section 8.2, we consider an alternative price-setting mechanism that was proposed by Burdett and Judd [1983] and that closely resembles the *request for quotes* (RFQ) protocol that is used on electronic trading platforms. Finally, in section 8.3, we consider a second alternative method of price determination that builds on the literature on competitive (or directed) search developed by Moen [1997] and Burdett, Shi, and Wright [2001], among others. According to these models, dealers post quotes and investors can direct their search toward the price they find most attractive, trading off execution speed and transaction costs.

8.1 Strategic Foundations of Nash Bargaining

In this section, we study the strategic microfoundations of the Nash bargaining outcome and show that it is an equilibrium of a sequential offer bargaining game between an investor and a dealer. To simplify the analysis, consider the special case in which investors have just two utility types: δ_H with probability f_H and $\delta_L < \delta_H$ with probability f_L. Assume that $f_H > s$ and conjecture that, as we established before, the marginal investor has utility type δ_H, implying that the interdealer price is equal to $P = R(\delta_H)$.

8.1.1 The Bargaining Game

In line with the strategic bargaining literature following Rubinstein [1982], we assume that, when a dealer and an investor meet, they engage in a sequential bargaining game over infinitely many periods of length h, and we will study the limit of the equilibrium as $h \to 0$.

In each period of bargaining, the investor incurs cost $c_I h$ and the dealer incurs cost $c_D h$. The sequence of events in each period is as follows. First, with probability λh, the investor meets and starts bargaining with a new dealer, leaving the incumbent with a payoff of zero. Second, with probability γh, the investor draws a new utility flow, which is δ_H with probability f_H or δ_L with probability f_L. Third, within each investor-dealer match, one of the two counterparties is chosen to be the proposer, which entitles it to make an offer. We assume that the investor is chosen with probability π_I and the dealer with probability $\pi_D = 1 - \pi_I$. The proposer can offer to trade the asset in exchange for a specific transfer; she can offer to wait until the next period, in which case the investor and dealer incur costs $c_I h$ and $c_D h$, respectively; or she can propose that they dissolve the match and quit bargaining altogether. The responder accepts or rejects and, in the case of rejection, decides whether to continue bargaining in the next period or to dissolve the match.

We focus on stationary Subgame Perfect Nash Equilibrium (SPNE) such that, in any given period, the players' strategies only depend on the utility flow of the investor and the identity of the proposer. Adapting the arguments of Merlo and Wilson [1998] to this environment with waiting costs, one can show that this bargaining game admits a stationary SPNE; that this SPNE is unique, in the sense that all stationary SPNE give players the same payoffs; and that all stationary SPNE are efficient, in the sense of maximizing the players' joint value. Moreover, there is a stationary SPNE in which the proposer makes an offer (to trade, wait, or dissolve the match) that is always accepted, and that makes the receiver indifferent between accepting and rejecting.

8.1.2 Equilibrium Trading Patterns and Terms of Trade

We guess and verify that, under parameter restrictions determined below, the trading patterns that we derived under the assumption of Nash bargaining continue to hold in the present strategic bargaining setting. Specifically, we conjecture that investors of type $(0, \delta_H)$ and $(1, \delta_L)$ trade immediately when they meet a dealer, while investors of type $(1, \delta_H)$ and $(0, \delta_L)$ do not trade and instead immediately dissolve the match.

MEETING BETWEEN A $(0, \delta_H)$ INVESTOR AND A DEALER

Under the assumption that the marginal investor has the high utility flow δ_H, the reservation value of the investor is equal to the interdealer price, so that the total surplus from trading is exactly equal to zero. It is then immediate to verify that the investor and the dealer find it optimal to trade immediately at a price $p(\delta_H) = P = R(\delta_H)$. The receiver in this case is always indifferent between trading and dissolving the match. Since there are waiting costs, and since the net utility of trading is zero for both counterparties, waiting yields strictly lower payoffs than quitting.

MEETING BETWEEN A $(1, \delta_L)$ INVESTOR AND A DEALER

We conjecture that in such a meeting, trade occurs immediately, and that the receiver is indifferent between trading and waiting. Let $p_I(\delta_L)$ ($p_D(\delta_L)$) denote the price offered by the investor (dealer) when selected, and let

$$p(\delta_L) \equiv \pi_I p_I(\delta_L) + \pi_D p_D(\delta_L) \tag{8.1}$$

denote the average price. As is standard, we determine these prices by stating that, in equilibrium, the receiver must be indifferent between accepting and rejecting. When the investor is the proposer and the dealer is the receiver, this indifference condition can be written as

$$P - p_I(\delta_L) = -c_D h + (1 - rh)(1 - \gamma f_H h - \lambda h)\left(P - p(\delta_L)\right) + o(h),$$

where $o(h)$ is a function with $\lim_{h \to 0} o(h)/h = 0$ that collects higher-order terms such as the approximation error for the discount factor, $e^{-rh} - (1 - rh)$, and the probability that a change of type and a dealer contact happen at the same time. The left-hand side of the equation above is the value of accepting the offer to trade at price $p_I(\delta_L)$. The right-hand side is the value of waiting: the dealer incurs the waiting cost $c_D h$ and trades during the next period as long as the investor has neither changed type nor met another dealer. This indifference condition can be simplified to

$$p_I(\delta_L) - p(\delta_L) = c_D h + (r + \gamma f_H + \lambda)\left(P - p(\delta_L)\right) h + o(h). \tag{8.2}$$

The left-hand side of this equation is the markup charged by the investor over the average price, which can be interpreted as the cost to the dealer of trading immediately. The right-hand side collects the various costs of waiting: the explicit cost, the cost of delaying the receipt of trading profits, and the expected loss if the trade does not occur, because the investor either changes type or meets another dealer.

Similarly, when the investor-owner is the receiver and the dealer is the proposer, the indifference condition of the investor can be written as

$$\begin{aligned} V(0,\delta_L)+p_D(\delta_L) &= (\delta_L-c_I)h \\ &\quad +(1-rh+o(h))\big((1-\gamma f_H h)(V(0,\delta_L) \\ &\quad +p(\delta_L))+\gamma f_H h V(1,\delta_H)\big), \end{aligned}$$

where we are careful to account for the utility flow δ_L enjoyed by the investor while waiting. Note that, unlike the indifference condition of the dealer, the probability λh of meeting a new dealer does not appear. This is because, when the investor starts bargaining with a new dealer, she has the same continuation value as with the previous one.

Proceeding as above shows that the indifference condition of the investor can be simplified to

$$\begin{aligned} p_D(\delta_L)-p(\delta_L) &= \big(\delta_L-c_I+\gamma f_H V(1,\delta_H)\big)\,h \\ &\quad -(r+\gamma f_H)\,\big(V(0,\delta_L)+p(\delta_L)\big)\,h+o(h). \end{aligned} \tag{8.3}$$

Using the Hamilton-Jacobi-Bellman (HJB) equation (3.17) of the $(1,\delta_L)$ investor yields

$$\begin{aligned} rV(1,\delta_L) &= \delta_L+\gamma f_H\,(V(1,\delta_H)-V(1,\delta_L)) \\ &\quad +\lambda\,\big(p(\delta_L)+V(0,\delta_L)-V(1,\delta_L)\big). \end{aligned}$$

Eliminating the term $\delta_L+\gamma f_H V(1,\delta_H)$ in (8.3) then yields

$$p(\delta_L)-p_D(\delta_L)=c_I h+(r+\gamma f_H+\lambda)\,\big(p(\delta_L)-R(\delta_L)\big)\,h+o(h), \tag{8.4}$$

where

$$R(\delta_L)\equiv V(1,\delta_L)-V(0,\delta_L)$$

is the reservation value of the investor. The interpretation of this expression is similar to that of (8.2). In particular, the left-hand side is the cost to the investor of trading immediately, while the right-hand side collects the various costs she incurs by trading later.

Given the definition of the average price in (8.1), it is clear that equations (8.2) and (8.4) form a system of two linear equations in two unknowns, $p_I(\delta_L)$ and $p_D(\delta_L)$. One can easily verify that this system has a unique solution when the period length h is sufficiently small. Moreover, we obtain the standard result that, as $h\to 0$, the dealer and the investor make the same offer. This is because the right-hand side of both (8.2) and

(8.4) goes to zero as $h \to 0$. To calculate this common offer made by the investor and the dealer in the limit, we multiply (8.2) by π_I, multiple (8.4) by π_D, take the difference between the two so that the left-hand sides cancel, and divide the resulting expression by the length of the period. This yields

$$0 = -\pi_I c_D + \pi_D c_I - (r + \gamma f_H + \lambda)\big(\pi_I P + \pi_D R(\delta_L) - p(\delta_L)\big) + o(1),$$

and solving for $p(\delta_L)$ leads to the pricing formula

$$p(\delta_L) = \pi_I \left(P + \frac{c_D}{r + \gamma f_H + \lambda}\right) + \pi_D \left(R(\delta_L) - \frac{c_I}{r + \gamma f_H + \lambda}\right). \tag{8.5}$$

Note that the formula is almost identical to the Nash bargaining solution, in which the price is a convex combination of the reservation values of the dealer and the investor. However, there are two important differences. First, the bargaining power of each counterparty is endogenous—in this case, it is equal to the probability that each side makes a price offer. Second, the reservation values of the two counterparties are adjusted for their respective waiting costs. This occurs even though these costs are never actually incurred in equilibrium. Intuitively, when the investor makes an offer, she can raise the price above the Nash bargaining solution because it is costly for the dealer to wait for the opportunity of making a counteroffer. In the formula, this effect is captured by adjusting the reservation value of the dealer up by $c_D/(r + \gamma f_H + \lambda)$, the present value of the waiting costs that the dealer would incur if the investor delays trade indefinitely, until she changes type or meets another dealer. The same logic implies that the dealer can lower the price, so that the reservation value of the investor is adjusted down by $c_I/(r + \gamma f_H + \lambda)$. Depending on the parameter values, the net effect can be negative or positive. If the expected present value of the investor's waiting costs is large (small) enough relative to that of the dealer, then the price is smaller (larger) than that implied by the generalized Nash bargaining formula.

Equation (8.5) is obtained by guessing that, when they receive an offer, the investor and dealer are both indifferent between trading or waiting. But this conjecture may not always be verified. For example, if the product $\pi_D c_I$ is large enough, then the average price in (8.5) can be strictly lower than the investor's reservation value $R(\delta_L)$, in which case the investor would strictly prefer quitting to trading. In such cases, the equilibrium has to be different. Specifically, one can show that trade continues to happen immediately, because equilibria must be efficient, but at an average price that makes the investors indifferent between trading and quitting, i.e., $p(\delta_L) = R(\delta_L)$. The opposite is true if $\pi_I c_D$ is large enough, in which case the average price must equal the dealer's reservation value, $p(\delta_L) = P$. See Exercise 8.8.

MEETINGS BETWEEN A $(1, \delta_H)$ OR A $(0, \delta_L)$ INVESTOR AND A DEALER

In the semicentralized model with Nash bargaining, there are no gains from trade when either a $(1, \delta_H)$ or a $(0, \delta_L)$ investor meets a dealer, and the trading counterparties are assumed to part ways. However, matters are more subtle in the model with strategic bargaining. The bargaining game allows investors to stay matched together by rejecting each other's offers, in effect creating a relationship. Indeed, if waiting costs are zero, it is easy to see that investors have a strict incentive to wait. For example, even though a $(1, \delta_H)$ investor does not gain from immediate trade with a dealer, she anticipates strictly positive gains from trade in the future, when she switches to a low type. If the waiting costs c_I and c_D are not too large, the investor and the dealer have incentives to remain matched until these gains materialize. However, if these costs are sufficiently large, then they both have incentives to dissolve the match.

To see this formally, conjecture that the proposer offers to quit bargaining when a $(1, \delta_H)$ investor and a dealer meet. To show that this offer is the basis of an equilibrium, it is sufficient to verify that, for both the dealer and the investor, this offer dominates waiting. The condition for the investor is

$$V(1, \delta_H) > \delta_H h + (1 - rh + o(h)) \left(-c_I h + \left(1 - \gamma f_L h\right) V(1, \delta_H) \right.$$
$$\left. + \gamma f_L h \left(V(0, \delta_L) + p(\delta_L)\right)\right),$$

whereas the condition for the dealer is

$$0 > (1 - rh + o(h)) \left(-c_D h + \gamma f_L h \left(P - p(\delta_L)\right)\right).$$

Since

$$p(\delta_H) = R(\delta_H) = V(1, \delta_H) - V(1, \delta_L),$$

the HJB equation (3.17) for a $(1, \delta_H)$ investor simplifies to

$$rV(1, \delta_H) = \delta_H + \gamma f_L \left(V(1, \delta_L) - V(1, \delta_H)\right).$$

Substituting this expression into the two indifference conditions reveals that, for h sufficiently small, these two inequalities hold if

$$c_I > \gamma f_L \left(p(\delta_L) - R(\delta_L)\right),$$
$$c_D > \gamma f_L \left(P - p(\delta_L)\right).$$

Intuitively, the left-hand side in each expression is the flow cost of waiting while the right-hand side is the flow benefit, defined as the product of the intensity of a change of the low utility type and the net utility of a trade. These inequalities make it clear that waiting costs are necessary for optimally dissolving the match: if $c_I = c_D = 0$, the same calculations lead to the conclusion that the investor and the dealer would want to stay matched and wait for a change of utility type.

Finally, the same calculations apply to the case of a $(0, \delta_L)$ investor, but they are easier. Indeed, in this case, when the investor switches to a high type, she buys the asset at price $P = R(\delta_H)$. Therefore, the net utility of trading in the future is zero for both the investor and the dealer, and there are no gains from waiting as long as the waiting costs are nonzero.

8.1.3 *Taking Stock*

The conditions above are derived based on conjectures regarding endogenous objects—the interdealer price and the reservation values. Next, we solve for these objects and offer conditions on exogenous parameters that validate these conjectures. First, proceeding as in chapter 4, we find that the reservation values solve

$$rR(\delta_H) = \delta_H + \gamma f_L \left(R(\delta_L) - R(\delta_H)\right),$$
$$rR(\delta_L) = \delta_L + \gamma f_H \left(R(\delta_H) - R(\delta_L)\right) + \lambda \left(p(\delta_L) - R(\delta_L)\right),$$

where we used that $p(\delta_H) = P = R(\delta_H)$. Substituting the expression (8.5) for the average price $p(\delta_L)$ and taking the difference between the two reservation value equations yields

$$R(\delta_H) - R(\delta_L) = \frac{\delta_H - \delta_L}{r + \gamma + \lambda\pi_I} - \frac{\lambda K}{r + \gamma + \lambda\pi_I},$$

where

$$K \equiv \frac{\pi_I c_D - \pi_D c_I}{r + \gamma f_H + \lambda}.$$

In the conjectured equilibrium, trading immediately or waiting must strictly dominate dissolving the match, so that $R(\delta_L) < p(\delta_L) < P$. With the explicit formula above, this condition reduces to

$$-\frac{\pi_I\left(\delta_H - \delta_L\right)}{r + \gamma} < K < \frac{\pi_D\left(\delta_H - \delta_L\right)}{r + \gamma + \lambda}. \tag{8.6}$$

In a meeting between a $(1, \delta_H)$ investor and a dealer, both parties find it optimal to dissolve the match without a transfer if the following conditions are satisfied:

$$c_I > \gamma f_L \frac{\pi_I(\delta_H - \delta_L) + (r + \gamma)K}{r + \gamma + \lambda\pi_I}, \tag{8.7}$$

$$c_D > \gamma f_L \frac{\pi_D(\delta_H - \delta_L) - (r + \gamma + \lambda)K}{r + \gamma + \lambda\pi_I}. \tag{8.8}$$

These conditions can be simultaneously satisfied in several natural cases; for example, if $\pi_I \in (0,1)$, $\pi_D c_I \simeq \pi_I c_D$, and (c_I, c_D) are sufficiently large. We summarize our findings in the following proposition.

Proposition 8.1: Assume that conditions (8.6), (8.7), and (8.8) hold. Then, in the semicentralized market with strategic bargaining, as the time between offers goes to zero, there exists an equilibrium in which, upon meeting a dealer,

1. Investors of type $(1, \delta_L)$ immediately sell at price
$$p(\delta_L) = \pi_I \left(P + \frac{c_D}{r + \gamma f_H + \lambda} \right) + \pi_D \left(R(\delta_L) - \frac{c_I}{r + \gamma f_H + \lambda} \right);$$
2. Investors of type $(0, \delta_H)$ immediately purchase the asset at price $P = R(\delta_H)$;
3. Investors of type $(0, \delta_L)$ and $(1, \delta_H)$ quit bargaining.

Proposition 8.1 provides conditions under which investors and dealers with no gains from trade endogenously choose to dissolve their match despite the fact that, in principle, our matching technology allows them to remain in contact and form a relationship. In this sense, as a by-product of our analysis, we have derived conditions under which the presence of costs implies that spot trading dominates relationship trading.

To facilitate the analysis of the bargaining game, we have limited our attention to the special case with only two utility types, $\delta_L < \delta_H$. The general case with a continuum of types is more difficult because condition (8.6) may only hold for a subset of types. In that case, pricing does not obey the formula in Proposition 8.1. Instead, the price must be take it or leave it: one of the counterparties receives zero surplus because she cannot credibly threaten to wait in order to make a counter offer. Thus, in the general case, one must solve for the endogenous set of types who accept these take-it-or-leave-it offers.

8.2 Request for Quotes as a Pricing Game

As OTC markets evolve, an increasingly popular mechanism for determining prices begins with a so-called request for quotes (RFQ). According to this protocol, an investor broadcasts a desired trade to dealers, typically via an electronic platform. After observing this request, dealers have a limited amount of time to respond with a quote. As in a classical auction, the investor observes these responses and decides whether or not to accept the best quote. Examples of OTC markets in which RFQs have become popular include the markets for corporate bonds, interest rate swaps, and credit default swaps; see Hendershott and Madhavan [2015], Fermanian, Guéant, and Pu [2016], and Riggs, Onur, Reiffen, and Zhu [2018] for detailed studies of these markets. In this section, we develop a stylized model of the RFQ protocol based on the pricing game of Burdett and Judd [1983].

8.2.1 A Model of RFQs

Consider the semicentralized market of chapter 4 but assume that, rather than meeting and bargaining with a single dealer, each investor periodically receives the opportunity to send an RFQ to $n \geq 2$ randomly selected dealers. Moreover, assume that dealers sometimes decline the request for idiosyncratic reasons, perhaps because they are busy with other clients. For example, in their study of the Credit Default Swaps (CDS) market, Riggs et al. [2018] find that dealers do not respond to an RFQ approximately 10 percent of the time.

If we let π denote the (independent) probability that each dealer does not reply to an RFQ, then it follows from the binomial formula that, conditional on receiving at least one quote, an investor receives $k \in \{1, 2, \ldots, n\}$ quotes with probability

$$\psi_k \equiv \mathbf{P}\left[k \text{ quotes} \middle| k \geq 1 \text{ quotes}\right] = \frac{1}{1-\pi^n}\binom{n}{k}(1-\pi)^k \pi^{n-k}. \tag{8.9}$$

In most markets, RFQs are not anonymous. To capture this feature in a simple way, we assume that dealers observe all relevant information about an investor who submits an RFQ, including her utility flow. In addition, dealers typically know the number of other dealers who will *receive* the RFQ, but they do not know how many other dealers will *respond* to it. Accordingly, we assume that dealers know the value of n, but they have to forecast the number of quotes that an investor will receive in response to her RFQ.

If a dealer chooses to offer a quote, then the investor will receive a *total of k quotes* if $k-1$ out of the $n-1$ other dealers respond. The binomial formula reveals that this event occurs with probability

$$\begin{aligned}\phi_k &\equiv \mathbf{P}\left[k-1 \text{ quotes from } n-1 \text{ dealers}\right]\\ &= \binom{n-1}{k-1}(1-\pi)^{k-1}\pi^{n-k}\\ &= \frac{k}{n(1-\pi)}\binom{n}{k}(1-\pi)^k\pi^{n-k} = \frac{k\psi_k}{\sum_{\ell=1}^{n}\ell\psi_\ell},\end{aligned}$$

where the third equality follows by expanding the binomial coefficient, and the last equality follows by substituting the expression for ψ_k given in (8.9) and using the fact that

$$\sum_{k=1}^{n} \phi_k = \sum_{m=0}^{n-1} \mathbf{P}\left[m \text{ quotes from } n-1 \text{ dealers}\right] = 1.$$

Given the expected number of replies from other dealers, each individual dealer formulates an optimal price offer (bid or ask). For the remainder of this section, suppose that the investor is a buyer, so that dealers in the RFQ must respond with an ask price (the case of an investor-seller is symmetric).

Consistent with our model of semicentralized trade, we denote by P the interdealer price and by $R(\delta)$ the reservation value function of investors. With this notation an RFQ posted by an investor with utility flow δ has gains from trade if and only if $P \leq R(\delta)$. In this case, it is clear that no dealer can find it optimal to quote a price outside of the interval $[P, R(\delta)]$. Therefore, without loss of generality, we can express a dealer's response as the choice of a constant $\theta \in [0, 1]$ that determines the price offer as a combination

$$\theta R(\delta) + (1-\theta)P \tag{8.10}$$

of the interdealer price and the investor's reservation value. As in our earlier analysis with generalized Nash bargaining between investors and dealers, θ can be interpreted as the share of the surplus appropriated by the dealer if his quote is accepted. However, in contrast to our earlier modeling where this parameter was exogenously fixed, θ is now endogenously determined by the RFQ parameters, n and π.

Let $G(\theta)$ denote the probability distribution over the values of $\theta \in [0, 1]$ quoted by dealers. The expected profit for an individual dealer offering an investor a quote $\theta \in [0, 1]$ is then

$$\Pi(\theta) = \theta\,(R(\delta) - P) \sum_{k=1}^{n} \phi_k \left(1 - G(\theta-)\right)^{k-1} \alpha_k(\theta).$$

The first term on the right-hand side, $\theta\,(R(\delta) - P)$, is the profit of the dealer in the event that his quote is accepted. The second term,

$$\sum_{k=1}^{n} \phi_k \left(1 - G(\theta-)\right)^{k-1} \alpha_k(\theta),$$

is the probability that the quote is accepted. This term can be understood as follows. First, with probability ϕ_k, the investor has a total of k offers in hand. Second, the offer θ is accepted only if all other quotes are worse, meaning that other dealers offer to appropriate a larger share of the surplus, which occurs with probability $(1 - G(\theta-))^k$. Third, the probability that θ is accepted conditional on all other offers being weakly larger is

$$\alpha_k(\theta) \equiv \sum_{j=0}^{k-1} \frac{1}{j+1} \binom{k-1}{j} \left[\frac{\Delta G(\theta)}{1-G(\theta-)}\right]^j \left[\frac{1-G(\theta)}{1-G(\theta-)}\right]^{k-1-j}.$$

Indeed, a concurrent offer is equal to θ with probability

$$\frac{\Delta G(\theta)}{1-G(\theta-)} = \frac{G(\theta)-G(\theta-)}{1-G(\theta-)},$$

and it is strictly greater than θ with probability

$$1 - \frac{\Delta G(\theta)}{1-G(\theta-)} = \frac{1-G(\theta)}{1-G(\theta-)}.$$

Hence, the probability of j other offers equal to θ and $k-1-j$ other offers strictly greater than θ is given by the binomial theorem. Finally, if there are j other price offers equal to θ, then the investor accepts one at random and the dealer sells with probability $1/(j+1)$.

8.2.2 *Equilibrium*

A symmetric equilibrium of the price-setting game can be summarized by a constant $\overline{\Pi}$ and a distribution of quotes $G(\theta)$ such that

$$\Pi(\theta) \leq \overline{\Pi}, \qquad \theta \in [0,1],$$

with equality for all $\theta \in \text{supp}(G)$. Our first result establishes that, if investors receive two or more quotes with strictly positive probability, the equilibrium must take one of two forms, illustrated in the right panel of figure 8.1: either all dealers set $\theta = 0$ and earn zero profits, or they all draw prices from a continuous distribution and earn positive profits.

Lemma 8.2: Assume that

$$\psi_1 = \frac{n(1-\pi)\pi^{n-1}}{1-\pi^n} < 1.$$

In equilibrium, either $G(\theta)$ is concentrated at $\theta = 0$ or it is continuous and strictly increasing over the support $[\underline{\theta}, 1]$, for some $\underline{\theta} > 0$.

Proof. If the equilibrium distribution $G(\theta)$ is not concentrated at the origin, then there exists some point $\theta > 0$ such that $G(\theta-) < 1$, and it follows that dealers must make strictly positive profits in the sense that $\overline{\Pi} = \Pi(\theta) > 0$. Given this, the lowest point $\underline{\theta}$

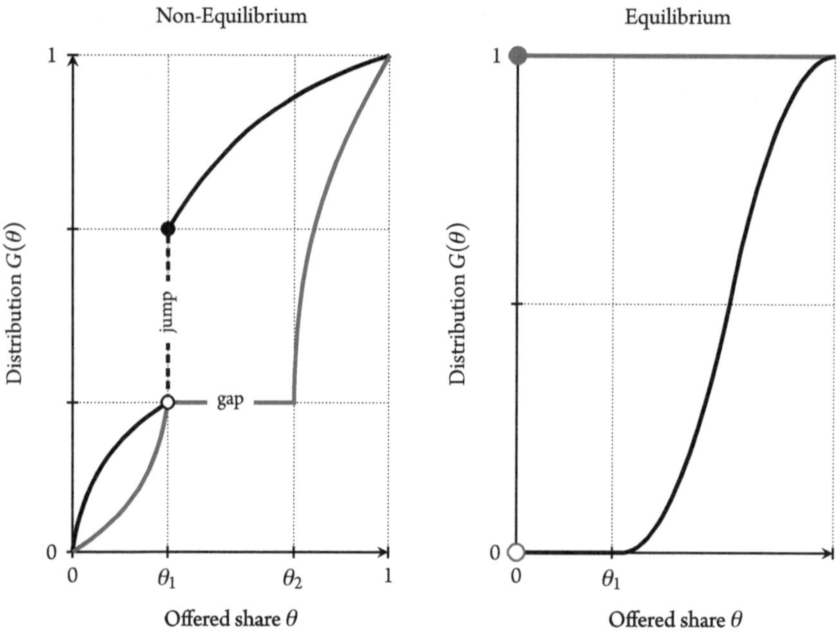

FIGURE 8.1. Equilibrium distribution of θ

The right panel of this figure illustrates the only two types of price offer distributions that can arise in equilibrium when $\psi_1 < 1$. The left panel illustrates two properties of the price offer distribution that can *not* arise in equilibrium.

in the support of the distribution must be bounded away from zero, as profits become vanishingly small as $\theta \to 0$. To see that the highest point $\overline{\theta}$ in the support of the distribution must be $\theta = 1$, it suffices to observe that if this is not then the case, then any price offer in $(\overline{\theta}, 1] \neq \emptyset$ would constitute a profitable deviation for the dealer, since it would improve her terms of trade while leaving her probability of trade unchanged.

We first show that, if it is not concentrated at zero, the distribution $G(\theta)$ must be continuous. Assume toward a contradiction that it has a discontinuity at some $\theta_1 > 0$, so that $\Delta G(\theta_1) > 0$, as illustrated by the top curve in the left panel of figure 8.1. We claim that in this case it cannot be optimal to quote θ_1. To see why, notice that a dealer who offers θ_1 can strictly increase his profits by reducing his ask by a small amount. Indeed, such a deviation eliminates all ties with other dealers posting θ_1 and thus increases the dealer's trade probability by a discrete amount, while only worsening her terms of trade by an arbitrarily small amount.

Finally, we argue that $G(\theta)$ is strictly increasing on $[\underline{\theta}, 1]$, so that there are no gaps in its support. Assume toward a contradiction that this property fails, so that $G(\theta)$ is constant over some nonempty interval $[\theta_1, \theta_2]$, as in the bottom curve of the left panel in figure 8.1. In this case, any dealer posting a quote in the interval (θ_1, θ_2) would strictly prefer quoting θ_2: such a deviation creates an arbitrarily small decrease in the trade probability, but a discrete increase in her trading profit conditional on her price offer being accepted. □

Following Burdett and Judd [1983], one can use the results in Lemma 8.2 to fully characterize the equilibrium set, as in the next proposition.

Proposition 8.3: There exists a unique equilibrium of the price-setting game.

1. If $\psi_1 = 1$, then $G(\theta)$ is concentrated at $\theta = 1$;
2. If $\psi_1 = 0$, then $G(\theta)$ is concentrated at $\theta = 0$;
3. If $\psi_1 \in (0, 1)$, then

$$G(\theta) = \max\left\{0, \frac{1 - \pi\theta^{\frac{1}{1-n}}}{1 - \pi}\right\} \tag{8.11}$$

is continuous and supported on the interval $[\phi_1, 1]$.

In all cases, the average transaction price for an investor-buyer with utility flow δ is given by equation (8.10) with $\theta = \psi_1$.

Proof. Let $\psi_1 = 0$ and assume toward a contradiction that the distribution is not concentrated at 0. In this case, we know from Lemma 8.2 that $G(\theta)$ is continuous over some support $[\underline{\theta}, 1]$. A dealer's profit is zero when she offers $\theta = 1$, since such an offer is never accepted. Alternatively, a dealer's profit is strictly positive when she offers $\underline{\theta}$, since the investor will surely accept this offer and $\underline{\theta} > 0$. Hence, the dealer is not indifferent between offering $\theta = \underline{\theta}$ and $\theta = 1$, and we have reached a contradiction.

Now let $\psi_1 \in (0, 1)$. A distribution concentrated at the origin, which leads to zero profits, cannot be an equilibrium. If it was, then a dealer would strictly prefer to offer any $\theta > 0$, as this would generate a strictly positive profit when it is the only offer received by the investor—an event that occurs with strictly positive probability when $\psi_1 > 0$.

Knowing that the distribution is continuous with support $[\underline{\theta}, 1]$, we can now characterize it as follows. Since dealers' profits are equalized over the support of the equilibrium distribution, it must be that

$$\overline{\Pi} = \Pi(1) = \phi_1 (R(\delta) - P) = \theta (R(\delta) - P) \sum_{k=1}^{n} \phi_k (1 - G(\theta))^{k-1}.$$

Canceling $R(\delta) - P$ from both sides reveals that $G(\theta)$is the unique solution to

$$\phi_1 = \theta \sum_{k=1}^{n} \phi_k \left(1 - G(\theta)\right)^{k-1}.$$

At the lower endpoint, $G(\underline{\theta}) = 0$ and the right-hand side of the equation above equals $\underline{\theta}$. This immediately implies that $\underline{\theta} = \phi_1 = \pi^{n-1}$. To obtain the explicit formula for the equilibrium distribution, divide both sides by ϕ_1 and use the definition of ϕ_k to obtain

$$\begin{aligned} 1 &= \sum_{k=1}^{n-1} \binom{n-1}{k-1} \left((1/\pi - 1)\left(1 - G(\theta)\right)\right)^{k-1} \theta \\ &= \sum_{k=1}^{n-1} \binom{n-1}{k-1} \left((1/\pi - 1)\left(1 - G(\theta)\right) \theta^{\frac{1}{n-1}}\right)^{k-1} \theta^{\frac{n-k}{n-1}}. \end{aligned}$$

An application of the binomial theorem implies that this equality holds if and only if the term in brackets satisfies

$$(1/\pi - 1)\left(1 - G(\theta)\right) \theta^{\frac{1}{n-1}} = 1 - \theta^{\frac{1}{n-1}},$$

and algebraic manipulations lead to the formula stated in (8.11).

To complete the proof, it now remains to determine the average transaction price. To do so, note that the law of large numbers implies that the expected net utility of an individual investor posting an RFQ is equal to the average net utility of a cross-section of such investors. This, in turn, equals the difference between the surplus and the average profit of the dealers selected to trade in the corresponding RFQs. The average profit is given by

$$\left(\sum_{\ell=1}^{n} \ell \psi_\ell\right) \phi_1 \left(R(\delta) - P\right) = \psi_1 \left(R(\delta) - P\right),$$

where the first term on the left-hand side is the number of quote requests that dealers collectively respond to, the second term is the expected profit per quote request, and the last equality follows from (8.9). The same result can also be obtained by direct calculation. Indeed, the cumulative distribution of the lowest θ offered by dealers is given by

$$H(\theta) \equiv \sum_{k=1}^{n} \psi_k \left\{1 - \left(1 - G(\theta)\right)^k\right\},$$

and integrating against this distribution yields

$$\int_{\phi_1}^{1} \theta\, dH(\theta) = \int_{\phi_1}^{1} \sum_{k=1}^{n} k\,\psi_k \theta\,(1 - G(\theta))^{k-1}\, dG(\theta)$$

$$= \left(\sum_{\ell=1}^{n} \ell \psi_\ell\right) \int_{\phi_1}^{1} \sum_{k=1}^{n} \phi_k \theta\,(1 - G(\theta))^{k-1}\, dG(\theta)$$

$$= \left(\sum_{\ell=1}^{n} \ell \psi_\ell\right) \phi_1 = \psi_1,$$

where the second and last equalities follow from (8.9). □

In the first case, dealers are *monopolistic* and only quote prices equal to the reservation value of the investor. This is the classic result of Diamond [1971]. In the second case, dealers quote the *competitive* price because investors always receive at least two simultaneous quotes, as in Bertrand competition. Finally, in the third case, dealers are neither monopolistic nor competitive and draw their price offers from a continuous distribution on the interval $[\phi_1, 1]$.

Using (8.9) it can be shown that the variable ψ_1, which determines the nature of the prevailing equilibrium, is decreasing in n and $1 - \pi$ (see Exercise 8.9 for details). Combining this observation with the result of Proposition 8.3 reveals that the endogenous share of the surplus that dealers in the RFQ expect to capture naturally decreases as competition strengthens, in the sense that either the number n of participating dealers or the probability that each individual dealer responds with a quote increases.

To conclude this section we want to stress that simply replacing the dealer bargaining power θ by the average share of surplus ψ_1 in the equilibrium of chapter 4 delivers the equilibrium of a market in which randomly selected dealers compete to trade through an RFQ each time that an investor makes contact with the market. Hence, the semicentralized model of chapter 4 is not a model of the past, when all trades in OTC markets occurred bilaterally: it applies equally well to the recent developments in OTC markets, in which a significant fraction of trades occur through RFQs.

8.3 Competitive Search

Up to this point, we have considered market environments in which prices between investors and dealers are determined *ex post*, i.e., after the parties have made contact. Such environments are arguably appropriate for studying opaque markets in which the trading interests of counterparties are not known in advance and investors must search for dealers to bargain over prices.

However, in several prominent OTC markets, new regulations and trading technologies have been implemented to promote greater price transparency. One convenient way to model a transparent price-setting protocol is to utilize models of competitive (or directed) search, in which investors can direct their orders toward specific prices posted by dealers. In particular, to capture a quote-driven OTC market, in this section we consider a model in which dealers commit to prices that are disseminated to all investors in the market, and investors direct their search toward the prices they find most attractive.

This theoretical setting captures an important aspect of many real-world OTC markets—namely, that dealers have *some* ability to attract order flow by offering better terms of trade. This ability could, for example, arise from the so-called dealer runs utilized in certain fixed-income markets, where dealers post indicative (but not binding) quotes reflecting their willingness to buy or sell. It could also arise from less formal channels, whereby some dealers have a reputation for offering better or worse terms. In either case, a key feature of the competitive search model is that investors face a trade-off between trading at a good price and trading quickly, as is often the case in real-world OTC markets (see, e.g., Li and Schürhoff [2019]).

Methodologically, we follow the seminal contribution of Moen [1997] and the large literature on competitive search that followed. As is well known from this literature, competitive search models have many attractive features. First, these models do not rely on ad hoc assumptions about agents' bargaining powers. Instead, the surplus-sharing rule is endogenously determined and, thus, depends on fundamentals. Second, in most settings, the surplus-sharing rule satisfies the Hosios [1990] condition, so that the number of dealers who post prices in equilibrium is efficient. Third, competitive search models tend to be highly tractable and amenable to a number of extensions, including the introduction of rich heterogeneity and alternative trading mechanisms. Lastly, as discussed above, such models offer a framework where equilibrium prices play an allocative role and investors face a trade-off between execution speed and trading costs.

8.3.1 The Market Setting

Our starting point is the semicentralized model introduced in chapter 4. There is a continuum of investors, with mass normalized to one, who can each hold zero or one unit of an asset and have utility flows $\delta \in \mathcal{D}$. Shocks to utility flows arrive at Poisson rate γ and trigger the draw of a new utility flow from a distribution F with support contained in $\mathcal{D}$. Investors search to trade through dealers, who can trade with each other instantly in a competitive interdealer market. We add three new features to this basic model.

First, we assume that dealers post and commit to a price at which they are willing to trade; for simplicity, we require that each dealer post at most one quote, that can be either to buy or to sell one unit of the asset. Dealers incur a cost κ to post a price quote, and the size of the dealer sector is determined by *free entry* (unlike in earlier chapters where it was exogenously fixed). The assumption that dealers have a limited capacity to post prices captures various costs, including the cost of time, the opportunity cost of mobilizing capital, and the costs of complying with regulation; see, e.g., Yueshen and Zou [2022] for an in-depth discussion of these costs.

As will become clear below, it is convenient to express the quotes posted by dealers as absolute markups or markdowns relative to the interdealer price, P. Specifically, we denote by m_1 a bid quote to purchase the asset from an investor-owner at price $P - m_1$. Likewise, we denote by m_0 an ask quote to sell the asset to an investor-nonowner at price $P + m_0$.

Our second departure from the semicentralized market model is that we assume the matching process between dealers' quotes and investors exhibits *congestion*. Namely, if a mass μ_d of dealers post a quote m and a mass μ_i of investors direct their orders to this quote, then we assume that transactions at this quote are executed at rate $\Xi(\mu_d, \mu_i)$. The function Ξ plays the same role as the matching function in other economic applications [see, e.g., Pissarides, 1985]. It is assumed to be homogeneous of degree one, strictly increasing in both arguments, strictly concave, twice continuously differentiable, and to satisfy the Inada conditions given by

$$\lim_{\mu_j \to 0} \frac{\partial \Xi}{\partial \mu_j} = \infty, \qquad \lim_{\mu_j \to \infty} \frac{\partial \Xi}{\partial \mu_j} = 0, \qquad \text{for all } \mu_{-j} > 0.$$

A classic example of a matching function satisfying those assumptions is the constant elasticity function given by

$$\Xi(\mu_d, \mu_i) = \Lambda \mu_d^{\alpha} \mu_i^{1-\alpha}$$

for some $\alpha \in (0, 1)$. We will use this highly tractable specification to illustrate the main features of the equilibrium later in this section.

If orders are executed at random, then our assumptions imply that investors who direct their orders to a quote posted by a mass μ_d of dealers and sought by a mass μ_i of investors effectively trade at Poisson rate

$$\frac{\Xi(\mu_d, \mu_i)}{\mu_i} = \Xi\left(\frac{\mu_d}{\mu_i}, 1\right) \equiv \lambda(\omega),$$

where $\omega \equiv \frac{\mu_d}{\mu_i}$ is the *market tightness* at this quote. On the other side of the market, a dealer who posts this quote trades at Poisson rate

$$\frac{\Xi(\mu_d, \mu_i)}{\mu_d} = \frac{\mu_i}{\mu_d}\,\Xi\left(\frac{\mu_d}{\mu_i}, 1\right) = \frac{\lambda(\omega)}{\omega}.$$

Note for later use that our assumptions on the matching function imply that the functions $\lambda(\omega)$ and $-\frac{\lambda(\omega)}{\omega}$ are twice continuously differentiable, strictly increasing, strictly concave with a derivative satisfying the Inada conditions, and map $[0, \infty]$ onto, respectively, $[0, \infty]$ and $[-\infty, 0]$.

8.3.2 Optimal Behavior and Equilibrium Definition

NOTATION

Let $\mathcal{M}_q = \mathbb{R}_+$ denote the feasible set of quotes a dealer can post to trade with investors holding $q \in \{0, 1\}$ units of the asset and $\mathcal{M}_q^\star \subset \mathcal{M}_q$ denote the set of quotes posted by dealers in equilibrium, where we simply take $\mathcal{M}_q^\star$ to be the empty set if dealers choose not to post any quote.

In addition, let $\Omega_q(m)$ denote the tightness of the market at quote m or, equivalently, the inverse of the length of the queue to trade at that quote. This function is to be determined in equilibrium and, importantly, needs to be defined for all possible quotes $m \in \mathcal{M}_q$, and not only for those in $\mathcal{M}_q^\star$. This is crucial to pin down the expectations of dealers about market tightness when they consider deviations from the set of equilibrium quotes.

DEALERS' OPTIMAL QUOTES AND ZERO PROFITS

Taking as given the market tightness function, $\Omega_q(m)$, the problem of a dealer is to choose a quote $m \in \mathcal{M}_q$ to offer investors who hold $q \in \{0, 1\}$ units of the asset in order to maximize the profit function:

$$\frac{\lambda(\Omega_q(m))}{\Omega_q(m)} m - \kappa.$$

The first term in this expression is the expected flow profit from posting quote m, whereas the second term is the flow cost. Given free entry, the equilibrium profits of dealers must be at most zero, so that

$$\frac{\lambda(\Omega_q(m))}{\Omega_q(m)} m \leq \kappa \text{ for all } m \in \mathcal{M}_q, \text{ with equality if } m \in \mathcal{M}_q^\star. \tag{8.12}$$

INVESTORS' RESERVATION VALUES

Next, we characterize the reservation values of investors, taking as given the market tightness $\Omega_q(m)$ at all quotes $m \in \mathcal{M}_q^\star$ for $q \in \{0, 1\}$. Proceeding as in previous chapters shows that the reservation value $R(\delta)$ of an investor with current utility flow δ satisfies

$$(r+\gamma)\,R(\delta) = \delta + \gamma \mathbf{E}^F\left[R(x)\right] + \max_{\mu \in \mathcal{M}_1^\star \cup \{n\}} \lambda(\Omega_1(\mu))\,(P - \mu - R(\delta)) - \max_{\mu \in \mathcal{M}_0^\star \cup \{n\}} \lambda(\Omega_0(\mu))\,(R(\delta) - P - \mu), \qquad (8.13)$$

with the convention that $\Omega_q(n) \equiv 0$ where n denotes the option of not seeking to trade. This equation for reservation values is similar to that which holds in the semicentralized market model of chapter 4, but there is one important difference: instead of continuously searching for dealers with whom to bargain over a trade, investors now choose whether to search and can direct their search efforts toward the best quotes, subject to a congestion friction.

MARKET TIGHTNESS FUNCTION

Given the reservation values of investors, we follow Chang [2018] and state the equilibrium conditions for the tightness functions as

$$\Omega_0(m) = \inf\Big\{\omega \geq 0 : \exists \delta \in \operatorname{supp}(F) \text{ such that } \lambda(\omega)\,(R(\delta) - P - m) > \max_{\mu \in \mathcal{M}_0^\star \cup \{n\}} \lambda(\Omega_0(\mu))\,(R(\delta) - P - \mu)\Big\} \qquad (8.14)$$

and

$$\Omega_1(m) = \inf\Big\{\omega \geq 0 : \exists \delta \in \operatorname{supp}(F) \text{ such that } \lambda(\omega)\,(P - m - R(\delta)) > \max_{\mu \in \mathcal{M}_1^\star \cup \{n\}} \lambda(\Omega_0(\mu))\,(R(\delta) - P - \mu)\Big\}, \qquad (8.15)$$

with the convention that $\inf \emptyset = \infty$. Acemoglu and Shimer [1999] interpret (8.14) and (8.15) in the spirit of subgame perfection. Namely, suppose that a dealer considers the possibility of deviating by posting a quote $m \notin \mathcal{M}_0^\star$ (the reasoning for bids is analogous). If the new quote is such that

$$R(\delta) - P - m \leq 0, \qquad \forall \delta \in \operatorname{supp}(F),$$

then no investor will seek to trade at m and, as a result, $\Omega_0(m) = \infty$; intuitively, if an investor were to seek that quote, then he would be alone in doing so and, thus, would obtain immediate execution. On the other hand, if the quote is attractive to some investors, in the sense that

$$R(\delta) - P - m > 0$$

for some $\delta \in \text{supp}(F)$, then these investors will seek to trade at m and the market tightness at that quote will fall—or the queue of investors will continue to grow—until the expected flow profits of all such investors from seeking to trade at m no longer exceed those they can obtain by seeking an optimally selected equilibrium quote $\mu \in \mathcal{M}_0^\star \cup \{n\}$.

Notice that we define the tightness functions $\Omega_0(m)$ and $\Omega_1(m)$ based on strict gains from trade, and not weak gains from trade: conditions (8.14) and (8.15) are stated in terms of strict inequalities and not weak inequalities. If, instead, they were defined in terms of weak inequalities, then the tightness functions would be identically zero. Indeed, investors who have just traded with dealers and have not yet changed utility flow have no gains from trade at equilibrium quotes. Hence, these investors have weak incentive to seek any quote such that $\omega = 0$. This implies that, if conditions (8.14) and (8.15) were based on weak inequalities, then $\omega = 0$ would belong to the sets, and evidently the market tightness functions would be zero as well.

The market tightness functions are a crucial input into the characterization of a competitive search equilibrium. Intuitively, suppose we break down each small interval into a two-stage game in which dealers first post quotes, and then investors direct their search to the desired quotes. Conditions (8.14) and (8.15) characterize a Nash equilibrium in the second-stage game: they require that the search strategies of investors be optimal, given the behavior of other investors and the quotes posted in the first stage. Moving to the first-stage game, conditions (8.14) and (8.15) are akin to demand and supply functions, respectively: taking as given the behavior of other dealers, they determine the flow of buy or sell orders from investors (that emerge in the second-stage game) from a dealer posting any quote. See Burdett, Shi, and Wright [2001] for explicit microfoundations of this two-stage game.

ASSET ALLOCATION AND MARKET CLEARING

A common result in competitive search models with heterogeneous agents is that the equilibrium features full separation. In our context this means that each quote $m \in \mathcal{M}_q^\star$ is optimally chosen by investors with $q \in \{0, 1\}$ units of the asset and a unique utility flow δ. Technically, this occurs because the (m, ω)—indifference curves of investors, which capture their willingness to trade off execution speed and trading costs, satisfy a single crossing property; see Moen [1997] and Acemoglu and Shimer [1999] for early instances of this result. Anticipating this property, we let $m_q(\delta)$ denote the quote $m \in \mathcal{M}_q^\star \cup \{n\}$ chosen by investors of type (q, δ) with the convention that investors who do not seek to trade choose the default option $m_q(\delta) = n$.

As before, we denote by $\Phi_q(\delta)$ the measure of investors with asset holdings $q \in \{0, 1\}$ and utility flow less than or equal to $\delta \in \mathcal{D}$. Again, these measures must satisfy three conditions. First, they must add up to the distribution of utility flows across the whole population:

$$\Phi_0(\delta) + \Phi_1(\delta) = F(\delta), \qquad \delta \in \mathcal{D}. \tag{8.16}$$

Second, they must be consistent with market clearing in the sense that the total measure of asset owners must equal the asset supply:

$$\Phi_1(\bar{\delta}) \equiv \lim_{\delta \uparrow \bar{\delta}} \Phi_1(\delta) = s.$$

Third, these cumulative measures must be consistent with stationarity, which requires that the inflow to and outflow from any given group of investors be equalized in the sense that

$$\int_B \gamma s dF(\delta) + \int_B \lambda(\Omega_0(m_0(\delta)))d\Phi_0(\delta) \tag{8.17}$$
$$= \int_B \gamma d\Phi_1(\delta) + \int_B \lambda(\Omega_1(m_1(\delta)))\, d\Phi_1(\delta),$$

for any Borel set $B \subseteq \mathcal{D}$. Lemma A.14 in appendix A.2 allows us to drop the explicit reference to Borel sets and heuristically write that the relationship holds at all utility flows:

$$\gamma s dF(\delta) + \lambda(\Omega_0(m_0(\delta)))\, d\Phi_0(\delta) = \gamma d\Phi_1(\delta) + \lambda(\Omega_1(m_1(\delta)))\, d\Phi_1(\delta).$$

Substituting (8.16) and solving yields

$$d\Phi_1(\delta) = \frac{\gamma s + \lambda(\Omega_0(m_0(\delta))}{\gamma + \lambda(\Omega_1(m_1(\delta))) + \lambda(\Omega_0(m_0(\delta)))}\, dF(\delta). \tag{8.18}$$

Note that condition (8.17) implies that the interdealer market automatically clears. In particular, evaluating this condition at $B = \mathcal{D}$ reveals that

$$\int_{\mathcal{D}} \lambda(\Omega_0(m_0(\delta)))d\Phi_0(\delta) = \int_{\mathcal{D}} \lambda(\Omega_1(m_1(\delta)))\, d\Phi_1(\delta),$$

where the left-hand side represents the flow of assets that dealers sell and the right-hand side represents the flow of assets that they buy. As in our earlier analysis, this result obtains because market clearing is an implication of stationarity: the only way that the mass of assets in the hands of investors remains constant is if the flow of purchases and the flow of sales are equalized.

DEFINITION OF EQUILIBRIUM

A *competitive search equilibrium* comprises an interdealer price P, an investor reservation value function $R(\delta)$, a pair of functions $m_0(\delta)$ and $m_1(\delta)$ for the quotes that an investor of current type (q, δ) finds optimal to seek, a pair of sets $\mathcal{M}_0^\star$ and $\mathcal{M}_1^\star$ for the ask and bid quotes that dealers find optimal to post, a pair of market tightness functions $\Omega_0(m)$ and $\Omega_1(m)$, and a pair of cumulative measures $\Phi_0(\delta)$ and $\Phi_0(\delta)$ that jointly solve equations (8.12)–(8.18).

8.3.3 An Alternative Representation of Reservation Values

To facilitate the equilibrium construction we start by deriving an alternative representation of reservation values. Specifically, we show that competition among dealers leads to quotes that maximize investors' option value of search, subject to the constraint that dealers make zero profit. As we show below, if this were not the case, dealers would be able to post quotes that are more attractive to investors and, thus, generate strictly positive profits.

Proposition 8.4: In a competitive search equilibrium the reservation value function of investors satisfies

$$(r+\gamma)\,R(\delta) = \delta + \gamma \mathbf{E}^F\left[R(x)\right] + \max_{\omega\geq 0}\left\{\lambda(\omega)\,(P - R(\delta)) - \kappa\omega\right\} \qquad (8.19)$$

$$- \max_{\omega\geq 0}\left\{\lambda(\omega)\,(R(\delta) - P) - \kappa\omega\right\}$$

for all utility flows $\delta \in \text{supp}(F)$.

Proof. To establish the result it suffices to show that, for any $\delta \in \text{supp}(F)$, the last two terms in (8.19) are equal to the last two terms of (8.13):

$$\max_{\mu\in\mathcal{M}_1^\star\cup\{n\}} \lambda(\Omega_1(\mu))\,(P - \mu - R(\delta)) = \max_{\omega\geq 0}\left\{\lambda(\omega)\,(P - R(\delta)) - \kappa\omega\right\},$$

$$\max_{\mu\in\mathcal{M}_0^\star\cup\{n\}} \lambda(\Omega_0(\mu))\,(R(\delta) - P - \mu) = \max_{\omega\geq 0}\left\{\lambda(\omega)\,(R(\delta) - P) - \kappa\omega\right\}.$$

Let us focus on the first equality, as the proof is the same for the second one. From the zero-profit condition (8.12) we deduce that

$$\lambda(\Omega_1(\mu))\,(P-\mu-R(\delta)) = \lambda(\Omega_1(\mu))\,(P-R(\delta)) - \kappa\Omega_1(\mu)$$
$$\leq \max_{\omega\geq 0}\{\lambda(\omega)\,(P-R(\delta)) - \kappa\omega\}$$

for all $\mu \in \mathcal{M}_1^{\star} \cup \{n\}$ and, therefore,

$$\max_{\mu\in\mathcal{M}_1^{\star}\cup\{n\}} \lambda(\Omega_1(\mu))\,(P-\mu-R(\delta)) \leq \max_{\omega\geq 0}\{\lambda(\omega)\,(P-R(\delta)) - \kappa\omega\}$$

for any $\delta \in \text{supp}(F)$. Now suppose toward a contradiction that this inequality is not an equality, so that there exist $\hat{\omega}$ and $\hat{\delta} \in \text{supp}(F)$ such that

$$\max_{\mu\in\mathcal{M}_1^{\star}\cup\{n\}} \lambda(\Omega_1(\mu))\left(P-\mu-R(\hat{\delta})\right) < \lambda(\hat{\omega})\left(P-R(\hat{\delta})\right) - \kappa\hat{\omega}. \tag{8.20}$$

Consider the quote $\hat{m}$ such that $\frac{\lambda(\hat{\omega})}{\hat{\omega}}\hat{m} = \kappa$, that is, the quote that achieves zero profits when the market tightness is exogenously set to $\hat{\omega}$. The definition of the tightness function (8.15) and (8.20) imply that we have

$$\lambda(\hat{\omega})\left(P-\hat{m}-R(\hat{\delta})\right) > \max_{\mu\in\mathcal{M}_1^{\star}\cup\{n\}} \lambda(\Omega_1(\mu))\left(P-\mu-R(\hat{\delta})\right)$$

and, therefore, $\Omega_1(\hat{\omega}) < \hat{\omega}$. Since the trading intensity of dealers is strictly increasing in the market tightness, this in turn implies

$$\frac{\lambda(\Omega_1(\hat{\omega}))}{\Omega_1(\hat{\omega})}\hat{m} - \kappa > \frac{\lambda(\hat{\omega})}{\hat{\omega}}\hat{m} - \kappa = 0,$$

which shows that quoting $\hat{m}$ generates strictly positive dealer profits and thus contradicts the zero-profit condition. □

The proposition establishes an equivalence between the competitive search model and an alternative model in which investors can choose the intensity with which they contact a centralized market where the asset is traded at the constant price P. More specifically, in a competitive search model, equilibrium search times are determined as if investors directly choose the market tightness subject to a linear cost—or, equivalently, as if they directly choose the intensity of contact with the centralized market, $\Lambda \equiv \lambda(\omega)$, subject to a convex cost given by $\kappa\lambda^{-1}(\Lambda)$. Of course, the competitive search equilibrium has a much richer structure than its search-intensity counterpart, since it also makes predictions about the equilibrium markups and markdowns charged by dealers, and their relationships with search times.

Note that since (8.19) holds at all points of $\text{supp}(F)$, we can replace the reservation value function by the solution to (8.19) posed over the whole set of utility flows without altering the reservation value of any actual investor in the market, at least if this solution is unique. Exercise 8.10 shows that this is indeed the case and also establishes that, as in previous chapters, the reservation value function is strictly increasing and absolutely continuous in utility flow.

8.3.4 Solving for Equilibrium

Proposition 8.4 provides the basis for the construction of equilibrium. As a first step, we note that the optimization problems in (8.19) are both strictly concave, and thus they admit unique optimal solutions that we denote by $\omega_1(\delta)$ and $\omega_0(\delta)$, respectively. This confirms our earlier conjecture that the equilibrium features full separation of utility types, so that each investor follows a *pure strategy* that directs her search toward a single quote at a time.

Differentiating (8.19) with respect to utility flow and using the envelope theorem shows that

$$R'(\delta) = \frac{1}{r + \gamma + \lambda(\omega_1(\delta)) + \lambda(\omega_0(\delta))} > 0. \tag{8.21}$$

This establishes that reservation values are strictly increasing in utility flow and implies that the optimizers $\omega_1(\delta)$ and $\omega_0(\delta)$ are strictly increasing and strictly decreasing, respectively. The interpretation of this result is clear: more extreme types have stronger incentives to trade, and thus optimally choose higher search intensities, $\lambda(\omega)$. However, with faster trading times come larger transaction costs that are explicitly given by

$$m_q(\delta) \equiv \frac{\kappa\, \omega_q(\delta)}{\lambda(\omega_q(\delta))}$$

as a result of the dealers' zero-profit condition.

Next, we observe that, as in previous chapters, the interdealer price P must lie in $(R(\underline{\delta}), R(\overline{\delta}))$, as otherwise the interdealer market would not clear. Since the reservation value function is continuous, there exists a marginal type $\delta^\star$ such that $R(\delta^\star) = P$, and it immediately follows that

$$\omega_0(\delta_0) = \omega_1(\delta_1) = 0, \qquad \forall \delta_0 \leq \delta^\star \leq \delta_1. \tag{8.22}$$

In other words, just as in the semicentralized market of chapter 4, owners (nonowners) do not trade if $\delta_1 \geq \delta^\star$ ($\delta_0 \leq \delta^\star$). This is intuitive: given that there is a cost to post a quote—or, under our alternative interpretation, a search intensity cost—investors never find it optimal to search on both sides of the market at the same time.

To determine the equilibrium tightness functions, we start by taking first-order conditions with respect to ω in (8.19). This gives

$$\kappa = \lambda'(\omega_1(\delta))(P - R(\delta)) = \lambda'(\omega_1(\delta)) \int_{\delta}^{\delta^\star} R'(x)dx, \qquad \delta \in (\underline{\delta}, \delta^\star],$$

$$= \lambda'(\omega_0(\delta))(R(\delta) - P) = \lambda'(\omega_0(\delta)) \int_{\delta^\star}^{\delta} R'(x)dx, \qquad \delta \in [\delta^\star, \overline{\delta}),$$

where the second equality follows from the fundamental theorem of calculus and the fact that $P = R(\delta^\star)$. Next, using (8.21) together with (8.22) to compute the two integrals, we obtain that the functions

$$\lambda'(\omega_0(\delta)) \int_{\delta^\star}^{\delta} \frac{dx}{r + \gamma + \lambda(\omega_0(x))} \tag{8.23}$$

and

$$\lambda'(\omega_1(\delta)) \int_{\delta}^{\delta^\star} \frac{dx}{r + \gamma + \lambda(\omega_1(x))} \tag{8.24}$$

are constant and equal to κ on $(\underline{\delta}, \delta^\star]$ and $[\delta^\star, \overline{\delta})$, respectively. Combining the first-order conditions and their respective derivatives with respect to utility flows, we obtain that

$$\omega_q(\delta) = T\left[((2q-1)(\delta^\star - \delta))^+\right] \tag{8.25}$$

for some strictly increasing function $T : \mathbf{R}_+ \to \mathbf{R}_+$ with $T(0) = 0$ that is described in the following lemma.

Lemma 8.5: The function $T(x)$ is the inverse of

$$S(y) \equiv \frac{\kappa\left(r + \gamma + \lambda(y) - y\lambda'(y)\right)}{\lambda'(y)}. \tag{8.26}$$

In particular, the equilibrium tightness functions are decreasing in (r, γ, κ).

Proof. Setting the derivatives of (8.23) and (8.24) to zero and using (8.25) shows that the function $T(x)$ must satisfy

$$T'(x) = -\frac{\lambda'(T(x))^2}{\kappa\lambda''(T(x))\left(r + \gamma + \lambda(T(x))\right)}, \tag{8.27}$$

subject to $T(0) = 0$. If the function $T(x)$ is a strictly increasing solution to this ordinary differential equation (ODE), then it admits a well-defined inverse $S(y)$ that satisfies

$$S'(y) = \frac{1}{T'(S(y))} = -\frac{\kappa\lambda''(y)\left(r+\gamma+\lambda(y)\right)}{\lambda'(y)^2}, \tag{8.28}$$

subject to the initial condition $S(0) = 0$. Integrating on both sides shows that $S(y)$ is given by (8.26). Conversely, the function $S(y)$ defined by (8.26) is strictly increasing since the intensity function $\lambda(\omega)$ is strictly increasing and strictly concave. Therefore, $S(y)$ admits a well-defined inverse $T(x)$, and a direct calculation using (8.28) shows that this inverse is a solution to the ODE (8.27) subject to $T(0) = 0$. The remaining claims in the statement follow from the implicit function theorem since $S(y)$ is increasing in y, r, γ, and κ. □

Having constructed the tightness functions in terms of the marginal type, we can plug them into (8.18) evaluated at the upper endpoint of $\mathcal{D}$ to state the market clearing condition as

$$\int_{\underline{\delta}}^{\delta^\star} \frac{\gamma s}{\gamma+\lambda\left(T(\delta^\star-\delta)\right)} dF(\delta) + \int_{\delta^\star}^{\overline{\delta}} \frac{\gamma s+\lambda\left(T(\delta-\delta^\star)\right)}{\gamma+\lambda\left(T(\delta-\delta^\star)\right)} dF(\delta) = s. \tag{8.29}$$

The following proposition completes the equilibrium construction by showing that this equation uniquely pins down the marginal type.

Proposition 8.6: Equation (8.29) admits a unique solution $\delta^\star \in \mathcal{D}$ and, as a result, there exists a unique competitive search equilibrium.

Proof. Equation (8.29) can be written compactly as

$$L(\delta^\star) \equiv \int_{\underline{\delta}}^{\overline{\delta}} \frac{\gamma s+\lambda\circ T\left((\delta-\delta^\star)^+\right)}{\gamma+\lambda\circ T\left(|\delta-\delta^\star|\right)} dF(\delta) = s.$$

Direct calculations show that the integrand is continuous in $(\delta, \delta^\star)$ and strictly decreasing in $\delta^\star$ for each fixed δ. Therefore, $L(\delta^\star)$ is a continuous as well as strictly decreasing function, and the result now follows from the intermediate value theorem by observing that $L(\overline{\delta}) < s < L(\underline{\pi})$. □

Example 8.7: To illustrate the features of the competitive search equilibrium, consider the case where the distribution of utility flows is uniform over the unit interval $\mathcal{D} = [0, 1]$ and assume that

$$\lambda(\omega) = \Lambda\omega^\alpha$$

for some $\Lambda > 0$ and $\alpha \in [0, 1]$. In this case, the inversion of $S(\theta)$ boils down to solving the nonlinear equation

$$x = S(T(x)) = \frac{\kappa}{\alpha\Lambda}(r+\gamma)\,T(x)^{1-\alpha} + \left(\frac{1}{\alpha} - 1\right)\kappa T(x)$$

for each $x \in [0, 1]$. This equation admits an explicit solution for specific parameter values. For example, if $\alpha = \frac{1}{2}$ then

$$T(x) = \left\{\sqrt{\left(\frac{r+\gamma}{\Lambda}\right)^2 + \frac{x}{\kappa}} - \frac{r+\gamma}{\Lambda}\right\}^2,$$

which implies that the equilibrium tightness functions $\omega_0(\delta)$ and $\omega_1(\delta)$ are explicitly given by

$$\omega_q(\delta) = T\left[(\delta - \delta^\star)^+ + q\,(\delta^\star - \delta)\right].$$

On the other hand, the fact that the distribution is uniform implies that the market clearing condition (8.29) can be written as

$$s = \int_0^{\delta^\star} \frac{\gamma s}{\gamma + \lambda\,(T(x))}dx + \int_0^{1-\delta^\star} \frac{\gamma s + \lambda\,(T(x))}{\gamma + \lambda\,(T(x))}dx.$$

In particular, if $s = \frac{1}{2}$ then a straightforward, albeit tedious, calculation shows that the marginal type is given by $\delta^\star = 1 - s = \frac{1}{2}$ independently of all the other parameters of the model. Taking advantage of this simplification, we plot in figure 8.2 the tightness functions $\omega_q(\delta)$, the distribution

$$\Phi_1(\delta) = \int_0^{\delta} \frac{\gamma s + \lambda(\omega_0(x))}{\gamma + \lambda(\omega_0(x)) + \lambda(\omega_1(x))}dx,$$

and the equilibrium trading intensities $\lambda(\omega_q(\delta))$ and $\frac{\lambda(\omega_q(\delta))}{\omega_q(\delta)}$ of investors and dealers for various values of the quote-posting cost parameter κ in a model with parameters $\alpha = s = \frac{1}{2}$ and $\Lambda = 3$.

The interpretation of Figure 8.2 is intuitive. Starting from the top left, the figure shows that the equilibrium tightness is larger for less favorable quotes and decreases in all open markets as the quote-posting cost κ decreases. This is natural since more attractive quotes are sought by more investors and because a lower cost implies that more dealers find it optimal to quote any given $m \in \mathcal{M}_q^\star$. As shown in the right panels of the figure, these features imply that investors with larger gains from trade obtain faster execution and that all investors trade faster as the quote-posting cost decreases, which in turn improves the overall efficiency of the equilibrium allocation. However,

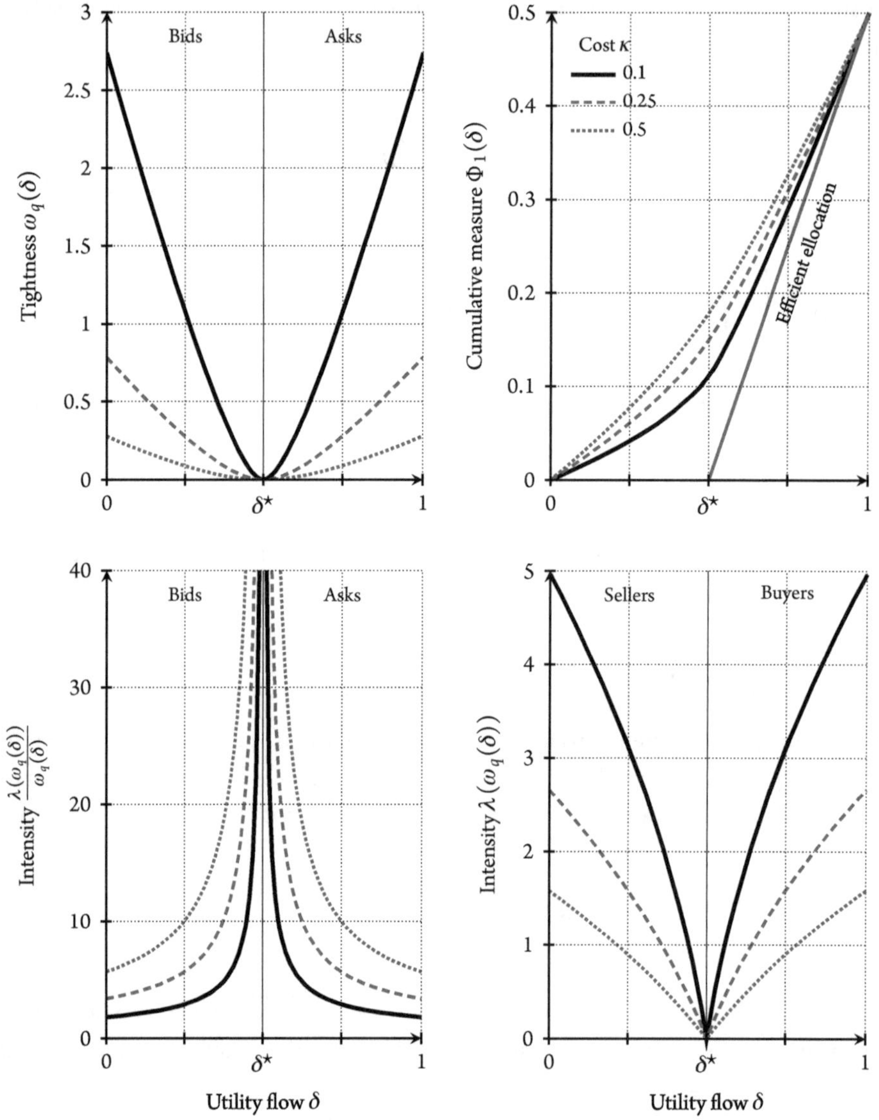

FIGURE 8.2. Competitive search equilibrium

This figure plots (clockwise from top left) the tightness functions, the distribution of utility flows among owners, and the equilibrium trading intensities of investors and dealers in a model with $F(\delta) = \delta$ on $\mathcal{D} = [0, 1]$, $s = \frac{1}{2}$, and $\lambda(\omega) = 3\sqrt{\omega}$ for different values of the quote-posting cost parameter κ.

the bottom right panel shows that these efficiency gains are made at the expense of active dealers who experience longer individual waiting times as a result of increased competition.

8.4 Exercises

Exercise 8.8: Consider a meeting between an investor of type $(1, \delta_H)$ and a dealer in the bargaining game of section 8.1. The goal of this exercise is to derive parameter restrictions such that, in a stationary SPNE, when the investor is a receiver, she is indifferent between accepting and quitting the bargaining table, while the dealer is indifferent between accepting and waiting.

1. Write the indifference condition of the investor and of the dealer and solve for $p_I(\delta_L)$ and $p_D(\delta_L)$.
2. Show that, if these indifference conditions hold, $p_I(\delta_L)$ and $p_D(\delta_L)$ converge to $R(\delta_L)$ as $h \to 0$. Provide intuition.
3. State the inequalities ensuring that the investor strictly prefers quitting over waiting, and the dealer strictly prefers waiting over quitting.
4. Show that these inequalities hold for all h small enough if

$$\frac{\pi_D c_I - \pi_I c_D}{r + \gamma f_H + \lambda} > \frac{\pi_I (\delta_H - \delta_L)}{r + \gamma}.$$

Exercise 8.9: Consider the model of RFQs developed in section 8.2 and recall that in equilibrium the average share of the surplus that a dealer captures when selected to trade is

$$\psi_1 = \frac{1-\pi}{\pi} \frac{n\pi^n}{1-\pi^n},$$

where $n \in \mathbf{N}$ is the number of dealers selected in each RFQ and $\pi \in (0, 1)$ is the probability that a dealer fails to respond.

1. Show that

$$\frac{\partial \psi_1}{\partial \pi} = \frac{(1-\pi^n)^2}{n\pi^{n-2}} f(\pi)$$

   for some decreasing function to be determined and use this result to prove that ψ_1 is increasing in π.
2. Regarding n as a continuous variable, show that

$$\frac{\partial \psi_1}{\partial n} = \frac{(1-\pi^n)^2}{\pi^n} g(n)$$

for some decreasing function to be determined. Use this result to prove that ψ_1 is decreasing in n.

Exercise 8.10: The goal of this exercise is to derive existence, uniqueness, and basic properties of the solution to the reservation value equation (8.19) in the competitive search model. Let

$$M_n(x) \equiv \sup_{\omega \leq n} \{\lambda(\omega)x - \kappa\omega\}, \qquad n \in [0, \infty],$$

and consider the parameterized family of equations

$$(r+\gamma)R(\delta) = S_n[R](\delta) \equiv \delta + \gamma \mathbf{E}^F[R(x)] + M_n(P - R(\delta)) - M_n(R(\delta) - P) \tag{8.30}$$

so that (8.19) corresponds to the case $n = \infty$.

1. Show that $M_n(x)$ is nondecreasing in (n, x) and convex in x with a derivative that takes values in $[0, \lambda(n)]$.
2. Show that $M_\infty(x) = \lambda(\omega^*(x))x - \kappa\omega^*(x)$ for some function $\omega^*(x) \geq 0$ that is equal to zero on $[-\infty, 0]$ and strictly increasing otherwise.
3. Show that if $R(x)$ is a solution to (8.30) for some $n \leq \infty$, then it is strictly increasing and such that

$$\underline{\delta} + M_\infty\left(\frac{\overline{\delta}}{r} - P\right) \leq rR(\delta) \leq \overline{\delta} + M_\infty\left(P - \frac{\underline{\delta}}{r}\right).$$

   Conclude that there exists $n^* < \infty$ such that $R(\delta)$ is a solution to (8.30) when $n = \infty$ if and only if it is also a solution when $n = n^*$.
4. Show that, for any $n < \infty$, the operator

$$T_n[R](\delta) \equiv \frac{2\lambda(n)R(\delta) + S_n[R](\delta)}{r + \gamma + 2\lambda(n)}$$

   satisfies Blackwell's conditions and maps

$$\left\{ R \in \mathcal{B}(\mathcal{D}) : \sup_{\delta \neq \delta'} \left| \frac{R(\delta) - R(\delta')}{\delta - \delta'} \right| \leq \frac{1}{r + \gamma + 2\lambda(n)} \right\}$$

   into itself. Argue that (8.30) with $n = \infty$ admits a unique solution that is bounded, strictly increasing, and Lipschitz continuous.

8.5 Notes and References

Following the seminal work of Rubinstein [1982], Binmore, Rubinstein, and Wolinsky [1986], and Rubinstein and Wolinsky [1987], multiple authors have offered strategic foundations for the bargaining solution in search-theoretic models. These include Trejos and Wright [1995] and Shi [1995] in monetary models and Hall and Milgrom [2008] in search and matching models of the labor market. In an OTC market framework, Duffie, Gârleanu, and Pedersen [2007] set up and solve an explicit bargaining game, but they do not address the incentives of investors to stay matched in order to capture future gains from trade. Appendix C of Lagos and Rocheteau [2008] considers strategic bargaining and explicitly addresses the investors' incentives to stay matched, but ultimately rules out this strategy by considering the limit in which the game is assumed to end infinitely fast. Similar assumptions are made by Farboodi, Jarosch, Menzio, and Wiriadinata [2018] and Li [2023], who consider explicit bargaining games in their OTC frameworks occurring in virtual time. In more recent work, Maciocco [2023] studies an environment in which investors and dealers engage in strategic bargaining and remain matched in relationships.

In the model we considered here, the equilibrium bargaining outcome can feature a delayed agreement because the value of the match may increase over time. For a more detailed discussion on bargaining games in a nonstationary environment, see Perry and Reny [1993], Merlo and Wilson [1995], and Coles and Wright [1998]. Note, however, that delays can also arise for other reasons, including asymmetric information. For an overview of bargaining games with private information and the induced possibility of delays, see Kennan and Wilson [1993]. A recent application to OTC markets can be found in Nozawa and Tsoy [2023], which is based on Tsoy [2018, 2019].

Section 8.2 is based on appendix B of Weill [2020]. Closely related pricing mechanisms are analyzed in Duffie, Dworczak, and Zhu [2017], Liu, Vogel, and Zhang [2018], Vogel [2019], and Glebkin, Shen, and Yueshen [2019]. Lester, Shourideh, Venkateswaran, and Zetlin-Jones [2023] extend this mechanism to a setting with asymmetric information about the value of the asset, while Garrett, Gomes, and Maestri [2018] consider a setting with asymmetric information about private valuations. Theoretically, Glebkin et al. [2019] consider an environment with an exogenous distribution of inventories across dealers, which generates a nonzero probability that a given dealer will decline a request—either because he does not have the necessary inventory or because he has reached capacity and can no longer buy. Yueshen and Zou [2022] study a related setting in which, as in the competitive search framework, it is costly for dealers to post quotes. In equilibrium, investors respond by choosing an optimal, finite number of dealers to contact. Wang [2003] provides a model in which dealers find it optimal to respond with a probability π strictly less than 1, and customers find it optimal to contact just two dealers.

Despite the vast literature on competitive or directed search (see the survey by Wright, Kircher, Julien, and Guerrieri [2021]), it is only recently that this framework has been incorporated into OTC market models. Most of the analysis in section 8.3 derives from results first explored in Lester, Rocheteau, and Weill [2015], who analyze competitive search in a semicentralized model of OTC markets with discrete utility types and divisible asset holdings. For other applications of competitive search models to OTC markets, see Guerrieri and Shimer [2014], Chang [2018], Armenter and Lester [2017], Hedlund [2016], Williams [2021], Chaumont [2018], Li [2018], Gabrovski and Kospentaris [2021], and Kargar, Passadore, and Silva [2021] among many others.

9

OTC Markets Under Stress

OTC markets have taken center stage in recent crises. For instance, the markets for various types of derivatives and asset-backed securities have often been identified as ground zero for the Global Financial Crisis (GFC) of 2007–2008 [see, for example, Brunnermeier, 2009]. More recently, at the onset of the COVID–19 crisis, the first important cracks in the U.S. financial system appeared in the OTC markets for Treasury, corporate, and municipal bonds [see, e.g., O'Hara and Zhou, 2022, for an overview.]. Given the central role that OTC markets play in the allocation of capital and the implementation of monetary policy, these events have naturally raised concerns among policymakers about the fragility of OTC markets and their ability to withstand stress. In particular, during these crises, many have argued that dealers should absorb more of the selling pressure in order to maintain a liquid market for investors.

To understand the incentives of dealers to provide liquidity in times of stress—and the subsequent resilience of OTC markets—this chapter studies trading activity in OTC markets in the aftermath of negative aggregate shocks that trigger a surge in selling pressure. From a methodological point of view, this requires us to step away from our usual focus on the steady state in order to study the temporal dynamics of the model *outside of the steady state*. Building on earlier work by Weill [2007] and Lagos, Rocheteau, and Weill [2011], we focus on several positive implications.

First, we derive conditions under which dealers find it optimal to provide liquidity by accumulating inventories during the stress event. To start, we show that both fluctuations in aggregate demand for assets and search frictions are necessary: when both of these ingredients are present, dealers optimally accumulate assets because they anticipate being able to resell them quickly to the investors who value them the most soon after the stress event subsides. In contrast, if either search frictions or fluctuations in aggregate asset demand are absent, then dealers have no incentive to provide liquidity to investors by accumulating inventories. While these ingredients are necessary, they are not sufficient. For example, if the stress period is expected to be sufficiently long lived, then dealers have little incentive to accumulate inventory and thus may not provide liquidity to market participants in equilibrium.

Second, we show that dealers accumulate assets in a falling market, i.e., that the asset price continues to fall as dealers purchase more and more assets. This seemingly counterintuitive outcome, where liquidity provision fails to stabilize prices, is a necessary characteristic of equilibrium, as it is precisely this feature that incentivizes dealers to build larger inventories, fully expecting that it will take longer to unwind these inventories.

9.1 A Negative Demand Shock and a Random Recovery

We consider the semicentralized OTC market model of chapter 4, modified to allow for aggregate fluctuations in demand. Specifically, we fix a set of utility flows $\mathcal{D} \subseteq \mathbf{R}_+$ and assume that at time $t = 0$, the market experiences a stress event: *all investors* in the market are hit by a negative preference shock that temporarily scales down all of their individual utility flows by a constant factor $\alpha \in [0, 1)$. This shock could represent, for example, an aggregate housing price shock that decreases the payoffs of all mortgage-backed securities, or an aggregate liquidity event that forces mutual funds to sell corporate bonds to redeem the shares of panicked investors.

After the initial shock, we assume that preferences revert to their preshock values at some exponentially distributed time τ_ρ with intensity $\rho > 0$. Figure 9.1 illustrates. Apart from the scaling down by α, the idiosyncratic utility flow process δ_t of an investor evolves as before: it is reset with intensity γ and new values are drawn from a distribution $F(\delta)$ on $\mathcal{D}$, which we assume for simplicity is strictly increasing and continuous.

As we show below, the occurrence of the stress event moves the market away from the steady state and, therefore, makes the reservation values of investors and the asset allocation change over time. Hence, whenever appropriate, we index all endogenous variables by time $t \geq 0$. Endogenous variables also depend on the state of market stress, i.e., on whether the preferences are still in the stressed state ($t < \tau_\rho$) or have recovered ($t \geq \tau_\rho$). Correspondingly, we use a hat (no hat) to denote endogenous variables during (after) the stress event. For example, we let $\hat{P}_t$ denote the interdealer price at time $t < \tau_\rho$ and P_t denote the interdealer price at time $t \geq \tau_\rho$. Although endogenous variables postrecovery are also functions of the realized recovery time, τ_ρ, we will keep this dependence implicit to simplify notations.

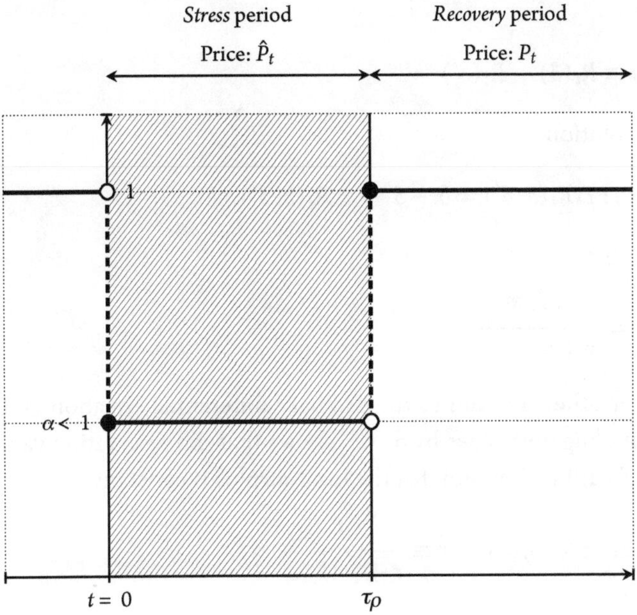

FIGURE 9.1. The timeline of the model

9.1.1 Reservation Values in the Recovery Period

Following the same steps as in previous chapters shows that, after the recovery time, the reservation value of investors satisfies

$$(r+\gamma)\, R_t(\delta) = \delta + \gamma \mathbf{E}^F\left[R_t(x)\right] + \lambda_\theta\, (P_t - R_t(\delta)) + \dot{R}_t(\delta), \tag{9.1}$$

where $\lambda_\theta = \lambda(1-\theta)$ denotes the bargaining-adjusted contact rate. The main difference between this equation and the one we derived in the steady-state environment of chapter 4 is that the interdealer price, P_t, now depends on time. As a result, the reservation value changes over time as well and, hence, the equation is augmented by a new term, $\dot{R}_t(\delta)$, that represents the partial derivative of the reservation value with respect to time. See section 3.4.3 for a discussion of time-dependent Hamilton-Jacobi-Bellman (HJB) equations.

A key observation is that the time variation induced by a changing price affects the reservation values of all investors in the same way, regardless of their utility flow. In particular, subtracting equation (9.1) evaluated at δ' from itself evaluated at $\delta \neq \delta'$ shows that

$$\Delta R_t(\delta,\delta') \equiv R_t(\delta) - R_t(\delta')$$

is a bounded solution to

$$(r+\gamma+\lambda_\theta)\,\Delta R_t(\delta,\delta') = \delta - \delta' + \Delta\dot{R}_t(\delta,\delta'),$$

and it follows that

$$\Delta R_t(\delta,\delta') = \frac{\delta-\delta'}{r+\gamma+\lambda_\theta}, \tag{9.2}$$

since any other other solution to the ordinary differential equation (ODE) diverges as $t \to \infty$. Dividing both sides by $\delta - \delta'$ shows that the reservation value function is differentiable in utility flow and that the local surplus is constant:

$$\sigma_t(\delta) = \lim_{\delta'\to\delta} \Delta R_t(\delta,\delta') = \sigma \equiv \frac{1}{r+\gamma+\lambda_\theta}. \tag{9.3}$$

Given this result we can now derive an explicit formula for reservation values. Indeed, the fact the local surplus is constant implies that

$$\mathbf{E}^F\left[R_t(x)\right] - R_t(\delta) = \mathbf{E}^F\left[\sigma\,(x-\delta)\right] = \sigma\left(\mathbf{E}^F\left[x\right] - \delta\right),$$

and substituting back into (9.1) shows that for each fixed $\delta \in \mathcal{D}$ the reservation value function satisfies

$$(r+\lambda_\theta)\,R_t(\delta) - \dot{R}_t(\delta) = \delta + \gamma\sigma\left(\mathbf{E}^F\left[x\right] - \delta\right) + \lambda_\theta P_t.$$

If the price path is uniformly bounded, then a direct calculation shows that the unique bounded solution to this equation is

$$R_t(\delta) = \frac{r}{r+\lambda_\theta} D(\delta) + \int_t^\infty \lambda_\theta e^{-(r+\lambda_\theta)(u-t)} P_u\, du,$$

where, as in chapter 4,

$$rD(\delta) \equiv \frac{r+\lambda_\theta}{r+\gamma+\lambda_\theta}\delta + \frac{\gamma}{r+\gamma+\lambda_\theta}\mathbf{E}^F\left[x\right].$$

This expression confirms that the reservation value function is continuous, differentiable, and strictly increasing in utility flow, as before. Moreover, under the maintained assumption that the price path is bounded, the reservation value is also an absolutely continuous function of time.

9.1.2 Reservation Values in the Stress Period

Similar steps show that during the stress period the reservation value function of investors satisfies

$$(r+\gamma)\hat{R}_t(\delta)=\alpha\delta+\gamma\mathbf{E}^F\left[\hat{R}_t(x)\right]+\lambda_\theta\left(\hat{P}_t-\hat{R}_t(\delta)\right) \\ +\rho\left(R_t(\delta)-\hat{R}_t(\delta)\right)+\dot{\hat{R}}_t(\delta). \tag{9.4}$$

There are two differences relative to the postrecovery equation (9.1). First, the utility flow is scaled down by $\alpha<1$ because of the demand shock. Second, the investor anticipates that the market will recover with intensity ρ, at which point her reservation value will jump from $\hat{R}_t(\delta)$ to $R_t(\delta)$.

Combining (9.3) with the same arguments as above reveals that the local surplus is also constant during the stress event, and equal to

$$\hat{R}_t'(\delta)=\hat{\sigma}\equiv\frac{\alpha+\rho\sigma}{r+\gamma+\rho+\lambda_\theta}=\sigma-\frac{1-\alpha}{r+\gamma+\rho+\lambda_\theta}<\sigma. \tag{9.5}$$

This shows that the marginal value of the asset jumps down for all investors upon the occurrence of the stress event and implies that the market experiences a surge in selling pressure.

9.2 When Dealers Cannot Accumulate Inventories

In this section, we analyze the model under the assumption that dealers must keep their individual asset positions equal to zero at all times and, thus, are unable to provide liquidity to investors by holding inventories. As in chapter 4, we assume that they can continue to facilitate trades by instantaneously matching the buyers and sellers who contact them.

We characterize the equilibrium and find that dealers may have incentives to hold inventory if they are allowed to do so. In particular, we show that such incentives exist only if there are both search frictions ($\lambda_\theta<\infty$) and aggregate fluctuations in demand ($\alpha<1$). Thus, the model predicts that liquidity provision arises in response to stress events precisely because of the existence of OTC market frictions.

9.2.1 Equilibrium

When dealers cannot hold inventories, the same arguments as in chapter 4 can be used to show that the marginal utility flow $\delta^\star$ remains constant over time and satisfies

$$s=1-F(\delta^\star).$$

This simple result obtains for two reasons. First, although investors derive lower utility flows during the stress event, they remain ranked in exactly the same way in the cross-section. Second, since dealers do not hold inventories, the supply held by investors is equal to s at all times.

Evaluating (9.1) and (9.4) at $\delta^\star$ reveals that the interdealer price remains constant during the stress period at some level $\hat{P} = \hat{R}(\delta^\star)$ and then jumps to its steady-state level $P = R(\delta^\star)$ once the market recovers. These constant price levels satisfy the linear system

$$rP = \gamma\sigma\left(\mathbf{E}^F[x] - \delta^\star\right) + \delta^\star, \tag{9.6}$$

$$r\hat{P} = \gamma\hat{\sigma}\left(\mathbf{E}^F[x] - \delta^\star\right) + \alpha\delta^\star + \rho\left(P - \hat{P}\right) \tag{9.7}$$

and solving yields

$$P - \hat{P} = \left(\sigma - \hat{\sigma}\right)\left[\left(\frac{\gamma}{r+\rho}\right)\mathbf{E}^F[x] + \left(1 + \frac{\lambda_\theta}{r+\rho}\right)\delta^\star\right].$$

Since the local surplus $\hat{\sigma} < \sigma$, this identity shows that, consistent with a surge in selling pressure, the stress event triggers an unambiguously negative jump in the interdealer price of the asset.

9.2.2 *Incentives for Inventory Accumulation*

The fact that $\hat{P} < P$ suggests that, if they could, dealers may have incentives to hold assets in inventory in order to earn the capital gain $P - \hat{P}$. However, it is not completely obvious that this strategy is profitable, because dealers cannot perfectly time the recovery: since they view τ_ρ as unpredictably random, they cannot buy the asset just before τ_ρ and sell it just after.

To better understand these incentives, assume that a dealer buys an asset at time 0 at the price $\hat{P}$ and holds it until time $\tau = \min\left\{\tau_\rho, \tau_\ell\right\}$, where τ_ρ is the time of the recovery and τ_ℓ is an independent exponential time with some intensity $\ell > 0$. If $\tau = \tau_\ell$ then the dealer is hit by a liquidity shock that forces him to sell his position at the interdealer price $\hat{P}$ before the market recovers. Otherwise, if $\tau = \tau_\rho$ then the dealer manages to hold on to his position until the recovery time, when he sells at the post-recovery price P. The expected discounted profit of this strategy is

$$\mathbf{E}\left[\mathbf{1}_{\{\tau=\tau_\rho\}}e^{-r\tau}P\right] + \mathbf{E}\left[\mathbf{1}_{\{\tau=\tau_\ell\}}e^{-r\tau}\hat{P}\right] - \hat{P} \tag{9.8}$$

$$= \frac{\rho P}{r+\rho+\ell} + \frac{\ell\hat{P}}{r+\rho+\ell} - \hat{P} = \frac{\rho P - (r+\rho)\hat{P}}{r+\rho+\ell},$$

where the first equality follows from Lemma A.18. Hence, we obtain that dealers have incentive to hold inventories if and only if

$$\rho\left(P-\hat{P}\right)>r\hat{P}. \tag{9.9}$$

The left-hand side is the expected growth rate of the price: with intensity ρ, the economy recovers and the price jumps from $\hat{P}$ to P. The right-hand side is the opportunity cost of buying the asset prior to the recovery. Indeed, if dealers were explicitly allowed to borrow and save at the rate r in some bank account, one would see that r is the rate that dealers pay to finance their asset purchases, or the rate that they forgo when investing in the assets instead of their bank accounts. Equation (9.9) is a classical condition for speculative demand to be positive in inventory problems [see, e.g., Deaton and Laroque, 1992].

Fluctuations in aggregate asset demand are clearly necessary for condition (9.9) to hold. Otherwise, if $\alpha=1$, then evidently $\hat{P}=P$, so that dealers never profit from buying, holding, and re-selling their inventories. One can also verify that condition (9.9) cannot hold absent frictions. Indeed, as frictions vanish we have that the local surplus $\hat{\sigma}\to 0$, and therefore

$$r\hat{P}=\alpha\delta^{\star}+\rho\left(P-\hat{P}\right)\geq\rho\left(P-\hat{P}\right)$$

as a result of (9.7). Next, we show that the expected profits of the dealer in (9.8) can be positive. To do so, let $\tau_\ell\equiv\tau_\theta$ denote the bargaining-adjusted contact time and observe that the price initially paid by the dealer is the reservation value of a marginal investor $\hat{P}=\hat{R}(\delta^{\star})$. Proceeding as in section 4.3.2 shows that this reservation value can be written as

$$\hat{R}(\delta^{\star})=\mathbf{E}_{\delta^{\star}}\left[\int_0^{\tau}e^{-rt}\alpha\delta_t dt+e^{-r\tau}\left(\mathbf{1}_{\{\tau=\tau_\theta\}}\hat{P}+\mathbf{1}_{\{\tau=\tau_\rho\}}R(\delta_{\tau_\rho})\right)\right],$$

and substituting this expression into the last term of (9.8) allows us to write the expected profits of the dealer as

$$-\mathbf{E}_{\delta^{\star}}\left[\int_0^{\tau}e^{-rt}\alpha\delta_t dt\right]+\mathbf{E}_{\delta^{\star}}\left[\mathbf{1}_{\{\tau=\tau_\rho\}}e^{-r\tau}\left(P-R(\delta_{\tau_\rho})\right)\right]. \tag{9.10}$$

This decomposition shows that the expected profits consist in two terms. The first term is negative and arises because the dealer does not enjoy the flow utility $\alpha\delta_t$ when holding the asset in inventory. Since these positive utility flows are capitalized in the interdealer price, they reduce the expected profits of the dealer. The second term can have either sign. It arises because the dealer can instantly resell the asset on the interdealer market at price P at the recovery time, whereas the investor must hold on to it with a continuation value equal to $R(\delta_{\tau_\rho})$ that is in general not equal to $P = R(\delta^\star)$, because an investor who was initially marginal may have changed utility flow by time τ_ρ. A direct calculation using (9.2) shows that

$$\mathbf{E}\left[\mathbf{1}_{\{\tau=\tau_\rho\}}e^{-r\tau}\left(P - R(\delta_{\tau_\rho})\right)\right] \propto \sigma\left(\delta^\star - \mathbf{E}^F[x]\right).$$

Hence the second term in the sequential representation (9.10) is positive if and only if $\mathbf{E}^F[x] < \delta^\star$ so that a marginal investor expects to switch to a lower utility flow upon his next preference shock, in which case the dealer's profits are positive if the loss fraction $1-\alpha$ is large enough.

We can go one step further and explicitly characterize the region of the parameter space for which dealers have strict incentives to provide liquidity. Indeed, (9.7) implies that

$$\rho P - (r+\rho)\hat{P} = -\alpha\delta^\star + \gamma\hat{\sigma}\left(\mathbf{E}^F[x] - \delta^\star\right),$$

and plugging in the explicit formula (9.5) for the local surplus $\hat{\sigma}$ during the stress period yields the following result.

Lemma 9.1: Let

$$\Psi \equiv \frac{\gamma}{r+\gamma+\lambda_\theta}\left(1 + \frac{\rho\left(\frac{1}{\alpha}-1\right)}{r+\gamma+\lambda_\theta+\rho}\right)\left(1 - \mathbf{E}^F\left[\frac{x}{\delta^\star}\right]\right).$$

Then dealers have strict incentives to accumulate inventories during the stress period if and only if the constant $\Psi > 1$.

The condition in Lemma 9.1 is easy to interpret. Dealers have stronger incentives to accumulate inventories if the interest rate r is small, because the cost of committing capital to buy assets is low; if the recovery rate ρ is large because the stress event is expected to be shorter lived; if the contact rate λ_θ is small, because the bargaining-adjusted frictions faced by investors are large; and if the loss fraction $1-\alpha$ is large, because investors derive less value from holding the asset during the stress period, which in turn makes them more willing to sell the asset at low prices that benefit dealers.

9.3 When Dealers Can Accumulate Inventories

We now solve for the equilibrium when dealers can hold inventories. To ensure that dealers have incentives to hold inventories, we suppose that $\mathbf{E}^F[x] < \delta^\star$ and make the simplifying assumption that $\alpha \to 0$. Technically, this means that, although the investor does not derive any utility from holding the asset during the stress period, her utility flow δ_t continues to evolve as before and determines her utility flow at the time of the recovery.

We solve for an equilibrium by working backwards, starting from after the recovery and then turning our attention to behavior and payoffs during the period of the stress event.

9.3.1 *After the Recovery*

Assume that, postrecovery, the interdealer price is a bounded and piecewise continuously differentiable function P_t. Consider a dealer who starts out at the recovery time τ_ρ with some inventory $I_{\tau_\rho} > 0$ accumulated during the stress period. The problem of this dealer is to choose a bounded variation path of inventories to maximize

$$-\int_{\tau_\rho}^{\infty} e^{-rt} P_t \, dI_t = I_{\tau_\rho} + \int_{\tau_\rho}^{\infty} e^{-rt} I_t \left(\dot{P}_t - rP_t\right) \, dt, \tag{9.11}$$

where the equality follows from integration by parts, just as in section 4.2. The integrand on the right-hand side of (9.11) can be interpreted as the profit that a dealer makes during a small interval of time. Indeed, when the representative dealer buys inventory I_t at time t and holds it until the later time $t+h$, she makes discounted profits equal to

$$I_t \left(e^{-r(t+h)} P_{t+h} - e^{-rt} P_t\right) \simeq e^{-rt} I_t \left(\dot{P}_t - rP_t\right) h.$$

The integrand in (9.11) can be maximized pointwise, leading to the optimal inventory policy given by

$$I_t = \begin{cases} +\infty & \text{if } \dot{P}_t - rP_t > 0, \\ \in \mathbf{R}_+ & \text{if } \dot{P}_t - rP_t = 0, \\ 0 & \text{if } \dot{P}_t - rP_t < 0. \end{cases}$$

In words, this equation shows that dealers want to hold infinite inventories if the price grows strictly faster than their discount rate, r, and no inventory if it grows strictly slower. In equilibrium, since the asset supply is finite, the asset demand must be finite as well, and so we must have $\dot{P}_t \leq rP_t$.

If the interdealer price were to adjust immediately to its steady-state level (9.6) at the recovery time, then we would have $\dot{P}_t = 0$ for all $t \geq \tau_\rho$, and the optimality condition above would imply that dealers want to instantly sell all their inventories at time τ_ρ. But this cannot be an equilibrium. Indeed, since investors must search for dealers to trade, they cannot instantly buy all of their inventories at the recovery time. As a result, the price will have to gradually adjust so that dealers are willing to sell their asset slowly, and the above optimality condition shows this can only happen if $\dot{P}_t = rP_t$ so that dealers have incentives to keep some assets in inventory.

Let us guess that dealers gradually liquidate their inventories between the recovery time τ_ρ and some time $\tau_\rho + T$, when the length of the liquidation interval will be determined endogenously. After time $\tau_\rho + T$ dealers hold no inventories. Therefore, going through the same steps as in section 9.2 shows that the interdealer price must have reached the postrecovery steady-state level and combining this boundary condition with the fact that the price grows at rate r we deduce that

$$P_t = e^{-r(T+\tau_\rho - t)} P, \qquad \forall t \in [\tau_\rho, \tau_\rho + T],$$

where the constant P is the steady-state price in (9.6).

Since the reservation value function is continuous and strictly increasing in utility flows, there is, as usual, a marginal investor who is indifferent between buying or not buying. However, because the price must continuously adjust to reflect the liquidation strategy of dealers, the utility flow $\delta_t^\star$ of this marginal investor is now changing over time. Specifically, the equation for reservation values evaluated at the point $\delta_t^\star$ implies that

$$rP_t = rR_t(\delta_t^\star) = \delta_t^\star + \gamma\sigma\left(\mathbf{E}^F[x] - \delta_t^\star\right) + \dot{R}_t(\delta_t^\star). \tag{9.12}$$

An application of the chain rule shows that

$$\dot{P}_t = \dot{R}_t(\delta_t^\star) + R_t'(\delta_t^\star)\dot{\delta}_t^\star = \dot{R}_t(\delta_t^\star) + \sigma\dot{\delta}_t^\star.$$

Plugging this expression back into (9.12) and using the fact that the price grows at rate r when dealers hold inventories, we deduce that

$$\dot{\delta}_t^\star = \gamma\mathbf{E}^F[x] + (r + \lambda_\theta)\,\delta_t^\star;$$

and solving this ODE subject to the terminal condition $\delta^\star_{\tau_\rho+T}=\delta^\star$ delivers an explicit solution for the marginal utility flow:

$$\delta^\star_t=\Delta\left(\tau_\rho+T-t\right)\equiv-\frac{\gamma\mathbf{E}^F[x]}{r+\lambda_\theta}+\left(\delta^\star+\frac{\gamma\mathbf{E}^F[x]}{r+\lambda_\theta}\right)e^{-(r+\lambda_\theta)(\tau_\rho+T-t)}. \quad (9.13)$$

Since the function $\Delta(z)$ is strictly decreasing, this expression shows that the marginal utility flow gradually increases as dealers sell inventories and reaches its steady-state level $\delta^\star$ once dealers have liquidated all their holdings. This is very natural. Indeed, since dealers sell inventories, investors must absorb more assets than in the steady state, and so the utility flow of the marginal investor must be lower than in the steady state.

The last step in the characterization of equilibrium after the recovery is to use the market clearing condition to determine T. The logic is similar to that in section 4.4.1. However, some additional care is required, since some assets are held by dealers instead of investors. As such, we must consider supply and demand originating from *both* investors and dealers. Indeed, during a small time interval of length h, the gross supply of assets is

$$\lambda h\,(s-I_t)+I_t.$$

The first term is the gross supply of assets originating from investors who collectively own $s-I_t$ assets and contact the market at rate λ. The second term is the gross supply originating from dealers. On the other side of the market, the gross demand is

$$\lambda h\left(1-F(\delta^\star_t)\right)+I_{t+h}.$$

Equating gross supply and gross demand, dividing by h and letting $h\to 0$, we obtain that inventories evolve according to

$$\dot{I}_t=\lambda\left(s-I_t-1+F(\delta^\star_t)\right).$$

Solving this ODE subject to the assumed initial condition and using (9.13) together with the change of variable $u=t-\tau_\rho$, we obtain that

$$I_{\tau_\rho+T}=0=I_{\tau_\rho}-\lambda\int_0^T\left(1-s-F\circ\Delta(T-u)\right)e^{\lambda u}du, \quad (9.14)$$

where the first equality follows from the fact that inventories must reach zero by the end of the liquidation period. Therefore, the above expression can be viewed as a single equation to determine the time T that dealers take to unwind their asset positions, as a function of the initial level of inventories I_{τ_ρ}.

Since $\Delta(z)\le\delta^\star$ is decreasing and the integrand is continuous, we have that the right-hand side of (9.14) is continuous as well as strictly decreasing in T and goes to minus infinity as T goes to infinity. Therefore, (9.14) has a unique solution $\mathcal{T}(I_{\tau_\rho})$, and it is easily checked that this solution is increasing in I_{τ_ρ}, so that dealers naturally take longer to unwind a larger asset position. As we will see next, the function $\mathcal{T}(I_{\tau_\rho})$ plays a key role in the characterization of the equilibrium during the stress period because it determines how long dealers hold inventories after the market recovers and, correspondingly, how depressed prices will be relative to the steady-state level.

9.3.2 During the Stress Period

We now solve for equilibrium during the stress period, taking as given our characterization of the equilibrium in the recovery period. The main difference relative to the previous section is that over that period the equilibrium does not evolve on a deterministic path, because market participants anticipate the recovery to arrive at rate ρ.

If the market recovers at time $\tau_\rho = s$, then the interdealer price of the asset immediately jumps up to

$$\mathcal{P}(I_s) \equiv e^{-r\mathcal{T}(I_s)}P, \tag{9.15}$$

where P is the steady-state price level of equation (9.6), and subsequently grows at the constant rate r until the inventories of dealers are depleted. Accordingly, if a dealer holds a unit of inventory during the time interval $[t, t+h]$, then her expected discounted profits can be written as

$$\rho h e^{-r(t+h)}\mathcal{P}(I_t) + (1-\rho h)e^{-r(t+h)}\hat{P}_{t+h} - e^{-rt}\hat{P}_t,$$

where the first term accounts for the fact that the dealer resells at $\mathcal{P}(I_t)$ if the market recovers and at $\hat{P}_{t+h}$ otherwise, and the second term accounts for the cost of acquiring the asset. Dealers are willing to hold a positive but finite inventory if the above expected profit is zero. Dividing both sides by h and letting $h \to 0$ allows us to write this condition as

$$r\hat{P}_t = \dot{\hat{P}}_t + \rho\left(\mathcal{P}(I_t) - \hat{P}_t\right). \tag{9.16}$$

As in the analysis above, the price must grow at an expected rate of r. However, the expected growth rate now has two components: the deterministic price change $\dot{\hat{P}}_t$ during the stress event and the upward jump $\mathcal{P}(I_t) - \hat{P}_t$ that occurs upon recovery. Solving this ODE subject to (9.15) and using the results of appendix A.3 shows that

$$\hat{P}_t = \int_t^\infty e^{-(r+\rho)(s-t)}\mathcal{P}(I_s)ds = \mathbf{E}_t\left[e^{-r(\tau_\rho - t)}\mathcal{P}(I_{\tau_\rho})\right], \qquad \forall t \in [0, \tau_\rho].$$

Hence, the price during the stress period is simply equal to the present value of reselling at time τ_ρ when the recovery occurs. Since $\mathcal{P}(i)$ is decreasing, it follows that if dealers accumulate inventories throughout the stress event in that $\dot{I}_t > 0$, then the expected price at the time of the recovery must fall, and the price during the stress period must fall as well, $\dot{\hat{P}}_t < 0$. The intuition is that dealers anticipate that their collective inventory accumulation will end up putting downward pressure on the price after the recovery and thus must be compensated by a lower price during the stress period.

To verify that dealers want to accumulate inventories, one must solve for the joint dynamics of I_t and the marginal utility flow $\hat{\delta}_t^\star$ that prevail during the stress period. Evaluating (9.4) at $\hat{\delta}_t^\star$ yields

$$r\hat{R}_t(\hat{\delta}_t^\star) - \dot{\hat{R}}_t(\hat{\delta}_t^\star) = \gamma\hat{\sigma}\left(\mathbf{E}^F[x] - \hat{\delta}_t^\star\right) + \rho\left(R_t(\hat{\delta}_t^\star) - \hat{R}_t(\hat{\delta}_t^\star)\right)$$

$$= \gamma\hat{\sigma}\left(\mathbf{E}^F[x] - \hat{\delta}_t^\star\right) + \rho\left(R_t(\hat{\delta}_t^\star) - \mathcal{P}(I_t)\right) + \rho\left(\mathcal{P}(I_t) - \hat{R}_t(\hat{\delta}_t^\star)\right),$$

where the second line obtains by adding and subtracting $\mathcal{P}(I_t)$. On the other hand, combining (9.5), (9.16), and

$$\mathcal{P}(I_t) = R_t(\delta_t^\star) = R_t(\Delta \circ \mathcal{T}(I_t))$$

with the prerecovery counterpart of (9.12), we obtain that prior to the recovery, the marginal utility flow $\hat{\delta}_t^\star$ evolves according to

$$\dot{\hat{\delta}}_t^\star = \gamma\mathbf{E}^F[x] + (r+\rho+\lambda_\theta)\,\hat{\delta}_t^\star - (r+\rho+\lambda_\theta+\gamma)\,\Delta \circ \mathcal{T}(I_t). \tag{9.17}$$

Finally, as in the analysis above, the market-clearing condition implies that the inventories of a representative dealer satisfy

$$\dot{I}_t = \lambda\left(s - I_t - 1 + F(\hat{\delta}_t^\star)\right). \tag{9.18}$$

Taken together, these ODEs can be studied in a phase diagram, as illustrated in figure 9.2. The downward-sloping dashed curve labeled *Isocline:* $\dot{\hat{\delta}}_t^\star = 0$ traces the locus of points $(\hat{\delta}_t^*, I_t)$ such that $\dot{\hat{\delta}}_t^\star = 0$ in equation (9.17). Likewise, the upward-sloping solid curve labeled *Isocline:* $\dot{I}_t = 0$ depicts the locus of points such that $\dot{I}_t = 0$ in equation (9.18). The intersection of the isoclines, when it exists, is a steady state of the dynamic system (9.17)–(9.18). The arrows summarize inventory and marginal investor dynamics in each region of the diagram: for example, a horizontal arrow pointing to the right (left) indicates that inventory is increasing (decreasing). Vertical arrows have a similar interpretation.

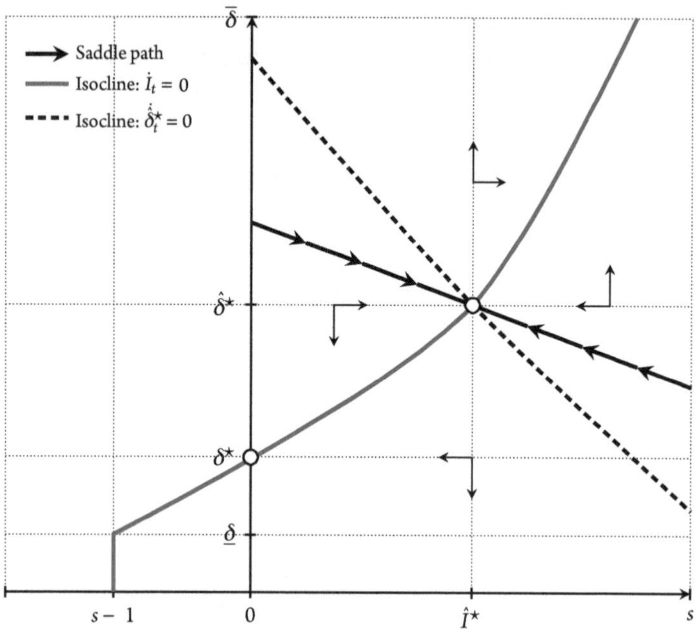

FIGURE 9.2. The phase plane diagram

The figure plots the phase plane diagram of the dynamic system formed by inventories and the utility flow of the marginal investor during the stress period.

Lagos, Rocheteau, and Weill [2011] provide a complete analysis of a closely related diagram. In particular, they show that the dynamic system has a unique solution, traditionally called the *saddle path,* that converges to the steady state. This saddle path gives the unique equilibrium during the stress period, while the steady state describes the asymptotic behavior of the market in the event that recovery never occurs. See Exercise 9.2 below for some results on the diagram associated to (9.17)–(9.18).

9.3.3 *Taking Stock*

Figure 9.3 illustrates the findings of this section. It shows the realized path of inventories and the interdealer price during the stress period and the ensuing recovery. The upper panel shows that dealers accumulate inventories throughout the stress period $[0, \tau_\rho]$. The lower panel shows that the price initially jumps down and continues to fall until τ_ρ so as to induce dealers to hold larger and larger inventories. When the economy recovers, dealers start unwinding their positions. Correspondingly, the interdealer

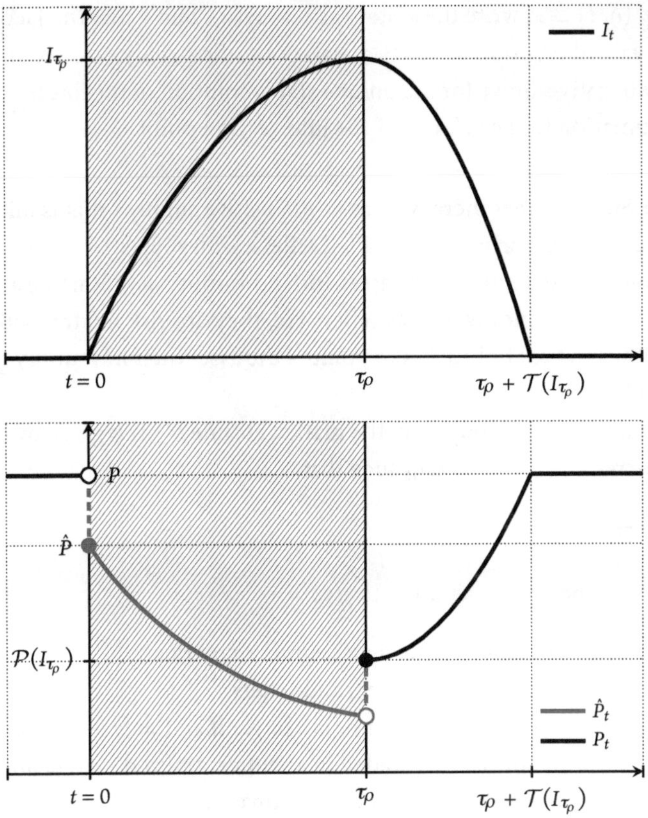

FIGURE 9.3. Inventory and price dynamics

The figure illustrates the time paths of a representative dealer's inventory (top panel) and the interdealer price (bottom panel) during the stress period (hatched region) and the ensuing recovery starting at time τ_ρ.

price jumps up at the recovery time and then grows at rate r until time $\tau_\rho + T$, at which point it has reached its steady-state level.

9.4 Exercises

Exercise 9.2: This exercise establishes some properties of the phase diagram corresponding to the dynamic system formed by (9.17) and (9.18).

1. Show that the two isoclines have a unique intersection with strictly positive inventories if and only if $\delta^\star > \mathbf{E}^F[x]$.

2. Letting $(\delta, I) \equiv x$, write the system as $\dot{x} = M(x)$. Show that the Jacobian of the vector valued function M has two real roots, one strictly positive and one strictly negative. Solve for the unique stable solution of the linear approximation to the ODE near the intersection point.

***Exercise* 9.3:** Suppose that there is an asset in positive supply s that is initially held by infinitely lived, risk-neutral investors, called sellers, with subjective discount rate $r > 0$. Sellers can hold $q \in \{0, 1\}$ unit of the asset with flow utility $q\delta_L$. Starting at time 0, buyers slowly enter the economy. Just as sellers are, they are risk neutral with a discount rate $r > 0$, but when they hold $q \in \{0, 1\}$ unit of the asset their flow utility $q\delta_H$ is higher than that of sellers.

Assume that the mass of buyers in the market at time $t \geq 0$ is given by a continuous and strictly increasing function μ_{Ht} such that

$$\lim_{t \to \infty} (\mu_{Ht} - s) > \mu_{H0} = 0$$

and denote by T_s the unique solution to $\mu_{Ht} = s$.

1. Assume that the asset is traded in a *centralized* market.
   a) Solve for the demand of buyers and sellers.
   b) Argue that the marginal investor is a buyer if and only if $t > T_s$.
2. Assume next that the asset is traded in a semicentralized market and that dealers are forbidden to hold any asset in inventory.
   a) Write the equations satisfied by the reservation values $R_t(\delta_H)$ and $R_t(\delta_L)$ of buyers and sellers.
   b) Show that $R_t(\delta_L) - R_t(\delta_H) = (\delta_H - \delta_L)/(r + \lambda_\theta)$.
   c) Argue that the marginal investor is a buyer if and only if $t > T_s$.
   d) Solve for the interdealer price over $[0, T_s)$ and (T_s, ∞). Compute the jump in the price at time T_s.
   e) Argue that dealers would have incentives to hold inventories if they were allowed to do so.
3. Assume finally that the asset is traded in a semicentralized market in which dealers are allowed to have inventories. Guess that there exist $t_1 < T_s < t_2$ such that dealers hold inventories for all $t \in [t_1, t_2]$. Note that the lower endpoint t_1 may or may not be equal to zero.
   a) Argue that the interdealer price must be continuous.
   b) Show that

$$\dot{I}_t = \lambda (s - \mu_{Ht}), \qquad \forall t \in [t_1, t_2].$$

Use this ODE to show that

$$\int_{t_1}^{t_2} (s - \mu_{Ht})\, e^{\lambda t}\, dt = 0.$$

c) Write the equations for $R_t(\delta_L)$, $R_t(\delta_H)$ and P_t, when $t \in [t_1, t_2]$.

d) Denote by

$$N_t = P_t - R_t(\delta_L)$$

the surplus in a match between a dealer and a seller at time t. Argue that $N_{t_2} = (\delta_H - \delta_L)/(r + \lambda_\theta)$ and that $N_{t_1} \geq 0$, with an equality if $t_1 \geq 0$. Solve for and verify that the latter condition can be written as

$$t_2 \leq t_1 + \frac{\log(\delta_H/\delta_L)}{r + \lambda_\theta} \text{ with "} = \text{" if } t_1 > 0.$$

e) Discuss comparative statics for the length of the inventory accumulation period $t_2 - t_1$.

9.5 Notes and References

The representation of a stress event studied in this chapter is due to Grossman and Miller [1988]. The main substantive difference is that, in Grossman and Miller [1988], dealers have no advantage in timing the market over investors, so they do not provide liquidity services. Instead, they provide risk-sharing services until the recovery materializes. Weill [2004, 2007] first introduced a Grossman and Miller [1988] shock in a search model of an OTC market. Lagos, Rocheteau, and Weill [2011] extended his analysis in two ways: they assume a random recovery, as in this chapter, and they allow for unrestricted asset holdings. Di Maggio [2013] shows that dealers can have destabilizing equilibrium strategies in anticipation of a negative shock.

The model in this chapter is closely related to these papers, yet still novel in that it considers a specification with indivisible holdings and a continuum of types. Weill [2004, 2007] and Lagos et al. [2011] go beyond the positive analysis of this chapter and derive normative implications. In particular, they show that, when the contact rate between investors and dealers is independent of the *ratio* of sellers to dealers, the equilibrium asset allocation maximizes welfare if and only if $\theta = 0$. Weill [2011] considers a market setting in which there are no search frictions but, instead, dealers face constraints on the flow of assets they can buy and sell from investors per unit of time. Duffie, Gârleanu, and Pedersen [2007], Feldhütter [2012], Trejos and Wright [2016], and Akin and Platt [2022] analyze the impact of shocks in OTC markets using models in which there are no dealers able to provide liquidity by holding inventories.

In this chapter, the stress event is modeled as a sudden increase in investors' demand for immediacy [Demsetz, 1968]. However, other types of negative shocks are also relevant. For example, during the 2007–2008 GFC, trading volume collapsed precisely in markets that were plagued by a surge in asymmetric information—namely, in asset-backed securities markets where investors had serious concerns about collateral quality. Camargo and Lester [2014] and Chiu and Koeppl [2016] have studied theoretically how the market recovers from such asymmetric information, and they have characterized welfare-improving policy interventions, while Zou [2019] considers dynamic information acquisition decisions.

There is also a large empirical literature studying the impact of stress events in OTC markets. In addition to studying large (but rare) events, the empirical literature has also analyzed smaller events in which the shock that generates stress is better identified. In particular, researchers have studied supply shocks created by the exclusion of a bond from an index when the bond crosses a maturity or credit threshold. The exclusion leads index funds to mechanically dispose of their holdings of the bond, creating a largely exogenous positive supply shock in the market; for example, see Bao, O'Hara, and Zhou [2018] and Dick-Nielsen and Rossi [2019]. The advantage of studying such supply shocks is that they are well identified. During a large stress event, such as the onset of the COVID-19 pandemic of March 2020, there are many shocks hitting the market at the same time—shocks that would impact the market even in the absence of liquidity frictions. In contrast, it is plausible that the impact of small supply shocks induced by index exclusion is only due to frictions.

Finally, recent research by Haddad, Moreira, and Muir [2021], Kargar et al. [2021], O'Hara and Zhou [2021], and Boyarchenko, Kovner, and Shachar [2022], among others, studies the behavior of the corporate bond market during the acute selling pressure that emerged at the onset of the COVID-19 crisis. Duffie [2020] and O'Hara and Zhou [2022] perform similar analyses of the Treasury and municipal bond markets, respectively. In general, they find that bond prices fell and transaction costs surged during the crisis period. However, several of these studies find that dealers did *not* accumulate inventories during these episodes. The theory above suggests conditions under which this can be the case; for example, if the stress event is expected to be long lived or if perceived frictions are small. Yet many have argued that dealers' unwillingness to absorb assets could be caused by other forces not modeled directly in this chapter. For example, Duffie [2022] argues that post-GFC regulations increased dealers' cost of holding assets, and thus made them less willing to lean against the wind. However, formal theoretical studies of this claim have only just begun; see, e.g., Cohen, Kargar, Lester, and Weill [2023].

10

Asymmetric Information: Private Values

In previous chapters, we studied frictions that make it difficult for investors to locate a counterparty, i.e., *search frictions*. But a commonly held view is that OTC markets are also plagued by *information frictions*; that is, OTC markets are often opaque, in the sense that investors have limited information about their counterparties and about prices. Moreover, this information is often asymmetric, in the sense that one counterparty knows payoff-relevant information that the other side does not.

While these canonical frictions have been studied extensively in isolation, chapters 10 and 11 introduce frameworks to study the way in which search and information frictions *interact*. The analysis is split across two chapters to treat two conceptually different types of asymmetric information. The first type, asymmetric information over *private values*, applies to situations in which one party cannot observe information relevant to the private payoff of the other party, such as preferences. The second type of asymmetric information, over *common values*, applies to situations in which one side of a trade cannot observe payoff-relevant characteristics of the asset being traded, as in the celebrated Lemons market of Akerlof [1970].

To study asymmetric information over private values, we start from a model of semi-centralized trade similar to that of chapter 4. However, we modify the model to account for the natural observation that, upon meeting a dealer, an investor may not have incentive to truthfully reveal her trading motives, as this could help the dealer extract more of the surplus. Specifically, we assume that dealers know the distribution of utility flows and asset holdings across the population of investors but cannot observe the individual utility flows of the investors they meet. Clearly, such an information friction only matters if dealers have some bargaining power because otherwise they would offer to trade at the interdealer price regardless of their counterparties.

The main insight that arises from the analysis of this model is that search frictions magnify the effects of asymmetric information over private values. To see why, note that under asymmetric information, dealers cannot condition their prices on the utility flow of their counterparties. As a result, they offer prices that some investors do not accept, despite the fact that there are gains from trade. In contrast, in chapter 4, trade always occurred when there were gains from trade. Search frictions exacerbate this inefficiency. In particular, we show that as search frictions worsen and meetings become less frequent, dealers' optimal price offers are accepted by a smaller fraction of investors. Hence, as search frictions become more severe, misallocation worsens for two reasons: because investors cannot rebalance their portfolios as frequently as they would like; and because dealers optimally set prices that customers reject more often, even though there are positive gains from trade.

10.1 The Model

10.1.1 The Semicentralized Market

Consider the semicentralized market of chapter 4. There are a unit measure of dealers who participate in a frictionless market, and a unit measure of risk-neutral investors who discount the future at rate $r > 0$ and can hold either zero or one unit of a durable asset in supply $s < 1$. Utility flows are iid across the population: the utility flow of an investor follows an idiosyncratic Markov jump process with intensity $\gamma > 0$ and reset distribution $F(\delta)$ on some bounded interval $\mathcal{D} = (\underline{\delta}, \overline{\delta})$. Each investor gets the opportunity to trade with a randomly selected dealer according to a Poisson process with intensity $\lambda > 0$.

Within this familiar framework, we add two new, crucial assumptions. First, while dealers observe whether the investors they meet want to buy or sell—and know the joint distribution of types across the populations of owners and nonowners—we assume that they *cannot* observe the utility flows of the investors they meet. Hence, there is asymmetric information about the *private* valuations of investors. Second, we assume that within each meeting dealers maximize their expected profits by making take-it-or-leave-it offers to investors.

For the sake of simplicity and clarity, in most of the analysis below we will assume that the distribution of utility flows, $F(\delta)$, is continuously differentiable with $F'(\delta) = f(\delta) > 0$ for all $\delta \in \mathcal{D}$. However, most of the results we derive in this section remain unchanged if we allow for more general distributions. We briefly cover an example with a discrete distribution in section 10.2.

10.1.2 Optimal Pricing by Dealers

Consider a meeting between a dealer and an investor-owner. The dealer knows that the investor is a potential seller but does not know her utility flow, δ. This makes it harder for the dealer to price discriminate. In particular, he cannot extract all the surplus by offering to buy from the investor at her reservation value, $R(\delta)$, as he would under complete information. Instead, the dealer chooses a price to maximize his expected profit, taking as given the interdealer price, P; the reservation values of investors; and the distribution of utility flows within the group of investor-owners, $\Phi_1(\delta)$.

If the dealer offers to buy at some *bid price* b, then the investor-owner weakly prefers to sell his asset if his reservation value $R(\delta) \geq b$. Hence, the dealer's optimization problem can be stated as

$$\max_{b \leq P} \left\{ (P-b) \int_{\underline{\delta}}^{\overline{\delta}} \mathbf{1}_{\{R(\delta)\leq b\}} \frac{d\Phi_1(\delta)}{\Phi_1(\overline{\delta})} \right\},$$

where the first factor is the profit that the dealer makes by buying from the investor at price b and reselling in the interdealer market at price P, and the second factor is the probability that the offer b is accepted. By the same logic, the optimization problem of a dealer who offers an *ask price* a to sell the asset can be stated as

$$\max_{a \geq P} \left\{ (a-P) \int_{\underline{\delta}}^{\overline{\delta}} \mathbf{1}_{\{R(\delta)\geq a\}} \frac{d\Phi_0(\delta)}{\Phi_0(\overline{\delta})} \right\},$$

where $\Phi_0(\delta)$ is the cumulative distribution of utility flows within the group of investors who do not hold the asset.

To simplify the formulation of these optimization problems, note that we can assume without loss of generality that the interdealer price P and the offered prices (a, b) lie in the range

$$\mathcal{R} \equiv \left\{ p \in \mathbf{R} : \underline{R} \equiv \min_{\delta \in \mathcal{D}} R(\delta) \leq p \leq \max_{\delta \in \mathcal{D}} R(\delta) \equiv \overline{R} \right\}.$$

of the reservation value function. Indeed, if $P \notin \mathcal{R}$ then the interdealer market cannot clear, because dealers are willing to trade with investors only in one direction. For example, if $P < \underline{R}$ then dealers are willing to sell to all investors but unwilling to buy from any. On the other hand, if the interdealer price $P \in \mathcal{R}$, then offering a price $p \notin \mathcal{R}$ cannot be optimal for the dealer. For example, bidding $b < \underline{R}$ is clearly weakly dominated by bidding any $b' \in [\underline{R}, P]$.

Using this observation, and conjecturing that the reservation value function is continuous and strictly increasing, we can reduce the dealers' problems to

$$\max_{\delta \in [\underline{\delta}, \delta^\star]} \Pi_b(\delta) \equiv \max_{\delta \in [\underline{\delta}, \delta^\star]} \left\{ \left(R(\delta^\star) - R(\delta)\right) \frac{\Phi_1(\delta)}{\Phi_1(\bar{\delta})} \right\} \tag{10.1}$$

and

$$\max_{\delta \in [\delta^\star, \bar{\delta}]} \Pi_a(\delta) \equiv \max_{\delta \in [\delta^\star, \bar{\delta}]} \left\{ \left(R(\delta) - R(\delta^\star)\right) \left(1 - \frac{\Phi_0(\delta)}{\Phi_0(\bar{\delta})}\right) \right\}, \tag{10.2}$$

where the utility flow $\delta^\star \in \mathcal{D}$ associated with the interdealer market price is implicitly defined by the requirement that $P = R(\delta^\star)$. In words, (10.1) and (10.2) show that, taking the reservation value function of investors as given, one can equivalently formulate the dealer's problem as one of choosing a price or as one of choosing the utility flow of the marginal investor-buyer or investor-seller, which in turn determines the ask and bid prices, respectively. To simplify the presentation, we accordingly say throughout this chapter that a dealer quotes a utility flow δ to mean that he quotes a price equal to the reservation value of an investor with that utility flow.

While the maxima in (10.1) and (10.2) are obviously attained, it is not clear a priori whether the maximizers are unique. In fact, we show below that, in equilibrium, there must be multiple maximizers among which dealers randomize their price offers. To explicitly allow for such mixed pricing strategies, we assume that, upon meeting an investor, a dealer offers to buy at a bid price $b \geq R(\delta)$ with probability $1 - B(\delta-)$ if the investor is an asset owner and to sell at an ask price $a \leq R(\delta)$ with probability $A(\delta)$ if the investor is a nonowner.

Since dealers never buy (sell) above (below) the interdealer market price, the distributions (A, B) must satisfy

$$\lim_{\delta \uparrow \delta^\star} A(\delta) = 1 - B(\delta^\star) = 0,$$

and we say that such a pair is optimal if

$$\operatorname{supp}(A) \subseteq \operatorname*{argmax}_{\delta \in [\delta^\star, \bar{\delta}]} \Pi_a(\delta), \tag{10.3}$$

$$\operatorname{supp}(B) \subseteq \operatorname*{argmax}_{\delta \in [\underline{\delta}, \delta^\star]} \Pi_b(\delta), \tag{10.4}$$

where $\operatorname{supp}(A) \subseteq \mathcal{D}$ and $\operatorname{supp}(B) \subseteq \mathcal{D}$ denote the *supports* of the ask and bid distributions, respectively. The interpretation is simply that all the prices that are offered in equilibrium must maximize dealers' profits.

Asymmetric-information pricing problems of this kind have been studied by many authors, including Myerson [1981] and Myerson and Satterthwaite [1983], but mostly in one-sided, partial equilibrium settings where reservation values and distributions are exogenously specified. In contrast, the model of this chapter considers a two-sided problem and embeds it into a dynamic search equilibrium where all objects are endogenously determined by the trading behavior that investors optimally adopt in response to the pricing strategies of dealers as in, e.g., Albrecht and Axell [1984].

10.1.3 Equilibrium Definition

Proceeding as in chapter 3 reveals that the reservation value function of an investor satisfies

$$\begin{aligned} rR(\delta) &= \delta + \gamma \mathbf{E}^F \left[R(x) - R(\delta) \right] \\ &\quad + \lambda \int_{\underline{\delta}}^{\overline{\delta}} (R(x) - R(\delta))^+ \, dB(x) - \lambda \int_{\underline{\delta}}^{\overline{\delta}} (R(\delta) - R(x))^+ \, dA(x) \end{aligned} \tag{10.5}$$

where the terms on the second line account for the fact that, upon meeting a dealer, the investor is offered to trade at price $R(x)$ with probability $dB(x)$ if he is an owner and with probability $dA(x)$ otherwise.

The following lemma establishes the existence of a unique solution to this equation and confirms our conjectures regarding its regularity.

Lemma 10.1: The unique solution to (10.5) satisfies

$$R(\delta) - R(\underline{\delta}) = \int_{\underline{\delta}}^{\delta} \frac{dx}{r + \gamma + \lambda\,(1 - B(x) + A(x))}. \tag{10.6}$$

In particular, the reservation value function is uniformly bounded, strictly increasing, and absolutely continuous on $\mathcal{D}$.

Proof. Existence, uniqueness, absolute continuity, and strict monotonicity follow from Proposition 3.6 and Corollary 3.8 in chapter 3. Since the reservation value function is absolutely continuous, we can change the order of integration to rewrite the integrals in (10.5) as

$$\begin{aligned} \int_{\underline{\delta}}^{\overline{\delta}} (R(x) - R(\delta))^+ dB(x) &= \int_{\delta}^{\overline{\delta}} \left(\int_{\delta}^{x} R'(y) dy \right) dB(x) \\ &= \int_{\delta}^{\overline{\delta}} R'(y) \left(\int_{y}^{\overline{\delta}} dB(x) \right) dy = \int_{\delta}^{\overline{\delta}} R'(y) \left(1 - B(y)\right) dy \end{aligned}$$

and

$$\int_{\underline{\delta}}^{\overline{\delta}} \left(R(\delta) - R(x)\right)^{+} dA(x) = \int_{\underline{\delta}}^{\delta} R'(y)A(y)dy,$$

so that

$$rR(\delta) = \delta + \gamma \left(\mathbf{E}^{F}[R(x)] - R(\delta)\right)$$
$$+ \lambda \int_{\delta}^{\overline{\delta}} R'(x)(1 - B(x))dx - \lambda \int_{\underline{\delta}}^{\delta} R'(x)A(x)dx.$$

Differentiating both sides and solving the resulting equation shows that the marginal reservation value $R'(x)$ is given by the integrand in (10.6), and the conclusion follows from the fundamental theorem of calculus. □

The joint distribution of utility flows and asset holdings can be characterized by imposing the usual stationarity conditions, subject to consistency and market clearing. As in chapter 4, the latter conditions be written as

$$F(\delta) = \Phi_0(\delta) + \Phi_1(\delta), \tag{10.7}$$

$$s = \Phi_1(\overline{\delta}), \tag{10.8}$$

whereas the former requires that

$$\int_G (\gamma + \lambda_1(\delta))\, d\Phi_1(\delta) = \int_G \left(\gamma \Phi_1(\overline{\delta}) dF(\delta) + \lambda_0(\delta) d\Phi_0(\delta)\right) \tag{10.9}$$

for any Borel set $G \subseteq \mathcal{D}$, where $\lambda_0(\delta)$ and $\lambda_1(\delta)$ denote the equilibrium trading intensities of nonowners and owners with utility flow $\delta \in \mathcal{D}$. In the current environment, these trading intensities are given by

$$\lambda_0(\delta) = \lambda A(\delta) \tag{10.10}$$

and

$$\lambda_1(\delta) = \lambda\,(1 - B(\delta)). \tag{10.11}$$

Note that the definition of the trading intensities assumes that nonowners trade when they are indifferent while owners do not. This assumption is clearly innocuous when $F(\delta)$ is continuous, but cannot be upheld in equilibrium if the distribution has atoms because in that case some randomization on either or both sides of the market may be required to ensure market clearing. See section 10.2 for an illustration in a model with three types.

Using Lemma A.14, we can drop the integral and the explicit reference to Borel sets to informally restate (10.9) pointwise as

$$(\gamma + \lambda_1(\delta))\, d\Phi_1(\delta) = \gamma \Phi_1(\bar{\delta}) dF(\delta) + \lambda_0(\delta) d\Phi_0(\delta). \tag{10.12}$$

Solving this equation subject to the consistency condition (10.7) then delivers the following characterization.

Lemma 10.2: The unique solution to (10.12) subject to (10.7) is

$$\Phi_1(\delta) = \Phi_1(\delta|m) \equiv \int_{\underline{\delta}}^{\delta} \frac{(\gamma m + \lambda_0(x))\, dF(x)}{\gamma + \lambda_0(x) + \lambda_1(x)}, \tag{10.13}$$

where m is the unique solution to $\Phi_1(\bar{\delta}|m) = m$ in $[0, 1]$ and the trading intensities are defined as in (10.11) and (10.10).

Proof. The first part follows by substituting (10.7) into (10.12) and solving the resulting equation for $d\Phi_1(\delta)$. The second part follows from the first by requiring that m coincides with the total mass of owners. □

Expanding the stationarity condition (10.9) for $G = \mathcal{D}$ and using the definition of the constant m reveals that

$$\int_{\underline{\delta}}^{\bar{\delta}} \lambda_1(\delta) d\Phi_1(\delta) = \int_{\underline{\delta}}^{\bar{\delta}} \lambda_0(\delta)\Phi_0(\delta),$$

where the left-hand side is the rate at which dealers buy and the right-hand side is the rate at which they sell. This identity shows that stationarity implies interdealer market clearing: the distribution of utility flows among owners and nonowners automatically adjusts to the pricing strategy of dealers in such a way that the interdealer market clears. This, in turn, implies that the mass of assets held by investors is constant over time, but it does *not* guarantee that this mass equals the asset supply. To obtain that property one must impose the additional market clearing condition (10.8).

Combining Lemmas 10.1 and 10.2 with the market clearing condition (10.8) and using the fact that the supports of the price distributions are separated by the inderdealer utility flow $\delta^\star$ (see (10.3) and (10.4)) reveals that the expected profits of a dealer can be expressed as

$$\Pi_a(\delta) = \int_{\delta^\star}^{\delta} \frac{dx}{r + \gamma + \lambda_0(x)} \int_{\delta}^{\bar{\delta}} \frac{\gamma\, dF(x)}{\gamma + \lambda_0(x)},$$

when he meets an owner and as

$$\Pi_b(\delta) = \int_{\delta}^{\delta^\star} \frac{dx}{r+\gamma+\lambda_1(x)} \int_{\underline{\delta}}^{\delta} \frac{\gamma \, dF(x)}{\gamma+\lambda_1(x)} \tag{10.14}$$

when he meets a nonowner. The first integral in each expression represents the dealer's profit per trade as a function of the offered price δ, and the second integral captures the probability that this offer is accepted.

With these elements in place, we are now ready to formally define a steady-state equilibrium for the semicentralized OTC market model with asymmetric information over private values.

Definition 10.3: A steady-state equilibrium consists of a pair of pricing strategies (A, B), a pair of cumulative measures (Φ_0, Φ_1), a reservation value function R, and an interdealer price $P = R(\delta^\star)$ such that

1. $R(\delta)$ solves (10.5) given A and B;
2. $\Phi_0(\delta)$ and $\Phi_1(\delta)$ satisfy (10.7), (10.8), and (10.12) given A and B;
3. A and B satisfy (10.3) and (10.4) given $R(\delta)$, $\Phi_0(\delta)$, $\Phi_1(\delta)$ and the price P.

An equilibrium is in pure strategies if the supports of A and B both consist of a single point. Otherwise, it is in mixed strategies.

10.2 A Detour: The Case with Three Types

Before proceeding to the analysis of the continuous case, we present a simple discrete example designed to illustrate some of the key insights.

10.2.1 Assumptions and Equilibrium Conjecture

Assume that the utility flows of investors present in the market are drawn from a discrete distribution with support given by

$$\text{supp}(F) = \{\delta_L, \delta_M, \delta_H\}$$

for some $\delta_L < \delta_M < \delta_H \in \mathcal{D}$. In addition, suppose that the mass of investors with the high utility flow exceeds the asset supply, so that

$$s < f_H \equiv \Delta F(\delta_H). \tag{10.15}$$

The results of chapter 4 imply that, under complete information, this simple model admits a unique steady-state equilibrium in which

i) The interdealer utility flow is $\delta^\star = \delta_H$;
ii) Asset owners with utility flow in the interval $\{\delta_L, \delta_M\}$ sell with probability 1 upon meeting a dealer;
iii) Nonowners with utility flow δ_H buy with some probability $\rho_{0H} \in (0, 1)$ upon meeting a dealer, and otherwise do not trade.

The main difference with the case of a continuous distribution is condition iii): because of atoms in the distribution, market clearing may require some randomization by investors who are indifferent between trading and not trading.

We conjecture, and later confirm, that an equilibrium with features similar to i)–iii) above continues to exist under private information. In particular, we consider a candidate equilibrium in which only investors with utility flow δ_H buy from dealers, so that there is no uncertainty about the utility type of buyers. As a result, as in the perfect information case, the distribution of ask prices is degenerate:

$$A(\delta) = \mathbf{1}_{\{\delta \geq \delta_H\}}. \tag{10.16}$$

On the other side of the market, however, dealers are unsure of the utility flows of the investors who want to sell. Formally, the optimization problem of a dealer who meets an owner can be stated as

$$\max_{x \in (\underline{\delta}, \delta_H]} \left\{ (R(\delta_H) - R(x)) \left(\psi_L \mathbf{1}_{\{x \geq \delta_L\}} + (1 - \psi_L) \mathbf{1}_{\{x \geq \delta_M\}} \right) \right\}, \tag{10.17}$$

where ψ_L denotes the fraction of sellers with utility flow δ_L.

Since utility flows lie in $\{\delta_L, \delta_M, \delta_H\}$ and the reservation value function is strictly increasing in utility flow, it is clear that the optimal strategy is to either bid δ_L or bid δ_M, or to randomize between these two bids. Accordingly, the bid distribution offered by dealers can be written as

$$B(\delta) = \begin{cases} 0, & \delta \in (\underline{\delta}, \delta_L), \\ \beta, & \delta \in (\delta_L, \delta_M), \\ 1, & \delta \in (\delta_M, \overline{\delta}), \end{cases} \tag{10.18}$$

for some $\beta \in [0, 1]$ that captures the probability of bidding δ_L.

To verify that this candidate is an equilibrium, we proceed in two steps. First, we solve for the reservation value function $R(\delta)$ and the asset allocation $\Phi_1(\delta)$, taking as given that dealers quote prices according to (10.16) and (10.18) for some constant $\beta \in [0, 1]$. Second, we determine β as the solution to a fixed-point problem, which ensures that given the reservation value and distribution functions induced by β, it is optimal for dealers to offer the price associated with the low utility flow with probability β.

10.2.2 Reservation Values

Given the offered price distributions, we can easily derive the reservation value of investors. In particular, (10.5) and (10.16)–(10.18) imply that

$$(r+\gamma)R(\delta) = \delta + \gamma \mathbf{E}^F\left[R(\delta_i)\right] - \lambda\left(R(\delta) - R(\delta_H)\right)^+ \\ + \lambda\beta(R(\delta_L) - R(\delta))^+ + \lambda(1-\beta)(R(\delta_M) - R(\delta))^+.$$

Solving this equation reveals that the gains from trade of potential sellers are simply given by

$$R(\delta_H) - R(\delta_M) = \frac{\delta_H - \delta_M}{r+\gamma} \tag{10.19}$$

and

$$R(\delta_H) - R(\delta_L) = \frac{\delta_H - \delta_M}{r+\gamma} + \frac{\delta_M - \delta_L}{r+\gamma+\lambda(1-\beta)}. \tag{10.20}$$

For δ_L investors, note that the probability β plays a role similar to the dealer bargaining power parameter in earlier chapters, in that it captures the share of the surplus that dealers appropriate when trading with δ_L investors. This reflects the fact that asymmetric information endogenously gives these investors what is commonly called an *information rent* by allowing them to sell at a price $R(\delta_M)$ that is strictly larger than their reservation value $R(\delta_L)$.

10.2.3 Asset Allocation

Given the bid and ask distributions it is straightforward to derive the induced asset allocation. To that end, let $\phi_{qi} \equiv \Delta\Phi_q(\delta_i)$ denote the measure of investors with asset holding $q \in \{0, 1\}$ and utility flow $\delta_i \in \{\delta_L, \delta_M, \delta_H\}$. With this notation, equations (10.9) and (10.16)–(10.18) imply that

$$\lambda\phi_{1L} + \gamma\phi_{1L} = \gamma s f_L, \tag{10.21a}$$

$$\lambda(1-\beta)\phi_{1M} + \gamma\phi_{1M} = \gamma s f_M, \tag{10.21b}$$

$$\gamma\phi_{1H} = \gamma s f_H + \lambda\rho_{0H}\phi_{0H}, \tag{10.21c}$$

subject to

$$s = \phi_{1L} + \phi_{1M} + \phi_{1H}, \tag{10.21d}$$

$$f_i = \phi_{1i} + \phi_{0i}, \qquad \forall i \in \{L, M, H\}, \tag{10.21e}$$

where ρ_{0H} is the probability that a nonowner with utility flow δ_H trades upon meeting a dealer. The constraints (10.21d) and (10.21e) ensure, respectively, that markets clear and that the distributions of utility flows among owners and nonowners are consistent with the distribution in the whole population.

Lemma 10.4: The unique solution to (10.21) is given by

$$\phi_{1L} = f_L - \phi_{0L} = \frac{\gamma s f_L}{\gamma + \lambda}, \tag{10.22}$$

$$\phi_{1M} = f_M - \phi_{0M} = \frac{\gamma s f_M}{\gamma + \lambda(1-\beta)}, \tag{10.23}$$

$$\phi_{1H} = f_H - \phi_{0H} = s - \frac{\gamma s f_L}{\gamma + \lambda} - \frac{\gamma s f_M}{\gamma + \lambda(1-\beta)}, \tag{10.24}$$

and

$$\rho_{0H} = \frac{\gamma}{\lambda} \frac{\phi_{1H} - s f_H}{\phi_{0H}} \tag{10.25}$$

and lies in the open set $(0, 1)^7$ for any value of $\beta \in [0, 1]$.

Proof. The solution and the fact that $\phi_{qi} \in (0, 1)$ for any $\beta \in [0, 1]$ follow from straightforward algebra. To complete the proof it thus suffices to show that $\rho_{0H} \in (0, 1)$. Substituting (10.24) into (10.25) shows that

$$\rho_{0H} = \frac{s\gamma^2 \beta f_M - s\gamma(\gamma + \lambda(1-\beta))(1 - f_H)}{(\gamma + \lambda(1-\beta))(s\lambda - (\lambda + \gamma(1-s))f_H) - \gamma s \lambda \beta f_M}$$

and the conclusion follows by observing that this expression is strictly decreasing as a function of β with

$$\rho_{0H}\Big|_{\beta=0} = \frac{\gamma s(1 - f_H)}{\gamma(1-s)f_H - \lambda(s - f_H))} < 1,$$

$$\rho_{0H}\Big|_{\beta=1} = \frac{\gamma s f_L}{\gamma(1-s)f_H + \lambda(f_H - s(1 - f_M))} > 0,$$

where the strict inequalities are due to (10.15). □

10.2.4 Equilibrium

Equations (10.17), (10.19), (10.20), and (10.22)–(10.24) imply that, taking as given the reservation values and the asset allocation induced by some $\beta \in [0,1]$, the dealer's optimal bidding strategy is

$$T(\beta) \equiv \begin{cases} 0, & \text{if } \psi_L(\beta) > \psi_L^*(\beta), \\ [0,1], & \text{if } \psi_L(\beta) = \psi_L^*(\beta), \\ 1, & \text{if } \psi_L(\beta) < \psi_L^*(\beta), \end{cases}$$

where

$$\begin{aligned} \psi_L(\beta) &\equiv \frac{\phi_{1L}}{\phi_{1L}+\phi_{1M}} \\ &= \frac{(\gamma+\lambda(1-\beta))f_L}{(\gamma+\lambda)f_M+(\gamma+\lambda(1-\beta))f_L} \end{aligned}$$

is the fraction of sellers with utility flow δ_L induced by β, and

$$\psi_L^*(\beta) \equiv \frac{R(\delta_H)-R(\delta_M)}{R(\delta_H)-R(\delta_L)} = \frac{(r+\gamma+\lambda(1-\beta))\,(\delta_H-\delta_M)}{(r+\gamma)(\delta_H-\delta_L)+\lambda(1-\beta)(\delta_H-\delta_M)}$$

denotes the fraction of sellers with utility flow δ_L that equates the profits from bidding either δ_L or δ_M. An equilibrium is then simply a fixed point of the operator $T:[0,1]\to[0,1]$, and straightforward manipulations lead to the following characterization of the equilibrium.

Proposition 10.5: Suppose that (10.15) holds and define

$$\Pi^* \equiv \left(1+\frac{\lambda}{\gamma}\right)\left(\frac{\delta_H-\delta_M}{\delta_M-\delta_L}\right)\frac{f_M}{f_L} > 0,$$

$$\Pi_* \equiv \left(1+\frac{\lambda}{r+\gamma}\right)\left(\frac{\delta_H-\delta_M}{\delta_M-\delta_L}\right)\frac{f_M}{f_L} \in (0,\Pi^*).$$

Then, there exists a unique equilibrium. The equilibrium price setting strategy of the dealer is given by (10.18) with the constant

$$\beta = \begin{cases} 0 & \text{if } 1 \le \Pi_*, \\ \frac{(\gamma+\lambda)(1-\Pi_*)}{\gamma(\Pi^*-\Pi_*)+\lambda(1-\Pi_*)} & \text{if } \Pi_* < 1 < \Pi^*, \\ 1 & \text{if } \Pi^* \le 1. \end{cases}$$

Moreover, if $\beta \in (0,1)$ then it is strictly decreasing in λ.

To analyze the combined effects of search and information frictions, let us first consider the different types of equilibria that can arise as we vary the meeting intensity. Given that

$$\frac{\partial \Pi^*}{\partial \lambda} = \left(1 + \frac{r}{\gamma}\right) \frac{\partial \Pi_*}{\partial \lambda} > 0$$

and

$$\lim_{\lambda \to 0} \Pi_* = \lim_{\lambda \to 0} \Pi^* = \Pi_0 \equiv \left(\frac{\delta_H - \delta_M}{\delta_M - \delta_L}\right) \frac{f_M}{f_L},$$

it is clear that only two cases may occur. If the parameters are such that $\Pi_0 \geq 1$, then dealers quote a single bid equal to δ_M irrespective of the meeting intensity. Alternatively, if $\Pi_0 < 1$, then all three types of equilibria may occur, depending on the meeting intensity: dealers only bid δ_L when λ is sufficiently low, they only bid δ_M when λ is sufficiently high, and otherwise they randomize between these two bids. See the top panels of figure 10.1 for an illustration.

In all cases, since $\lim_{\lambda \to \infty} \Pi_* = \infty$, the only type of equilibrium that can occur as search frictions vanish is one in which dealers bid δ_M with probability 1. In this limit, owners with the intermediate utility flow sell with probability 1 but do not receive any of the gains from trade, and $\beta \to 0$ so that owners with the low utility flow also sell with probability 1. Interpreting β as the effective bargaining power of dealers with δ_L investors shows that δ_L investors are able to extract ever-larger information rents as search frictions vanish. Hence, relative to the symmetric information case of chapter 4 with monopolistic dealers ($\theta = 1$), the effects of information frictions persist as search frictions vanish.

Information frictions can distort the allocation over and beyond the effect of search frictions. In particular, if $\beta > 0$ then at each instant there are owners with intermediate utility flow who receive a bid of δ_L and do not sell. As a result, the mass ϕ_{1M} of such investors is larger than its full-information counterpart and, since the mass of owners with low utility flow is the same in both models, it follows that the mass ϕ_{0H} of misallocated nonowners is higher under asymmetric information. If instead $\beta = 0$, then the equilibrium allocation under asymmetric information is the same as under complete information because nonowners with low or intermediate utility flows trade with probability 1 upon meeting a dealer. Together with Proposition 10.5, these observations imply that asymmetric information magnifies the allocative effects of search frictions only if the meeting intensity is sufficiently low.

Information frictions also distort the prices at which the asset is traded. In particular, the interdealer market price $R(\delta_H)$ under asymmetric information is higher than

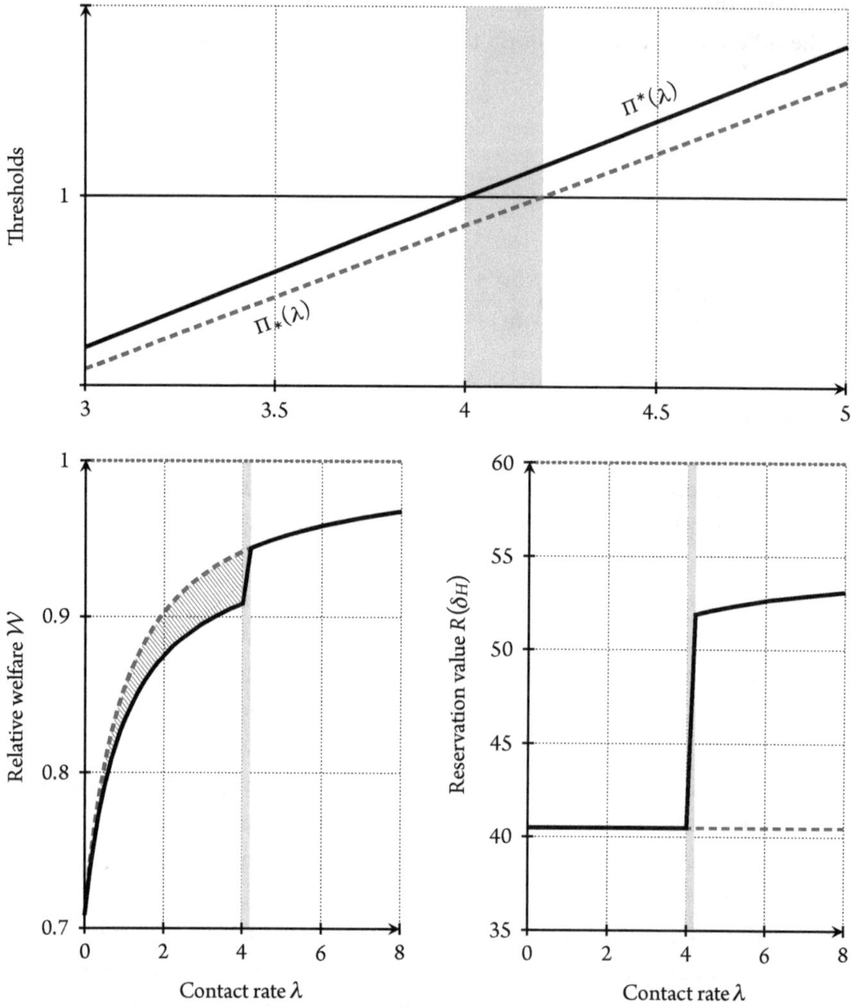

FIGURE 10.1. Search and information frictions

The top panel plots the tresholds Π_* and Π^* as functions of the contact rate. The bottom panels plot the relative welfare and the interdealer price as functions of the contact rate in the semicentralized market with search and information frictions (solid), the semicentralized market with search frictions (dashed), and the frictionless market (dotted). In each panel the shaded region indicates the interval of meeting intensities for which the equilibrium is in mixed strategies. The parameters used to produce the figure satisfy condition (10.15) and $\Pi_0 < 1$.

in the complete-information setting of chapter 4 with dealer bargaining power $\theta = 1$, but lower than its frictionless counterpart δ_H/r, even as $\lambda \to \infty$; see the bottom right panel of figure 10.1 for an illustration. As explained in section 4.4.3, the fact that the asset trades at a discount is a consequence of search frictions and the condition $f_H > s$, which implies that the marginal type $\delta^\star = \delta_H$ is higher than the average utility flow. The novel feature in the present chapter is that asymmetric information results in a strictly smaller discount as soon as the meeting intensity is large enough to ensure that $\beta < 1$. This occurs because in an equilibrium with $\beta < 1$, owners with low utility flow extract information rents by being able to sell at δ_M with strictly positive probability. These rents increase the option value of selling and, thereby, increase the reservation value of all investors. Note, however, that this comparative static heavily depends on the assumption that dealers make take-it-or-leave-it offers, and thus may not be robust to alternative trading protocols.

How do the effects of information frictions depend on the severity of search frictions? To answer this question, we need to understand how the pricing behavior of dealers depends on the meeting rate, λ. From Proposition 10.5 we know that β is weakly decreasing in λ, so that dealers bid δ_M more often as search frictions weaken, as illustrated in the top right panel of figure 10.1. This occurs for two reasons. First, an increase in λ skews the distribution of utility flows among owners toward the intermediate utility flow, which provides dealers with an incentive to bid δ_M more frequently. Second, given $\beta < 1$, an increase in λ causes the spread

$$R(\delta_M) - R(\delta_L) = \frac{\delta_M - \delta_L}{r + \gamma + \lambda(1 - \beta)}$$

to decrease, which makes it less attractive for dealers to target potential sellers with the low utility flow.

The fact that the low bid probability β decreases in λ implies that misallocation declines as search frictions become less severe. This occurs for two reasons that mirror the frictions at play in the model. First, more frequent meetings allow investors to adjust their holdings more often, which naturally reduces misallocation. Second, private information implies that dealers are more likely to quote δ_M as the meeting intensity increases, which improves the allocation by ensuring that a greater fraction of positive-surplus matches result in trade. To illustrate this effect, the bottom left panel of figure 10.1 plots the steady-state welfare relative to the frictionless benchmark

$$\mathcal{W} \equiv \frac{1}{s\delta_H} \sum_i \delta_i \phi_{1i}$$

as a function of the meeting intensity with and without private information. The area between the frictionless benchmark (dotted) and the full information benchmark (dashed) accounts for the efficiency losses due to search frictions, whereas the hatched area between the full- and private-information welfare (solid) accounts for the additional losses due to the information friction.

10.3 Back to the Continuously Differentiable Case

After this detour through the discrete case, we now return to the smooth case in which the distribution of utility flows is continuously differentiable with $F'(\delta) = f(\delta) > 0$ for all $\delta \in \mathcal{D}$.

10.3.1 Necessary Conditions

Our earlier analysis shows that, when $F(\delta)$ is continuous, the dealer's expected profits from quoting $\delta \in \mathcal{D}$ are respectively given by

$$\Pi_a(\delta) = \int_{\delta^\star}^{\delta} \frac{dx}{r+\gamma+\lambda A(x)} \int_{\delta}^{\overline{\delta}} \frac{\gamma\, dF(x)}{\gamma+\lambda A(x)}$$

when meeting a buyer and

$$\Pi_b(\delta) = \int_{\delta}^{\delta^\star} \frac{dx}{r+\gamma+\lambda(1-B(x))} \int_{\underline{\delta}}^{\delta} \frac{\gamma\, dF(x)}{\gamma+\lambda(1-B(x))}$$

when meeting a seller. To narrow down the search for an equilibrium, we establish several properties that must hold in any equilibrium.

Proposition 10.6: In any equilibrium,

1. The interdealer utility flow $\delta^\star \in \mathcal{D}$.
2. The supports of the price distributions are such that $\text{supp}(B) \subset (\underline{\delta}, \delta^\star)$ and $\text{supp}(A) \subset (\delta^\star, \overline{\delta})$.
3. The price distributions are atomless and thus continuous. In particular, all equilibria are in mixed strategies.

Proof. To establish the first assertion, assume toward a contradiction that there exists an equilibrium in which $\delta^\star = \underline{\delta}$. In such an equilibrium dealers never buy, because the mass of investors with utility flow $\underline{\delta}$ is equal to zero. Since the interdealer market must clear, it follows that dealers never sell either. But this cannot be an equilibrium because, in the absence of trade,

$$\Pi_a(\delta) = \frac{(\delta - \underline{\delta})(1 - F(\delta))}{r + \gamma}$$

is strictly positive on $\mathcal{D}$. Symmetrically, in an equilibrium with $\delta^\star = \overline{\delta}$, dealers never sell and, thus, never buy. However, this cannot be optimal because, absent trade, the expected dealer profit is

$$\Pi_b(\delta) = \frac{(\overline{\delta} - \delta)F(\delta)}{r + \gamma} > 0, \qquad \delta \in \mathcal{D}.$$

To prove the second assertion, assume toward a contradiction that there exists an equilibrium in which $\underline{\delta} \in \operatorname{supp}(B)$. Because the expected profit function is by definition constant over the latter set, it must be that

$$\max_{\delta \in [\underline{\delta}, \delta^\star]} \Pi_b(\delta) = \Pi_b(\underline{\delta}) = 0.$$

However, since reservation values are strictly increasing and

$$\Phi_1'(\delta) = \frac{(\gamma s + \lambda A(\delta)) f(\delta)}{\gamma + \lambda(1 - B(\delta) + A(\delta))} > 0,$$

we can find $\delta \in (\underline{\delta}, \delta^\star) \neq \emptyset$ such that $\Pi_b(\delta) > 0$, and the required contradiction follows. Similarly, if there exists an equilibrium in which $\delta^\star \in \operatorname{supp}(B)$, then condition (10.4) implies that

$$\max_{\delta \in [\underline{\delta}, \delta^\star]} \Pi_b(\delta) = \Pi_b(\delta^\star) = 0,$$

and the same arguments as above deliver a contradiction by showing that we may find $\delta \in (\underline{\delta}, \delta^\star) \neq \emptyset$ such that $\Pi_b(\delta) > 0$.

Let us now turn to the last assertion and assume toward a contradiction that there exists an equilibrium in which $\Delta B(z) > 0$ for some $z \in \operatorname{supp}(B)$. Since B is right-continuous and $f = F'$ is continuous, we have that the expected profit in (10.14) is differentiable with

$$\Pi_b'(\delta) = \frac{f(\delta) L(\delta)}{\gamma + \lambda(1 - B(\delta))} - \frac{K(\delta)}{r + \gamma + \lambda(1 - B(\delta))}, \tag{10.26}$$

where the functions

$$K(\delta) \equiv \int_{\underline{\delta}}^{\delta} \frac{\gamma f(x)dx}{\gamma + \lambda(1 - B(x))},$$

$$L(\delta) \equiv \int_{\delta}^{\delta^\star} \frac{\gamma\, dx}{r + \gamma + \lambda(1 - B(x))},$$

are continuous. Using this expression shows that the first-order condition of optimality at a point $z \in \text{supp}(B)$ can be written as

$$\Pi_b'(z) \leq 0 \leq \lim_{\delta \uparrow b} \Pi_b'(\delta) = \frac{f(z)L(z)}{\gamma + \lambda(1 - B(z-))} - \frac{K(z)}{r + \gamma + \lambda(1 - B(z-))},$$

where the limit exists because B is nondecreasing and thus admits left-limits at all points of $\mathcal{D}$. The required contradiction follows by observing that these inequalities cannot both hold if z is an atom of the bid distribution. Indeed, if the second inequality holds, then (10.26) implies that

$$\frac{K(z)}{f(z)L(z)} \leq \frac{r + \gamma + \lambda(1 - B(z-))}{\gamma + \lambda(1 - B(z-))} < \frac{r + \gamma + \lambda(1 - B(z))}{\gamma + \lambda(1 - B(z))},$$

where the strict inequality follows from the fact that $\Delta B(z) > 0$. Substituting this inequality into (10.26) yields

$$\Pi_b'(z) = \frac{f(z)L(z)}{r + \gamma + \lambda(1 - B(z))} \left(\frac{r + \gamma + \lambda(1 - B(z))}{\gamma + \lambda(1 - B(z))} - \frac{K(z)}{f(z)L(z)} \right) > 0,$$

which contradicts the first inequality. The proof of the corresponding results for the ask distribution is similar. □

The proposition offers the striking conclusion that there are no equilibria in pure strategies when the distribution is continuously differentiable; that is, there are no equilibria in which the support of either or both of the price distributions is reduced to a point. To see why, consider an equilibrium in which dealers offer a single bid price b. In such an equilibrium, owners with reservation values $R(\delta) > b$ never sell. As a result, such owners are relatively abundant in equilibrium, and this endogenous selection implies that raising the bid is profitable because, when the density is continuous, the induced increase in the mass of accepted offers more than compensates for the higher price that the dealer pays for each asset. Similarly, since owners with $R(\delta) \leq b$ always sell upon meeting a dealer, there are relatively few such investors in equilibrium, and this endogenous selection makes it profitable to reduce the bid because the lower

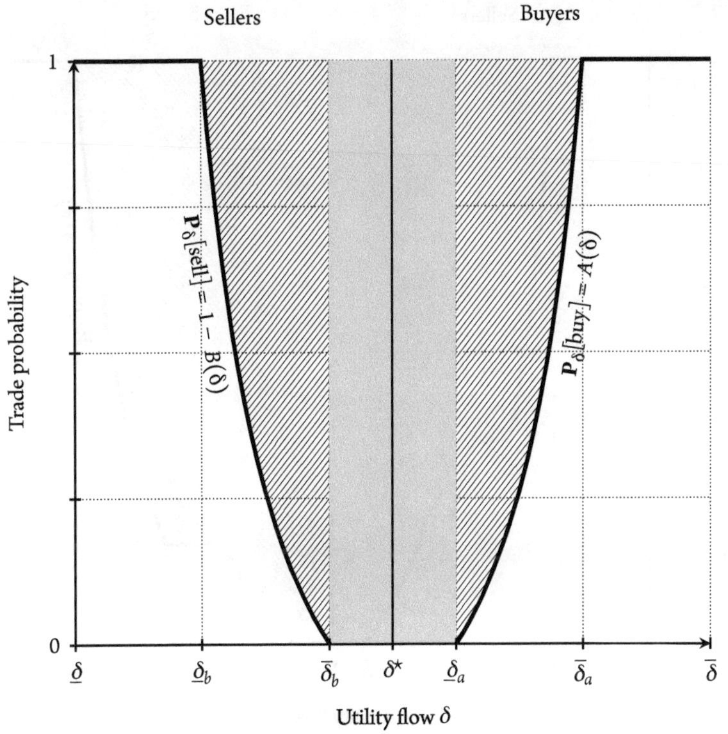

FIGURE 10.2. Equilibrium trade probabilities

This figure illustrates the probability that an owner with utility flow $\delta \leq \delta^\star$ sells upon meeting a dealer (left panel) and the probability that a nonowner with utility flow $\delta \geq \delta^\star$ buys upon meeting a dealer (right panel). The shaded areas indicate utility flows whose trades would occur with probability 1 under complete information but may be delayed ▨ or impossible ▭ under asymmetric information.

price paid for each asset more than compensates for the induced decrease in the mass of accepted offers.

The necessary conditions of Proposition 10.6 have important implications for the trading experience of investors in the market. In particular, as illustrated in figure 10.2, these conditions imply that the pricing strategies of dealers endogenously split the population into three groups. Owners with low utility flows $\delta < \underline{\delta}_b$ and nonowners with large utility flows $\delta > \overline{\delta}_a$ have the largest potential gains from trade with dealers and, therefore, are willing to pay a premium to trade fast. With this in mind, dealers optimally offer bid prices in $[\underline{\delta}_b, \overline{\delta}_b]$ and ask prices in $[\underline{\delta}_a, \overline{\delta}_a]$ so that, upon meeting a dealer, these investors trade with probability 1.

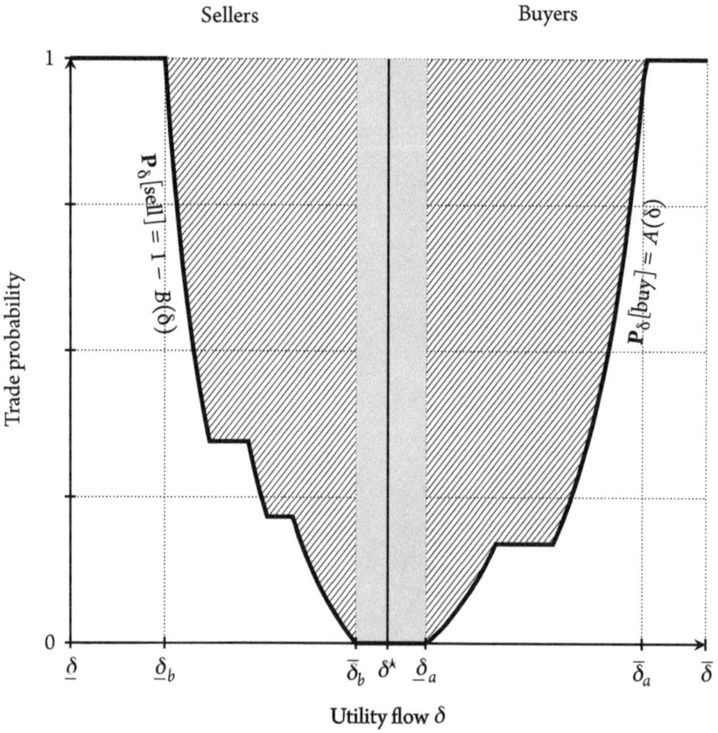

FIGURE 10.3. Equilibrium trade probabilities with bunching

This figure illustrates the probability that an owner with utility flow $\delta \leq \delta^\star$ sells upon meeting a dealer (left panel) and the probability that a nonowner with utility flow $\delta \geq \delta^\star$ buys upon meeting a dealer (right panel). The shaded areas indicate utility flows whose trades would occur with probability 1 under complete information but may be delayed ▨ or impossible ▭ under asymmetric information.

Next, owners with utility flows $\delta \in [\underline{\delta}_b, \overline{\delta}_b]$ and nonowners with utility flows $\delta \in [\underline{\delta}_a, \overline{\delta}_a]$ have intermediate gains from trade and, thus, may be willing to forgo immediacy in the hope of better terms. In equilibrium, dealers exploit this by quoting random prices that offer such investors the possibility of gains from trade but may result in delays if the realized price is not accepted. Importantly, and in contrast to the full-information case where dealers capture the whole surplus in every match, investors in these first two groups retain a strictly positive share of the surplus in every trade they execute and, thus, enjoy *information rents* that mitigate the market power of dealers within each match. Finally, dealers ensure their profit margin by bounding their bid and ask prices away from the interdealer price so that trade breaks down for owners with utility flows $\delta \in (\overline{\delta}_b, \delta^\star]$ and nonowners with utility flows $\delta \in [\delta^\star, \underline{\delta}_a)$, who offer the smallest potential gains from trade.

If the trade probabilities are as depicted in figure 10.2, then the equilibrium is fully separating in the sense that utility flows that are not excluded from trading effectively face different terms. However, Proposition 10.6 does not preclude the possibility of holes in the support of the equilibrium bid and ask distributions, as illustrated in figure 10.3, where instead of being connected, the support of the bid (ask) distribution is the union of two (three) disjoint intervals. In the mechanism design literature, such situations are referred to as *bunching* [e.g., Mussa and Rosen, 1978; Guesnerie and Laffont, 1984; Laffont and Martimort, 2001] because investors whose utility flows fall in a given hole of the distribution are offered equivalent terms of trade and, thus, either all accept or all refuse a given offer under the equilibrium pricing strategy. To exclude bunching a priori, and thus greatly simplify the equilibrium analysis, we need to impose additional conditions on the distribution of utility flows. The following result provides a convenient sufficient condition that holds for a large class of distributions.

Proposition 10.7: If the density $f(\delta)$ is log concave, then the supports of A and B are connected in equilibrium and, hence, there is no bunching.

Proof. See section 10.4.1. □

The class $\mathcal{L}$ of distributions with log-concave densities has found applications in multiple areas of economics, statistics, and operations research. For example, the uniform distribution, the exponential and double exponential distributions, the normal distribution, the power distribution with exponent $p \geq 1$, and the beta distributions with parameters $a, b \geq 1$ (as well as the truncation of any of these distributions to an interval) all belong to the class $\mathcal{L}$. See Saumard and Wellner [2014] for a review of the theory of log-concave functions, An [1998]; Ewerhart [2013], and Bagnoli and Bergstrom [2006] for surveys of applications in economics and statistics, and appendix A.4 for properties of $\mathcal{L}$ that are relevant for our purposes.

A distinctive feature of $\mathcal{L}$ is that its members are *unimodal* in the sense that, for any F in this class there exists an m such that $f(\delta)$ is increasing below m and decreasing above it. To understand why bunching is likely if this property fails, suppose that the density $f(\delta)$ is bimodal over the interval $(\underline{\delta}, \delta^\star]$ associated with sellers, so that the conditional distribution $F(\delta)/F(\delta^\star)$ is strictly convex on two separate regions, as in figure 10.4. Assume further that the point $\delta_0 \in \text{supp}(B)$ and consider the possibility of bidding more than δ_0. The fact that the distribution changes from concave to convex at τ implies that there are very few owners with utility flows in the interval $[\delta_0, \delta_1]$. Therefore, offering prices

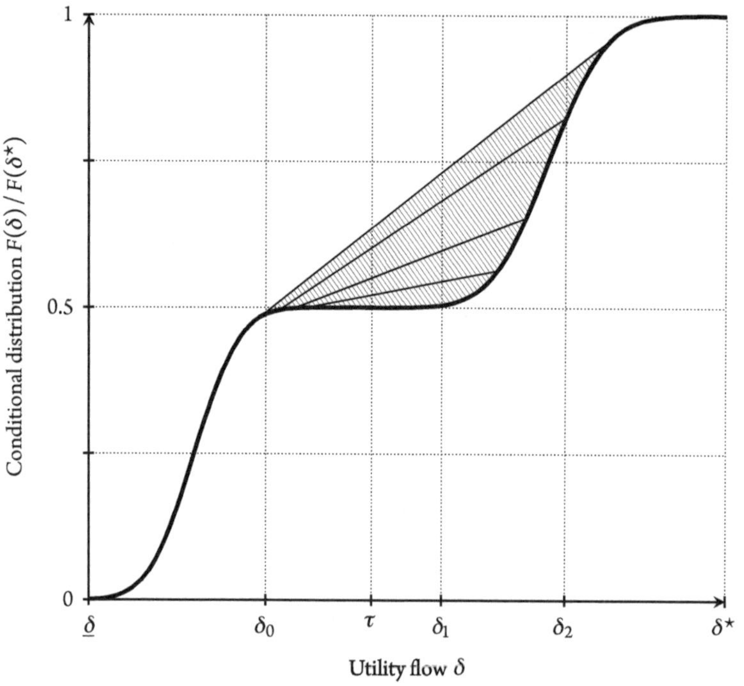

FIGURE 10.4. A distribution of utility flows $F \notin \mathcal{L}$

This figure illustrates a case in which the conditional density $f(\delta)/F(\delta^\star)$ of utility flows among investors with utility flows below $\delta^\star$ is bimodal so that the distribution includes two convex pieces: one starting at the left endpoint $\underline{\delta}$ and another starting at τ. The endpoints of the straight lines represent pairs satisfying condition (10.50).

in that interval is unlikely to be optimal, as it would reduce the dealer's profits per trade without significantly increasing the numbers of trades. By contrast, bidding prices to the right of δ_1 may keep the dealer indifferent because the convexity of the distribution over $[\delta_1, \delta_2]$ may generate a sufficiently large increase in the number of trades to offset the higher cost of buying each asset. Combining these observations suggests that the bid distribution is likely to be flat over some interval spanning τ, and this intuition is upheld by the straight lines in the figure whose endpoints provide examples of thresholds (α, β) satisfying the bunching condition (10.50) in the proof of Proposition 10.7.

10.3.2 Fully Separating Equilibria

To focus on equilibria that do not involve bunching, we assume from now on that the distribution of utility flows $F \in \mathcal{L}$.

The necessary conditions of Propositions 10.6 and 10.7 restrict the sets of bid and ask distributions over which to search for equilibria. However, since these distributions are likely to have kinks on the boundary of their supports, it is more convenient to characterize the equilibrium in terms of the auxiliary functions

$$\begin{aligned}\mathbf{A}(q) &\equiv 1-\frac{\Phi_0(F^{-1}(q))}{1-s}\\ &= 1-\frac{q-\Phi_1(F^{-1}(q))}{1-s}=\int_q^1 \frac{\gamma\, d\theta}{\gamma+\lambda A(F^{-1}(\theta))}\end{aligned} \tag{10.27}$$

and

$$\begin{aligned}\mathbf{B}(q) &\equiv \frac{\Phi_1(F^{-1}(q))}{s}\\ &= \int_{\underline{\delta}}^{F^{-1}(q)} \frac{\gamma F'(x)dx}{\gamma+\lambda(1-B(x))}=\int_0^q \frac{\gamma\, d\theta}{\gamma+\lambda(1-B(F^{-1}(\theta)))}.\end{aligned} \tag{10.28}$$

These two distributions represent, respectively, the fraction of nonowners who agree to buy at an ask price that a fraction $q \geq 1-F(\delta^\star)$ of the population would accept and the fraction of owners who agree to sell at a bid price that a fraction $q \leq F(\delta^\star)$ of the population would accept.

The fact that the equilibrium price distributions are continuous implies that the functions $\mathbf{A}$ and $\mathbf{B}$ must be continuously differentiable and this property opens the way for a differential characterization of equilibrium. As a first step toward this characterization, we make explicit the relationship between (A, B) and $(\mathbf{A}, \mathbf{B})$ by providing necessary and sufficient conditions under which the integrals in (10.27) and (10.28) can be inverted, to recover the former from the latter. To simplify the presentation of this result, we start with a definition. For any given $\delta^\star \in \mathcal{D}$ we denote by $\mathcal{P}(\delta^\star)$ the set of functions $\mathbf{A}, \mathbf{B} : [0,1] \to [0,1]$ with the following properties:

($\mathcal{P}_1$) $\mathbf{A}(1)=\mathbf{B}(0)=0$.
($\mathcal{P}_2$) $\mathbf{A}$ and $\mathbf{B}$ are continuously differentiable.
($\mathcal{P}_3$) There exist utility flows

$$\underline{\delta}_b < \overline{\delta}_b < \delta^\star < \underline{\delta}_a < \overline{\delta}_a$$

such that $\mathbf{A}$ is strictly convex on the set $F[\underline{\delta}_a, \overline{\delta}_a] \equiv [F(\underline{\delta}_a), F(\overline{\delta}_a)]$, $\mathbf{B}$ is strictly convex on the set $F[\underline{\delta}_b, \overline{\delta}_b]$, and

$$-\mathbf{A}'(q) = \mathbf{B}'(p) = \begin{cases} 1, & (p,q) \in [F(\overline{\delta}_b), 1] \times [0, F(\underline{\delta}_a)], \\ \frac{\gamma}{\gamma+\lambda}, & (p,q) \in [0, F(\underline{\delta}_b)] \times [F(\overline{\delta}_a), 1]. \end{cases} \tag{10.29}$$

With this definition at hand, we have the following result.

Lemma 10.8: A pair of distributions (A, B) verifies the conditions of Propositions 10.6 and 10.7 for some fixed $\delta^\star$ if and only if

$$\lambda(A(\delta), 1 - B(\delta)) = \gamma \left(-\frac{1 + \mathbf{A}'(F(\delta))}{\mathbf{A}'(F(\delta))}, \frac{\mathbf{B}'(F(\delta)) - 1}{\mathbf{B}'(F(\delta))} \right) \tag{10.30}$$

for some functions $(\mathbf{A}, \mathbf{B}) \in \mathcal{P}(\delta^\star)$.

Proof. See Exercise 10.15. □

Since $F'(\delta) > 0$ by assumption, it is clear that the quantile map $F^{-1}(q)$ is strictly increasing. Therefore, maximizing the expected bid profit function over utility flows $\delta \in (\underline{\delta}, \delta^\star]$ is equivalent to maximizing

$$\begin{aligned} \hat{\Pi}_b(q) &\equiv \Pi_b(F^{-1}(q)) \\ &= \left[\int_{\underline{\delta}}^{F^{-1}(q)} \frac{\gamma F'(x) dx}{\gamma + \lambda(1 - B(x))} \right] \cdot \left[\int_{F^{-1}(q)}^{\delta^\star} \frac{dx}{r + \gamma + \lambda(1 - B(x))} \right] \end{aligned} \tag{10.31}$$

over $q \in [0, F(\delta^\star)]$. Changing variables from x to $F^{-1}(\theta)$ in the integrals and substituting (10.30) simplifies this expression to

$$\hat{\Pi}_b(q) = \mathbf{B}(q) \int_q^{F(\delta^\star)} \frac{\ell(\theta) \mathbf{B}'(\theta)}{r\mathbf{B}'(\theta) + \gamma} d\theta,$$

where the function $\ell(q) \equiv 1/F'(F^{-1}(q))$ denotes the derivative of the quantile map. By the same token, the ask problem can be stated as

$$\Pi_a^\star = \max_{\delta \in [\delta^\star, \overline{\delta})} \Pi_a(\delta) = \max_{q \in [F(\delta^\star), 1]} \hat{\Pi}_a(q),$$

with the modified objective

$$\hat{\Pi}_a(q) \equiv \Pi_a(F^{-1}(q)) = \mathbf{A}(q) \int_{F(\delta^\star)}^{q} \frac{\ell(\theta)\mathbf{A}'(\theta)}{r\mathbf{A}'(\theta) - \gamma} d\theta. \tag{10.32}$$

In view of (10.27) and (10.28), the functions **A** and **B** are entirely determined by their restrictions to the sets $F[\underline{\delta}_a, \overline{\delta}_a]$ and $F[\underline{\delta}_b, \overline{\delta}_b]$ over which they are strictly convex. Therefore, to obtain a characterization of equilibrium, it suffices to find conditions on these objects that are necessary and sufficient to ensure that markets clear and that the intervals $F[\underline{\delta}_a, \overline{\delta}_a]$ and $F[\underline{\delta}_b, \overline{\delta}_b]$ are contained in the sets of maximizers of $\hat{\Pi}_a(q)$ and $\hat{\Pi}_b(q)$, respectively. Such conditions are provided by the following theorem.

Theorem 10.9: A triple $(A, B, \delta^\star)$ forms an equilibrium if and only if (10.30) holds for some $(\mathbf{A}, \mathbf{B}) \in \mathcal{P}(\delta^\star)$ that solve

$$r\mathbf{A}'(q) = \gamma - \frac{\ell(q)}{\Pi_a^\star}\mathbf{A}(q)^2, \qquad q \in F[\underline{\delta}_a, \overline{\delta}_a], \tag{10.33a}$$

$$r\mathbf{B}'(q) = \frac{\ell(q)}{\Pi_b^\star}\mathbf{B}(q)^2 - \gamma, \qquad q \in F[\underline{\delta}_b, \overline{\delta}_b], \tag{10.33b}$$

subject to

$$\mathbf{A}(F(\underline{\delta}_a)) = F'(\underline{\delta}_a)\left(\underline{\delta}_a - \delta^\star\right), \tag{10.34a}$$

$$\mathbf{B}(F(\overline{\delta}_b)) = F'(\overline{\delta}_b)\left(\delta^\star - \overline{\delta}_b\right), \tag{10.34b}$$

and the market clearing condition

$$s\left(F(\overline{\delta}_b) - \mathbf{B}(F(\overline{\delta}_b))\right) = (1-s)\left(1 - F(\underline{\delta}_a) - \mathbf{A}(F(\underline{\delta}_a))\right), \tag{10.35}$$

where the constants

$$\Pi_a^\star = \frac{\gamma(1 - F(\overline{\delta}_a))^2}{(\gamma+\lambda)(r+\gamma+\lambda)F'(\overline{\delta}_a)} = \frac{F'(\underline{\delta}_a)(\underline{\delta}_a - \delta^\star)^2}{r+\gamma}, \tag{10.36a}$$

$$\Pi_b^\star = \frac{\gamma F(\underline{\delta}_b)^2}{(\gamma+\lambda)(r+\gamma+\lambda)F'(\underline{\delta}_b)} = \frac{F'(\overline{\delta}_b)(\delta^\star - \overline{\delta}_b)^2}{r+\gamma}, \tag{10.36b}$$

give an individual dealer's equilibrium expected profit from a match with a nonowner and an owner, respectively.

Proof. See section 10.4.2. □

Theorem 10.9 derives necessary and sufficient conditions for an equilibrium but proves neither existence nor uniqueness. For a given $(\underline{\delta}_b, \overline{\delta}_a)$, it can be shown that the Riccati equations (10.33) subject to (10.36) and the initial conditions (10.34) admit unique solutions that depend continuously on the thresholds. What is a priori less clear is whether these functions are convex, and whether the system of equations obtained by requiring that these functions also satisfy (10.35) and (10.29) admits a solution. The dimension, nonlinearity, and implicit nature of this system make its analysis quite intricate for a general distribution of utility flows. However, in section 10.3.3 we show that this system admits an explicit solution when the distribution is uniform. Before turning to that example, we first discuss some implications of Theorem 10.9.

The natural benchmarks against which to gauge the equilibrium effects of private information are the outcomes of an otherwise similar semicentralized market with full information. From the results of chapter 4, we know that the equilibrium asset allocation, the reservation values of investors, and the interdealer price in such an environment are given by

$$\Phi_1^{\#}(\delta) = \frac{\gamma}{\gamma+\lambda} sF(\delta) + \frac{\lambda}{\gamma+\lambda}\left(F(\delta) - (1-s)\right)^+,$$

$$R^{\#}(\delta) = \frac{r+\lambda(1-\theta)}{r\left(r+\gamma+\lambda(1-\theta)\right)}\delta + \frac{\gamma \mathbf{E}^F[\delta]}{r\left(r+\gamma+\lambda(1-\theta)\right)},$$

and

$$P^{\#} = R^{\#}(\delta^{\#}) = R^{\#}\left(F^{-1}(1-s)\right),$$

where $\theta \in [0,1]$ denotes the bargaining power of dealers relative to investors and the superscripts distinguish these objects from their private-information counterparts. In particular, the case of take-it-or-leave-it offers by dealers can be obtained by letting $\theta = 1$, in which case reservation values are independent of the contact rate and given by the autarky values:

$$R^{\#}(\delta)\big|_{\theta=1} = \frac{\delta}{r+\gamma} + \frac{\gamma \mathbf{E}^F[\delta]}{r(r+\gamma)} = \mathbf{E}_\delta\left[\int_0^\infty e^{-rt}\delta_t dt\right]. \tag{10.37}$$

Intuitively, the fact that dealers have full information and all the bargaining power grants them monopoly power within every match. As a result, the possibility of trading with dealers becomes worthless to investors, which, in turn, implies that their reservation values are equal to the autarky values irrespective of the contact rate. This leads to the well-known Diamond [1971] paradox: local monopoly power by a continuum of dealers leads to the fully discriminating monopolistic outcome, even with arbitrarily large contact rates.

By contrast, the results of Proposition 10.6 and Theorem 10.9 show that private information allows some investors to retain a strictly positive share of the surplus generated by their trades and, thereby, provides a simple resolution of the paradox. Indeed, the fact that dealers have incomplete information forces them to screen counterparties by offering a nonzero share of the surplus to investors with sufficiently large gains from trades and excluding all others. Since some matches with strictly positive surpluses no longer result in trade, this pricing strategy implies that the asset allocation is less efficient than it is with full information, i.e., that $\Phi_1^{\#}(\delta) \leq \Phi_1(\delta)$. However, it also implies that an investor's expected gains from buying

$$\int_{\underline{\delta}}^{\overline{\delta}} (R(\delta) - R(x))^+ \, dA(x) = \int_{\underline{\delta}_a}^{\max\{\delta, \underline{\delta}_a\}} \frac{A(x)dx}{r + \gamma + \lambda A(x)}$$

and from selling

$$\int_{\underline{\delta}}^{\overline{\delta}} (R(x) - R(\delta))^+ \, dB(x) = \int_{\max\{\delta, \underline{\delta}_b\}}^{\overline{\delta}_b} \frac{(1 - B(x))dx}{r + \gamma + \lambda(1 - B(x))}$$

are strictly positive and depend on the intensity of the search friction over the set of utility flows $\mathcal{D} \backslash [\overline{\delta}_b, \underline{\delta}_a]$ that traded in equilibrium.

Going one step further, the next proposition shows that, as search frictions vanish, private information drives the profits of dealers to zero so that the outcomes of the semi-centralized market with private information converge to those of a frictionless market with full information.

Proposition 10.10: Assume that $f(\delta)$ is uniformly bounded from above and away from zero. Then, along a sequence of equilibria indexed by λ,

$$\lim_{\lambda \to \infty} \Pi^{\star}_{a,b} = 0, \tag{10.38}$$

$$\lim_{\lambda \to \infty} \Phi_1(\delta) = \Psi_1(\delta) = (F(\delta) - (1 - s))^+, \tag{10.39}$$

$$\lim_{\lambda \to \infty} \left(\underline{\delta}_a, \overline{\delta}_b, \delta^{\star}\right) = \delta^{\#}, \tag{10.40}$$

and the reservation values of all investors converge to $\delta^{\#}/r$.

Proof. See section 10.4.3. □

The intuition behind Proposition 10.10 is that when contacts with investors are instantaneous, every dealer effectively competes against all others for each trade. Indeed, in this limit investors can instantaneously contact infinitely many dealers. Therefore, it is clear that a nonowner with utility flow larger than $\delta^\star$ will sample successive dealers until he receives an offer to buy at the lowest price $R(\underline{\delta}_a)$ in the support of the ask price distribution, which occurs with probability 1 by the law of large numbers. Moreover, this price must be equal to the interdealer price; otherwise an individual dealer could deviate by offering to sell at $a < R(\underline{\delta}_a)$ and make a strictly positive profit. Similarly, an owner with utility flow below $\delta^\star$ will instantaneously contact dealers until she receives an offer to sell at the largest price in the support of the bid distribution, and this price must equal the interdealer price because otherwise a dealer could outbid all others and still make strictly positive profits. As a result, dealers' profits are driven to zero, which implies that no types are excluded from trade and guarantees that the allocation is efficient.

The intuitive arguments above also apply to the semicentralized market with full information. However, in that case the equilibrium converges to its frictionless counterpart, as search frictions vanish *only if* $1-\theta>0$ so that investors have strictly positive bargaining power. Indeed, if dealers have full information and all the bargaining power, then reservation values are given by the autarky values (10.37), independently of λ, so that neither the reservation values nor the interdealer price can converge to their frictionless counterparts.

In order to establish the existence and uniqueness of the equilibrium and to discuss comparative statics, we now consider the explicitly solvable special case where utility flows are uniformly distributed.

10.3.3 Uniformly Distributed Utility Flows

Assume that utility flows are uniformly distributed on the unit interval, so that $f(\delta)=\ell(q)=1$. Substituting these functions into Theorem 10.9 shows that the equilibrium requirements simplify to

$$r\mathbf{A}'(\delta)=\gamma-\frac{\mathbf{A}(\delta)^2}{\Pi_a^\star}, \qquad \delta\in[\underline{\delta}_a,\overline{\delta}_a], \tag{10.41a}$$

$$r\mathbf{B}'(\delta)=\frac{\mathbf{B}(\delta)^2}{\Pi_b^\star}-\gamma, \qquad \delta\in[\underline{\delta}_b,\overline{\delta}_b], \tag{10.41b}$$

subject to the boundary conditions

$$\mathbf{A}(\underline{\delta}_a) = \underline{\delta}_a - \delta^\star, \tag{10.42a}$$

$$\mathbf{B}(\overline{\delta}_b) = \delta^\star - \overline{\delta}_b. \tag{10.42b}$$

$$-\mathbf{A}'(\overline{\delta}_a) = \mathbf{B}'(\underline{\delta}_b) = \tfrac{\gamma}{\gamma+\lambda}. \tag{10.42c}$$

and the market clearing condition

$$s(2\overline{\delta}_b - \delta^\star) = (1-s)(\delta^\star + 1 - 2\underline{\delta}_a), \tag{10.43}$$

where the constants

$$\Pi_a^\star = \frac{\gamma(1-\overline{\delta}_a)^2}{(\gamma+\lambda)(r+\gamma+\lambda)} = \frac{(\underline{\delta}_a - \delta^\star)^2}{r+\gamma}, \tag{10.44a}$$

$$\Pi_b^\star = \frac{\gamma \underline{\delta}_b^2}{(\gamma+\lambda)(r+\gamma+\lambda)} = \frac{(\delta^\star - \overline{\delta}_b)^2}{r+\gamma}, \tag{10.44b}$$

give the expected equilibrium profits of a dealer. Standard results on Riccati equations (see for example Reid [1972]) based on the transformation

$$(\mathbf{A}(q), \mathbf{B}(q)) = -r\left(\Pi_a^\star \frac{\alpha'(q)}{\alpha(q)}, \Pi_b^\star \frac{\beta'(q)}{\beta(q)}\right)$$

show that the general solutions to (10.41) are given by

$$\mathbf{B}(\delta) = \left(\frac{2\gamma\underline{\delta}_b}{r\xi_\lambda}\right) \frac{b + e^{\left(\frac{\xi_\lambda}{\underline{\delta}_b}\right)(\delta - \underline{\delta}_b)}}{b - e^{\left(\frac{\xi_\lambda}{\underline{\delta}_b}\right)(\delta - \underline{\delta}_b)}}, \tag{10.45}$$

$$\mathbf{A}(\delta) = \left(\frac{2\gamma(1-\overline{\delta}_a)}{r\xi_\lambda}\right) \frac{a + e^{\left(\frac{\xi_\lambda}{1-\overline{\delta}_a}\right)(\overline{\delta}_a - \delta)}}{a - e^{\left(\frac{\xi_\lambda}{1-\overline{\delta}_a}\right)(\overline{\delta}_a - \delta)}}, \tag{10.46}$$

with

$$\xi_i \equiv \frac{2}{r}\sqrt{(\gamma+i)(r+\gamma+i)} \tag{10.47}$$

for some constants $a, b \in \mathbf{R}$. Inserting these solutions into (10.42), (10.43), and (10.44) gives a system of seven equations. Solving that system for (a, b) and the equilibrium thresholds $(\underline{\delta}_b, \overline{\delta}_b, \delta^\star, \underline{\delta}_a, \overline{\delta}_b)$ provides an explicit solution for the unique equilibrium. To state the result, we denote by $\cosh(x) \equiv \left(e^x + e^{-x}\right)/2$ the hyperbolic cosine function.

Proposition 10.11: If utility flows are uniformly distributed on the unit interval, then the equilibrium is uniquely given by

$$A(\delta) = \begin{cases} 0, & \delta \le \underline{\delta}_a, \\ \frac{r}{2\lambda} \cosh\left(\eta_\lambda + \xi_\lambda \cdot \frac{\overline{\delta}_a - \delta}{1-\overline{\delta}_a}\right) - \frac{r}{2\lambda}\left(\eta_0 + \xi_0\right), & \delta \in [\underline{\delta}_a, \overline{\delta}_a], \\ 1, & \delta \ge \overline{\delta}_a, \end{cases}$$

$$B(\delta) = \begin{cases} 0, & \delta \le \underline{\delta}_b, \\ \frac{r}{2\lambda}\left(\eta_\lambda - \xi_\lambda\right) - \frac{r}{2\lambda} \cosh\left(\eta_\lambda - \xi_\lambda \cdot \frac{\delta - \underline{\delta}_b}{\underline{\delta}_b}\right), & \delta \in [\underline{\delta}_b, \overline{\delta}_b], \\ 1, & \delta \ge \overline{\delta}_b, \end{cases}$$

and the thresholds

$$\delta^\star = 1 - s,$$

$$\underline{\delta}_a = 1 - \frac{s\left(\eta_0 + \eta_\lambda + \xi_\lambda\right)}{\eta_0 + \eta_\lambda + \xi_0 + \xi_\lambda}, \quad \overline{\delta}_a = 1 - \frac{s\xi_\lambda}{\eta_0 + \eta_\lambda + \xi_0 + \xi_\lambda},$$

$$\underline{\delta}_b = \frac{(1-s)\xi_\lambda}{\eta_0 + \eta_\lambda + \xi_0 + \xi_\lambda}, \quad \overline{\delta}_b = \frac{(1-s)\left(\eta_0 + \eta_\lambda + \xi_\lambda\right)}{\eta_0 + \eta_\lambda + \xi_0 + \xi_\lambda},$$

with the nonnegative constants defined by

$$\eta_i \equiv \log\left(1 + \frac{2(\gamma + i)}{r} - \xi_0 + \mathbf{1}_{\{i>0\}}\left(\xi_0 + \xi_i\right)\right)$$

and (10.47) for any given $i \ge 0$.

Proof. Given Theorem 10.9 it suffices to verify that **A** and **B** are strictly convex on $[\underline{\delta}_a, \overline{\delta}_a]$ and $[\underline{\delta}_b, \overline{\delta}_b]$, respectively. Substituting the stated solutions into (10.45) and (10.46) shows that on these intervals

$$\mathbf{B}(\delta) = \left(\frac{2\gamma\underline{\delta}_b}{r\xi_\lambda}\right) \frac{1 + e^{-\eta_\lambda + \xi_\lambda\left(\frac{\delta}{\underline{\delta}_b} - 1\right)}}{1 - e^{-\eta_\lambda + \xi_\lambda\left(\frac{\delta}{\underline{\delta}_b} - 1\right)}}, \tag{10.48}$$

$$\mathbf{A}(\delta) = \left(\frac{2\gamma(1-\overline{\delta}_a)}{r\xi_\lambda}\right) \frac{1 + e^{\eta_\lambda + \xi_\lambda\left(\frac{\delta - \overline{\delta}_b}{1-\overline{\delta}_b}\right)}}{1 - e^{\eta_\lambda + \xi_\lambda\left(\frac{\delta - \overline{\delta}_b}{1-\overline{\delta}_b}\right)}}. \tag{10.49}$$

Differentiating (10.49) shows that $\mathbf{A}'(\delta) < 0$. Since $\mathbf{A}(\overline{\delta}_a) > 0$, this implies that $\mathbf{A}(\delta) > 0$ for all $\delta \in [\underline{\delta}_a, \overline{\delta}_a]$, and differentiating a second time gives

$$\mathbf{A}''(\delta) = -\frac{r}{2\gamma}\left(\frac{\xi\lambda}{1-\overline{\delta}_a}\right)^2 \mathbf{A}(\delta)\mathbf{A}'(\delta) > 0.$$

Similarly, differentiating (10.48) shows that B is strictly positive as well as strictly increasing, and differentiating a second time gives

$$\mathbf{B}''(\delta) = \frac{r}{2\gamma}\left(\frac{\xi\lambda}{\underline{\delta}_b}\right)^2 \mathbf{B}(\delta)\mathbf{B}'(\delta) > 0,$$

which completes the proof. □

By symmetry we have that the ratio of the mass of excluded investors to the mass of unaffected investors is the same for buyers and sellers. Furthermore, (10.44) implies that this ratio is given by

$$w \equiv \frac{\delta^\star - \overline{\delta}_b}{\underline{\delta}_b} = \frac{\underline{\delta}_a - \delta^\star}{1-\overline{\delta}_a} = \frac{\sqrt{\gamma(r+\gamma)}}{\sqrt{(\gamma+\lambda)(r+\gamma+\lambda)}},$$

and a direct calculation shows that

$$\frac{\partial w}{\partial \lambda} \leq 0 \leq \frac{\partial w}{\partial \gamma}, \frac{\partial w}{\partial r}.$$

To further illustrate the properties of the equilibrium, figure 10.5 plots the equilibrium thresholds and the width of the equilibrium price distributions as functions of the arrival rate of preference shocks (left panels) and the contact rate between investors and dealers (right panels).

The top panels of the figure show that dealers tend to offer better trading terms—i.e., lower asks and higher bids—as the contact rate λ increases or the reset rate γ decreases. Intuitively, this occurs because either variation tends to limit the potential gains from trade with investors by making the steady-state distributions of asset holdings and utility flows more selected, which partly offsets the market power of dealers. Dealers also tend to exclude fewer investors as λ increases or γ decreases, and the numbers are significant. For example, the equilibrium pricing strategy of dealers excludes about 16% of the investor population in the base case, and this percentage grows to 24% in the limit where the reset rate $\gamma \to \infty$ or the contact rate $\lambda \to 0$.

Comparing the top panels of the figure shows that the mass of investors who are subject to trading delays, i.e., those whose utility flows lie in the support of the price distributions, are more affected by the reset rate than by the contact rate. In fact, the top

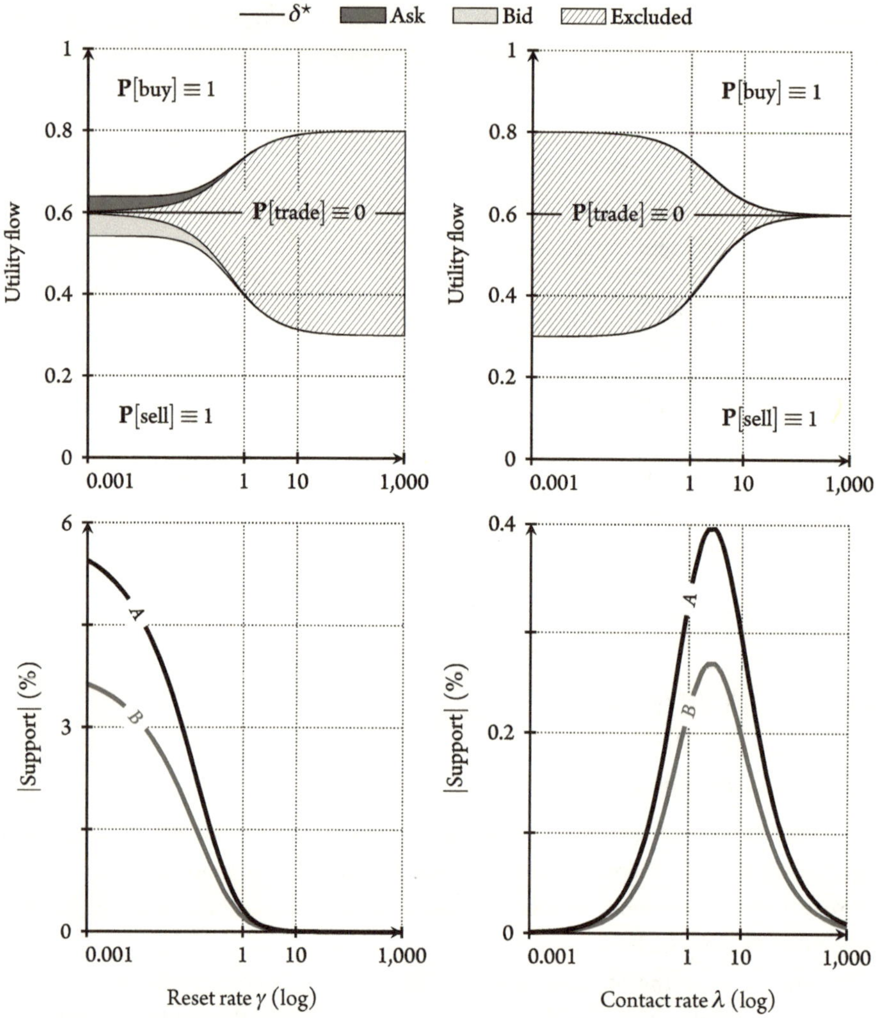

FIGURE 10.5. Equilibrium thresholds

The left panels plot the equilibrium thresholds (top) and the width of support of the equilibrium price distributions (bottom) as functions of the arrival rate γ of preference shock in a model with contact rate $\lambda = 1$, asset supply $s = 0.4$, interest rate $r = 5\%$, and a uniform distribution of utility flows on the unit interval. The right panel plots the same quantities as functions of the contact rate λ between investors and dealers when the arrival rate of preference shocks is set to $\gamma = 1$.

right panel may even give the impression that the supports of the equilibrium price distributions are reduced to a point, but this is not so. As a confirmation, the bottom panels plot the width of the support of the bid and ask distributions expressed in percentages of the population. In both panels the qualitative behavior is the same: The width of the supports is decreasing in the reset rate and bell shaped in the contact rate, with the ask distribution slightly more spread out than the bid. The latter feature is directly related to the fact that the figure is constructed with an asset supply $s = 0.4$, which favors the position of sellers.

10.4 Omitted Proofs

10.4.1 Proof of Proposition 10.7

Assume toward a contradiction that, in some equilibrium, there exist $\alpha, \beta \in \text{supp}(B)$ such that the interval $(\alpha, \beta) \notin \text{supp}(B)$. Since f and B are continuous it is clear that Π_b, defined in (10.14), is continuously differentiable. Combining this property with the fact that $\alpha, \beta \in \text{supp}(B)$, we deduce that

$$\Pi_b(\alpha) - \Pi_b(\beta) = \Pi_b'(\alpha) = \Pi_b'(\beta) = 0.$$

Exercise 10.12 shows that these conditions can only hold if the density of utility flows is such that $f(\alpha) \neq f(\beta)$, in which case they imply

$$f(\beta)f(\alpha)(\beta - \alpha)^2 = (F(\beta) - F(\alpha))^2.$$

It remains to show that this equality cannot hold under the stated assumptions. To this end, we first observe that since $\beta > \alpha$,

$$\log\left(\tfrac{1}{\beta-\alpha}\int_\alpha^\beta f(t)dt\right) > \tfrac{1}{\beta-\alpha}\int_\alpha^\beta \log f(t)dt$$

$$= \tfrac{1}{\beta-\alpha}\int_\alpha^\beta \log f\left(\tfrac{\beta-t}{\beta-\alpha}\cdot\alpha + \tfrac{t-\alpha}{\beta-\alpha}\cdot\beta\right)dt$$

$$\geq \tfrac{1}{\beta-\alpha}\int_\alpha^\beta \left(\tfrac{\beta-t}{\beta-\alpha}\log f(\alpha) + \tfrac{t-\alpha}{\beta-\alpha}\log f(\beta)\right)dt = \log\sqrt{f(\alpha)f(\beta)},$$

where the strict inequality follows from Jensen's inequality and the assumption that f is not constant on $[\alpha, \beta]$, the second inequality follows from the log concavity of f, and the last equality follows by computing the integral. Multiplying both sides by two and exponentiating the result shows that

$$(F(\beta)-F(\alpha))^2=\left(\int_\alpha^\beta f(t)dt\right)^2>(\beta-\alpha)^2 f(\alpha)f(\beta), \tag{10.50}$$

which completes the proof. The corresponding result for the ask distribution can be proved using similar steps. □

10.4.2 Proof of Theorem 10.9

PROOF OF NECESSITY

Assume that $(A, B, \delta^\star)$ forms an equilibrium. By Lemma 10.8 and Propositions 10.6 and 10.7, this implies that (10.30) holds for some $(\mathbf{A},\mathbf{B}) \in \mathcal{P}(\delta^\star)$ with thresholds $(\underline{\delta}_b, \overline{\delta}_b, \underline{\delta}_a, \overline{\delta}_a)$. Substituting (10.30) into (10.8) and computing the integrals gives (10.35), and it now remains to show the necessity of (10.33), (10.34), and (10.36).

Since $(A, B; \delta^\star)$ is an equilibrium, we have that $\hat{\Pi}_b(q)$ is maximal and, thus, constant on the interval $F[\underline{\delta}_b, \overline{\delta}_b]$. Because $\hat{\Pi}_b(q)$ is continuously differentiable, this property is equivalent to

$$\hat{\Pi}_b'(q)=0, \qquad q\in F[\underline{\delta}_b,\overline{\delta}_b],$$

$$\hat{\Pi}_b(\theta)\le \Pi_b^\star=\hat{\Pi}_b(q), \qquad q\in F[\underline{\delta}_b,\overline{\delta}_b],\theta\notin F[\underline{\delta}_b,\overline{\delta}_b].$$

The latter condition and (10.31) imply that

$$\frac{\Pi_b^\star}{\mathbf{B}(q)}=\int_q^{F(\delta^\star)}\frac{\ell(\theta)\mathbf{B}'(\theta)}{r\mathbf{B}'(\theta)+\gamma}d\theta, \qquad q\in F[\underline{\delta}_b,\overline{\delta}_b].$$

Substituting this identity into $\hat{\Pi}_b'(q)$ gives

$$\begin{aligned}0=\hat{\Pi}_b'(q)&=\mathbf{B}'(q)\int_q^{F(\delta^\star)}\frac{\ell(\theta)\mathbf{B}'(\theta)}{r\mathbf{B}'(\theta)+\gamma}d\theta-\frac{\ell(q)\mathbf{B}(q)\mathbf{B}'(q)}{r\mathbf{B}'(q)+\gamma}\\ &=\frac{\mathbf{B}'(q)\Pi_b^\star}{\mathbf{B}(q)}-\frac{\ell(q)\mathbf{B}(q)\mathbf{B}'(q)}{r\mathbf{B}'(q)+\gamma}, \qquad q\in F[\underline{\delta}_b,\overline{\delta}_b],\end{aligned}$$

from which we deduce that **B** solves (10.33b). Evaluating this equation at the endpoints of its domain and using (10.29) then shows that (10.36b) holds and that **B** satisfies (10.34b). Similar arguments establish the necessity of the corresponding properties of the function **A**. □

PROOF OF SUFFICIENCY

Assume that $(\mathbf{A}, \mathbf{B}; \delta^\star)$ satisfies the conditions of the theorem and let $(\underline{\delta}_b, \overline{\delta}_b, \underline{\delta}_a, \overline{\delta}_a)$ denote the corresponding thresholds. By Lemma 10.8 we have that the price distributions (A, B) defined by (10.30) satisfy the conditions of Propositions 10.6 and 10.7. On the other hand, substituting (10.30) into (10.13) shows that the market clearing condition (10.8) can be stated as

$$s = \Phi_1(\overline{\delta}) = \int_{\underline{\delta}}^{\overline{\delta}_b} \frac{\gamma s f(x) dx}{\gamma + \lambda(1 - B(x))}$$

$$+ \int_{\overline{\delta}_b}^{\underline{\delta}_a} s f(x) dx + \int_{\underline{\delta}_a}^{\overline{\delta}} \frac{(\gamma s + \lambda A(x)) f(x)}{\gamma + \lambda A(x)} dx$$

$$= s\mathbf{B}(F(\overline{\delta}_b)) + s\left(F(\underline{\delta}_a) - F(\overline{\delta}_b)\right) + 1 - F(\underline{\delta}_a) - (1 - s)\mathbf{A}(F(\underline{\delta}_a)),$$

which is equivalent to (10.35). To complete the proof it now remains to show that the price distributions are optimal, i.e., that $F[\underline{\delta}_a, \overline{\delta}_a]$ and $F[\underline{\delta}_b, \overline{\delta}_b]$ are included in the set of maximizers of $\hat{\Pi}_a(q)$ and $\hat{\Pi}_b(q)$, respectively. Consider first the case of the bid distribution. Substituting (10.29) into (10.31) and using the differential equation (10.33b) we deduce that

$$\hat{\Pi}_b(q) = \begin{cases} \frac{\gamma q}{\gamma + \lambda}\left(\frac{\underline{\delta}_b - F^{-1}(q)}{r + \gamma + \lambda} + \frac{\Pi_b^\star}{\mathbf{B}(F(\underline{\delta}_b))}\right), & q \leq F(\underline{\delta}_b), \\ \Pi_b^\star, & q \in F[\underline{\delta}_b, \overline{\delta}_b], \\ \frac{\delta^\star - F^{-1}(q)}{r + \gamma}\left(q + \mathbf{B}(F(\overline{\delta}_b)) - F(\overline{\delta}_b)\right), & q \geq F(\overline{\delta}_b). \end{cases} \tag{10.51}$$

Differentiating the first line at $q = F(\delta)$ shows that

$$\hat{\Pi}_b'(F(\delta)) \propto \pi_b(\delta) \equiv \underline{\delta}_b + \frac{(r + \gamma + \lambda)\Pi_b^\star}{\mathbf{B}(F(\underline{\delta}_b))} - \delta - \frac{F(\delta)}{f(\delta)}, \qquad \delta \in (\underline{\delta}, \underline{\delta}_b].$$

Since f is log concave we have that F/f is nondecreasing. Therefore, the function $\pi_b(\delta)$ is decreasing on $(\underline{\delta}, \underline{\delta}_b]$ and, since

$$\pi_b(\underline{\delta}_b) = \underline{\delta}_b + \frac{(r + \gamma + \lambda)\Pi_b^\star}{\mathbf{B}(F(\underline{\delta}_b))} - \underline{\delta}_b - \frac{F(\overline{\delta}_b)}{F'(\overline{\delta}_b)} = 0$$

due to (10.29) and (10.36b), we conclude that $\hat{\Pi}_b(q)$ is increasing on $[0, F(\underline{\delta}_b)]$. Next, differentiating the third line of (10.51) and using the boundary condition (10.34b), we obtain that

$$\operatorname{sign}\left(\hat{\Pi}_b'(F(\delta))\right) = \operatorname{sign}\left(\kappa_b(\overline{\delta}_b) - \kappa_b(\delta)\right), \qquad \delta \in [\overline{\delta}_b, \delta^\star],$$

with the function

$$\kappa_b(\delta) \equiv F(\delta) - f(\delta)\left(\delta^\star - \delta\right) = F(\delta)\left(1 - \frac{f(\delta)}{F(\delta)}(\delta^\star - \delta)\right).$$

It now suffices to show that $\kappa_b(\delta)$ is increasing on $[\overline{\delta}_b, \delta^\star]$. Since f is log concave, we have that f/F is decreasing. This implies that the bracketed term in the definition of $\kappa_b(\delta)$ is increasing and, since $F(\delta)$ is strictly increasing, the desired result now follows by observing that

$$\begin{aligned}
\kappa(\overline{\delta}_b) &= F(\overline{\delta}_b) - \mathbf{B}(F(\overline{\delta}_b)) = F(\underline{\delta}_b) - \mathbf{B}(F(\underline{\delta}_b)) + \int_{F(\underline{\delta}_b)}^{F(\overline{\delta}_b)} \left(1 - \mathbf{B}'(\theta)\right) d\theta \\
&\geq F(\underline{\delta}_b) - \mathbf{B}(F(\underline{\delta}_b)) + \left(1 - \mathbf{B}'(\overline{\delta}_b)\right) \int_{F(\underline{\delta}_b)}^{F(\overline{\delta}_b)} d\theta \\
&= F(\underline{\delta}_b) - \mathbf{B}(F(\underline{\delta}_b)) = \frac{\lambda F(\underline{\delta}_b)}{\gamma + \lambda} > 0,
\end{aligned}$$

where the first equality is due to (10.34b), the inequality is due to the strict convexity of $\mathbf{B}$ on $F[\underline{\delta}_b, \overline{\delta}_b]$, the third equality is due to (10.29), and the last equality follows from the combination of (10.29) and $(\mathcal{P}_1)$.

Likewise, substituting (10.29) into (10.32) and using (10.33a), we deduce that the expected ask profit satisfies

$$\hat{\Pi}_a(q) = \begin{cases} \frac{F^{-1}(q)-\delta^\star}{r+\gamma}\left(F(\underline{\delta}_a) - q + \frac{(r+\gamma)\Pi_a^\star}{\underline{\delta}_a-\delta^\star}\right), & q \leq F(\underline{\delta}_a), \\ \Pi_a^\star, & q \in F[\underline{\delta}_a, \overline{\delta}_a], \\ \frac{\gamma(1-q)}{\gamma+\lambda}\left(\frac{F^{-1}(q)-\overline{\delta}_a}{r+\gamma+\lambda} + \frac{\Pi_a^\star}{\mathbf{A}(F(\overline{\delta}_a))}\right), & q \geq F(\overline{\delta}_a). \end{cases} \tag{10.52}$$

Differentiating the third line at $q = F(\delta)$ shows that

$$\hat{\Pi}_a'(F(\delta)) \propto \pi_a(\delta) \equiv \frac{1 - F(\delta)}{f(\delta)} - \delta + \overline{\delta}_a - \frac{\Pi_a^\star}{\mathbf{A}(F(\overline{\delta}_a))}, \qquad \delta \in [\overline{\delta}_a, \overline{\delta}).$$

Since f is log concave we have that $1 - F$ is also log concave, and it follows that the ratio $(1 - F)/f$ is nondecreasing; see Proposition A.21. This implies that the function $\pi_a(\delta)$

is decreasing on the interval $[\overline{\delta}_a, \overline{\delta})$ and, since we also have

$$\pi_a(\overline{\delta}_a) = \frac{1 - F(\overline{\delta}_a)}{f(\overline{\delta}_a)} - \frac{\Pi_a^\star}{\mathbf{A}(F(\overline{\delta}_a))} = 0$$

due to (10.29) and (10.36a), we conclude that $\hat{\Pi}_a(q)$ is decreasing on $[F(\overline{\delta}_a), 1]$. Next, differentiating the first line of (10.52) and using the boundary condition (10.34a), we deduce that

$$\text{sign}\left(\hat{\Pi}_a'(F(\delta))\right) = \text{sign}\left(\kappa_a(\underline{\delta}_a) - \kappa_a(\delta)\right), \qquad \delta \in [\delta^\star, \underline{\delta}_a],$$

with the function

$$\kappa_a(\delta) \equiv F(\delta) + f(\delta)(\delta - \delta^\star), \tag{10.53}$$

and it remains to show that $\kappa_a(\delta)$ is increasing on $[\delta^\star, \underline{\delta}_a]$.

Since the density $f(\delta) > 0$ is log-concave, it admits a *right* derivative $f'(\delta)$ that is nonnegative on $(\underline{\delta}, m]$ for some $m \in \text{cl}(\mathcal{D})$ and such that $f'(\delta)/f(\delta)$ is decreasing. Differentiating (10.53) and using these properties we deduce that

$$\frac{\kappa_a'(\delta)}{f(\delta)} = 2 + \frac{f'(\delta)}{f(\delta)}\left(\delta - \delta^\star\right) \geq 2 + \frac{f'(\underline{\delta}_a)}{f(\underline{\delta}_a)}\left(\delta - \delta^\star\right), \qquad \delta \in [\delta^\star, \underline{\delta}_a].$$

If $\underline{\delta}_a \leq m$ then $f'(\underline{\delta}_a) \geq 0$, so that the right-hand side is strictly positive and the proof is complete. If instead $\underline{\delta}_a > m$ then $f'(\underline{\delta}_a) \leq 0$, in which case the inequality implies that

$$\frac{\kappa_a'(\delta)}{f(\delta)} \geq 2 + \frac{f'(\underline{\delta}_a)}{f(\underline{\delta}_a)}\left(\underline{\delta}_a - \delta^\star\right), \qquad \delta \in [\delta^\star, \underline{\delta}_a].$$

To show that the right-hand side is positive, consider (10.33a). Since $\mathbf{A}(q)$ and $\ell(q)$ are convex on $F[\underline{\delta}_a, \overline{\delta}_a]$, they both admit right derivatives on that interval. Combining these properties with (10.33a) shows that $\mathbf{A}$ admits a second right derivative that satisfies

$$\begin{aligned} 0 \leq r\Pi_a^\star \mathbf{A}''(q) &= -\frac{d}{dq}\left(\ell(q)\mathbf{A}(q)^2\right) \\ &= -\ell'(q)\mathbf{A}(q)^2 - 2\mathbf{A}(q)\mathbf{A}'(q)\ell(q), \qquad \delta \in [\delta^\star, \underline{\delta}_a]. \end{aligned}$$

Evaluating this inequality at the point $q = F(\underline{\delta}_a)$ and substituting conditions (10.29) and (10.34a), we finally obtain that

$$0 \leq r\Pi_a^\star \mathbf{A}''(\underline{\delta}_a) = \frac{f'(\underline{\delta}_a)\mathbf{A}(F(\underline{\delta}_a))^2}{f(\underline{\delta}_a)^3} - \frac{2\mathbf{A}(F(\underline{\delta}_a))\mathbf{A}'(F(\underline{\delta}_a))}{f(\underline{\delta}_a)}$$
$$= (\underline{\delta}_a - \delta^\star)\left(2 + \frac{f'(\underline{\delta}_a)}{f(\underline{\delta}_a)}(\underline{\delta}_a - \delta^\star)\right),$$

and the proof is complete. □

10.4.3 Proof of Proposition 10.10

Using (10.36a) we deduce that

$$0 = \lim_{\lambda\to\infty} \frac{\gamma(r+\gamma)}{(\gamma+\lambda)(r+\gamma+\lambda)} = \lim_{\lambda\to\infty} \frac{f(\underline{\delta}_a)f(\overline{\delta}_a)\left(\underline{\delta}_a - \delta^\star\right)^2}{(1-F(\overline{\delta}_a))^2}$$
$$\geq \lim_{\lambda\to\infty} \underline{\varepsilon}^2\left(\underline{\delta}_a - \delta^\star\right)^2,$$

where $\underline{\varepsilon} > 0$ is a uniform lower bound on $f(\delta)$. This implies that $\underline{\delta}_a - \delta^\star \to 0$ and, circling back to (10.36a), implies that

$$0 \leq \lim_{\lambda\to\infty} \Pi_a^\star = \lim_{\lambda\to\infty} \frac{f(\underline{\delta}_a)\left(\underline{\delta}_a - \delta^\star\right)^2}{r+\gamma} \leq \lim_{\lambda\to\infty} \frac{\overline{\varepsilon}\left(\underline{\delta}_a - \delta^\star\right)^2}{r+\gamma} = 0,$$

where $\overline{\varepsilon} > 0$ is a uniform upper bound on $f(\delta)$. Applying similar arguments to the expected profits from offering a bid price reveals that

$$\lim_{\lambda\to\infty}\left(\delta^\star - \overline{\delta}_b\right) = \lim_{\lambda\to\infty} \Pi_b^\star = 0,$$

and it follows that $\overline{\delta}_b$, $\underline{\delta}_a$, and $\delta^\star$ converge to a common limit $\hat{\delta}$. To determine this limit, note that the definition of $(\mathbf{A}, \mathbf{B})$ and condition (10.7) imply that

$$\Phi_1(\delta) = \begin{cases} s\mathbf{B}(F(\delta)), & \delta \leq \overline{\delta}_b, \\ s(F(\delta) - F(\overline{\delta}_b) + \mathbf{B}\left(F(\overline{\delta}_b)\right), & \delta \in (\overline{\delta}_b, \underline{\delta}_a), \\ F(\delta) + (1-s)(\mathbf{A}(F(\delta)) - 1), & \delta \geq \underline{\delta}_a. \end{cases}$$

Letting the contact rate $\lambda \to \infty$ on both sides of this equality, and using the fact that $\underline{\delta}_a - \overline{\delta}_b \to 0$, reveals that

$$\lim_{\lambda\to\infty} \Phi_1(\delta) = \lim_{\lambda\to\infty} \mathbf{1}_{\{\delta\leq\overline{\delta}_b\}} s\mathbf{B}(F(\delta))$$
$$+ \lim_{\lambda\to\infty} \mathbf{1}_{\{\delta\geq\overline{\delta}_a\}}(F(\delta) + (1-s)\left(\mathbf{A}(F(\delta)) - 1\right)).$$

Since the functions **B** and $-\mathbf{A}$ are decreasing, it follows from (10.34) and the first part of the proof that we have

$$0 \le \lim_{\lambda\to\infty} \mathbf{1}_{\{\delta\le\bar\delta_b\}}\mathbf{B}(F(\delta)) \le \lim_{\lambda\to\infty} \mathbf{1}_{\{\delta\le\bar\delta_b\}}\mathbf{B}(F(\bar\delta_b))$$
$$\le \lim_{\lambda\to\infty} \mathbf{1}_{\{\delta\le\bar\delta_b\}}\overline{\varepsilon}\left(\delta^\star - \bar\delta_b\right) = 0,$$
$$0 \le \lim_{\lambda\to\infty} \mathbf{1}_{\{\delta\ge\bar\delta_a\}}\mathbf{A}(F(\delta)) \le \lim_{\lambda\to\infty} \mathbf{1}_{\{\delta\ge\bar\delta_a\}}\mathbf{A}(F(\underline\delta_a))$$
$$\le \lim_{\lambda\to\infty} \mathbf{1}_{\{\delta\ge\bar\delta_a\}}\overline{\varepsilon}\left(\underline\delta_a - \delta^\star\right) = 0,$$

and combining these inequalities we conclude that

$$\begin{aligned}\lim_{\lambda\to\infty} \Phi_1(\delta) &= \lim_{\lambda\to\infty} \mathbf{1}_{\{\delta\ge\bar\delta_a\}}\left(F(\delta) - (1-s)\right)\\ &= \mathbf{1}_{\left\{\delta\ge\hat\delta\right\}}\left(F(\delta) - (1-s)\right).\end{aligned} \tag{10.54}$$

Since the left-hand side is nonnegative it follows that $\hat\delta \ge \delta^\#$. Alternatively, combining (10.54) and (10.7) shows that

$$\lim_{\lambda\to\infty} \Phi_0(\delta) = F(\delta) - \lim_{\lambda\to\infty} \Phi_1(\delta) = F(\delta) + \mathbf{1}_{\left\{\delta\ge\hat\delta\right\}}\left(1 - s - F(\delta)\right).$$

Because the left-hand side is nondecreasing we deduce that $F(\hat\delta) \le 1-s$, which is equivalent to $\hat\delta \le \delta^\#$. Substituting $\hat\delta = \delta^\#$ into (10.54) gives (10.39), and it remains to establish the claim regarding reservation values.

Integrating by parts in (10.5) and using Lemmas 10.1 and 10.2, we deduce that the smallest and largest reservation values, respectively, satisfy

$$\begin{aligned} rR(\underline\delta) = \underline\delta &+ \int_{\underline\delta}^{\bar\delta_b} \frac{\gamma(s - F(\delta)\Phi_1'(\delta))}{\gamma s + r\Phi_1'(\delta)} d\delta \\ &+ \int_{\bar\delta_b}^{\underline\delta_a} \underline\kappa(\delta) d\delta + \int_{\underline\delta_a}^{\bar\delta} \frac{\gamma\delta(1-F(\delta))(1-\Phi_1'(\delta))}{\gamma(1-s) + r(1-\Phi_1'(\delta))} d\delta, \end{aligned} \tag{10.55}$$

$$\begin{aligned} rR(\bar\delta) = \bar\delta &- \int_{\underline\delta}^{\bar\delta_b} \frac{\gamma F(\delta)\Phi_1'(\delta)}{\gamma s + r\Phi_1'(\delta)} d\delta \\ &- \int_{\bar\delta_b}^{\underline\delta_a} \overline\kappa(\delta) d\delta - \int_{\underline\delta_a}^{\bar\delta} \frac{\gamma(1-F(\delta))\Phi_1'(\delta) + \gamma(F(\delta)-s)}{\gamma(1-s) + r(1-\Phi_1'(\delta))} d\delta, \end{aligned} \tag{10.56}$$

for some uniformly bounded functions $\underline{\kappa}(\delta)$ and $\overline{\kappa}(\delta)$. Before passing to the limit in this expression we claim that

$$\lim_{\lambda\to\infty} \Phi_1'(\delta) = \Psi_1'(\delta) \equiv \mathbf{1}_{\{\delta\geq\delta^\#\}} f(\delta). \tag{10.57}$$

Indeed, (10.39) implies that

$$0 = \lim_{\lambda\to\infty} (\Phi_1(\delta) - \Psi_1(\delta)) = \lim_{\lambda\to\infty} \int_{\underline{\delta}}^{\delta} \left(\Phi_1'(x) - \Psi_1'(x)\right) dx$$

for all $\delta \in \mathcal{D}$ and, since the integrand is uniformly bounded from above and below, we may apply Fatou's lemma twice to obtain

$$\int_{\underline{\delta}}^{\delta} \limsup_{\lambda\to\infty} \left(\Phi_1'(x) - \Psi_1'(x)\right) dx \leq 0 \leq \int_{\underline{\delta}}^{\delta} \liminf_{\lambda\to\infty} \left(\Phi_1'(x) - \Psi_1'(x)\right) dx,$$

from which the claim follows. Now, letting $\lambda \to \infty$ in (10.55)–(10.56), and using (10.57) together with (10.40) and the dominated convergence theorem, we obtain that

$$rR(\underline{\delta}) = \underline{\delta} + \int_{\underline{\delta}}^{\delta^\#} d\delta = \delta^\# = \overline{\delta} - \int_{\delta^\#}^{\overline{\delta}} d\delta = rR(\overline{\delta}),$$

and the desired result follows by observing that the reservation value function is nondecreasing. □

10.5 Exercises

Exercise 10.12: Assume that in some equilibrium there exists $\alpha, \beta \in \text{supp}(B)$ such that the interval $(\alpha, \beta) \notin \text{supp}(B)$.

1. Show that there are constants $M_0, N_0 > 0$ such that

   $$\Pi_b(\delta) = (M_0 + M_1(\delta))\,(N_0 + N_1(\delta))$$

   for all $\alpha \in [\alpha, \beta]$ where

   $$(M_1(\delta), N_1(\delta)) \equiv \left(\frac{\gamma\,(F(\delta) - F(\alpha))}{r + \lambda(1 - B(\alpha))}, \frac{\beta - \delta}{r + \gamma + \lambda(1 - B(\alpha))}\right).$$

2. Show that the condition $\Pi_b(\alpha) = \Pi_b(\beta)$ is equivalent to

   $$M_0 N_1(\alpha) = N_0 M_1(\beta).$$

3. Show that the condition $\Pi_b'(\alpha) = \Pi_b'(\beta) = 0$ is equivalent to the system of equations

$$N_1'(\alpha)M_0 + M_1'(\alpha)N_0 = -M_1'(\alpha)N_1(\alpha), \tag{10.58}$$

$$N_1'(\beta)M_0 + M_1'(\beta)N_0 = -M_1(\beta)N_1'(\beta). \tag{10.59}$$

4. Equations (10.58) and (10.59) can be viewed as a linear system of two equations for the two unknown constants (M_0, N_0). Show that this system admits a solution only if $f(\alpha) \neq f(\beta)$.
5. Apply Cramer's rule to the system (10.58)–(10.59) to calculate M_0/N_0 and use the result to show that

$$f(\alpha)f(\beta)\,(\beta - \alpha)^2 = (F(\beta) - F(\alpha))^2$$

is necessary for $\Pi_b(\alpha) - \Pi_b(\beta)$ and $\Pi_b'(\alpha) = \Pi_b'(\beta) = 0$.

Exercise 10.13: Assume that $F(\delta)$ is continuously differentiable. Show that the equilibrium bid and ask distributions converge to single point distributions to be specified as either the contact rate $\lambda \to 0$ or the reset rate $\gamma \to \infty$.

Exercise 10.14: Show that the limits in (10.38), (10.39), and (10.40) also hold as the reset rate $\gamma \to 0$. What happens to reservation values in that limit?

Exercise 10.15: Denote by $B(\delta)$ an arbitrary distribution on the set $\mathcal{D}$ and define the function $\mathbf{B}(q)$ as in equation (10.28).

1. Show that if B is continuous then $\mathbf{B}$ is strictly convex on $\text{supp}(B)$.
2. Show that if B is supported on $[\underline{\delta}_b, \overline{\delta}_b] \subset (\underline{\delta}, \delta^\star)$ then $\mathbf{B}$ satisfies (10.29).
3. Conversely, show that if $\mathbb{B} : [0,1] \to [0,1]$ with $\mathbb{B}(0) = 0$ is continuously differentiable, strictly convex on some interval $F[\underline{\delta}_b, \overline{\delta}_b] \subset (0, F(\delta^\star))$, and such that if (10.29) is satisfied then

$$\hat{B}(\delta) \equiv 1 + \frac{\gamma}{\lambda}\left(1 - \frac{1}{\mathbb{B}'(F(\delta))}\right)$$

defines a continuous distribution that is supported on $[\underline{\delta}_b, \overline{\delta}_b]$.

10.6 Notes and References

The material of this chapter is to a large extent drawn from Hugonnier, Lester, and Weill [2024a], which incorporates the search problem with asymmetric information over private values [first studied by Albrecht and Axell, 1984] into the semicentralized OTC market model. Other studies that introduce asymmetric information over private values into search-theoretic models include Gehrig [1993], Spulber [1996], Zhu [2011], Cujean and Praz [2013], Mäkinen and Palazzo [2017], Garrett, Gomes, and Maestri [2018], Lester, Shourideh, Venkateswaran, and Zetlin-Jones [2023], Akin and Platt [2022], and Glebkin, Shen, and Yueshen [2019].

Two papers that are closely related to the content of this chapter are Bethune, Sultanum, and Trachter [2019] and Zhang [2017]. Bethune et al. [2019] study the trading and issuance of assets in a decentralized market, much like the interdealer market of chapter 7, but assume that participants do not observe each other's utility flows. Zhang [2017] studies a semicentralized market with private information that is closer to the model of this chapter, but only considers the nongeneric case in which the distribution of utility flows admits a density that is symmetric around the asset supply $s = 1/2$. A key difference with both papers is that, instead of assuming that one party quotes a price upon meeting, Bethune et al. [2019] and Zhang [2017] both adopt a mechanism design approach. Specifically, these authors assume that one of the parties offers a direct mechanism that specifies a price $P(\delta)$ and probability of execution $\pi(\delta)$ as functions of the utility flow reported by the other party and rely on incentive compatibility to elicit truthful revelation. In such an approach, the terms of trade are known in advance, and uncertainty affects the trade execution. By contrast, in our formulation the price itself is random, and this randomness generates uncertainty over trade execution. The fact that investors have quasilinear preferences implies that the two approaches are equivalent despite this difference; Zhang [2017] notes this connection but does not provide a differential characterization of the equilibrium.

Finally, note that the competitive, or directed, search model of section 8.3 already accommodates asymmetric information about private values. That is, in the equilibrium we constructed, it is not necessary to assume that dealers observe investors' utility flows when they post quotes. Instead, dealers in that model post quotes and have rational expectations about the utility flows of the investors who find it optimal to choose their quotes.

11

Asymmetric Information: Common Values

In this section, we explore a second type of private information in which there are two types of assets being traded—say, low- and high-quality assets—as in the classic lemons market studied by Akerlof [1970]. We assume that owners of an asset can observe its quality but nonowners cannot distinguish its quality ex ante. Since, as we describe below, all agents prefer high-quality to low-quality assets, we refer to this case as the *common value* case.

This case received a lot of attention in the aftermath of the 2007–2008 Global Financial Crisis (GFC), which began with a sudden bout of illiquidity in the OTC markets for various types of asset-backed securities. For example, as housing prices declined in the run-up to the GFC, the value of some (but not all) mortgage-backed securities fell dramatically. As these values were difficult to discern, many attributed the subsequent market breakdown or freeze to asymmetric information regarding the value of the assets, as in Akerlof [1970]. A number of pressing questions ensued: To what extent were the frictions associated with asymmetric information over the assets' quality amplified (or mitigated) by the trading frictions in OTC markets? What was the optimal policy to unfreeze these markets? Could forcing these markets to transition from OTC to centralized exchanges prevent future crises?

Answering these questions requires a model that incorporates both search frictions and asymmetric information over common values, which we develop below. As is well known, models of this type are much more complicated than models with perfect information, and often are considerably more difficult to solve than models with asymmetric information regarding private values. In particular, equilibrium is not guaranteed to exist for all parameter values [Rothschild and Stiglitz, 1976], and multiplicity of equilibrium often emerges, giving rise to a need for equilibrium refinements. Hence, unlike in previous chapters, where we strove for generality, much of the analysis in this chapter is conducted within the context of a special case of our general framework. This allows us to connect our results to those in the existing literature, where similar simplifying assumptions are common, and to highlight our key insights.

Studying the effects of asymmetric information in a dynamic search model reveals several insights. In general, the opportunity to resell an asset after purchasing it generates interesting interactions between current and future market conditions. In some regions of the parameter space, this means that reducing search frictions can ease the harmful effects of adverse selection; that is, increasing the frequency of trade can allow the market to transition from a *freeze* equilibrium—where only low-quality assets are effectively traded—to a *liquid* equilibrium where both low- and high-quality assets trade.

Dynamic complementarities also create scope for multiple equilibria in this dynamic setting. Specifically, when opportunities to retrade are sufficiently frequent, freeze and liquid equilibria can coexist. In the former case, investors anticipate low prices in the future, which drives down their reservation values and ensures low prices in the current period. In the latter case, reservation values are higher—as the option value of selling in the event of acquiring a low-quality asset is positive—which in turn supports higher prices and more liquidity in the current period. Hence, reducing search frictions can also increase the possibility of multiple, self-fulfilling equilibria.

11.1 Environment

We consider an environment with a measure 1 of investors who can hold either zero or one unit of an asset. Unlike in the analysis in previous chapters, we assume that there are two types of assets, indexed by $j \in \{\ell, h\}$, where ℓ and h denote low and high-quality, respectively. Let s_j denote the supply of type j assets and let $s = s_\ell + s_h$ denote the total supply of assets. In keeping with much of the literature on this topic, we assume that, upon acquiring an asset and becoming an owner, an investor immediately learns its quality. However, a nonowner cannot distinguish between the two types of asset.

As in previous chapters, investors are heterogeneous with respect to the utility they derive from holding a unit of either type of the asset. Specifically, we assume that an investor with utility type $\delta \in \mathcal{D}$ receives utility flow $\delta - z_j$ from holding one unit of an asset of quality j, where $z_\ell > z_h$. As before, investors periodically receive iid shocks to their utility type: at Poisson arrival rate γ, investors draw a new utility flow δ' from an exogenously fixed cumulative distribution function $F(\delta')$.

11.1.1 Simplifying Assumptions

We impose two additional assumptions to simplify the analysis. First, unlike in the semicentralized framework studied in chapter 4, we assume that there are no dealers.

Instead, investors can directly access a competitive market at Poisson arrival rate λ. This allows us to abstract from the bargaining problem between investors and dealers, and focus directly on the interactions between asymmetric information and search frictions. Note that introducing a similar assumption in the framework of chapter 10 would eliminate the inefficiencies that derive from asymmetric information regarding private valuations, as these only arise in a setting with dealers who have some market power. However, as we will establish below, allowing investors direct access to a competitive market (at random arrival times) does *not* eliminate the inefficiencies that arise from asymmetric information over common values.

Second, we focus our attention on the special case of two utility flows where the distribution is given by

$$F(\delta) = \begin{cases} 0 & \text{if } \delta < \delta_L, \\ f_L & \text{if } \delta_L \leq \delta < \delta_H, \\ 1 = f_L + f_H & \text{if } \delta \geq \delta_H. \end{cases}$$

Along with parametric restrictions made explicit below, this assumption allows us to easily identify the marginal investors and focus on the relationship between their trading behavior and equilibrium prices and allocations.

11.1.2 Notation

Let $\phi_{q,j}(\delta)$ denote the mass of investors with utility type $\delta \in \{\delta_L, \delta_H\}$ who hold $q \in \{0, 1\}$ units of a type $j \in \{\ell, h\}$ asset and $\Phi_{q,j}(\delta)$ denote the associated *cumulative* distribution. As we describe below, taking these distributions and a price P as given, nonowners will formulate beliefs about the steady-state fraction $\psi_j \in (0, 1)$ of type j assets for sale in the market.

Let $V(1, \delta, z_j)$ denote the value function of an investor with utility type δ who holds one unit of a type $j \in \{\ell, h\}$ asset, $V(0, \delta)$ denote the value function of a nonowner with utility type δ, and

$$R(\delta, z_j) = V(1, \delta, z_j) - V(0, \delta), \qquad \text{for } j \in \{\ell, h\},$$

denote the reservation value function of an investor with utility type δ for one unit of a type j asset. As in the perfect-information benchmark, given an asset price P, an owner's optimal selling strategy can be summarized by the function

$$\alpha_j(P, \delta) = \begin{cases} 0 & \text{if } P < R(\delta, z_j), \\ [0, 1] & \text{if } P = R(\delta, z_j), \\ 1 & \text{if } P > R(\delta, z_j). \end{cases} \tag{11.1}$$

In words, for a given price P, an investor who owns an asset of type $j \in \{\ell, h\}$ and has utility type δ will sell with probability $\alpha_j(P, \delta)$.

A nonowner who has the opportunity to buy a unit of the asset cannot distinguish between the two types of assets being sold but, in equilibrium, infers that the fraction of low-quality assets being sold is ψ_ℓ. Let

$$R_b(\delta; \psi_\ell) = \psi_\ell R(\delta, z_\ell) + (1 - \psi_\ell) R(\delta, z_h) \tag{11.2}$$

denote the reservation value function of such a buyer, and

$$\alpha_b(P, \delta; \psi_\ell) = \begin{cases} 0 & \text{if } P > R_b(\delta; \psi_\ell), \\ [0, 1] & \text{if } P = R_b(\delta; \psi_\ell), \\ 1 & \text{if } P < R_b(\delta; \psi_\ell), \end{cases} \tag{11.3}$$

denote the probability that this investor will purchase the asset at price P. In what follows, we will often suppress the dependence of R_b and α_b on ψ_ℓ to economize on notation, but it should be understood that these functions depend on the composition of the pool of assets being sold in the market.

11.1.3 Reservation Values

Following the same steps that we used in earlier chapters, one easily arrives at the following Hamilton-Jacobi-Bellman equation for the reservation value of an investor for an asset of quality $j \in \{\ell, h\}$:

$$\begin{aligned} rR(\delta, z_j) = \delta - z_j + \gamma \mathbf{E}^F \left[R(\delta', z_j) - R(\delta, z_j) \right] \\ + \lambda \alpha_j(P, \delta) \left(P - R(\delta, z_j) \right) - \lambda \alpha_b(P, \delta) \left(R_b(\delta) - P \right). \end{aligned} \tag{11.4}$$

The reservation value equation (11.4) is similar to the reservation value we derived under perfect information, but there is an important difference. Specifically, under private information, an investor's decision to sell depends on the reservation value of the asset she owns, $R(\delta, z_j)$, while her decision to buy depends on the average reservation value defined in (11.2). If $\psi_\ell \in (0, 1)$, so that

$$R(\delta, z_\ell) < R_b(\delta) < R(\delta, z_h),$$

this feature creates the possibility that an investor with utility type δ may have strict incentives to buy and sell at the same time if she owns a low-quality asset, or to neither buy nor sell if she owns a high-quality asset. In contrast, with perfect information, investors always prefer to either buy or sell.

The following lemma establishes fundamental properties of the reservation value functions, along with several implications for optimal behavior.

Lemma 11.1: The reservation value function $R(\delta, z)$ is increasing in δ and decreasing in z. In particular,

1. $R_b(\delta; \psi_\ell)$ is increasing in δ and such that $R(\delta, z_\ell) \leq R_b(\delta; \psi_\ell) \leq R(\delta, z_h)$ for any constant $\psi_\ell \in [0, 1]$, with at least one inequality holding strictly.
2. If an owner of a high-quality asset is at least weakly willing to sell at price P, then an owner of a low-quality asset will strictly prefer to sell at that same price. That is, $\alpha_h(P, \delta) > 0 \Rightarrow \alpha_\ell(P, \delta) = 1$.
3. Trading behavior follows a threshold pattern in the sense that

$$\exists\, \delta \in [\delta_L, \delta_H) : \alpha_b(P, \delta) > 0 \Rightarrow \alpha_b(P, \delta') = 1,$$

$$\exists\, (j, \delta) \in \{\ell, h\} \times (\delta_L, \delta_H] : \alpha_j(P, \delta) > 0 \Rightarrow \alpha_j(P, \delta'') = 1,$$

for all utility types $\delta' > \delta > \delta''$.

Proof. Standard arguments from earlier chapters (see, e.g., section 5.2.2) can be used to establish that the reservation value function is Lipschitz continuous. Therefore, an application of the envelope theorem to (11.4) [see Theorem 1 in Milgrom and Segal, 2002] shows that

$$(r + \gamma) R_\delta(\delta, z_j) = 1 - \lambda \alpha_j(P, \delta) R_\delta(\delta, z_j) - \lambda \alpha_b(P, \delta) \mathbf{E}^\Psi[R_\delta(\delta, z)],$$

where

$$\mathbf{E}^\Psi[R_\delta(\delta, z)] \equiv \int_{\underline{\delta}}^{\overline{\delta}} R_\delta(\delta, z) d\Psi(z)$$

denotes an expectation under the distribution of the quality of assets for sale in the market. Solving for the derivative and simplifying gives

$$R_\delta(\delta, z_j) = \frac{1}{r + \gamma + \lambda \alpha_j(P, \delta)} \left(1 + \frac{\alpha_b(P, \delta) \mathbf{E}^\Psi[R_\delta(\delta, z)]}{r + \gamma + \lambda \alpha_j(P, \delta)}\right)^{-1},$$

which is clearly strictly positive. The steps to prove that $R(\delta, z_j)$ is decreasing in the second argument are similar, though slightly easier since the value function of a nonowner does not depend on z. We leave this section of the proof as an end-of-chapter exercise (see Exercise 11.4). □

11.1.4 Distributions

Given the investors' optimal trading behavior, we can now derive the joint distributions of asset holdings and utility types. Note that, in previous chapters where we worked with an arbitrary distribution, it was convenient to focus on the cumulative measures. However, with just two utility types, it is easier and more transparent to characterize the masses $\phi_{1,j}(\delta)$ and $\phi_0(\delta)$.

For $\delta \in \{\delta_L, \delta_H\}$ and $\neg\delta = \{\delta_L, \delta_H\} \setminus \delta$, the mass of nonowners in a steady-state equilibrium must satisfy

$$0 = \gamma\big(\phi_0(\neg\delta)f(\delta) - \phi_0(\delta)f(\neg\delta)\big) \qquad (11.5)$$
$$- \lambda\alpha_b(P,\delta)\phi_0(\delta) + \lambda \sum_{j\in\{\ell,h\}} \alpha_j(P,\delta)\phi_{1,j}(\delta),$$

where the terms on the first line capture the net inflow from preference shocks while those on the second line represent the net inflow from trading. Similar logic reveals that the measure $\phi_{1j}(\delta)$ must satisfy

$$0 = \gamma\big(\phi_{1,j}(\neg\delta)f(\delta) - \phi_{1,j}(\delta)f(\neg\delta)\big) \qquad (11.6)$$
$$+ \lambda\psi_j\alpha_b(P,\delta)\phi_0(\delta) - \lambda\alpha_j(P,x)\phi_{1,j}(\delta).$$

Notice in equation (11.6) that the inflow of type j assets from trade depends on the fraction ψ_j of these assets in the market. Finally, we must have

$$s_\ell = \phi_{1,\ell}(\delta_L) + \phi_{1,\ell}(\delta_H), \qquad (11.7)$$
$$s_h = \phi_{1,h}(\delta_L) + \phi_{1,h}(\delta_H),$$

and

$$f(\delta) = \phi_0(\delta) + \phi_{1,j}(\delta) + \phi_{1,j}(\delta) \qquad (11.8)$$

to ensure that the measures are consistent with market clearing and with the distribution of utility types in the whole population.

11.1.5 Equilibrium Definition

A steady-state equilibrium consists of a price P, a composition of assets being sold ψ_j, a pair of reservation value functions $R(\delta, z_j)$ and $R_b(\delta; \psi_\ell)$, a pair of decision rules $\alpha_j(P,\delta)$ and $\alpha_b(P,\delta;\psi_\ell)$, and masses of investors $\{\phi_0(\delta), \phi_{1,j}(\delta)\}$, such that

1. The reservation value functions satisfy (11.2) and (11.4).
2. The decision rules satisfy (11.1) and (11.3).
3. The distributions satisfy (11.5)–(11.8).
4. The price P clears the market:

$$\mathbf{S}(P) \equiv \sum_{(j,x)} \alpha_j(P,x)\phi_{1,j}(x) = \sum_x \alpha_b(P,x)\phi_0(x) \equiv \mathbf{D}(P).$$

5. The composition of assets being sold satisfies

$$\psi_j = \frac{\sum_{x\in\{\delta_L,\delta_H\}} \alpha_j(P,x)\phi_{1,j}(x)}{\sum_{j\in\{\ell,h\}}\sum_{x\in\{\delta_L,\delta_H\}} \alpha_j(P,x)\phi_{1,j}(x)}.$$

Note that the market clearing condition $\mathbf{S}(P) = \mathbf{D}(P)$ is, in fact, implied by the stationarity conditions imposed on the distribution of asset holdings and utility types. In particular, the fact that the measure of owners remains constant over time implies that the flows of purchases and sales are equal at all times.

11.1.6 Parametric Assumption

To further simplify the analysis, we will make the additional assumption that $f_H = 1 - f_L$ is sufficiently large, relative to the asset supply, so that investors with the high utility type δ_H are the marginal buyers. In particular, we establish in Lemma 11.2 below that

$$1 > f_H > 2s_\ell + s_h \tag{11.9}$$

is a sufficient condition to ensure that nonowners with utility type δ_H are the marginal buyers in *any* equilibrium. While this assumption reduces the number of cases we have to study, the steps required to characterize the equilibrium in other regions of the parameter space are similar.

Lemma 11.2: If condition (11.9) is satisfied then

$$P = \psi_\ell R(\delta_H, z_\ell) + \psi_h R(\delta_H, z_h) \equiv R_b(\delta_H; \psi_\ell) \tag{11.10}$$

in any steady-state equilibrium.

Proof. Suppose $P < R_b(\delta_H; \psi_\ell)$. At such a price, $\mathbf{D}(P) \geq \lambda\phi_0(\delta_H)$, since all nonowners with utility type δ_H would strictly prefer to buy. On the other side of the market, the quantity supplied $\mathbf{S}(P) \leq \lambda\left[s_\ell + \phi_{1,h}(\delta_L)\right]$, since owners of high-quality assets with utility type δ_H would strictly prefer not to sell at such a price. However, demand will strictly exceed supply, since

$$\begin{aligned} f_H > 2s_\ell + s_h &\Rightarrow f_H > s_\ell + s_h + \phi_{1,\ell}(\delta_H) \\ &\Rightarrow f_H > s_\ell + \phi_{1,h}(\delta_L) + \phi_{1,h}(\delta_H) + \phi_{1,\ell}(\delta_H) \\ &\Rightarrow \phi_0(\delta_H) > s_\ell + \phi_{1,h}(\delta_L) \\ &\Rightarrow \mathbf{D}(P) > \mathbf{S}(P), \end{aligned}$$

where the first two implications follow from (11.7) and the third implication follows from (11.8). Alternatively, if $P > R_b(\delta_H; \psi_\ell)$, then $\mathbf{D}(P) = 0$ and $\mathbf{S}(P) > 0$, so that supply strictly exceeds demand. □

11.2 The Special Case with $\lambda = 0$

Before proceeding to the general case, we first characterize the set of equilibria in an essentially static or one-shot setting, where we allow all agents to trade at $t = 0$ but assume that they never have the opportunity to trade again. Analyzing this special case is helpful for at least two reasons. First, many of the key steps in the construction of this type of equilibrium are useful in the analysis of the dynamic model, with $\lambda > 0$, which follows. Second, our derivation with $\lambda = 0$ allows us to introduce a well-known source of equilibrium multiplicity in static, competitive environments with asymmetric information [see Wilson, 1980] and to propose an equilibrium selection rule. This is important because, in the next section, we establish that multiplicity can arise in the dynamic model with $\lambda > 0$ *even after* this equilibrium selection rule is imposed; that is, we show how and why multiplicity arises in dynamic markets with asymmetric information even after eliminating this well-known source of multiplicity in static market settings.

11.2.1 *Equilibrium Characterization*

In an environment in which $\lambda = 0$, the steady-state allocation of assets across investors is random and given by

$$\begin{aligned} &\phi_{1,j}(\delta) = s_j f(\delta), \\ &\phi_0(\delta) = (1-s) f(\delta). \end{aligned} \qquad (11.11)$$

Moreover, normalizing $z_h = 0$ and solving the reservation value equation when $\lambda = 0$ we obtain that

$$R(\delta, z_\ell) = R(\delta, z_h) - z_\ell \qquad (11.12)$$

for $\delta \in \{\delta_L, \delta_H\}$, and

$$R(\delta_H, z_h) = \delta_H - \gamma f_L \frac{\delta_H - \delta_L}{r+\gamma}, \tag{11.13}$$

$$R(\delta_L, z_h) = \delta_L + \gamma f_H \frac{\delta_H - \delta_L}{r+\gamma} = \delta_H - (r + \gamma f_L) \frac{\delta_H - \delta_L}{r+\gamma}. \tag{11.14}$$

Under assumption (11.9), nonowners with utility type δ_H are the marginal buyers, so that the price is given by (11.10). At this price, it must be that

$$\alpha_\ell(P, \delta_L) - 1 = \alpha_h(P, \delta_H) = \alpha_b(P, \delta_L) = 0.$$

Hence, deriving an equilibrium requires solving for the strategies $\alpha_\ell(P, \delta_H), \alpha_h(P, \delta_L)$, $\alpha_b(P, \delta_H)$, and the induced composition of assets

$$\psi_\ell = \frac{\phi_{1,\ell}(\delta_L) + \alpha_\ell(P, \delta_H)\phi_{1,\ell}(\delta_H)}{\phi_{1,\ell}(\delta_L) + \alpha_\ell(P, \delta_H)\phi_{1,\ell}(\delta_H) + \alpha_h(P, \delta_L)\phi_{1,h}(\delta_L)},$$

subject to the requirements that these strategies be optimal given the asset price in (11.10) and that markets clear. The market clearing condition requires that

$$\alpha_b(P, \delta_H)\phi_0(\delta_H) = \phi_{1,\ell}(\delta_L) + \alpha_\ell(P, \delta_H)\phi_{1,\ell}(\delta_H) + \alpha_h(P, \delta_L)\phi_{1,h}(\delta_L),$$

where the left-hand side represents the asset demand while the right-hand side represents the asset supply.

The following lemma describes the set of equilibria of the static model. We refer to the equilibrium in which all owners of high-quality assets with utility type δ_L sell as the *liquid equilibrium*. In this equilibrium, we have that

$$\psi_\ell = \widetilde{\psi}_\ell \equiv \frac{s_\ell}{s_\ell + s_h f_L} < 1 = \alpha_h(P, \delta_L) = 1, \tag{11.15}$$

so that the price is given by

$$\widetilde{P} = \widetilde{\psi}_\ell R(\delta_H, z_\ell) + \left(1 - \widetilde{\psi}_\ell\right) R(\delta_H, z_h). \tag{11.16}$$

Alternatively, we refer to the equilibrium in which only low-quality assets trade, so that $\alpha_h(P, \delta_L) = 0$ and $\psi_\ell = 1$, as the *freeze equilibrium*.

Lemma 11.3: Let $z_h \equiv 0$ and define

$$\underline{Z}_\ell \equiv \frac{r}{r+\gamma}(\delta_H - \delta_L) < \underline{Z}_\ell / \widetilde{\psi}_\ell \equiv \overline{Z}_\ell.$$

Under condition (11.9), the set of equilibria is as follows:

1. A freeze equilibrium exists for all $z_\ell \geq \underline{Z}_\ell$.
2. A liquid equilibrium exists for all $z_\ell \leq \overline{Z}_\ell$.
3. An equilibrium that is neither freeze nor liquid exists for all $z_\ell \in \left(\underline{Z}_\ell, \overline{Z}_\ell\right)$ and has both $\alpha_h(P, \delta_L) \in (0, 1)$ and $\psi_\ell \in \left(\widetilde{\psi}_\ell, 1\right)$.

Proof. Consider first a candidate freeze equilibrium, with

$$P = R(\delta_H, z_\ell),$$

$$0 = 1 - \psi_\ell = \alpha_h(P, \delta_L).$$

Since owners of type ℓ assets with utility type δ_H are indifferent, any value of $\alpha_\ell(P, \delta_H)$ is consistent with optimal behavior. The same is true for $\alpha_b(P, \delta_H)$, since uninformed buyers correctly anticipate that only low-quality assets are for sale. Therefore, we must only confirm that $\alpha_h(P, \delta_L) = 0$ is optimal, which requires that $P = R(\delta_H, z_\ell) \leq R(\delta_L, z_h)$. Using (11.12) and (11.14), one can easily confirm that this condition is satisfied if and only if $z_\ell \geq \underline{Z}_\ell$. Next consider the candidate liquid equilibrium with

$$P = \widetilde{P},$$

$$0 = 1 - \alpha_h(P, \delta_L) = \psi_\ell - \widetilde{\psi}_\ell.$$

In this case $\alpha_\ell(P, \delta_H) = \alpha_b(P, \delta_H) = 1$ is optimal because

$$R_b(\delta_H) = \widetilde{P} > R(\delta_H, z_\ell).$$

Hence, it is again sufficient to check that $\alpha_h(P, \delta_L) = 1$ is optimal, which requires that $\widetilde{P} \geq R(\delta_L, z_h)$. Using (11.12) and (11.13), one can easily confirm that this condition is satisfied if and only if $z_\ell \leq \overline{Z}_\ell$. Finally, in an equilibrium that is neither liquid nor freeze, it must be that

$$P = R(\delta_L, z_h) = \Psi_\ell(\alpha_h) R(\delta_H, z_\ell) + (1 - \Psi_\ell(\alpha_h))\, R(\delta_H, z_\ell), \tag{11.17}$$

where

$$\Psi_\ell(\alpha_h) = \frac{s_\ell}{s_\ell + \alpha_h s_h f_L}.$$

Since buyers are indifferent at this price, any value of $\alpha_b(P, \delta_H) \in [0, 1]$ is consistent with optimality. Moreover, since $\Psi_\ell(\alpha_h) < 1$ for all values of the constant $\alpha_h \in (0, 1)$, we have that $P > R(\delta_H, z_\ell)$, and it follows that the strategy $\alpha_\ell(P, \delta_H) = 1$ is optimal. Hence, it remains to solve for the value of $\alpha_h \in (0, 1)$ such that (11.17) is satisfied.

Using (11.12) and (11.13), one can easily confirm that such a value exists if and only if $z_\ell \in (\underline{Z}_\ell, \overline{Z}_\ell)$. □

Since the thresholds $\underline{Z}_\ell < \overline{Z}_\ell$, we have that the unique equilibrium is a *freeze equilibrium* when

$$z_\ell \geq \overline{Z}_\ell \Leftrightarrow \frac{\delta_H - \delta_L}{r+\gamma} - \left(\frac{z_\ell}{r}\right) \frac{s_\ell}{s_\ell + s_h f_L} \leq 0.$$

The first term on the left-hand side of the second inequality represents the gains from trade in a perfect-information setting, i.e., the discounted expected value of transferring an asset from an investor with a low utility type to one with a high utility type. The second term is the expected loss from acquiring a low-quality asset: the product of the net present value of the discount associated with acquiring a low-quality asset, z_ℓ, and the probability that an asset for sale is low-quality. Hence, as one might expect, a freeze equilibrium is the unique equilibrium when the gains from trade are small relative to the expected losses from acquiring a low-quality asset, i.e., when the lemons problem is severe.

The unique equilibrium is the *liquid equilibrium* when $z_\ell \leq \underline{Z}_\ell$, i.e., when the perfect-information gains from trade are sufficiently large relative to the difference in asset quality, $z_\ell - z_h$. Finally, there exist moderate values of the parameter z_ℓ such that there are three equilibria: the freeze equilibrium, the liquid equilibrium, and a *semiliquid equilibrium* in which some but not all owners of high-quality assets with utility type δ_L sell.

This multiplicity of equilibria stems from the nature of demand in markets with asymmetric information. In particular, a nonowner's payoff from buying an asset, $R_b - P$, depends negatively on the price P but also depends on the composition of assets in the market, which skews toward higher-quality assets as the price increases. Hence, a nonowner's payoff is indirectly increasing in the asset price, in that

$$\frac{d(R_b - P)}{dP} = (R(\delta_H, z_h) - R(\delta_H, z_\ell)) \frac{\partial \psi_h}{\partial P} - 1 \geq -1.$$

If the first effect is sufficiently positive, then the demand curve can be upward sloping and multiple equilibria can emerge.

The left panel of figure 11.1 plots the demand correspondence in the case where $z_\ell \in (\underline{Z}_\ell, \overline{Z}_\ell)$. When the price $P \leq R(\delta_H, z_\ell)$, nonowners correctly infer that only low-quality assets will be sold, since

$$z_\ell > \underline{Z}_\ell \Rightarrow R(\delta_H, z_\ell) < R(\delta_L, z_h).$$

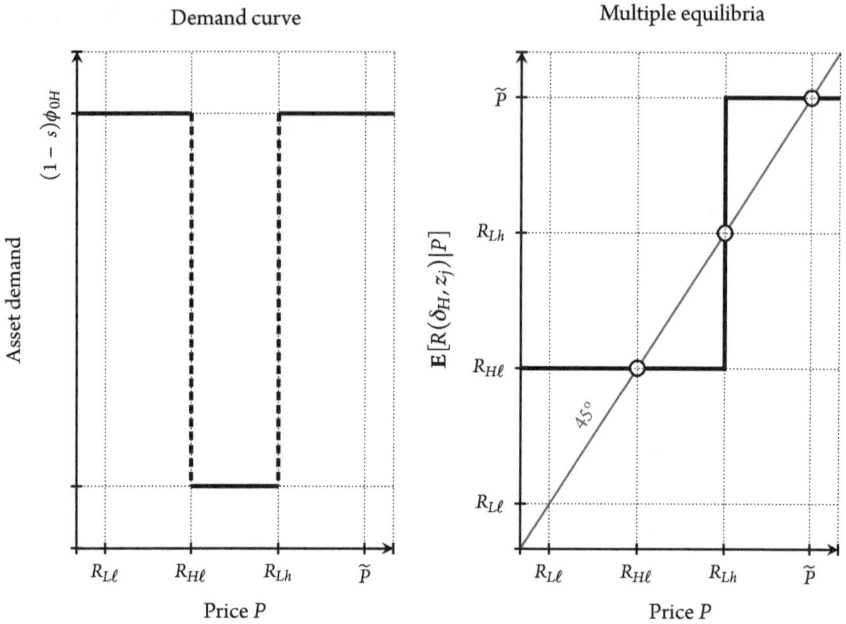

FIGURE 11.1. Equilibrium multiplicity $z_\ell \in (\underline{Z}_\ell, \overline{Z}_\ell)$

This figure illustrates the nature of equilibrium multiplicity in the static model. To increase readability, we denote by ϕ_{0H} the equilibrium measure of high-type nonowners and by $R_{ij} \equiv R(\delta_i, z_j)$ the reservation value of an investor with utility flow $\delta_i \in \{\delta_L, \delta_H\}$ for an asset of quality $z_j \in \{z_\ell, z_h\}$.

Hence, $\alpha_b(P, \delta_L) = 1$ in this price range so all nonowners are willing to buy. When the price $P \in (R(\delta_H, z_\ell), R(\delta_L, z_h))$, demand falls to zero, as the price exceeds the nonowners' reservation value since $\psi_\ell = 1$. The demand curve is thus downward sloping for prices $P < R(\delta_L, z_h)$.

However, the demand curve is *upward sloping* at the point $P = R(\delta_L, z_h)$. In particular, with only two utility types, a marginal increase in the price at this indifference point causes a marginal deterioration in the terms of trade that a buyer faces, but a discrete improvement in the average quality of the assets being sold. As nonowners infer the change in the composition of assets being sold, demand increases with the price.

The right panel of figure 11.1 shows how the nonmonotonicity of demand translates into multiple equilibria. Recall that, under the assumption that nonowners with utility type δ_H are the marginal buyers, the equilibrium is a fixed point in which the price induces a certain composition of owners to sell—that is, P induces decision rules $\alpha_j(P, \delta)$—and the induced composition of sellers implies a price equal to a nonowner's expected payoffs, $\mathbf{E}\left[R(\delta_H, z_j)|P\right]$.

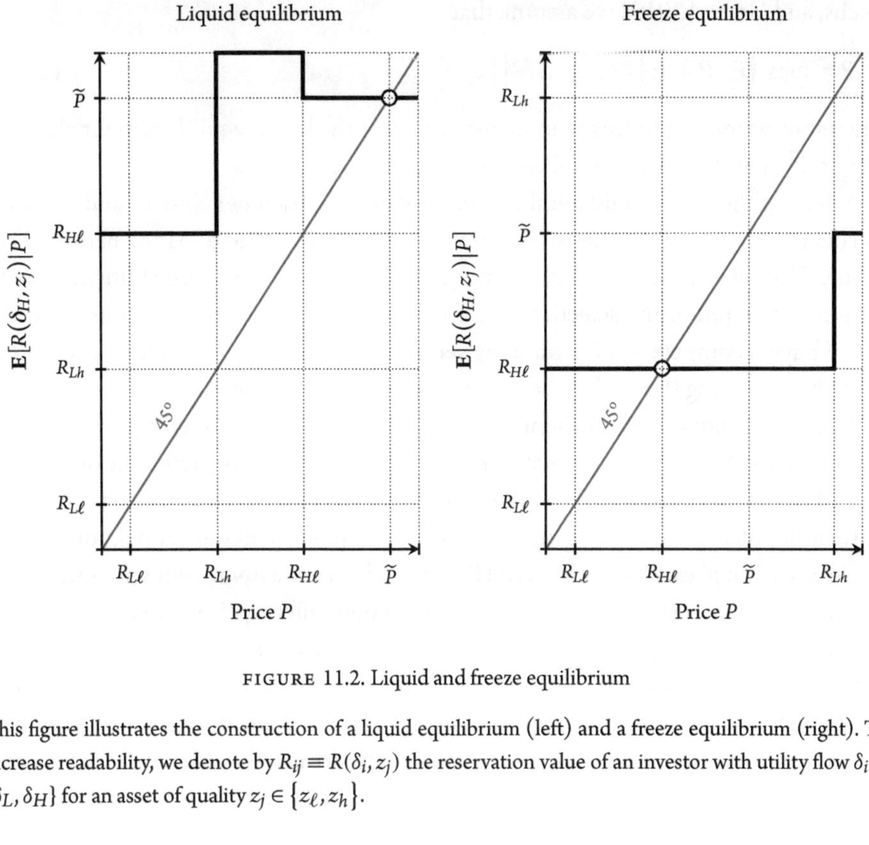

FIGURE 11.2. Liquid and freeze equilibrium

This figure illustrates the construction of a liquid equilibrium (left) and a freeze equilibrium (right). To increase readability, we denote by $R_{ij} \equiv R(\delta_i, z_j)$ the reservation value of an investor with utility flow $\delta_i \in \{\delta_L, \delta_H\}$ for an asset of quality $z_j \in \{z_\ell, z_h\}$.

Figure 11.2 illustrates the liquid and freeze equilibria. In the liquid equilibrium (left panel), when the gains from trade between utility types δ_H and δ_L are large relative to the differences in asset quality, demand exceeds supply when the price is low; even when nonowners anticipate only low-quality assets for sale, they are willing to pay a price that induces owners of high-quality assets with utility type δ_L to sell. As a result, the unique equilibrium pools both low- and high-quality assets. Alternatively, in a freeze equilibrium (right panel), when the lemons problem is severe, the pooling price $\widetilde{P}$ that nonowners are willing to pay is not sufficient to compensate owners of high-quality assets with utility type δ_L to sell.

11.2.2 Equilibrium Selection

To focus on equilibrium multiplicity that arises because of dynamic forces, and to understand how search frictions affect these forces, we will employ an equilibrium selection rule that selects the *most liquid* equilibrium. In particular, following Asriyan,

Fuchs, and Green [2019] we assume that

$$P = \max\left\{P : P = \mathbf{E}\left[R(\delta_H, z_j)|P\right]\right\}. \tag{11.18}$$

Therefore, according to this refinement, we select the liquid equilibrium for all values of $z_\ell \le \overline{Z}_\ell$ and the freeze equilibrium for all $z_\ell > \overline{Z}_\ell$.

Selecting the most liquid equilibrium provides a natural benchmark and allows us to concentrate on the sources of illiquidity that are due to the dynamic nature of our model. However, as discussed in Asriyan et al. [2019], there are also strategic foundations for this equilibrium selection rule. In particular, this refinement captures the idea that if buyers compete à la Bertrand by setting prices, then they should not be able to profit by increasing their offer above the candidate equilibrium price.

Consider a thought experiment in which a nonowner with utility type δ_H is able to post a price offer and assume that, if multiple types of owners prefer her offer to the candidate equilibrium price, then one of these owners is chosen at random according to their population weights. If there are multiple equilibria in our model, then a profitable deviation p' exists whenever $\alpha_h(P, \delta_L) < 1$ because a nonowner with utility type δ_H would achieve a strictly higher payoff if she could offer a price $R(\delta_L, z_h) < P' < \widetilde{P}$, where $\widetilde{P}$ denotes the price in the liquid equilibrium as defined in equation (11.16). Note that this bid would be accepted both by owners of low-quality assets and by owners of high-quality assets with utility type δ_L. Hence, the selection rule we employ ensures that our static equilibrium concept is robust to an alternative, equally plausible setting in which prices are determined by buyers posting strategic offers, as opposed to a nonstrategic Walrasian auctioneer.

11.3 The General Case with $\lambda > 0$

We now return to the task of characterizing equilibria in the dynamic model where the contact rate $\lambda > 0$. We maintain assumption (11.9), which ensures that nonowners with utility type δ_H are the marginal buyers. We also apply the refinement in (11.18) to select a unique equilibrium in the competitive market at each point in time, taking as given the distributions and reservation values that arise in the dynamic steady-state equilibrium. In this section, we will characterize the parameter values such that the market is always in the freeze equilibrium or always in the liquid equilibrium; we discuss additional types of *nonstationary* equilibria later in the chapter.

11.3.1 Equilibrium Characterization

The steps required to characterize equilibria when $\lambda > 0$ are similar to those required to characterize equilibria in the static case. In particular, for each type of equilibrium (freeze or liquid), we derive the steady-state distributions and reservation values induced by the candidate price P and decision rules $\alpha_j(P,\delta)$, for $j \in \{\ell, h\}$ and $\delta \in \{\delta_L, \delta_H\}$. Then, we derive conditions such that the candidate satisfies our criteria for an equilibrium, taking as given these distributions and reservation values. The following lemma summarizes the results of this procedure.

Lemma 11.4: Suppose that $z_h \equiv 0$ and let

$$\underline{\mathcal{Z}}_\ell(\lambda) \equiv \frac{\delta_H - \delta_L}{r+\gamma}\left(\frac{r}{\widetilde{\psi}_\ell} + \frac{\gamma\lambda f_L}{r+\gamma+\lambda}\right), \tag{11.19}$$

$$\overline{\mathcal{Z}}_\ell(\lambda) \equiv \frac{\delta_H - \delta_L}{r+\gamma}\left(\frac{r+\lambda(1-\widehat{\psi}_\ell)}{\widehat{\psi}_\ell} + \frac{\gamma\lambda f_L}{r+\gamma+\lambda}\right),$$

where the constant $\widetilde{\psi}_\ell < 1$ is defined as in (11.15) and

$$\widehat{\psi}_\ell \equiv \frac{s_\ell}{s_\ell + \frac{\gamma}{\gamma+\lambda} s_h f_L}.$$

Given (11.2) and (11.18), a freeze equilibrium exists for all $z_\ell \geq \underline{\mathcal{Z}}_\ell(\lambda)$ and a liquid equilibrium exists for all $z_\ell \leq \overline{\mathcal{Z}}_\ell(\lambda)$.

Proof. Consider first a freeze equilibrium with

$$\alpha_h(P,\delta_L) = P - R(\delta_H, z_\ell) = 0. \tag{11.20}$$

In this candidate equilibrium, the steady-state distribution of owners of high-quality assets with utility type δ_L is $\phi_{1,h}(\delta_L) = s_h f_L$ as in the static case; since these assets never trade, it should not be surprising that they are allocated randomly across investors. The reservation values for high-quality assets are also the same as in the static case, so that $R(\delta_H, z_h)$ and $R(\delta_L, z_h)$ are given by (11.13) and (11.14), respectively. Intuitively, the value of owning a high-quality asset is the same in an economy where owners never get the chance to trade and in an economy where they have opportunities to trade but do not.

In contrast, the reservation value of owning a low-quality asset depends on the contact rate. Indeed, solving (11.20) yields

$$R(\delta_H, z_\ell) = \delta_H - z_\ell - \frac{\gamma f_L}{r+\gamma+\lambda}(\delta_H - \delta_L).$$

Since both buyers and owners of low-quality assets with utility type δ_H are indifferent between trading or not trading in a candidate freeze equilibrium, any $\alpha_b(P,\delta_H)$ and $\alpha_\ell(P,\delta_H)$ with values in $[0,1]$ are consistent with optimality. Hence, to ensure the existence of a freeze equilibrium given the refinement in (11.18), we must check that $\alpha_h(P, \delta_L) = 0$ is optimal in the candidate equilibrium, and rule out the existence of a liquid equilibrium given the steady-state distribution of assets across investors and reservation values derived above. The first task follows immediately from the observation that

$$z_\ell \geq \underline{Z}_\ell(\lambda) \Rightarrow R(\delta_H, z_\ell) < R(\delta_L, z_h).$$

For the second, note that the fraction of low-quality assets in the market would be $\widetilde{\psi}_\ell$ at the pooling price $P = \widetilde{\psi}_\ell R(\delta_H, z_\ell) + \left(1 - \widetilde{\psi}_\ell\right) R(\delta_H, z_h)$. This price fails to define an equilibrium if and only if owners of high-quality assets with utility type δ_L are not willing to sell at this price because

$$R(\delta_L, z_h) > \widetilde{\psi}_\ell R(\delta_H, z_\ell) + \left(1 - \widetilde{\psi}_\ell\right) R(\delta_H, z_h). \tag{11.21}$$

Substituting the reservation values into (11.21), one can show that the right-hand side (RHS) is strictly greater than the left-hand side (LHS) at $z_\ell = z_h = 0$; that the LHS is independent of z_ℓ, while the RHS is continuous and strictly decreasing in z_ℓ; and that the RHS is strictly less than the LHS for sufficiently large values of z_ℓ. Hence, it follows from the intermediate value theorem that there exists a unique threshold $\underline{Z}_\ell > 0$ such that (11.21) is satisfied, and solving for this threshold yields (11.19).

Now consider the liquid equilibrium in which

$$\max\left\{R(\delta_L, z_h), R(\delta_H, z_\ell)\right\} \leq P = \psi_\ell R(\delta_H, z_\ell) + (1 - \psi_\ell) R(\delta_H, z_h)$$

for some $\psi_\ell < 1$ and $\alpha_h(P, \delta_L) = \alpha_\ell(P, \delta_H) = 1$.

Using (11.5)–(11.7), one easily obtains that

$$\phi_{1,h}(\delta_L) = s_h \frac{\gamma f_L}{\gamma + \lambda},$$

and it immediately follows that the fraction of low-quality assets being sold in the candidate equilibrium is equal to $\widehat{\psi}_\ell$. Given the composition of assets, we have to check that the pooling price is sufficiently high to compensate owners of high-quality assets with utility type δ_L in the sense that

$$R(\delta_L, z_h) \leq \widehat{\psi}_\ell R(\delta_H, z_\ell) + \left(1 - \widehat{\psi}_\ell\right) R(\delta_H, z_h). \tag{11.22}$$

Since $z_h = 0$, one can show that

$$\widehat{\psi}_\ell R(\delta_H, z_\ell) + \left(1 - \widehat{\psi}_\ell\right) R(\delta_H, z_h) - R(\delta_L, z_h)$$

is a decreasing function of z_ℓ, strictly positive when $z_\ell = 0$, and strictly negative for z_ℓ sufficiently large. Hence, it follows from the intermediate value theorem that there

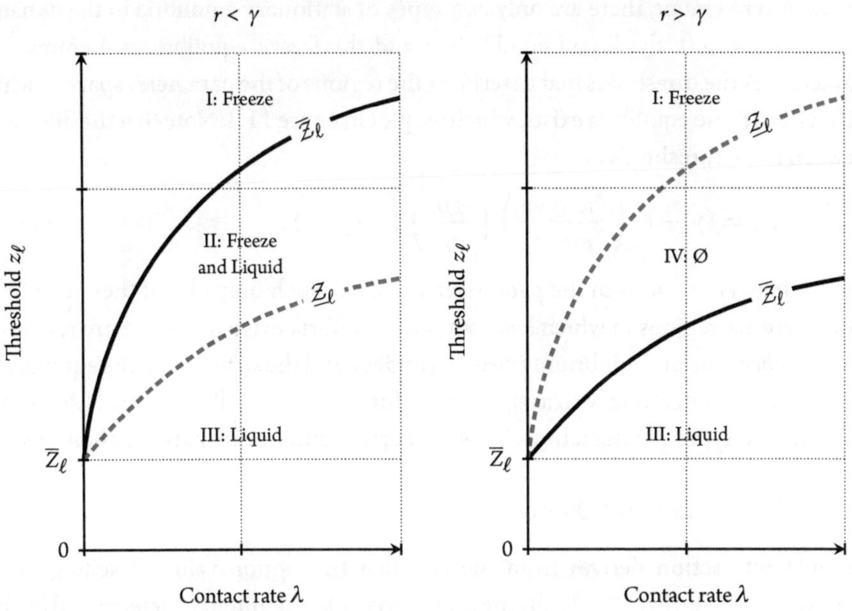

FIGURE 11.3. Equilibrium regions when $\lambda > 0$

This figure illustrates the types of equilibrium that exist depending the sign of $r - \gamma$, the contact rate λ, and the position of z_ℓ relative to $(\underline{\mathcal{Z}}_\ell, \overline{\mathcal{Z}}_\ell)$.

is a threshold $\overline{\mathcal{Z}}_\ell$ such that (11.22) is satisfied for all $z_\ell \leq \overline{\mathcal{Z}}_\ell$. To characterize this threshold, note that

$$P = R(\delta_L, z_h) > R(\delta_H, z_\ell)$$

when (11.22) holds with equality. Plugging in the reservation value equations and solving, one sees that $R(\delta_H, z_h)$ and $R(\delta_L, z_h)$ are unchanged from (11.13) and (11.14). Alternatively, when equation (11.22) holds with equality, the reservation value of investors with low-quality assets is

$$rR(\delta_H, z_\ell) = \delta_H - z_\ell - \frac{\gamma f_L}{r + \gamma + \lambda}(\delta_H - \delta_L) + \lambda\,(R(\delta_L, z_h) - R(\delta_H, z_\ell)), \tag{11.23}$$

and solving the system yields the explicit expression for $\overline{\mathcal{Z}}_\ell$ reported in the statement of the lemma. □

We leave it as an exercise (see Exercise 11.7) to prove that an equilibrium with $\alpha_h(P, \delta) \in (0, 1)$ does not exist given the equilibrium refinement in (11.18). Hence, given our refinement, there are only two types of stationary equilibria in the dynamic setting with $\lambda > 0$: the liquid equilibrium and the freeze equilibrium. Lemma 11.4 characterizes the thresholds that determine the regions of the parameter space in which each type of these equilibria exists, which we plot in figure 11.3. Note that the difference between these thresholds is

$$\overline{Z}_\ell - \underline{Z}_\ell = (\gamma - r)\left(\frac{\delta_H - \delta_L}{r+\gamma}\right)\left(\frac{s_h f_L}{s_\ell}\right)\left(\frac{\lambda}{\lambda+\gamma}\right). \tag{11.24}$$

Hence, there are regions of the parameter space in which only one of these equilibria exist; there are regions in which *both* types of equilibria exist; and there are regions in which *neither* type of equilibrium exists. To understand the structure of the equilibrium set in our dynamic setting with asymmetric information, we follow Maurin [2018] and highlight two types of interactions between current and future market conditions.

11.3.2 The Resale and Quality Effects

The first interaction derives from the fact that the option value of selling in the future—what Maurin [2018] calls the *resale effect*—is not uniquely determined by fundamentals in a market with asymmetric information about common values. Instead, there is a self-fulfilling relationship between an investor's current reservation value and her expectations of future prices; we highlight this resale effect in equation (11.23), but it also appears in the reservation value of investors in state (δ_L, z_ℓ).

In particular, in a freeze equilibrium buyers anticipate lower prices in the future, which drives down their reservation value and makes them unwilling to pay a high price today. Hence, expectations of a freeze equilibrium in the future allow for the existence of a freeze equilibrium today. Likewise, in a liquid equilibrium, expectations of high prices in the future introduce a liquidity premium for low-quality assets, which reduces the penalty from acquiring a lemon and increases an investor's current willingness to pay. Therefore, expectations of future liquidity create conditions that allow for a liquid equilibrium today.

The second interaction between current and future economic conditions operates through the relationship between prices and the composition of assets potentially for sale—what Maurin [2018] calls the *quality effect*. Specifically, when the price is low, owners of high-quality assets with utility type δ_L do not sell, and the stock of *potential* sellers of high-quality assets is relatively large. When the price is high, owners of high-quality assets with utility type δ_L sell, and the average quality of potential sellers is worse. This effect explains why $\widehat{\psi}_\ell > \widetilde{\psi}_\ell$, i.e., why the fraction of low-quality assets sold at a candidate pooling price is larger in the liquid equilibrium than in the freeze equilibrium.

11.3.3 Liquidity Fluctuations and Endogenous Volatility

To summarize, the resale effect generates a dynamic complementarity between future market conditions and current willingness to pay, and thus provides a force for multiple equilibria. This resale effect is strongest when investors are patient—i.e., when r is small—so that investors' future payoffs have sufficient impact on their current reservation value. The quality effect, in contrast, creates a negative relationship between future market conditions and current prices. This effect requires investors' types to be persistent—i.e., for γ to be small—to create a sufficiently tight relationship between investors' current decision rules and the future composition of assets potentially for sale.

From (11.24), it is easy to see that the resale effect dominates when $r < \gamma$, in which case multiple equilibria arise for $z_\ell \in (\underline{\mathcal{Z}}_\ell, \overline{\mathcal{Z}}_\ell)$. Asriyan et al. [2019] consider a discrete time model with *no* persistence in types, which corresponds in our environment to a very large value of γ. They show that the emergence of multiple, self-fulfilling equilibria can generate what they call *sentiment equilibria*, where investors' expectations of future market conditions can fluctuate according to an extrinsic random variable or sunspot. Hence, the interaction between asymmetric information and the option value of resale can generate endogenous fluctuations in liquidity, prices, volume, and welfare without changes in the underlying fundamentals.

Alternatively, when $r > \gamma$, the quality effect dominates and there are no stationary equilibria when the parameter $z_\ell \in (\underline{\mathcal{Z}}_\ell, \overline{\mathcal{Z}}_\ell)$. Instead, as Maurin [2018] shows, the equilibrium features *cycles*. In these cycles, there are intervals of time in which the market experiences freeze equilibria, when high-quality assets do not trade and $\phi_{1,h}(\delta_L)$ increases. Then, when the stock of potential sellers of high-quality assets is sufficiently large, the market transitions to a liquid equilibrium and the composition of assets for sale skews back toward low quality. Hence, when preference shocks are sufficiently persistent to rule out multiple steady-state equilibria, our OTC market model with asymmetric information suggests a second reason for excess volatility and endogenous fluctuations corresponding to predictable changes in the allocation of assets across investors.

11.3.4 Liquidity and Search Frictions

Notice immediately that

$$\lim_{\lambda\to 0} \underline{\mathcal{Z}}_\ell = \lim_{\lambda\to 0} \overline{\mathcal{Z}}_\ell = \overline{Z}_\ell,$$

so that the structure of the equilibrium set is continuous in λ. In particular, when search frictions are severe and opportunities to trade are very infrequent, the equilibrium is unique almost everywhere: only low-quality assets trade when the expected loss from acquiring a lemon is large relative to the perfect information gains from trade, and the liquid (or pooling) equilibrium arises otherwise. This result highlights, again, that multiple equilibria arise because of the option value of future trading opportunities.

As the contact rate increases, the effect on equilibrium outcomes depends on the sign of $\gamma - r$. The left panel of figure 11.3 depicts the effect of λ on the structure of the equilibrium set when $\gamma > r$. In this case, since

$$\operatorname{sign}\frac{\partial \overline{\mathcal{Z}}_\ell}{\partial \lambda} = \operatorname{sign}\left[\frac{\gamma - r}{(\gamma+\lambda)^2}\left(\frac{\gamma s_h f_L}{s_\ell}\right) + \frac{\gamma f_L(r+\gamma)}{(r+\gamma+\lambda)^2}\right],$$

it is clear that $\overline{\mathcal{Z}}_\ell$ is unambiguously increasing, as is $\underline{\mathcal{Z}}_\ell$. Hence, as λ increases, the region in which the liquid equilibrium exists expands and the region in which the freeze equilibrium exists contracts. In this sense, *reducing trading frictions eases the illiquidity effects of adverse selection.* Intuitively, when investors are sufficiently patient, the opportunity to resell an asset when they acquire a lemon increases their current willingness to pay. If these opportunities are sufficiently frequent, the reservation values of investors increase enough to support a liquid equilibrium. For similar reasons, the region of multiplicity expands as λ increases, too, because the existence of more opportunities to trade strengthens the resale effect and thus creates a greater degree of complementarity between current and future market conditions.

The effects of search frictions on liquidity are more subtle in the case where $\gamma < r$, because the sign of $\frac{\partial \overline{\mathcal{Z}}_\ell}{\partial \lambda}$ is then ambiguous. For example, when $\gamma \approx r$ or s_ℓ is large relative to s_h, then the threshold $\overline{\mathcal{Z}}_\ell$ is increasing and the effects of the contact rate on the set of liquid and freeze equilibrium are similar to the case in which $\gamma > r$. Moreover, since $\underline{\mathcal{Z}}_\ell$ is unambiguously increasing, the region in which the freeze equilibrium exists is shrinking as λ gets larger. However, it is possible that $\overline{\mathcal{Z}}_\ell$ is decreasing in λ in some regions of the parameter space. In this case, an increase in λ can strengthen the quality effect and, thus, expand the region where neither a liquid nor a freeze equilibrium exists, i.e., the region where we conjecture that there are nonstationary cycles, oscillating between liquid and freeze states.

11.3.5 Interventions in Frozen Markets

Given the harmful effects associated with *frozen* financial markets, a natural question is whether government interventions can help restore liquidity. One specific intervention that has been studied is the effect of government asset purchases, which were utilized in several markets after the GFC. Chiu and Koeppl [2016] study this intervention in a related model and find that the mere promise of asset purchases in the future can cause an increase in current reservation values through the resale effect. If this effect is strong enough, the announcement of asset purchases alone can be sufficient to transition the market from a freeze equilibrium to a liquid equilibrium.

The optimal timing of such an intervention is subtle, however, and can depend on the degree of search frictions. For example, studying nonstationary dynamics in a frictional market with adverse selection, Camargo and Lester [2014] and Fuchs and Skrzypacz [2015] show that frequent opportunities to trade in the future can induce owners of low-quality assets to wait for prices to improve, rather than selling their assets. This slows down the improvement in the composition of assets, through the quality effect, and hence the process by which the market unfreezes. Hence, as Fuchs and Skrzypacz [2015] emphasize, sometimes frictions that limit future trading opportunities—such as search frictions—can be welfare improving.

11.4 Exercises

Exercise 11.5: Prove that the function $R(\delta, z)$ is decreasing in z.

Exercise 11.6: Prove that the steady-state distributions and reservation values converge to (11.11) and (11.12) as $\lambda \to 0$.

Exercise 11.7: In the dynamic model with $\lambda > 0$, prove that there does not exist a stationary equilibrium with $\alpha_h(P, \delta_L) \in (0, 1)$ that survives the equilibrium refinement defined in (11.18).

Exercise 11.8: Suppose $r < \gamma$, $z_h = 0$, and $z_\ell \in \left(\underline{Z}_\ell, \overline{Z}_\ell\right)$.

1. Solve explicitly for the price P^1 in the liquid equilibrium and P^0 in the freeze equilibrium. Prove that $P^1 > P^0$.
2. Consider an intervention in which the government offers to buy unlimited quantities of the asset at a price $P \in \left(P^0, P^1\right)$. How does this intervention change the set of possible equilibria?
3. Calculate the cost of such a policy to the government.

11.5 Notes and References

The material of this chapter draws heavily from Hugonnier, Lester, and Weill [2024b], which builds on a large literature that studies the effects of asymmetric information in decentralized markets. Though we do not attempt to provide an exhaustive review here, several papers are worth mentioning. Chiu and Koeppl [2016] were among the first to introduce asymmetric information over asset quality into the framework of Duffie, Gârleanu, and Pedersen [2005], to characterize the steady-state equilibrium, and to highlight the possibility of multiple equilibria. Earlier papers that introduced uncertainty over asset quality into models of decentralized trade include Blouin [2003], Inderst [2005], and Moreno and Wooders [2010]. Maurin [2018] studies a related discrete-time environment. He identifies the resale and quality effects, explores how their relative strength depends on the persistence of preference shocks, and illustrates the implications for equilibrium outcomes. Asriyan, Fuchs, and Green [2019] study a dynamic setting with asymmetric information, too, but assume that preference shocks are not persistent at all. In this setting, they show that multiple, self-fulfilling equilibria can arise and explore how sunspots can generate endogenous fluctuations.

A second, related literature studies the nonstationary dynamics of prices and allocations in frictional markets when the idiosyncratic value or quality of an asset cannot be observed by potential buyers; see Janssen and Roy [2002], Camargo and Lester [2014], and Fuchs and Skrzypacz [2015], among others. These papers highlight that investors who own low-quality assets have lower reservation values—and thus tend to sell faster—which leads to improving asset quality over time. In a related setting, Zou [2019] allows investors to acquire information before making an offer, and shows that endogenizing this margin can lead to so-called liquidity traps.

Similar topics have also been explored in environments where prices and allocations are determined subject to the frictions and price-setting protocols of competitive search models. In these models, owners of different-quality assets tend to sort themselves into different submarkets based on prices and trade probabilities, so that separation occurs endogenously. See Kim [2012], Guerrieri and Shimer [2014], Chang [2018], Williams [2021], and Auster and Gottardi [2019]. Nozawa and Tsoy [2023] take a different approach, based on Tsoy [2018, 2019], that allows them to consider two-sided private information. However, as in the papers cited above, in their approach there are trading delays in equilibrium that endogenously depend on asset quality.

Finally, there is a long history of studying information aggregation and learning about the *aggregate* state in decentralized trading environments, going back to (at least) Wolinsky [1990] and Blouin and Serrano [2001]. In contrast to our environment—where uninformed agents know the aggregate distribution of asset quality but cannot observe the quality of any individual asset—these papers study an environment where the uninformed are trying to learn about the quality of *all* assets. More recent contributions to this literature include Duffie and Manso [2007], Duffie, Malamud, and Manso

[2009], Golosov, Lorenzoni, and Tsyvinski [2014], Lauermann and Wolinsky [2016], Lauermann, Merzyn, and Gábor [2018], and Kaya and Kim [2018].

Though many of the papers cited above explore the effects of information frictions in decentralized models of trade, few study the *interaction* between search and information frictions. Lester, Shourideh, Venkateswaran, and Zetlin-Jones [2019] study this interaction explicitly in a frictional setting based on the search-theoretic framework of Burdett and Judd [1983]. They find that reducing search frictions can make it more difficult for buyers to make offers that separate owners of low and high assets, and that this can ultimately lead to a reduction in ex ante welfare. In a dynamic model of OTC trading through dealers, Lester, Shourideh, Venkateswaran, and Zetlin-Jones [2023] also show that reducing search frictions can have unexpected effects in the presence of asymmetric information. In particular, they show that reducing frictions can slow down the speed with which dealers learn about the aggregate state, leading to a reduction in market liquidity as dealers set wider bid-ask spreads to compensate for their informational disadvantage.

12

OTC vs. Centralized Markets

The existence of OTC markets may seem puzzling. After all, technologies such as centralized limit-order books—that closely resemble idealized Walrasian auctions—have been available for decades and would seemingly produce more efficient economic outcomes. The existence of OTC markets becomes even more puzzling when such markets coexist with more centralized exchanges; see, e.g., the discussion of bond trading in Biais and Green [2019]. In such instances, despite the availability of a centralized exchange, we observe some participants *choosing* to trade OTC instead. These observations have given rise to two open questions: why did OTC trading arrangements emerge, and why have they persisted to this day?

These theoretical questions have important practical implications as well. For instance, inspired by the belief that OTC markets can produce undesirable outcomes, regulators have introduced measures to make such markets more centralized. As a concrete example, the Dodd-Frank Wall Street Reform and Consumer Protection Act of 2010 mandated that swaps be traded on centralized, multilateral platforms called Swap Execution Facilities (SEFs). Similarly, the European Market Infrastructure Regulation (EMIR), adopted by the European Union in 2012, aims at enhancing transparency and limiting credit risk by requiring most derivatives trades to be centrally cleared and reported. What are the consequences, intended or otherwise, of migrating trading activity from OTC markets to more centralized venues?

To satisfactorily answer these questions, one needs to model the demand of investors for trading in OTC vs. centralized markets. In doing so, one could focus on a variety of distinctions between OTC and centralized markets. These include differences in pretrade price transparency and competition for order flow; different methods of price determination and settlement in bilateral vs. multilateral trading arrangements; or differences in the way that information is revealed to other market participants after a trade has occurred. In this chapter, we develop a very simple search-theoretic model of venue choice that focuses on differences in the time it takes to locate a counterparty in OTC markets, relative to centralized exchanges.

In this model, we assume that investors can either search for a dealer to trade with in a semicentralized OTC market or pay an exogenous cost to trade instantly in a centralized market. To endogenize the contact rate in the OTC market, we assume that dealers choose whether to enter the market. Within this model, we characterize the equilibrium and determine the set of investors who find it optimal to trade in OTC vs. centralized markets. We find that concentration of volume in OTC markets can, in some cases, be a self-fulfilling phenomenon. Finally, we conduct a welfare analysis to study whether OTC markets are too large. We find that, relative to the social optimum, investors participate too little in the OTC market and that dealers enter either too little or too much, depending on their bargaining power.

12.1 The Market Setting

To introduce a meaningful trade-off between OTC and centralized markets, we modify the semicentralized market model of chapter 4 in two ways. First, we endogenize the contact rate by assuming that there is free entry of dealers in the OTC market. Second, we assume that investors can pay a fixed cost to participate directly in the competitive interdealer market. We borrow the assumption of a fixed participation cost from the work of Spulber [1996], Hall and Rust [2003], and Miao [2005]. This device is perhaps the simplest way to create a trade-off between OTC and centralized markets, but it also captures an important aspect of real-world markets. For example, Allen and Wittwer [2023] argue that fixed costs of trading are an important determinant of the decision to participate in the OTC or the centralized market for Canadian government bonds. In the Notes and References of this chapter, we review papers that have explored other determinants of this tradeoff.

To simplify the analysis we assume throughout this chapter that the asset supply is $s = \frac{1}{2}$ and that the distribution of investors' utility flows admits a density that is symmetric around the mean

$$m \equiv \mathbf{E}^F[x] = \int_{\underline{\delta}}^{\overline{\delta}} x f(x) dx = \frac{1}{2}\left(\underline{\delta} + \overline{\delta}\right)$$

in the sense that

$$f(\delta) = g\left(|m - \delta|\right) \tag{12.1}$$

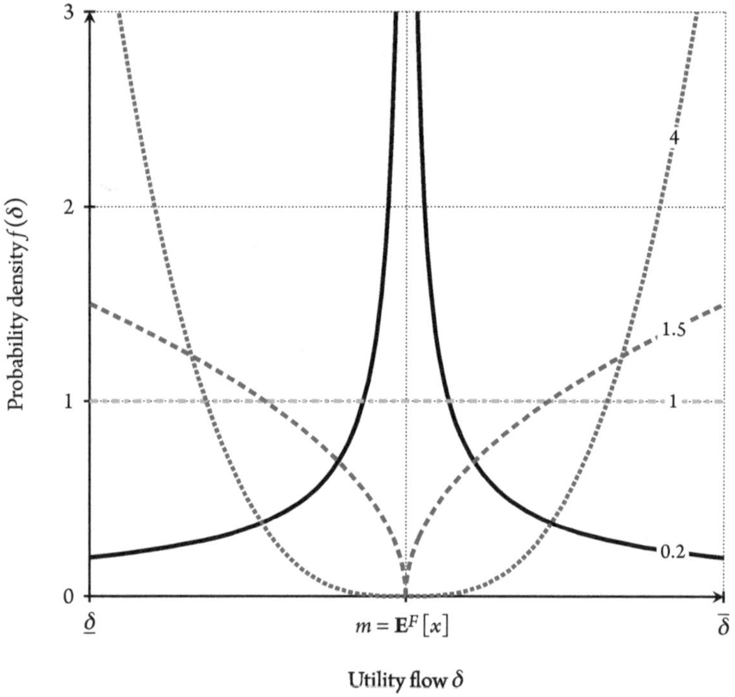

FIGURE 12.1. Symmetric power distributions

This figure illustrates the family of symmetric densities obtained from (12.1) by using the function $g_b(x)$ of (12.2) with $b \in \{0.2, 1, 1.5, 2, 4\}$.

for some nonnegative function such that $g(x) = 0$ for $x \geq \underline{\delta} - m$ and that integrates to $\frac{1}{2}$ on $[0, \underline{\delta} - m]$. As illustrated in figure 12.1, a flexible class of such distributions can be obtained from (12.1) by using the family of power functions defined by

$$g_b(x) \equiv \mathbf{1}_{\{m+x\leq\bar{\delta}\}} \frac{b}{|\mathcal{D}|^b} |2x|^{b-1} \tag{12.2}$$

for some $b > 0$. We will use this particular functional form in our illustrations of the properties of the equilibrium later in the chapter.

The asset is initially allocated randomly across investors. As a result, the density of utility flows among investors with $q \in \{0, 1\}$ assets is

$$\phi_{q0}(\delta) = \big(qs + (1-q)(1-s)\big) f(s).$$

At time $t=0$, each dealer decides once and for all whether to enter the OTC market by paying a cost $c>0$. We assume that customers meet dealers more frequently in the OTC market when more dealers enter. Specifically, investors' contact rate with dealers is given by

$$\lambda \equiv \Lambda(\mu_d),$$

where μ_d is the measure of dealers in the OTC market and $\Lambda(\mu)$ is a continuous, strictly increasing, strictly concave, and continuously differentiable function such that $\Lambda(0)=0$. The economic meaning of concavity is that the meeting technology has decreasing returns to scale: when more dealers enter, the flow rate of meetings *per dealer*, $\Lambda(\mu_d)/\mu_d$, is decreasing.

Investors can trade in two ways. First, they can at any time pay a fixed cost $\kappa>0$ to trade instantly in the interdealer market. Second, they can trade indirectly through dealers as in the semicentralized market model of chapter 4: they contact a randomly selected dealer with Poisson intensity λ defined as above and bargain over the terms of trade. As in previous chapters, the bargaining power of the dealer is denoted by $\theta \in [0,1]$.

We solve for an equilibrium in two steps. First, in section 12.2 we solve for the equilibrium price and allocation, taking as given the search intensity in the OTC market induced by dealer entry. Second, in section 12.3, we endogenize the search intensity via the dealers' free entry condition. In section 12.4 we compare the equilibrium outcome to the social optimum.

12.2 Equilibrium Given Dealer Entry

Our symmetry assumption allows us to guess and verify that there exists an equilibrium in which the interdealer price P immediately reaches its steady-state level at time $t=0$. Since, in semi-centralized markets, investors' decisions may depend on time only through the interdealer price, this in turn implies that their value functions are time invariant.

12.2.1 Reservation Values

Let $\mathcal{P}_q \subseteq \mathcal{D}$ denote the set of utility flows such that investors who hold q unit of the asset find it optimal to participate in the centralized market. For nonowners, $\mathcal{P}_0$ is the set of utility flows such that

$$V(0,\delta)=V(1,\delta)-(P+\kappa) \tag{12.3}$$

and

$$rV(0,\delta) \geq \gamma \mathbf{E}^F \left[V(0,x) - V(0,\delta)\right] + \lambda_\theta \left(R(\delta) - P\right)^+, \tag{12.4}$$

where $\lambda_\theta \equiv \lambda(1-\theta)$ denotes the bargaining-adjusted rate at which an investor contacts a dealer, $V(q,\delta)$ denotes the value function of an investor with utility flow $\delta \in \mathcal{D}$ and asset holdings $q \in \{0,1\}$, and

$$R(\delta) \equiv V(1,\delta) - V(0,\delta)$$

denotes her reservation value. Condition (12.3) requires that the value function $V(0,\delta)$ of a nonowner who finds it optimal to participate in the centralized market be equal to the cost of acquiring the asset at price $P+\kappa$ and continuing with the value function $V(1,\delta)$. On the other hand, condition (12.4) requires that the value function of a nonowner with utility flow in $\mathcal{P}_0$ be at least as large as the value associated with the decision of searching in the OTC market instead of participating in the centralized market.

Consider a nonowners with utility flow $\delta \in \mathcal{P}_0$. Equation (12.3) and the strict positivity of the participation cost imply that

$$V(0,\delta) + (P-\kappa) = V(1,\delta) - 2\kappa < V(1,\delta).$$

Therefore, $\delta \in \mathcal{P}_0 \Rightarrow \delta \notin \mathcal{P}_1$. In words, if a nonowners finds it optimal to participate in the centralized market, then an owner with the same utility flow cannot find it optimal to do the same. This intuitive result means that it cannot be optimal to buy and sell at the same time, as this would incur the strictly positive *round trip* cost 2κ. In addition, it implies that the value function of an owner with $\delta \in \mathcal{P}_0$ equals the value of searching:

$$rV(1,\delta) = \delta + \gamma \mathbf{E}^F \left[V(1,x) - V(1,0)\right] + \lambda_\theta \left(P - R(\delta)\right)^+. \tag{12.5}$$

Combining (12.3), (12.4), and (12.5) shows that for $\delta \in \mathcal{P}_0$ the reservation value function satisfies

$$P+\kappa = R(\delta) \geq P-\kappa$$

and

$$rR(\delta) \leq \delta + \gamma \mathbf{E}^F \left[R(x) - R(\gamma)\right] + \lambda_\theta \left(P - R(\delta)\right).$$

A similar analysis for utility flows in the sets $\mathcal{P}_1$ and $\mathcal{D} \backslash (\mathcal{P}_0 \cup \mathcal{P}_1)$ allows us to establish the following result.

Lemma 12.1: The reservation value function of investors is the unique solution to the variational inequality

$$rR(\delta) = \min\Big\{r(P+\kappa), \max\{r(P-\kappa),$$
$$\delta + \gamma \mathbf{E}^F[R(x) - R(\delta)] + \lambda_\theta (P - R(\delta))\}\Big\}.$$

In particular, the reservation value function is bounded from below by $P-\kappa$ and from above by $P+\kappa$, nondecreasing, and absolutely continuous.

Proof. The result follows from contraction mapping arguments similar to those of chapter 3. See Exercise 12.6 for details. □

Lemma 12.1 shows that the reservation value function solves the usual equation from chapter 4, adjusted for the option of trading in the centralized market at a fixed cost. Importantly, the reservation value of an investor can never be smaller than $P-\kappa$ or larger than $P+\kappa$, because if it was, the investor would then find it optimal to pay the fixed cost and instantly trade in the centralized market at the interdealer market price.

As in previous chapters, in equilibrium, there must be some marginal utility flow $\delta^\star \in \mathcal{D}$ such that $P = R(\delta^\star)$, for otherwise the market would not clear because all investors would be on the same side of both markets. This in turn implies that some investors must find it optimal not to participate in the centralized market and that $\mathcal{D} \setminus (\mathcal{P}_0 \cup \mathcal{P}_1)$ is an interval $(\delta_s, \delta_b) \ni \delta^\star$. For all utility flows in that set, searching in the OTC market is optimal for both owners and nonowners, meaning that

$$(r+\gamma)R(\delta) = \delta + \gamma \mathbf{E}^F[R(x)] + \lambda_\theta (P - R(\delta)).$$

In particular, differentiating both sides with respect to δ shows that on this interval $R'(\delta) = 1/(r+\gamma+\lambda_\theta)$. Combining this result with the fact that the reservation value of a marginal investor is equal to the interdealer price, we deduce that

$$R(\delta) = P + \frac{\delta - \delta^\star}{r+\gamma+\lambda_\theta}, \qquad \delta \notin \mathcal{P}_0 \cup \mathcal{P}_1. \tag{12.6}$$

Substituting this expression into the value-matching conditions $R(\delta_s) = P - \kappa$ and $R(\delta_b) = P + \kappa$ gives a system of two equations that explicitly characterizes the participation decisions of investors.

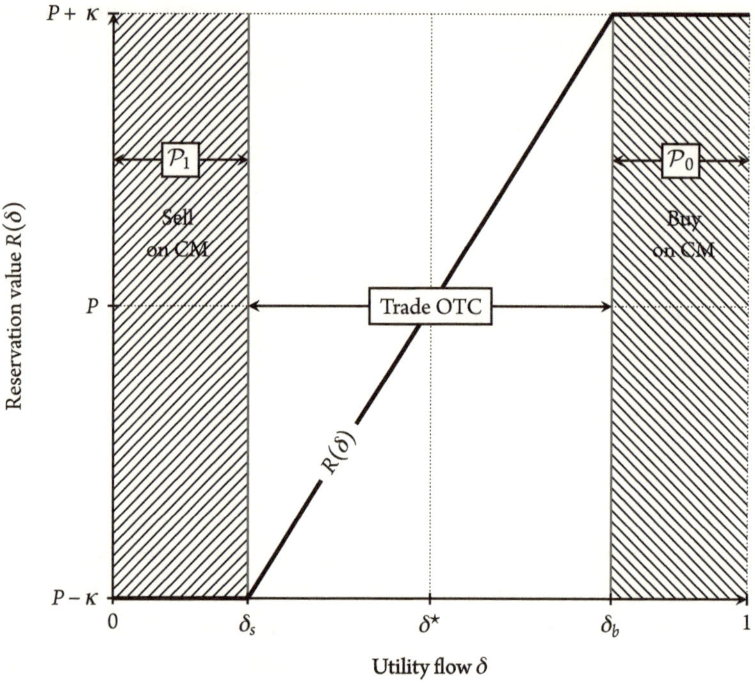

FIGURE 12.2. The reservation value function

This figure illustrates the shape of the reservation value function and the optimal participation decisions of investors in the centralized (CM) and OTC markets. The parameters of the model used to generate the figure are $\mathcal{D} = (0, 1)$, $r = 0.05$, $\theta = 0.5$, $\gamma = 1$, $\lambda = 80$, $\kappa = 0.008$, and $P = 10$.

Lemma 12.2: Let

$$\delta_s \equiv \max\left\{\underline{\delta}, \delta^\star - \kappa\,(r + \gamma + \lambda_\theta)\right\}, \tag{12.7a}$$

$$\delta_b \equiv \min\left\{\overline{\delta}, \delta^\star + \kappa\,(r + \gamma + \lambda_\theta)\right\}. \tag{12.7b}$$

Then the sets of investors who find it optimal to participate in the centralized market are given by $\mathcal{P}_1 = (\underline{\delta}, \delta_s]$ and $\mathcal{P}_0 = [\delta_b, \overline{\delta})$.

Investors find it optimal to participate in the centralized market if and only if their trade surplus

$$\frac{|\delta - \delta^\star|}{r + \gamma + \lambda_\theta} \tag{12.8}$$

exceeds the fixed participation cost κ. Hence, an owner participates if her utility flow is sufficiently small while a nonowner participates if her utility flow is sufficiently large; see figure 12.2 for an illustration. Furthermore, the explicit expression of the thresholds (δ_s, δ_b) shows that the set of participants in the centralized market naturally shrinks as the participation cost κ increases and as the interest rate r, the switching rate γ, or the bargaining-adjusted contact rate λ_θ increase, since any such change results in a lower trade surplus. In particular, if

$$\kappa\,(r+\gamma+\lambda_\theta) \geq \max\left\{\overline{\delta}-\delta^\star, \delta^\star-\underline{\delta}\right\},$$

then no investor participates in the centralized market, because the cost is too large and/or the marginal surplus is too small.

12.2.2 Symmetric Equilibrium

Given our assumptions that the asset supply $s=\frac{1}{2}$ and that the probability density of utility flows is symmetric around its mean, it is natural to conjecture that in equilibrium the marginal utility flow that determines the interdealer price is equal to the mean utility flow: $\delta^\star = m$. To justify this conjecture we need to verify that markets clear at all times.

INITIAL MARKET CLEARING

At time $t=0$, owners with $\delta<\delta_s$ and nonowners with $\delta>\delta_b$ pay the participation cost to instantly trade in the centralized market. Keeping in mind that the asset is initially allocated randomly, the market clearing condition can thus be stated as

$$sF(\delta_s) = (1-s)\,(1-F(\delta_b)), \tag{12.9}$$

and one can easily verify that this condition holds because $s=1-s$ and the thresholds (δ_s, δ_b) in (12.7) are symmetric around $m=\delta^\star$.

MARKET CLEARING AT $t>0$

After the initial date, owners with utility flows in $[\delta_s, \delta^\star]$ search to sell in the OTC market, and all owners immediately pay κ to sell in the centralized market if they switch to a utility flow $\delta<\delta_s$. Likewise, nonowners with utility flows in $[\delta^\star, \delta_b]$ search to buy in the OTC market, and all nonowners pay κ to instantly buy in the centralized market if they switch to a utility flow $\delta>\delta_b$. Taken together, these observations show that after the initial time, the market clearing condition is given by

$$\gamma sF(\delta_s) + \lambda\int_{\delta_s}^{\delta^\star}\phi_{1t}(x)dx = \gamma\,(1-s)\,(1-F(\delta_b)) + \lambda\int_{\delta^\star}^{\delta_b}\phi_{0t}(x)dx.$$

On each side of this condition, the first term collects the flow of investors who trade in the centralized market, whereas the second term captures the flow of investors who trade with a dealer in the OTC market. To see that this condition holds when $\delta^\star = m$, observe that the first terms on each side are equal due to the initial market clearing condition (12.9) and that, in a symmetric equilibrium, the densities of utility flows must be such that

$$\phi_{1t}(\delta) = \phi_{0t}(2\delta^\star - \delta), \qquad \delta \in \mathcal{D},$$

to ensure the symmetry of the asset allocation.

We close this section by deriving the equilibrium densities of utility flows among owners and nonowners, which we will need to study both entry by dealers and the social planner's problem.

Proposition 12.3: In equilibrium

$$\phi_{1t}(\delta) = f(\delta) - \phi_{0t}(\delta) = f(\delta) \cdot \begin{cases} 0, & \delta \leq \delta_s, \\ \frac{\gamma + \lambda e^{-(\gamma+\lambda)t}}{2(\gamma+\lambda)}, & \delta \in (\delta_s, \delta^\star], \\ 1 - \frac{\gamma+\lambda e^{-(\gamma+\lambda)t}}{2(\gamma+\lambda)}, & \delta \in [\delta^\star, \delta_b), \\ 1, & \delta \geq \delta_b, \end{cases} \tag{12.10}$$

for any value $\lambda \equiv \Lambda(\mu_d)$ of the contact rate with dealers.

Proof. The first equality in (12.10) follows from the fact that the densities must sum up to $f(\delta)$. Since owners with $\delta \leq \delta_s$ and nonowners with $\delta \geq \delta_b$ instantly trade in the centralized market, it is clear that $\phi_{1t}(\delta) = f(\delta) - \phi_{0t}(\delta)$ must be equal to zero for all $\delta \leq \delta_s$ and to $f(\delta)$ for all $\delta \geq \delta_b$.

Over the interval $(\delta_s, \delta^\star]$ of owners who find it optimal to search in the OTC market, we have that the density evolves according to

$$\dot{\phi}_{1t}(\delta) = \gamma s f(\delta) - \gamma \phi_{1t}(\delta) - \lambda \phi_{1t}(\delta),$$

where the first two terms on the right account for the inflow and outflow due to type switching, while the third term accounts for the outflow due to trade with dealers. Solving this ordinary differential equation subject to $\phi_{10}(\delta) = sf(\delta)$ gives the second line in (12.10). By symmetry we then deduce that

$$\phi_{0t}(\delta) = \phi_{1t}(2\delta^\star - \delta) = \frac{\gamma + \lambda e^{-(\gamma+\lambda)t}}{2(\gamma + \lambda)} f(\delta)$$

on the interval $[\delta^\star, \delta_b)$ of nonowners who find it optimal to search in the OTC market, and the third line in (12.10) now follows from the fact that the densities sum up to the population density $f(\delta)$. □

12.3 Free Entry of Dealers

Next, we study the equilibrium arrival rate of meetings with dealers in the OTC market, assuming that dealers can enter at a fixed cost c.

To formulate the free entry condition, recall that when a dealer meets an investor with utility flow $\delta \in \mathcal{D}\backslash(\mathcal{P}_0 \cup \mathcal{P}_1)$, she appropriates a fraction θ of the surplus and thus makes a profit equal to

$$\theta|R(\delta) - P| = \frac{\theta\,|\delta - \delta^\star|}{r + \gamma + (1-\theta)\Lambda(\mu_d)},$$

where the equality follows from (12.6) and the definition of the contact rate. At time $t \geq 0$, the flow rate of such trades *per dealer* is

$$\Gamma_t\,(\delta, \mu_d) \equiv \Lambda(\mu_d)\,\left(\mathbf{1}_{\{\delta<\delta^\star\}}\phi_{1t}(\delta) + \mathbf{1}_{\{\delta>\delta^\star\}}\phi_{0t}(\delta)\right)/\,\mu_d,$$

where the numerator represents the aggregate flow of trades and the denominator is the measure of dealers. Therefore, aggregating across utility flows and over time shows that the *free entry condition* is given by

$$c \geq \int_0^\infty e^{-rt}\left(\int_{\delta_s(\mu_d)}^{\delta_b(\mu_d)} \frac{\theta\,|x - \delta^\star|\,\Gamma_t\,(x, \mu_d)}{r + \gamma + (1-\theta)\,\Lambda(\mu_d)}dx\right)dt,$$

with equality if $\mu_d > 0$. Substituting the densities of Proposition 12.3 into this expression, integrating, and rearranging, we obtain that the free entry condition can be equivalently stated as

$$\frac{C(\lambda)}{\lambda} \geq \theta S\,(\lambda(1-\theta))\,M(\lambda), \quad \text{with equality if } \lambda > 0, \tag{12.11}$$

where the function

$$C(x) \equiv c\Lambda^{-1}\,(x)$$

captures the total entry costs incurred by the dealer sector when the contact rate with investors is equal to λ, and

$$S(x) \equiv \int_0^{\kappa(r+\gamma+x)} \frac{yg(y)\,dy}{r\,(r+\gamma+x)},$$

$$M(x) \equiv \frac{r+\gamma}{r+\gamma+x}.$$

The left-hand side of (12.11) is the average cost of search intensity incurred by the dealer sector. The right-hand side is the profit per unit of search intensity, which is the product of two terms. The first term, $\theta S(\lambda(1-\theta))$, is the present discounted value of dealers' profits when they trade with investors, assuming a constantly random distribution of assets among those investors who find it optimal to search in the OTC market (with utility flows in δ_s, δ_b). The second term, $M(\lambda) \leq 1$, adjusts this present value down to properly account for the fact that assets do not, in fact, remain allocated at random: over time, the OTC market allocates more and more assets to investors with $\delta \geq \delta^\star$, so dealers meet fewer and fewer investors in (δ_s, δ_b) with whom they have gain from trade.

The free entry condition (12.11) reveals that there are several forces creating *strategic substitutability* in the entry decisions of dealers. First, when λ increases, the average cost of search intensity, $C(\lambda)/\lambda$, increases as well, making it more costly to enter. Second, $M(\lambda)$ decreases: the fact that the asset is better allocated when λ is larger implies that there are fewer investors who gain from trading with dealers. Third, since investors can meet dealers more frequently going forward, the trade surplus in (12.8) decreases for all utility flows, which in turn implies a reduction in the profits that dealers make in every OTC trade.

However, the free entry condition also reveals the existence of a force for *strategic complementarity* stemming from the participation decisions of investors. Namely, when λ increases, investors participate more in the OTC market and less in the centralized market because their trade surplus (12.8) decreases. This extensive margin effect may lead to increased dealer profits, especially if the increase in the contact rate λ induces a large mass of investors to migrate from the centralized to the OTC market.

Proposition 12.4: There exists an equilibrium. Moreover,

1. If the map $\lambda \mapsto \theta S(\lambda(1-\theta))M(\lambda)$ is increasing in some interval of λ, then there are cost functions such that multiple equilibria exist.
2. If the map $x \mapsto xg(x)$ is strictly decreasing, then the equilibrium is unique and the equilibrium measure of dealers is increasing in θ and κ.

Proof. To prove the existence claim, note first that if

$$C'(0) = \lim_{\lambda \to 0} \frac{C(\lambda)}{\lambda} \geq \theta S(0)M(0).$$

then there exists an equilibrium in which no dealer enters. Otherwise, using the fact that $g(y) = 0$ for all sufficiently large $y > 0$, we deduce that

$$\lim_{\lambda \to \infty} \theta S(\lambda(1-\theta))M(\lambda) = 0, \tag{12.12}$$

and existence follows from an application of the intermediate value theorem because the functions C, S, and M are clearly continuous.

To establish the existence of multiple equilibria, suppose that the condition of the statement holds so that there exists $\lambda_1 < \lambda_2$ such that

$$\theta S(\lambda_1(1-\theta))M(\lambda_1) < \theta S(\lambda_2(1-\theta))M(\lambda_2).$$

Combining this property with (12.12) and the intermediate value theorem shows that there exists $\lambda_3 > \lambda_2$ such that

$$\mathfrak{c} \equiv \theta S(\lambda_1(1-\theta))M(\lambda_1) = \theta S(\lambda_3(1-\theta))M(\lambda_3),$$

and it follows that both λ_1 and λ_3 are equilibria for $C(\lambda) \equiv \mathfrak{c}\lambda$. Finally, a direct calculation using (A.20) shows that

$$S'(x) = \int_0^{\kappa(r+\gamma+x)} \frac{\kappa\,(r+\gamma+x)\,g(\kappa(r+\gamma+x)) - yg(y)}{r+\gamma+x} dy.$$

If the map $y \mapsto yg(y)$ is strictly decreasing, then this derivative is strictly negative. Since the function $M(\lambda)$ is also strictly decreasing, this shows that the right-hand side of (12.11) is strictly decreasing, and uniqueness follows. The remaining comparative statics follow from straightforward algebra. □

The first result of the proposition establishes the possibility of multiple equilibria, as illustrated in figure 12.3. In this numerical example, there are three equilibria. In the first equilibrium $\lambda = 0$, so that no dealer enters the OTC market and the free entry condition holds as a strict inequality. In the intermediate equilibrium, some dealers enter the OTC market, and investors are active in both the OTC and centralized markets. Finally, in the equilibrium with the highest value of λ, even more dealers enter the OTC market and, as a result, no investors participate in the centralized market.

The existence of multiple equilibria sheds light on certain historical patterns in the data. For example, Biais and Green [2019] document that bond trading migrated from a centralized exchange to an OTC market in the mid-1940s and conjecture that this change may have been due to liquidity spillovers. In particular, they write, "as institutions and dealers became more prevalent in bond trading, they tipped the balance in favor of the OTC markets" (p. 251). Our analysis offers a more formal, yet nuanced, description of this transition. To see why, note that an increase in the prevalence of dealers is not, in and of itself, sufficient to tip the balance toward OTC trading. Indeed, as more dealers enter, the pool of profitable trades shrinks and transaction costs decline,

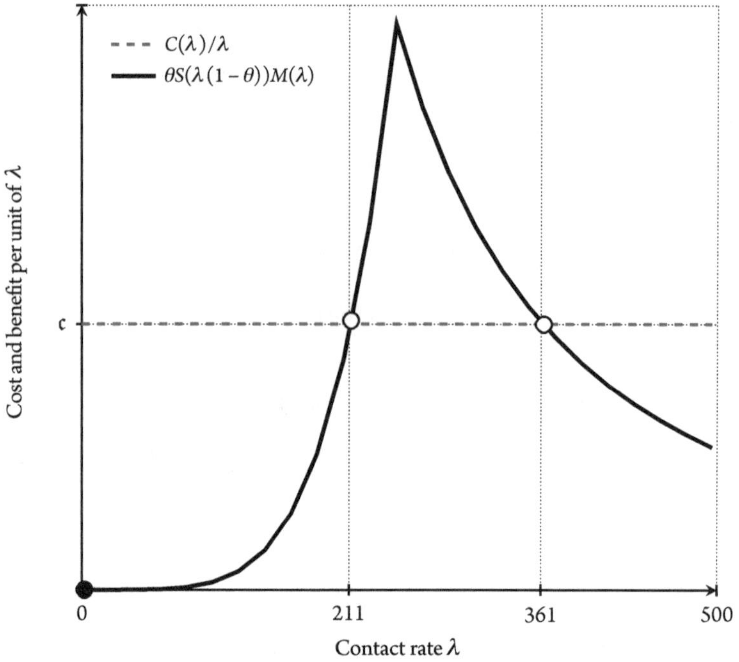

FIGURE 12.3. Multiplicity of entry equilibria

This figure illustrates the existence of multiple equilibria in a model with a linear cost function $C(\lambda) = \mathfrak{c}\lambda$, the same parameters as in figure 12.2, and a probability density of utility flows obtained from the function $g_b(x)$ defined in (12.2) by setting $b = 7$. The ∘ indicates an equilibrium with entry while the • indicates the equilibrium where no dealer enters the OTC market. The kink in the solid curve corresponds to the lowest contact rate such that all investors find it optimal to participate in the OTC market.

thus discouraging further entry. Hence, for the balance to tip toward OTC trading, it is necessary that the entry of dealers attract a large mass of high-surplus investors that one could interpret as the large institutions that Biais and Green [2019] argue were becoming more prevalent during that time period.

The second result in Proposition 12.4 provides a condition for equilibrium uniqueness. Intuitively, this condition requires that the total utility flow of marginal OTC market participants, $xg(x)$, decrease as participation increases. Under this condition, the strategic complementarity induced by the participation margin is sufficiently weak that multiplicity does not arise. Finally, the third result in the proposition establishes that more dealers find it optimal to enter the OTC market when they have more bargaining power and when participation costs in the centralized market are large.

12.4 Welfare Analysis

Given the above description of the equilibrium, we now turn to the normative task of characterizing the socially optimal market structure. We address this problem in two steps. First, we solve for the socially optimal participation and trade decisions at all times, taking as given any measure of dealers μ_d or, equivalently, any contact rate λ. Second, we solve for the socially optimal level of dealers entry at the initial time $t = 0$.

12.4.1 *Socially Optimal Participation and Trade*

The planner chooses feasible trades for all investors but is bound to the same trading technology. As a result, trades in the OTC market must occur at rate λ, while trades in the centralized market can be arranged instantly but incur a fixed cost κ. Using optimal control as in Weill [2007], one can show that the solution of the planner's problem has the same structure as the above equilibrium. Specifically, it is socially optimal for investors to trade in the centralized market if their utility flow satisfies $|\delta - \delta^\star| > \beta$ and to trade OTC otherwise, where $\delta^\star = m$ and β is a participation threshold to be determined.

As a first step, we note that for a given contact rate λ the social welfare function can be written as

$$\begin{aligned} W(\beta|\lambda) &= \int_0^\infty e^{-rt} \left(\int_{\delta^\star}^{\bar{\delta}} \delta f(\delta) d\delta \right) dt \\ &+ \int_0^\infty e^{-rt} \left(\int_{\delta^\star - \beta}^{\delta^\star} \delta \phi_{1t}(\delta) d\delta - \int_{\delta^\star}^{\delta^\star + \beta} \delta \phi_{0t}(\delta) d\delta \right) dt \\ &- \kappa \left(1 + \gamma \int_0^\infty e^{-rt}\, dt \right) \left(sF(\delta^\star - \beta) + (1 - s)(1 - F(\delta^\star + \beta)) \right), \end{aligned}$$

where the densities of utility flows $\phi_{1t}(\delta)$ and $\phi_{0t}(\delta)$ among owners and nonowners are given as Proposition 12.3 but with the investor thresholds (δ_s, δ_b) replaced by the planner's thresholds.

Taken together, the terms on the first two lines represent the present value of utility flows enjoyed by investors, in deviation from the frictionless allocation, which prescribes that the asset be held by investors with $\delta \geq \delta^\star$. Namely, the first line is the present value of utility flows enjoyed by investors in the frictionless allocation. The two terms on the second line account for the fact that the allocation is not frictionless: the first term adds the utility flows enjoyed by investors with $\delta < \delta^\star$ who actually hold assets but should not, and the second term subtracts the utility flows that are not actually enjoyed because some investors with $\delta \geq \delta^\star$ do not hold assets. The terms on the last line give the present value of the trading costs incurred by investors, at time 0 and whenever they switch to utility flows crossing the participation thresholds.

Combining our symmetry assumptions with the explicit expressions of the densities in (12.10), one can show that

$$W(\beta|\lambda) = W^\star - \frac{r+\gamma}{r}\int_0^\beta \frac{xg(x)}{r+\gamma+\lambda}dx - \frac{r+\gamma}{r/\kappa}\left(\frac{1}{2} - G(\beta)\right), \tag{12.13}$$

where the constant $W^\star$ is the welfare generated by the frictionless allocation and $G(\beta)$ is the cumulative distribution derived from $g(x)$. The second term is the cost of misallocation, while the third term is the cost of participation in the centralized market. Taking derivatives with respect to β yields

$$\frac{\partial W}{\partial \beta}(\beta|\lambda) = \frac{r+\gamma}{r}g(\beta)\left(\kappa - \beta\left(r+\gamma+\lambda\right)\right).$$

The second term in the bracket is negative because increasing OTC market participation increases misallocation, whereas the first term is positive because investors incur lower fixed costs as participation in the OTC market increases. Using this first-order condition, one can clearly see that the socially optimal threshold is explicitly given by

$$\beta^\star(\lambda) \equiv \kappa\left(r+\gamma+\lambda\right) > \kappa\left(r+\gamma+\lambda(1-\theta)\right).$$

This inequality shows that, in equilibrium, investors participate too little in the OTC market whenever $\theta > 0$, i.e., whenever dealers have some bargaining power. The reason is that, when formulating their participation decisions, investors calculate their reservation values based on the bargaining-adjusted contact rate $\lambda(1-\theta)$ instead of the actual contact rate λ.

This finding can be interpreted using the celebrated results of Hosios [1990], who provided a condition on bargaining shares for efficient participation. To intuitively explain this condition, consider a search market between two types of agents, A and B, in respective measures μ_A and μ_B. Assume that the contact rate between types A and B is given by a matching function $\mathcal{M}(\mu_A, \mu_B)$ that is homogeneous of degree one. In such a setting, Hosios [1990] showed that, under fairly general conditions, equilibrium participation by agents of type A is efficient if their bargaining power θ_A is equal to the elasticity of the matching function with respect to μ_A:

$$\theta_A \equiv \frac{\mu_A}{\mathcal{M}} \cdot \frac{\partial \mathcal{M}}{\partial \mu_A}.$$

The intuition that is commonly given in the literature is that efficient entry requires that agents of type A capture a share of the surplus equal to their contribution to the matching process, as measured by the marginal increase in the number of matches generated by additional entry of type A agents.

In our model, the condition of Hosios [1990] can be applied as follows. Since dealers have already made their entry decisions at the initial time, the only participation decisions lie with investors. Therefore, the matching function between dealers and any group of investors of size μ_A is $\lambda\mu_A$, and the elasticity of this function with respect to μ_A is one. Therefore, the reasoning of Hosios [1990] dictates that investors should have all the bargaining power, which in turn implies that the participation of investors in the OTC market is inefficient unless the bargaining power of dealers is $\theta = 0$.

12.4.2 *Socially Optimal Entry of Dealers*

Next, we determine the socially optimal mass of dealers in the OTC market by maximizing the social welfare function (12.13) net of entry costs when investors participate optimally, i.e., by solving

$$\max_{\lambda\geq 0}\left\{W\left(\beta^{\star}(\lambda)\middle|\lambda\right)-C(\lambda)\right\}.$$

An application of the envelope theorem shows that at the optimum of this problem we must have

$$C'(\lambda)\geq\frac{\partial W}{\partial\lambda}\left(\beta^{\star}(\lambda)\middle|\lambda\right)=S(\lambda)M(\lambda)\ \text{ with equality if }\lambda>0. \tag{12.14}$$

This necessary condition is similar to the free entry condition (12.11), but with three differences. First, one sees on the left-hand side that the planner uses the marginal cost of search intensity, $C'(\lambda)$, instead of the average cost in the free-entry equilibrium. Equivalently, given that

$$C(\lambda)=c\Lambda^{-1}(\lambda), \tag{12.15}$$

the planner cares about the marginal increase, $\Lambda'(\mu_d)$, in the contact rate with investors, whereas an individual dealer's profits are determined by the average meeting rate, $\Lambda(\mu_d)/\mu_d$. Second, the right-hand side is not multiplied by the bargaining power of dealers because the planner considers the full benefit of entry, not just the share of profit that accrues to dealers. Third, participation in the centralized market is chosen in a socially optimal way, so that the argument of the function $S(x)$ on the right-hand side is λ instead of $\lambda\,(1-\theta)$.

These differences imply that, in general, it is not possible to achieve, at the same time, socially optimal entry of dealers in the OTC market and socially optimal participation of investors in the centralized market. Given socially optimal entry by dealers, attaining socially optimal participation of investors requires setting the dealers' bargaining power to zero. However, if $\theta = 0$, then dealers make no profits ex post and hence do not enter ex ante. Likewise, taking the ratio of (12.11) to (12.14) at equality, one obtains that, given socially optimal participation of investors in the centralized market, attaining socially optimal entry of dealers in the OTC market requires

$$\theta = \frac{C(\lambda)}{\lambda C'(\lambda)} = \frac{\mu_d \Lambda'(\mu_d)}{\Lambda(\mu_d)},$$

where the second equality follows from (12.15). This is again the condition of Hosios [1990], but applied to dealers instead of investors. It states that the bargaining power of dealers must equal the elasticity of the meeting technology, $\mu_d \Lambda'(\mu_d)/\Lambda(\mu_d)$. This occurs because the entry decisions of dealers are based on the average number of matches they create, whereas the planner cares about the marginal increase in the number of matches or, equivalently, about the marginal cost of search intensity.

If the map $x \mapsto xg(x)$ is strictly decreasing, then the free entry equilibrium is unique and the planner's first-order condition (12.14) is sufficient, which facilitates their comparison.

Proposition 12.5: Assume that the map $x \mapsto xg(x)$ is strictly decreasing and denote by $(\lambda_P, \lambda_E(\theta))$ the contact rates in, respectively, the planner's problem and the free entry equilibrium when the dealers' bargaining power equals θ. If $\lambda_P > 0$ then

1. There exists $\theta_P > 0$ such that $\lambda_E(\theta) < \lambda_P$ if and only if $\theta < \theta_P$.
2. $\lambda_E(\theta)(1-\theta) < \lambda_P$ for all $\theta \in [0, 1]$.

Proof. To establish the first claim, recall from Proposition 12.4 that under the stated condition, $S(x)$ is strictly decreasing and $\lambda_E = \lambda_E(\theta)$ is increasing in θ. As the bargaining power of dealers decreases we clearly have

$$\lim_{\theta \to 0} (\lambda_P - \lambda_E(\theta)) = \lambda_P > 0.$$

On the other hand, the convexity of the cost function, the strict decrease of $S(x)$, and the assumption of the statement jointly imply that

$$\lim_{\lambda \to 0} \frac{C(\lambda)}{\lambda} \le \frac{C(\lambda_P)}{\lambda_P} \le C'(\lambda_P) = S(\lambda_P)M(\lambda_P) < S(0)M(0).$$

This shows that $\lambda_E(1) > 0$, so that (12.11) holds as an equality when $\theta = 1$. Using this property together with the convexity of the cost function then gives

$$C'(\lambda_E(1)) \geq \frac{C(\lambda_E(1))}{\lambda_E(1)} = S(0)M(\lambda_E(1)) > S(\lambda_E(1))M(\lambda_E(1)).$$

This shows that the increasing function $C'(x) - S(x)M(x)$ is strictly positive at $\lambda_E(1)$, and since it is zero at $\lambda_P > 0$, we must have that $\lambda_E(1) > \lambda_P$. Taking stock, we have shown that

$$\lambda_E(0) < \lambda_P < \lambda_E(1),$$

and the desired result now follows from the intermediate value theorem and the strict monotonicity of the map $\theta \mapsto \lambda_E(\theta)$.

To establish the second claim, assume toward a contradiction there exists some $\theta \in [0, 1]$ such that $\lambda_E(\theta)(1-\theta) = \lambda_P$, so that the planner's first-order condition and the free entry condition can be written as

$$C'(\lambda_P) = S(\lambda_P)M(\lambda_P)$$

and

$$\frac{C(\lambda_P/(1-\theta))}{\lambda_P/(1-\theta)} = \theta S(\lambda_P)M(\lambda_P/(1-\theta)).$$

Taking the ratio between the two and rearranging gives

$$\begin{aligned}\frac{M(\lambda_P/(1-\theta))}{M(\lambda_P)} C'(\lambda_P)\frac{\theta\lambda_P}{1-\theta} &= C(\lambda_P/(1-\theta)) \\ &\geq C(\lambda_P) + C'(\lambda_P)\frac{\theta\lambda_P}{1-\theta},\end{aligned}$$

which contradicts the fact that the function $M(x)$ is strictly decreasing and thus establishes the desired result. □

The first result in the proposition shows that, to induce efficient entry of dealers in the OTC market, dealers must have strictly positive bargaining power. As discussed above, this generates inefficiently low participation of investors in the centralized market. Moreover, the second result shows that, irrespective of the dealers' bargaining power, it is not possible to induce socially optimal participation in the centralized market, even at the cost of creating excessive entry of dealers in the OTC market.

12.5 Exercises

Exercise 12.6: Consider the equation for reservation values in Lemma 12.1.

1. In the text we verified that this equation has to hold on the set $\mathcal{P}_0$. Verify that it also holds on the sets $\mathcal{P}_1$ and $\mathcal{D}\backslash(\mathcal{P}_0 \cup \mathcal{P}_1)$.
2. Consider the equation obtained by adding $(\gamma + \lambda_\theta)R(\delta)$ to both sides of the reservation equation in Lemma 12.1 and dividing by $r + \gamma + \lambda_\theta$. Show that this modified equation defines a contraction on the set of bounded functions on $\mathcal{D}$.
3. Show that the reservation value equation admits a unique bounded solution and that this solution is both continuous and nondecreasing.

12.6 Notes and References

The model in this chapter is original. Some technical comments about our assumptions are in order. To start, the symmetry assumptions regarding the asset supply, the utility flow distribution, and the initial distribution of assets help with tractability: they keep the allocation symmetric and ensure that the equilibrium interdealer price immediately adjusts to its steady-state level at time $t = 0$. Similar symmetry assumptions are made by Farboodi, Jarosch, and Shimer [2022]. Another important simplification is that entry is a static decision made at the initial time, as otherwise, maximizing social welfare would require solving for dealers' optimal *dynamic* entry decisions, which is a much more difficult optimization problem.

While reminiscent of Diamond [1982], the multiplicity result of Proposition 12.4 arises for different reasons. Indeed, in Diamond [1982], multiplicity is driven by increasing returns in the matching technology, which implies that dealers match with investors more frequently when more dealers enter. OTC market models that explore liquidity spillovers induced by similar matching technologies with increasing returns include Vayanos and Wang [2007], Weill [2008], Vayanos and Weill [2008], Sambalaibat [2018], Li and Song [2023], and Coppola, Krishnamurthy, and Xu [2023]. However, this source of strategic complementarity is not present in the model studied here because the matching function $\Lambda(\mu_d)$ is concave: as more dealers enter, they match with investors *less* frequently since $\Lambda(\mu_d)/\mu_d$ is decreasing in μ_d. Instead, the multiplicity in our model is driven by the fact that both sides of the market make an extensive margin decision, so that dealers' entry can encourage investors' participation in OTC markets [see Rocheteau and Wright, 2013, for a related result].

To highlight the distinction between exchanges and OTC trading platforms, the model of this chapter allows investors to choose between a centralized and a semicentralized trading venue. Several papers in the existing literature allow investors to choose between different venues with the *same* market structure in order to study competition across trading platforms. For example, Pagnotta and Philippon [2018] assume that investors commit ex ante to trade forever in one of two semicentralized venues, and that venues compete by investing in speed and setting fees. In Back, Celebi, Kakhbod, and Reppen [2022], investors are allowed to choose between two semicentralized venues as their utility type changes over time.

Another key, simplifying assumption in this chapter is that investors must pay some exogenous fixed cost in order to participate in the centralized market. The recent literature has developed models to explain why, in reality, it can indeed be more costly to trade in centralized than in OTC markets, based on detailed analysis of price-setting mechanisms and informational frictions.

In particular, Rostek and Weretka [2015] argue that centralized markets are often thin because they involve a finite (often small) number of participants. In thin markets, investors no longer take prices as given, as in frictionless markets. Instead, they rationally anticipate that their trades have price impact, raising the price when they want to buy and lowering it when they want to sell. Investors who anticipate price impact trade less aggressively than they do absent frictions; this situation creates misallocation. In that context, Malamud and Rostek [2017], Babus and Parlatore [2022], Chen and Duffie [2021], Rostek and Yoon [2021], and Wittwer [2021] have shown that breaking down the centralized market into fragmented venues can sometimes improve welfare.

To gain some intuition on the welfare impact of fragmentation, let us briefly elaborate on the paper by Chen and Duffie [2021]. In their work, fragmentation has two opposing effects. On the one hand, smaller marketplaces imply greater price impact, which leads investors to trade even less aggressively. On the other hand, since investors are able to split their orders across markets, the larger price impact now affects a smaller quantity of infra-marginal units. Chen and Duffie [2021] show that it is possible to choose the level of fragmentation that implements the efficient allocation of assets.

In the above papers, centralized markets are imperfect because of market thinness and price impact. Another crucial consideration when evaluating the merits of centralized vs. OTC markets is the presence and interaction of market structure with information frictions. In particular, since OTC markets traditionally exhibit less pretrade and posttrade price transparency, information is potentially transmitted (or leaked) more slowly in OTC markets relative to centralized exchanges. Following Kyle [1985], there is a large literature in finance studying how concerns over information leakage affect investors' trading behavior; see, for example, Burdett and O'Hara [1987], Easley and O'Hara [1987], and Seppi [1990].

Recent attempts to study how market structure affects information leakage and trading activity include Hendershott and Madhavan [2015], Kawakami [2010, 2017], and

Baldauf and Mollner [2024]. For example, Kawakami [2010, 2017] considers a setting with ex ante identical investors who receive an idiosyncratic endowment of a risky asset, and some independent private information about the fundamental value of that asset. He shows that gains from trade are a hump-shaped function of N, the number of investors trading in the market. When N is very small, adverse selection destroys gain from trade, as in Bhattacharya and Spiegel [1991]. When N is large, the Hirshleifer [1971] effect causes the price to become almost perfectly revealing of the true payoff. As a result, there is almost no risk left to share, which also destroys ex ante gains from trade. Fragmentation emerges endogenously: competitive trading platforms offer investors the opportunity to trade in small exclusive markets.

The idea that trading frictions can be welfare improving in the presence of asymmetric information emerges in several other recent papers, including Lester, Shourideh, Venkateswaran, and Zetlin-Jones [2019] and Glode and Opp [2019]. For example, Glode and Opp [2019] show that, when the asymmetry of information between customers is severe, moderately informed agents can be natural intermediaries. They also endogenize market structure in a network formation game where investors choose ex ante to form chains of bilateral meetings along which trading occurs ex post.

Others have highlighted additional dimensions along which centralized markets can be imperfect (and OTC markets can create value). Vogel [2019] takes the view that, in markets such as the corporate bond market, existing centralized platforms allow investors to quickly query the entire market but only attract a random number of quotes from dealers. The OTC market, by contrast, allows investors to receive quotes from all dealers, but only sequentially and by incurring nontrivial search costs. In Dugast, Üslü, and Weill [2022], trading large quantities requires some capacity, either in the centralized or in the OTC market. These capacities represent investors' access to funding, collateral, or trading expertise. In equilibrium, large-capacity investors endogenously play the role of dealers in the OTC market by providing intermediation services to small-capacity investors. Intermediate-capacity investors sort themselves into the multilateral centralized market. Altermatt and Gottardi [2023] also study sorting but generate a form of trading capacity endogenously by imposing collateral requirements. Farboodi, Jarosch, and Shimer [2022] study a search model in which investors make an ex ante choice of search intensity. They find that the equilibrium features mixed strategies: investors choose heterogeneous intensities. Interestingly, under some conditions on the cost of intensity, some investors endogenously choose an infinite intensity, and so they resemble the dealers in models of semicentralized OTC markets.

13

Conclusion

There are several compelling reasons to study OTC markets. First, OTC markets are large; as we discuss in chapter 2, the overall market capitalization of securities traded in OTC markets is actually larger than that in centralized limit-order books. Second, OTC markets play a crucial role in the modern financial ecosystem; indeed, the most recent two episodes of financial market stress, in 2008 and again in 2020, began with disruptions to trade (and, eventually, government interventions) in key OTC markets. Last, despite a variety of technological advancements, OTC markets appear to be here to stay. In fact, even in markets where investors can freely choose between different trading mechanisms—including centralized limit-order books—OTC trade remains a popular trading arrangement [see, e.g., Riggs, Onur, Reiffen, and Zhu, 2018].

The study of OTC markets raises a number of unique challenges and questions. To start, it is important to identify potential sources of trading delays and price dispersion in OTC markets, and the connections between these frictions, asset prices, and the allocation of the asset across different types of investors. Second, one needs to estimate the size of these frictions, and to quantitatively evaluate the welfare implications of various trading mechanisms. Identifying and estimating these fundamentals are crucial to address a variety of pressing concerns for academics, policymakers, and practitioners alike. For example, what are the characteristics of investors who end up serving as intermediaries? How do different trading protocols affect who trades with whom, and at what price? What are the advantages of OTC markets, relative to centralized exchanges? Would we be better off forcing certain assets to trade on exchanges?

To overcome the challenges highlighted above and provide answers to these questions requires developing a conceptual framework that captures the key features of OTC markets. The foundations of such a framework were established decades ago, with the partial equilibrium search models found in Stigler [1961], McCall [1970], and Garbade and Silber [1976], and the equilibrium search models developed in Diamond [1982] and Rubinstein and Wolinsky [1985, 1987]. More recently, the seminal work of Duffie, Gârleanu, and Pedersen [2005, 2007] assembled these building blocks into a tractable, coherent equilibrium framework focused on financial markets. Since then, theoretical advancements and empirical work have continued to leapfrog one another: as empiricists have used more detailed, richer data sets to uncover new stylized facts, theorists have modified and extended the existing frameworks to confront these facts and pose new questions for the data.

Though further advancements are surely on the horizon, the purpose of this book is to outline some of the basic facts that motivate the study of OTC markets (chapter 2); to provide a detailed introduction to the basic building blocks of the search-theoretic approach to studying decentralized trade (chapter 3); and to use these building blocks to develop two workhorse models of OTC markets in depth (chapters 4 and 5).

Next, going beyond these initial chapters, we have covered extensions and applications that are well established in the literature. For example, the case of divisible asset holdings treated in chapter 6 was developed by Lagos and Rocheteau [2009] and Gârleanu [2009] in order to study the relationships between trading frictions, trade size, and transaction costs, among other things. The model of frictional intermediation presented in chapter 7 was developed in Hugonnier, Lester, and Weill [2020] to study the patterns of trade in the customer-dealer *and the interdealer* markets that are prevalent in various OTC markets, such as the corporate and municipal bond markets. The extension to alternative pricing mechanisms introduced in chapter 8, such as directed search with price posting, was developed in Lester, Rocheteau, and Weill [2015] to study the empirical relationship between, e.g., trading costs and execution speed. Finally, the analysis of OTC markets under stress, covered in chapter 9, was first explored in Weill [2007] and Lagos, Rocheteau, and Weill [2011] to study the performance and resilience of OTC markets in response to large aggregate shocks. Despite the clear antecedents in the literature, these chapters still contain some new results. For example, the conditions derived in section 4.6 that determine whether investors prefer spot vs. relationship trading provide new insights into the determinants of market microstructure. As a second example, the closed-form characterization of prices in section 8.2 provides an ideal setting for studying the proliferation of electronic trading platforms in several OTC markets, and the potential ramifications for prices and allocations.

The last few chapters offer extensions that contain a larger degree of novelty. Our analysis of OTC markets with asymmetric information in chapters 10 and 11 provides new frameworks to study the effects of transparency and adverse selection in financial markets. While this analysis draws on a variety of results from the existing literature, our synthesis of these results with the benchmark models of OTC markets is relatively new [see Hugonnier, Lester, and Weill, 2024a,b]. In the same vein, the framework introduced in chapter 12 provides a solid foundation for the comparison of OTC markets and centralized exchanges.

And yet, despite the significant progress of the past two decades, many fundamental questions remain unanswered. We conclude with a short discussion of just a few of these questions. To start, though our understanding of different market structures has certainly improved, we still do not fully understand why some assets trade on OTC markets and other, seemingly similar assets do not—a puzzle clearly articulated in Rust and Hall [2003]. This question is only magnified in markets with multiple trading venues, where we observe that some trades are executed via bilateral, often voice-based interactions while others are executed through more centralized, multilateral trading platforms. What characteristics of an investor, or of the trade, determine the venue where the trade is executed? If both types of trading arrangements offer some value to investors, what is the impact of forcing all trade to migrate from OTC markets to more centralized exchanges, as some policymakers have advocated?

A second line of questions focuses more squarely on the behavior of dealers. More specifically, models of OTC markets can potentially offer a deeper understanding of the *interaction* between investors' demand for liquidity and dealers' willingness to supply it. In the traditional market microstructure literature, dealers' behavior took center stage, while demand for liquidity from investors often received short shrift. In contrast, the models developed in this book provide a formal derivation of the determinants of investors' intertemporal demand for liquidity, but more work remains to be done in understanding the incentives of dealers to supply it—both in "normal times" and in times of stress. Of particular interest is understanding the effect of regulations on the costs that dealers face when providing intermediation services, and the subsequent emergence of nonbank financial intermediaries.

All of these questions, and many more, are being actively studied both theoretically and empirically. More generally, we anticipate this exciting literature to continue to grow and develop, as new methodologies and better data continue to emerge.

APPENDIX A

Mathematical Tools

A.1 Fixed Point Results

Let $\mathcal{X}$ be a subset of $\mathbf{R}^n$ and denote by $\mathcal{B} = \mathcal{B}(\mathcal{X})$ the Banach space of real valued, bounded functions on $\mathcal{X}$ equipped with the norm

$$\|f\| = \sup_{x \in \mathcal{X}} |f(x)|.$$

Let further $T : \mathcal{B} \to \mathcal{B}$ be an operator that maps $\mathcal{B}$ onto itself and consider the problem of finding a solution $f \in \mathcal{B}$ to the fixed point equation $f = Tf$. The following results are of repeated use throughout the book.

Definition A.1: A contraction on $\mathcal{B}$ is an operator $T : \mathcal{B} \to \mathcal{B}$ such that

$$\|Tf - Tg\| \leq c\|f - g\|$$

for some $c < 1$ and all functions $f, g \in \mathcal{B}$.

The following result is often very useful to prove that a given operator is a contraction.

Proposition A.2 (Blackwell's conditions): Assume that $T : \mathcal{B} \to \mathcal{B}$ is nondecreasing and that there exists $c < 1$ such that the discounting condition

$$T[a + f] \leq ca + T[f], \qquad \forall (a, f) \in \mathbf{R}_+ \times \mathcal{B}. \tag{A.1}$$

holds. Then T is a contraction on $\mathcal{B}$.

Proof. Since $f \leq g + \|f - g\|$ it follows from the weak increase of T and the discounting condition (A.1) that $Tf \leq Tg + c\|f - g\|$. Exchanging the roles of f and g then gives the desired result. □

Theorem A.3 (Banach fixed point theorem): If T is a contraction on $\mathcal{B}$ then it admits a unique fixed point in $\mathcal{B}$, and this fixed point can be obtained as the limit $\lim_n T^n g$ starting from any function $g \in \mathcal{B}$.

Proof. Define a sequence by setting $f_0 = g$ and $f_{n+1} = Tf_n$ for some arbitrary but fixed $g \in \mathcal{B}$. Since T is a contraction we have that

$$\begin{aligned}\|f_{n+1} - f_n\| &= \|Tf_n - Tf_{n-1}\| \\ &\le c\|f_n - f_{n-1}\| = c\|Tf_{n-1} - Tf_{n-2}\| \\ &\le c^2\|f_{n-1} - f_{n-2}\| = c^2\|Tf_{n-2} - Tf_{n-3}\| \\ &\le c^3\|f_{n-2} - f_{n-3}\| \le \cdots \le c^n\|f_1 - f_0\|,\end{aligned}$$

and therefore

$$\begin{aligned}\|f_m - f_n\| &\le \|f_m - f_{m-1}\| + \|f_{m-1} - f_{m-2}\| + \cdots + \|f_{n+1} - f_n\| \\ &\le \left(c^m + c^{m-1} + \cdots + c^n\right)\|f_1 - f_0\| \\ &\le \frac{c^n}{1-c}\|f_1 - f_0\|, \qquad \text{(A.2)}\end{aligned}$$

where the last inequality follows from the fact that

$$\sum_{k=n}^{m} c^k = \frac{c^n - c^{1+m}}{1-c} \le \frac{c^n}{1-c}.$$

By assumption $c \in (0, 1)$. Therefore, (A.2) implies that for any $\varepsilon > 0$ there exists $N_\varepsilon \in \mathbf{N}$ such that

$$\|f_m - f_n\| \le \varepsilon, \qquad \forall m \ge n \ge N_\varepsilon.$$

This shows that $(f_n)_{n=1}^{\infty}$ is a Cauchy sequence in the Banach space $(\mathcal{B}, \|\cdot\|)$ and thus converges to some limit $f \in \mathcal{B}$. Since T is a contraction it is by definition Lipschitz continuous. In particular, we have

$$f = \lim_n f_n = \lim_n Tf_{n-1} = T\left(\lim_n f_{n-1}\right) = Tf,$$

so that f is a fixed point of T, and uniqueness follows by noting that if f' is another such fixed point then

$$\|f' - f\| = \|Tf' - Tf\| \le c\|f' - f\| < \|f' - f\|,$$

which is impossible. □

Corollary A.4: Assume that T is a contraction on $\mathcal{B}$. If T maps $\mathcal{B}$ onto some closed subset $\mathcal{B}^*$ then its unique fixed point $f \in \mathcal{B}^*$.

Proof. Since $T^n g \in \mathcal{B}^*$ and $\mathcal{B}^*$ is closed, we have that $f = \lim_n T^n g \in \mathcal{B}^*$, and the result now follows from Theorem A.3. □

Corollary A.5: Assume that T is a nondecreasing contraction on $\mathcal{B}$ with its fixed point $f \in \mathcal{B}$ and that $g \in \mathcal{B}$ is such that $Tg \leq g$. Then $f \leq g$.

Proof. Iterating the assumed inequality by repeated applications of the nondecreasing operator T on both sides shows that $g \geq Tg \geq T^2 g \geq \cdots \geq T^n g$, and the result follows from Theorem A.3 by letting $n \to \infty$. □

The next corollary offers easily verifiable conditions to rank the fixed point of different contractions and is very useful when studying the comparative statics of solutions to dynamic programming equations.

Corollary A.6: Assume that $T \leq S$ are contractions on $\mathcal{B}$ and denote their respective fixed points by f and g. If the operator S is nondecreasing then $f \leq g$.

Proof. Since $T \leq S$ and f is the fixed point of T, we have that $f = Tf \leq Sf$. Iterating this inequality by repeated applications of the nondecreasing operator S on both sides then shows that $f \leq Sf \leq S^2 \leq \cdots \leq S^n f$, and the desired result now follows from Theorem A.3 by letting $n \to \infty$. □

A.2 Random Variables and Distributions

Consider a *probability space* defined as a triple $(\Omega, \mathcal{F}, \mathbf{P})$, where Ω is a set that we refer to as the sample space, $\mathcal{F}$ is a σ-algebra of subsets of the sample space (i.e., a collection of subsets that includes the empty set and that is closed under complements and countable unions), and $\mathbf{P} : \mathcal{F} \to [0, 1]$ is a probability measure on $\mathcal{F}$.

Definition A.7: A random variable with values in an open interval $\mathcal{D} = (\underline{\delta}, \overline{\delta})$ such that $-\infty \leq \underline{\delta} < \overline{\delta} \leq \infty$ is a map $x : \Omega \to \mathcal{D}$ that is $\mathcal{F}$-measurable in that

$$\{\omega \in \Omega : x(\omega) \in A\} \in \mathcal{F}$$

for any Borel set $A \subseteq \mathbf{R}$.

Each random variable induces a probability measure

$$\nu(A) = \mathbf{P}\left[\{\omega \in \Omega : x(\omega) \in A\}\right], \quad \text{with} \quad \nu(\mathcal{D}) = 1,$$

that represents the likelihood that $x(\omega)$ falls into the Borel set $A \subseteq \mathbf{R}$, and the left-tail of this probability measure

$$F(\delta) = \nu((\underline{\delta}, \delta]) = \mathbf{P}\left[\{\omega \in \Omega : x(\omega) \leq \delta\}\right]$$

is referred to as the cumulative distribution function (CDF). With this in place we say that $F : \mathcal{D} \to \mathbf{R}$ is a *distribution* if it is the CDF of a random variable with values in $\mathcal{D}$. The following lemma gathers basic properties of distributions.

Lemma A.8: Assume that F is a distribution. Then F is nonnegative, weakly increasing, and right continuous. Furthermore,

$$\lim_{\delta \downarrow \underline{\delta}} F(\delta) = 1 - \lim_{\delta \uparrow \overline{\delta}} F(\delta) = 0,$$

so that F can be extended to $\mathrm{cl}(\mathcal{D}) = [\underline{\delta}, \overline{\delta}]$ by setting $F(\underline{\delta}) = 1 - F(\overline{\delta}) = 0$.

Proof. Nonnegativity and monotonicity follow from the definition. To establish right-continuity note that

$$\begin{aligned}\lim_{\delta \downarrow \delta_0} F(\delta) &= \lim_{\delta \downarrow \delta_0} \mathbf{E}\left[\mathbf{1}_{\{x \leq \delta\}}\right] \\ &= \mathbf{E}\left[\lim_{\delta \downarrow \delta_0} \mathbf{1}_{\{x \leq \delta\}}\right] = \mathbf{E}\left[\mathbf{1}_{\{x \leq \delta_0\}}\right] = F(\delta_0)\end{aligned}$$

for all $\delta_0 \in \mathcal{D}$, where the second equality follows by dominated convergence and the third follows from the fact that the function $\delta \mapsto \mathbf{1}_{\{x(\omega) \leq \delta\}}$ is right continuous for each $\omega \in \Omega$. By the same token,

$$F(\underline{\delta}+) = \mathbf{E}\left[\lim_{\delta \downarrow \underline{\delta}} \mathbf{1}_{\{x \leq \delta\}}\right] = \mathbf{E}\left[\mathbf{1}_{\{x \leq \underline{\delta}\}}\right] = 0$$

at the lower end, and

$$F(\overline{\delta}-) = \mathbf{E}\left[\lim_{\delta \uparrow \overline{\delta}} \mathbf{1}_{\{x \leq \delta\}}\right] = \mathbf{E}\left[\lim_{\delta \uparrow \overline{\delta}} \mathbf{1}_{\{\overline{\delta} \neq x \leq \overline{\delta}\}}\right] = \mathbf{E}\left[\mathbf{1}_{\{x < \overline{\delta}\}}\right] = 1$$

at the upper end, where the last equality of each line follows from the fact that the random variable takes values in $\mathcal{D}$. $\square$

In the above lemma the assumption that $\mathcal{D}$ is an *open* interval is necessary to establish that $F(\underline{\delta}+) = 1 - F(\overline{\delta}-) = 0$ because in its absence the underlying random variable may assign strictly positive probability to either or both of the endpoints. Note, however, that this assumption is without generality, as one can embed any closed or half-closed interval into an open interval.

Example A.9: If $\underline{\delta} < \delta_0 < \delta_1 < \cdots < \overline{\delta}$ and $(p_i)_{i=1}^{\infty}$ is a sequence of strictly positive numbers that sum to one, then

$$F(\delta) = \sum_{i=0}^{\infty} \mathbf{1}_{\{\delta_i \le \delta_i\}} p_i$$

defines a distribution function. In this example the distribution function is piecewise constant between the points δ_i, and its jumps

$$\Delta F(\delta_i) = F(\delta_i) - F(\delta_{i-}) = p_i$$

capture the probability that the distribution of the underlying discrete random variable puts on each of these atoms. Examples of such distributions that we use in the text include the binomial distribution with

$$F(\delta) = \sum_{i=0}^{N} \mathbf{1}_{\{i \le \delta\}} \binom{i}{N} q^i (1-q)^{N-i}$$

for some $N \in \mathbf{N}$ and $q \in (0, 1)$, and the Poisson distribution with

$$F(\delta) = \sum_{i=0}^{\infty} \mathbf{1}_{\{i \le \delta\}} \frac{e^{-\lambda} \lambda^i}{i!}$$

for some $\lambda > 0$ that gives both the mean and the variance of the distribution. In the binomial case we may take for $\mathcal{D}$ any open set that includes $\{0, \ldots, N\}$, while in the Poisson case we may take any set of the form $(\underline{\delta}, \infty)$ for some fixed $\underline{\delta} < 0$.

Example A.10: If $f : \mathcal{D} \to \mathbf{R}_+$ is integrable, $\mathcal{D}$ then

$$F(\delta) = \int_{\underline{\delta}}^{\delta} f(x) dx$$

defines a distribution provided that $\int_{\mathcal{D}} f(x) dx = 1$. In such cases the associated random variable is said to be continuous, and its probability density function is given by the derivative $F' = f$. This class includes all the standard examples of absolutely continuous distribution functions such as the uniform distribution on a compact interval,

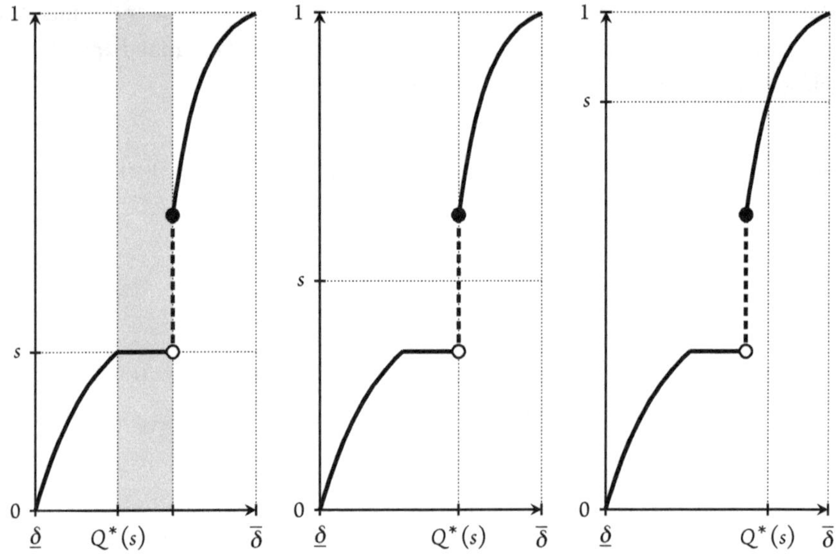

FIGURE A.1. The quantile map

This figure illustrates the determination of the set of quantiles of a distribution function. In the last two panels the set is reduced to the singleton $\{Q^*(s)\}$, whereas in the first one it is given by the whole shaded interval.

the exponential distribution on the positive real line (see below for more details), and the normal distribution on $\mathbf{R}$.

Example A.11: As is easily seen, the class of distribution functions defines a convex set of functions. Therefore, it follows from the two previous examples that any function of the form

$$F(\delta) = \sum_{i=1}^{\infty} \mathbf{1}_{\{\delta_i \le \delta\}} p_i + \int_{\underline{\delta}}^{\delta} f(x)dx$$

defines a distribution function, provided that the point masses $(p_i)_{i=1}^{\infty}$ and the probability density f are such that $F(\overline{\delta}) = 1$. In each of the above examples the distribution is at least piecewise absolutely continuous, but this need not be the case in general, as there exist nondecreasing functions that are continuous but singular. See Corbae, Stinchcombe, and Zeman [2009, chap. 7.9] for a discussion.

In some situations it is necessary to invert a given distribution function. For that purpose, we consider the set-valued mapping

$$Q(s) \equiv \{\delta \in \mathrm{cl}(\mathcal{D}) : F(\delta-) \leq s \leq F(\delta)\},$$

whose elements give the quantile(s) of the distribution at the level $s \in [0, 1]$. As illustrated in figure A.1, this set reduces to a singleton unless the distribution is constant and equal to s over some open set. The following lemma provides a simple change variable that shows that, even in such nongeneric cases, the function

$$Q^*(s) = \inf Q(s) = \inf \{\delta \in \mathrm{cl}(\mathcal{D}) : s \leq F(\delta)\}$$

provides a generalized inverse of the original distribution.

Lemma A.12: $Q^*(s) \leq \delta$ if and only if $F(\delta) \geq s$ for any $(s, \delta) \in [0, 1] \times \mathcal{D}$. In particular, if the random variable u is uniformly distributed on the unit interval, then the random variable $Q^*(u)$ is distributed according to F on $\mathcal{D}$.

Proof. If $s \leq F(\delta)$ then

$$\delta \in \Theta(s) \equiv \{x \in \mathrm{cl}(\mathcal{D}) : s \leq F(x)\},$$

and therefore $Q^*(s) \leq \delta$. Conversely, if $Q^*(s) \leq \delta$ then $F(Q^*(s)) \leq F(\delta)$ because the distribution function is nondecreasing. Now choose an sequence $(\delta_n)_{n=1}^{\infty} \subseteq \Theta(s)$ that decreases to $Q^*(s)$. Since $\delta_n \in \Theta(s)$ we have $s \leq F(\delta_n)$, and the result follows by observing that

$$F(Q^*(s)) = F\left(\lim_{n\to\infty} \delta_n\right) = \lim_{n\to\infty} F(\delta_n)$$

due to the right-continuity of the distribution. Applying the first part at $s = u$ and taking expectations then shows that $\mathbf{P}\left[Q^*(u) \leq \delta\right] = \mathbf{P}\left[u \leq F(\delta)\right] = F(\delta)$, which completes the proof. □

Since any distribution function is bounded and nondecreasing, it follows from classical results (see for example Protter and Morrey [1977, chap. 12]) that the Lebesgue–Stieltjes integral

$$\mathbf{E}\left[\phi(x)\right] = \int_{\Omega} \phi(x(\omega))d\mathbf{P} = \int_{\underline{\delta}}^{\overline{\delta}} \phi(\delta)dF(\delta)$$

against the induced Borel measure exists for a large class of integrands that includes all bounded measurable functions. Given this definition it is natural to wonder under what conditions one can to rank the expectations associated with different distributions. The following result provides an easily applicable answer to this question and is of repeated use throughout the book.

Proposition A.13: Assume that F and G are distributions on $\mathcal{D}$. Then the following conditions are equivalent:

1. $F(\delta) \leq G(\delta)$ for all $\delta \in \mathcal{D}$.
2. The associated quantile functions satisfy $Q_G^*(s) \leq Q_F^*(s)$ for all $s \in [0, 1]$.
3. The inequality

$$\int_{\underline{\delta}}^{\overline{\delta}} \phi(\delta) dF(\delta) \geq \int_{\underline{\delta}}^{\overline{\delta}} \phi(\delta) dG(\delta).$$

holds for any nondecreasing $\phi \in \mathcal{B}$.

If either of these equivalent conditions hold, then we say that F first-order stochastically dominates G and we write $F \succ G$.

Proof. If condition 1 holds, then $s \leq F(Q_F^*(s)) \leq G(Q_F^*(s))$ for all $s \in [0, 1]$, and it follows that $Q_G^*(s) \leq Q_F^*(s)$ for all $s \in [0, 1]$, which is condition 2. Conversely, if condition 2 holds, then Lemma A.12 implies that

$$\{F(\delta) \geq s\} = \left\{Q_F^*(s) \leq s\right\} \subseteq \left\{Q_G^*(s) \leq s\right\} = \{G(\delta) \geq s\}$$

for all $(s, \delta) \in [0, 1] \times \mathcal{D}$, and condition 1 follows. Now assume that condition 1 holds and fix a nondecreasing function $\phi \in \mathcal{B}$. By standard approximation results we have that there exists a sequence of step functions

$$\phi_n(\delta) = \sum_{k=1}^{n} a_{nk} \mathbf{1}_{\{\delta > \delta_{nk}\}} \leq \phi(\delta)$$

that increases pointwise to the function ϕ. For any approximating function along that sequence we have that

$$\begin{aligned} \int_{\underline{\delta}}^{\overline{\delta}} \phi_n(\delta) dF(\delta) &= \sum_{k=1}^{n} a_{nk}(1 - F(\delta_{nk})) \\ &\geq \sum_{k=1}^{n} a_{nk}(1 - G(\delta_{nk})) = \int_{\underline{\delta}}^{\overline{\delta}} \phi_n(\delta) dG(\delta), \end{aligned}$$

where the inequality follows from condition 1. Using the dominated convergence to pass to the limit then shows that

$$\int_{\underline{\delta}}^{\overline{\delta}} \phi(\delta)dF(\delta) = \lim_{n\to\infty} \int_{\underline{\delta}}^{\overline{\delta}} \phi_n(\delta)dF(\delta)$$

$$\geq \lim_{n\to\infty} \int_{\underline{\delta}}^{\overline{\delta}} \phi_n(\delta)dG(\delta) = \int_{\underline{\delta}}^{\overline{\delta}} \phi(\delta)dG(\delta),$$

and it now follows from the arbitrariness of ϕ that condition 3 holds. Conversely, suppose that condition 3 holds and consider the weakly increasing function $\phi(\delta) = \mathbf{1}_{\{\delta>\delta_0\}}$ for some $\delta_0 \in \mathcal{D}$. For this function we have that condition 3 reads as

$$1 - F(\delta_0) = \int_{\underline{\delta}}^{\overline{\delta}} \phi(\delta)dF(\delta) \geq \int_{\underline{\delta}}^{\overline{\delta}} \phi(\delta)dG(\delta) = 1 - G(\delta_0),$$

which implies condition 1. □

Given two distributions on $\mathcal{D}$, we say that G is absolutely continuous with respect to F if, for any Borel set $B \subseteq \mathcal{D}$, $F(B) = 0$ implies that $G(B) = 0$. We then have the following lemma.

Lemma A.14: Suppose that (F, G) are distributions such that

$$\int_B \alpha(\delta)\, dF(\delta) = \int_B \beta(\delta)\, dG(\delta), \tag{A.3}$$

for all Borel sets $B \subseteq \mathcal{D}$, and some integrable functions such that $\alpha(\delta) \geq 0$ and $\beta(\delta) \geq \varepsilon > 0$. Then

a) G is absolutely continuous with respect to F.
b) The nonnegative function $\alpha(\delta)/\beta(\delta)$ is the Radon-Nikodym derivative of G with respect to F in the sense that

$$G(B) = \int_B \frac{\alpha(\delta)}{\beta(\delta)} dF(\delta),$$

for all Borel sets $B \subseteq \mathcal{D}$, and we write $dG(\delta) = (\alpha(\delta)/\beta(\delta))\, dF(\delta)$.

Proof. If $B \subseteq \mathcal{D}$ is a Borel set such that $F(B) = 0$, then the assumptions of the statement imply that we have

$$G(B) \leq \frac{1}{\varepsilon} \int_B \beta(\delta) dG(\delta) = 0,$$

and therefore $G(B) = 0$. This proves a), and it now follows from the Radon-Nikodym theorem (see Theorem 7.11 in Stokey and Lucas [1989]) that there exists an integrable function $\gamma(\delta) \geq 0$ that is F-almost everywhere unique and such that

$$G(B) = \int_B \gamma(\delta)\, dF(\delta)$$

for all Borel sets $B \subseteq \mathcal{D}$. Substituting in (A.3), we obtain that

$$\int_B h(\delta)\, dF(\delta) = 0, \text{ where } h(\delta) \equiv \beta(\delta) \left(\frac{\alpha(\delta)}{\beta(\delta)} - \gamma(\delta) \right)$$

for all Borel sets $B \subseteq \mathcal{D}$. To conclude the proof we evaluate the above condition using the Borel sets defined by

$$B^{\pm} \equiv \left\{ \delta \in \mathcal{D} : h(\delta)^{\pm} > 0 \right\}.$$

This gives

$$\int_{B^{\pm}} |h(\delta)|\, dF(\delta) = 0,$$

which implies that $F(B^{\pm}) = 0$ since $|h(\delta)| > 0$ on $B^{\pm}$ and, thereby, confirms that $h(\delta) = 0$ for F-almost every $\delta \in \mathcal{D}$. □

A.3 Exponential Random Variables

A positive random variable τ is exponential with rate $\lambda > 0$ if its distribution function is given by

$$F(t) = \mathbf{P}[\tau \leq t] = 1 - e^{-\lambda t}, \qquad \forall t \geq 0. \tag{A.4}$$

In the text we use exponential random variables to model the arrival date of random events, in which case $\lambda^{-1} = \mathbf{E}[\tau]$ represents the expected arrival date. In this context a key feature of this class of random variables is that they are memoryless: if the event has not arrived by some given date, then the time remaining until its arrival is exponentially distributed with the same rate as the unconditional arrival.

Lemma A.15 (Memoryless property): If the random variable τ is exponential with rate λ and $t > 0$ then, conditional on the event $\{\tau > t\}$, the random variable $\tau - t$ is exponential with rate λ.

Proof. This follows from Bayes' rule and (A.4) by noting that

$$\mathbf{P}[\tau - t \le s | \tau > t] = 1 - \frac{\mathbf{P}[\tau > t+s]}{\mathbf{P}[\tau > t]} = 1 - e^{-\lambda s}$$

for all $s \ge 0$. □

The following lemmas collect properties of exponential random variables that are of repeated use throughout the text.

Lemma A.16: If τ is an exponential random variable with rate $\lambda > 0$, then $(\lambda/\phi)\tau$ is an exponentially distributed random variable with rate $\phi > 0$.

Proof. Simply observe that $\mathbf{P}[(\lambda/\phi)\tau \le t] = \mathbf{P}[\tau \le (\phi/\lambda)t] = e^{-\phi t}$. □

Lemma A.17: If τ is an exponential random variable with rate $\lambda > 0$ and $f : \mathbf{R}_+ \to \mathbf{R}$ is a bounded function, then

$$\mathbf{E}\left[e^{-r\tau} f(\tau)\right] = \int_0^\infty e^{-(r+\lambda)t} \lambda f(t) dt = \mathbf{E}\left[\int_0^\tau e^{-rt} \lambda f(t) dt\right]$$

for any discount rate $r > 0$. In particular,

$$\mathbf{E}\left[e^{-r\tau}\right] = \frac{\lambda}{r+\lambda} = \mathbf{E}\left[\int_0^\tau e^{-rt} \lambda dt\right]$$

for any discount rate $r > 0$.

Proof. The first equality follows by direct calculation from the definition of the cumulative distribution

$$\begin{aligned}\mathbf{E}\left[e^{-r\tau} f(\tau)\right] &= \int_0^\infty e^{-rt} f(t) \mathbf{P}[\tau \in dt] \\ &= \int_0^\infty e^{-rt} f(t) d\mathbf{P}[\tau \le t] = \int_0^\infty e^{-(r+\lambda)t} \lambda f(t) dt.\end{aligned}$$

The second equality follows by observing that

$$\begin{aligned}\mathbf{E}\left[\int_0^\tau e^{-rt} f(t) dt\right] &= \mathbf{E}\left[\int_0^\infty e^{-rt} \mathbf{1}_{\{\tau > t\}} f(t) dt\right] \\ &= \int_0^\infty e^{-rt} \mathbf{P}[\tau > t] f(t) dt = \int_0^\infty e^{-(r+\lambda)t} f(t) dt.\end{aligned}$$

The last part of the statement follows by letting $f = 1$. □

Lemma A.18: Assume that $(\tau_i)_{i=1}^n$ are independent exponential random variables with rates $(\lambda_i)_{i=1}^n$. Then $\tau = \min_i \tau_i$ is exponential with rate $\sum_j \lambda_j$ and

$$\mathbf{E}\left[e^{-r\tau}\mathbf{1}_{\{\tau=\tau_i\}}\right] = \frac{\lambda_i}{r+\sum_j \lambda_j}$$

for any discount rate $r > 0$.

Proof. The first part follows from (A.4) and the independence assumption by noting that

$$\begin{aligned}\mathbf{P}\left[\tau > t\right] &= \mathbf{P}\left[\{\tau_1 > t\} \cap \{\tau_2 > t\} \cap \cdots \cap \{\tau_n > t\}\right] \\ &= \prod_{i=1}^n \mathbf{P}\left[\tau_i > t\right] = \prod_{i=1}^n e^{-\lambda_i t} = e^{-\sum_i \lambda_i t}.\end{aligned}$$

To establish the second part let $\lambda = \sum_j \lambda_j$ and observe that

$$\begin{aligned}\mathbf{E}\left[e^{-r\tau}\mathbf{1}_{\{\tau=\tau_i\}}\right] &= \mathbf{E}\left[e^{-r\tau_i}\mathbf{1}_{\{\min_{j\neq i}\tau_j > \tau_i\}}\right] \\ &= \mathbf{E}\left[e^{-r\tau_i}\mathbf{E}\left[\mathbf{1}_{\{\min_{j\neq i}\tau_j > \tau_i\}}\middle|\tau_i\right]\right] \\ &= \mathbf{E}\left[e^{-(r+\lambda-\lambda_i)\tau_i}\right] = \frac{\lambda_i}{r+\lambda-\lambda_i+\lambda_i} = \frac{\lambda_i}{r+\lambda}.\end{aligned}$$

where the second equality follows from the law of iterated expectations, the third equality follows from the first part applied to $(\tau_j)_{j\neq i}$, and the last equality follows from Lemma A.17 applied to τ_i. □

Lemma A.19: Assume that $(\tau_i)_{i=1}^n$ are independent exponential random variables with rates $(\lambda_i)_{i=1}^n$; then

$$\mathbf{P}\left[\sum_{k=1}^n \tau_k \in dt\right] = \frac{e^{-\lambda t}\lambda^n t^{n-1}}{(n-1)!}dt,$$

which is known as the Erlang distribution with parameters (n, λ).

Proof. Let $\sigma_n = \sum_{k=1}^n \tau_k$. Lemma A.17 and the assumed independence between the terms of the sum imply that

$$\mathbf{E}\left[e^{-\beta\sigma_n}\right]=\prod_{k=1}^{n}\mathbf{E}\left[e^{-\beta\tau_k}\right]=\left(\frac{\lambda}{\lambda+\beta}\right)^n,$$

and the desired result follows by inverting this Laplace transform. See Schiff [1999, ex. 1.28] for a detailed argument. □

A.4 Distributions with Log-Concave Densities

Continuous distributions that admit a density whose logarithm is concave play a key role in the solution of problems with asymmetric information. In this section we state some properties of such distributions that are used in the text. A review of the theory of log-concave functions can be found in Saumard and Wellner [2014].

Definition A.20: A continuous distribution F is of class $\mathcal{L}$ if it admits a density $f=F'$ such that $\log f$ is a concave function.

Proposition A.21: Assume that $F\in\mathcal{L}$. Then

1. The function F is log concave.
2. The survival function $1-F$ is log concave.
3. $\exists m\in \mathrm{cl}(\mathcal{D})$ such that $F(\delta)$ is convex on $(\underline{\delta},m]$ and concave on $[m,\underline{\delta})$.

Proof. Since $\log f$ is concave, we have that $f>0$ is absolutely continuous and admits a weak derivative $f'=F''$ such that

$$\frac{f'(\delta)}{f(\delta)}=\frac{F''(\delta)}{F'(\delta)}$$

is nonincreasing. This immediately implies the validity of assertion 3. To establish assertions 1 and 2 we need to show that f/F and $-f/(1-F)$ are both nonincreasing or, equivalently, that

$$F(\delta)^2\frac{d}{d\delta}\left(\frac{f(\delta)}{F(\delta)}\right)=f'(\delta)F(\delta)-f(\delta)^2\leq 0$$

and

$$(1-F(\delta))^2\frac{d}{d\delta}\left(\frac{f(\delta)}{1-F(\delta)}\right)=f'(\delta)(1-F(\delta))+f(\delta)^2\geq 0.$$

To prove these two inequalities note that since the ratio f'/f is nonincreasing due to log-concavity, we have that

$$\frac{f'(\delta)}{f(\delta)}F(\delta)=\frac{f'(\delta)}{f(\delta)}\int_{\underline{\delta}}^{\delta}f(x)dx\leq\int_{\underline{\delta}}^{\delta}f'(x)dx\leq f(\delta)-f(\underline{\delta})\leq f(\delta)$$

and

$$\frac{f'(\delta)}{f(\delta)}(1-F(\delta))=\frac{f'(\delta)}{f(\delta)}\int_{\delta}^{\overline{\delta}}f(x)dx\geq\int_{\delta}^{\overline{\delta}}f'(x)dx\geq -f(\delta),$$

where on each line the last inequality follows from the fact that the density is strictly positive. □

A.5 Stochastic Processes

Assume that time is continuous and indexed by $t \geq 0$. Let $\mathcal{D}=(\underline{\delta},\overline{\delta})$ denote an open interval of the real line with $|\overline{\delta}-\overline{\delta}|\leq\infty$ and fix a probability space $(\Omega,\mathcal{F},\mathbf{P})$ as defined in Appendix A.2.

Definition A.22: A $\mathcal{D}$-valued stochastic process is a collection $(\delta_t)_{t\geq 0}$ of $\mathcal{D}$-valued random variables that is measurable in the sense that

$$\{\omega\in\Omega:\delta_t(\omega)\in A\}\in\mathcal{F}$$

for each $t\geq 0$ and every Borel set $A\subseteq\mathbf{R}$.

To capture the gradual revelation of uncertainty that is inherent to the temporal nature of economic phenomena, we equip the probability space with a family $\mathbb{F}=\{\mathcal{F}_t\}_{t\geq 0}$ of σ-algebras such that

$$\mathcal{F}_t\subseteq\mathcal{F}_{t+u}\subseteq\mathcal{F},\qquad \forall t,u\geq 0.$$

The family $\mathbb{F}$ is referred to as a *filtration*, and the usual interpretation is that $\mathcal{F}_t$ models the collection of events that are known at date $t\geq 0$. In this context the monotonicity condition guarantees that no information is lost, so that the total amount of available information only grows over time. To ensure that the stochastic process is consistent with this interpretation, we need to impose the following progressive measurability condition:

Definition A.23: A stochastic process $(\delta_t)_{t\geq 0}$ is adapted to the filtration $\mathbb{F}$ if the random variable δ_t is $\mathcal{F}_t$-measurable for every date $t\geq 0$.

There are usually several possible choices of filtration. In particular, the simplest filtration with respect to which a given stochastic process is adapted is the natural filtration

$$\mathcal{F}_t^{(\delta)} = \sigma\{\delta_s : 0 \le s \le t\}$$

that it generates over time. When referring to this filtration we interpret the property that $A \in \mathcal{F}_t^{\delta}$ as meaning that an agent who continuously observes the process knows by date t whether the event A has occurred.

The following definitions and examples cover some classes of stochastic processes that we frequently encounter in the text.

Definition A.24: An $\mathbb{F}$-adapted process $(\delta_t)_{t\ge 0}$ with $\delta_0 = 0$ is a Poisson process with intensity λ if it has right-continuous and piecewise constant paths with jumps of size one and if for any $0 \le s \le t$ the random variable $\delta_t - \delta_s$ is independent of $\mathcal{F}_s$ and Poisson distributed with parameter $\lambda(t-s)$.

Example A.25: Here is a simple construction of the Poisson process. Let $(\tau_n)_{n=1}^{\infty}$ be a sequence of iid exponential random variables with rate λ and consider the stochastic process defined by

$$\delta_t = \max\left\{k \in \mathbf{N}_0 : \sigma_k = \sum_{n=1}^{k} \tau_n \le t\right\}, \tag{A.5}$$

with its natural filtration $\mathbb{F} = \mathbb{F}^{(\delta)}$. This process has right-continuous and piecewise constant paths with jumps of size one. Therefore, all we need to prove that $(\delta_t)_{t\ge 0}$ is a Poisson process is to compute

$$\mathcal{P} = \mathbf{P}[\delta_t - \delta_s = k | \delta_s = i] = \frac{\mathbf{P}[\{\delta_s = i\} \cap \{\delta_t = i+k\}]}{\mathbf{P}[\delta_s = i]}$$

for arbitrary $0 \le s \le t$ and $i, k \in \mathbf{N}_0$. Assume first that $k = 0$. Using (A.5) and Lemma A.19 shows that in this case the numerator is given by

$$\begin{aligned}\mathbf{P}[\delta_s = \delta_t = i] &= \mathbf{P}[\{\sigma_i \le s\} \cap \{\sigma_i + \tau_{i+1} > t\}] \\ &= \mathbf{E}\left[\mathbf{1}_{\{\sigma_i \le s\}} e^{-\lambda(t-\sigma_i)}\right] = \int_0^s \frac{e^{-\lambda t}\lambda^i u^{i-1} du}{(i-1)!} = \frac{e^{-\lambda t}(\lambda s)^i}{i!},\end{aligned}$$

and setting $t = s$ shows that the denominator is

$$\mathbf{P}[\delta_s = i] = \frac{e^{-\lambda s}(\lambda s)^i}{i!}.$$

Now assume that $k \geq 1$. Since $a = \tau_{i+k+1}$ and $b = \tau_{i+1}$ are both exponentially distributed with rate λ, and the random variables a, b, σ_i, and $c = \sigma_{i+k} - \sigma_{i+1}$ are independent, we have that

$$\begin{aligned}
\mathbf{P}\left[\{\delta_s = i\} \cap \{\delta_t = k\}\right] &= \mathbf{P}\left[\{\sigma_i \leq s < \sigma_{i+1}\} \cap \{\sigma_{i+k} \leq t < \sigma_{i+k} + a\}\right] \\
&= \mathbf{E}\left[\mathbf{1}_{\{\sigma_i \leq s < \sigma_{i+1}\}} \mathbf{1}_{\{\sigma_{i+k} \leq t\}} e^{-\lambda(t - \sigma_{i+k})}\right] \\
&= \mathbf{E}\left[\mathbf{1}_{\{\sigma_i \leq s < \sigma_i + b\}} \mathbf{1}_{\{b + c + \sigma_i \leq t\}} e^{-\lambda(t - b - c - \sigma_i)}\right] \\
&= \mathbf{E}\left[\mathbf{1}_{\{\sigma_i \leq s\}} \mathbf{1}_{\{c \leq t - s\}} \lambda(t - s - c) e^{-\lambda(t - c - \sigma_i)}\right] \\
&= \mathbf{E}\left[\mathbf{1}_{\{\sigma_i \leq s\}} e^{\lambda \sigma_i}\right] \mathbf{E}\left[\mathbf{1}_{\{c \leq t - s\}} \lambda(t - s - c) e^{\lambda(c - t)}\right].
\end{aligned}$$

Applying Lemma A.19 to σ_i and c then gives

$$\mathbf{E}\left[\mathbf{1}_{\{\sigma_i \leq s\}} e^{\lambda \sigma_i}\right] = \int_0^s \frac{\lambda^i u^{i-1} du}{(i-1)!} = \frac{(\lambda s)^i}{i!},$$

$$\begin{aligned}
\mathbf{E}\left[\lambda(t - s - c)^+ e^{\lambda c}\right] &= \mathbf{1}_{\{k=1\}} \lambda(t - s) \\
&\quad + \mathbf{1}_{\{k \geq 2\}} \int_0^{t-s} \frac{\lambda^k u^{k-2} (t - s - u) du}{(k-2)!} \\
&= \mathbf{1}_{\{k=1\}} \lambda(t - s) + \mathbf{1}_{\{k \geq 2\}} \frac{\lambda^k (t - s)^k}{k!} = \frac{(\lambda(t - s))^k}{k!},
\end{aligned}$$

and putting everything back together we conclude that

$$\mathcal{P} = \frac{e^{-\lambda(t-s)} (\lambda(t - s))^k}{k!}.$$

This shows that, conditional on δ_s, the increment $\delta_t - \delta_s$ is a Poisson random variable with mean $\lambda(t - s)$. Since this distribution does not depend on δ_s, this in turn implies that the increment $\delta_t - \delta_s$ is independent of $\mathcal{F}_s$, and it finally follows that $(\delta_t)_{t \geq 0}$ is a Poisson process.

Definition A.26: An $\mathbb{F}$-adapted stochastic process $(\delta_t)_{t \geq 0}$ is a Markov process if

$$\mathbf{P}\left[\delta_{t+s} \in A | \mathcal{F}_t\right] = \mathbf{P}\left[\delta_{t+s} \in A | \delta_t\right]$$

for all $s, t \geq 0$ and every Borel set $A \subseteq \mathbf{R}$. If, in addition, the right-hand side of the above identity only depends on δ_t and the time increment s, then the Markov process is said to be homogeneous.

Example A.27: Let $(F(\cdot|\delta))_{\delta\in\mathcal{D}}$ be a collection of distributions on $\mathcal{D}$. A Markov chain on $\mathcal{D}$ with transition function $F(\cdot|\delta)$ is a process such that

$$\mathbf{P}\left[\delta_t = \delta_{[\![t]\!]}\right] = 1$$

for all $t \geq 0$ and

$$\mathbf{P}\left[\delta_n \leq \delta | \delta_{n-1}\right] = F(\delta|\delta_{n-1})$$

for all $n \in \mathbf{N}$, where $[\![\cdot]\!]$ denotes the integer part. The interpretation of this construction is clear: the process starts at $\delta_0 \in \mathcal{D}$ and remains constant until $t = 1$, where it jumps to a value δ_1 that is drawn from the distribution $F(\cdot|\delta_0)$ and from which the same cycle begins anew. As we will see below in Appendix A.6, processes of this type can be used as building blocks to construct a rich class of jump processes.

Definition A.28: A stochastic process $(\delta_t)_{t\geq 0}$ is a (super/sub)martingale with respect to the filtration $\mathbb{F}$ if it is adapted to $\mathbb{F}$ and such that

$$\mathbf{E}|\delta_t| < \infty \quad \text{and} \quad \mathbf{E}\left[\delta_t|\mathcal{F}_t\right] = \delta_s \ (\leq/\geq)$$

for all $0 \leq s \leq t$.

Example A.29: If $g \in \mathcal{B}$ is a differentiable function and $(N_t)_{t\geq 0}$ is a Poisson process with intensity $\lambda > 0$, then

$$\int_0^t g(s)(dN_s - \lambda ds) = \sum_{s\leq t} \mathbf{1}_{\{\Delta N_s \neq 0\}} g(s) - \int_0^t \lambda g(s) ds$$

is a martingale. In particular, setting $g \equiv 1$ shows that $N_t - \lambda t$ is a martingale. To prove this result let $u \leq t$ and observe that

$$\begin{aligned}\int_u^t g(s) dN_s &= g(t)N_t - g(u)N_u - \int_u^t g'(s) N_{s-} ds \\ &= g(t)N_t - g(u)N_u - \int_u^t g'(s)(N_s - N_u) ds - \int_u^t g'(s) N_u ds \\ &= g(t)(N_t - N_u) - \int_u^t g'(s)(N_s - N_u) ds,\end{aligned}$$

where the first equality follows by differentiating $g(t)N_t$ and the second follows from the fact that the jumps of N_t take place on sets of Lebesgue measure 0. Taking conditional expectations on both sides shows that

$$\mathbf{E}\left[\int_u^t g(s)dN_s \middle| \mathcal{F}_u\right] = g(t)\mathbf{E}\left[N_t - N_u|\mathcal{F}_u\right] - \int_u^t g'(s)\mathbf{E}\left[N_s - N_u|\mathcal{F}_u\right] ds$$

$$= \lambda g(t)(t-u) - \int_u^t \lambda g'(s)(s-u)ds$$

$$= \int_u^t \lambda g(s)ds,$$

where the second equality follows from the fact that the increment $N_s - N_u$ has mean $\lambda(s-u)$ independently of $\mathcal{F}_u$.

A.6 Markov Jump Processes

Throughout the text we model the time-varying type of an economic agent as a Markov process that is constant between exponentially distributed times at which its value is randomly reset. Such processes are referred to as Markov jump processes and are formally defined as follows:

Definition A.30: Assume that $(\delta_t)_{t\geq 0}$ is an homogeneous $\mathcal{D}$-valued Markov process and define

$$Ag(\delta) = \lim_{h\to 0} \frac{1}{h}\mathbf{E}\left[g(\delta_{t+h}) - g(\delta_t)\middle|\delta_t = \delta\right], \tag{A.6}$$

where the limit is with respect to the norm on $\mathcal{B}$. Then the process $(\delta_t)_{t\geq 0}$ is said to be a Markov jump process if

$$Ag(\delta) = \gamma(\delta)\int_{\underline{\delta}}^{\overline{\delta}} \left(g(x) - g(\delta)\right) dF(x|\delta), \qquad \forall g \in \mathcal{B}, \tag{A.7}$$

for some nonnegative $\gamma \in \mathcal{B}$ and some collection $\mathbf{F} = (F(\cdot|\delta))_{\delta\in\mathcal{D}}$ of distribution functions on $\mathcal{D}$.

An intuitive interpretation of the definition of the infinitesimal generator is that $Ag(\delta_t)$ specifies the expected rate of change of the process $g(\delta_t)$ over the next infinitesimal time interval given its current value δ_t. Indeed, it follows from (A.6) that for any sufficiently regular function,

$$\mathbf{E}\left[g(\delta_{t+h}) - g(\delta_t)\middle|\delta_t\right] = Ag(\delta_t)h + o(h),$$

where $o(h)$ denotes a quantity that converges to zero faster than h. Applying this relation to the test function

$$g(x) = \mathbf{1}_{\{x \leq z\}} \mathbf{1}_{\{x \neq \delta\}}$$

with $z \in \mathcal{D}$ shows that for a Markov jump process;

$$\mathbf{P}\left[\delta_t \neq \delta_{t+h} \leq z | \delta_t\right] = h \int_{\underline{\delta}}^{z} \mathbf{1}_{\{x \neq \delta_t\}} \gamma(\delta_t) dF(x|\delta_t) + o(h). \tag{A.8}$$

This identity provides a description of the local behavior of the process and allows for a clear interpretation of the functions γ and $F(\cdot|\delta)$ that appear in the definition of A. Indeed, letting $z \uparrow \bar{\delta}$ in (A.8) shows that the flow probability of a jump occurring over the next instant is

$$\lim_{h \to 0} \frac{1}{h} \mathbf{P}\left[\delta_t \neq \delta_{t+h} | \delta_t\right] = \gamma(\delta_t) \left(1 - \Delta F(\delta_t | \delta_t)\right), \tag{A.9}$$

and substituting this expression back into (A.8) then shows that, conditional on the arrival of a jump, the cumulative distribution of the new value of the process is given by the rescaled distribution

$$\lim_{h \to 0} \mathbf{P}\left[\delta_{t+h} \leq z | \delta_{t+h} \neq \delta_t\right] = \frac{F(z|\delta_t) - \mathbf{1}_{\{\delta_t \leq z\}} \Delta F(\delta_t|\delta_t)}{1 - \Delta F(\delta_t|\delta_t)}. \tag{A.10}$$

The product on the right of (A.9) and the rescaling in (A.10) jointly reflect the fact that, conditional on the current state of the process, the arrival of the next reset date is exponentially distributed with rate $\gamma(\delta_t)$ but only leads to an actual jump if the newly drawn value differs from the previous one, which occurs with probability

$$\int_{\underline{\delta}}^{\bar{\delta}} \mathbf{1}_{\{x \neq \delta_t\}} dF(x|\delta_t) = 1 - \Delta F(\delta_t|\delta_t).$$

The distinction between the reset dates and the jump times of a Markov jump process is also apparent in the fact that the action of the generator in (A.7) only depends on $\gamma(\delta)$ and $dF(x|\delta)$ through their product at points $x \neq \delta$. This invariance gives us some degrees of freedom in the specification of a Markov jump process. In particular, starting from an arbitrary $\gamma(\delta)$ and $F(x|\delta)$ one can obtain either an equivalent specification with a constant arrival rate of resets by replacing the original parameters with

$$\gamma^*(\delta) = \|\gamma\|, \tag{A.11}$$

$$F^*(x|\delta) = \frac{\gamma(\delta)}{\|\gamma\|} F(x|\delta) + \left(1 - \frac{\gamma(\delta)}{\|\gamma\|}\right) \mathbf{1}_{\{\delta \leq x\}}; \tag{A.12}$$

or an equivalent specification in which every reset automatically triggers a jump by replacing the original parameters with

$$\gamma^{\sharp}(\delta) = \gamma(\delta)(1 - \Delta F(\delta|\delta)),$$

$$F^{\sharp}(x|\delta) = \frac{1}{1 - \Delta F(\delta|\delta)}(F(x|\delta) - \mathbf{1}_{\{\delta \leq x\}}\Delta F(\delta|\delta)).$$

Which equivalent specification is most convenient depends on the question at hand. For example, in the proof of the following existence result it is easiest to work with a constant arrival rate, as this allows us to explicitly construct the process by running a Markov chain according to a random clock modeled as a Poisson process.

Proposition A.31: Assume that $\gamma \in \mathcal{B}$ is nonnegative and that $\mathbf{F} = (F(\cdot|\delta))_{\delta \in \mathcal{D}}$ is a collection of distribution functions on $\mathcal{D}$. Then there exists a Markov process with the infinitesimal generator given by (A.7).

Proof. Assume that $\|\gamma\| = \sup_\delta \gamma(\delta) > 0$, for otherwise there is nothing to prove. As discussed above, the action of the generator remains unchanged if we replace $(\gamma, F(\cdot|\delta))$ by (A.11) and (A.12) so that

$$Ag(\delta) = \|\gamma\| \int_{\underline{\delta}}^{\overline{\delta}} (g(x) - g(\delta))dF^*(x|\delta).$$

Now, let $(Y_t)_{t \geq 0}$ be a Markov chain on $\mathcal{D}$ as in Example A.27 and define

$$\delta_t = Y_{N_t}$$

where the random time change $(N_t)_{t \geq 0}$ is an independent Poisson process with intensity $\gamma = \|\gamma\|$ obtained as in Example A.25. To prove that this construction defines a Markov process, it suffices to show that

$$\mathbf{E}\left[g(\delta_{t+h})\middle|\mathcal{F}_t\right] = \mathbf{E}\left[g(\delta_{t+h})\middle|\delta_t\right] \tag{A.13}$$

for all $g \in \mathcal{B}$ and $t, h \geq 0$ where $\mathcal{F}_t = \mathcal{F}_t^{(\delta)} \vee \mathcal{F}_t^{(N)}$. Indeed, if this property holds, then the law of iterated expectations implies that

$$\begin{aligned}\mathbf{E}\left[g(\delta_{t+h})\middle|\mathcal{F}_t^{(\delta)}\right] &= \mathbf{E}\left[\mathbf{E}\left[g(\delta_{t+h})\middle|\mathcal{F}_t\right]\middle|\mathcal{F}_t^{(\delta)}\right] \\ &= \mathbf{E}\left[\mathbf{E}\left[g(\delta_{t+h})\middle|\delta_t\right]\middle|\mathcal{F}_t^{(\delta)}\right] = \mathbf{E}\left[g(\delta_{t+h})\middle|\delta_t\right],\end{aligned}$$

and the $\mathbb{F}^{(\delta)}$-Markov property now follows from Definition A.26. To establish the validity of equation (A.13) let

$$Pg(y) = \mathbf{E}\left[g(Y_{n+1})\,\middle|\,Y_n = y\right] = \int_{\underline{\delta}}^{\overline{\delta}} g(x)dF(x|y) \tag{A.14}$$

denote the one-step transition operator of the underlying Markov chain and observe that for any $g \in \mathcal{B}$ and $B \in \mathcal{F}_t$,

$$\begin{aligned}
\mathbf{E}\left[\mathbf{1}_{\{B\}}g(\delta_{t+h})\right] &= \mathbf{E}\left[\mathbf{1}_{\{B\}}g\left(Y_{N_t+[N_{t+h}-N_t]}\right)\right] \\
&= \mathbf{E}\left[\mathbf{1}_{\{B\}}\sum_{n=0}^{\infty} e^{-\gamma h}\frac{(\gamma h)^n}{n!}g\left(Y_{N_t+n}\right)\right] \\
&= \mathbf{E}\left[\mathbf{1}_{\{B\}}\sum_{n=0}^{\infty} e^{-\gamma h}\frac{(\gamma h)^n}{n!}P^n g\left(Y_{N_t}\right)\right] \\
&= \mathbf{E}\left[\mathbf{1}_{\{B\}}\sum_{n=0}^{\infty} e^{-\gamma h}\frac{(\gamma h)^n}{n!}P^n g(\delta_t)\right],
\end{aligned}$$

where the first and last equalities follow from the definition of δ_t, the second equality follows from basic properties of the Poisson process, and the third equality follows from (A.14). This shows that our construction defines a time-homogenous Markov process such that

$$\mathbf{E}\left[g(\delta_{t+h})\,\middle|\,\delta_t = \delta\right] = \mathbf{E}\left[g(\delta_h)\,\middle|\,\delta_t = \delta\right] = \sum_{n=0}^{\infty} e^{-\gamma h}\frac{(\gamma h)^n}{n!}P^n g(\delta_t),$$

and the result now follows by observing that

$$\begin{aligned}
\left|\frac{1}{h}\mathbf{E}\left[g(\delta_{t+h}) - g(\delta_t)\,\middle|\,\delta_t\right] - Ag(\delta_t)\right| &= \left|\sum_{n=2}^{\infty} e^{-\gamma h}\frac{\gamma^n h^{n-1}}{n!}(P^n - I)g(\delta_t)\right| \\
&\leq 2\|g\|\left|\sum_{n=2}^{\infty} e^{-\gamma h}\frac{\gamma^n h^{n-1}}{n!}\right| \\
&= 2\|g\|\left(1 - e^{-\gamma h}\right)
\end{aligned}$$

for all $g \in \mathcal{B}$ and letting $h \to 0$. □

The following proposition establishes a martingale property that is often used as an alternative characterization of a Markov jump process.

Proposition A.32: Assume that $(\delta_t)_{t\geq 0}$ is a Markov jump process with the generator A as in definition A.30. Then the process

$$M_t = e^{-rt}g(\delta_t) + \int_0^t e^{-rs}(rg(\delta_s) - Ag(\delta_s))ds$$

is a bounded $\mathbb{F}^{(\delta)}$-martingale for all $p \in \mathcal{B}$ and $r > 0$.

Proof. Let $g \in \mathcal{B}$ be fixed. Since $\|Ag\| \leq 2\|\gamma\|\,\|g\|$ we have that

$$|M_t| \leq \|g\| + \int_0^t e^{-rs}\|Ag - rg\|ds$$
$$\leq \|g\| + \int_0^t e^{-rs}(2\|\gamma\| + r)\|g\|ds \leq 2\left(1 + \frac{\|\gamma\|}{r}\right)\|g\|,$$

and it follows that the process $(M_t)_{t\geq 0}$ is bounded. Now define a family of time-indexed operators by setting

$$T_\eta h(\delta) = \mathbf{E}\left[h(\delta_{t+\eta})\,\middle|\,\delta_t = \delta\right] = \mathbf{E}\left[h(\delta_\eta)\,\middle|\,\delta_0 = \delta\right]$$

for all $\eta \geq 0$ and $h \in \mathcal{B}$. Since $g \in \mathcal{B}$, we know from Lemma A.33 below that the map $\eta \mapsto T_\eta g$ is differentiable with $(d/d\eta)T_\eta g = T_\eta Ag$. Therefore, a direct calculation using the assumed homogeneity of the Markov process shows that

$$\frac{d}{d\eta}(e^{-r\eta}T_\eta g)(\delta) = e^{-r\eta}\left(T_\eta Ag - rT_\eta g\right)(\delta)$$
$$= e^{-r\eta}\mathbf{E}\left[(Ag - rg)(\delta_\eta)\,\middle|\,\delta_0 = \delta\right]$$
$$= e^{-r\eta}\mathbf{E}\left[(Ag - rg)(\delta_{t+\eta})\,\middle|\,\delta_t = \delta\right].$$

Integrating over the time increment η between $\eta = 0$ and $\eta = \theta - t$ on both sides of this relation then gives

$$\mathbf{E}\left[e^{-r(\theta-t)}g(\delta_\theta)\,\middle|\,\mathcal{F}_t^{(\delta)}\right] - g(\delta_t) = \mathbf{E}\left[e^{-r(\theta-t)}g(\delta_\theta)\,\middle|\,\delta_t\right] - g(\delta_t)$$
$$= T_{\theta-t}g(\delta_t) - T_0 g(\delta_t)$$
$$= \int_0^{\theta-t} e^{-r\eta}\mathbf{E}\left[(Ag - rg)(\delta_{t+\eta})\,\middle|\,\delta_t\right]d\eta$$
$$= \int_t^{\theta} e^{-r(s-t)}\mathbf{E}\left[(Ag - rg)(\delta_s)\,\middle|\,\delta_t\right]ds$$
$$= \int_t^{\theta} e^{-r(s-t)}\mathbf{E}\left[(Ag - rg)(\delta_s)\,\middle|\,\mathcal{F}_t^{(\delta)}\right]ds,$$

and the required martingale property now follows from the boundedness of the function $Ag - rg$, which justifies the application of Fubini's theorem required to interchange the integral and the expectation in the rightmost term. □

Lemma A.33: Assume that $(\delta)_{t\geq 0}$ is a Markov jump process with the generator A as in definition A.30. Then the mapping

$$\mathbf{R}_+ \ni \eta \mapsto T_\eta h = \mathbf{E}\left[h(\delta_\eta)\,\middle|\,\delta_0 = \cdot\right] \in \mathcal{B} \tag{A.15}$$

is differentiable for any $h \in \mathcal{B}$ with

$$\frac{d}{d\eta}\left(T_\eta h\right) = \lim_{s\to 0} \frac{1}{s}\left(T_{\eta+s}h - T_\eta h\right) = T_\eta A h,$$

where the limit is with respect to the norm on $\mathcal{B}$.

Proof. Fix an arbitrary $h \in \mathcal{B}$. As a first step we claim that the map in (A.15) is strongly continuous at the origin. Indeed, if this property fails, then there exist a constant $\varepsilon^* > 0$ and a decreasing sequence $(\eta_n)_{n=1}^{\infty} \to 0$ such that

$$\inf_{n\in\mathbf{N}} \|T_{\eta_n}h - h\| = \inf_{n\in\mathbf{N}} \|T_{\eta_n}h - T_0 h\| \geq \varepsilon^*.$$

On the other hand, since the functions $\frac{T_{\eta_n}h - h}{\eta_n}$ converge to Ah in the norm of $\mathcal{B}$, we have that for any $\varepsilon > 0$ there exists an index m such that

$$\sup_{n\geq m} \left\| \frac{T_{\eta_n}h - h}{\eta_n} - Ah \right\| \leq \varepsilon.$$

Combining the two inequalities gives

$$\frac{\varepsilon^*}{\eta_n} \leq \left\| \frac{T_{\eta_n}h - h}{\eta_n} \right\| \leq \left\| \frac{T_{\eta_n}h - h}{\eta_n} - Ah \right\| + \|Ah\| \leq \varepsilon + 2\|\gamma\|\,\|h\|$$

for all $n \geq m$, and the contradiction follows by letting $n \to \infty$. Turning to the proof of the statement, we start by observing that the Markov property and the law of iterated expectations jointly imply that

$$\begin{aligned} T_{\eta+s}h(\delta_0) &= \mathbf{E}\left[h(\delta_{\eta+s})\,\middle|\,\delta_0\right] \\ &= \mathbf{E}\left[\mathbf{E}\left[h(\delta_{\eta+s})\,\middle|\,\mathcal{F}_\eta^{(\delta)}\right]\middle|\,\delta_0\right] \\ &= \mathbf{E}\left[\mathbf{E}\left[h(\delta_{\eta+s})\,\middle|\,\delta_\eta\right]\middle|\,\delta_0\right] = T_\eta T_s h(\delta_0) \end{aligned}$$

for all $s, \eta \geq 0$. Combining this property with the definition of the left and right derivatives then shows that for all $s > 0$ we have

$$\begin{aligned}\left\|\frac{T_{\eta+s}h - T_\eta h}{s} - T_\eta Ah\right\| &= \left\|T_\eta\left(\frac{T_s h - h}{s} - Ah\right)\right\| \\ &\leq \left\|\frac{T_s h - h}{s} - Ah\right\| \end{aligned} \tag{A.16}$$

and

$$\begin{aligned}\left\|\frac{T_{\eta-s}h - T_\eta h}{-s} - T_\eta Ah\right\| &= \left\|T_{\eta-s}\left(\frac{T_s h - h}{s} - T_s Ah\right)\right\| \\ &\leq \left\|\frac{T_s h - h}{s} - T_s Ah\right\| \\ &\leq \|T_s Ah - Ah\| + \left\|\frac{T_s h - h}{s} - Ah\right\|, \end{aligned} \tag{A.17}$$

where the inequality in (A.16) and the first inequality in (A.17) follow from the fact that $\|T_\tau k\| \leq \|k\|$ for all $\tau \geq 0$ and $k \in \mathcal{B}$. Letting $s \to 0$ and using the definition of A in conjunction with the strong continuity established in the first part then shows that the left and right derivative are both equal to $T_\eta Ah$, which completes the proof. □

Remark A.34: Let $\mathcal{C} = \mathcal{C}(\mathcal{D})$ denote the set of continuous functions on $\mathcal{D}$. For some of the results in the text it is necessary to assume that

$$h \mapsto \gamma(\delta) \int_{\underline{\delta}}^{\overline{\delta}} h(x) dF(x|\delta) \text{ maps } \mathcal{C} \text{ into itself.} \tag{A.18}$$

This property is sometimes referred to the Feller property (see, e.g., Stokey and Lucas [1989, p. 220]) and can be ensured by assuming that the intensity function $\gamma \in \mathcal{C}$ and that the map $\delta \mapsto dF(\cdot|\delta)$ from $\mathcal{D}$ into the set of probability measures defined on $\mathcal{D}$ is weakly continuous. By the so-called Portmanteau theorem the latter weak continuity is equivalent to the requirement that

$$\limsup_{n\to\infty} \int_{\underline{\delta}}^{\overline{\delta}} \mathbf{1}_{\{x\in C\}} \left(dF(x|\delta_n) - dF(x|\delta)\right) \leq 0$$

for any closed subset $C \subseteq \mathcal{D}$ as $\delta_n \to \delta$, which is in turn equivalent to the requirement that

$$\lim_{n\to\infty} \int_{\underline{\delta}}^{\overline{\delta}} h(x) \left(dF(x|\delta_n) - dF(x|\delta)\right) = 0$$

for any function $h \in \mathcal{C}$ as $\delta_n \to \delta$.

Example A.35: Consider the Markov jump process on $\mathcal{D} = \mathbf{R}$ with the infinitesimal generator given by

$$Ag(\delta) = \gamma\left(g(\delta+1) - g(\delta)\right)$$

for some constant $\gamma > 0$. Starting from a given $\delta_0 \in \mathbf{R}$, this process is piecewise constant between jumps of size one whose interarrival times are exponential with rate γ. Therefore, one naturally expects that $(\delta_t - \delta_0)_{t\geq 0}$ constitutes a Poisson process with intensity γ, and we verify this property in Example A.39 below by computing the transition density of the process.

Example A.36: Let $\underline{\delta} < \delta_1 < \delta_2 < \cdots < \overline{\delta}$ be distinct points and $(p_{ij})_{i,j=1}^{\infty}$ be a collection of nonnegative numbers such that $p_{ii} = 0$ and $\sum_j p_{ij} = 1$. Consider the Markov jump process with generator given by

$$Ag(\delta) = \gamma(\delta)\sum_{j=1}^{\infty}\left(g(\delta_j) - g(\delta)\right)\sum_{i=1}^{\infty}\mathbf{1}_{\{\delta=\delta_i\}}p_{ij}$$

for some nonnegative function $\gamma \in \mathcal{B}$. The behavior of this process depends on its initial value. If the process starts from some $\delta \notin (\delta_i)_{i=1}^{\infty}$, then it remains constant forever since $Ag(\delta) = 0$. Otherwise, if the process starts from $\delta = \delta_i$ for some i, then it behaves like a continuous-time Markov chain that lives on the countable state space $(\delta_j)_{j=1}^{\infty}$ and transitions from state δ_i to state δ_j according to an exponential random variable with rate $\gamma(\delta_i)p_{ij}$.

The remainder of this section provides formulas for computing expectations along the path of a Markov jump process.

Proposition A.37: Let $c \in \mathcal{B}$ and assume that $(\delta_t)_{t\geq 0}$ is a Markov jump process with generator A. Then

$$g(\delta) = \mathbf{E}\left[\int_t^{\infty} e^{-r(s-t)}c(\delta_s)ds\,\middle|\,\delta_t = \delta\right] \tag{A.19}$$

is the unique solution to $rg = c + Ag$ in $\mathcal{B}$ for any $r > 0$. Furthermore, if $c \in \mathcal{C}$ and (A.18) holds, then $g \in \mathcal{C}$.

Proof. Let $c \in \mathcal{B}$ be fixed. Since

$$c(\delta) + (A-r)g(\delta) = c(\delta) - (r+\gamma(\delta))g(\delta) + \int_{\underline{\delta}}^{\overline{\delta}} g(x)dF(x|\delta),$$

we have that the set of solutions $g \in \mathcal{B}$ to the equation in the statement coincides with the set of fixed points of the operator

$$Sg(\delta) = \frac{c(\delta)}{r+\gamma(\delta)} + \frac{\gamma(\delta)}{r+\gamma(\delta)} \int_{\underline{\delta}}^{\overline{\delta}} g(x)dF(x|\delta). \tag{A.20}$$

This operator clearly maps $\mathcal{B}$ into itself. Furthermore, a direct calculation shows that

$$\|Sg - Sh\| = \sup_{\delta \in \mathcal{D}} \left| \frac{\gamma(\delta)}{r+\gamma(\delta)} \int_{\underline{\delta}}^{\overline{\delta}} (g-h)(x)dF(x|\delta) \right| \le \frac{\|\gamma\| \|f-g\|}{r+\|\gamma\|}.$$

Since $r > 0$, this shows that S is a contraction and thus admits a unique fixed point $g \in \mathcal{B}$ by application of Theorem A.3. To show that this fixed point coincides with the expectation in (A.19) and thus complete the proof, we argue as follows. Because g is a solution to $rg - Ag = c$, it follows from Proposition A.32 that the process

$$\begin{aligned} M_t &= e^{-rt} g(\delta_t) + \int_0^t e^{-rs} \left(rg(\delta_s) - Ag(\delta_s) \right) ds \\ &= e^{-rt} g(\delta_t) + \int_0^t e^{-rs} c(\delta_s) ds \end{aligned}$$

is a bounded $\mathbb{F}^{(\delta)}$-martingale. In particular, we have that

$$\begin{aligned} M_t &= e^{-rt} g(\delta_t) + \int_0^t e^{-rs} c(\delta_s) ds \\ &= \mathbf{E}\left[M_\eta \middle| \mathcal{F}_t^{(\delta)} \right] = \mathbf{E}\left[e^{-r\eta} g(\delta_\eta) + \int_0^\eta e^{-rs} c(\delta_s) ds \middle| \mathcal{F}_t^{(\delta)} \right] \end{aligned}$$

for all $0 \le t \le \eta$ and therefore

$$g(\delta_t) = \mathbf{E}\left[e^{-r(\eta-t)} g(\delta_\eta) + \int_t^\eta e^{-r(s-t)} c(\delta_s) ds \middle| \mathcal{F}_t^{(\delta)} \right]. \tag{A.21}$$

Now, since $r > 0$ and the functions $c, g \in \mathcal{B}$ we have that

$$\lim_{\eta \to \infty} e^{-r\eta} |g(\delta_\eta)| \le \lim_{\eta \to \infty} e^{-r\eta} \|g\| = 0$$

and

$$\left| e^{-r(\eta-t)} g(\delta_\eta) + \int_t^\eta e^{-r(s-t)} c(\delta_s) ds \right| \le \|g\| + \frac{1}{r} \|c\|.$$

Therefore, letting $\eta \to \infty$ in (A.21) gives (A.19) by application of the dominated convergence theorem. To complete the proof, assume that $c \in \mathcal{C}$ and that (A.18) holds. In this case it is easily seen from (A.20) that S maps $\mathcal{C}$ onto itself, and the conclusion now follows from Corollary A.4 by observing that $\mathcal{C}$ is a closed subset of $\mathcal{B}$. □

Corollary A.38: Assume that $c \in \mathcal{B}$ is nondecreasing, that $\gamma(\delta) = \gamma$ is constant, and that the map $\delta \mapsto F(\cdot|\delta)$ is is nonincreasing. Then the function $g \in \mathcal{B}$ defined by (A.19) is nondecreasing.

Proof. When the intensity function is constant, the operator S in the proof of Proposition A.37 simplifies to

$$Sg(\delta) = \frac{c(\delta)}{r+\gamma} + \frac{\gamma}{r+\gamma}\int_{\underline{\delta}}^{\overline{\delta}} f(x)dF(x|\delta).$$

Proposition A.13 implies that under the stated monotonicity assumption, S maps the set of nondecreasing bounded functions into itself, and the desired result now follows from Corollary A.4 by noting that this set is closed in $\mathcal{B}$. □

Example A.39: Consider the Markov jump process defined in Example A.35 and let $c(\delta) = \mathbf{1}_{\{\delta \le k\}}$ for some $k \in \mathbf{R}$. By Proposition A.37 the function g associated with this source term is the unique bounded solution to

$$\gamma g(\delta+1) = (r+\gamma)g(\delta) - \mathbf{1}_{\{\delta \le k\}}.$$

To solve this equation we first note that any solution must vanish for all $\delta > k$, because otherwise

$$\lim_{n\to\infty} \gamma g(\delta+n) = \lim_{n\to\infty} (r+\gamma)^n g(\delta) = +\infty,$$

which contradicts the boundedness of the required solution. Proceeding by backward induction from the terminal condition $g(1 + [\![k]\!]) = 0$, it is then easily shown that the solution is given by

$$g(\delta) = \frac{1}{r+\gamma}\sum_{n=0}^{\infty} \mathbf{1}_{\{n \le k-\delta\}} \left(\frac{\gamma}{r+\gamma}\right)^n.$$

Now, observing that

$$g(\delta) = \int_0^\infty e^{-ru}\mathbf{P}\left[\delta_{t+u} \le k | \delta_t = \delta\right] du$$

is the Laplace transform in $\langle r|u\rangle$ of the conditional distribution of the process and inverting the transform reveals that

$$\mathbf{P}\left[\delta_s \le k | \delta_t = \delta\right] = \sum_{n=0}^{\infty} \mathbf{1}_{\{n \le k-\delta\}} e^{-\gamma(s-t)} \frac{(\gamma(s-t))^n}{n!}.$$

This shows that the increment $\delta_s - \delta_t$ is Poisson distributed with mean $\gamma(s-t)$ independently of $\mathcal{F}_t^{(\delta)}$ for all $s \ge t \ge 0$, and it follows that $(\delta_t - \delta_0)_{t\ge 0}$ is a Poisson process with intensity γ.

Corollary A.40: Assume that $F(\cdot|\delta) = F(\cdot)$ for all $\delta \in \mathcal{D}$. Then the bounded function defined in (A.19) is given by

$$g(\delta) = \frac{c(\delta)}{r+\gamma(\delta)} + \frac{\gamma(\delta)}{r+\gamma(\delta)} \left(\int_{\underline{\delta}}^{\overline{\delta}} \frac{c(x)dF(x)}{r+\gamma(x)} \right) \Big/ \left(\int_{\underline{\delta}}^{\overline{\delta}} \frac{rdF(x)}{r+\gamma(x)} \right)$$

and further simplifies to

$$g(\delta) = \left(1 - \frac{\gamma}{r+\gamma}\right) \frac{c(\delta)}{r} + \left(\frac{\gamma}{r+\gamma}\right) \int_{\underline{\delta}}^{\overline{\delta}} \frac{c(x)}{r} dF(x)$$

when the intensity function $\gamma(\delta) = \gamma$ is constant.

Proof. The same arguments as in the proof of Proposition A.37 show that under the stated assumptions the unknown function satisfies

$$g(\delta) = Sg(\delta) = \frac{c(\delta)}{r+\gamma(\delta)} + \frac{\gamma(\delta)}{r+\gamma(\delta)} \int_{\underline{\delta}}^{\overline{\delta}} g(x)dF(x)$$

for all $\delta \in \mathcal{D}$. Integrating against the distribution function $dF(\delta)$ on both sides and solving the resulting equation gives

$$\int_{\underline{\delta}}^{\overline{\delta}} p(x)dF(x) = \left(\int_{\underline{\delta}}^{\overline{\delta}} \frac{c(x)dF(x)}{r+\gamma(x)} \right) \Big/ \left(\int_{\underline{\delta}}^{\overline{\delta}} \frac{rdF(x)}{r+\gamma(x)} \right),$$

from which the result follows by substitution. □

Corollary A.41: Assume that $F(\cdot|\delta) = F(\cdot)$ and $\gamma(\delta) = \gamma$ for all $\delta \in \mathcal{D}$. Then the cumulative distribution of the process is given by

$$\mathbf{P}\left[\delta_t \le x | \delta_0\right] = F(x) + e^{-\gamma t}\left(\mathbf{1}_{\{\delta_0 \le x\}} - F(x)\right)$$

and converges to $F(x)$ as $t \to \infty$.

Proof. Corollary A.40 with $c(\delta) = \mathbf{1}_{\{\delta \le x\}}$ shows that the Laplace transform of the cumulative distribution with respect to time is given by

$$\int_0^\infty e^{-rt}\mathbf{P}\left[\delta_t \le x|\delta_0\right] dt = \frac{1}{r+\gamma}\left(\mathbf{1}_{\{\delta_0 \le x\}} + \frac{\gamma}{r}F(x)\right)$$

for all values of $r > 0$, and the desired conclusions now follow by inverting this elementary transform. □

BIBLIOGRAPHY

Daron Acemoglu and Robert Shimer. Holdups and efficiency with search frictions. *International Economic Review*, 40:827–851, 1999.

Tobias Adrian, Nina Boyarchenko, and Or Shachar. Dealer balance sheets and bond liquidity provision. *Journal of Monetary Economics*, 89(C):92–109, 2017.

Gara Afonso, Roc Armenter, and Benjamin Lester. A model of the federal funds market: Yesterday, today, and tomorrow. *Review of Economic Dynamics*, 33:177–204, 2019.

Gara Afonso, Anna Kovner, and Antoinette Schoar. Trading partners in the interbank market. Federal Reserve Bank of New York Staff Report No. 620, 2014.

Gara Afonso and Ricardo Lagos. Trade dynamics in the market for federal funds. *Econometrica*, 83:263–313, 2015a.

Gara Afonso and Ricardo Lagos. The over-the-counter theory of the fed funds market: A primer. *Journal of Money, Credit and Banking*, 47:127–154, 2015b.

George A. Akerlof. The market for "lemons": Quality uncertainty and the market mechanism. *Quarterly Journal of Economics*, 84(3):488–500, 1970.

Nuray Akin and Brennan C. Platt. Transition dynamics in equilibrium search. *American Economic Journal: Microeconomics*, 14(4):158–199, 2022.

James Albrecht and Bo Axell. An equilibrium model of search unemployment. *Journal of Political Economy*, 92(5):824–840, 1984.

Jason Allen, Robert Clark, and Jean-Francois Houde. Search frictions and market power in negotiated price markets. *Journal of Political Economy*, 127:1550–1598, 2019.

Jason Allen and Milena Wittwer. Centralizing over-the-counter markets? *Journal of Political Economy*, 131: 3310–3351, 2023.

Lukas Altermatt and Piero Gottardi. Market choice in asset trading: The role of collateral. Working paper, University of Essex, 2023.

Yakov Amihud and Haim Mendelson. Dealership market: Marketmaking with inventory. *Journal of Financial Economics*, 8:31–53, 1980.

Yakov Amihud and Haim Mendelson. Asset pricing and the bid-ask spread. *Journal of Financial Economics*, 17:223–249, 1986.

Yakov Amihud and Haim Mendelson. Liquidity, maturity, and the yield on U.S. Treasury securities. *Journal of Finance*, 46:479–486, 1991.

Yakov Amihud, Haim Mendelson, and Lasse H. Pedersen. Liquidity and asset prices. *Foundations and Trends in Finance*, 4:270–364, 2005.

Mark Yuying An. Logconcavity versus logconvexity: A complete characterization. *Journal of Economic Theory*, 80(2):350–369, 1998.

Yu An. Competing with inventory in dealership markets. Working paper, Johns Hopkins University, 2019.

Yu An and Zeyu Zheng. Immediacy Provision and Matchmaking. *Management Science*, 69(2):1245–1263, 2023.

Andrew Ang, Vineer Bhansali, and Yuhang Xing. The muni bond spread: Credit, liquidity, and tax. Columbia Business School Research Paper No. 14.37, 2014.

Roc Armenter and Benjamin Lester. Excess reserves and monetary policy implementation. *Review of Economic Dynamics*, 23:212–235, 2017.

Navneet Arora, Priyank Gandhi, and Francis A. Longstaff. Counterparty credit risk and the credit default swap market. *Journal of Financial Economics*, 103(2):280–292, 2012.

David M. Arseneau, David E. Rappoport, and Alexandros P. Vardoulakis. Private and public liquidity provision in OTC markets. *Theoretical Economics*, 15(4):1669–1712, 2020.

Adam Ashcraft and Darrell Duffie. Systemic illiquidity in the federal funds market. *American Economic Review, Papers and Proceedings*, 97:221–225, 2007.

Paul Asquith, Thom Covert, and Parag Pathak. The effects of mandatory transparency in financial market design: Evidence from the corporate bond market. National Bureau of Economic Research Working Paper No. 19417, 2013.

Vladimir Asriyan, William Fuchs, and Brett Green. Liquidity sentiments. *American Economic Review*, 109 (11):3813–3848, 2019.

Andrew Atkeson, Andrea Eisfeldt, and Pierre-Olivier Weill. Entry and exit in OTC derivatives markets. *Econometrica*, 83(6):2231–2292, 2015.

Sarah Auster and Piero Gottardi. Competing mechanisms in markets for lemons. *Theoretical Economics*, 14(3):927–970, 2019.

Ana Babus and Cecilia Parlatore. Strategic fragmented markets. *Journal of Financial Economics*, 145:876–908, 2022.

Kerry Back, Oguzhan Celebi, Ali Kakhbod, and A. Max Reppen. Segmented trading markets. Boston University Questrom School of Business Research Paper No. 4119978, 2022.

Mark Bagnoli and Ted Bergstrom. Log-concave probability and its applications. In Charalambos D. Aliprantis, Rosa L. Matzkin, Daniel L. McFadden, James C. Moore, and Nicholas C. Yann, eds., *Rationality and Equilibrium*, Studies in Economic Theory, pp. 217–241. Springer, 2006.

Markus Baldauf and Joshua Mollner. Competition and information leakage. *Journal of Political Economy*, 132(5):1603–1641, 2024.

Jack Bao, Maureen O'Hara, and Alex Zhou. The Volcker rule and market making in times of stress. *Journal of Financial Economics*, 130:95–113, 2018.

Jack Bao, Jun Pan, and Wang Jiang. The illiquidity of corporate bonds. *Journal of Finance*, 66:911–946, 2011.

Richard Bellman. *Dynamic programming*. Dover Publications, 1957.

Paula Beltran. A lending network under stress: A structural analysis of the money market funds industry. Working paper, UCLA, 2021.

Dimitri Bertsekas and Steven Shreve. *Stochastic optimal control : The discrete time case*. Academic Press, 1978. http://hdl.handle.net/1721.1/4852.

Hendrik Bessembinder, Stacey Jacobsen, William Maxwell, and Kumar Venkataraman. Capital commitment and illiquidity in corporate bonds. *Journal of Finance*, 73:1615–1661, 2018.

Hendrik Bessembinder and William Maxwell. Markets: Transparency and the corporate bond market. *Journal of Economic Perspectives*, 22:217–234, 2008.

Hendrik Bessembinder, William Maxwell, and Kumar Venkataraman. Market transparency, liquidity externalities, and institutional trading costs in corporate bonds. *Journal of Financial Economics*, 82:251–288, 2006.

Hendrik Bessembinder, Chester Spatt, and Kumar Venkataraman. A survey of the microstructure of fixed-income markets. *Journal of Financial and Quantitative Analysis*, 55(1):1–45, 2020. https://doi.org/10.1017/S0022109019000231.

Zachary Bethune, Bruno Sultanum, and Nicholas Trachter. Asset issuance in over-the-counter markets. *Review of Economic Dynamics*, 33:4–29, 2019.

Utpal Bhattacharya and Matthew Spiegel. Insiders, outsiders, and market breakdowns. *Review of Financial Studies*, 4:255–282, 1991.

Bruno Biais and Richard C. Green. The microstructure of the bond market in the 20th century. *Review of Economic Dynamics*, 33:250–271, 2019.

Bruno Biais, Johan Hombert, and Pierre-Olivier Weill. Equilibrium pricing and trading volume under preference uncertainty. *Review of Economic Studies*, 81:1401–1437, 2014.

Bruno Biais and Pierre-Olivier Weill. Liquidity shocks and order book dynamics. Working paper, Toulouse School of Economics and UCLA, 2009.

Javier Bianchi and Saki Bigio. Banks, liquidity management, and monetary policy. *Econometrica*, 9:391–454, 2022.

Javier Bianchi, Saki Bigio, and Charles Engel. Payments, liquidity, and exchange rates. Working paper, UCLA, 2018.

Saki Bigio and Yuliy Sannikov. A model of credit, money, interest, and price. Working paper, UCLA, 2019.

Ken Binmore, Ariel Rubinstein, and Asher Wolinsky. The Nash bargaining solution in economic modelling. *RAND Journal of Economics*, 17(2):176–188, 1986.

Max R. Blouin. Equilibrium in a decentralized market with adverse selection. *Economic Theory*, 22:245–262, 2003.

Max R. Blouin and Roberto Serrano. A decentralized market with common values uncertainty: Non-steady states. *Review of Economic Studies*, 68:323–346, 2001.

Vladimir I. Bogachev. *Measure theory*. Springer, 2007.

Nina Boyarchenko, Anna Kovner, and Or Shachar. It's what you say and what you buy: A holistic evaluation of the corporate credit facilities. *Journal of Financial Economics*, 144(3):695–731, 2022.

Giulia Brancaccio and Karam Kang. Search frictions and product design in the municipal bond market. NBER Working Paper No. 30775, 2022.

Giulia Brancaccio, Dan Li, and Norman Schurhoff. Learning by trading: The case of the U.S. market for municipal bonds. Working paper, Cornell University, 2017.

Pierre Brémaud. *Point processes and queues*. Springer, 1981.

Markus K. Brunnermeier. Deciphering the liquidity and credit crunch 2007–2008. *Journal of Economic Perspectives*, 23(1):77–100, 2009.

Greg Buchak, Gregor Matvos, Tomas Piskorski, and Amit Seru. Why is intermediating houses so difficult? Evidence from ibuyers. NBER Working Paper No. 28252, 2022.

Kenneth Burdett and Kenneth L. Judd. Equilibrium price dispersion. *Econometrica*, 51(4):955–969, 1983.

Kenneth Burdett and Dale T. Mortensen. Wage differentials, employer size, and unemployment. *International Economic Review*, 39:257–273, 1998.

Kenneth Burdett and Maureen O'Hara. Building blocks: An introduction to block trading. *Journal of Banking and Finance*, 11:193–212, 1987.

Kenneth Burdett, Shouyong Shi, and Randall Wright. Pricing and matching with frictions. *Journal of Political Economy*, 109:1060–1085, 2001.

Braz Camargo and Ben Lester. Trading dynamics in decentralized markets with adverse selection. *Journal of Economic Theory*, 153:534–568, 2014.

Michael Carter and Bruce Van Brunt. *The Lebesgue-Stieltjes integral: a practical introduction*. Springer, 2000.

Briana Chang. Adverse selection and liquidity distortion. *Review of Economic Studies*, 85(1):275–306, 2018.

Briana Chang and Shengxing Zhang. Endogenous market making and network formation. Working paper, University of Wisconsin–Madison and London School of Economics, 2018.

Huifeng Chang. A macroeconomic model with bond market liquidity. Working paper, Fudan University School of Management, 2022.

Alain Chateauneuf, Michèle Cohen, and Isaac Meilijson. Four notions of mean-preserving increase in risk, risk attitudes and applications to the rank-dependent expected utility model. *Journal of Mathematical Economics*, 40:547–571, 2004.

Gaston Chaumont. Sovereign debt, default risk, and the liquidity of government bonds. Working paper, University of Rochester, 2018.

Daniel Chen and Darrell Duffie. Market fragmentation. *American Economic Review*, 111:2247–2274, 2021.

Hui Chen, Rui Cui, Zhiguo He, and Konstantin Milbradt. Quantifying liquidity and default risks of corporate bonds over the business cycle. *Review of Financial Studies*, 31:852–897, 2018.

Jonathan Chiu and Thor Koeppl. Trading dynamics with adverse selection and search: Market freeze, intervention and recovery. *Review of Economic Studies*, 83:969–1000, 2016.

Jaewon Choi, Yesol Huh, and Sean Seunghun Shin. Customer liquidity provision: Implications for corporate bond transaction costs. *Management Science*, 70(1):187–206, 2024.

Jamie Coen and Patrick Coen. A structural model of liquidity in OTC markets. Working paper, Toulouse School of Economics, 2022.

Jamie Coen and Patrick Coen. A structural model of interbank network formation and contagion. Working paper, Toulouse School of Economics, 2023.

Assa Cohen, Mahyar Kargar, Benjamin Lester, and Pierre-Olivier Weill. Inventory, market making and liquidity in OTC markets. *Journal of Economic Theory*, 222:105917, 2024.

Melvyn G. Coles and Eric Smith. Marketplaces and matching. *International Economic Review*, 39:239–254, 1992.

Melvyn G. Coles and Randall Wright. A dynamic equilibrium model of search, bargaining, and money. *Journal of Economic Theory*, 78(1):32–54, 1998.

Jean-Edouard Colliard and Gabrielle Demange. Asset dissemination through dealer markets. *Management Science*, 67:6211–6234, 2021.

Antonio Coppola, Arvind Krishnamurthy, and Chenzi Xu. Liquidity, debt denomination, and currency dominance. Working paper, Stanford University, 2023.

Dean Corbae, Maxwell B. Stinchcombe, and Juraj Zeman. *An introduction to mathematical analysis for economic theory and econometrics*. Princeton University Press, 2009.

Ben Craig and Yiming Ma. Intermediation in the interbank lending market. *Journal of Financial Economics*, 145:179–207, 2022.

Wei Cui and Sören Radde. Search-based endogenous asset liquidity and the macroeconomy. *Journal of the European Economic Association*, 18:2221–2269, 2020.

Julien Cujean and Rémy Praz. Asymmetric information and inventory concerns in over-the-counter markets. Working paper, University of Bern, 2013.

Adrien d'Avernas. Disentangling credit spreads and equity volatility. Working paper, Stockholm School of Economics, 2017.

M. H. A. Davis. Martingale methods in stochastic control. In *Stochastic control theory and stochastic differential systems*, volume 16 of *Lecture notes in control and information sciences*, pp. 85–117. Springer, 1979.

Angus Deaton and Guy Laroque. On the behaviour of commodity prices. *Review of Economic Studies*, 59 (1):1–23, 01 1992.

Harold Demsetz. The cost of transacting. *Quarterly Journal of Economics*, 82:33–53, 1968.

Peter A. Diamond. A model of price adjustment. *Journal of Economic Theory*, 3(2):156–168, 1971.

Peter A. Diamond. Aggregate demand management in search equilibrium. *Journal of Political Economy*, 90 (5):881–894, 1982.

Jens Dick-Nielsen. How to clean enhanced TRACE data. Working paper, Copenhagen Business School, 2014.

Jens Dick-Nielsen, Peter Feldhütter, and David Lando. Corporate bond liquidity before and after the onset of the subprime crisis. *Journal of Financial Economics*, 103(3):471–492, 2012.

Jens Dick-Nielsen and Marco Rossi. The cost of immediacy for corporate bonds. *Review of Financial Studies*, 32:1–41, 2019.

Jens Dick-Nielsen. How to clean academic trace data. Working paper, Copenhagen Business School, 2019.

Marco Di Maggio. Market turmoil and destabilizing speculation. Working paper, MIT, 2013.

Marco Di Maggio, Amir Kermani, and Zhaogang Song. The value of trading relations in turbulent times. *Journal of Financial Economics*, 124:266–284, 2017.

Randall Dodd. Financial markets: Exchange or over-the-counter. International Monetary Fund: Back to Basics, 2012. https://www.imf.org/en/Publications/fandd/issues/Series/Back-to-Basics/Financial-Markets.

Darrel Duffie. Marketmaking under the proposed Volcker rule. Working paper, Stanford University, 2012a.

Darrell Duffie. *Dark markets*. Princeton University Press, 2012b.

Darrell Duffie. Still the world's safe haven: Redesigning the U.S. treasury market after the COVID-19 crisis. Technical Report 62, Hutchins Center Working Paper, 2020.

Darrell Duffie. *Fragmenting markets: Post-crisis bank regulations and financial market liquidity*. Walter de Gruyter, 2022.

Darrell Duffie, Piotr Dworczak, and Haoxiang Zhu. Benchmarks in search markets. *Journal of Finance*, 72(5):1983–2044, 2017.

Darrell Duffie, Nicolae Gârleanu, and Lasse H. Pedersen. Securities lending, shorting, and pricing. *Journal of Financial Economics*, 66:307–339, 2002.

Darrell Duffie, Nicolae Gârleanu, and Lasse H. Pedersen. Over-the-counter markets. *Econometrica*, 73: 1815–1847, 2005.

Darrell Duffie, Nicolae Gârleanu, and Lasse H. Pedersen. Valuation in over-the-counter markets. *Review of Financial Studies*, 20:1865–1900, 2007.

Darrel Duffie, Semyon Malamud, and Gustavo Manso. Information percolation with equilibrium search dynamics. *Econometrica*, 77(5):1513–1574, 2009.

Darrell Duffie and Gustavo Manso. Information diffusion in large populations. *American Economic Review, Papers and Proceedings*, 97, 2007.

Jérôme Dugast. Unscheduled news and market dynamics. *Journal of Finance*, 78:2537–2586, 2018.

Jérôme Dugast, Semih Üslü, and Pierre-Olivier Weill. A theory of participation in OTC and centralized markets. *Review of Economic Studies*, 89:3223–3266, 2022.

David Easley and Maureen O'Hara. Price, trade size, and information in securities markets. *Journal of Financial Economics*, 19(1):69–90, 1987.

Amy K. Edwards, Lawrence E. Harris, and Michael S. Piwowar. Corporate bond market transaction costs and transparency. *Journal of Finance*, 62(3):1421–1451, 2007.

Jens Eisenschmidt, Yiming Ma, and Anthony Lee Zhang. Monetary policy transmission in segmented markets. *Journal of Financial Economics*, 151:103738, 2024.

Andrea Eisfeldt, Bernard Herskovic, Srimam Rajan, and Emil N. Siriwardane. OTC intermediaries. *Review of Financial Studies*, 128:615–677, 2023.

Nicole El Karoui. Les aspects probabilistes du controle stochastique. In *Ecole d'Eté de Probabilités de Saint-Flour IX-1979*, pp. 73–238, Springer, 1981.

Christian Ewerhart. Regular type distributions in mechanism design and ρ-concavity. *Economic Theory*, 53:591–603, 2013.

Maryam Farboodi, Gregor Jarosch, Guido Menzio, and Ursula Wiriadinata. Intermediation as rent extraction. Technical report, MIT, Princeton, New York University, and IMF, 2018.

Maryam Farboodi, Gregor Jarosch, and Robert Shimer. The emergence of market structure. *Review of Economic Studies*, 90(1):261–292, 2022.

Peter Feldhütter. The same bond at different prices: Identifying search frictions and selling pressures. *Review of Financial Studies*, 25(4):1155–1206, 2012.

Jean-David Fermanian, Olivier Guéant, and Jiang Pu. The behavior of dealers and clients on the European corporate bond market: The case of multi-dealer-to-client platforms. *Market Microstructure and Liquidity*, 2, 2016.

Nathan Foley-Fisher, Stefan Gissler, and Stéphane Verani. Over-the-counter market liquidity and securities lending. *Review of Economic Dynamics*, 33:272–294, 2019.

Thierry Foucault, Marco Pagano, and Ailsa Roell. *Market liquidity*. Oxford University Press, 2013.

Nils Friewald, Rainer Jankowitsch, and Marti G. Subrahmanyam. Illiquidity or credit deterioration: A study of liquidity in the US corporate bond market during financial crises. *Journal of Financial Economics*, 105(1):18–36, 2012.

Nils Friewald and Florian Nagler. Over-the-counter market frictions and yield spread changes. *Journal of Finance*, 74(6): 3217–3257, 2019.

William Fuchs and Andrzej Skrzypacz. Government interventions in a dynamic market with adverse selection. *Journal of Economic Theory*, 158:371–406, 2015.

Miroslav Gabrovski and Ioannis Kospentaris. Intermediation in over-the-counter markets with price transparency. *Journal of Economic Theory*, 198:105364, 2021.

Kenneth D. Garbade and William L. Silber. Price dispersion in the government securities market. *Journal of Political Economy*, 84(4):721–740, 1976.

Nicolae Gârleanu. Portfolio choice and pricing in illiquid markets. *Journal of Economic Theory*, 144:532–564, 2009.

Mark Garman. Market microstructure. *Journal of Financial Economics*, 3:257–275, 1976.

Daniel F. Garrett, Renato Gomes, and Lucas Maestri. Competitive screening under heterogeneous information. *Review of Economic Studies*, 86(4):1590–1630, 12 2018.

Alessandro Gavazza. The role of trading frictions in real asset markets. *American Economic Review*, 101(4): 1106–1143, 2011a.

Alessandro Gavazza. Leasing and secondary markets: Theory and evidence from commercial aircraft. *Journal of Political Economy*, 119(2):325–377, 2011b.

Alessandro Gavazza. An empirical equilibrium model of a decentralized asset market. *Econometrica*, 84: 1755–1798, 2016.

Thomas Gehrig. Intermediation in search markets. *Journal of Economics and Management Strategy*, 2:97–120, 1993.

Athanasios Geromichalos and Lucas Herrenbrueck. Monetary policy, asset prices and liquidity in over-the-counter markets. *Journal of Money, Credit, and Banking*, 48(1):35–79, 2016.

Athanasios Geromichalos, Lucas Herrenbrueck, and Kevin Salyer. A search-theoretic model of the term premium. *Theoretical Economics*, 11:897–935, 2016.

Athanasios Geromichalos and Kuk Mo Jung. An over-the-counter approach to the forex market. *International Economic Review*, 59:859–905, 2018.

Sergei Glebkin, Ji Shen, and Bart Zhou Yueshen. Simultaneous multilateral search. *Review of Financial Studies*, 36(2):571–614, 2023.

Vincent Glode and Christian C. Opp. Over-the-counter vs. limit-order markets: The role of traders' expertise. *Review of Financial Studies*, 33(2):866–915, 2019.

Michael Gofman. A network-based analysis of over-the-counter markets. Working paper, University of Rochester, 2014.

Michael Gofman. Efficiency and stability of a financial architecture with too-interconnected-to-fail institutions. *Journal of Financial Economics*, 124:113–14, 2017.

Michael A. Goldstein, Edith S. Hotchkiss, and Erik R. Sirri. Transparency and liquidity: A controlled experiment on corporate bonds. *Review of Financial Studies*, 20(2):235–273, 2007.

Mikhail Golosov, Guido Lorenzoni, and Aleh Tsyvinski. Decentralized trading with private information. *Econometrica*, 82:1055–1091, 2014.

Richard Green, Burton Hollifield, and Norman Schürhoff. Financial intermediation and the costs of trading in an opaque market. *Review of Financial Studies*, 20:275–314, 2006.

Richard Green, Burton Hollifield, and Norman Schürhoff. Dealer intermediation and price behavior in the aftermarket for new bond issues. *Journal of Financial Economics*, 86(3):643–682, 2007.

Sanford J. Grossman and Merton H. Miller. Liquidity and market structure. *Journal of Finance*, 43:617–637, 1988.

Veronica Guerrieri and Robert Shimer. Dynamic adverse selection: A theory of illiquidity, fire sales, and flight to quality. *American Economic Review*, 104:1875–1908, 2014.

Roger Guesnerie and Jean-Jacques Laffont. A complete solution to a class of principal-agent problems with an application to the control of a self-managed firm. *Journal of Public Economics*, 25(3):329–369, 1984.

Valentin Haddad, Alan Moreira, and Tyler Muir. When selling becomes viral: Disruptions in debt markets in the COVID-19 crisis and the Fed's response. *Review of Financial Studies*, 34:5309–5351, 2021.

George Hall and John Rust. Middlemen versus market makers: A theory of competitive exchange. *Journal of Political Economy*, 111:353–403, 2003.

Robert E. Hall and Paul Milgrom. The limited influence of unemployment on the wage bargain. *American Economic Review*, 98:1653–1674, 2008.

Lu Han and William C. Strange. The microstructure of housing markets: Search, bargaining, and brokerage. *Handbook of Regional and Urban Economics*, 5:813–886, 2015.

Larry Harris. *Trading and exchanges: Market microstructure for practitioners*. Oxford University Press, 2003.

J. Michael Harrison and David M. Kreps. Speculative behavior in a stock market with heterogenous expectations. *Quarterly Journal of Economics*, 92:323–336, 1978.

Joel Hasbrouck. *Empirical market microstructure: The institutions, economics, and econometrics of securities trading*. Oxford University Press, 2007.

Zhiguo He, Paymon Khorrami, and Zhaogang Song. Commonality in credit spread changes: Dealer inventory and intermediary distress. *Journal of Financial Economics*, 35:4630–4673, 2022.

Zhiguo He and Konstantin Milbradt. Endogenous liquidity and defaultable bonds. *Econometrica*, 82: 1443–1508, 2014.

Aaron Hedlund. The cyclical dynamics of illiquid housing, debt, and foreclosures. *Quantitative Economics*, 7(1):289–328, 2016.

Terrence Hendershott, Dan Li, Dmitry Livdan, and Norman Schürhoff. Relationship trading in OTC markets. *Journal of Finance*, 75(2):683–734, 2020.

Terrence Hendershott and Ananth Madhavan. Click or call? Auction versus search in the over-the-counter market. *Journal of Finance*, 70:419–447, 2015.

Jack Hirshleifer. The private and social value of information and the reward to inventive activity. *American Economic Review*, 61:561–574, 1971.

Burton Hollifield, Artem Neklyudov, and Chester Spatt. Bid-ask spreads, trading networks and the pricing of securitizations: 144a vs. registered securitization. *Review of Financial Studies*, 30:3048–3085, 2017.

Arthur J. Hosios. On the efficiency of matching and related models of search and unemployment. *Review of Economic Studies*, 57(1):279–298, 1990.

Julien Hugonnier. Speculative behavior in decentralized markets. Working paper, Swiss Finance Institute, EPFL, 2012.

Julien Hugonnier, Benjamin Lester, and Pierre-Olivier Weill. Frictional intermediation in over-the-counter markets. *Review of Economic Studies*, 87:1432–1469, 2020.

Julien Hugonnier, Benjamin Lester, and Pierre-Olivier Weill. Heterogeneity in decentralized asset markets. *Theoretical Economics*, 7:1313–1356, 2022.

Julien Hugonnier, Benjamin Lester, and Pierre-Olivier Weill. OTC markets with asymmetric information: The private value case. EPFL Working paper, 2024a.

Julien Hugonnier, Benjamin Lester, and Pierre-Olivier Weill. OTC markets with asymmetric information: The common value case. EPFL Working paper, 2024b.

Julien Hugonnier, Semyon Malamud, and Erwan Morellec. Capital supply uncertainty, cash holdings, and investment. *Review of Financial Studies*, 28:391–445, 2015.

Roman Inderst. Matching markets with adverse selection. *Journal of Economic Theory*, 121:145–166, 2005.

Maarten C. W. Janssen and Santanu Roy. Dynamic trading in a durable good market with asymmetric information. *International Economic Review*, 43(1):257–282, 2002.

Mahyar Kargar, Benjamin Lester, David Lindsay, Shuo Liu, Pierre-Olivier Weill, and Diego Zúñiga. Corporate bond liquidity during the COVID-19 crisis. *Review of Financial Studies*, 34:5352–5401, 2021.

Mahyar Kargar, Benjamin Lester, Sébastien Plante, and Pierre-Olivier Weill. Sequential search for corporate bonds. Working paper, UCLA, 2023.

Mahyar Kargar, Juan Passadore, and Dejanir Silva. Liquidity and risk in OTC markets: A theory of asset pricing and portfolio flows. Working paper, University of Illinois, 2021.

Kei Kawakami. *The formation of exchanges: Risk sharing and information aggregation*. PhD dissertation, University of California, Los Angeles, 2010.

Kei Kawakami. Welfare consequences of information aggregation and optimal market size. *American Economic Journal: Microeconomics*, 9(4):303–323, 2017.

Ayça Kaya and Kyungmin Kim. Trading dynamics with private buyer signals in the market for lemons. *Review of Economic Studies*, 85(4):2318–2352, 2018.

John Kennan and Robert Wilson. Bargaining with private information. *Journal of Economic Literature*, 31 (1):45–104, 1993.

Kyungmin Kim. Endogenous market segmentation for lemons. *The RAND Journal of Economics*, 43(3): 562–576, 2012.

Pèter Kondor and Gàbor Pinter. Clients' connections: Measuring the role of private information in decentralized markets. *Journal of Finance*, 77(1):505–544, 2022.

Oleg Korenok, Ioannis Kospentaris, and John Lightle. An experimental evaluation of the over-the-counter search model. Working paper, Department of Economics, VCU School of Business, 2024.

Julian Kozlowski. Long-term finance and investment with frictional asset markets. *American Economic Journal: Macroeconomics*, 13(4):411–448, 2021.

Albert S. Kyle. Continuous auctions and insider trading. *Econometrica*, 53(6):1315–1336, 1985.

Jean-Jacques Laffont and David Martimort. *The theory of incentives: the principal-agent model.* Princeton University Press, 2001.

Ricardo Lagos and Gastón Navarro. Monetary policy operations: Theory, evidence, and tools for quantitative analysis. NBER Working Paper No. 31370, 2023.

Ricardo Lagos and Guillaume Rocheteau. Liquidity in asset markets with search frictions. Technical report, Working paper, Federal Reserve Bank of Minneapolis, 2008.

Ricardo Lagos and Guillaume Rocheteau. Liquidity in asset markets with search frictions. *Econometrica*, 77:403–426, 2009.

Ricardo Lagos, Guillaume Rocheteau, and Pierre-Olivier Weill. Crises and liquidity in OTC markets. *Journal of Economic Theory*, 146:2169–2205, 2011.

Ricardo Lagos and Shengxing Zhang. Monetary exchange in bilateral over-the-counter markets. *Review of Economic Dynamics*, 2019a.

Ricardo Lagos and Shengxing Zhang. The limit of onetary economics: On money as a constraint on market power. *Econometrica*, 90(3):1177–1204, 2022.

Ricardo Lagos and Shengxing Zhang. Turnover liquidity and the transmission of monetary policy. *American Economic Review*, 110:1635–1672, 2020.

Stephan Lauermann, Wolfram Merzyn, and Virág Gábor. Learning and price discovery in a search model. *Review of Economic Studies*, 85:1159–1192, 2018.

Stephan Lauermann and Asher Wolinsky. Search with adverse selection. *Econometrica*, 84(1):243–315, 2016.

Lucie Lebeau. Credit frictions and participation in over-the-counter markets. *Journal of Economic Theory*, 189:105100, 2020.

Stephen F. LeRoy and John Krainer. Equilibrium valuation of illiquid assets. *Economic Theory*, 19:223–242, 2002.

Benjamin Lester, Guillaume Rocheteau, and Pierre-Olivier Weill. Competing for order flow in OTC markets. *Journal of Money, Credit and Banking*, 47(S2):77–126, 2015.

Benjamin Lester, Ali Shourideh, Venky Venkateswaran, and Ariel Zetlin-Jones. Screening and adverse selection in frictional markets. *Journal of Political Economy*, 127(1):338–377, 2019.

Benjamin Lester, Ali Shourideh, Venky Venkateswaran, and Ariel Zetlin-Jones. Market-making with search and information frictions. *Journal of Economic Theory*, 212:105714, 2023.

Dan Li and Norman Schürhoff. Dealer networks. *Journal of Finance*, 74(1):91–144, 2019.

Jessica S. Li. Strategic bargaining and portfolio choice in intermediated markets. Working paper, University of Chicago, 2023.

Jessica S. Li, Maureen O'Hara, Andreas C. Rapp, and Xing Alex Zhou. Bond market illiquidity: Is portfolio trading the solution? SMU Cox School of Business Research Paper No. 23–09, 2023.

Jian Li and Haiyue Yu. Investor composition and the liquidity component in the U.S. corporate bond market. Working paper, Columbia University, 2021.

Qi Li. Security design without verifiable retention. *Journal of Economic Theory*, 200:105381, 2022.

Wei Li and Zhaogang Song. Asset heterogeneity, market fragmentation, and quasi-consolidated trading. Working paper, Johns Hopkins University, 2023.

Yiting Li. Middlemen and private information. *Journal of Monetary Economics*, 42:131–159, 1998.

Shuo Liu. Dealer's search intensity in U.S. corporate bond markets. Working paper, UCLA, 2020a.

Shuo Liu. Socially optimal search intensity in over-the-counter markets. *Review of Economic Dynamics*, 53:224–282, 2024.

Ying Liu, Sebastian Vogel, and Yuan Zhang. Electronic trading in OTC markets vs. centralized exchange. Working paper, Swiss Finance Institute, 2018.

Lars Ljungqvist and Thomas J. Sargent. *Recursive macroeconomic theory*. 3rd ed. MIT Press, 2012.

Alex Maciocco. Trading relationships in over-the-counter markets. Working paper, University of California, Irvine, 2023.

Taneli Mäkinen and Francesco Palazzo. Adverse selection and search congestion in over-the-counter markets. *Journal of Monetary Economics*, 146:103577, 2024.

Semyon Malamud and Marzena Rostek. Decentralized exchange. *American Economic Review*, 107:3320–3362, 2017.

Semyon Malamud and Andreas Schrimpf. Intermediation markups and monetary policy pass-through. Working paper, EPFL and BIS, 2017.

Semyon Malamud and Andreas Schrimpf. An intermediation-based model of exchange rates. Working paper, EPFL and BIS, 2018.

Adrian Masters. Middlemen in search equilibrium. *International Economic Review*, 48:343–362, 2007.

Fabrizio Mattesini and Ed Nosal. Liquidity and asset prices in a monetary model with OTC asset markets. *Journal of Economic Theory*, 164:187–217, 2016.

Vincent Maurin. Liquidity fluctuations in over-the-counter markets. *Journal of Finance*, 77(2):1325–1369, 2022.

John J. McCall. Economics of information and job search. *Quarterly Journal of Economics*, 84(1):113–126, 1970.

Antonio Merlo and Charles Wilson. A stochastic model of sequential bargaining with complete information. *Econometrica*, 63(2):371–399, 1995.

Antonio Merlo and Charles Wilson. Efficient delays in a stochastic model of bargaining. *Economic Theory*, 11:39–55, 1998.

Jianjun Miao. A search model of centralized and decentralized trade. *Review of Economic Dynamics*, 9(1):68–92, 2005.

Konstantin Milbradt. Asset heterogeneity in over-the-counter markets. Working paper, Northwestern University, Kellogg School of Management, 2017.

Paul Milgrom and Ilya Segal. Envelope theorems for arbitrary choice sets. *Econometrica*, 70:583–601, 2002.

Espen R. Moen. Competitive search equilibrium. *Journal of Political Economy*, 105:385–411, 1997.

Diego Moreno and John Wooders. Decentralized trade mitigates the lemons problem. *International Economic Review*, 51(2):383–399, 2010.

Michael Mussa and Sherwin Rosen. Monopoly and product quality. *Journal of Economic Theory*, 18(2): 301–317, 1978.

Roger B. Myerson. Optimal auction design. *Mathematics of Operations Research*, 6(1):58–73, 1981.

Roger B. Myerson and Mark A. Satterthwaite. Efficient mechanisms for bilateral trading. *Journal of Economic Theory*, 29(2):265–281, 1983.

Artem Neklyudov. Bid-ask spreads and the over-the-counter interdealer markets: Core and peripheral dealers. *Review of Economic Dynamics*, 33:57–84, 2019.

Yigal S. Newman and Michael A. Rierson. Illiquidity spillovers: Theory and evidence from European telecom bond issuance. Stanford University, 2003.

Ed Nosal and Guillaume Rocheteau. *Money, payments and liquidity*. MIT Press, 2011.

Yoshio Nozawa and Anton Tsoy. Over-the-counter markets for non-standardized assets. Working paper, University of Toronto, 2023.

Maureen O'Hara. *Market microstructure theory*. Blackwell, 1995.

Maureen O'Hara and Alex Zhou. Anatomy of a liquidity crisis: corporate bonds in the COVID-19 crisis. *Journal of Financial Economics*, 142:46–68, 2021.

Maureen O'Hara and Alex Zhou. Mutual fund fragility, dealer liquidity provisions and the pricing of municipal bonds. *Management Science*, 70(7):4802–4823, 2022.

Marco Pagano. Trading volume and asset liquidity. *Quarterly Journal of Economics*, 104: 255–274, 1989.

Emiliano S. Pagnotta and Thomas Philippon. Competing on speed. *Econometrica*, 86(3): 1067–1115, 2018.

Mariano J. Palleja. Filters for the academic trace database. Working paper, UCLA, 2022.

Juan Passadore and Yu Xu. Illiquidity in sovereign debt markets. *Journal of International Economics*, 137:103618, 2022.

Motty Perry and Philip J. Reny. A non-cooperative bargaining model with strategically timed offers. *Journal of Economic Theory*, 59(1):50–77, 1993.

Nicolas Petroky-Nadeau and Etienne Wasmer. *Labor, credit, and goods markets: The macroeconomics of search and unemployment*. MIT Press, 2017.

Barbara Petrongolo and Christopher A. Pissarides. Looking into the black box: A survey of the matching function. *Journal of Economic Literature*, 39(2):390–431, 2001.

Gabor Pinter and Semih Üslü. Comparing search and intermediation frictions across markets. Working paper, Bank of England and Johns Hopkins University, 2021.

Gabor Pinter, Chaojun Wang, and Junyuan Zou. Size discount and size penalty: Trading costs in bond markets. Working paper, Bank of England, University of Pennsylvania, the Wharton School, and INSEAD, 2021.

Christopher Pissarides. Short-run equilibrium dynamics of unemployment, vacancies, and real wages. *American Economic Review*, 75:676–690, 1985.

Christopher Pissarides. *Equilibrium unemployment theory*. 2nd ed. MIT Press, 2000.

Fabien Postel-Vinay and Jean-Marc Robin. Equilibrium wage dispersion with worker and employer heterogeneity. *Econometrica*, 6:2295–2350, 2002.

Rémy Praz. Equilibrium asset pricing with both liquid and illiquid markets. Working paper, Swiss Finance Institute, EPFL, 2015.

Murray H. Protter and Charles B. Morrey. *A first course in real analysis*. Springer, 1977.

W. T. Reid. *Riccati Differential Equations*. Academic Press, 1972.

Lynn Riggs, Esen Onur, David Reiffen, and Haoxiang Zhu. Swap trading after Dodd-Frank: Evidence from index CDs. *Journal of Financial Economics*, 137(3):857–886, 2020.

Guillaume Rocheteau and Randall Wright. Liquidity and asset-market dynamics. *Journal of Monetary Economics*, 60(2):275–294, 2013.

Hee Su Roh. Repo specialness in the transmission of quantitative easing. Working paper, Stanford University, 2019.

Marzena Rostek and Marek Weretka. Dynamic thin markets. *Review of Financial Studies*, 28: 2946–2992, 2015.

Marzena Rostek and Ji Hee Yoon. Exchange design and efficiency. *Econometrica*, 89:2887–2928, 2021.

Ioanid Rosu. A dynamic model of the limit order book. *Review of Financial Studies*, 22(11): 4601–4641, 2009.

Michael Rothschild and Joseph Stiglitz. Equilibrium in competitive insurance markets: An essay on the economics of imperfect information. *Quarterly Journal of Economics*, 90(4): 629–649, 1976.

Ariel Rubinstein. Perfect equilibrium in a bargaining model. *Econometrica*, 50:97–109, 1982.

Ariel Rubinstein and Asher Wolinsky. Equilibrium in a market with sequential barganing. *Econometrica*, 53:1133–1150, 1985.

Ariel Rubinstein and Asher Wolinsky. Middlemen. *Quarterly Journal of Economics*, 102(3): 581–593, 1987.

John Rust and George Hall. Middlemen versus market makers: A theory of competitive exchange. *Journal of Political Economy*, 111(2):353–403, 2003.

Jacob S. Sagi. Asset-level risk and return in real estate investments. *Review of Financial Studies*, 34:3647–3694, 2021.

Batchimeg Sambalaibat. Endogenous specialization in dealer networks. Working paper, Indiana University, Kelley School of Business, 2018.

Batchimeg Sambalaibat. A theory of liquidity spillover between bond and CDS markets. *Review of Financial Studies*, 35:2525–2569, 2022.

Adrien Saumard and Jon A. Wellner. Log-concavity and strong log-concavity: A review. *Statistics Surveys*, 8:45–114, 2014.

Joel L. Schiff. *The Laplace transform: Theory and applications*. Springer, 1999.

Duane J. Seppi. Equilibrium block trading and asymmetric information. *Journal of Finance*, 45(1):73–94, 1990.

Ji Shen, Bin Wei, and Hongjun Yan. Financial intermediation chains in an OTC market. *Management Science*, 67:4623–4642, 2020.

Andrei Shevchenko. Middlemen. *International Economic Review*, 45:1–25, 2004.

Shouyong Shi. Money and prices: A model of search and bargaining. *Journal of Economic Theory*, 67(2): 467–496, 1995.

Robert Shimer. *Labor Markets and Business Cycles* (CREI Lectures in Macroeconomics). Princeton University Press, 2010.

Rafael Silveira and Randall Wright. Search and the market for ideas. *Journal of Economic Theory*, 145(4): 1550–1573, 2010.

Emil N. Siriwardane. Limited investment capital and credit spreads. *Journal of Finance*, 74(5):2303–2347, 2019.

Daniel F. Spulber. Marketmaking by price-setting firms. *Review of Economic Studies*, 63:559–580, 1996.

George J. Stigler. The economics of information. *Journal of Political Economy*, 63:213–225, 1961.

Nancy L. Stokey and Robert E. Lucas. *Recursive methods in economic dynamics*. Harvard University Press, Cambridge, 1989.

Francesco Trebbi and Kairong Xiao. Regulation and market liquidity. *Management Science*, 65(5):1949–1968, 2017.

Alberto Trejos and Randall Wright. Search, bargaining, money, and prices. *Journal of Political Economy*, 103(1):118–141, 1995.

Alberto Trejos and Randall Wright. Search-based models of money and finance: An integrated approach. *Journal of Economic Theory*, 164:10–31, 2016.

Chung-Yi Tse and Yujing Xu. Inter-dealer trades in OTC markets—Who buys and who sells? *Review of Economic Dynamics*, 39:220–257, 2021.

Anton Tsoy. Alternating-offer bargaining with the global game game information structure. *Theoretical Economics*, 13:869–931, 2018.

Anton Tsoy. Bargaining over a non-standardized asset. Working paper, University of Toronto, 2019.

Semih Üslü. Pricing and liquidity in decentralized asset markets. *Econometrica*, 87(6):2079–2140, 2019.

Semih Üslü and Güner Velioğlu. Liquidity in the cross section of OTC assets. Working paper, Johns Hopkins University, 2019.

Dimitri Vayanos and Tan Wang. Search and endogenous concentration of liquidity in asset markets. *Journal of Economic Theory*, 136:66–104, 2007.

Dimitri Vayanos and Pierre-Olivier Weill. A search-based theory of the on-the-run phenomenon. *Journal of Finance*, 63:1361–1398, 2008.

Sebastian Vogel. When to introduce electronic trading platforms in over-the-counter markets? Working paper, Swiss Finance Institute, EPFL, 2019.

Neng Wang. Caballero meets Bewley: The permanent income hypothesis in general equilibrium. *American Economic Review*, 93:927–936, 2003.

Pierre-Olivier Weill. Essays on liquidity in financial markets. PhD dissertation, Stanford University, 2004.

Pierre-Olivier Weill. Leaning against the wind. *Review of Economic Studies*, 74:1329–1354, 2007.

Pierre-Olivier Weill. Liquidity premia in dynamic bargaining markets. *Journal of Economic Theory*, 140: 66–96, 2008.

Pierre-Olivier Weill. Liquidity provision in capacity constrained markets. *Macroeconomic Dynamics*, 15:119–144, 2011.

Pierre-Olivier Weill. The search theory of over-the-counter markets. *Annual Review of Economics*, 12:747–773, 2020.

Basil Williams. Search, liquidity, and retention: Screening multidimensional private information. *Journal of Political Economy*, 129(5):1487–1507, 2021.

Charles Wilson. The nature of equilibrium in markets with adverse selection. *Bell Journal of Economics*, 11(1):108–130, 1980.

Milena Wittwer. Connecting disconnected financial markets? *American Economic Journal: Microeconomics*, 13:252–282, 2021.

Asher Wolinsky. Information revelation in a market with pairwise meetings. *Econometrica*, 58:1–23, 1990.

Tsz-Nga Wong and Mengbo Zhang. Disintermediating the federal funds market. Working paper, Federal Reserve Bank of Richmond, 2022.

World Federation of Exchanges database. Stocks traded, turnover ratio of domestic shares (%) - United States. World Bank, n.d. https://data.worldbank.org/indicator/CM.MKT.TRNR?name_desc=true&locations=US

Randall Wright, Philipp Kircher, Bruno Julien, and Veronica Guerrieri. Directed and competitive search: A guided tour. *Journal of Economic Literature*, 59(1):90–148, 2021.

Botao Wu. Post-crisis regulations, trading delays, and increasing corporate bond liquidity premium. Working paper, NYU Stern School of Business, 2021.

Ming Yang and Yao Zeng. The coordination of intermediation. Working paper, Duke University and University of Washington, 2019.

Abdullah Yavaş. Marketmakers versus matchmakers. *Journal of Financial Intermediation*, 2:33–58, 1992.

Bart Zhou Yueshen and Junyuan Zou. Less is more. Working paper INSEAD, 2022.

Shengxing Zhang. Liquidity missallocation in an over-the-counter market. *Journal of Economic Theory*, 174:16–56, 2017.

Haoxiang Zhu. Finding a good price in opaque over-the-counter markets. *Review of Financial Studies*, 25: 1255–1285, 2011.

Junyuan Zou. Information acquisition and liquidity traps in over-the-counter markets. Working paper, INSEAD, 2019.

INDEX

References in *Italics* refer to figures.